W9-BWI-459

66-23695 (2-21-68)

HISTORY OF THE UNITED STATES
FROM THE COMPROMISE OF 1850

CLASSIC AMERICAN HISTORIANS

Paul M. Angle, GENERAL EDITOR

History of the UNITED STATES

from the Compromise of 1850

by James Ford Rhodes

abridged and edited by Allan Nevins

THE UNIVERSITY OF CHICAGO PRESS   Chicago & London

WINGATE COLLEGE LIBRARY
WINGATE, N. C.

The selections in this book are taken from the first five volumes of the 1907 printing of James Ford Rhodes's *History of the United States from the Compromise of 1850 to the Final Restoration of Home Rule in the South in 1877,* published by the Macmillan Company.

Library of Congress Catalog Card Number: 66–23695
THE UNIVERSITY OF CHICAGO PRESS, CHICAGO & LONDON
The University of Toronto Press, Toronto 5, Canada
Abridged edition © 1966 by The University of Chicago
All rights reserved
Published 1966. Printed in the United States of America

General Editor's Preface

FEW TODAY read the great American historians. Few can. If a reader limited himself to those chosen for inclusion in this series—Prescott, Parkman, Bancroft, McMaster, Moses Coit Tyler, Henry Adams, Nicolay and Hay, and Rhodes—he would find himself straining his eyes eight hours a day for at least a year. This, in the modern world, is an impossible requirement.

Yet that the works of these men should remain unknown is deplorable. Something is better than nothing. From that conviction this series was born. But what should that "something" be? A series of condensations? How can one condense the sixteen volumes of Parkman, or the nine volumes of Henry Adams, into one volume without doing inexcusable violence to the whole? On the other hand, representative selections, each of substantial length, can convey a good idea of point of view, breadth of treatment, narrative skill, and style. This was the method chosen.

After this choice was made, the general editor came across a relevant pronouncement which John Hay made during the serialization of *Abraham Lincoln: A History*. "The only question," Hay wrote to Richard Watson Gilder, editor of the *Century*, "is whether you want the Life to run three years or four. If the former, you must take heroic measures. Leaving out a chapter here and there, or retrenching an adjective, will do

37920

no good. . . . You must cut great chunks of topics out. . . . Neither Nicolay nor I can write the work over again for the purpose of saving a half chapter here and there." Nor, we submit, can anyone else.

The books in this series were designed for reading, not research. All documentation has therefore been eliminated. Editors of individual volumes have used their discretion in retaining expository footnotes. Such footnotes as they have added are identified by their initials. The typographical style, punctuation, and spelling of the original texts have been followed.

PAUL M. ANGLE

Introduction

THE career of James Ford Rhodes was quite remarkable. He was a successful businessman who, at the height of his lucrative enterprises, gave up moneymaking, and although he possessed no special training for literary work, threw off all commercial connections, changed his residence, immersed himself in books, and embarked upon a deliberate and persistent effort to make himself a historian. Charles W. Eliot later remarked that by this very unusual shift from trade to letters, a shift completed in 1885 at the age of thirty-seven, he "rendered great service to American scholarship and the country." It was an example which might more frequently be followed. He himself took some pride in it. He wrote Frederic Bancroft that he ought to be given credit for withdrawing from business when he was rapidly accumulating a fortune, because "I thought I ought to devote myself to something higher"; and equal credit for the fact that, having withdrawn, "I did not become an intellectual dawdler or a European sojourner." He had worked hard in managing his coal and iron business, but he was pleased to record that, without any spur of necessity, he later worked much harder upon his history.

In this abandonment of self to pursue a higher ambition we may see the strain of idealism which not infrequently mingled with the hard practical realism of sons of the Western Reserve, who were Puritans at a second remove. Many strains went into

Rhodes's character and training. His father, Dan Rhodes, was a Vermonter by birth and a cousin of Stephen A. Douglas. All accounts emphasize his roughness of tongue and manner, but they likewise credit him with ability and character. Certainly he made a success of his various enterprises in coal, iron, and lake shipping; certainly he showed a marked respect for education and spent money generously to school his son. The mother, Sophia Lord Russell, was a serious-minded woman of Connecticut origin, who gave much time to church and charities. Rhodes never forgot that he was of pure New England stock, a fact to be remembered in appraising his history; and when he took up literature it seemed more natural for him to go to Boston than to New York or Washington.

Yet he had imbibed at an early age the hustling, progressive, hopeful spirit of Cleveland. Mark Hanna became a brother-in-law; John Hay was a friend; he knew and admired John D. Rockefeller. He also imbibed from his early surroundings a spirit of breadth and tolerance in both politics and religion. Although his schoolmates were chiefly Republicans, his father was a staunch Douglas Democrat. His mother was an Episcopalian, his father was a Deist, and his early teachers were fervent Congregationalists.

This breadth of outlook was a fortunate element in the training of the future historian; nor was his rather desultory education without great value. In grammar school and the very superior Cleveland high school he found two men as teachers whom he thought inspiring. In the University of the City of New York, where he studied in 1865–66, he met another, Benjamin N. Martin, who specially fostered his taste for history. Rhodes and the other students mastered Guizot's *General History of Civilization in Europe,* a text with a high concentration of facts and liberal ideas, so completely that they could have given a full abstract of the book. Another text they employed was Georg Weber's *Outlines of Universal History*. Martin not only encouraged wide reading, but insisted that his students give much time to essay writing. He introduced young Rhodes to Macaulay, whose essays delighted the lad, and to Tocqueville, whose analysis of the democratic system in America and France, and defense of it as a historical necessity, were equally pleasing.

"And," wrote Rhodes later, "I read two books that mark an epoch in my intellectual life—Buckle's *History of Civilization,* and Draper's *Intellectual History of Europe.* I shall never forget the interest and even excitement with which I turned the pages of Buckle's two volumes. Such purely intellectual emotion does not often fall to one. I was mastered. In my mind I became a disciple of Buckle. How I regretted his untimely death! But it seemed to me that earth had no purer pleasure to offer than to be able to produce such a book; and death seemed robbed of its terror after having achieved such celebrity. The story was then current that Buckle's last words were, 'Oh, my book, my book!' And under the influence excited by those two volumes no story could have been more pathetic As I read the last words of the second volume, May 16, 1866, I resolved some day to write a history."

Not completing his course at New York University, Rhodes spent the following year at the old University of Chicago, where he read the Scottish philosophers, heard Robert Collyer preach, gained his first acquaintance with Herbert Spencer's ideas, and was given a warm love for English literature by another inspiring teacher, William Matthews. Here, too, he was captivated by the brilliant political articles and scholarly reviews of the *Nation,* recently founded by E. L. Godkin. Then came six months in Paris, where he saw the Exposition of 1867, listened to a course of lectures by Edouard Laboulaye, and wrote some letters on French affairs for the *Chicago Times.* A short period of study at the School of Mines in Berlin followed, after which he made a tour of the principal iron and steel works of western Germany and the British Isles. When he came home to Cleveland in 1868, his father lost little time in packing him off to investigate the coal and iron resources of North Carolina, Georgia, and eastern Tennessee (1869), a horseback journey which took him into the heart of Reconstruction unrest. It is clear that although Rhodes's training was unsystematic, it was remarkably varied, practical, and stimulating, and that even as a boy he learned much outside books—much of men, of affairs, of different scenes and social environments.

The fifteen years of business life which occupied him from 1870 to 1885 were clearly irksome—he spoke of letting his partners bear the main burden—and might have been intellectually deadening. But he refused to give up mental stimuli. He laid out a systematic course of reading in which the historians bulked large; he devoured novels and plays; he joined the Vampire Club, a literary group in which John Hay was the dominant figure; and he continued to train himself in writing. His ambition gradually became fixed. "One evening in 1877," he states, "while reading Hildreth's *History of the United States,* I laid down my book and said to myself, Why should I not write a History of the United States? From that time my reading, though desultory and often interrupted by the pressure and anxieties of business and the claims of society, had this end in view. I began making notes. I resolved that as soon as I gained a competence I would retire from business, and devote myself to history and literature. This resolution was sometimes shaken, and sometimes lost sight of, but it would not entirely down." When in 1885 he crossed the Rubicon, he began contributing articles and reviews to the *Magazine of Western History.* Meanwhile, he gave nearly a year and a half to rest and travel. Then, returning temporarily to Cleveland in 1887, he began reading for his first two volumes, and on November 30, 1891, submitted them to Harper & Brothers.

Rhodes was always explicit in stating his historical aims. He meant to write a great narrative in the style of Thucydides and Macaulay, trying to delve broadly into the sentiment and spirit of his period, and to present its principal figures and scenes with memorable power, but not desiring to penetrate to the economic and philosophical roots of events. The idea of a philosophy of history did not attract him; he distrusted historical laws. He copied into his first notebook a sentence from George William Curtis: "In writing history the vital necessity is the historical sense, the ability to conceive the spirit of a time and to interpret it with candor." His models in English letters were Gibbon, Macaulay, and Lecky rather than Freeman or Stubbs; in American letters he thought that Motley's *Rise of the Dutch Republic* and Fiske's *Discovery of America* were the two greatest books produced up to 1892. He defined his ambitions rather carefully in 1907, when his work was practically done, in a letter to Charles Francis Adams:

You owe me no apology whatever for saying that "no well and philosophically considered narrative of the [Civil War] struggle has yet appeared," as the remark did not disturb me in the least. For a philosophical narrative was not my aim. There is use for the philosophy of history, and it will ever have an attraction for busy and profound thinkers, and addiction to it does not necessarily preclude good narrative work. Lecky did little but philosophize in his History of Morals, but that did not prevent his writing a good narrative of the Eighteenth Century. You yourself who are given to philosophy wrote a gem of a biography in the life of your Father; and that and your essay based on the Fish papers show that you need yield to no American historian in the matter of a narrative style. But a purely narrative historian should, so far as he can, put all philosophic conditions aside. His aim is to tell a story and leave philosophy to others. One great merit of Macaulay, said Justin Winsor, is that his narrative carries his philosophy along with it. This was not strictly true of Macaulay in all cases, nor is it of my volumes, but such was my aim, and what little philosophizing I have indulged in has diminished as my volumes have grown.

He added, referring to a criticism which Adams had just written in the *Proceedings of the Massachusetts Historical Society* (October, 1905) of the fifth volume of his history:

A concrete case will show why one with my method should avoid if possible all philosophic theory. Did I believe with you (which I do not) that the "blockade was the controlling condition of Union success," that "the blockade was the determining factor, as cotton was the dynamic factor of the struggle," I would not have "woven the narrative over this philosophical skeleton." For had I done so, such is the constitution of the human mind, at any rate my own, that as I went through the mass of my material I would have seized upon all the facts that made for my theory and marshalled them in its support while those that told against me I would have unconsciously and undoubtedly quite honestly neglected. As William James said of H. Spencer, he has a great avidity for facts that support his theory and amasses them in a surprising manner; but he has no eye for the others. My aim was to get rid so far as possible of all preconceived notions and theories.

In short, Rhodes wished to analyze historical transactions and to appraise historical personages, much as he would have analyzed business affairs and appraised contemporary figures in the Cleveland business world; to present a straightforward, objective, and if possible vivid story of events, without much theorizing and no use whatever of abstract ideas; to avoid tendentious and dogmatic writing on the one side, and writing detached from reality on the other. The principal engines in his arsenal were his hard common sense, his honesty, and his immense industry. He warmly prized Theodore Roosevelt's commendation of him as "a great historian who understood practical affairs," and one "in such wise superior to Lecky." He frankly admitted that in his *History* he avoided writing on subjects for which he lacked special and expert competence, skirting the question of sea power because "I have not the basic knowledge," refusing to go into considerations of military strategy because he lacked the "competence," and abstaining from any discussion of fine points of international law.

He stood squarely on his position as a judicial-minded, hardheaded, shrewd-eyed, and perfectly candid narrator, who founded his story—and it was always first and foremost a story—upon diligent labor by himself and trained assistants in the available sources. His principal helpers were Professor E. G. Bourne of Western Reserve University, Miss Alice Wyman of the Boston Athenaeum, and Mr. D. M. Matteson of Cambridge, Massachusetts, and he knew how to employ their talents to supplement his own. They contributed to his masses of data, and sometimes to his interpretation, but never to his dominant ideas or style. Matteson has testified: "Whatever went into the melting pot, the gold that came out—and it was gold—was all Rhodes."

Rhodes is properly to be judged as a historian in the light of his avowed aims, and in the light also of the materials that he was able to use. When he began writing his *History* in 1887, the events of 1850–60 (covered in the first two volumes) were as near him as the events of the decade 1940–50 are near Americans today. Many valuable works on the period had been published, but they were naturally for the most part political and military; other works did not appear until after Rhodes had completed his writing, and books furnishing social and economic materials, in particular, were delayed. In one postscript after another, as his successive volumes came out, Rhodes lamented the fact that various writings had emerged too late for his use.

Thus at the close of his second volume he remarks that when W. P. Trent's valuable *Life of William Gilmore Simms* and Thomas Nelson Page's less useful but colorful book *The Old South* had been published, his printer's work was so far advanced that he could not levy upon them. He tried to look fairly on the Southern side, but Trent and Page presented some considerations that he had missed; and he particularly commended to his readers Trent's chapter called "Romantic Dreams and Political Nightmares," and three chapters by Page on the social and intellectual history of the South. In his volumes on the war, Rhodes was prevented from giving due space to naval operations by the fact that the *Naval Records* had not been published. Rhodes had the benefit of Nicolay and Hay's *Lincoln,* but not of any of the more thorough and candid work on Lincoln which was inaugurated by Miss Tarbell's two volumes in 1900. He had the benefit of Jefferson Davis's *Rise and Fall of the Confederate Government,* but not of any biography of Davis worth mentioning. Gideon Welles's *Diary* was not published until long years after Rhodes had passed Welles's period of service (1911). An immense mass of memoirs, including such indispensable items as the autobiography of Carl Schurz, and the reminiscences of Jacob D. Cox, James Harrison Wilson, and Henry Villard, was poured out after Rhodes had finished. Indeed, that stream has continued into our own day. What good use Rhodes might have made of the classic *Diary* of George Templeton Strong, for example!

When he came to the Reconstruction years, Rhodes labored under an even greater disability in the thinness of his sources. The fifth and sixth volumes of his history appeared in 1906. Everyone could see that they emphasized political history, omitting many topics of cardinal importance on the economic and social side; and some of their deficiencies in this respect were rather glaringly revealed when in 1906–7 W. L. Fleming published his *Documentary History of Reconstruction,* a two-volume work which comprehended the cultural, social, and economic history of the South from 1865–77 as well as the political. Had Rhodes written after and not before the publication of Fleming's source work, had he possessed as well the admirable monographs on Reconstruction which William A. Dunning's students were soon pouring out at Columbia University, his fifth and sixth volumes might have been very different in content. Critics must distinguish between deficiencies which were his fault, and those which a general historian, unable to wait on the slow wheels of time or to halt long enough for monographic delving, could not avoid.

The reception given the first two volumes, by both scholars and the general public, was highly gratifying. Such a history of the events leading to the Civil War had been eagerly desired, though few had expected it to appear in so interesting and authoritative a form, and none could have predicted that it would come from a retired businessman. "Nearly everybody had thought some writer like Dunning of Columbia or Albert Bushnell Hart of Harvard would step forward," Frederic Bancroft later recalled. "Great was the astonishment to learn that a for-

mer coal and iron merchant held the pen." Great, too, was the
pleasure of most readers in finding that the ideas imbuing the
work were those of laissez-faire liberals of the free-soil school.

"There was one universal acclaim of praise," wrote John T.
Morse, Jr., of Boston—a statement true of the North though not
of the South. Many people liked the work for its eulogistic
treatment of Clay, Webster, Lincoln, and (with sharp reserva-
tions) Seward; nearly everybody admired the gusto and verve
with which Rhodes recounted the battle over the Compromise
of 1850, the Northern revolt against the Fugitive Slave Act,
Harriet Beecher Stowe's production of *Uncle Tom's Cabin,* the
woes of Bleeding Kansas, John Brown's melodramatic career,
Preston Brook's assault upon Sumner in the Senate chamber,
and the other lurid events down to Fort Sumter. Rhodes's assertion that slavery was the root cause of the Civil War commanded general assent. His portraiture of the leading statesmen was always graphic; and the episodes which he brought to
life were the more effective because they had been dimly remembered by millions from childhood days.

When the eminent W. E. H. Lecky, author of the penetrating
history of morals and the monumental work upon eighteenth–
century Britain just mentioned, praised Rhodes for his manifest desire "to do justice to all sides and to tell the exact truth,"
and when the British legal authority, A. V. Dicey, pronounced
his work "the most just and the most comprehensive account"
of the period, he could hope that they anticipated the judgment
of posterity. Rhodes was especially pleased by a magisterial
review in the *Nation,* which declared that the chapter on
slavery was a model summary of a difficult subject; that the
charitable estimate of Stephen A. Douglas was shrewd and fair;
and that the volumes promised "a noteworthy and valuable
addition to our solid literature." The one critique that gave
Rhodes deep pain was an unsigned review in the *Atlantic
Monthly*. He readily discerned that it was written by a Southerner, though he could not know that the man was Woodrow
Wilson. Sales of the two volumes were so substantial, despite

the depression following the Panic of 1893, that a new edition appeared in the autumn of 1895.

From this triumph Rhodes pressed on to the completion of his Civil War narrative, permitting no interruptions save those imposed by some uncertainties of health and a normally busy social life. His third volume appeared in 1895, his fourth in 1899, and his fifth in 1904. That they were the best volumes of his whole work, a distinct advance upon the first two, no discriminating reader could doubt. Carrying Rhodes into the full current of the Civil War and a little beyond its triumphant end, they exalted his spirit as the Peloponnesian War had exalted the heart of Thucydides. He received the praise and encouragement of national leaders like Theodore Roosevelt, of fellow historians like James Schouler and John Fiske, of literary critics like Barrett Wendell—who ranked him with Thucydides and Tacitus—and of such scholars in other fields as William James, who termed his books "admirable." Once more the usually reserved *Nation* praised him warmly. He possessed in remarkable degree, it said, the principal requirements of a modern historian: unflagging industry, accurate judgment, clarity, impartiality, and balance. H. Morse Stephens, who treated the French Revolution in a rigidly scientific spirit, asserted that among living and active writers of American history the first place undoubtedly belonged to Rhodes. As he pressed on, though with flagging energy and some signs of failing power, to complete his narrative down to the year 1877 in seven volumes, sales of his work showed a sustained appeal to both students and general readers.

By the year 1890 he had begun to spend much time in the East. He took a place for several summers at Hyannis Port on Cape Cod; he made friends throughout New England. In the autumn of 1891 he leased a house in Cambridge from Professor Adams Sherman Hill of Harvard, who had been an efficient war correspondent for Greeley's *Tribune*—and who let Rhodes use his manuscript correspondence with Sydney Howard Gay, the managing editor of the paper. Two Harvard historians, Albert

Bushnell Hart and the librarian Justin Winsor, became fast friends. A little later, in 1895, Rhodes moved to Boston, enlarging his circle. Election to the Massachusetts Historical Society in 1893, the oldest and most famous of such American organizations, pleased him so much that the title pages of his sixth and seventh volumes, published in 1906, recorded his membership along with his honorary degrees. Charles Francis Adams, Henry Cabot Lodge, Robert Grant, and William Roscoe Thayer were enrolled among his intimates. He joined the Tavern Club, and it was at a club dinner that he made a speech of welcome to George Macaulay Trevelyan, an English historian whom he came to know as well as he knew James Bryce and John Morley.

Yet most involvements outside his history Rhodes avoided to the last. "I cannot make a speech," he wrote Frederic Bancroft. "I would be a poor presiding officer. 'Shoemaker, stick to your last.' My tastes are essentially those of the student. The best work I do is that in the library." The First World War put an end to his foreign travels, except for a brief sojourn in Nice–Cimiez in 1922. He took a keen interest in current affairs but kept quite aloof from politics—which was fortunate, for his letters reveal an excessively Republican and conservative set of judgments. He died in Brookline, Massachusetts, in 1927.

By two papers on the writing of history and the profession of historian in his *Historical Essays,* Rhodes made it clear that the models whom he most admired were Herodotus, Thucydides, and Tacitus among the ancients; Ernst Curtius, S. R. Gardiner, and J. R. Green along with Carlyle, Gibbon, and Macaulay among the moderns. His taste, in short, was for the great story-tellers, usually of rich literary gifts, who might be candidly partisan but must never be as inaccurate as Froude or as tedious as George Bancroft. He was frankly old-fashioned and spoke slightingly of the new ideas of innovators like Bernard Shaw. It seems probable that he was more influenced in his historical writing by Macaulay than anybody else. At any rate,

he followed Macaulay's doctrine that history ought to emphasize the concrete, the individual, and the dramatic. Let history,
wrote Macaulay, be like a novel, with the difference that it is
true while novels are fictitious; let it be capable of "interesting
the affections, and presenting pictures to the imagination";
let it "invest with the reality of flesh and blood beings whom
we are too much inclined to consider as personified qualities."
Macaulay's plan caused him to work on a minute scale, painting characters life-size, relating events with fullness, sustaining
the interest with biographical anecdotes, and keeping up, as
Cotter Morison says, "a vigilant liveliness of narrative which
simulated the novel of adventure." Setting out to cover a century and a half, Macaulay actually traversed in five large
volumes a period of about fifteen years. In the same way,
Rhodes treated events copiously, gave close attention to vivid
character portraiture, introduced a constant succession of lively
incidents, and kept an element of suspense alive in his books.
The story never halts; it sweeps steadily onward, without pause
for philosophizing, social and institutional analysis, or scientific inquiry. And in his five fundamental volumes Rhodes, like
Macaulay, covers just fifteen years—1850-65.

As narrative history these volumes remain a remarkable
achievement. The first two, dealing with the eventful decade
1850-60, are the most rapid in pace. Their subject matter is
almost exclusively political. In a thousand pages Rhodes pauses
only once for a chapter static in quality and concerned with
social and economic forces rather than with public affairs, his
seventy-five pages on slavery; and even this contains narrative
elements, for it includes an account of the publication of *Uncle
Tom's Cabin,* its reception and influence, and the Southern
rejoinders to it. The remainder of the first two volumes is pure
story, flowing from year to year, event to event, with clear,
direct, and often impetuous force. It is like a broad historical
romance, with the characters and events all real. Rhodes pauses
but briefly to set his scenes, and gives us none of that elaborate

tableau painting which some devotees of narrative history, like Claude G. Bowers, offer. He uses newspapers with unprecedented thoroughness. These, with letters, memoirs, and public documents, are carefully studied to present the most striking characters—from Calhoun, Clay, Webster, and Zachary Taylor down to Buchanan, Sumner, Seward, Douglas, and finally Lincoln—in graphic strokes and with generally astute summarizations. The brief portraits of minor personages like Lewis Cass, Edward Everett, Pierre Soulé, W. L. Marcy, and Robert J. Walker are also done with finish and vigor.

But it is always the story of events which is most vital to Rhodes—the external and obvious story given with too little attention to the forces behind it, but told with a dash, a sweep, and a sense of its heroic quality which makes it absorbing. Errors of proportion, such as the devotion of nearly fifteen pages to an account of the yellow fever epidemic of 1853 in New Orleans, are few. Courage is shown in the forcible assertion of new and unpopular interpretations. Most of Rhodes's early readers were shocked, for example, by his defense of Webster's Seventh of March Speech in advocacy of the Compromise of 1850; by his treatment of Douglas's Kansas-Nebraska Bill of 1854 as an honest attempt to heal the sectional breach by a statesmanlike measure, not as a dishonest piece of demagogy; and by his frank exposition of Seward's numerous errors of judgment and faults of temper. More recent research has shown that he was correct in taking these positions. When Rhodes comes to a dramatic story like the campaign of 1856, warfare in Kansas, or John Brown's raid in Virginia, he relates it with a full but not hectic or exaggerated sense of its exciting quality. Each chapter ends on a note of suspense, and the reader is carried irresistibly forward until the two volumes 1850-60 close with events that show them to be but the prologue to a still greater drama. Lincoln has been elected; the South is in revolt; a fever of nationalism is seizing the free North and Northwest. The footlights are about to flash up more intensely, the orchestra to burst into "The Star Spangled Banner," and the curtain to rise on the First Inaugural, Bull Run, and Ball's Bluff.

The great conflict is equally well covered. No mere scientist can ever be a worthy historian of the bloody battles, the passionate political contests, and the anxious diplomacy of the Civil War period. The writer who essays a satisfactory treatment of its intricacies must have some of the qualities which Thomas Hardy brought to *The Dynasts,* Stephen Vincent Benét to *John Brown's Body,* and—most of all—those James Ford Rhodes brought to the first five volumes of his *History.* We may reproach Rhodes with lack of philosophic depth and scientific thoroughness; but we must concede to him a sweep, a vigor, and a sense of the soul-stirring quality of a great critical period such as few historians provide us. It is true that he was highly partisan. He wrote as a son of New England transplanted to northern Ohio, and as a child of the great Free Soil movement. His bias led him at times, as in his excessively severe treatment of the fire-eating advocates of slavery expansion, his contempt for Buchanan, and his condemnation of efforts at new compromises, into a somewhat misleading interpretation of men and events. Later he was too ready to make Lincoln the masterful hero of the war, and to overlook his deficiencies as organizer and administrator. To wartime administration, indeed, Rhodes gives singularly little attention, and he almost wholly ignores the greatest Northern organizer of the conflict, the redoubtable quartermaster general, Montgomery C. Meigs.

But let us recognize also that a certain amount of partisanship is indispensable to high narrative interest. The romancer creates a world in which hero is pitted against villain; the romantic narrative historian finds it necessary to identify himself with forces of right arrayed valiantly against men and institutions representing wrong. Rhodes saw in the free institutions, the democratic temper, and the reforming ideals of the North a set of protagonists fighting against evils that threatened the very life of the nation. In the broad view he was right. In some details he pushed this attitude too far, but a more balanced and impartial position would have robbed his history of half its narrative power—and might not have brought him much nearer the truth.

The historian tried to look at both sides of nearly every moot issue, and to show faults and virtues alike in the men he treated. The looming hero of his third and fourth volumes is Lincoln. Rhodes stands by him and his policies as against the Copperheads on one side and the Jacobins on the other; he demonstrates just how the election of 1864 vindicated the President's course. Nevertheless, he severely criticizes Lincoln for assenting to gross violations of civil liberties by permitting arbitrary arrests, the suppression of newspapers, and other extra-judicial procedures that Rhodes terms "inexpedient, unnecessary, and wrong." By well-marshaled evidence, again, Rhodes proves McClellan unfit for the chief command against Lee. McClellan's dilatory moves, exaggeration of the strength of the enemy, and timid underestimate of his own power brought about the failure of his campaign on the Peninsula. Yet the author pronounces Lincoln's removal of McClellan with no better replacement than Burnside a mistake. Rhodes never lacked opinions, and was seldom swayed by partialities.

Doubtlessly because economic topics did not lend themselves to the dramatic treatment that could be given political combats and martial campaigns, Rhodes instinctively left them out of his volumes. Because the discussion of organization and administration possesses no narrative color, he omitted it from his work. When Reconstruction began, the central concern of the United States swung to industry, transportation, and mercantile activity, so that Rhodes's indifference to these subjects fatally crippled his sixth and seventh volumes. He was hampered, too, by a lack of monographic work in these fields that only time could remedy.

Obviously, Rhodes had more taste, insight, and literary dexterity than George Bancroft; but, like Bancroft, he conceived of his narrative as a highly colored and frequently dramatic work that approached the character of a prose epic. Bancroft had written of colonial history as tending toward one titanic event, the establishment of American freedom, political, economic, and social, in the Revolution. That concept gave his work force, dignity, and climactic power, but it resulted in a deplorable warping of the materials. Although it had some literary justification, from the scientific point of view it was a highly inadequate approach. Rhodes similarly resolved to make his history a sweeping but well-unified narrative of the sectional conflict over slavery, in which the details of events and phases should be subordinated to the grand impact of the central theme. As the Revolution had seemed to Americans born in the next generation after Yorktown the most titanic and thrilling of struggles, so the Civil War seemed to Rhodes an epic whole, a tremendous tidal thrust in the development of democracy, which should be treated as fervently as Macaulay had treated the thrust of Whiggish forces and aims culminating in the Revolution of 1688, and with as much unity as Carlyle had achieved in his massive, million-word work on Frederick the Great.

Memories of boyhood days in Cleveland, when he had hung excitedly upon the news of battles and political clashes, intensified in Rhodes's mind the epic or histrionic view of American history from 1850 to 1877. "This period," he wrote in the first page of his *History,* "the brief space of a generation, was an era big with fate for our country, and for the American must remain fraught with the same interest that the war of the Peloponnesus had for the ancient Greek, or the struggle between the Cavalier and the Puritan had for their descendants." To give unity to his narrative, Rhodes naturally had to suppress many facts which were irrelevant to the central theme; to make this theme appear really epic, he had to simplify many other facts and movements. His first six volumes are essentially a history of the rise, development, and termination of the sectional conflict, and are very far from a history of the whole

American people, in all their interests and activities, in that generation. This meant of course a distinct distortion of fact. From many points of view, the Civil War was merely an interrupting episode, not an overriding central movement, in the nineteenth-century history of America. From other points of view—the industrial, for example—it was an accelerating impulse, but nothing more.

In sum, we may say that Rhodes was at fault in this limited concept of his work, and was also at fault in the bias or preconception with which he approached his subject. To be sure, he labored to tell the impartial truth, and always disclaimed any prejudices. At some points he believed that he had leaned backward to do justice to the South. Yet he could not escape the ingrained ideas, the fundamental postulates, natural to a Yankee son of the Western Reserve growing into adolescence in the years of battle, victory, and reconstruction. Vigorously avowing his moral abhorrence of slavery, he made it plain that he would not bring an understanding temper to the Yancey–Toombs–Davis contention that Southerners had a right to carry their peculiar type of property into the Western territories that belonged to the whole nation. Though nowhere did he show the intolerant bias of his contemporary Hermann von Holst, he was basically subjective rather than objective.

This attitude comes out clearly in such matters as his over-emphatic condemnation of the Fugitive Slave Act ("the mere statement of the provisions of this law is its condemnation"), in his denunciation of the Southern oligarchy, in his acrid comparison of Southern cultural deficiencies with the cultural achievements of New England, and above all in his acceptance of the contemporaneous Free Soil concept of the wickedness of the Kansas-Nebraska Act. Few contrasts in our historical literature are more glaring than that between the fifth chapter in his history, dealing with the beginnings of the Pierce Administration and the struggle over the Kansas-Nebraska bill, and the third chapter of Volume II of Albert J. Beveridge's *Abraham Lincoln*, treating the same topics. The man who reads both at the present day will rub his eyes, wondering if the two writers can really be examining the same men and events; and if he studies the evidence, he will soon conclude that Rhodes's preconceptions led him astray. Bias was the product of Rhodes's principal fault, his lack of depth in studying the American nation.

The defects of such a work inevitably grow. Rhodes's first five volumes, coming down to Reconstruction, are by far his best; but even they become, year by year, more antiquated in point of view and faulty in factual detail. His style, sometimes pedestrian and seldom illumined by felicity of phrase or brilliance of imagery, lacks the preservative quality found in the style of Prescott, Parkman, and Henry Adams. For his own generation he did an extremely useful work. His research was wide and conscientious. To newspapers especially he continued to the end to give remarkable study. Not content with examining merely the most important journals, he delved into files East and West, North and South, using organs of all parties and the independent presses to obtain a grasp of public opinion. At the same time, he knew literature unusually well. He had read much in the poetry, fiction, essays, and travel writings of the period, though with excessive emphasis on New England books, and had so arranged their salient contents in his mind and notebooks (for he used old-fashioned notebooks and not loose classifiable sheets) that their material was readily available to his pen. This material brightened many a page. But readers of a later day find his frame too narrow and his studies deficient in depth.

His sustained examination of slavery early in his *History* is an instance of this fact. Treating the system itself, its effects on master and family, upon the slave, and upon the community, summarizing the views of those who arraigned it and the apologies of its defenders, he gave the Americans of 1893 a far more judicial study of the institution than they could find elsewhere. Even after the books of Ulrich B. Phillips, Frank L. Owsley, and others, down to Kenneth M. Stampp, this treatise retains points of interest and significance. Yet on such complex subjects as the nature of slavery among yeoman farmers and the psychology of the slave, he is quite inadequate. The third volume has an entertaining discussion of social change in the 1850's, correct in pointing to immense activity in all kinds of reform and a generally high standard of ethics, and full of interesting facts. Yet how loose and superficial it seems after the recent dissections of rural and urban sociology by specialized students! In his fourth volume the treatment of British sentiment and diplomacy during the Civil War constitutes another long essay, which was remarkably fresh and illuminating when Rhodes wrote it. It was he, for example, who first proved that Great Britain did not yield to threats in preventing the armored rams from leaving Liverpool in 1863; the Ministry had acted to stop them before Charles Francis Adams's famous warning, "My lord, this is war." Yet the volumes of Ephraim D. Adams on *Great Britain and the American Civil War* inaugurated a series of studies which have given us a surer understanding of the diplomacy of the war period. We now know just where Austria, Spain, and Russia, as well as Britain and France, stood.

It should be pointed out that Rhodes's grasp of character and motive was usually excellent, and that his portraits of many of the personages of the time remain valid. Indeed, his handling of the personal element in history is far surer and more vigorous than that of von Holst, Schouler, or McMaster. His picture of Douglas, which was more sympathetic and admiring than that previously drawn by Northern writers, is striking; he shows that Douglas grew with the demands of his times, and that the Little Giant of the Lecompton battle was a much stronger man in every way than the Little Giant of 1854. His presentation of Lincoln, illustrating his sagacity, patience, magnanimity, foresight, and spiritual power with apt incident and quotation, is discerning and convincing. His analysis of Southern fire-eaters has never been surpassed. He was perhaps too severe upon Seward, upon the "mingled folly and rashness" of the secessionist leaders, and upon the Congressional Radicals; in dealing with Andrew Johnson he erred painfully. Yet, on the whole, he has given us the best portrait gallery, the closest approach to the studies of leadership in crisis written by Lord Clarendon and George Otto Trevelyan, to be found in any American work.

In short, Rhodes was a great historian, limited to some extent by stylistic shortcomings, and to a greater degree by inherited restrictions of understanding and outlook, but most of all by the fact that he wrote before an array of new weapons had been supplied by the nascent social studies and the rising generation of monograph writers. With the opportunities and means available to him, he executed a magnificent piece of narrative history that offers a larger combination of enjoyment and profit than any but a few historians provide. All citizens interested in our national past should read it.

The selections in this book have been taken from Rhodes's first five volumes, his truly significant work. Since he did not give his chapters titles, I have supplied my own. For the text I have used the 1907 edition.

ALLAN NEVINS

Contents

HISTORY OF THE UNITED STATES
FROM THE COMPROMISE OF 1850

Chicago Historical Society

I T *seemed a happy hour for the American republic when, on a September morning in 1847, as a bright sun gilded the snowy heights of Popocatapetl, silent crowds of Mexicans watched from the rooftops, and battle-hardened lines of troops lined the city plaza, a detachment of General Winfield Scott's men raised their starry banner over the central palace of Mexico City. A rapid, easy, spectacular war had closed in victory. It had vastly enlarged the area of the nation. The millions of mechanics, factory hands, clerks, and farmers had room for expansion into what would soon be new territories and states. The next Congress, which would meet in December to find Jefferson Davis of Mississippi and Stephen A. Douglas of Illinois among new Senate members, and Abraham Lincoln holding a seat in the House, was the first to find the flag waving over three million square miles, and the whole Pacific coast from Puget Sound to the Gulf of California.*

Yet, although the national future seemed immeasurably widened, not all the results of the war gave men pleasure. Begun under a Democratic president, James K. Polk, it had placed the principal laurels of victory upon two Whig generals, Scott and Zachary Taylor; and it had strengthened the party which opposed it, while it had divided and weakened the supporting party. The fact was that the war had been bitterly unpopular in much of the Union, especially in New England and New York. Hence it was that although Southern Democrats hoped to see slavery expand over much of the new acquisitions, most Democrats in the Northeast and many in the Middle West opposed its growth in extent or power. A Democratic Representative from Pennsylvania, David Wilmot, had introduced in 1846 an amendment to an appropriation bill stipulating that, in territory gained from Mexico, slavery should never exist. The House at once passed it, but it never got through the Senate.

Rhodes begins his History *with the Compromise of 1850. All beginnings are more or less artificially selected. To make his narrative more understandable, however, he might well have begun with the debate of 1847-48 on the prolongation of the Mexican War, which elicited from John C. Calhoun a protest* against fighting on to acquire lands south of California and New Mexico, and with the ratification (March 10, 1848) of a reasonable treaty of peace. New Mexico then included present-day Nevada and Utah. As early as 1848 Congress, considering the organization of Oregon Territory, took up the great constitutional issue that lay underneath the emerging debates on the future of the West. Did Congress have power to regulate or prohibit slavery in the territories that it organized? When Congress passed its Oregon bill in late summer, it was with a prohibition of slavery. But although everybody knew that climate forbade slavery in that area, the debate had aroused passionate feeling.

Rhodes gives us graphic and accurate portraits of some of the more arresting figures—Calhoun, William Lloyd Garrison, John Quincy Adams, and a group of senators including Seward of New York, Sumner of Massachusetts, and Ben Wade of Ohio. These men appear in different circumstances covering twenty years or more. Calhoun stands against the background of Jackson's first administration. Garrison emerges in connection with the launching of the Liberator in 1831, the journal he used for thirty-five years to attack slavery. John Quincy Adams, erratic but unswervingly courageous, appears battling against slavery expansion and for the right to present antislavery petitions to Congress. Then we leap forward to view Seward, Sumner, and Wade in the struggle over the Compromise of 1850.

The historian labors hard to furnish an impartial view of all these men. Later writers would give a different estimate of Calhoun. They would emphasize more strongly his position as a political theorist, and particularly his theories upon state rights, and the importance of a "concurrent majority" as distinguished from a numerical majority, and they would rate him more highly as a thinker. More recent writers would also treat Garrison differently. Two views of him can be defended. One is sharply critical, the other favorable. Both, however, make much more use of psychoanalytic knowledge than was possible when Rhodes wrote. Sumner, also, challenges the psychoanalyst. Not so with Ben Wade, a one-dimensional *personality whom most recent historians would dismiss as a man responsive only to two chords of feeling: personal ambition and sectional vindictiveness.*

A Gallery of Passionate Leaders

THE Palmetto State had no manufactures, nor could she expect to build up any with her system of labor. Her interest being to buy manufactured articles as cheaply as possible, she could have no sympathy with legislation that had for its purpose the fostering of home industries. The favorite idea was to exchange cotton for English goods, with no restrictions whatever on this reciprocal trade. For the production of cotton, slave labor was then thought to be necessary; and free trade and negro slavery, therefore, became associate and fundamental tenets in the South Carolina political catechism.

The enactment of the tariff of 1828 created great excitement in South Carolina, and public meetings were held all over the State, denouncing the law in unmeasured terms. Nullification was threatened, and, while the majority did not seem ready to take that step, the sentiment in favor of nullification simply needed a leader to give it shape and direction; and a leader was at hand in the person of the Vice-President, John C. Calhoun. His opinions marked him out for the guide of his native State. He had hitherto been intensely national in his feelings, and in favor of giving a liberal construction to the Constitution. "He is," wrote John Quincy Adams in his diary, "above all sectional and factious prejudices, more than any other statesman of this Union with whom I have ever acted." He was then "a man of fair and candid mind, of enlarged philosophical views, and of ardent patriotism." But, according to the same keen observer, that was when Calhoun felt sanguine as to his prospects for the presidency; and this hope had a reasonable basis, for the Northern States in 1824 voted almost in a body for him for Vice-President. Even Webster at one time

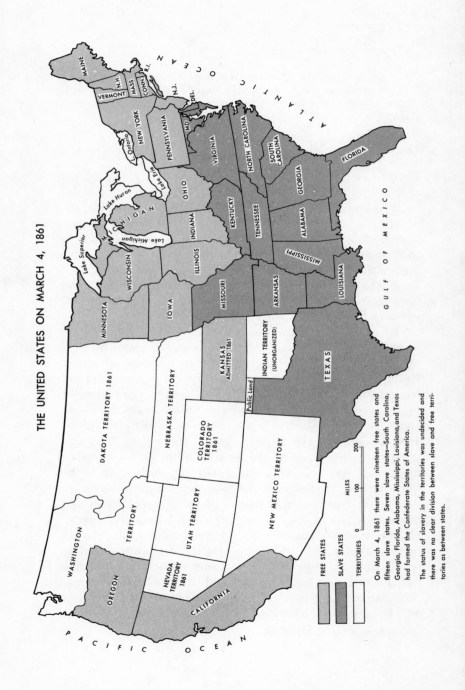

THE UNITED STATES ON MARCH 4, 1861

On March 4, 1861 there were nineteen free states and fifteen slave states. Seven slave states—South Carolina, Georgia, Florida, Alabama, Mississippi, Louisiana, and Texas had formed the Confederate States of America.

The status of slavery in the territories was undecided and there was no clear division between slave and free territories as between states.

FREE STATES
SLAVE STATES
TERRITORIES

MILES
0   100   200

was strongly inclined to support him for the highest office in the country. In 1828 Calhoun had by no means renounced this ambition. He was candidate for Vice-President on the same ticket with General Jackson; and for another term he hoped to have the influence of the great popular hero in favor of his own elevation to the higher place. He was now drawn in two directions—in one by the sentiment of his own State, in the other by his feeling of nationality and restless craving for the presidency. He would retain his support at the North, and yet he wished to lead the public sentiment of South Carolina. He was equal to the occasion. He did nothing until after election, when he had a handsome majority of the electoral votes for Vice-President; but in December the legislature printed a paper which he had prepared under the title of "The South Carolina Exposition and Protest on the Subject of the Tariff." This was a mild document, and merely a plain argument to show the great injury of a protective tariff to the "staple States"; and while the right of interposing the veto of the State is asserted, no threat is made, but, on the contrary, it is deemed advisable to allow time for further consideration and reflection, in the hope of a returning sense of justice on the part of the majority. After this deliverance the excitement in South Carolina subsided.

The next act of the drama took place in the national theatre. Desiring to know how the country would receive the bare doctrine of nullification, Senator Hayne was put forward to deliver the prologue, but Calhoun was the prompter behind the scenes. Hayne asserted that, in case of a palpable violation of the Constitution by the general government, a State may interpose its veto; that this interposition is constitutional, and the State is to be the sole judge when the federal government transcends its constitutional limit. The senator's speeches were not remarkable, and would never have been remembered, had not his most labored effort given Webster the occasion for one of those rare bursts of eloquence that astonish and delight the world. On the morning of the day when this masterpiece of American oratory was delivered, a fellow-senator said to Webster: "It is a critical moment, and it is time, it is high time, that the people of this country should know what this Constitution *is*." "Then," answered Webster, "by the blessing of Heaven, they shall learn this day before the sun goes down what I understand it to be." An abstract of this speech, which, as a literary production, has been compared to the oration of Demosthenes on the Crown, need not detain us. Webster's oration itself is familiar to students of American history, to lovers of English literature, and to all those whose admiration is kindled by eloquence in any tongues. Its famous peroration was soon declaimed from every college and school platform, and it still retains its place among such pieces of oratory by virtue of its earnest feeling and classic style. A large audience heard the speech, but the interest in the question was so great that the brilliant crowd that gathered in the Senate chamber was but a fraction of the people over whom his words were to have lasting power. He spoke to the whole country, and to the American people of future ages. The principles he laid down are fundamental truths. It took a long war to establish them; but now, sealed in blood, they are questioned by none save Southerners of the past generation.

That the argument crushed nullification was public opinion in the Northern, Western, and many of the Southern States. It settled the question for the moment, and probably would have done so for a generation had not there occurred about this time a complete change in the political fortunes of Calhoun. General Jackson quarrelled with him, and this blasted his hopes for the presidency. Adams called him "a drowning man." He no longer needed to halt between two opinions. He could abandon his national ideas and devote himself to the seeming interests of his native State. His talents were well adapted to the work. The South had special interests based upon her peculiar system of labor. The North was growing much faster than the South, and the large immigration from Europe, just beginning, was being directed entirely to the free States. The

South attracted none of this, for the reason that freemen would not work with slaves. The stubborn fact came home to every Southern politician that she was losing political power. A theory of the Constitution was therefore needed which should give the minority an absolute check on the majority. Calhoun was by nature and education as well fitted to construct a narrow and sectional hypothesis as Webster was adapted to develop a broad national one. After 1830, we look in vain to Calhoun for any exhibition of that pervasive patriotism that was so distinguishing a feature in the characters of Webster, Clay, and Jackson.

Calhoun now bent all his energies to the task, and worked out the fine-spun theory of nullification. He elaborated it in subtle language, and supported it by ingenious, metaphysical reasoning. Brave in the closet when developing his theories, on the stage of action he shrank from putting them in practice. He became a man of one idea; he lacked that commerce with the world which would have modified the opinions he elaborated in the study. "Calhoun is mind through and through," said Lieber; and Harriet Martineau was struck by his "utter intellectual solitude," by his harangues at the fireside as if he were in the Senate, and, observing that he was full of his nullification doctrine, wrote, "I never saw any one who so completely gave me the idea of possession." An impracticable theorist, he neglected the obvious application of his country's Constitution, of the constitutions of the different States, and of the English Constitution. . . . William Lloyd Garrison began the abolitionist movement by the establishment of the *Liberator* at Boston, January 1st, 1831. Although he had for several years been advocating anti-slavery ideas, his denunciations of slavery had attracted as little attention at the national capital as Paul's preaching excited in the palace of the Cæsars. At this time, in the slave States, the opinion prevailed that slavery in the abstract was an evil. Miss Martineau conversed with many hundreds of persons in the South on the subject, but she met only one person who altogether defended the institution. Everybody justified its present existence, but did so on the ground of the impossibility of its abolition, although forecasts were sometimes given of the position the South would in the future be forced to take. Senator Hayne, in the celebrated debate, argued that slavery in the abstract was no evil; but, in the course of the same discussion, Benton had addressed himself to the people of the North and with truthful emphasis assured them that "slavery in the abstract had but few advocates or defenders in the slave-holding states." The sentiment at the North was well portrayed by Webster in his reply to Hayne. "The slavery of the South," he said, "has always been regarded as a matter of domestic policy left with the States themselves, and with which the federal government had nothing to do. . . . I regard domestic slavery as one of the greatest evils, both moral and political. But whether it be a malady and whether it be curable, and if so, by what means; or, on the other hand, whether it be the *vulnus immedicabile* of the social system, I leave it to those whose right and duty it is to inquire and decide. And this I believe is, and uniformly has been, the sentiment of the North."

More than forty years had now passed since the establishment of the government. The hopes of its founders had not been realized, for the number of slaves was fast increasing; slavery had waxed strong and had become a source of great political and social power. While optimists, looking for a sign from heaven and a miracle, hoped that, by some occult process, the slaves would be freed voluntarily by the next generation, the abolitionists believed that reform from within the system could not be expected, but that its destruction must come from influences from the outside. The vital point was to convince the Northern people that negro slavery was a concern of theirs; that as long as it existed in the country without protest on their part, they were partners in the evil; and although debarred from legislative interference with the system, that was no reason why they should not think right on the subject, and bear testimony without ceasing against its hateful character.

The apostle who had especial fitness for the work, and who now came forward to embody this feeling and rouse the national conscience from the stupor of great material prosperity, was Garrison. Adopting the Stoic maxim, "My country is the world," he added its corollary, "My countrymen are all mankind," and with the change of *my* to *our* he made it the motto of the *Liberator*. In his salutatory address he said: "I shall strenuously contend for the immediate enfranchisement of our slave population. . . . *I will be* as harsh as truth and as uncompromising as justice. . . . I am in earnest—I will not equivocate—I will not excuse—I will not retreat a single inch—and I will be heard." In one of the succeeding issues he said: "Everybody is opposed to slavery, O, yes! there is an abundance of philanthropy among us. . . . I take it for granted slavery *is* a crime—a damning crime; therefore, my efforts shall be directed to the exposure of those who practise it." Soon the *Liberator* appeared with a pictorial heading that displayed the national capitol, floating from whose dome was a flag inscribed "Liberty"; in the foreground is seen a negro, flogged at a whipping-post, and the misery of a slave auction. This journal began in poverty; but in the course of the first year the subscription list reached five hundred. Garrison wrote the leading articles and then assisted to set them up in type and did other work of the printer.

In August of this year (1831) occurred the Nat Turner insurrection in Virginia, which seemed to many Southerners a legitimate fruit of the bold teaching of Garrison, although there was indeed between the two events no real connection. But this negro rising struck terror through the South and destroyed calm reason. The leader, Nat Turner, a genuine African of exceptional capacity, knowing the Bible by heart, prayed and preached to his fellow-slaves. He told them of the voices he heard in the air, of the visions he saw, and of his communion with the Holy Spirit. An eclipse of the sun was a sign that they must rise and slay their enemies who had deprived them of freedom. The massacre began at night and continued for forty-eight hours; women and children were not spared, and before the bloody work was checked sixty-one whites were victims of negro ferocity. The retribution was terrible. Negroes were shot, hanged, tortured, and burned to death, and all on whom suspicion lighted met a cruel fate. In Southampton County, the scene of the insurrection, there was a reign of terror, and alarm spread throughout the slave States.

This event, and the thought that it might be the precursor of others of the same kind, account for much of the Southern rage directed against Garrison and his crusade. Nor, when we reflect on the sparsely settled country, the wide distance between plantations—conditions that made a negro insurrection possible—and when we consider what it was for planters to have hanging over their heads the horrors of a servile war, will it seem surprising that judicial poise of temper was impossible when Southerners discussed the work of Garrison. They regarded it as an incitement for their slaves to revolt. But they did injustice to Garrison, for Nat Turner had never seen a copy of the *Liberator,* and the paper had not a single subscriber south of the Potomac. Nor did Garrison ever send a pamphlet or paper to any slave, nor advocate the right of physical resistance on the part of the oppressed. He was a non-resistant, and did not believe that force should be used to overturn legal authority, even when unjustly and oppressively exercised. The assertion that slavery is a damning crime is one thing; the actual incitement of slaves to insurrection is another. The distinction between the two was not appreciated at the South. Stringent laws were made against the circulation of the *Liberator,* and vigilance committees sent their warnings to any who were supposed to have a part in spreading its doctrines. In North Carolina Garrison was indicted for a felony, and the legislature of Georgia offered a reward of five thousand dollars for the arrest and conviction of the editor or publisher. One voice went abroad from public officials, popular meetings, and from the press of the South, demanding that the governor of

Massachusetts or the mayor of Boston should suppress the "infernal *Liberator*."

The people of Virginia had often struggled to free themselves from the coils of slavery, and the Nat Turner insurrection furnished the occasion for another attempt. At the following session of the Legislature a proposition was made to inquire into the expediency of some plan of gradual emancipation. In the debate that took place on the subject, the evil of slavery was characterized in terms as strong as an abolitionist could have used. The alarm excited all over the South by the negro rising in Southampton County was not, one member explained, from the fear of Nat Turner, but it was on account of "the suspicion eternally attached to the slave himself—a suspicion that a Nat Turner might be in every family, that the same bloody deed might be acted over at any time, and in any place; that the materials for it were spread through the land, and were always ready for a like explosion."

But a majority of the House of Representatives, in which the project was discussed, could not be had for ordering an inquiry, and the further consideration of the subject was indefinitely postponed. It has sometimes been asserted that had not the abolitionist agitation begun, this Virginia movement would have resulted in the gradual emancipation of slaves in that state; but there is, in truth, no reason for thinking that anything more would have come of it than from previous abortive attempts in the same direction. On many pages of Virginia history may one read of noble efforts by the noble men towards freeing their State from slavery. But the story of the end is a repeated tale; the seeds sown fell among thorns, and the thorns sprung up and choked them.

Meanwhile Garrison and his little band continued the uphill work of proselyting at the North, and especially in Boston. Merchants, manufacturers, and capitalists were against the movement, for trade with the South was important, and they regarded the propagation of abolition sentiments as injurious to the commercial interests of Boston. Good society turned the back upon the abolitionists. Garrison had no college education to recommend him to an aristocracy based partly upon wealth and partly upon culture. The churches were bitterly opposed to the movement. . . .

Meanwhile, a champion for the abolition cause appeared in the House of Representatives in one who had gained reputation in the field of diplomacy, whose many years as Secretary of State had caused to shine more brightly the lustre he had ac-quired abroad, who had served with honor one term as Presi-dent, but to whose destiny it fell to win his greatest renown and to render the country his greatest service in the popular branch of Congress. This was John Quincy Adams. He had from time to time presented petitions for the abolition of slavery and the slave-trade in the District of Columbia, and they had gone through the usual parliamentary forms without remark. But they were coming too thick and fast for Southern sentiments, and in January, 1836, when Adams presented a petition in the usual language, a member from Georgia moved that it be not received. A heated discussion of some days followed, and months were spent in the concoction of a scheme by which these abolition ideas might be excluded from the halls of Congress. The result was the adoption of the famous gag rule. This pro-vided that whereas the agitation of the subject was disquieting and objectionable, "all petitions, memorials, resolutions, or papers relating in any way, or to any extent whatsoever, to the subject of slavery or the abolition of slavery, shall, without being either printed or referred, be laid upon the table, and that no further action whatever shall be had thereon."

This, for the Southern leaders, was the beginning of the madness that the gods send upon men whom they wish to destroy; for, instead of making the fight on the merits of the question, they shifted the ground. Had they simply resisted the abolition of slavery in the District, the vast preponderance of Northern sentiment would have been with them; but, with a fatuitous lack of foresight, they put Adams in a position where his efforts in the anti-slavery cause were completely over-shadowed in his contest for the right of petition. At each session of Congress, "the old man eloquent," for he had gained this name, presented petition after petition for the abolition of slavery and the slave-trade in the District of Columbia, and each time they were disposed of under the gag rule. The anti-slavery people of the country, fully alive to the fact that a representative had appeared who would present such prayers, busied themselves in getting up and forwarding to him peti-tions, and those he presented must be numbered by thousands, and they were signed by 300,000 petitioners. Never had there been such a contest on the floors of Congress. One man, with no followers and no adherents, was pitted against all the represent-atives from the South. It was a contest that set people to think-ing. The question could not fail to be asked, If the slave power now demands that the right of petition must be sacrificed, what will be the next sacred republican principle that must be given up in obedience to its behests? Yet the merchants and manu-facturers of Boston had no sympathy with the efforts of Adams; they did not approve of his stirring up the question. But the district he represented was the Plymouth, and, true to the sacred memories of freedom its name suggests, its voters sent him for eight successive terms to the House, and he died there with the harness on his back.

Adams was a master of sarcasm and invective, and his use of these weapons of argument was unsparing and effective. A man without friends, his enemies were many. While not an orator in the highest sense of the term, he was ever ready to speak, and kept a cool head in the midst of the heat and excitement that his efforts aroused. His is a character on whom the historian would fain linger. His honesty of purpose and fearless bearing atone manifold for his cold heart and repellent exterior. It is not given to us to see many public men as we see John Quincy Adams. In his famous diary he jots down his impressions of men and events, and discloses his inmost thoughts and feel-ings. His record is a crucial test of character. No one can rise

WINGATE COLLEGE LIBRARY
WINGATE, N. C.

from a perusal of that diary without an increased feeling of admiration for the man. We may discern foibles we had not looked for, but we see with greater force the virtues. The honesty, the sincerity and strength of character give us a feeling of pride that such a man was an American.

While Adams appeared with a bold front in public, he was in reality torn by conflicting emotions. He confides to his diary: "The abolitionists generally are constantly urging me to indiscreet movements which would ruin me, and weaken and not strengthen their cause. My own family, on the other hand, exercise all the influence they possess to restrain and divert me from all connection with the abolitionists and their cause. Between these adverse impulses my mind is agitated almost to distraction. The public mind in my own district and State is convulsed between the slavery and abolition questions, and I walk on the edge of a precipice in every step that I take." Another entry made in the diary in the same year is a faithful representation of the state of public opinion on what had now become the all-absorbing question. "It is also to be considered," he wrote, "that at this time the most dangerous of all the subjects for public contention is the slavery question. In the South it is a perpetual agony of conscious guilt and terror, attempting to disguise itself under sophistical argumentation and braggart menaces. In the North the people favor the whites and fear the blacks of the South. The politicians court the South because they want their votes. The abolitionists are gathering themselves into societies, increasing their numbers, and in zeal they kindle the opposition against themselves into a flame; and the passions of the populace are all engaged against them."

In 1837, Webster, in a speech at New York, described the anti-slavery sentiment of the country in felicitous words. "The subject" (of slavery), said he, "has not only attracted attention as a question of politics, but it has struck a far deeper-toned chord. It has arrested the religious feeling of the country; it has taken strong hold on the consciences of men. He is a rash man indeed, and little conversant with human nature, and especially has he a very erroneous estimate of the character of the people of this country, who supposes that a feeling of this kind is to be trifled with or despised." It no longer required the martyr spirit to be an abolitionist in the eastern part of the country, and yet there were few accessions from the influential part of the community. It was an affair of great moment, when Wendell Phillips and Edmund Quincy, representatives of the wealth, culture, and highest social position of Boston, joined the anti-slavery society. Wendell Phillips became an abolitionist from seeing Garrison dragged through the streets of Boston by a mob; and Quincy's action was decided by the martyrdom of Lovejoy, who persisted in publishing an anti-slavery paper at Alton, Ill., and was shot down by a pro-slavery mob. . . .

The Thirty-second Congress met on December 1st. There was little change in the relative strength of the political parties in the Senate; the Democrats had made a slight gain. Charles Sumner, of Massachusetts, and Benjamin F. Wade, of Ohio, took their seats in the Senate; they resembled each other in nothing but personal courage and hatred of slavery. Sumner was a graduate of Harvard, a representative of the culture of Boston, and the intimate friend of nearly every one of that brilliant set of scholars, poets, and *literati* to whose productions during the twenty years before the civil war we may point with a just feeling of pride. Himself a ripe scholar, he loved the classics; he was a profound student of history, delving into the past so earnestly that his desire to visit the old countries grew into a passion. He went abroad furnished with letters from the wise and influential of America to the men of distinction across the sea, and returned with a mind broadened by contact with the thinkers, writers, and politicians of Europe. He had charming manners and rare social accomplishments; he and Chase were considered the handsomest men in the Senate. A favorite child of fortune, kind friends ever stood ready to give their help; opportunities were made for him. Sumner was not a great lawyer; the bent of his mind was towards politics rather than law. Possessed of strong moral feelings, politics especially attracted him on account of the moral element that now entered into public questions. From an early day he had hated slavery; the *Liberator* was the first paper he had ever subscribed for, having read it since 1835, yet he was opposed to Garrison's doctrines on the Constitution and the Union. A Whig until 1848, he then became a Free-soiler, and by a well-managed coalition of the Free soilers and Democrats he was this year elected senator.

Benjamin F. Wade, also a son of New England, was in character of the rugged heroic type. Born of poor parents, he worked on the western Massachusetts farm in the summer, and had only the common schooling of two or three months in the winter. His religious education was wholly under the guidance of his pious mother; he read the Bible with diligence, and knew the Westminster Catechism by heart. When twenty-one, he went to Ohio and took up his home on the Western Reserve. The problem then with him was how to get a living in this new rough country. He worked as a drover and as a common laborer; but finally deciding to adopt law as a profession, he studied in a lawyer's office, was admitted to the bar, and was fortunate in forming a partnership with Joshua R. Giddings, a leading lawyer in northeastern Ohio. Only by a strong effort of the will was Wade able to overcome his constitutional diffidence in public speaking, which at the outset threatened to defeat his intention of becoming an advocate; but he grew to be a vigorous speaker.

His second legal associate, Rufus P. Ranney, became the best lawyer and soundest judge of Ohio, taking rank with the most carefully trained legal minds of the country. The bar of the Western Reserve was an able body of men; they had but few law-books, and those they mastered; their literature was the Bible and Shakespeare, and their forensic contests were apt displays of logic, invective, and wit. In that community influence went for nothing; if a man rose to the top it was through ability and industry. In those days the best lawyers went to the legislature and sat on the bench. There they took great interest in the enactment of necessary measures, and were careful that the phraseology should be simple and exact, considering the deliberate yet positive expounding of the law a grave and solemn duty. It was an honor to be a member of the legislature, and an honor to be a judge.

Wade had been a State circuit judge, had served in the legislature, and was this year elected to the Senate as a Whig of well-known anti-slavery principles. He was thoroughly honest; his manners were rough, and his style of address was abrupt.

There were now five men in the Senate who, though differing in party antecedents, were ready to work together in opposing the extension of slavery: Seward, of New York; Chase and Wade, of Ohio; Sumner, of Massachusetts; and Hale, of New Hampshire. Their ages were respectively fifty, forty-three, fifty-one, and forty-five. The absence of Benton from this Senate was conspicuous; after thirty years of eminent service he had failed to secure a re-election because he would not sacrifice his principles one jot at the dictation of the pro-slavery Democrats of Missouri.

ZACHARY TAYLOR, *the rough-and-ready general elected by the Whigs on a wave of popular emotion for a war hero, announced that he meant to leave legislation to Congress, an astonishing (and untenable) abdication of power. He had neither political experience nor knowledge of government, and even his best friends expected little of him. He appointed a commonplace Cabinet that was totally unable to give him guidance or fruitful counsel. The result was that Senator William M. Seward of New York, who with his associate Thurlow Weed had a tremendous fund of political experience and savoir faire, and who was as tactful as he was shrewd, became Taylor's principal adviser. He knew just how to make himself useful to the green president. Then, too, New York was the Empire State, and a great deal of Whig Party strength resided there.*

By 1850 the organization of territorial government in California and the Utah–New Mexico region could no longer be postponed. Gold had been discovered in California, a flood of settlers had poured in, and President Taylor among others felt that mere justice demanded action. But questions of the gravest importance were bound up in any legislation. Wilmot's Proviso of 1846 had not passed, but it had angered and frightened the South. It had called forth from Calhoun a set of resolutions asserting that slaves, as property, could not be barred from any territory under the American flag. A question of equilibrium was also involved. The annexation of Texas had given the Union fifteen slave states to thirteen free states. Then the admission of Oregon and Wisconsin had restored a balance. What of the doctrine of sectional equality if California entered, as seemed certain, as another free state?

Since the President could offer little leadership, the problem went to Congress. Above all, it went into the Senate, where the debate was conducted by four leaders of the passing generation, Henry Clay, Calhoun, Webster, and Thomas Hart Benton, and by some energetic young spirits, the chief being Jefferson Davis and Stephen A. Douglas. Every clear-headed man knew that sectional schism would wreck the Union. To avert such a breach, Clay claimed the

*center of the stage at the beginning of 1850. He
offered a comprehensive plan, based upon various
pieces of legislation already introduced, and embracing features that balanced the gains and losses of
the Free Soil area and the slaveholding area.*

*Rhodes tells his story of the ensuing parliamentary
battle as a warm sympathizer with the antislavery
cause, declaring that such a sympathizer "can most
truly write the story." Subsequent historians have
been less partisan. They have given due weight to the
honest apprehensions that dominated such Southern
leaders as Calhoun, Robert Toombs, and Alexander
H. Stephens. They feared what Toombs called "degradation and injury" in their political and economic
position and, more fundamentally, that the nation
might take precipitate measures giving the Negro a
premature social equality with Southern whites. Recent historians have laid greater emphasis upon the
incompetence of the Taylor administration, the un-
reasonableness of both radical Northerners and fire-
eating Southerners, and the wisdom of the moderates
who rallied behind Clay. It was these moderates,
supported by such journals as the* National Intelligencer *and the* Union *in Washington, and the*
Tribune *in New York, who carried the day for the
Compromise. Recent histories have also allotted
Douglas a larger credit for the result than Rhodes gave
him. They have been as emphatic as Rhodes, however, in their commendation of the statesmanlike
stand by Webster and in their praise of his brave
Seventh-of-March Speech, so unjustly condemned by
the poet Whittier.*

The Struggle over the
Compromise of 1850

ZACHARY TAYLOR was inaugurated March 5th, 1849. He was
sincerely honest, a man of good judgment, pure morals, great
energy, of independent and manly character, and possessed

rare moral as well as physical courage. He had little education and many prejudices. But he was in every sense of the word a patriot and nothing of a partisan. Doubt had for a time, indeed, prevailed regarding his political opinions, for he had never voted. The party managers induced him to say, finally, that he was a Whig; but General Taylor at the same time insisted that if elected "he would not be the President of a party, but the President of the whole people."

He was, as we have seen, nominated by the regular Whig convention; but while the campaign was in progress he had discomfited his Northern adherents by accepting the nomination of a Democratic meeting at Charleston, which preferred him to Cass, as he was deemed safer on the slavery question. Taylor was from Louisiana, and owned a large sugar plantation there, with several hundred slaves. As the Whig convention had adopted no declaration of principles, what course the newly-elected President would take on the question of slavery in the territories was problematical. It had, however, been asserted with confidence at the North during the campaign that he would not veto any anti-slavery legislation which should receive the assent of congress. While the President, in his inaugural address, did not touch upon the question which had distracted the legislature of the country, nevertheless his guarded expressions seemed to indicate that his Northern supporters had fairly outlined his policy. But his cabinet appointments were favorable to the Southern section of his party; four of them were from the slave and three from the free States. The prominent members were John M. Clayton, of Delaware, Secretary of State; Thomas Ewing, of Ohio, Secretary of the Interior; Reverdy Johnson, of Maryland, Attorney-General; and Jacob Collamer, of Vermont, Postmaster-General. Collamer was the only man of marked anti-slavery sentiments.

The problem which the country had to solve called for its wisest statesmanship. It demanded the full measure of the time and ability of the President and his advisers, but they were not able to devote their attention immediately to the exigency of the State. The executive power had passed from one political party to the other; the Democrats, therefore, must be turned out of the offices to make room for the faithful Whigs. "To the victors belong the spoils" was a doctrine first put in practice by the Democratic party. But the Whigs were apt pupils, and as there were about fifty thousand places in the civil service, a horde of hungry office-seekers flocked to Washington. General Taylor was a man of business habits. His long service in the army, and his experience in the management of a large plantation, had taught him that merit and fitness were the proper and only tests that should be applied to subordinates, and his mind was still firm in this conviction when he delivered his inaugural address. He said: "I shall make honesty, capacity, and fidelity indispensable prerequisites to the bestowal of office." Although the President had good business ideas, he was ignorant of party management, and soon allowed himself to be guided by those who had all their lives wrought in the sphere of practical politics. General Taylor had a high respect for the Vice-President, Millard Fillmore, of New York, and, until undeceived a short time before his arrival at Washington, he thought that the Vice-President could be *ex officio* a member of his cabinet. He was nevertheless disposed to rely upon the experience of Fillmore in all important matters, and nothing at first seemed so important as the New York patronage. But in this State there were two divisions of the Whig party, one headed by Fillmore and the other by William H. Seward, who had recently been elected to the Senate; and, to forestall differences that might naturally arise, Thurlow Weed, a common friend, had them both dine with him at Albany when they were on their way to Washington. "Here," as Weed himself relates, "everything was pleasantly arranged. The Vice-President and the Senator were to consult from time to time, as should become necessary, and agree upon the important appointments to be made in our State." Fillmore, however, seems to have had the better of the arrangement; for the first knowledge that came to Seward of the New York custom-house appointments was when their names were read in executive session of the Senate.

The President also appointed anti-Seward Whigs to other lucrative offices in the State. Seward, as Lincoln afterwards said, "was a man without gall," and did not openly resent the infraction of the agreement. He did not retire to his tent, but patiently bided his time. He voted for the confirmation of his adversaries, and then went to work with serenity to supplant his rival in the favor of the President. In this he was much assisted by his friend Weed, who had great influence, for he was one of the first to look to General Taylor as a presidential candidate. Their efforts were successful, and soon Seward became the directing spirit of the administration.

Thurlow Weed relates with great satisfaction that the President "became convinced that the significance of a zealous and patriotic movement of the people, which overthrew Democratic supremacy, meant something more than the election of a Whig President and the appointment of a Whig cabinet." "I did not think it wise or just," the President himself remarked, "to kick away the ladder by which I ascended to the presidency; colonels, majors, captains, lieutenants, sergeants, and corporals are just as necessary to success in politics as they are to the discipline and efficiency of an army." On another occasion the President inquired of the Secretary of the Treasury "whether you think our friends are getting their share of the offices." The Secretary answered that he "had not thought of the matter in that light." "Nor," rejoined the President, "have I until recently. But if the country is to be benefited by our services, it seems to me that you and I ought to remember those to whose zeal, activity, and influence we are indebted for our places. There are plenty of Whigs, just as capable and honest, and quite as deserving of office, as the Democrats who have held them through two or three presidential terms. Rotation in office, provided good men are appointed, is sound Republican doctrine."

The Democratic newspapers of the day are full of derisive

taunts at the wholesale removals from office. The Whigs either defended them as the work of reform, or else retorted by recriminations. Yet many of the leading Whigs were far from being satisfied. Clay complained that the good positions went to those who had been instrumental in bringing about the nomination of General Taylor,* and Webster grieved bitterly over the refusal of the administration to grant his request for an office of "small pecuniary consideration" for his only son. Abraham Lincoln was an urgent applicant for the office of Commissioner of the General Land Office. He solicited support from his late friends in Congress, and endeavored to have his claim advocated in the party newspapers, but his efforts were without fruit. The Postmaster-General Collamer, in a letter to his friend John J. Crittenden, laments not having been able to carry out Crittenden's wishes in reference to the appointment of the local mail agent at Louisville. But the President had taken the matter out of his hands, and as he was "but a subaltern," he had to obey. The Secretary of State found fault with Collamer, and wrote: "Our friend Collamer is behind; he is a glorious fellow, but *too tender* for progress. He has been often, indeed, at his wits' end, frightened about removals and appointments, but I cry courage to them all, and they will go ahead *all*, by and by! Taylor has all the moral as well as physical courage needed for the emergency." Yet the President, whose knowledge of literature went not "much beyond good old Dilworth's spelling-book," unwittingly did the cause of letters a great service in the removal of Nathaniel Hawthorne from the surveyorship of the Salem custom-house, for on the afternoon of the day on which the gifted author was deprived of his place he began to write "The Scarlet Letter." He lost his salary of twelve hundred dollars a year, but he gave to his country its greatest romance.

While Congress was still in session Calhoun was busy in working up a sentiment that should fire the Southern heart with

* Clay's *Private Correspondence,* p. 587. "It is undeniable that the public patronage has been too exclusively confined to the original supporters of General Taylor, without sufficient regard to the merits and just claims of the great body of the Whig party."

zeal to defend the rights which were in supposed jeopardy. A convention of Southern members of Congress issued an address drawn up by Calhoun. In this declaration they complained of the difficulties in recovering fugitive slaves; they found fault with the systematic agitation of the slavery question by the abolitionists; they demanded the right of emigrating into the territories with their slaves; and they inveighed bitterly against the House for its action in regard to New Mexico and California. More than eighty members participated in the meeting when this address was adopted, but only about half of that number affixed their signatures to the instrument. It was published throughout the South with a flourish of trumpets; and soon it was hailed by its authors as the second declaration of independence. Except in South Carolina, however, the address did not make a deep impression. For the moment Calhoun seemed to have lost influence. His intellectual vagaries had become tiresome, and his over-refinement of phrase proved tedious even to those whose sympathy was ardent with the Southern cause.

Of greater moment were the resolutions of the Virginia legislature. They affirmed that "the adoption and attempted enforcement of the Wilmot proviso" would present two alternatives to the people of Virginia; one of "abject submission to aggression and outrage," and the other "of determined resistance at all hazards and to the last extremity." The sovereign people of Virginia, as they valued their rights of property and dearest privileges, could have no difficulty in making a choice between the two alternatives. It was likewise resolved that the abolition of slavery or of the slave-trade in the District of Columbia would be a direct attack upon the institution of the Southern States. These resolutions were carried by a large majority; and this official utterance of the most powerful State in the South was an incitement to Southern feeling and a guide to the way of evincing it. The resolutions were approved at many public meetings held over the South; they were endorsed by several Democratic state conventions; and they formed the basis of similar expressions from other legislatures.

The excitement was especially great in Missouri. The legislature of this State had passed resolutions protesting against the principle of the Wilmot proviso, and instructing her senators and representatives to act in hearty co-operation with the members from the slave-holding States. This was a shaft aimed at Senator Benton, who was opposed to the extension of slavery. He accepted the challenge, repaired to Missouri when the Senate adjourned, and made a noble fight against the slavery extensionists. He spoke at meeting after meeting, defending his own course and making an aggressive warfare on Calhoun and his Missouri disciples.

The feeling was at fever heat in Tennessee. The address of the Democratic State Central Committee to the voters said, "The encroachments of our Northern brethren have reached a point where forbearance on our part ceases to be a virtue." In Kentucky, Clay had written a letter intended to influence the constitutional convention about to assemble, in which he favored a plan of gradual emancipation of the slaves in his State. A people's meeting held in Trimble County, Ky., requested him to resign his place as senator in consequence of the sentiments avouched in this letter. The question of freeing the slaves was made an issue and discussed in every county of the State, but not one avowed emancipationist was elected to the convention. The convention itself not only failed to adopt any plan of gradual emancipation, but, on the contrary, the new constitution asserted, in the strongest terms, the right of property in slaves and their increase.

In the cotton States the feeling was more intense than in the border States. The Virginia resolutions were everywhere endorsed. The prevailing sentiment of South Carolina was shown at a dinner to Senator Butler, when "Slavery," "Our territorial acquisitions from Mexico," and "A Southern Confederacy" were toasted amid great enthusiasm. The Democrats were more outspoken than the Whigs, but party lines were beginning to be merged and swallowed up in the community of sectional interest. Yet the Northern Whigs tried to think that they and the

Southern members of their party could meet on a common ground. The New York *Tribune* maintained that "the Southern Whigs want the great question settled in such a manner as shall not humble and exasperate the South; the Southern Locofocos (i. e., Democrats) want it so settled as to conduce to the extension of the power and influence of slavery." But, in truth, when a question of practical legislation arose, the interest of section was stronger than the hold of party.

The feeling in the North was as deeply stirred as in the South. The conflict of sentiment was well shown in the reception given to the letter of Clay which favored the gradual emancipation of the slaves in Kentucky. In the North it was universally approved; in the South, outside of his own State, it was just as emphatically condemned. Every one of the legislatures of the free States, except Iowa, passed resolutions to the effect that Congress had the power, and that it was its duty, to prohibit slavery in the territories. Many States also requested their senators and representatives to use their utmost influence to abolish slavery and the slave-trade in the District of Columbia. Party lines were not considered; they had no influence upon this action. Some of the legislatures were strongly Whig; in others the Democrats were greatly in the ascendant. But the parties seemed to vie with each other in taking advanced anti-slavery ground, and in some of the legislatures the resolutions were passed by a nearly unanimous vote. As a body, the Whigs were more pronounced in their views than were the regular Democrats. Greeley maintained that the Whigs of New York State recognized "the restriction of slavery within its present limits as one of the cardinal principles of our political faith," but the Free-soilers, comprising for the most part those who had supported Van Buren the previous year, were strenuous in their demands that the general government should forbid slavery where it had the power. Charles Sumner came to the front in a Free-soil convention at Worcester, Mass., and wrote the vigorous address which proclaimed "opposition to slavery wherever we are responsible for it," demanded its prohibition in the new territories, and its abolition in the District of Columbia. The Democrats of Ohio felt very powerfully the impulse of the anti-slavery movement, and in February the legislature, by a combination of two Free-soilers, who held the balance of power, with the Democrats, elected Salmon P. Chase to the United States Senate. He was a strong opposer of slavery; was of partially Democratic antecedents, and had presided over the Free-soil convention which nominated Van Buren for the presidency. At Cleveland an enthusiastic convention of Free-soilers was held on the 13th of July to celebrate the passage of the Ordinance of 1787. Clay was invited to be present, but declined on account of other engagements; he seemed to think, however, that the commemoration was ill-timed as being liable "to increase the prevailing excitement."

General Cass tried to stem the current of popular opinion in the West. He held that Congress had no right to legislate upon slavery in the territories; and, while the legislature of Michigan elected him to the Senate—for they could not forget the part he had played in the material development and civil organization of their State—yet the same body of men resolved that Congress ought to prohibit slavery in New Mexico and California. The Cleveland *Plain Dealer,* which had loyally supported Cass for President, expressed the opinion of the majority of Ohio Democrats when it declared that "the institution of slavery is bound to be the death of Democracy in this country, unless the Democratic party as a body eschew its requirements."

The position which President Taylor was gradually taking proved a source of gratification to the anti-slavery people. When he came to Washington his Southern sympathies were strong, and he had the notion that the Northerners were encroaching on the rights of the South. A short experience in the executive office served to convince him that the encroachment was from the opposite direction, and he had the manliness to act contrary to the supposed interests of his own section. The influence of Seward, moreover, was a potent factor in the President's actual envisagement of the situation. Complaint had been made at the

South that a majority of the cabinet were in favor of the principle of the Wilmot proviso; and this dissatisfaction was heightened by a speech of the President at Mercer, Pa., in August, when he said: "The people of the North need have no apprehension of the further extension of slavery; the necessity of a third party organization on this score would soon be obviated." State and congressional elections took place during the spring, summer, and fall, but they afforded no indication of the direction of popular sentiment. On the whole, the Whigs lost some advantages as compared with the Presidential election. Party divisions were rigidly observed, but the slavery question was nowhere at issue in any of the States at the North. The Van Buren and the Cass Democrats had generally united on the State tickets—in some States on an anti-slavery platform, in others by ignoring the national question. The New York *Tribune,* however, explained that the result of the elections in Tennessee and Kentucky was due to the fact that the Whigs "were cried down in those States as an anti-slavery party." It is indubitable that the Northern sentiment was wholesome and thoroughly imbued with the desire to check the extension of slavery.

Towards the latter part of the year speculations as to the action of Congress began to be made; the opinion prevailed that at the next session the question would be settled, and there was little doubt of its settlement in a manner that would satisfy Northern sentiment. It seemed as if this feeling needed only discretion in its guidance, and nerve in the assertion of its claims, to become embodied in legislative acts that should fix the vital principle at issue.

Meanwhile, from action which was taking place in California, one bone of contention seemed likely to be removed. After this territory had been taken possession of by the Americans, it was placed under a quasi-military government, and this was continued after the treaty of peace was proclaimed. Before his inauguration General Taylor had been anxious that Congress should decide upon some plan of government for

California; he said that "he desired to substitute the rule of law and order there for the bowie-knife and revolvers." A month after his inauguration he sent T. Butler King, a Whig congressman from Georgia, to California, as a confidential agent of the administration, to assist the growing movement towards the formation of a State government, and to work in conjunction with the military governor. California, which, when acquired, had been deemed an insignificant province, had now become the El Dorado of the world. Nine days before the treaty of peace between the United States and Mexico was signed, gold was discovered in the foot-hills of the Sierras. Only a few persons in California were aware of the find, and none in the United States or Mexico knew of it when the treaty was ratified. "The accursed thirst of gold" was to work out the destiny of this territory; but it was not until well into May, 1848, that scepticism in San Francisco gave way to faith in this discovery. By the middle of the summer the news was believed everywhere, and from all parts people flocked to the gold diggings. When it became known at Monterey, Colton relates that every one began to make preparations to go to the mines. Blacksmiths, carpenters, masons, farmers, bakers, tapsters, boarding-house keepers, soldiers, and domestics—all left their occupations. That writer, who was the alcalde of Monterey, reports that he only had a community of women left, a gang of prisoners, and a few soldiers.* So it was everywhere in the territory. The country was in a state of frenzy. The hunger of wealth had taken hold of the whole population. Laborers demanded ten dollars a day and carpenters sixteen dollars. Privates from the army and sailors from the naval ships deserted and repaired to the gold diggings. A private could make more money in the mines in a day than he received in the service in a month.

At that time it required about forty days for the transmission of the mails from San Francisco to New York. The fabu-

---

* "A general of the U. S. Army, the commander of a man-of-war, and Alcalde of Monterey, in a smoking kitchen, grinding coffee, toasting a herring, and peeling onions!" *Three Years in California,* Colton, p. 248.

lous stories were at first doubted in the eastern part of the country, but were soon accepted with fervid belief. The news had soon reached all parts of the civilized world, and then began an emigration to California for which nowhere could there be found a likeness save in a tale of legendary Greece. The thirsters after gold, the seekers of El Dorado, were Argonauts in search of the golden fleece. Yet the resemblance fails when we come to consider the character of the California emigrants. While they numbered many good men, especially from the Western States, there were many outlaws and criminals among them. From all parts of the world outcasts and vagrants swelled the crowd that undertook the hardships of the dangerous journey for the sake of bettering their condition and their fortunes. In truth, the journey was one that only the hardy could endure. If the emigrant chose to go by sailing vessel from New York around Cape Horn, he had to brave the perils and discomforts of the most dangerous of ocean voyages. He could, indeed, go by the Isthmus of Panama, but, as the railroad was not then built, the crossing of the isthmus was attended with great hazard. Arriving at Panama, on the Pacific side, the travellers had to wait for days, and even weeks, in an atmosphere whose every breath was laden with pestilential spores. On more than one occasion, when the steamship arrived which was to take them to the Golden Gate, it was found that the expectant passengers largely exceeded the capacity of the boat, and men scrambled and fought to get on board to secure their paid-for passage.

There was still left the overland route. This was a wagon journey of more than two thousand miles, through a country of great variety in its physical features. Warm, pleasant valleys were succeeded by bleak and almost impassable mountains; thence the route proceeded down into miasmatic swamps, then across forbidding alkali wastes and salt flats, baked and cracked by the sun. The travellers were stifled with heat and dust, yet were likewise sure to encounter drenching rains. It was often necessary to cross flooded lowlands and sweeping river currents; as if the misery were not complete, they met with occasional chilling blasts and suffocating simoons. They were not only subject to these changes of climate and altitude, but they were in constant fear of the savages. Whether by starvation, disease, or violence, many of the overland emigrants perished on the way. Nevertheless, in spite of all these obstacles, there arrived in California, in the year 1849, 39,000 souls by sea and 42,000 overland. These were "the inflowing Argonauts," known to this day as "forty-niners," from the year in which they made their journey. Discouraging and conflicting reports came home from the emigrants, but the rush continued; and some years later, in England, the telling pen of De Quincey was enlisted to decry California. "She," said the brilliant Englishman, "is going ahead at a rate that beats Sindbad and Gulliver." Its story reads "to the exchanges of Europe like a page from the 'Arabian Nights.' "*

What was the government of this community? How was law administered? There was the military governor, who had no authority save such as he might choose to assume; and there were the alcaldes, a survival of the Mexican officials, with duties that were partly judicial and partly executive; their business was to maintain order, punish crime, and redress injuries. Some of the old Mexican alcaldes still held their sway, and others had been chosen by the communities over which they presided. Walter Colton was appointed alcalde of Monterey by the commodore of the naval ship which was stationed at that port. But on the whole the territory was bordering on a state of anarchy. There were no land laws; mining titles were disputed and sometimes fought over. A deserted wife at San Francisco complained that there was no power to give her a legal divorce. The habit of carrying weapons was universal;

---

* The romantic side of the California fever did not escape the notice of George Ticknor. He writes to Sir Charles Lyell, in 1849, that it is evidence that there is "in our Anglo-Saxon blood more of a spirit of adventure and romance than belongs to the age."—*Life of George Ticknor*, vol. ii. p. 241. Only three years previously American fellow-travellers of Lyell had told him in their journey from New York to Boston that they hoped to see in their lifetime a population of fifteen thousand souls in California and Oregon. Sir Charles Lyell's *Second Visit*, vol. ii. p. 265.

drunken brawls were common; the Indians made raids on the settled communities and stole horses and cattle; the vineyards and orchards of San José and Santa Clara were destroyed by immigrants; it was complained that San Luis Obispo had become a "complete sink of drunkenness and debauchery"; ruffians united themselves in bands to rob, and the convoys from the mines were their especial prey; murders were common, and lynch law was put into execution not infrequently; yet murder was deemed a lesser time than theft; and when law-breakers were put in prison, the alcalde was in constant fear that a mob would break in and release the prisoners. The cry that went out of Macedonia for help was no louder than that which went from the majority of Californians to Congress to give them a territorial government. Yet, if Congress would not help them, they determined to help themselves. The first immigration was largely from Mexico, Peru, Chili, China, and the Hawaiian Islands, and the food-supply of the miners came in considerable portion from this group. But as the American population increased, and as men of better antecedents joined the fortune-seekers, that knack at political organization which is so prominent a trait of our national character, appeared, and it was determined to establish a civil government. Meetings were held at many places in the territory, and a convention to frame a government was called to meet May 6th, 1849; so that in case Congress adjourned March 4th without making any provision for them, they could go ahead and institute a government of their own. They were assisted in this movement by the military governor and the confidential agent of the administration. Forty-eight members were chosen for the convention, of whom twenty-two were from the Northern States, fifteen from the slave States, seven were native Californians, and four foreign-born. Party or sectional opinions had not entered into the choice of the delegates, but it was supposed that their action would be controlled by Southern men. The meeting of the convention was postponed from time to time; but at last it met at Monterey on the 3d of September, with the object of forming a State. The convention was by no means destitute of ability, although an assemblage of young men. Scarcely a gray head could be seen. There were fourteen lawyers, twelve farmers, seven merchants; the remainder were engineers, bankers, physicians, and printers. The idea of forming an original constitution did not enter into their heads. There were men from various states who were familiar with the provisions of their own organic law; but the Constitution was largely modelled after those of New York and Iowa. To the astonishment of Northern men, no objection whatever was made to the clause in the bill of rights which forever prohibited slavery in the state. The members of the convention worked diligently day and night; on the 13th of October their labors were at an end and they affixed their signatures to the Constitution. One month later it was adopted by the vote of the people. The legislature which it constituted met in December, and by a compromise arrangement, elected John C. Frémont and William M. Gwin senators; Frémont held anti-slavery and Gwin pro-slavery opinions.

When Congress met on the first Monday of December, 1849, the vastly preponderating sentiment in the free States was that California and New Mexico should remain free territory. On the other hand, the sentiment was equally strong in the South against any congressional legislation that should interfere with their supposed right of taking their slaves into the new territories. In other words, a population of thirteen millions demanded that the common possession should be dedicated to freedom; a population of eight millions demanded the privilege of devoting it to slavery. California, by the unanimous vote of a convention regularly chosen, whose action was ratified by an honest vote of her people, had cast her lot on the side of the free States.

Congress met December 3d. The House was made up of 112 Democrats, 105 Whigs, and 13 Free-soilers, and its organization first demanded attention. The candidate of the Whigs for speaker was Winthrop, of Boston, an able and honorable gen-

tleman, of fine birth and breeding, who had been speaker of
the previous Congress. Eight of the Free-soilers, however, under the lead of Joshua R. Giddings, refused their support on
the ground that he had not during his term as speaker recognized the anti-slavery sentiment in the appointment of the
committees, nor would he pledge himself to do so should he be
chosen at this session. Giddings represented a district of northeastern Ohio composed of several of the counties of the Western
Reserve; with the exception of the Plymouth, it was the most
liberty-loving district in the country. He had served many terms
in the House, and had distinguished himself, battling by the
side of John Quincy Adams for the right of petition and for
the anti-slavery cause. Although not a man of great ability, he
had great zeal; and as he felt himself untrammelled by the
shackles of party, he served his district to its full satisfaction,
and made an enviable record as an advocate of freedom. Yet
eleven years of legislative experience had failed to teach him
that, while it is true there are now and then political principles
that must not be bated a jot, even though the heavens fall, it is
equally true that for the most part in public life one should
sacrifice his ideal good for the best attainable. It was so in this
case. If Giddings and his associates had voted for Winthrop,
he would have been chosen speaker. They did not choose to do
so, and finally Howell Cobb, of Georgia, was elected. His devotion to slavery and Southern interests was the distinguishing
feature of his character, and he made up the committees in a
way extremely favorable to the South and the slave interest.
"He loves slavery," said Horace Mann; "it is his politics, his
political economy, and his religion." Horace Mann had gained
a wide and well-deserved reputation as an educator; but on
the death of John Quincy Adams he was prevailed upon to fill
the vacant place of representative of the Plymouth district. He
was wiser than his Ohio colleague, for he voted steadily for
Winthrop "as the best man we could possibly elect." The acme
of logical adherence to a fixed idea, in spite of surrounding
circumstances, was reached when Giddings and his followers

voted for Brown, of Indiana, for speaker, a Democrat of the straitest sect, because he agreed to make the constitution of certain committees satisfactory to them; and that, too, while, as Giddings himself said, "Neither the moral nor political character of Mr. Brown recommended him to the favor of just and honorable men." The balloting for speaker lasted nearly three weeks, and the excitement occasioned by the protracted organization of the House boded no good for the Northern cause. Between the ballots animated discussions sometimes took place, and the Southern bluster was loud and menacing. Disunion was emphatically threatened in case the principle of the Wilmot proviso was insisted upon, or if the attempt were made to abolish slavery in the District of Columbia. Robert Toombs and Alexander Stephens, both Whigs from Georgia, were the most vehement in their threats to the North and their appeals to the South. Contemptuous epithets were bandied to and fro; at one time the lie was given, and only the interference of the sergeant-at-arms with his mace of office prevented a fist-fight on the floor of the House.

As soon as the House was organized, the President sent his message to Congress. He touched briefly on the important question, but his words were carefully weighed. The latest advices from California gave him reason to believe that she had framed a Constitution, established a state government, and would shortly apply for admission into the Union. This application was recommended to the favorable consideration of Congress. It was likewise believed that at a time not far distant the people of New Mexico would present themselves for admission into the Union. He counselled Congress to await their action, for that would avert all causes of uneasiness, and good feeling would be preserved. It was his opinion, moreover, that "we should abstain from the introduction of those exciting topics of sectional character which have hitherto produced painful apprehensions in the public mind."

The great intellectual contest was to take place in the Senate. There Webster, Clay, and Calhoun appeared together for the last time. They were all of them born during the Revolutionary War, and were of that school of statesmen who had the privilege of learning their lessons in constitutional law from the lips of many of the fathers of the government themselves. It was the last scene they were to play upon the political stage; but before they made their exit they saw the entrance of the rising class of statesmen whose mission was to proclaim that slavery was sectional, that freedom was national, and who were more imbued with the sacred notions of liberty that the founders of the republic at first maintained than were Webster and Clay, whose contact had been actual with Jefferson and Adams, with Madison and Marshall. Seward and Chase now appeared in the Senate for the first time, while Hale entered upon his third year of service.

It is now in order to describe Clay more fully. He was a man of large natural ability, but he lacked the training of a systematic education. He learned early to appreciate his heaven-born endowments, and to rely upon them for success in his chosen career. Of sanguine temperament, quick perception, irresistible energy, and enthusiastic disposition, he was well fitted to be a party advocate, and was the greatest parliamentary leader in our history. He was, however, inclined to "crack the whip" over those of his supporters who exhibited a desire to hang back and question whither his impetuous lead would tend. He knew men well, but he had no knowledge of books. The gaming-table had for him allurements that he could not find in the library. According to the manners of his time, he drank to excess. His warm heart made him a multitude of friends; his impulsive action and positive bearing raised up enemies; yet at his death he left not an enemy behind him. He was withal a man of inflexible integrity. Straitened in pecuniary circumstances during a large part of his Congressional career, he nevertheless held himself aloof from all corruption. Other Americans have been intellectually greater, others have been more painstaking, others still have been greater benefactors to their country; yet no man has been loved as the people of the United States loved Henry Clay.

In his declining years his thoughts took on a serious cast, and he embraced the Christian religion. It is noteworthy that he began his speech on the compromise resolutions with words not only solemn, but tinctured with religious fervor. He had not been consistent on the slavery question; yet when we consider that he was a slave-holder and that he represented a slave State, his impulsive outbursts for the cause of freedom are more to be admired than his occasional truckling to the slave power is to be condemned. At this time, he was keenly alive to his own importance. His forty years of public life, in which his name had been identified with measures of the utmost significance, impelled him to think that no legislative act of far-reaching moment would be complete unless he had a hand in its framework. Nearly eight years of retirement had only made him more anxious to act a leading part when he came again upon the scene of action. Before going to Washington, he had been flattered by hearing indirectly that the administration was counting much on his exertions at the approaching session. On his arrival at the capital he was unquestionably disappointed that President Taylor did not receive him with open arms and ask and take his advice regarding the policy of the administration. "My relations to the President," writes Clay, "are civil and amicable, but they do not extend to any confidential consultations in regard to public measures." It is possible that had General Taylor put himself under the guidance of Clay, Clay might himself have adopted the President's plan with some elaboration and extension, but it was contrary to his nature and to the whole course of his life to give unreserved adherence to the scheme of another. He could lead, but he could not follow. Especially was it impossible for him to follow the President, whose political ability he despised; nor could he rid his inmost heart of the notion that Taylor occupied the place which rightfully belonged to himself. A feeling of pique influenced him as he went to work to concoct his scheme; but as he became more deeply engaged in the labor, the overmastering sentiment of his mind was certainly that of sincere patriotism. He believed that the Union was in danger. Such was the constitution of his mind that, while he was blind to the merits of the plan of another, the benefits of his own dazzled him to the sight of all objections. He honestly felt that he was the man beyond all others to devise a scheme which should save the Union. It is true that his talents as a constructive statesman were of high rank. His hope was that this compromise would give peace to the country for thirty years, even as the Missouri Compromise had done. The plan was perfected by the last of January, and on the 29th Clay introduced it into the Senate in the form of a series of resolutions which were intended to be a basis of compromise, and whose object was to secure "the peace, concord, and harmony of the Union." Their provisions were as follows:

1. The admission of California with her free Constitution.

2. As slavery does not exist by law and is not likely to be introduced into any of the territory acquired from Mexico, territorial governments should be established by Congress without any restriction as to slavery.

3. The boundary between Texas and New Mexico, which was in dispute, was determined.

4. Directs the payment of the *bona fide* public debt of Texas contracted prior to the annexation, for which the duties on foreign imports were pledged, upon the condition that Texas relinquish her claim to any part of New Mexico.

5. Declares that it is inexpedient to abolish slavery in the District of Columbia without the consent of Maryland, of the peope of the district, and without just compensation to the owners of slaves.

6. Declares for the prohibition of the slave-trade in the District of Columbia.

7. More effectual provision should be made for the rendition of fugitive slaves.

8. Declares that Congress has no power to interfere with the slave-trade between the States.

A few days after the introduction of the resolutions, Clay obtained the floor of the Senate and made a set speech in their favor. He was a persuasive speaker, his magnetism was great; the impassioned utterance and the action suited to the word aroused the enthusiasm of the moment, and carried everything resistlessly before him, whether he addressed the tumultuous mass-meeting or his cultivated audience of the Senate. Yet he can hardly be ranked as among the half-dozen great orators of the world. It is true that his speeches in print convey no idea of the effect of their delivery, and, in the reading, one loses the whole force of his fine physical presence, and fails to appreciate the strength derived from his supremely nervous temperament. He began in an egotistical vein, referring in the most natural way to his long absence from the Senate, explained that his return was simply "in obedience to a stern sense of duty," and disclaimed any higher object of personal ambition than the position he now occupied. None could doubt his sincerity. He had given up all hope of attaining the presidency, which he had so long and so ardently desired. Age and ill-health, for his body was racked by a cruel cough, served to remind him that the sands of his earthly career were almost run. On this day that he was to speak for the cause of the Union, he was so weak that he could not mount the steps of the Capitol without leaning on the arm of his companion and stopping to rest. Although the floor of the Senate was crowded and the galleries were filled with a brilliant audience of grace, beauty, and intelligence,* his expression of opinion was as honest and frank as if he were talking to a confidential friend. He was thoroughly impressed with the dangers that beset the country. He speaks of never before having been "so appalled and so anxious"; he calls his theme "the awful subject." As an

* "Mr. Clay's unrivalled popularity has again secured him an audience such as no other statesman, no matter however able and respected, has ever before obtained here. To get within hearing of his voice I found to be impossible."—Washington correspondence of New York *Tribune*.

evidence of the intense party feeling, he alluded to the fact
that the House had spent one whole week in the vain attempt
to elect a doorkeeper because the point at issue was "whether
the doorkeeper entertained opinions upon certain national
measures coincident with this or that side of the House." He
thus described the manifestations of the excitement prevalent
in the country: "At this moment we have in the legislative
bodies of this capitol and in the States twenty odd furnaces in
full blast, emitting heat and passion and intemperance, and
diffusing them throughout the whole extent of this broad land."
His endeavor had been to "form such a scheme of accommodation" as would obviate "the sacrifice of any great principle"
by either section of the country, and he believed that the series
of resolutions which he presented accomplished the object.
Concession by each side was necessary, "not of principle, but
of feeling, of opinion in relation to matters in controversy between them." The admission of California as a State would,
under the circumstances, be simply the recognition of a time-
honored precedent of the government. The North insisted on
the application of the Wilmot proviso to the rest of the territory acquired from Mexico; yet slavery did not exist there by
law, and the orator in a few pregnant questions stated the case
in the most powerful manner: "What do you want who reside
in the free States? You want that there shall be no slavery introduced into the territories acquired from Mexico. Well, have
you not got it in California already, if admitted as a State?
Have you not got it in New Mexico, in all human probability,
also? What more do you want? You have got what is worth a
thousand Wilmot provisos. You have got nature itself on your
side. You have the fact itself on your side." It was, however,
necessary to institute a territorial government for New Mexico.
It· was not right to allow matters to run along without interference from Congress, to establish a regular system. The orator
referred to the fact that in the previous September the people
of New Mexico had held a convention, had chosen a delegate
to Congress, and had instructed him to represent to that body

that their actual government was "temporary, doubtful, uncertain, and inefficient in character and operation," that they were "surrounded and despoiled by barbarous foes, and ruin appears inevitably before us, unless speedy and effectual protection be extended to us by the United States."

Of only one other item of the compromise resolutions is it necessary to speak in detail. The settlement of the Texas boundary may be regarded as an eminently proper one, although the payment of the Texas debt was open to objection as being a measure not free from corruption. As there "was money in it," that feature might be looked upon as intending to win support for the entire project. In the provisions regarding the District of Columbia, a concession was made to the demands of each side.

There remained, then, the declaration in favor of a provision for the more effectual rendition of fugitive slaves. Until he reached this point, Clay's leaning had evidently been more to the Northern than to the Southern side of the controversy, although he tried to hold the balance level between them, and endeavored to blend appeal and argument equally to each section. But on this point he took extreme Southern ground. The Fugitive Slave law, passed in the first years of the government, required the aid and countenance of the State magistrates as well as judges of the United States for its execution; but, as the sentiment on the slavery question diverged more widely between the two sections, there arose a strong feeling in the Northern States against lending their assistance to restore fugitive slaves. The legislature of Massachusetts enacted a law, making it penal for her officers to perform any duties under the act of Congress of 1793 for their surrender. Pennsylvania passed an act forbidding her judicial authorities to take cognizance of any fugitive-slave case. The border States especially complained of the difficulties encountered in reclaiming their runaway negroes. And as it had been decided by the United States Supreme Court that the Constitution had conferred on Congress an exclusive power to legislate concerning their extradition, it was demanded by those Southerners who were willing to compromise the matters in dispute that a more effectual law for the recovery of fugitive slaves should be a part of the arrangement. So much explanation is necessary to understand Clay's very positive expressions. "Upon this subject," he said, "I do think that we have just and serious cause of complaint against the free States. . . . It is our duty to make the law more effective; and I shall go with the senator from the South who goes furthest in making penal laws and imposing the heaviest sanctions for the recovery of fugitive slaves and the restoration of them to their owners."

After touching upon each one of his resolutions in order, Clay offered some general considerations: "There have been, unhappily, mutual causes of agitation furnished by one class of the States as well as by the other, though, I admit, not in the same degree by the slave States as by the free States." Yet he had "an earnest and anxious desire to present the olive branch to both parts of this distracted and at the present moment unhappy country." He made an appeal to both sides to do something to quiet the clamors of the nation; depicting, in lively colors, the vast extent of the country, its present prosperity and wealth, the success of the government, as having proceeded from the Union. If these great blessings were worth conserving, mutual concessions should certainly be made to save the Union from dissolution. "War and dissolution of the Union are identical," he exclaimed. The orator closed with a prophecy that events have completely falsified. Should the Union be dissolved and war follow, he declared, it would be a war more ferocious and bloody, more implacable and exterminating, than were the wars of Greece, the wars of the Commoners of England, or the revolutions of France. And after a war—"not of two or three years' duration, but a war of interminable duration . . . some Philip or Alexander, some Cæsar or Napoleon, would arise and cut the Gordion knot and solve the problem of the capacity of man for self-government, and crush the liberties of both the severed portions of this common empire."

The floor of the Senate was assigned to Calhoun for the 4th of March, to speak on the compromise resolutions. Long battle with disease had wasted his frame, but, swathed in flannels, he crawled to the Senate chamber to utter his last words of warning to the North, and to make his last appeal for what he considered justice to his own beloved South. He was too weak to deliver his carefully written speech. At his request, it was read by Senator Mason. Calhoun sat, with head erect and eyes partly closed, immovable in front of the reader; and he did not betray a sense of the deep interest with which his friends and followers listened to the well-matured words of their leader and political guide. This was Calhoun's last formal speech; before the end of the month he had passed away from the scene of earthly contention. The speech is mainly interesting as stating with precision the numerical preponderance of the North, the reasons of Southern discontent, and the forebodings of his prophetic soul in reference to the future. He admitted that universal discontent pervaded the South. Its "great and primary cause is that the equilibrium between the two sections hase been destroyed." It was the old story that the North had grown faster in population than the South. Every one knows that it was slavery which kept back the South in the race; but this Calhoun could not see, and he sought the cause in remote and unsubstantial reasons. When Calhoun said the South, he meant the slave power, and the South had not held pace with the North because, first, in his opinion, the Ordinance of 1787 and the Missouri Compromise had excluded her from territory that should have been left "open to the emigration of masters with their slaves"; second, the tariff and internal-improvements system had worked decidedly against her interests; and, third, the gradual yet steady assumption of greater powers by the federal government at the expense of the rights of the States had proved an inestimable injury to the South. "The cords that bind the States together," said the senator, "are not only many, but various in character. Some are spiritual or ecclesiastical; some political, others social." The strongest are those of a religious nature, but they have begun to snap. The great Methodist Episcopal Church has divided; there is a Methodist Church North and a Methodist Church South, and they are hostile. The Protestant organization next in size, the Baptist Church, has likewise fallen asunder. The cord which binds the Presbyterian Church "is not entirely snapped, but some of its strands have given way. That of the Episcopal Church is the only one of the four great Protestant denominations which remains unbroken and entire. . . . If the agitation goes on, the same force, acting with increased intensity, will finally snap every cord"—political and social as well as ecclesiastical—"when nothing will be left to hold the States together except force." It is undeniable that the Union is in danger. How can it be saved? Neither the plan of the distinguished senator of Kentucky nor that of the administration will save the Union. It rests with the North, the stronger party, whether or not she will take the course which will effect this devoutly to-be-wished-for consummation. The North must give us equal rights in the acquired territory; she must return our fugitive slaves; she must cease the agitation of the slave question; and she must consent to an amendment to the Constitution "which will restore to the South, in substance, the power she possessed of protecting herself before the equilibrium between the two sections was destroyed by the action of this government." The admission of California will be the test question. If you admit her, it will be notice to us that you propose to use your present strength and to add to it "with the intention of destroying irretrievably the equilibrium between the two sections."

The latter part of Calhoun's speech is important solely because it defines the position of the extreme Southern party. The mildness of his language, and the almost pathetic appeal to Northern senators, did not veil the arrogance of his demands. He did not now explain the nature of the constitutional amendment which in his judgment was required, but in a posthumous essay, which was designed as his political testament, he entered upon the matter fully. The amendment was to pro-

vide for the election of two Presidents, one from the free States
and one from the slave States; either was to have a veto on all
congressional legislation. He held until the end to the fanciful
Roman analogy. He saw in his mind's eye the Southern tribune
checking the power of the Northern consul and of Congress;
and while he remembered that the tribunes of Rome became as
despots with absolute power, this did not lessen his wish for
a like authority as a safeguard of Southern interests. Intellectual vagary can go to no extremer length in politics than
to propound a scheme which is alike impossible of adoption,
and would be utterly impracticable in operation. The constitutional amendment suggested by Calhoun was generally regarded at the South as a utopian scheme; yet he had a following of something like fifty members of Congress, who, even if
they did not subscribe to his vague ideas in the science of
government, were willing to follow him to the extreme length
of secession from the Union, if the dispute could not be settled
to their liking. These members represented fairly the feeling
of their slave-holding constituents.

Before proceeding to the further consideration of the debate
on the compromise resolutions, we should satisfy ourselves
whether the Union was indeed in danger. The proceedings of
Congress had certainly intensified the excitement. The contest
for speaker, the clashes between the representatives of the opposing views, the threats on one side and defiance on the other,
had added gravity to a situation already grave. "Two months
ago," said Clay, "all was calm in comparison to the present
moment. All now is uproar, confusion, and menace to the existence of the Union and to the happiness and safety of the
people." Yet Clay had great difficulty in making up his mind
as to how much of the danger was real, and how much only
apparent. He writes, "My hopes and fears alternate." Calhoun's speech was as sincere as a death-bed utterance, and
leaves no doubt that he believed the country on the eve of
disunion. Webster was as much perplexed as Clay. In the middle of February he did not fear dissolution of the Union nor

the breaking-up of the government. He writes: "I think that the clamor about disunion rather abates. I trust that if on our side we keep cool, things will come to no dangerous pass. California will probably be admitted just as she presents herself." Three weeks later he had materially modified his opinion. Still, there was not so much change in the actual situation as in one's apprehension of it. For it was a time of seething commotion; the political atmosphere was highly charged; one's settled opinions of to-day were liable to be disturbed by violent collision of opposing notions to-morrow; and the impetuous speech of some Southern Hotspur might shake the resolution of timorous Northern men. Yet the fears were not all confined to the national capital. Scott, the general of the army, who was stationed at New York, thought that "our country was on the eve of a terrible civil war." Senator Benton, however, ridiculed the idea of danger. Seward thought the threats of disunion "too trivial for serious notice." Chase was not in the least alarmed at "the stale cry of disunion." Giddings thought the "cry of dissolution was gasconade." . . . It has been the *dernier ressort* of Southern men for fifty years whenever they desired to frighten dough-faces into a compliance with their measures. In general, the Northern anti-slavery men treated the Southern threats as bravado and as hardly worth serious notice.* Yet there was one notable exception to this universal opinion. Horace Mann believed that if the North insisted upon passing the Wilmot proviso for the territories, some of the Southern

---

* "Our Northern friends are blind, absolutely blind, to the real dangers by which we are surrounded."—Letter of C. S. Morehead, Whig representative from Kentucky, to John J. Crittenden, March 30th, *Life of Crittenden,* vol. i. p. 363. The opinion at that time of the extreme abolitionist was well stated by Theodore Parker in a sermon delivered in 1852. He combated strenuously the idea that there was any danger of dissolution of the Union in 1850. "We have," he said, "the most delicate test of public opinion—the state of the public funds, the barometer which indicates any change in the political weather;" but during all this discussion "the funds of the United States did not go down one mill." "The Southern men know well that if the Union were dissolved their riches would take to itself legs and run away—or firebrands, and make a St. Domingo out of South Carolina! They cast off the North! They set up for themselves! Tush! tush! Fear boys with bugs!"

States would rebel. Still, there was an earnest feeling at the North, and especially in New England, that if there were a risk in insisting that slavery should go no further, it was a risk well worth taking.

Carefully weighing the contemporary evidence, and looking on it in the light of subsequent history, I think that little danger of an overt act of secession existed while General Taylor was in the presidential chair. The power of a determined executive to resist the initial steps towards casting off allegiance to the general government was great. While diverse constitutional interpretations and different views as to the force of various precedents might puzzle the President, he was certain to discern betimes any move towards rebellion; and that he was resolved to put down with all the force at his command.*

An incident occurring at this time shows to what stern determination General Taylor had come. The extreme pro-slavery Whigs from the Southern States took the position that they were willing to admit California, provided that in the rest of the territory in question the government would protect and recognize property in slaves, even as other property was protected and recognized. But until this condition was formally acknowledged they were utterly opposed to the admission of California with her free constitution, and, with the assistance of the Southern Democrats, they prevented by filibustering the consideration of a bill in the House which had that for its object. While this obstruction was in progress, Alexander H. Stephens and Robert Toombs, both Southern Whig representatives, called to see the President to discuss his policy and to demand that he, as their party's chief, should use his influence and power to favor the end which they had in view. The President plainly informed them that he would sign any constitutional law which Congress might pass. The direct intimation was that he would sign a bill which provided unconditionally

---

* "The malcontents of the South mean to be factious; and they expect to compel compromise. I think the President as willing to try conclusions with them as General Jackson was with the nullifiers."—Seward to Weed, Nov. 30th, 1849, *Life of Seward,* vol. ii. p. 112.

for the admission of California; and they were indirectly given to understand that he would approve the application of the Wilmot proviso to the territories. As a reply to this outline of future action, the Southern congressmen threatened dissolution of the Union, whereupon the President became angry and said that, if it were necessary, he would take the field himself to enforce the laws of his country; and if these gentlemen were taken in rebellion against the Union, he would hang them with as little mercy as he had hanged deserters and spies in Mexico.

In the midst of the mutual recrimination accompanying this inevitable sectional controversy, there can be no better evidence as to whence came the aggression than the complete change that had taken place in the sentiments of General Taylor since he had occupied the executive office. Before he was nominated for President, he had written an emphatic letter to his son-in-law, Jefferson Davis, in which he had maintained that the South must resist boldly and decisively the encroachments of the North; and the Southerners had counted much on his assistance. He now, however, looked upon several Southern members as conspirators, and Jefferson Davis as their chief. If we lay aside the speeches in Congress as merely threats of irate Southerners, and get at Southern sentiment from legislative resolutions, from expressions in the press, and from public meetings, it is undeniable that had the Wilmot proviso passed Congress, or had slavery been abolished in the District of Columbia, the Southern convention for which arrangements were making would have been a very different affair from the one that actually did assemble at Nashville. Steps would undoubtedly have been taken towards disunion; and while resolute action of the President was certain to arouse the dormant Union feeling in the South, his task would have been more difficult than was that of General Jackson, for he would have to contend with more States than South Carolina.

A change in Southern sentiment is, however, noticeable shortly after the introduction of Clay's compromise resolutions. This was assisted by a vote in the House of Representatives, laying on the table a resolution which provided for the application of the Wilmot proviso to the territory east of California. Clay's speech influenced powerfully the opinion of Southern Whigs. From the beginning of February, it is easy to trace the growth of a Southern sentiment favorable to the admission of California, if only the Wilmot proviso were not insisted upon for New Mexico, and slavery were allowed to remain in the District of Columbia. This by no means pleased the knot of Southern disunionists, who desired nothing better than the passage by Congress of the Wilmot proviso. In that event they had well-grounded hopes that they could unite the South in their views; then they would give their ultimatum, and, if it were rejected, they would dissolve the Union. Efforts, indeed, were made by the extreme Southern Democrats to check the slowly rising Union sentiment. Their aim was to resist the admission of California, and to make the resistance a sectional shibboleth in place of opposition to the Wilmot proviso.

While, thus, the fear of a formal secession from the Union, such as took place eleven years later, had not at this time sufficient foundation, there was danger in the adjournment of Congress without provision for the matters in dispute.* The war of legislative declarations, of resolutions, of public meetings, would continue, and inflammatory writing in the press would not cease. Northern legislative action, supported by public sentiment, would not only make it difficult, but impossible, to recover a fugitive slave. On the other hand, it was probable that most of the Southern States would by way of retaliatory legislation pass laws to prevent the sale of Northern products by retail in their limits. The governor of Virginia, John B. Floyd, proposed to his legislature a system of taxation of the products of those states which would not deliver up fugi-

---

* "In the Senate there are eight Southern senators and in the House thirty members from the same section who are organized as disunionists and are opposed to any compromise whatever looking to the perpetuity of the Union."—Washington correspondence New York *Tribune*, Feb. 2d, 1850.

tive slaves. A suspension of intercourse between the two sections would follow, and the situation would be strained to the utmost. If, indeed, armed conflicts at various points did not result from the excited feeling, it was certain that the harmony which should subsist between the parts of a federal Union would be utterly destroyed; and after months or even years of such a state of mutual repulsion, it could only end in compromise, peaceful separation, or war.*

Two of the great senatorial triumvirate had spoken; the Senate and the country had yet to hear the greatest of them all. Daniel Webster spoke on the compromise resolutions the 7th of March. In the course of this work, whenever possible, his precise words have been used, in narration and illustration; for in intellectual endowment Webster surpassed all of our public men. No one understood the fundamental principles of our polity better; no one approached his wonderful power of expression. It seemed that the language of the constitutional lawyer who laid down principles of law that the profound legal mind of Marshall fixed in an immutable judicial decision, and who, at the same time, could make abstruse points clear and carry conviction to the understanding of men who were untrained in logic or in law, was best fitted to guide us through the maze of constitutional interpretation in which our history abounds. Indeed, the political history of the country for twenty-seven years preceding 1850 might be written as well and fully from the speeches, state papers, and letters of Webster as the story of the latter days of the Roman republic from the like material of Cicero which has come down to us.

As an orator, Webster has been compared in simplicity to Demosthenes and in profundity to Burke. This is the highest praise. The wonderful effect of his oratory is strikingly told by George Ticknor, who, fresh from a long intercourse with the

* "I am not one of those who, either at the commencement of the session or at any time during its progress, have believed that there was present any actual danger to the existence of the Union. But I am one of those who believe that, if this agitation is continued for one or two years longer, no man can foresee the dreadful consequences."—Clay, *Senate*, May 21st.

most distinguished men in England and on the Continent, went to hear Webster deliver his Plymouth oration. Ticknor writes: "I was never so excited by public speaking before in my life. Three or four times I thought my temples would burst with the gush of blood"; and, though from his youth an intimate friend of Webster's, he was so impressed that "when I came out I was almost afraid to come near him. It seemed to me as if he was like the mount that might not be touched, and that burned with fire." Thomas Marshall, of Kentucky, heard the reply to Hayne, and when Webster came to the peroration he "listened as to one inspired, and finally thought he could see a halo around the orator's head like what one sees in the old pictures of saints and martyrs."

The diction of Webster was formed by a grateful study of Shakespeare and Milton; through his communion with these masters, his whole soul was thoroughly attuned to the highest conceptions and purest harmonies of our literature. He is one of the few orators whose speeches are read as literature. He was our greatest lawyer, yet in a bad cause he was not a good advocate, for he had not the flexibility of mind which makes the worse appear the better reason; but in cases apparently hopeless, with the right on his side, he won impossible triumphs. He was our greatest Secretary of State. He had, said Sumner, "by the successful and masterly negotiation of the treaty of Washington" earned the title of "Defender of Peace."

The Graces presided at his birth. His growth developed the strong physical constitution with which nature had endowed him equally with a massive brain. His was a sound mind in a sound body. His physical structure was magnificent, his face handsome; he had the front of Jove himself. "He is," said Carlyle, "a magnificent specimen. . . . As a logic-fencer, or parliamentary Hercules, one would incline to back him at first sight against all the extant world." "Webster," said Henry Hallam, "approaches as nearly to the beau ideal of a republican senator as any man that I have ever seen in the course of my life." Josiah Quincy speaks of him as a "figure cast in heroic mould, and which represented the ideal of American manhood." He was well described by the bard he loved so well: "How noble in reason! how infinite in faculties! in form and moving, how express and admirable! in action, how like an angel! in apprehension, how like a god!" On the basis of this extraordinary natural ability was built the superstructure of a systematic education. His devoted father mortgaged the New Hampshire farm to send him to college, and three years of laborious study of law followed the regular course at Dartmouth. Years afterwards he repaid his Alma Mater for her gifts when he pleaded, and not in vain, for her chartered rights in invincible logic before the most solemn tribunal of the country. Intellectually, Webster was a man of slow growth. The zenith of his power was not reached until he made the celebrated reply to Hayne, and he was then forty-eight years old.

In union with this grand intellect were social qualities of a high order. His manners were charming, his nature was genial, and he had a quick sense of seemly humor. Carlyle speaks of him as "a dignified, perfectly bred man." Harriet Martineau says "he would illuminate an evening by telling stories, cracking jokes, or smoothly discoursing to the perfect felicity of the logical part of one's constitution." Ticknor, who was so impressed with the majestic delivery of the orator, speaks of his being "as gay and playful as a kitten." The social intercourse between Webster and Lord Ashburton, while they were at work on the Washington treaty, is one of those international amenities that grace the history of diplomacy. This treaty, by which we gained substantial advantages and England made honorable concessions, was not negotiated through stately protocols, but was concluded through a friendly correspondence and during the interchange of refined social civilities. During this transaction Ashburton was impressed with "the upright and honorable character" of Webster. As late as 1845 there might be seen engravings which were an indication of the popular notion that honesty was his cardinal virtue.

He had strong domestic feelings. He honored his father,

loved his brother, and was devoted to his wife and children; his affection for his many friends was pure and disinterested. He had during his life a large share of domestic affliction, and his deep and sincere grief shows that he had a large heart as well as a great head. He had a constant belief in revealed as well as natural religion.

His healthy disposition was displayed even in his recreations. He was a true disciple of Izaak Walton, and he also delighted in the chase. Few men have loved nature more. Those grand periods that will never cease to delight lovers of oratory were many of them conned at his Marshfield retreat, where he worshipped the sea and did reverence to the rising sun. After a winter of severe work in his declining years, he gets to Marshfield in May, and writes: "I grow strong every hour. The giants grew strong again by touching the earth; the same effect is produced on me by touching the salt sea-shore."

The distinctive virtue of Webster was his patriotism. He loved his country as few men have loved it; he had a profound reverence for the Constitution and its makers. He spoke truly when he said: "I am an American, and I know no locality but America; that is my country"; and he was deeply in earnest when he gave utterance to the sentiment, "I was bred, indeed I might also say I was born, in admiration of our political institutions." Webster's great work was to inspire the country with a strong and enduring national feeling; and he impressed upon the people everywhere, except in the cotton States, a sacred love for the Union. How well his life-work was done was seen, less than nine years after he died, in the zealous appeal to arms for the defence of the nation. In the sleepless nights before his death, no sight was so welcome to his eyes as the lantern he saw through the windows placed at the mast-head of the little shallop, in order that he might discern, fluttering at the mast, the national flag, the emblem of the Union to which he had consecrated the best thoughts and purest efforts of his life.

During the last twenty years of his career Webster had a

great desire to be President. Three times he was exceedingly anxious for the Whig nomination, and thought his chances were good for getting it; but the nomination never came to him. Indeed, he always overrated the probabilities of his success. He was of that class of statesmen who were stronger before the country than before the political convention. Had he ever been named as his party's choice, he would unquestionably have been a strong candidate; but he never had the knack of arousing the enthusiasm of the party, which Clay possessed in so eminent degree. Nor did his frequent action independent of political considerations commend him to the men who shaped the action of the party convention. George Ticknor said, in 1831, Webster "belongs to no party; but he has uniformly contended for the great and essential principles of our government on all occasions"; and this was to a large extent true of him during his whole life. His tendency to break away from party trammels was shown more than once during his long career. In 1833, as we have seen, he supported with enthusiasm the Democratic President, and would not assent to the compromise devised by the leader of his party. But the crowning act of independence was when he remained in the cabinet of President Tyler, when all his colleagues resigned. The motive for this action was the desire to complete the negotiation of the Ashburton treaty for Webster felt that he of all men was best fitted for that work; and his heart was earnestly enlisted in the effort to remove the difficulties in the way of a peaceful settlement, and to avert a war between England and the United States. His course, although eminently patriotic, was certain to interfere with his political advancement. For he resisted the imperious dictation of Clay, he breasted the popular clamor of his party, and he pursued his own ideas of right despite the fact that he had to encounter the tyranny of public opinion which De Tocqueville has so well described.

The French, who make excuses for men of genius as the Athenians were wont to do, have a proverb, "It belongs to great men to have great defects." Webster exemplified this maxim. He was fond of wine and brandy, and at times drank deep; he was not scrupulous in observing the seventh commandment. Though born and reared in poverty, he had little idea of the value of money and of the sacredness of money obligations. He had no conception of the duty of living within his means, and he was habitually careless in regard to the payment of his debts. His friends more than once discharged his obligations; besides such assistance, he accepted from them at other times presents of money, but he would have rejected their bounty with scorn had there gone with it an expectation of influencing his public action. This failing was the cause of serious charges being preferred against him. He was accused of being in the pay of the United States Bank, but this was not true; and he was charged with a corrupt misuse of the secret service fund while Secretary of State under Tyler, but from this accusation he was fully and fairly exonerated.

Considering that it was only by strenuous effort that the son of the New Hampshire farmer obtained the highest rank in political and social life, it is hard to believe that he was constitutionally indolent, as one of his biographers states. When sixty-seven years old it was his practice to study from five to eleven in the morning; he was in the Supreme Court from eleven to three, and the rest of the day in the Senate until ten in the evening. When he had the time to devote himself to his legal practice, his professional income was large.

Such, in the main, if Daniel Webster had died on the morning of the seventh day of March, 1850, would have been the estimate of his character that would come down to this generation. But his speech in the Senate on that day placed a wide gulf between him and most of the men who were best fitted to transmit his name to posterity. Partisan malignity has magnified his vices, depreciated his virtues, and distorted his motives.

Let us now consider this speech, which the orator himself thought the most important effort of his life. The most signal event in the long session of Congress we are at present considering, it was almost as momentous in the history of the country as it was in the life of Webster. It is the only speech in our history which is named by the date of its delivery, and the general acquiescence in this designation goes to show that it was a turning-point in the action of Congress, in popular sentiment, and in the history of the country.

Webster began: "I wish to speak to-day, not as a Massachusetts man, nor as a Northern man, but as an American. . . . It is not to be denied that we live in the midst of strong agitations, and are surrounded by very considerable dangers to our institutions and government. The imprisoned winds are let loose. The East, the North, and the stormy South combine to throw the whole sea into commotion, to toss its billows to the skies, and disclose its profoundest depths. . . . I speak to-day for the preservation of the Union. 'Hear me for my cause.'" He spoke of the Mexican war as having been "prosecuted for the purpose of the acquisition of territory. . . . As the acquisition was to be south of the United States, in warm climates and countries, it was naturally, I suppose, expected by the South that whatever acquisitions were made in that region would be added to the slave-holding portion of the United States. Very little of accurate information was possessed of the real physical character either of California or New Mexico, and events have not turned out as was expected. Both California and New Mexico are likely to come in as free States, and therefore some degree of disappointment and surprise has resulted. . . . It is . . . the prohibition of slavery which has contributed to raise . . . the dispute as to the propriety of the admission of California into the Union under this Constitution."

The orator then proceeded to discuss slavery from a general historical standpoint, whence an allusion followed naturally to the different view taken of the institution at the North and at the South. It is too long to quote, but it is a fair, dispassionate statement, and rises to the level of a judgment by a philosophical historian. He regrets the separation of the Methodist Episcopal Church. Speaking with the utmost feeling on the subject, he expresses the opinion that the schism might have been prevented; and he then comments upon the matter in words pregnant with wisdom that not only applied with force to the slavery question in 1850, but have a meaning for all controversies to all time.

At the time the Constitution was adopted, there was, he said, "no diversity of opinion between the North and the South upon the subject of slavery. It will be found that both parts of the country held it equally an evil, a moral and political evil. . . . The eminent men, the most eminent men, and nearly all the conspicuous politicians of the South held the same sentiments—that slavery was an evil, a blight, a scourge, and a curse. . . . There was, if not an entire unanimity, a general concurrence of sentiment running through the whole community, and especially entertained by the eminent men of all parts of the country. But soon a change began at the North and the South, and a difference of opinion showed itself; the North growing much more warm and strong against slavery, and the South growing much more warm and strong in its support." The reason that the South ceased to think it an evil and a scourge, but, on the other hand, maintained that it was "a great religious, social, and moral blessing," was "owing to the rapid growth and sudden extension of the cotton plantations of the South."

In reply to Calhoun's statement that "there has been a majority all along in favor of the North," Webster averred that "no man acquainted with the history of the Union can deny that the general lead in the politics of the country, for three-fourths of the period that has elapsed since the adoption of the Constitution, has been a Southern lead." He directed attention to the events that brought about the annexation of Texas, referred at length to the joint resolution which allowed four more States to be formed out of her territory; and laid great stress upon the stipulation that the States which would be created south of the line of 36° 30′—and this embraced nearly the whole of Texas—were permitted to have slavery, and would without question be slave States. To that "this government is solemnly pledged by law and contract . . . and I for one mean to fulfil it, because I will not violate the faith of the government. . . . Now as to California and New Mexico, I hold slavery to be excluded from those territories by a law even superior to that which admits and sanctions it in Texas. I mean the law of nature, of physical geography, the law of the formation of the earth. That law settles forever, with a strength beyond all terms of human enactment, that slavery cannot exist in California or New Mexico. . . . What is there in New Mexico that could by any possibility induce anybody to go there with slaves? There are some narrow strips of tillable land on the borders of the rivers; but the rivers themselves dry up before midsummer is gone. . . . And who expects to see a hundred black men cultivating tobacco, corn, cotton, rice, or anything else, on lands in New Mexico, made fertile only by irrigation?" Considering that "both California and New Mexico are destined to be free, . . . I would not take pains uselessly to reaffirm an ordinance of nature, nor to re-enact the will of God. I would put in no Wilmot proviso for the mere purpose of a taunt or reproach. . . . Wherever there is a substantive good to be done, wherever there is a foot of land to be prevented from becoming slave territory, I am ready to assert the principle of the exclusion of slavery. I am pledged to it from the year 1837; I have been pledged to it again and again; and I will perform those pledges; but I will not do a thing unnecessarily that wounds the feelings of others, or that does decredit to my own understanding."

As regards the non-rendition of fugitive slaves, Webster thought that the complaints of the South were just, and that the North had lacked in her duty; and he proposed, with some amendments, to support the fugitive slave bill which had been drawn up and introduced by Senator Mason of Virginia. He referred to the abolition societies at the North, and did not "think them useful. I think their operations for the last twenty years have produced nothing good or valuable. . . . The violence of the Northern press is complained of." But "the press is violent everywhere. There are outrageous reproaches in the North against the South, and there are reproaches as vehement in the South against the North." There is, however, "no solid grievance presented by the South within the redress of the government . . . but the want of a proper regard to the injunction of the Constitution for the delivery of fugitive slaves."

It is near the close of the speech that occurs the fine passage depicting the utter impossibility of peaceable secession. "Sir, he who sees these States, now revolving in harmony around a common centre, and expects them to quit their places and fly off without convulsion, may look the next hour to see the heavenly bodies rush from their spheres, and jostle against each other in the realms of space, without causing the wreck of the universe." And in his peroration, which in eloquence almost equals that of his reply to Hayne, he adjured the Senate and the country, "instead of speaking of the possibility or utility of secession, instead of dwelling in those caverns of darkness, instead of groping with those ideas so full of all that is horrid and horrible, let us come out into the light of day; let us enjoy the fresh air of liberty and union. Never did there devolve on any generation of men higher trusts than now devolve upon us for the preservation of this Constiution, and the harmony and peace of all who are destined to live under it. Let us make our generation one of the strongest and brightest links in the golden chain which is destined, I fondly believe, to grapple the people of all the States to this Constitution for ages to come."

This speech of Webster had been long and anxiously awaited. The desire was great to know what position he would take; the curiosity was intense to know whether he would support the compromise or would join the anti-slavery Whigs and approve the plan of the President. It had been rumored that he, in connection with some Southern senators, was intending to prepare a scheme of adjustment; on the other hand, Giddings and other Free-soilers thought that he would sustain their doctrines.

Horace Mann did not believe that Webster would compromise the great question. All this conjecture was idle. More than six weeks before he made the declaration in public, he had given Clay to understand that he would support substantially the Kentucky senator's scheme of compromise. Before concurring in all the details, he desired to give the subject careful consideration; and between the time of his interview with Clay on January 21st and the delivery of his speech he consulted with men of diverse views. He heard every side advocated; he saw the subject in all its bearings. As the result of his mature and carefully considered judgment, he determined to follow his own first impressions, and devote himself to the advocacy of Clay's plan, "no matter what might befall himself at the North."

The speech produced a wonderful sensation; none other in our annals had an immediate effect so mighty and striking. The reply to Hayne and the reply to Calhoun have more permanent value, and their influence has been lasting; the 7th of March speech dealt with slavery, and when the slavery question ceased to be an issue the discourse of Webster lost all but the historical interest. A careful reading of the speech now fails to disclose the whole reason of its harsh reception at the North. It is probable that the matured historical view will be that Webster's position as to the application of the Wilmot proviso to New Mexico was statesmanship of the highest order. In 1846, 1847, and 1848, the formal prohibition of slavery in the territory to be acquired, or which was acquired from Mexico, seemed a vital and practical question. The latitude of the territory in in dispute gave reason to suppose that its products would be those of the cotton States, and that it would naturally gravitate towards slave institutions. While many believed that the Mexican law sufficed to preserve freedom in California and New Mexico, it nevertheless was good policy to make extraordinary appropriations for the war only on condition of an express understanding that the territory acquired should be free. But in 1850 the question had changed. California had decided for herself; and the more important half of the controversy was

cut off by the action of the people interested. There remained
New Mexico.* The very fact that California had forbidden
slavery was an excellent reason for believing that New Mexico
would do likewise. It had now become known that while the
latitude of New Mexico assigned her to the domain of slavery,
the altitude of the country gave her a different climate from
that of the slave States, and subjected her to different economical conditions. It was understood that neither cotton, tobacco,
rice, nor sugar could be raised, and no one in 1850 maintained
that slave labor was profitable save in the cultivation of those
products. The correspondence between Webster and the delegate to Congress from New Mexico shows that any one conversant with the facts knew that slavery had not the smallest
chance of being established in that territory.† The people themselves proved that no Wilmot proviso was needed, for in convention assembled in May they formed a State government,
and declared for the absolute prohibition of slavery. It seems

---

* New Mexico then comprised the westerly portions of New Mexico as
at present bounded, and Colorado, Nevada, and Utah, most of Arizona, and
the southwesterly part of Wyoming. *Narrative and Critical History of
America,* Justin Winsor, vol. vii. p. 552.

† This correspondence was published in many of the newspapers of the
day, and may be found in Webster's *Works,* vol. vi. p. 548. Hugh N. Smith,
the delegate from New Mexico, under date of April 9th, wrote: "New
Mexico is an exceedingly mountainous country, Santa Fé itself being twice
as high as the highest point of the Alleghanies, and nearly all the land
capable of cultivation is of equal height, though some of the valleys have
less altitude above the sea. The country is cold. Its general agricultural
products are wheat and corn, and such vegetables as grow in the Northern
States of this Union. It is entirely unsuited for slave labor. Labor is exceedingly abundant and cheap. It may be hired for three or four dollars a
month, in quantity quite sufficient for carrying on all the agriculture of the
territory. There is no cultivation except by irrigation, and there is not a
sufficiency of water to irrigate all the land.

"As to the existence at present of slavery in New Mexico, it is the general understanding that it has been altogether abolished by the laws of
Mexico; but we have no established tribunals which have pronounced as
yet what the law of the land in this respect is. It is universally considered,
however, that the territory is altogether a free territory. I know of no
persons in the country who are treated as slaves, except such as may be
servants to gentlemen visiting or passing through the country. I may add
that the strongest feeling against slavery universally prevails throughout
the whole territory, and I suppose it quite impossible to convey it there,
and maintain it by any means whatever."

that Webster had studied this territorial question more deeply, knew the facts better, and saw clearer than his detractors. It certainly is no lack of consistency in a public man to change his action in conformity to the circumstances. The end desired was to have California and New Mexico free; and if that could be gained by the action of these communities, it was surely as well as to have it determined by a formal act of Congress. To insist upon a rigid principle when it is no longer applicable or necessary is not good politics; yet great blame has been attached to Webster because he did not now insist on the Wilmot proviso. Anti-slavery writers have pointed to the legislative establishment of slavery in New Mexico in 1859 as proof that Webster made in 1850 a fatal error of judgment. But the practice never actually existed in that territory, and the act of 1859 was the work of a coterie, passed for political effect.

The historian whose sympathies are with the anti-slavery cause of 1850—and it seems clear that he can most truly write the story—can by no means commend the whole of the 7th-of-March speech. The orator dwelt upon the conditions of the annexation of Texas at too great a length, for the bad bargain and the manner in which it was made were not a pleasant recollection to the North. It was not necessary to lay great stress upon the fact that more slave States could be created out of Texas, for, while it is obvious that the intention was to remind the South how well they had fared in the Union, the orator's mode of treating the subject was of a nature to irritate the North; and all the more, because his argument could not legally be impugned. Webster's reference to the abolition societies and their work brought a storm of indignation upon his head from people who were not used to suppress their voice or mince their meaning. Webster was wrong in his estimate of the abolitionists. Yet similar judgments were common; and for ten years more we find the same pleas against the agitating of slavery. The complete answer to this deprecation was given by Lowell for once and all: "To be told that we ought not to agitate the question of slavery, when it is that which is forever agitating us, is like telling a man with the fever and ague on him to stop shaking, and he will be cured."

But what grieved the old supporters of Webster the most was his severe censure of the North for their action in regard to fugitive slaves. The bill of Mason, which, with some amendments, he proposed to support, was a stringent measure; and while Webster's own idea was that the fugitive ought to have a jury trial in case he denied owing service to the claimant, there is no doubt that he would have voted for the Mason bill pure and simple, or, had he been in the Senate that the time, for the actual Fugitive Slave law passed in September, rather than that the compromise should fail. It was thus that the country regarded, and rightly, his position. Webster's remarks on this subject are those of an advocate bound to the letter of the law, fettered by technicality and overborne by precedent. He does not take a broad, statesmanlike view, drawn indeed from the written law, but adapted to changing sentiments and keeping pace with the progress of the century; he who had taught us to seize the essential and eternal principles underlying the record is not true to the standard which he himself erected. Webster could see "an ordinance of Nature," and the "will of God" written on the mountains and plateaus of New Mexico, but he failed to see an ordinance of Nature and the will of God implanted in the hearts of men that led them to refuse their assistance in reducing to bondage their fellows, whose only crime had been desire for liberty and escape from slavery. These feelings in the minds of men of Massachusetts were, in Webster's opinion, "local prejudices" founded on "unreal ghostly abstractions." He could detect the "taunt and reproach" to the South in the Wilmot proviso, but could not discover that a rigorous fugitive slave act was equally a taunt and reproach to the North.

Other points in this discourse occasioned much comment at the time, but the principal ones, and all that are necessary to a comprehension of what will follow, have been touched upon. It now remains to relate how the country received this speech.

The Massachusetts Legislature was in session discussing the national question, but dropped the subject in its general aspect to consider their great senator's relation to it. One member said that Webster was "a recreant son of Massachusetts who misrepresented her in the Senate." Henry Wilson "declared that Webster in his speech had simply, but hardly, stated the Northern and national side of the question, while he had earnestly advocated the Southern and sectional side; that his speech was Southern altogether in its tone, argument, aim and end." The anti-slavery Whigs and Free-soil members were anxious to instruct Webster formally to support the Wilmot proviso and vote against Mason's Fugitive Slave bill; and a resolution with that purport was introduced by Wilson, but they had not the strength to carry it through the legislature. The speech was received in a like manner by the majority of the Northern representatives in Congress. No one of the New England Whig members agreed with him. Horace Mann especially was bitter. He writes: "Webster is a fallen star! Lucifer descending from heaven!" "There is a very strong feeling here [at Washington] that Mr. Webster has played false to the North." "He has not a favorable response from any Northern man of influence." Giddings represented the anti-slavery sentiment of Ohio when he says, "By this speech a blow was struck at freedom and the contitutional rights of the free States which no Southern arm could have given."

A public meeting in Faneuil Hall condemned the action of Webster. Theodore Parker, who was one of the principal speakers, said: "I know no deed in American history done by a son of New England to which I can compare this but the act of Benedict Arnold. . . . The only reasonable way in which we can estimate this speech is as a bid for the presidency." In the main, the Northern Whig press condemned the salient points of the speech. The New York *Tribune* was especially outspoken, and doubted whether Webster would carry with him a Northern Whig vote. A large proportion of the Whig newspapers of New England felt obliged to dissent from the opinion of him whose arguments they had heretofore received with avidity and spread with zeal. It was regarded as an indication of great weight when the Boston *Atlas,* whose editor was a warm personal friend of Webster, combated unreservedly the important positions of the 7th-of-March speech; and although this respectful criticism was expressed in emphatic terms, the editor spoke more in sorrow than in anger. Those of the Whig journals who, after the flush of surprise, came to their leader's support could only advocate his principles in a lukewarm manner; and it was evident that devotion to Webster, and not to the cause he had made his own, was the spring of their action. Nearly all the religious papers of the North vented their disapproval. Whittier, in a song of plaintive vehemence called "Ichabod," mourned for the "fallen" statesman whose faith was lost, and whose honor was dead.

Curtis and Theodore Parker, who agree in nothing else, are of the same mind about public sentiment. "This speech," writes Curtis, "was received by probably a great majority of Mr. Webster's constituents, if not by a majority of the whole North, with disfavor and disapprobation." "I think," said Parker, "not a hundred prominent men in all New England acceded to the speech."

This was the instant outburst of opinion; but friends for Webster and his cause came with more deliberate reflections. Some prominent Democratic journals approved from the first his position, and there were many Whigs in New England, and especially in Boston, who were sure to follow Webster whithersoever he led. The majority, indeed, would have preferred that he had spoken differently, but their personal devotion induced them to espouse his side. His moral and intellectual influence in the free States was greater than that of any man living, for the people had confidence that his gigantic intellect would discover the right, and that his intellectual honesty would impel him to follow it. The country has listened to but two men on whose words they have hung with greater reverence than on those of Webster. The intellectual force and moral greatness of Washington and of Lincoln were augmented by their high office and the gravity of the existing crises. When the first excitement had subsided, the friends of Webster bestirred themselves, and soon testimonials poured in, approving the position he had taken. The most significant of them was the one from eight hundred solid men of Boston, who thanked him for "recalling us to our duties under the "Constitution," and for his "broad, national, and patriotic views." The tone of many of the Whig papers changed, some to positive support, others to more qualified censure.

IT *is profitable to compare Rhodes's picture of South-*
ern society before the Civil War with that found in
the pages of various British observers. They, too,
tried to achieve impartiality.

Harriet Martineau, for example, included in her
Society in America *a section entitled "Morals of*
Slavery." Asking what social morals were possible in
a society marked by such injustice, she identified sev-
eral. The most obvious, she thought, was compassion
or mercy. Nowhere could more appealing instances of
that virtue be found than in slaveholding areas where
the whites were in a constant relationship with
helpless, improvident, and dependent Negro wards.
There, she writes, "I saw endless manifestations of
mercy. . . . The thoughtfulness of masters, mistresses,
and children about not only the comforts, but the in-
dulgences of their slaves, was a frequent subject of
admiration with me." She saw them make large sac-
rifices for the social and intellectual advantage of
their people. In South Carolina a planter of her ac-
quaintance, for example, when cholera ravaged the
district, refused to leave his estates, and remained to
labor all day among his sick slaves, nursing them with
his own hands, bathing them, and cheering them.

Another virtue inculcated by slavery was patience.
"Nothing," Harriet Martineau writes, "struck me
more than the patience of slaveowners. In this virtue
they probably surpass the whole Christian world."
The slaves, ignorant, indolent, and often of childlike
impulses, would try the patience of a saint. Miss Mar-
tineau noted that people from New England and
Europe, on becoming slaveholders, were usually more
severe than native Southerners. Such newcomers
could not see meals delayed, infants neglected, live-
stock maltreated, and crops carelessly ruined, their
property wasted and plans thwarted, without explo-
sions of anger. The better Southerners had learned
restraint. "It seems to me," Miss Martineau declared,
"that every slaveholder's temper is subjected to a dis-
cipline which must either ruin or perfect it." By im-
plication, she suggested the virtues of the habit of
command that slavery gave to masters, Washington's
career presenting an example.

Rhodes gives a balanced depiction of both the

brighter and darker aspects of Southern society,
which was more novel and courageous at the begin-
ning of the 1890's for Northerners brought up on
Olmsted's volumes of Southern travel and Uncle
Tom's Cabin *than it seems today. He was neither*
very well informed nor penetrating on the econom-
ics of slavery, and subsequent writers have added
much to his treatment of this aspect of Southern life,
as to his study of Southern psychology. A greater
progressivism was appearing in parts of the South
when the storm of the Civil War broke, and it held
elements of both social and moral promise in a seem-
ingly stagnant and brutal society.

Southern Society

It is not surprising that the Southerners shone in the political
sphere. Their intellect tended naturally to public affairs; they
had the talent and leisure for politics which a landed aristocracy is apt to have under a representative government; and
when the slavery question assumed importance at Washington,
their concern for shaping the course of national legislation became a passion, and seemed necessary for the preservation of
their order. But it was only in law and politics that the South
was eminent. She did not give birth to a poet, nor to a philosopher after Jefferson, and his philosophy she rejected. She could
lay claim only to an occasional scientist, but to no great historian; none of her novelists or essayists who wrote before the
war has the next generation cared to read. Whoever, thinking
of the opportunities for culture in the ancient world given by
the existence of slavery, seeks in the Southern community a
trace even of that intellectual and artistic development which
was the glory of Athens, will look in vain. Had the other causes
existed, the sparse settlements of the South, the lack of a compact social body, made utterly impossible such results as mark
Grecian civilization. The physical and economic conditions
of the South presented insuperable obstacles to any full devel-

opment of university education. While efforts were made to promote the establishment of colleges, the higher fields of scientific and literary research were not cultivated with eminent success; for the true scientific spirit could never have free play in a community where one subject of investigation of all-pervading influence must remain a closed book.

When one thinks of the varied forms under which the intellect of New England displayed itself, and remembers the brilliant achievements there in the mind's domain which illumine the generation before the war, he cannot but feel the prominence of the South in politics, after the great Virginia statesmen had left the stage, was held at too great cost, if it was maintained at the sacrifice of a many-sided development such as took place at the North.

The great majority of the slave-holders lacked even ordinary culture. Nothing illustrates this better than the experience of Olmsted while on a horseback journey of three months, from the banks of the Mississippi to the banks of the James. In the rural districts of that country there were no inns. The traveller's stopping-places for the night were the houses of the farmers along his route, many of whom made it a practice to accommodate strangers and were willing to accept in payment for their trouble the price which would have been demanded by an inn-keeper. A majority of Olmsted's hosts in this journey were slave-holders, and a considerable proportion cotton-planters. He observed that certain symbols of civilization were wanting. "From the banks of the Mississippi to the banks of the James," he writes, "I did not (that I remember) see, except perhaps in one or two towns, a thermometer, nor a book of Shakespeare, nor a piano-forte or sheet of music, nor the light of a Carcel or other good centre-table or reading lamp, nor an engraving or copy of any kind of a work of art of the slightest merit."

The lack of schools was painfully apparent. The deficiency in the rudiments of education among the poor whites and smaller slave-holders was recognized, and attracted attention from the Southern newspapers, and occasionally from those high in office. Much vain declamation resulted, but no practical action. Indeed, the situation was one of difficulty. To plant schools in a sparsely settled country, among a people who have not the desire of learning and who do not appreciate its value, requires energy, and this energy was lacking. Moreover, there must have been among the slave-holding lords a secret satisfaction that the poor whites were content to remain in ignorance;* for in the decade before the war great objections were made to school-books prepared and printed at the North, and yet there were no others. In the beginning of the abolitionist agitation, Duff Green, perceiving that the benefits of slavery ought to be taught to the young, obtained a charter from South Carolina for a Southern Literary Company, whose object was to print school-books adapted to a slave-holding community; but this company had apparently not achieved its purpose, for in *De Bow's Review*, in 1855, there is a complaint that "our text-books are abolition books." The chapter on slavery in Wayland's Moral Science "was heretical and unscriptural." We are using "abolition geographies, readers, and histories," which overrun "with all sorts of slanders, caricatures, and blood-thirsty sentiments." "Appletons' Complete Guide of the World" is "an elegant and comprehensive volume," but contains "hidden lessons of the most fiendish and murderous character that enraged fanaticism could conceive or indite." "This book and many other Northern school-books scattered over the country come within the range of the statutes of this State [Louisiana], which provide for the imprisonment for life or the infliction of the penalty of death upon any person who

---

* "We imagine that the propriety of shooting a Yankee schoolmaster, when caught tampering with our slaves, has never been questioned by any intelligent Southern man. This we take to be the unwritten law of the South. . . . Let all Yankee schoolmasters who purpose invading the South, endowed with a strong nasal twang, a long Scriptural name, and Webster's lexicographic book of abominations, seek some more congenial land, where their lives will be more secure than in 'the vile and homicidal slave States.' "—Richmond *Examiner*, 1854, cited in a pamphlet entitled "A Bake-pan for Doughfaces," published at Burlington, Vt., by C. Goodrich.

shall 'publish or distribute' such works; and were I a citizen of New Orleans," adds the writer, "this work should not escape the attention of the grand jury." A year later, a writer in the same review maintains that "our school-books, especially, should be written, prepared, and published by Southern men"; and he inveighs against the readers and speakers used in the schools, and gives a list of those which are objectionable. One of them was the "Columbian Orator," and it is interesting to know that this was the first book which the slave, Frederick Douglass, bought. In it were speeches of Chatham, Sheridan, and Fox, and in reading and pondering these speeches the light broke in upon his mind, showing him that he was a victim of oppression, and that, if what they said about the rights of man was true, he ought not to be a slave. The writer in the *Review* complained that these books contained poems of Cowper and speeches of Webster which Southern children should not read, and he was certain that if parents knew their whole contents "they would demand expurgated editions for the use of their children." All schoolboys know that the kind of books complained of contain, for the most part, the choice selections of English literature—works that have survived owing to their elevation of thought and beauty of expression. Such attacks were a condemnation of literature itself, for from Homer down the master-spirits of many ages have reprobated slavery.

History, as well as literature, needed expurgation before it was adapted to the instruction of Southern youth. Peter Parley's "Pictorial History of the United States" was complained of, because the author, although a conservative Whig and far from being an abolitionist, deemed it necessary, in the course of his narrative, to mention slavery, the attempts at colonization, and the zeal with which some people labored "in behalf of immediate and universal emancipation."

It was likewise necessary to prepare the historical reading of adults with care. In an editorial notice in *De Bow's Reveiw* of the current number of *Harper's Magazine*, which had a large circulation at the South, it was suggested that the notice of the Life of Toussaint "had been better left out, so far as the South is concerned." To what absurdities did this people come on account of their peculiar institution! Touissant, as a brilliant historian of our day has told us, exercised on our history "an influence as decisive as that of any European ruler." He was, alike with Napoleon and Jefferson, one of the important links of that historical chain which secured for us Louisiana and New Orleans.

It is not from a periodical published in a corner, and carrying no influence, that these comments have been cited. *De Bow's Review* was devoted to economical and social matters; it was one of the most powerful organs of the thinking people and best society of the South. Moreover, it had received the endorsement of fifty-five Southern senators and representatives in Congress for the "ability and accuracy of its exposition of the working of the system of polity of the Southern States." De Bow was professor of political economy in the University of Louisiana, and his *Review* was published in the commercial metropolis of the South. Indeed, the provision for education in harmony with their institutions was a subject of grave consideration by thinking men, and a thoroughly representative body—the Southern commercial convention which was held at Memphis in 1853—paid it marked attention. The convention earnestly recommended to the citizens of the Southern States: "The education of their youth at home, as far as practicable; the employment of native teachers in their schools and colleges; the encouragement of a home press; and the publication of books adapted to the educational wants and the social condition of these States."

It is no wonder such recommendations were thought necessary, for many delegates must have remembered the difficulty which attended the publication of the works of Calhoun, although South Carolina appropriated ten thousand dollars for the purpose. A Charleston newpaper complained: "The writings of Mr. Calhoun were edited in Virginia; the stereotyped plates were cast in New York; they were then sent to Colum-

bia, where the impressions were struck off; the sheets were
thence transferred to Charleston in order that the books might
be bound; and now that they are bound, there is really no publisher in the State to see to their circulation."

If we contrast the North and the South in material prosperity, the South will appear to no better advantage than it does
in respect of intellectual development. Yet the superiority of
the North in this regard was by no means admitted. The thinking men of the South felt, if this were proved, a serious draw-
back to their system would be manifest. We find, therefore, in
the Southern literature many arguments to show that the contrary was true; most of them take the form of statistical demonstrations, in which the census figures are made to do strange
and wondrous duty. Parson Brownlow, of Tennessee, in a joint
debate at Philadelphia, where he maintained that American
slavery ought to be perpetuated, brought forward an array of
figures which demonstrated to his own satisfaction that the
material prosperity of the South was greater than that of the
North; and the time he was speaking it seemed to him that his
section was smiling with good fortune, while the Northern industries were crippled by the loss of Southern trade and by the
financial panic of 1857. A favorite method of argument was to
make a comparison between two representative States. Georgia
and New York were contrasted in the light of the census of
1850, with the result of convincing the Southern mind that in
social, political, and financial conditions Georgia was far superior to New York. A paper was read before the Mercantile
Society of Cincinnati to demonstrate that, as between Maryland and Massachusetts, Virginia and New York, Kentucky
and Ohio, the slave States were the more prosperous. "Virginia," says the author, "instead of being poor and in need of
the pity of the much poorer population of the North, is perhaps
the richest community in the world." After a comparison of the
census figures, the conclusion is that the free people of the
slave-holding States are much richer than those of the non-
slave-holding States. De Bow, in introducing this paper to his

public, said that, although it had been angrily assailed by the abolition press, it had never been refuted or invalidated in any material respect. Arguments, of which these are examples, are made by men who go with preconceived ideas to the statistics, and select therefrom what they deem will sustain their thesis. Such reasoning does not proceed from earnest seekers after truth. The speciousness of its deductions was shown over and over again. Indeed, it needed no extensive marshalling of statistics to prove that the welfare of the North was greater than that of the South. Two simple facts, everywhere admitted, were of so far-reaching moment that they amounted to irrefragable demonstration. The emigration from the slave States to the free States was much larger than the movement in the other direction; and the South repelled the industrious emigrants who came from Europe, while the North attracted them. "Leave us in the peaceable possession of our slaves," cried Parson Brownlow, "and our Northern neighbors may have all the paupers and convicts that pour in upon us from European prisons." This remark found general sympathy, because the South ignored, or wished to ignore, the fact that able-bodied men with intelligence enough to wish to better their condition are the most costly and valuable products on earth, and that nothing can more redound to the advantage of a new country than to get men without having been at the cost of rearing them.* This was occasionally appreciated at the South, and sometimes the greater growth in wealth and population of the North would break in upon the mind of Southern thinkers with such force that they could not hold their peace. Sometimes the truth would be owned, but its dissemination was prevented, for fear that the admission of it would furnish arguments to the abolitionists.

Two of the most careful observers who ever considered the differences between the South and the North are unimpeach-

* One of the imports of the United States, "that of adult and trained immigrants, . . . would be in an economical analysis underestimated at £ 100,000,000 a year."—Thorold Rogers, Lectures in 1888, *Economic Interpretation of History,* p. 407.

able witnesses to the greater prosperity of the latter. Washington noted, in 1796, that the prices of land were higher in Pennsylvania than in Virginia and Maryland, "although they are not of superior quality." One of the important reasons for the difference was that Pennsylvania had passed laws for the gradual abolition of slavery, which had not been done in the other two States; but it was Washington's opinion that "nothing is more certain than that they must, at a period not far remote," take steps in the same direction.

De Tocqueville was struck with the external contrast between the free and the slave States. "The traveller who floats down the current of the Ohio," he wrote, "to the point where that river joins the Mississippi may be said to sail between liberty and slavery; and he only needs to look around him in order to decide in an instant which is the more favorable to humanity. On the Southern bank of the river the population is thinly scattered; from time to time one descries a gang of slaves at work, going with indolent air over the half-desert field; the primeval forest unceasingly reappears; one would think that the people were asleep; man seems to be idle, nature alone offers a picture of activity and life. From the Northern bank, on the contrary, there arises the busy hum of industry which is heard afar off; the fields abound with rich harvests; comfortable homes indicate the taste and care of the laborer; prosperity is seen on all sides; man appears rich and content; he labors." The difference was greater when De Tocqueville visited this country than in Washington's day; and it was greater in 1850 than when the philosophic Frenchman recorded his observations in the book which is a classic in the science of politics. The difference was of a nature that must become intensified with the years.

What was the reason of the marked diversity between the two sections of the country? The only solution of the question is that which presented itself to the mind of De Tocqueville. "Almost all the differences which may be remarked between the Southerners and Northerners had their origin in slavery"; for the settlers of both sections of the country belonged "to the same European race, had the same customs, the same civilization, the same laws, and their shades of difference were very slight." It is true that the Cavalier colonized Virginia, and the Puritan in England began coming nearer together, until, by the middle of the nineteenth century, there was no longer a line of demarcation. After the American Revolution, however, the difference between the Virginian and the man of Massachusetts increased so that it became the remark of travellers, the theme of statesmen, and finally a subject for the arbitrament of the sword. In that contest the Scotch-Irishman of South Carolina fought on one side, and the Scotch-Irishman of Pennsylvania fought on the other; but in the seventeenth century, on their native soil, they would have stood shoulder to shoulder in a common cause.

Nor will the diversity of climate account in any considerable degree for the difference between the South and the North in material prosperity and intellectual development. The climate of Virginia and Kentucky was like that of Pennsylvania and Ohio; yet the contrast was seen in a marked degree between those communities. The climate of the slave States as a whole was not warmer than that of Italy or Spain, and those countries have been the seat of an energetic and intellectual people.* An illustration showing that the physical conditions of the South did not require slavery was seen in the German colony settled in Texas. By 1957 the Germans made up nearly one-half of the white population of Western Texas, and constituted a community apart. They believed in the dignity of labor; those who had not land were willing to work for the proprietors, and those who had capital would not purchase slaves. They were industrious, thrifty, fairly prosperous, and contented. They brought from their homes some of the flowers of civilization, and were an

* "Contemplated in the mass, facts do not countenance the current idea that great heat hinders progress."—*Sociology,* Herbert Spencer, vol. i. p. 19. "High degrees of moral sentiment control the unfavorable influences of climate; and some of our grandest examples of men and of races come from the equatorial regions—as the genius of Egypt, of India, and of Arabia."—Emerson's *Lecture on Civilization.*

oasis in the arid desert of slavery. Olmsted had a happier experience among these people than in his journey from the Mississippi to the James, where he failed to see the common indications of comfort and culture. Among the Germans of Texas, he wrote, "you are welcomed by a figure in blue flannel shirt and pendent beard," quoting Tacitus; you see "Madonnas upon log walls;" coffee is served you "in tin cups upon Dresden saucers;" and you hear a symphony of Beethoven on a grand piano. These Germans loved music and hated slavery. In 1854, after their annual musical festival at San Antonio, they resolved themselves into a political convention, and declared that slavery was an evil which ought eventually to be removed.

In giving the South credit for producing able politicians, we have not exhausted the subject of the virtues of her social system. The little aristocracy, whose nucleus was less than eight thousand large slave-holders, had another excellence that deserves high esteem. While in the North their manners were often agressive, in their own homes they displayed good breeding, refined manners, and dignified deportment. And these were more than outside show; the Southern gentleman was to the manner born. In society and conversation he appeared to the best advantage. He had self-assurance, an easy bearing, and to women a chivalrous courtesy; he was "stately but condescending, haughty but jovial." Underneath all were physical courage, a habit of command, a keen sense of honor, and a generous disposition. The Southerners were fast friends, and they dispensed hospitality with an open hand. They fitted themselves for society, and looked upon conversation as an art. They knew how to draw out the best from their guests; and, with all their high self-appreciation, at home they did not often indulge in distasteful egotism. They amused themselves with literature, art, and science; for such knowledge they deemed indispensable for prolonging an interesting conversation. They were cultivated, educated men of the world, who would meet their visitors on their own favorite ground.

If we reckon by numbers, there were certainly more well-bred people at the North than at the South; but when we compare the cream of society in both sections, the palm must be awarded to the slave-holding community. The testimony of English gentlemen and ladies, few of whom have any sympathy with slavery, is almost unanimous in this respect. They bear witness to the aristocratic bearing of their generous hosts. Between the titled English visitors and the Southern gentlemen there was, indeed, a fellow-feeling, which grew up between the two aristocracies separated by the sea. There was the concord of sentiments. The Southern lord, like his English prototype, believed that the cultivation of the soil was the finest and noblest pursuit. But nearly all educated Englishmen, whether belonging to the aristocracy or not, enjoyed their intercourse with Southerners more than they did the contact with the best society at the North, on account of the high value which they placed on good manners. The men and women who composed the Brook farm community, and the choice spirits whom they attracted, were certainly more interesting and admirable than any set of people one could meet in Richmond, Charleston, or New Orleans; but society, properly so called, is not made up of women with missions and men who aim to reform the world. The little knot of literary people who lived in Boston, Cambridge, and vicinity were a fellowship by whom it was an honor to be received; but these were men of learning and wisdom; they were "inaccessible, solitary, impatient of interruptions, fenced by etiquette"; and few of them had the desire, leisure, or money to take part in the festive entertainments which are a necessary accompaniment of society.

When the foreign visitors who came here during the generation before the war compared Northern and Southern society, they had in their minds the people whom they met at dinners, receptions, and balls; the Northern men seemed frequently overweighted with business cares, and, except on the subjects of trade, politics, and the material growth of the country, were not good talkers. The merchant or manufacturer of Boston, New York, or Philadelphia was a busy man; he had not the leisure of his Southern brother to cultivate the amenities of life, and he lacked that abandon of manners which Englishmen found so charming in the slaveholding lords.

This superiority of the best Southern society undoubtedly grew out of the social system of which slavery was the basis; but there went with it two drawbacks. In these circles where conversation was a delight, one subject must be treated with the utmost delicacy. The Englishman could argue with his Southern host that a monarchy was better than a republic, but he might not exult over the emancipation of the slaves in the West Indies. The German could deny the inspiration of the Bible, but he might not question that the institution of slavery was divine. One was made to feel in the most emphatic manner that his host desired no expression on the subject other than an opinion that the relation which existed between the whites and the blacks at the South was the necessary one.

The high sense of personal worth, the habit of command, the tyranny engendered by the submission of the prostrate race, made the Southern gentleman jealous in honor, sudden and quick in quarrel. While the duello was not an outgrowth of slavery, its practice in the South was more savage and bloody than anywhere else in the civilized world. The custom of going about fully armed to be prepared for an enemy, the readiness with which pistols were used on slight provocation, the frequent occurrence of deadly street fights, were an anomaly among a people so urbane and generous; but they were the result of slavery.

From youth the slave-holder was accustomed to have his word regarded as law; when he insisted, others yielded. Accustomed to irresponsible power over his dependants, he could not endure contradiction, he would not brook opposition. When one lord ran against another in controversy, if the feelings were deeply engaged the final argument was the pistol. The smaller slave-holders, influenced partly by the same reason and partly actuated by imitation of the aristocracy, settled their disputes in like manner, but more brutally, for they also used the bowie-knife in their encounters. The poor whites aped their betters.

The consequence was a condition of society hardly conceivable in a civilized, Christian, Anglo-Saxon community. In the new States of the Southwest, it was perhaps explainable as incident to the life of the frontier; but when met with in the old communities of Virginia and the Carolinas, it could admit but of one influence—that it was primarily due to slavery. But slavery itself and these attendant phenomena were survivals in the South, more than in any other contemporary enlightened community, of a passing militant civilization.

I have endeavored to describe slavery and its effects as it might have appeared to an honest inquirer in the decade before the war. There was no difficulty in seeing the facts as they have been stated, or in arriving at the conclusions drawn. There was a correct picture of the essential features of slavery in *Uncle Tom's Cabin,* the book which everybody read. The author of it had "but one purpose, to show the institution of slavery truly just as it existed." While she had not the facts which a critical historian would have collected—for the *Key to Uncle Tom's Cabin* was not compiled until after the novel was written—she used with the intuition of genius the materials gained through personal observation, and the result was what she desired. If we bear in mind that the novelist, from the very nature of the art, deals with characteristic and not with average persons, the conclusion is resistless that Mrs. Stowe realized her ideal. Fanny Kemble wrote to the *London Times* that she could bear witness to the truth and moderation of *Uncle Tom's Cabin* as a representation of the slave system in the United States, and added that her testimony was "the experience of an eye-witness, having been a resident in the Southern States, and having opportunities of observation such as no one who has not lived on a slave estate can have." It was certain, she proceeded, that the incident of Uncle Tom's death was not only possible, but it was unfortunately a very probable occurrence. Olmsted came to the conclusion that cases like the Red River episode were not extremely rare.

The fidelity of truth of that portion of the novel was sometimes questioned in a curious way. Bishop Polk assured an English clergyman that he "had been all over the country on Red River, the scene of the fictitious sufferings of Uncle Tom, and that he had found the temporal and spiritual welfare of the negroes well cared for. He had confirmed thirty black persons near the situation assigned to Legree's estate."

A Northern doctor of divinity who wrote a book in defence of slavery based on a three months' sojourn at the South, admitted that "some of the warmest advocates of slavery [at the South] said that they could parallel most of the abuses in slavery mentioned in the book out of their own knowledge; and on speaking of some bad master and wishing to express his tyrannical character and barbarous conduct, they would say, 'He is a real Legree'; or, 'He is worse than Legree.'" A Southern Presbyterian preacher who published a book of speeches and letters to maintain that "slavery is of God," and ought "to continue for the good of the slave, the good of the master, and the good of the whole American people," said: "I have admitted, and do again admit, without qualification, that every fact in 'Uncle Tom's Cabin' has occurred in the South"; and again he speaks of it as "that book of genius, true in all its facts, false in all its impressions." The great desire of the author to be impartial was evident from the description of slave-holders; the humane and generous men were even more prominent in the story than the inhuman ones. She did justice to the prevailing and correct sentiment at the South that Northerners were harder masters than Southern men, by making Legree, whose name became a synonym for a brutal slave-holder, a son of New England.

Mrs. Stowe was felicitous in her description of the negro character. There was a fitness in the secondary title of the book, "Life among the Lowly." It was the life she had studied with rare human sympathy, and in its portrayal the author's genius is seen to the best advantage. Some critics objected that Uncle Tom was an impossible character, and that the world, in weeping at the tale of his ill-treatment and sufferings, exhibited a mawkish sentimentality. But the author knew his prototype. Frederick Douglass also describes a colored man whose resemblance to Uncle Tom was "so perfect that he might have been the original of Mrs. Stowe's Christian hero." Rev. Noah Davis, who wrote in a little book the narrative of his own life, certainly equalled Uncle Tom in piety, self-denial, and industry.*

The author's most conspicuous failure as a portrayer of manners is in the descriptions of the best society at the South. Nor is this surprising. Her life was an earnest working one, and she had no conception of a society where dinner-parties, receptions, and balls made up the lives of its votaries. Her associates were ministers, devoted to their calling, and hard-working college professors, who esteemed learning above all; their thoughts were so engrossed in their serious occupations that the lighter graces of life seemed like folly and idleness. It is, then, no wonder that the subtle charm which exquisite manners spread over plantation life and New Orleans society completely eluded the observation of the author.

The Southern people desired to stand well at the great tribunal of modern civilization. As their peculiar institution was under the ban of the most enlightened portion of the world, they made repeated efforts to set themselves in the right. As long as the argument followed the line of admitting the evil, while averring that for the present, at least, slavery seemed the most advantageous relation between the two races at the South, the slave-holders had much sympathy from the North and from England. It was conceded that if the slaves were freed, civil rights must eventually be accorded them. This condition staggered many who hated slavery. In those Northern States where the negro had the right to vote, that right was exercised only with great difficulty and some danger; and the blacks were few in number, and patiently submitted to a practical annulling of their privilege. But the fact was appreciated that at the South,

* A Narrative of the Life of Noah Davis, a colored man, written by himself, published at Baltimore, 1859. I am informed by a colored man who knew him well that Davis was truly a religious man, and had the confidence and respect of all classes of citizens.

owing to the great number of negroes, the problem would be a fair different one. There was, therefore, considerable sympathy with the opinion of McDuffie, that if the slaves were freed and made voters, no rational man could live in such a state of society. Basil Hall, who travelled in this country in 1827 and 1828, believed that the slave-holders were "a class of men who are really entitled to a large share of our indulgence"; that no men were more ready than were most of the American planters to grant "that slavery is an evil in itself and eminently an evil in its consequences;" but to do away with it seemed "so completely beyond the reach of any human exertions that I consider the abolition of slavery as one of the most profitless of all possible subjects of discussion." The difficulty did not escape the philosophic mind of De Tocqueville. "I am obliged to confess," he wrote, "that I do not regard the abolition of slavery as a means of putting off the struggle between the two races in the southern States. . . God forbid that I should justify the principle of negro slavery, as some American writers have done; but I only observe that all the countries which formerly adopted that execrable principle are equally able to abandon it at the present time."

Owing, however, to the efforts which Southern statesmen made for the extension of slavery, it became necessary to maintain the proposition that slavery is a positive good. The logic of the abolitionists likewise had influence in goading the Southern reasoners to this position. "Twenty years ago," wrote W. Gilmore Simms, "few persons in the South undertook to justify negro slavery, except on the score of necessity. Now, very few persons in the same region question their perfect right to the labor of their slaves; and, more, their moral obligation to keep them still subject as slaves, and to compel their labor, so long as they remain the inferior beings which we find them now, and which they seem to have been from the beginning. This is a great good, the fruit wholly of the hostile pressure."

The book from which this passage is taken contains all that can be said in favor of slavery. The jurist, the statesman, the *littérateur,* and the educator—the most distinguished writers of the Southern States united in a publication of collected essays which they had written for Southern magazines, and gave them to the world under the title of *The Pro-slavery Argument.* As I have already had occasion to refer many times to this work, an extended abstract of it would be profitless. In the light of our day it is melancholy reading. It is the waste of varied ability in a doomed cause.

Chancellor Harper devotes the larger part of his essay to arguing the good of slavery as an abstract question. Governor (afterwards Senator) Hammond applies himself to proving two texts: First, that the domestic slavery of these States is "not only an inexorable necessity for the present, but a moral and humane institution, productive of the greatest political and social advantages;" and, "I endorse without reserve the much-abused sentiment of Governor McDuffie, that 'slavery is the corner-stone of our republican edifice;' while I repudiate, as ridiculously absurd, that much lauded but nowhere accredited dogma of Mr. Jefferson, that 'all men are born equal.' " Simms's contribution to this volume, entitled "Morals of Slavery," was a criticism of Harriet Martineau's description of the peculiar institution. He felt that, as a candid man, he must make some damaging admissions, and that ultimately he would be obliged to resort to recrimination; he therefore fortified his reasoning in advance by demanding, "Why should we account to these people? What are they, that they should subject us to the question? . . . The Southern people form a nation, and, as such, it derogates from their dignity that they should be called to answer at the tribunal of any other nation. When that call shall be definitely or imperatively made, they will answer with their weapons, and in no other language than that of war to the knife"*

---

* *Pro-slavery Argument,* p. 384. This essay of Prof. Dew was a review of the debate in the Virginia legislature, 1831–32 (see p. 57), attracted much attention, and had great influence on public sentiment in Virginia at the time. The argument was regarded as convincing, and worthy of publication in connection with essays of a later date.

Dew, the professor of history, metaphysics, and political law at William and Mary College, Virginia, propounded two questions: "Can these two distinct races of people, now living together as master and servant, be ever separated?" and "will the day ever arrive when the black can be liberated from his thraldom and mount upward in the scale of civilization and rights, to an equality with the white?" He answered both of these questions with a decided negative; his article, full of deductions from history and law, and abounding in wealth of illustration, essayed to prove that any such consummation was either undesirable or impossible. He narrowed the question to Virginia; but the inference was plain that what applied to Virginia could with greater force be urged in reference to most of the other slave States. The author arrived at this conclusion: "There is slave property of the value of $100,000,000 in the State of Virginia, and it matters but little how you destroy it, whether by the slow process of the cautious practitioner, or with the frightful despatch of the self-confident quack; when it is gone, no matter how, the deed will be done, and Virginia will be a desert."

We can only regard with pity these arguments that were retailed in the select circles of the South, and used to persuade willing Northern and English visitors. When we meet them in their naked form, we can only turn away with disgust. A representative from Louisiana, during the debate on the compromise of 1850, said in the House: "A union is not worth a curse as long as distinction exists between negroes and horses." "Niggers are property, sir," an illiterate slave-holder told Olmsted, "the same as horses and cattle; and nobody has anymore right to help a negro that has run away than he has to steal a horse."

A writer in *De Bow's Review* maintained that slavery of the negro was no worse than slavery of the ass. "God made the world," he tells us. "God gave thee there thy place, my hirsute brother; and, according to all earthly probabilities and possibilities, it is thy destiny therein to remain, bray as thou wilt. From the same great power have our sable friends, Messrs. Sambo, Cuffee & Co., received their position also . . . Alas, 'my poor black brother!' thou, like the hirsute, must do thy braying in vain. Where God has placed thee there must thou stay." A unique book of several hundred closely printed pages was published at Natchez in 1852, entitled *Studies on Slavery, in Easy Lessons*. A considerable portion of it was devoted to combating the views of Wayland as found in his "Moral Science," and of Channing as elaborated in his treatise on "Slavery." The author takes issue with Channing on the statement, "Now, I say, a being having rights cannot justly be made property; for this claim over him virtually annuls all his rights." The Southern apostle rejoins: "We see no force of argument in this position. It is also true that all domestic animals held as property have rights. 'The ox knoweth his owner, and the ass his master's crib.' They all have 'the right of petition,' and ask in their way for food; are they the less property?"

So long as Southern reasoners maintained that the negro race was inferior to the Caucasian, their basis was scientific truth, although their inference that this fact justified slavery was cruel as well as illogical. But the assertion that the negro does not partake of the nature of mankind is as repugnant to science as it is to common-sense. The chimpanzee is not so near in intellect to the blackest Congo as is this negro to Daniel Webster. The common possession of language creates a wide gulf between man and the highest of the other animals.

The chief argument in favor of slavery was drawn from the Bible. The Mosaic law authorized the buying and holding of bondmen and bondmaids; it was therefore argued that if God's chosen people were not only permitted but enjoined to possess slaves, slavery must certainly be an institution of the Deity. Texts of approval from the New Testament were more difficult to find. Although slavery in the Roman empire was an obtrusive fact, Christ was silent on the subject. The apologists of slavery made the utmost of Paul's exhortation to servants to obey their masters; yet of all the writings of the apostle of the Gentiles, the one of chief value to these special pleaders was his shortest epistle. It was used as a triumphant justification of the Fugitive

Slave law. Paul sent back the runaway slave Onesimus to his master Philemon, the inclination to retain him being outweighed by the justice of his owner's claim.

The weighty scriptural argument, however, was that based on the curse of Canaan. This reasoning had been used by the fathers of the Christian church, but its force was vastly greater as employed to justify negro slavery. It seems amazing that a few verses of a chapter of Genesis should be sincerely deemed sufficient warrant for the degradation of more than three million human beings. The unscientific use of the Bible in the nineteenth century to defend slavery finds a striking parallel in its use in the seventeenth and eightenth centuries to defend the belief in witchcraft against the attacks of science. Jefferson Davis, in the debate upon the compromise measures, asserted that slavery "was established by decree of Almighty God" and that "through the portal of slavery alone has the descendant of the graceless son of Noah ever entered the temple of civilization." The persistence with which these statements were made, and the fact that they were believed in good faith, gave the institution a rooted strength which it could not have gained from reasoning based only on human considerations. When doubts of the right to hold slaves would rise in the minds of religious men at the South, they were checked by the thought that this was to question the mysterious ways of an inscrutable Providence. Noah had said, presumably with authority from on high: "Cursed be Canaan [the son of Ham]; a servant of servants shall he be unto his brethren." Blessed be Shem, and blessed be Japeth, and Canaan shall be their servant.

Nor was the influence of this argument confined to the South. It seemed to many Christians at the North that it was flying in the face of Providence to wish a change in the divinely ordered relation of master and slave between the descendant of Japheth and the descendant of Ham. Stranger yet does it seem to us, who are willing to accept the conclusions about the origin of race which have been arrived at by the patient and brilliant investigators of our day, that Emerson, who was to go

beyond the letter and grasp the spirit, should have been so profoundly swayed by the Mosic explanation of the blackness of
the negro. "The degradation of that black race," he said,
"though now lost in the starless spaces of the past, did not come
without sin."

But the biblical argument in favor of slavery did not remain
unchallenged. Between 1850 and 1860, the anti-slavery people
received large accessions from Christian ministers and teachers,
and with as firm faith in the inspiration of the Bible as the
Southern religionists, they took up the gauntlet and joined issue
on the chosen ground. Whether the Bible and the Christian
religion sanctioned slavery, was a prominent topic in the joint
debates that were held in Northern cities. The anti-slavery literature is full of such discussions. On the logical point, there is
no question that the Northern reasoners had altogether the better of the argument. The spirit of Christianity was certainly opposed to slavery; under the Roman empire it had ameliorated
the condition of the slaves, and during the middle ages it had
been the chief influence in the abolition of slavery in Europe.

The fact that the slaves had their material wants supplied
and were without anxiety for the morrow was urged without
ceasing as one of the benefits of the system. When Seward visited
Virginia he was told that they were the "happiest people in the
world." Frederika Bremer was convinced that under a good
master the slaves were "much better provided for than the poor
working people in many parts of Europe." Lyell quotes the observations of a Scotch weaver who had spent several weeks on
cotton plantations in Alabama and Georgia, and who asserted
that he had not there witnessed one fifth of the real suffering he
had seen in manufacturing establishments in Great Britain.
This agreed with Lyell's own experience. Lady Wortley was
impressed by the fact that the slaves "seemed thoroughly happy
and contented." Mackay was convinced that the slaves were
"better clad, fed, and cared for than the agricultural laborers of
Europe or the slop tailors and semstresses of London and Liverpool." Achille Murat, who became a Florida planter, maintained
that the slaves were happier than the laborers in the large En-

glish manufacturing towns and than European peasants in general; and he wrote further that slavery, when viewed from afar, has quite a different physiognomy from that which presents itself when viewed on the spot; "that which appears rigorous by law becomes lenient by custom."

The opinions of these foreign travellers, with the exception of the Scotch weaver who supported himself by manual labor and only saw the lower society, were greatly influenced by the generous hospitality of Southern gentlemen. Harriet Martineau had found that hospitality so remarkable and grateful that she discerned in it the lurking danger of blinding many to the real evils of slavery. In those spacious country-houses everything was so "gay and friendly," there was "such a prevailing hilarity and kindness," that one forgot the misery on which this open-handed way of living was based. The liberality and heartiness of Southern entertainments made a powerful impression on Lyell, who has left a graceful testimony of "the perfect ease and politeness with which a stranger is made to feel himself at home."

The character in which the slave-holding lord wished to appear to the world is well illustrated by a fanciful account in *The Southern Literary Journal* of a visit by a nineteenth-century Addison to Sir Roger de Coverley's plantation. The Carolina de Coverley is described as having all the virtues of the famous English knight, whose faithful old domestics, grown gray-headed in the service, are paralled by "healthy, laughing, contented" negroes, who are "comfortably provided for," whose "sleep is sweet," and who "care not for the morrow." The devotion of the ancient servants to the English Sir Roger, their joyful welcome when he returned from a journey, the mixture of the father and the master of the family in his conduct to his dependants, is likened to the "endearing relation" which exists between the slaves and the Carolina lord.* But the imitator of

---

* "In 'the days that are no more,' so confiding and affectionate was the relation of the master and the slave, and we, who personally loved many of them, cannot now easily become reconciled to the attitude of alienation in which the negroes stand towards us."—Mrs. Davis in 1890, *Memoirs of Jefferson Davis*, vol. i. p. 311.

this most graceful of sketches unwisely draws beyond the lines
of his model, and fouls with the dark blot of slavery a bright
and charming picture of rural life. "Cleanliness is indispensable
to health," says Sir Roger de Coverley of Carolina, "and makes
the slave prolific. I have at this time a hundred and fifty of these
people; and their annual increase may be estimated as adding
as much to my income as arises from all other sources." The
love of art as well as the love of liberty would have prevented
Joseph Addison from putting such words into the mouth of his
knight; for had Sir Roger spoken them, he would have been no
longer the old-fashioned country gentleman of high honor and
rare benevolence that remains as one of the characteristic crea-
tions of English literature.

A well-known result of slavery was the denial of free speech
at the South. While Southern advocates of the rightfulness of
slavery were heard willingly at the North in joint debate,˙or
from the lyceum platform, Garrison and Parker would have
forfeited their lives had they gone South and attempted to get
a hearing. The circulation of anti-slavery newspapers and
books was suppressed as far as possible. One book, however,
and the most dangerous of all, found many readers. The desire
to read *Uncle Tom's Cabin* was too great to be crushed by
the usual efforts at repression.

It must, however, be confessed that reason enough existed
for the denial of free speech and a free press. The first duty of
a society is self-preservation. Whether or not the danger of slave
insurrections was great, it is certain that the fear of them was
real and ever present. "I speak from facts," said John Randolph,
"when I say that the night bell never tolls for fire in Richmond,
that the frightened mother does not hug her infant the more
closely to her bosom, not knowing what may have happened. I
have myself witnessed some of the alarms in the capital of
Virginia." De Tocqueville was struck by the inevitable danger
of a struggle between the blacks and whites in the slave States.
While he found the subject discussed freely at the North, it was
ignored at the South; yet the tacit foreboding of servile insur-

rection in that community seemed more dreadful than the expressed fears of his Northern friends. Men in the slave States were wont to deny the danger, but Fanny Kemble testified that all Southern women to whom she had spoken about the matter admitted that they lived in terror of their slaves. Never elsewhere had she known "anything like the pervading timidity of tone," and it was her belief that the slave-holders lived in a "perpetual state of suspicion and apprehension." Olmsted saw "more direct expression of tyranny in a single day and night at Charleston than at Naples under Bomba, in a week."

A SHOWY *Jacksonian Democrat who had risen to be brigadier general in the Mexican War without fighting any battles, Franklin Pierce was elected president in 1852 as a dark-horse candidate who, like Polk before him, had been nominated when the jealousies of more experienced men made their selection impossible. He carried all but four states against the unappealing Whig leader Winfield Scott, though his popular majority fell below fifty thousand. He was a weak executive. Without great ability or force of character, he hoped to score a brilliant success in foreign affairs, acquiring Cuba and making it a member of the Union. Fortunately for the country, he got nowhere with this plan, for Spain continued to hold Cuba tightly.*

Rhodes offers an effective narrative of the Pierce administration. He might have made it clearer that Pierce committed a disabling error at the outset when he tried to please all the Democratic factions by giving each a representative in the Cabinet. William L. Marcy of New York, the secretary of state, came in as a devoted Unionist and an opponent of slavery expansion. Jefferson Davis, the secretary of war, had lately been ready to break up the Union if not permitted to widen the bounds of slavery. Caleb Cushing of Massachusetts, a man of few moral convictions and complete subservience to slavery interests, was made attorney general. The border slave states gained control of the treasury by the appointment of James Guthrie of Kentucky as secretary. Altogether the administration leaned strongly to the Southern side. Thomas Hart Benton later declared it an administration in which the president was powerless, "and in which nullifiers, disunionists, and renegades used his name . . . for their own audacious and criminal purposes."

By his maladroit tactics, Pierce quickly made enemies. Meanwhile, as Rhodes shows, the strongest man in his Cabinet proved not to be the elderly Marcy but the brilliant and energetic Jefferson Davis, who did more than anybody else to control the president. By the end of 1853 it was plain that the government was drifting. It had no strong hand at the helm. The three great leaders of the Senate, who had done so much to make that chamber powerful and enlightened—Henry Clay, John C. Calhoun, and Daniel Webster,—had died. Since Pierce had failed to impress the Democratic leaders or catch the imagination of the country, a new president would have to be chosen in 1856. Rhodes might have made it clearer that the Democratic party was torn by dissension because Pierce had given it no common ground of principle; and that party dissensions and the feeling of most people that a strong new governmental policy was needed gave an opening to some leader who could offer a fresh and dramatic course of action. Such a leader was soon to lift his voice in Congress.

One of the most stirring parts of Rhodes's History *is his long chapter describing the debate upon the bill for the organization of the Nebraska area which Senator Stephen A. Douglas introduced in Congress at the beginning of 1854. This was to prove the most important and disastrous enactment of the Pierce administration. Douglas had seen that the drifting government needed some strong new lead, and that a dramatic stroke might rescue the administration from the doldrums into which it had fallen. A formula was needed to open the trans-Missouri West to railroads and settlement; he moved all too precipitately to offer it. The result was the wildest storm that the slavery issue had yet created and a drastic realignment of American politics.*

The main reasons for the storm were simple. The so-called Nebraska country covered a tremendous area, extending from the 40th parallel northward to the Canadian line, and from the Missouri River westward to the Continental Divide. Bill after bill had been introduced, beginning in 1850, to give it territorial organization. All had been defeated, chiefly because of Southern opposition. Stubborn proslavery leaders, seeing that the country lay north of the Missouri Compromise line, refused to budge. When Douglas reported his new bill from the committee on territories, he at first hoped to evade the slavery question. Southern interests, however, insisted that the legis-

lation should include an explicit repeal of the Miss-
ouri Compromise and thus open the Western reaches
to all settlers who wished to carry slaves into them.

Pierce's Administration

WHILE the term "the solid South" had not come into use, politicians were beginning to think what a force there might be in
the fact. The South would have one hundred and seventeen
votes in the next convention, and, since it was pretty well understood that there was no chance of the nomination of a Southern
man, it was evident that if this strength could be concentrated
on a favorite son of the North, it would, added to his home support, assure him the nomination. Thoughts and calculations
like these must have passed through Douglas's mind during his
trip of recreation to Europe the preceding summer; and when
he came to Washington to survey the ground, one way was manifest in which he might commend himself to Southern favor. The
acquisition of Cuba was out of his province. While free trade
was popular at the South, the senator had no taste for economical questions, and the Pacific railroad was a Western measure.
But the organization of the new territories might be handled in
a satisfactory manner; this, moreover, was the favorite field of
Douglas, and he was chairman of the committee on territories.
A bill for the organization of the territory of Nebraska had
passed the House at the previous session and was reported to
the Senate. This bill was in the usual form, but made no reference whatever to slavery. It encountered opposition in the Senate, as involving bad faith with the Indians; and as it came up
late in the session, there was not sufficient time for its consideration, so it failed to become a law. The same bill was introduced
into the Senate in December, 1853, and referred to the committee on territories. On the 4th of January, 1854, Douglas made
a report which was the introduction to a project whose importance cannot be overestimated. The territory Nebraska com-

prised what is now the States of Kansas, Nebraska, the Da-
kotas, Montana, part of Colorado, and Wyoming. It was part
of the Louisiana purchase, and contained four hundred and
eighty-five thousand square miles, a territory more than ten
times as large as New York, and larger by thirty-three thousand
square miles than all the free States then in the Union east of
the Rocky Mountains. In this magnificent domain were less
than one thousand white inhabitants; but as soon as it should
be opened to settlement by proper legislation, there was certain to be a large immediate increase of population.*

This report of Douglas's began with the announcement of the
discovery of a great principle which had been established by
the compromise measures of 1850. They "were intended to have
a far more comprehensive and enduring effect than the mere
adjustment of difficulties arising out of the recent acquisition
of Mexican territory. They were designed to establish certain
great principles, which would not only furnish adequate remedies for existing evils, but, in all time to come, avoid the perils
of similar agitation by withdrawing the question of slavery from
the halls of Congress and the political arena, committing it to
the arbitration of those who were immediately interested in,
and alone responsible for, its consequences. . . . A question has
arisen in regard to the right to hold slaves in the territory of
Nebraska, when the Indian laws shall be withdrawn and the
country thrown open to emigration and settlement. . . . It is a
disputed point whether slavery is prohibited in the Nebraska
country by valid enactment. . . . In the opinion of those eminent
statesmen who hold that Congress is invested with no rightful
authority to legislate upon the subject of slavery in the territories, the eighth section of the act preparatory to the admission
of Missouri is null and void." The reader may be reminded that

---

* One of the objections made to the organization of the territory was
on account of insufficient population, but it was not well taken. Douglas
was well informed on this point, and showed clearly that if the restrictions
in favor of the Indians were removed, there would be a large influx of
settlers. Benton, who opposed the Nebraska bill of Douglas, was positive
that a territorial government ought to be at once established for Nebraska.
See *Harper's Magazine*, Dec., 1853, p. 121.

the gist of the Missouri Compromise lay in this eighth section, which provided that slavery should be prohibited in all the Louisiana territory lying north of 36°30' north latitude, not included within the limits of the State of Missouri. Douglas's report continued: "The prevailing sentiment in large portions of the Union sustains the doctrine that the Constitution of the United States secures to every citizen an inalienable right to move into any of the territories with his property, of whatever kind and description, and to hold and enjoy the same under the sanction of law." Yet the committee did not propose to recommend the affirmation or the repeal of the eighth section of the Missouri act. The report concluded with the statement, "The compromise measures of 1850 affirm and rest upon the following propositions:

"First—That all questions pertaining to slavery in the territories, and the new States to be formed therefrom, are to be left to the decision of the people residing therein, by their appropriate representatives, to be chosen by them for that purpose.

"Second—That 'all cases involving title to slaves' and 'questions of personal freedom' are to be referred to the jurisdiction of the local tribunals, with the right of appeal to the Supreme Court of the United States.

"Third—That the provision of the Constitution of the United States in respect to fugitives from service is to be carried into faithful execution in all 'the organized territories,' the same as in the States."

The bill reported by the committee as first printed contained the provision that the territory of Nebraska, or any portion of the same, when admitted as a State or States, "shall be received into the Union with or without slavery, as their Constitution may prescribe at the time of their admission." This language was borrowed from the Utah and New Mexico bills, which were a part of the compromise of 1850. Three days after the bill was first printed another section was added, which incorporated into the bill these closing propositions of the committee's report.

Douglas professed to have discovered a way by which the

slavery question might be put to rest. But everybody North and South, as well as Douglas himself, knew that this report would certainly open up again the agitation. The country was at peace. Business was good; evidences of smiling prosperity were everywhere to be seen. The spirit of enterprise was rampant; great works were in progress, others were projected. Political repose was a marked feature of the situation. The slavery question seemed settled, and the dream of the great compromisers of 1850 seemed to be realized. Every foot of land in the States or in the territories seemed to have, so far as slavery was concerned, a fixed and settled character. The obnoxious part of the compromise to the North, the Fugitive Slave law, was no longer resisted. Another era of good feeling appeared to have set in. The earnest hope of Clay, that the work in which he had so large a share would give the country rest from slavery agitation for a generation, did not seem vain. There has been restored, said the President in his message, "a sense of repose and security to the public mind throughout the confederacy." This quiet was ruthlessly disturbed by Douglas's report, which, though professing in one part not to repeal the Missouri Compromise, closed with a proposition which certainly set it aside. The Missouri Compromise forever prohibited slavery in what was now the territory of Nebraska. Douglas proposed to leave to the inhabitants of Nebraska the decision as to whether or not they would have slavery. From the circumstances under which the Missouri Compromise was enacted, from the fact that it received the seal of constitutionality from an impartial President and a thoroughly representative cabinet, it had been looked upon as having the moral force of an article of the Constitution itself. For what purpose was the repose of the country disturbed by throwing a doubt on the constitutionality and application of an act which had been acquiesced in and observed by both parties to the compact for thirty-four years?

The motives which actuate men who alter the current of their time are ever an interesting study; and in this case no confidential letters or conversations need be unearthed to arrive at a

satisfactory explanation. We may use the expression of the Independent Democrats in Congress and say that the dearest interests of the people were made "the mere hazards of a presidential game"; or we may employ the words of John Van Buren, an
astute politician who was in the secrets of the party, and ask,
"Could anything but a desire to buy the South at the presidential shambles dictate such an outrage?" And this true statement and the inference from this trenchant question explain the
motives prompting Douglas to this action. Even those who were
very friendly to the measure did not scruple openly to express
this opinion. One wrote that Douglas had betrayed "an indiscreet and hasty ambition"; another granted that the object of
Douglas "was to get the inside track in the South." The defences
made by Douglas and his friends at the time and in the succeeding years, when his political prospects depended upon the
justification of his course, are shuffling and delusive. None are
satisfactory, and it may with confidence be affirmed that the
action of the Illinois senator was a bid for Southern support in
the next Democratic convention. In truth, Douglas might have
used the words of Frederick the Great when he began the unjust
war against Austria for the conquest of Silesia: "Ambition, interest, the desire of making people talk about me, carried the
day, and I decided" to renew the agitation of slavery.

Douglas subsequently, veiling his own ambition under the
wish to promote the interests of the Democratic party, confessed
in part the truth of this impeachment. He said that his party, in
the election of Pierce, had consumed all its powder, and therefore, without a deep-reaching agitation, it would have no more
ammunition for its artillery. Yet it was patent to every one—
and none knew it better than Douglas, for he was the ablest
politician of the party—that the Democrats needed to make no
fresh issue; that to let things drift along and not turn them into
new channels was the safest course, and that appeals to past history were the best of arguments. An economical administration,
a reduction of the tariff, a vigorous and just foreign policy, were
certain to keep the Democrats in power as long as man could

foresee. There was, it is true, one element of uncertainty. The factions quarrel in New York had led to defeat at the last State election; but the party was so strong that even without the Empire State it could retain its ascendency in the nation, and there was, moreover, good reason to hope that this trouble would be patched up before another presidential election.

To become the acknowledged and dominating leader of so strong a party seemed to an ardent partisan an object worthy of any exertion and any sacrifice. It was the ambition of Douglas to hold the same position among the Democrats that Clay had held among the Whigs. Clay attained that position by being the originator of important legislative measures and by carrying them to a successful issue. The ability of Douglas lay in this direction, and he, like Clay, was a natural leader of men. Indeed, they were men of similar parts, strong natures whose private vices were hardly hidden. But Clay had profound moral convictions which, although sometimes set at naught in the heat of partisan conflict, were of powerful influence in his political career; in the view of Douglas, moral ideas had no place in politics.

Douglas prepared the bill without consultation with any Southern men. It was submitted first to two Western senators, and, after their approval was given, was shown to their Southern friends.* It became the object of some of those opposed to the Nebraska bill to show that the project was dictated by the

---

* This was the statement of Douglas in the Senate in 1856, *Congressional Globe,* vol. xxxiii. p. 393. I have never seen any well-attested evidence which contradicts this statement. Butler, of South Carolina, said in the Senate during the debate: "I have had very little to do with this bill, and I believe the South has had very little to do with the provisions of the bill." At the time of the greatest unpopularity of this legislation, Douglas said in the Senate (Feb. 23d, 1855): "The Nebraska bill was not concocted in any conclave, night or day. It was written by myself, at my own house, with no man present. Whatever odium there is attached to it, I assume it. Whatever of credit there may be, let the public award it where they think it belongs." The earliest premonition of the report which I have found is in the New York *Herald* of Jan. 2d, 1854: "It is understood that the territory of Nebraska is to be admitted into the confederacy upon such terms as will leave it at the option of her people to make it either a slave or free territory."

South. Much credence was given to a boast of Senator Atchison, made under the inspiration of the invisible spirit of wine, that he had forced Douglas to bring in such a bill. It was also charged that Toombs and Stephens had been the potent influence which had brought about the action. The Illinois senator, in April, 1856, denied both of these imputations, and all the circumstances support the truth of this denial.* Douglas was a man of too much independence to suffer the dictation of Atchison, Toombs, or Stephens. He always wanted to lead, and was never content to follow.

Immediately on the publication of the report the anti-slavery people of the North took alarm. The newspapers which were devoted to freedom saw the point at once and made clear the scheme which was in progress. One journal said it was a "proposition to turn the Missouri Compromise into a juggle and a cheat"; it was "presented in so bold and barefaced shape that it is quite as much an insult as it is a fraud." Another called it an overt attempt to override the Missouri Compromise. Another termed the project low trickery, which deluded the South with the idea that it would legalize slavery in Nebraska, and at the same time cheated the North "with a thin pretence of not repealing the existing prohibition." The anti-slavery press responded more quickly than the people whose sentiment they both represented and led. The people of the South were as much surprised at the report as those of the North. Not counting upon Douglas as one of their adherents through thick and thin, they at first viewed the proposition with distrust, and some even regarded it as "a snare set for the South." But the senators and representatives from the slave-holding States understood the matter better than the people and the press, and knew that Douglas had taken a long stride in their direction. As he could

* In 1886, Jefferson Davis, in a letter to a friend, said: "So far as I know and believe, Douglas and Atchison never were in such relation to each other as would have caused Douglas to ask Atchison's help in preparing the bill, and I think the whole discussion shows that Douglas originated the bill, and for a year or two vaunted himself on its paternity."—*Memoirs of Jefferson Davis,* by his wife, vol. i. p. 671.

not retrace his steps, he could therefore be easily influenced to alter his bill in a manner that should make it conform pretty nearly to their cherished wish.

On Monday, the 16th of January, Dixon, a Whig senator from Kentucky, who was filling the unexpired term of Henry Clay, offered an amendment to the Nebraska act, which provided in set terms for the repeal of the slavery-restriction feature of the Missouri Compromise. The Senate was astonished and Douglas was startled. He went at once to Dixon's seat and remonstrated courteously against the amendment. He said that in his bill he had used almost the same words which were employed in the Utah and New Mexico acts; and as they were a part of the compromise measures of 1850, he hoped that Dixon, who had been a zealous friend of that adjustment, would do nothing to interfere with it or weaken it before the country. Dixon replied that it was precisely because he was a zealous friend of the compromise of 1850 that he had introduced the amendment; in his view, the Missouri Compromise, unless expressly repealed, would continue to operate in the Territory of Nebraska; and while the bill of Douglas affirmed the principle of non-intervention, this amendment was necessary to carry it legitimately into effect. That being the well-considered opinion of Dixon, he was determined to insist upon his amendment.

On the 17th of January, Sumner offered an amendment to the Nebraska act which expressly affirmed the slavery restriction of the Missouri Compromise.

A few days after Dixon had surprised the Senate, Douglas called to see him and invited him to take a drive. The conversation turned upon the subject which was uppermost in their minds, and, to the great delight of Dixon, the Illinois senator proposed to take charge of his amendment and incorporate it in the Nebraska bill. As Dixon reports the familiar talk, Douglas in substance said: "I have become perfectly satisfied that it is my duty, as a fair-minded national statesman, to co-operate with you as proposed in securing the repeal of the Missouri

Compromise restriction. It is due to the South; it is due to the Constitution, heretofore palpably infracted; it is due to that character for *consistency* which I have heretofore labored to maintain. The repeal, if we can effect it, will produce much stir and commotion in the free States of the Union for a season. I shall be assailed by demagogues and fantastics there, without stint or moderation. Every opprobrious epithet will be applied to me. I shall probably be hung in effigy in many places. It is more than probable that I may become permanently odious among those whose friendship and esteem I have heretofore possessed. This proceeding may end my political career. But, acting under the sense of duty which animates me, I am prepared to make the sacrifice; I will do it." Dixon relates that Douglas spoke in an earnest and touching manner; the Kentucky senator was deeply affected and showed emotion in the reply that he made. "Sir," he said, "I once recognized you as a demagogue, a mere party manager, selfish, and intriguing. I now find you a warm-hearted and sterling patriot. Go forward in the pathway of duty as you propose, and though all the world desert you, *I never will.*"

It was a pretty comedy. The words of Douglas are those of a self-denying patriot, and not those of a man who was sacrificing the peace of his country, and, as it turned out, the success of his party, to his own personal ambition. Between the Monday on which the amendment repealing the Missouri Compromise was introduced, and the day of the drive with Dixon, Douglas resolved to take a further step in the path on which he had entered. Of course, all sorts of influences were brought to bear upon him by Southern men, and there was one powerful argument from the Democratic point of view. While the difference between Democrats and Whigs at the South was no longer essential, the party organizations remained intact, and each endeavored to win an advantage over the other by taking more pronounced ground in the interest of slavery. It would not do, therefore, to have a measure of so obvious advantage to the South fathered by a Whig, even by one who truly felt, as he afterwards stated in the Senate: "Upon the question of slavery, I know no Whiggery and I know no Democracy." This argument and others undoubtedly had their influence on Douglas; but, in truth, he had laid out his course when he made the report of the 4th of January. He had then crossed the Rubicon; he was now preparing to burn his bridges behind him.

Unquestionably Douglas would have preferred to stand on the proposition as at first introduced. It is the testimony of two personal and political friends that he was reluctant to incorporate in his bill a clause virtually repealing the Missouri Compromise. The ambiguous character of the first project was not without design, and suited his purpose exactly. At the South it could be paraded as a measure in her interest, while at the North there might be honest differences of opinion whether or not the slavery restriction was set aside; and in the inception of this movement it is probable that Douglas thought that, no matter what legislation was had, none but free States would be formed out of this territory. This was certainly his opinion in 1850, when he maintained that "the Missouri Compromise had no practical bearing upon the question of slavery—it neither curtailed nor extended it an inch. Like the ordinance of 1787, it did the South no harm, the North no good." And in the same speech he expressed the opinion that the Nebraska territory would be forever free, and out of it would be formed at least six free States. It was rumored at the time, and was always believed by many of the friends of Douglas, that what finally decided him to shape the bill in accordance with Dixon's views was because he had reason to believe that if he did not take that step Cass would forestall him, support the repeal of the Missouri Compromise, and thereby gain an important advantage in the race for the Democratic nomination.

Douglas had written his report and prepared his first bill without any consultation with the President, but the rising tide of Northern sentiment against the measure, and the certainty that the murmur would become a roar, admonished him that nothing could be safely omitted which would aid the passage of the act through both houses of Congress. He felt confident that success in the Senate was certain, but the power and influence of the administration might be necessary to insure a majority in the House. He sought, therefore, the assistance of the President. Pierce, through his own organ, the Washington *Union*, which faithfully represented his opinions, had approved the report of the committee on territories; but he did not regard with favor the amendment of Dixon, and on January 20th the *Union* argued against it.*

On Sunday morning, January 22d, Douglas, in company with other gentlemen, members of Congress, called on Jefferson Davis, and stated to him the proposed change in the Nebraska bill. They further desired that he would procure them on that day an interview with the President, who, as they knew, was strictly opposed to receiving visits or discussing political affairs on Sunday; but it was highly important to introduce the substitute on the following day, and Douglas would not do so without consulting the President. Davis went with them to the White House. He stood on such friendly footing with Pierce that the door was always open to him, and, leaving his companions in the reception-room, he proceeded at once to the private apartments of the President and unfolded the object of their visit. Afterwards the President met the gentlemen, listened to the reading of the bill, gave attention to the arguments of Douglas explanatory of the proposed alteration, and in the end promised the support of the administration. We may feel certain, however, that it was the persuasion of Davis at the private interview which induced the President to give his approval. He could not have forgotten that, less than two months

---

* "To repeal the Missouri Compromise might, and according to our view would, clear the principle of congressional non-intervention of all embarrassment; but we doubt whether the good thus promised is so important that it would be wise to seek it through the agitation which necessarily stands in our path. Upon a calm review of the whole ground, we yet see no such reasons for disturbing the compromise of 1850 as could induce us to advocate either of the amendments proposed to Mr. Douglas's bill."— Washington *Union*, Jan. 20th. The amendments referred to are Dixon's and Sumner's.

previously, when in his message he mentioned that in regard to the slavery and sectional question there had been "restored a sense of repose and security to the public mind throughout the confederacy," he had added, "That this repose is to suffer no shock during my official term, if I have power to avert it, those who placed me here may be assured." On this Sunday he had the power to fulfil the solemn pledge he had given the nation and its representatives; but his hankering after a renomination made him easily susceptible to the influences which were brought to bear upon him.

Douglas had reckoned wisely when he applied to Davis for help in gaining the President. There were two opposing influences in the administration, one represented by the Secretary of State and the other by the Secretary of War, and Douglas knew that in this affair it was Davis that he should call upon. Pierce loved and trusted Davis, who had, moreover, the backing of the Southern Democracy, which the President was now anxious to conciliate in order to effectually contradict reports current in the South that the administration was tinctured with Free-soilism. Yet Pierce was also solicitous for the support of Marcy in this affair, and requested Douglas and his companions to call upon him for consultation. This wish was, of course, complied with, but the Secretary of State was not found at home.

On Monday, January 23d, Douglas offered a substitute for his preceding bill. It differed from the other in two particulars. It affirmed that the slavery restriction of the Missouri Compromise "was superseded by the principles of the legislation of 1850, commonly called the compromise measures, and is hereby declared inoperative"; and it divided the great territory into two parts, calling the northern portion Nebraska, and the southern Kansas. The northern and southern boundaries of Kansas were the same as those of the present State, but the western limit was the Rocky Mountains, and the total area one hundred and twenty-six thousand square miles.

We cannot clearly trace the ways leading up to this division of Nebraska, which apparently formed no part of the original plan. Nor is the explanation of Senator Douglas sufficient. It is almost certain that if there had been no question of slavery, this change would not have been made. A steadfast Northern follower of Douglas has acknowledged that the purpose which he had in view by this division was to make one slave and one free State; and there is much in the contemporaneous evidence to lead one to this conclusion. In the summer and fall of 1853, a movement began in western Missouri with the avowed object of making Nebraska slave territory. In that portion of the State there were fifty thousand slaves, worth perhaps twenty-five millions of dollars, and the interests of their owners seemed to demand that the contiguous country should be devoted to slavery. Senator Atchison urged this view warmly, showing that the only obstacle to their wishes lay in the Missouri Compromise. Coming to Washington on the opening of Congress, he felt that he had an aggressive sentiment behind him which demanded the repeal of the slavery restriction. His eyes, and those of his constituents, were cast longingly on the country which is now Kansas, and in which they hoped slavery might gain the foothold it had in Missouri. The Missouri border abounded in adventurous spirits who were ready for any enterprise; Atchison and his fellow slave-holders were confident that if the restriction were removed, these men could be used to advantage in establishing a slave State. Kansas was all they wanted, and the territory, if divided, would be easier to manage. That all this was known to the Southern Democrats and Whigs in Congress and to Senator Douglas is indisputable. The supporters of the Nebraska bill came together so frequently in caucus and conference that, if all the features of the situation were not discussed, they must certainly have been well understood. Indeed, the expectation that Kansas would become a slave State was openly expressed on the floor of the House. It follows plainly enough, therefore, that the division of the territory was in the interest of slavery; and if Douglas had not been brought to the point of actually conceding that Kansas should be a slave State, he at least knew that there was a well-devised scheme in progress to make it one.

Tuesday, the 24th of January, was a notable day in the history of the Kansas-Nebraska bill. Dixon stated in the Senate that he was entirely satisfied with the amendment Douglas had incorporated in his bill; and the Washington *Union* had a carefully written editorial which was the fruit of the conference of the preceding Sunday. After endorsing the substitute of the committee on territories, the organ of the President went on to say: "We cannot but regard the policy of the administration as directly involved in the question. That policy looks to fidelity to the compromise of 1850 as an essential requisite in Democratic orthodoxy. The proposition of Mr. Douglas is a practical execution of the principles of that compromise, and, therefore, cannot but be regarded by the administration as a test of Democratic orthodoxy. The union of the Democracy on this proposition will dissipate forever the charge of Free-soil sympathies so recklessly and pertinaciously urged against the administration by our Whig opponents; while it will take from disaffection in our ranks the last vestige of a pretext for its opposition."

On this same day (January 24th) was published the "Appeal of the Independent Democrats in Congress to the People of the United States." Chase wrote the paper from a draft made by Giddings, and it received some verbal corrections from Sumner and Gerrit Smith. These men signed it, as did also Edward Wade and Alexander De `Witt, representatives from Ohio and Massachusetts. All of the signers were Free-soilers. Like so many political manifestoes, composed in the midst of agitating events and under the influence of powerful emotion, the Appeal of the Independent Democrats is strong in expression; but few partisan documents will stand so well the test of time. It expresses earnest feeling, but it relates truthful history. The historical argument is incontrovertible. The reasoning is earnest, but the writers felt that, having history and justice on their side, they needed only to make fair statements, and that the straining of any point was unnecessary. Viewing it in the calm light of the present, criticism is silent. Had the language been less strong, the writers would not have shown themselves equal to the occasion. It is a brave, truthful, earnest exposition.

It should be remarked that all of the address except the post-script was written before Douglas introduced his substitute of January 23d, and has reference to the report and first bill of the committee on territories. The Appeal states at the outset that, should the project receive the sanction of Congress, it "will open all the unorganized territory of the Union to the ingress of slavery." Therefore, "We arraign this bill as a gross violation of a sacred pledge; as a criminal betrayal of precious rights; as part and parcel of an atrocious plot to exclude from a vast unoc-cupied region immigrants from the Old World and free laborers from our own States, and convert it into a dreary region of despotism inhabited by masters and slaves." The history of the Missouri Compromise is then related, and the truthful state-ment is made: "For more than thirty years—during more than half the period of our national Constitution—this compact [i. e., the Missouri Compromise] has been universally regarded and acted upon as inviolable American law." And now it is proposed to cancel this compact. "Language fails to express the senti-ments of indignation and abhorrence" which the Nebraska act inspires. "It is a bold scheme against American liberty worthy of an accomplished architect of ruin. . . . Shall a plot against humanity and democracy so monstrous, and so dangerous to the interest of liberty throughout the world, be permitted to suc-ceed? We appeal to the people. We warn you that the dearest interests of freedom and the Union are in imminent peril. . . . Let all protest, earnestly and emphatically, by correspondence, through the press, by memorials, by resolutions of public meet-ings and legislative bodies, and in whatever other mode may seem expedient, against this enormous crime."

The postscript, which was written just before the Appeal was given to the press, relates to the substitute of January 23d. The truth of the emphatic statements with which it closes has never been successfully impugned, and they may justly receive the seal of impartial history. "This amendment," the Appeal says, "is a manifest falsification of the truth of history. . . . Not a man in Congress, or out of Congress, in 1850 pretended that the compromise measures would repeal the Missouri prohibition. Mr. Douglas himself never advanced such a pretence until this session. His own Nebraska bill, of last session, rejected it. It is a sheer afterthought. To declare the prohibition inoperative may, indeed, have effect in law as a repeal, but it is a most discreditable way of reaching the object. Will the people permit their dearest interests to be thus made the mere hazards of a presidential game, and destroyed by false facts and false inferences?"

This appeal was published in nearly all the newspapers of the free States. The field had been well prepared for the sowing of this seed. Connected with the journals of this time were many able and earnest men full of enthusiasm for a righteous cause. Almost without exception, the conspicuous editors at the North took ground from the first against the Nebraska act, and their papers abounded in sharp criticisms of the author of the measure and in entreaties to the friends of freedom not to permit the consummation of the infamy. Some regarded the measure with anger, others with grief, and all with apprehension. The public mind was in a state that could not fail to be profoundly affected by an authoritative and impressive protest from Washington. It is true that the Free-soil congressmen had not a large political following; but their arguments were so cogent that they convinced and roused many men who had been accustomed to regard the authors of the Appeal with mistrust. If the politicians at Washington, wrote one earnest journalist, have any doubt about the public opinion, let them put their ears to the ground and they "will hear the roar of the tide coming in."

When Douglas came into the Senate on the morning of January 30th, he was a prey to angry excitement, and shortly after his entrance he took the floor to open the debate on the Kansas-Nebraska bill. The reason of his rage was soon apparent. It was caused by the Appeal of the Independent Democrats and by the indications of public sentiment which had already reached

Washington, and which Douglas was inclined to attribute wholly to the prompting of this address. In deference to the wishes of Chase and Sumner, he had postponed the consideration of the bill for six days, and now he charged Chase with having come to him "with a smiling face and the appearance of friendship," begging for delay, merely in order to get a wide circulation for the Appeal and forestall public opinion before an exposition of the measure was made by its author. The address, he said, grossly misrepresented the bill, arraigned the motives and calumniated the characters of the members of the committee, and the postscript applied coarse epithets to himself by name. Chase endeavored to interrupt the speaker, and an excited colloquy followed; Douglas lost his temper completely, and emphatic language was used by both senators, so that they were at different times called to order by the president. This, one may gather from the official report in the *Congressional Globe;* but it was stated that Douglas carefully corrected his remarks before publication, and struck out many opprobrious words he had used. Several Washington correspondents agree in their description of the manner and language of Douglas. One speaks of his "senatorial billingsgate," and of the "vulgarity and vehemence of the abuse which he poured out upon Senator Chase"; another described the scene as one of "intemperate violence," and maintained that the course of Douglas was "indecorous and a most reprehensible violation of the dignity of the body," and that his style of attack was "more becoming a pot-house than the Senate"; and another spoke of his speech as "violent and abusive." In spite of the fact that the display of temper at the outset lost Douglas in a certain degree the respect of his audience, the speech was conceded by his opponents to be able and ingenious, indeed the very best that could be made in a very bad cause. An earnest abolitionist paid a tribute to the remarkable force and adroitness of the argument.

Douglas stated that by the Missouri Compromise of 1820 a geographical line had been established, north of which slavery was prohibited, and south of which it was permitted. When

New Mexico and California were acquired, a logical adherence to that principle required the extension of this line to the Pacific Ocean. On his motion in 1848, the Senate had adopted such a provision; but it failed in the House, being defeated "by Northern votes with Free-soil proclivities." This refusal to extend the Missouri Compromise line to the Pacific Ocean gave rise to a furious slavery agitation, which continued until it was quieted by the compromise measures of 1850. In that series of acts, the principle established was: "Congressional non-intervention as to slavery in the territories; that the people of the territories . . . were to be allowed to do as they pleased upon the subject of slavery, subject only to the provisions of the Constitution." Although the only territorial bills which were a part of the plan of 1850 were those organizing Utah and New Mexico, yet the Missouri Compromise line, in all the unorganized territory not covered by those bills, was superseded by the principles of that compromise. "We all know," said the senator, "that the object of the compromise measures of 1850 was to establish certain great principles, which would avoid the slavery agitation in all time to come. Was it our object simply to provide for a temporary evil? Was it our object just to heal over an old sore and leave it to break out again? Was it our object to adopt a mere miserable expedient to apply to that territory, and that alone, and leave ourselves entirely at sea, without compass, when new territory was acquired or new territorial organizations were to be made? Was that the object for which the eminent and venerable senator from Kentucky [Clay] came here and sacrificed even his last energies upon the altar of his country? Was that the object for which Webster, Clay, and Cass, and all the patriots of that day, struggled so long and so strenuously? Was it merely the application of a temporary expedient in agreeing to stand by past and dead legislation that Baltimore platform pledged us to sustain the compromise of 1850? Was it the understanding of the Whig party when they adopted the compromise measures of 1850 as an article of political faith, that they were only agreeing to that which was past and had no reference

to the future?" By no means. In the legislation of 1850 a
principle was adopted—the principle of congressional non-
interference with slavery, and when the two party conventions
resolved to acquiesce in the compromise measures, they were
giving pledges that in their future action they would carry out
that principle. Now it is necessary to organize the territory of
Nebraska. The Missouri Compromise restriction is inconsistent
with this later principle and should give place to it. "The legal
effect of this bill," continued Douglas, "is neither to legislate
slavery into these territories nor out of them, but to leave the
people do as they please. . . . If they wish slavery, they have a
right to it. If they do not want it, they will not have it, and you
should not force it upon them."

Did Douglas describe the workings of his own mind between
January 4th and 23d, when he said, in graphic words: "I know
there are some men, Whigs and Democrats, who . . . would be
willing to vote for this principle, provided they could do so in
such equivocal terms that they could deny that it means what it
was intended to mean, in certain localities." But he went on to
say: "I do not wish to deal in any equivocal language. If the
principle is right, let it be avowed and maintained. If it is
wrong, let it be repudiated. Let all this quibbling about the
Missouri Compromise . . . be cast behind you; for the simple
question is, will you allow the people to legislate for themselves upon the question of slavery? Why should you not?" For
the benefit, probably, of what he called "tender-footed Democrats," he maintained that it was worse than folly to think of
Nebraska being a slave-holding country. Nor did the manifestations of public sentiment averse to the measure frighten
Douglas. "This tornado," he said, "has been raised by abolitionists, and abolitionists alone."

The senator made an argument based on the fact that the
boundary lines of New Mexico and Utah, as constituted, annulled the Missouri Compromise in a part of the territory to
which it applied. While this at the time was considered ingenious reasoning, it was effectually refuted by Chase and Everett,

and Douglas did not allude to it in his speech which closed the debate; nor was this the argument he relied on in the many defences he made of his present course in after-years.

When Douglas sat down, Chase obtained the floor and made a defence of the Appeal of the Independent Democrats. They meant exactly what they said; it was not an occasion for soft words; they considered the Missouri Compromise a sacred pledge, and its proposed abrogation "a criminal betrayal of precious rights." "What rights are precious," demanded the senator, "if those secured to free labor and free laborers in that vast territory are not?" The attempt of Douglas to shield himself under the ægis of Clay and Webster was not overlooked; the Illinois senator knew it to be a strong point, and in after-years elaborated it into a statement that he had given the "immortal Clay," lying on his death-bed, a pledge that his energies should be devoted to the vindication of the principle of leaving each State and territory free to decide its institutions for itself, and he had also given the same pledge to the "godlike Webster." On the day when this justification was first broached, Chase must have felt that if he held his peace, the stones would cry out against it, and he emphatically asserted: "When the senator vouches the authority of Clay and Webster to sustain him, he vouches authorities which would rebuke him could those statesmen speak from their graves."

On the 3d of February, Chase made his mark in an elaborate speech against the Kansas-Nebraska bill, and on that day he took a place in the foremost ranks of the statesmen who devoted themselves to anti-slavery principles.

He was, with perhaps the exception of Sumner, the handsomest man in the Senate, and as he rose to make his plea for the maintenance of plighted faith, all felt the force of his commanding presence. More than six feet high, he had a frame and figure proportioned to his height; with his large head, massive brow, and smoothly shaven face, he looked like a Roman senator; and the similitude was heightened by his coming to plead against the introduction of Punic faith into the Congress of the

United States. He appreciated the gravity of the situation, and attributed the crowded galleries, the thronged lobbies and the full attendance of the Senate to the transcendent interest of the theme. Chase was not a fluent and easy speaker; he had less of the spirit of the orator than Douglas; he could not sway an audience of the Senate as could the Little Giant. Nevertheless, the dignity of his manner and the weight of his words obtained him a careful hearing, and he was listened to with attention by senators and visitors.

When Congress met, he said, "no agitation seemed to disturb the political elements." The two great political parties "had announced that slavery agitation was at an end;" the President "had declared his fixed purpose to maintain the quiet of the country. . . . But suddenly all is changed. . . . And now we find ourselves in an agitation the end and issue of which no man can foresee. Who is responsible for this renewal of strife and controversy? . . . It is slavery. . . . And what does slavery ask for now? It demands that a time-honored and sacred compact shall be rescinded—a compact which has endured through a whole generation; a compact which has been universally regarded as inviolable, North and South; a compact the constitutionality of which few have doubted, and by which all have consented to abide." The ground on which it is proposed to violate this compact is supposed to be found in the doctrine that the restriction of the Missouri Compromise is superseded by the principles of the compromise measures of 1850. This is a "statement untrue in fact and without foundation in history." It is, continued the senator, "a novel idea. At the time when these measures were before Congress in 1850, when the questions involved in them were discussed from day to day, from week to week, and from month to month, in this Senate Chamber, who ever heard that the Missouri prohibition was to be superseded? What man, at what time, in what speech, ever suggested the idea that the acts of that year were to affect the Missouri Compromise? . . . Did Henry Clay, in the report made by him as chairman of the committee of thirteen, or in any speech in support of the compromise acts, or in any conversation, in the committee or out of the committee, ever even hint at this doctrine of supersedure? Did any supporter or any opponent of the compromise acts ever vindicate or condemn them upon the ground that the Missouri prohibition would be affected by them? Well, sir, the compromise acts were passed. They were denounced North and they were denounced South. Did any defender of them at the South ever justify his support of them upon the ground that the South had obtained through them the repeal of the Missouri prohibition? Did any objector to them at the North ever even suggest, as a ground of condemnation, that that prohibition was swept away by them? No, sir! No man, North or South, during the whole of the discussion of those acts here, or in that other discussion which followed their enactment throughout the country, ever intimated any such opinion." After effectually refuting the argument of Douglas drawn from the constitution of the boundaries of New Mexico and Utah, and giving an account of the anti-slavery opinions of the fathers of the government, Chase related briefly and correctly the history of the Missouri Compromise, and in a few words he stated the obligations which that act imposed on the South. He said: "A large majority of Southern senators voted for it."

To *a great body of Northerners the repeal of the Missouri Compromise was an outrage not to be brooked. The country above the Compromise line had enjoyed exemption from the crippling institution for thirty-four years, a full generation. To carry slavery into it was, in Lincoln's graphic imagery, to put snakes into the beds of the children of the Western country. When Senators Sumner of Massachusetts, Seward of New York, and Chase of Ohio denounced Douglas's bill as "a gross violation of a sacred pledge" and "a criminal betrayal of sacred rights," they felt a passionate anger against the "slave power." The presidency was in the hands of a weak man who sympathized with the South; the strongest Cabinet members were Southerners or Southern sympathizers; Congress was dominated by Southern groups. Feeling that the republic was in danger of a fatal perversion, a host of determined men awoke to the clarion of battle.*

Rhodes's narrative of this exciting part of our political history has had the substantial endorsement of most subsequent historians, although scholars of Southern sympathies have dissented from its strong Free Soil point of view and have questioned parts of its interpretation of Douglas's motives. Douglas perhaps thought that climate would exclude slavery from the Nebraska country anyway; he soon learned that the only way he could get the bill passed was by repeal of the Compromise. Rhodes might well have explained more fully the multiplicity of the forces pressing Douglas to his rash step. They included his desire to assist his friend David Atchison politically, his interest in helping Chicago and northern Illinois gain new railroad advantages, his pride in his historic rolé as the chief figure in organizing and developing new territories, and his realization that the inept Pierce Administration needed a firm new path. His moral obtuseness to the evils of slavery—for he did not care whether it was voted up or voted down—and his natural impetuosity were large elements in his course. If he hoped to become president, a legitimate ambition, he soon found that he had taken the wrong road.

Douglas and the Kansas-Nebraska Act

W HEN the scope of the Kansas-Nebraska act came to be thoroughly understood, when it was noted that the friends of Southern institutions in Congress were earnest in its favor and that the abolitionists were vehemently opposed to it, the newspapers began to praise Douglas warmly and to advocate his measure with zeal. The exceptions were few, and were practically confined to New Orleans and the commercial cities of the border States. While some observers reported a feeling of indifference in regard to the measure, this arose from the fact that it was not perfectly understood, or because its passage would be regarded as a barren victory. There was no doubt, however, that the Charleston *Courier* faithfully represented Southern opinion when it remarked, "We cherish slavery as the apple of our eye, and are resolved to maintain it, peaceably if we can, forcibly if we must"; and it may confidently be stated that when the Kansas-Nebraska bill was understood to be of benefit to slavery, Southern sentiment at that moment became concentrated in its favor. "The South flies to the bill," wrote Francis Lieber from South Carolina, "as moths to the candle."

The legislatures of the slave States were slower to act than those of the North. Before the bill passed the Senate, only Georgia had spoken. Her House unanimously, and the Senate with only three dissenting votes, adopted resolutions strongly in favor of the bill, and instructed her delegation to vote in Congress accordingly. In Tennessee the Senate endorsed the principles of the Kansas-Nebraska act, but the House laid a similar resolution on the table. Not until after the bill had passed the United States Senate did the legislatures of Mississippi and Louisiana adopt resolutions approving it.

And now the day had come when a vote on the bill was to be taken. The Senate met on the 3d of March at the usual hour, and an animated discussion of the measure consumed the afternoon and evening. The floor was full and the galleries were crowded when Douglas rose, a half an hour before midnight, to close the debate. He offered to waive his privilege in order that they might proceed to vote; but many senators protested, and begged him to go on. The importance of the occasion and the influence which this speech might have on his future career might well make even as ready a speaker as Douglas tremble when he thought what he must confront. The bill had passed to a third reading the day previous by a vote of twenty-nine to twelve, so that argument in the Senate was needless; but the people of the North were almost unanimously against the measure and its author, and it was to them that Douglas spoke with extraordinary energy and ability, persuading and imploring them to reverse their verdict. A feeling of regret that he had provoked this controversy must have mingled with the excitement of the combatant in the contest; but there was no trace of it in his manner as he applied himself vigorously to the work of justifying himself, of defending his bill, and of hurling defiance at his opponents.

The appearance of Douglas was striking. Though very short in stature, he had an enormous head, and when he rose to take arms against the sea of troubles which opposed him, he was the very picture of intellectual force. Always a splendid fighter, he seemed this night like a gladiator who contended against great odds; for while he was backed by thirty-seven senators, among his fourteen opponents were the ablest men of the Senate, and their arguments must be answered if he expected to ride out the storm which had been raised against him. Never in the United States, in the arena of debate, had a bad cause been more splendidly advocated; never more effectively was the worse made to appear the better reason.

The opponents of the bill, he said, had misrepresented the issue to the country; they wished the people to believe that the paramount object of the bill was to repeal the Missouri Compromise. "That which is a mere incident they choose to consider the principle. They make war on the means by which we propose to accomplish an object instead of openly resisting the object itself. The principle which we propose to carry into effect is this: *That Congress shall neither legislate slavery into any territories or State, nor out of the same; but the people shall be left free to regulate their domestic concerns in their own way, subject only to the Constitution of the United States.* In order to carry this principle into practical operation, it becomes necessary to remove whatever legal obstacles might be found in the way of its free exercise. It is only for the purpose of carrying out this great fundamental principle of self-government that the bill renders" the Missouri restriction inoperative and void.

Douglas then went on to show, by extracts from his speeches, that as he thought now, so had he thought in 1850; and at that time the legislature of his State believed that the principle should be so applied. We are ccntending, he maintained, for "the great fundamental principle of popular sovereignty"; and as the Missouri restriction is inconsistent with that principle, it ought to be abrogated. Instead of the opponents of this bill talking about "the sanctity of the Missouri Compromise and the dishonor attached to the violation of plighted faith, . . . why do they not meet the issue boldly and fairly and controvert the soundness of this great principle of popular sovereignty in obedience to the Constitution?" It is because "the doctrine of the abolitionists—the doctrine of the opponents of the Nebraska and Kansas bill and of the advocates of the Missouri restriction —demands congressional interference with slavery, not only in the territories, but in all the new States to be formed therefrom. It is the same doctrine, when applied to the territories and new States of this Union, which the British government attempted to enforce by the sword upon the American colonies. It is this fundamental principle of self-government which constitutes the distinguishing feature of the Nebraska bill. . . . The onward march of this great and growing country," he continued, made it necessary for the committee on territories to give a government to Nebraska; and then we met this question of slavery.

It could be settled on the principle of 1820, which was congressional interference, or on the principle of 1850, which was non-interference. "We chose the latter for two reasons; first, because we believed that the principle was right; and, second, because it was the principle adopted in 1850, to which the two great political parties of the country were solemnly pledged." If we will adopt this principle, the senator further argued, "it will have the effect to destroy all sectional parties and sectional agitators." If the slavery question is withdrawn from the political arena and removed to the States and territories, each to decide for itself, there can be no more agitation of slavery. If this vexed question is removed from politics, the agitators will be deprived of their vocation. There will be no further necessity for bargains between the North and the South.

"I have not," said Douglas at the close of his argument, "brought this question forward as a Northern man or as a Southern man. I am unwilling to recognize such divisions and distinctions. I have brought it forward as an American senator, representing a State which is true to this principle, and which has approved of my action with respect to the Nebraska bill. I have brought it forward not as an act of justice to the South more than to the North. I have presented it especially as an act of justice to the people of those territories, and of the States to be formed therefrom, now and in all time to come. I have nothing to say about Northern rights or Southern rights. I know of no such divisions or distinctions under the Constitution. The bill does equal and exact justice to the whole Union, and every part of it; it violates the rights of no State or territory, but places each on a perfect equality, and leaves the people thereof to the free enjoyment of all their rights under the Constitution."

The foregoing extracts will give an idea of the line of argument which Douglas pursued; but nearly the whole speech must be read to comprehend the skill with which specious arguments were urged, and duly to estimate the dexterity with which an historical account of the Missouri Compromise and succeeding events was used. The kindly feeling of the audience towards him

from the first was increased by his audacity, and with artful
management he gained their sympathy. He told how he had
been maligned all over the country. He had been burned in
effigy in all the abolition towns of Ohio because they believed
the misrepresentations of Chase; he had been hanged in effigy
in Boston, owing to the influence of Sumner; but that he considered an honor, for this same Boston had closed Faneuil Hall
to the immortal Webster. A remonstrance had been presented to
the Senate in which he was called "a traitor to his country, to
freedom, and to God, worthy only of everlasting infamy"; and
he had even received insulting letters from Ohio, rejoicing at
his domestic bereavements,* and praying that still greater
calamities might befall him. The state of public sentiment of
which these were the manifestations was, the senator averred,
due to the misrepresentations of his opponents, and particularly
to those which were contained in the Appeal of the Independent
Democrats.

In spite of his warmth of argument and vehemence of attack,
Douglas showed the most perfect courtesy to his antagonists.
When Seward, Chase, or Sumner, to whom he especially addressed himself, desired to interrupt him to correct a statement
or briefly reply to an argument, Douglas cheerfully yielded the
floor; but every rejoinder showed that in debate he was more
than a match for any one of these senators. The politeness with
which he complied with their requests for a hearing, and the
force of his answers, caused Seward to burst out, in admiration,
"I have never had so much respect for the senator as I have
to-night."

In the course of his speech, Douglas took up Everett's argument, and showed by the construction he put upon Webster's
7th-of-March speech that he could twist the language of the
clearest of speakers to his purpose as well as he could distort
the facts of history.

While the suavity of Douglas during the whole night was remarkable, he did not propose to let Chase and Sumner off as

* The wife of Douglas died Jan. 19th, 1853.

easily as he had Seward and Everett. Their charge that his measure was offered as a bid for Presidential votes was a ranking wound, and he demanded with a show of sincere indignation if they were "incapable of conceiving that an honest man can do a right thing from worthy motives?" Nor did he think that these senators were proper judges of his character or principles, for he intimated that they had obtained their seats in the Senate "by a corrupt bargain or dishonorable coalition." This angered Chase, who met it with an indignant denial, and Sumner made a calm refutation. In the excited colloquy which followed between Chase and a Democrat from California, who insisted on charging directly that Douglas had only implied, the "Little Giant" was cool, and, restraining the impetuosity of his supporter, continued the defence of his own motives; and, with the address of a master of parliamentary art, he made it appear, by the most delicate implication, that he was a self-sacrificing patriot, while Chase was actuated by an "unworthy ambition."

Douglas spoke until daybreak, and the crowd remained to hear the last words of the giant, who was flushed with victory and seemed to exult in his strength. Senator Houston explained why he could not consent to a violation of the Missouri Compromise; and then the vote was taken. The Senate was composed of sixty-one members,* of whom fifty-one were present, and the vote stood 37 in favor to 14 against the bill. There were recorded in the affirmative fourteen Northern Democrats, fourteen Southern Democrats, and nine Southern Whigs; while four Northern Democrats, six Northern Whigs, two Free-soilers, one Southern Whig, and one Southern Democrat voted in the negative. The negative vote is a roll of legislative honor, and deserves detailed mention. It was composed of Dodge of Wisconsin, Hamlin of Maine, James of Rhode Island, Walker of Wisconsin, Houston of Texas, Democrats; Fessenden of Maine, Fish and Seward of New York, Foot of Vermont, Smith of Connecticut, Wade of

* There were thirty-one States, but there was one vacancy.

Ohio, and Bell of Tennessee, Whigs; and Chase and Sumner, Free-soilers.

As the senators went home on this sombre March morning, they heard the boom of the cannon from the navy-yard proclaiming the triumph of what Douglas called popular sovereignty. Chase and Sumner, who were devoted friends, walked down the steps of the Capitol together, and as they heard the thunders of victory, Chase exclaimed: "They celebrate a present victory, but the echoes they awake will never rest until slavery itself shall die."

Before the bill passed, an amendment of Badger of North Carolina was incorporated in it to the effect that nothing in the act should be construed to revive the old Louisiana law which protected slavery in the whole of that territory. An amendment of Clayton was likewise adopted, which provided that only citizens of the United States should have the right of suffrage and of holding office in the territories. This was intended to work against emigrants from Europe who might settle there. The amendment was only carried by a vote of 22 to 20; and it is noticeable, as indicating the feeling towards the foreign population, that all the senators but one who favored this amendment were from the slave States, and all who opposed it were from the free States, Douglas voting with Chase, Seward, Sumner, and Wade.

This speech of Douglas, which closed the debate, has been considered at length, for it was an epoch-making event in the decade of 1850-60. Cass was the author of the doctrine which Douglas so warmly embraced, but until now it had been known as congressional non-intervention, or squatter sovereignty. Douglas this night gave it the name of popular sovereignty, and the name was a far greater invention than the doctrine. The ardent advocacy of the sovereignty of the people was certain to have a powerful influence; and while at this moment the fate of Douglas seemed trembling in the balance, he was destined to rise above the wave of popular indignation which now threatened to overwhelm him. Using his principle of popular sovereignty to oppose the encroachments of slavery, he would in the future enlist under that banner many who now regarded his work with execration.

The doctrine of popular sovereignty died with slavery. At the best it was a makeshift. As expounded by Douglas, it meant that Congress, which represented the political wisdom of an educated people, should abdicate its constitutional right of deciding a question, which demanded the most sagacious statesmanship, in favor of a thousand, or perhaps ten thousand, pioneers, adventurers, and fortune-seekers who should happen to locate in a territory. As an expedient to settle an angry controversy, and as one of a series of compromises, congressional non-intervention in Utah and New Mexico was justified in 1850; but, used as a principle to unsettle a time-honored settlement, it can receive at the bar of history only an unqualified condemnation.

A spirit had been roused by the introduction of this bill which the politicians must reckon with. On the 13th of March, Hamilton Fish, senator from New York, presented a petition, signed by clergymen of different denominations in New York City and its vicinity, remonstrating against the passage of the Kansas-Nebraska act. The bishop of the Episcopal Church headed the memorial, which was subscribed by a majority of the clergymen of New York City. This petition attracted no attention, and it was ordered to lie upon the table in the usual manner. But the next day Everett presented a remonstrance against the passage of the Nebraska bill, signed by three thousand and fifty clergymen of all denominations and sects in the different States of New England. There were in that section of country three thousand eight hundred ministers, and this memorial was therefore the expression of the sentiments of a very large part of the whole number.

The petition was couched in strong language. It said: "The undersigned, clergymen of different religious denominations in New England, hereby, in the name of Almighty God, and in his presence, do solemnly protest against the passage of what is known as the Nebraska bill. . . . We protest against it as a great moral wrong, as a breach of faith eminently unjust to the moral principles of the community, and subversive of all confidence in national engagements; as a measure full of danger to the peace and even the existence of our beloved Union, and exposing us to the righteous judgments of the Almighty."

The reading of this memorial created a sensation in the Senate. Douglas made some fierce and sarcastic remarks, and rebuked the clergymen for quitting their proper vocation and meddling in an affair which they did not understand. They had, he said, "desecrated the pulpit and prostituted the sacred desk to the miserable and corrupting influence of party politics."

Somewhat more than a month later, Douglas himself presented a petition against the bill of five hundred and four clergymen of the Northwestern States, which emanated from Chicago, and which was similar in language to the New England petition. He made this the text of a speech which criticised severely the interference of preachers in affairs of State.

Douglas and the Southern senators might cry down these manifestations, but in truth they were the inception of a movement which was destined to have a powerful influence towards the abolition of slavery. On the compromise measures clergymen had been divided; indeed, many of high station had counselled submission to the Fugitive Slave law. Now, however, they were practically united, and they considered it their duty to preach sermons against what they believed to be a violation of plighted faith.*

It will be generally conceded that on political questions which are those of mere expediency the minister should be silent. It would to-day shock the church-going community to hear from the pulpit arguments directed to show that a high tariff or free trade was demanded by the law of God; but when the paramount political issue becomes intertwined with a sacred moral

---

* Douglas said that on one day in New England fifteen hundred to two thousand sermons were preached against the bill. Appendix, *Congressional Globe*, vol. xxix. p. 656. The religious and secular newspapers of this time are full of reports of sermons on the subject.

principle, it is the duty of the preacher to declare that principle, and to urge his hearers to make their political action conform to the behests of the moral law. The slavery question had a moral as well as a political side. The ministers would have been recreant to their calling had they not proclaimed from their pulpits what the spirit of their religion prompted them to speak. This widespread agitation from the pulpit is a striking evidence of the deeply stirred-up feeling at the North. It was patent that the preachers spoke to willing listeners, and that their congregations would stand by them in the position they had taken.

The bill now went to the House of Representatives, and the first action of this body showed that it paid attention to the demonstrations of popular sentiment which the Senate had depreciated and disregarded. On the 21st of March, the Senate Kansas-Nebraska bill came up in order, and Richardson, who was thoroughly devoted to Douglas and his interests, moved that it be referred to the committee on territories, of which he was the chairman. Cutting, a member from New York City, who belonged to the faction of "Hards," at once moved that it be referred to the committee of the whole on the state of the Union, and demanded the previous question. He stated that he was in favor of the principle of the bill; but the representatives owed it to the country to consider this "grave and serious question" carefully, to correct whatever imperfections there were in the measure as it had come from the Senate, and to make plain to the people of the North what was intended by this legislation; for it was undeniable that, "since its introduction into Congress, the North would seem to have taken up arms, and to have become excited into a sort of civil insurrection." In spite of the protest of Richardson that such a reference of the bill "would be killing it by indirection," Cutting's motion prevailed by a vote of 110 to 95. This action was a defeat for the friends of the measure, and especially incensed Breckenridge, of Kentucky, who said that, having been done "under the guise of friendship to the bill, it was the act of a man who throws his arm in apparently friendly embrace around another saying, 'How is it with thee, brother?' and at the same time covertly stabs him to the heart." Some of the opponents of the bill were disposed to think that it had no chance of passing the House at this session; but those who had the best knowledge and clearest judgment thought, with the New York *Tribune,* that the snake was scotched, not killed. As a matter of fact, this reference placed the bill at the foot of the calendar; there were fifty bills ahead of it, and it could not be reached in the regular course of legislation.

The shrewd anticipation of Douglas, that the help of the administration would be needed to carry the measure through the House, was realized. Marcy, however, who had more influence with the representatives than any other member of the cabinet, was indifferent to the fate of the measure. Indeed, after Douglas introduced the substitute, Marcy's apprehensions of the effect of it on the Democratic party were so grave that he entertained the idea of resigning his position, and took advice from his personal and political friends regarding his line of duty. The drift of their opinion was that he ought to remain. The "Softs" had now an equal amount of the patronage and influence of New York State; but should Marcy retire, it was feared that the "Hards" would gain the supremacy. It may be presumed that in Marcy's mind a higher motive was mixed with the lower, and that he felt that, if he resigned, a secretary of state might be chosen who would truckle to the Southern propaganda, and give them effective aid in carrying out schemes prejudicial to the country.

The vacillation of the President undoubtedly caused uneasiness among the supporters of the measure. When under the influence of Davis and Cushing, he was an enthusiastic friend of it, and expressed himself warmly in favor of the principle of the bill; when chilled by the doubts of Marcy, he wavered. "You ask me," wrote Dix, "what General Pierce's opinion is. I do not know. Some say he is for the repeal of the Missouri Compromise—others as confidently that he is against it." The result of the New Hampshire election might well make him halt be-

tween the two opinions. His native State, which had given him
a handsome majority for President, was now only carried with
great difficulty by the Democratic governor; and, what was of
more importance, the lower House of the legislature was so
strongly anti-Nebraska that it would insure the choice of two
opposition senators in the place of Norris and Williams, who
had voted for the Kansas-Nebraska act. But, in spite of internal
dissensions and the unsteadiness of the President, the authoritative public expressions of the administration were all one
way. It was announced that the patronage would be used in the
interest of those representatives who voted for the bill; and the
morning after the House had consigned it to the committee of
the whole, the *Union* declared that the Kansas-Nebraska project had become a prominent measure of President Pierce's administration. "If it be defeated in the House, it will, it must be
admitted, be a defeat of the administration." Important appointments were withheld in order that they might be used to
reward the constant friends of the bill; alluring bait was held out
to those who were lukewarm, and threats were employed to
coerce the representatives who were disposed to rebel against
the dictates of the party leaders. All the members of the cabinet,
except Marcy and McClelland, were working for the measure,
and Davis and Cushing were earnest and indefatigable advocates.

As the bill slept in the committee of the whole, some of its
friends and some of its enemies began to think that the project
would not be revived this session. But they little knew Douglas
who thought one check would daunt him. He thoroughly understood the situation. He was aware that many Northern Democratic representatives would secretly delight if the bill were
never brought to a vote in the House, yet these same men would
feel constrained to give it their voice when the question was
actually put. They would not dare to resist the power of the administration and that party discipline which, having been instituted by Jefferson, had gained force by use, and was never
so powerful as now.

On the 8th of May the result of the pressure became manifest. On that day Richardson, the trusted lieutenant of Douglas, obtained the floor after the reading of the journal, and moved that the House resolve itself into the committee of the whole on the state of the Union. He frankly avowed that his object was to have the committee lay aside all bills which had the precedence of the Kansas-Nebraska bill, so that they might at once proceed to its consideration. While the Senate act had been placed at the foot of the calendar, there were but eighteen bills ahead of the House bill, which had been reported by the House committee of territories, and which was the same as the Senate bill before it had been amended. Richardson now moved to lay aside one by one these bills. The question was put eighteen times, and each time the majority voted with their leader. The House Kansas-Nebraska bill was then reached, when Richardson proposed as a substitute a bill which was the same as the Senate act, with the exception of the Clayton amendment. This was, the next two days, debated in committee. On Thursday, May 11th, Richardson obtained the floor almost immediately after the reading of the journal, moved that the debate close the next day at twelve o'clock, and on that motion called for the previous question. At this, the pent-up feeling of the opponents of the measure broke forth. They implored Richardson for more time; they protested against this summary closing of debate as rank injustice. An informal discussion was permitted by the speaker, in order to see whether an understanding could not be arrived at; but the feeling was so intense that heated expressions were not avoided, and the breach became wider. One member roused the wrath of others by calling the bill a "swindle." Alexander H. Stephens expressed the willingness of the majority to give the minority a reasonable time for debate, provided they would then allow a vote to be taken; but he emphatically declared that if factious opposition were made, it would be met "as factious opposition in this House has always been met." Lewis D. Campbell cried, amidst shouts of approval: "I will resist the further progress of this bill by all the means which the

rules of the House place in my power, even though gentlemen may call it faction." Then filibustering under the leadership of Campbell began. Motions to adjourn, motions to
adjourn to a fixed time, motions for a call of the House,
followed one another. Then a member would ask to be excused from voting, and a friend would move that he be excused; and on all these motions the yeas and nays were called
for. In short, all kinds of dilatory motions were used with
skill by men who thoroughly understood the rules of the House,
and they were supported by a determined minority. The session continued all day Thursday, all of Thursday night, and all
day Friday, without reaching any result. At times the monoto-
nous call of the yeas and nays would cease, and attempts would
be made by the more moderate of both sides to come to some
arrangement, when a remark would be interjected by some
member which would provoke an angry reply, and the uproar
and confusion would begin again. Douglas was on the floor of
the House a large share of the time for the purpose of directing
his followers, but he and Richardson did little but watch and
wait for a subsidence of the excited feeling. It was after eleven
o'clock on Friday night when, as a result of a talk between
Campbell and Richardson, the latter stated that, as a number
of the opponents of the bill had signified their desire that they
might have until the next day for deliberation, he would move
an adjournment. The House was now in a very excited state.
The nervous tension caused by loss of sleep, irregular hours,
and powerful emotion was manifest. Those who were accustomed to use stimulants in times of excitement were inflamed by
strong drink. It had been freely talked that a disturbance was
liable to occur, and many members came to the House armed
for the fray. A spark only was needed to produce an explosion.

Hunt, a Whig from Louisiana opposed to the measure, who
many times had tried to pour oil upon the troubled waters, now
made a patriotic and amicable appeal to Richardson to give his
friends until Monday for consideration. Richardson made a
courteous reply, saying it was beyond his power to grant the
request, but hoped that on the morrow a desirable result might

be reached. Had the speaker then put the question, trouble would have been avoided; but, with praiseworthy intentions, he permitted a desultory discussion, during which Alexander Stephens made some fiery remarks. This brought Campbell to his feet, who had started to reply when he was called to order by Seward, of Georgia. It must be understood that this discussion was by unanimous consent, no debatable question being before the House, and no member could speak if called to order by another. The interposition of Seward was unfair, and cries of order went up from all parts of the hall. Above the confusion could be heard the voice of Campbell: "I shall resist this measure to the bitter end. I say so, never minding the gentleman who calls me to order." Amidst repeated shouts of "Order!" Seward retorted: "There are other places instead of this where personal difficulties may be settled." Confusion was now confounded. Members crowded around Campbell. Many got on the tops of the desks. Above the din Campbell vehemently exclaimed: "I tell you, gentlemen, that I shall resist this measure with all the power that I can to the bitter end." Members still continued to crowd around Campbell, and it was reported that weapons were drawn, and that an attempt was made to use one by Edmundson, of Virginia. The speaker did his best to preserve order; he prayed all lovers of order to assist him, and he commanded the sergeant-at-arms to use the emblem of authority. The sergeant-at-arms, advancing with the mace of the House, arrested Edmundson, compelled members to resume their seats, and was successful in partially restoring order. The speaker then cut off all further attempts at discussion, and, as soon as possible, put the motion of Richardson, and declared the House adjourned. By his prompt action he undoubtedly prevented a bloody affray. It deserves to be noted that among the gentlemen who effectually assisted the speaker in preventing a disgraceful brawl were Aiken and Keitt of South Carolina. The sitting came to a close at twenty-seven minutes before midnight, the House having been in continuous session nearly thirty-six hours.

The next day's session of the House was short, and nothing

was done. On this Saturday, May 13th, an enthusiastic anti-Nebraska meeting of five thousand people was held in the City Hall Park, New York City, the assemblage being composed chiefly of mechanics. The speeches were heard attentively, and the resolutions responded to with earnestness. One of these declared that they would vote for no representative who gave his voice in Congress for the repeal of the Missouri Compromise.

On Monday, May 15th, Richardson proposed to give until Saturday for debate. This offer would undoubtedly have been made before, had not a special order on the Pacific Railroad bill stood in the way. To postpone this now, a suspension of the rules was necessary, and eighteen Northern Democrats, who had hitherto voted in the opposition, gave their voices on the side of the majority, which made the requisite two-thirds vote; and it was then decided that the debate should close on the Saturday following. The action of these Democrats was severely criticised by the Whigs, and they were charged with being recreant to principle and dominated by party considerations; but, in truth, such questioning of motives was liable to be unjust. It must always occur to some congressmen of the minority, as it does to the philosophic observer, that filibustering is an inane mode of accomplishing an object. It rarely defeats the aim of the majority, although indeed it may postpone action. It is true that there was abundant reason to suppose that if action were not reached on the Kansas-Nebraska bill this session, it would not be revived at the next; but it was also true that the majority was large enough and determined enough to keep the House in session until the measure was passed. The assertion of the minority that the majority wanted to stifle debate was, of course, a subterfuge. Already, Richardson stated, eighty speeches had been made in the House on the question, which was more than had ever been made on any previous measure; and before the bill came to a vote this number was increased to one hundred.

The discussion proceeded quietly the remaining days of the week, the House holding long sessions. On Saturday, the 20th, the members came together at nine o'clock. The debate closed soon after twelve; the opposition badgered the minority the rest of the day by offering amendments and speaking to them under the five-minute rule. On Monday, May 22d, the House met and went immediately into committee. Stephens then moved to strike out the enacting clause of the bill, avowing that his object was to cut off all amendments, and have the bill reported to the House so that a vote might be taken on it. This unusual proceeding caused a great sensation. Indeed, Stephens had great difficulty in getting the leaders to agree to this mode of action. One member declared that it was apparent the majority purposed to ride rough-shod over the minority. Another, in the midst of the excitement, called upon his friends not to vote upon the question, and cried: "Oppose tyranny by revolution!" The motion to strike out the enacting clause was, however, agreed to. The committee rose and reported to the House. Then ensued a stubborn contest. The minority used every means in their power to prevent a vote; but the management of Richardson was skilful, and he had Douglas at hand to prompt him. The House refused to concur in the report of the committee, which struck out the enacting clause of the bill. Well might Stephens write, "I took the reins in hand, applied whip and spur, and brought the 'wagon' out." It was nearly midnight when a vote was reached. The Kansas-Nebraska bill was then passed by 113 yeas to 100 nays. Forty-four Northern and fifty-seven Southern Democrats voted for the bill, and these were reinforced by twelve Whigs from the slave States; against the bill were forty-five Whigs and forty-two Democrats from the North, two Democrats and seven Whigs from the slave States. The names of these nine, with whom respect for plighted faith was more powerful than the supposed interest of their section, deserve a record. They were: Puryear and Rogers of North Carolina, Bugg, Cullom, Etheridge, and Taylor of Tennessee, Hunt of Louisiana, Whigs; and Millson of Virginia and Thomas H. Benton, Democrats.

No man in either House of Congress brought so much intelligence and experience to bear upon his vote as did Benton. He had come into political life on the Missouri Compromise. His State had kept him in the Senate for thirty years; and when the legislature would no longer elect him, he had appealed to the people of his district and they had sent him to the House. He was not only a statesman of experience, but he was writing a history of the events in which he had been an actor and on which he had looked as a spectator. Certainly his protest should have been regarded. He spoke as a statesman whose memory and judgment were enlightened by the investigation of an historian. He declared that the movement for the abrogation of the Missouri Compromise began "without a memorial, without a petition, without a request from a human being"; that this scheme was directed against a compromise which was not a "mere statute to last for a day," but one which "was intended for perpetuity, and so declared itself." When he came to analyze the Kansas-Nebraska bill, he referred to the explanation which Douglas had incorporated in his substitute in words which were remembered as long as Douglas was a candidate for the presidency.*

As the House bill had left out the Clayton amendment, it was necessary that it should go to the Senate before becoming a law. An interesting debate of two days occurred, in which important revelations were made of the efforts used to dragoon a few objecting Southern Whigs into support of the measure. The difference, moreover, in the construction of the act by its friends became again apparent. Judged by the succeeding events, the most remarkable expressions came from Sumner, for he had an insight into the future. This bill, he said, "is at once the worst and the best bill on which Congress ever acted. It is the worst bill, inasmuch as it is a present victory of slavery. . . . It is the best bill, . . . for it prepares the way for that 'All hail hereafter,' when slavery must disappear. It annuls all past compromises

---

* Benton said that the clause "It being the true intent and meaning of this act, etc.," was "a little stump speech injected in the belly of the bill."

with slavery, and makes all future compromises impossible. Thus it puts freedom and slavery face to face, and· bids them grapple. Who can doubt the result?"

The bill, as it had come from the House, was ordered to a third reading by a vote of 35 to 13, and passed the Senate May 25th. It was approved by the President May 30th.

It is safe to say that, in the scope and consequences of the Kansas-Nebraska act, it was the most momentous measure that passed Congress from the day that the senators and representatives first met to the outbreak of the civil war. It sealed the doom of the Whig party; it caused the formation of the Republican party on the principle of no extension of slavery; it roused Lincoln and gave a bent to his great political ambition. It made the Fugitive Slave law a dead letter at the North; it caused the Germans to become Republicans; it lost the Democrats their hold on New England; it made the Northwest Republican; it led to the downfall of the Democratic party.

It may be asserted with confidence that no man in the country except Douglas could have carried this measure through the necessary stages of becoming a law. Five years later, in familiar talk with his Boswell, he said: "I passed the Kansas-Nebraska act myself. I had the authority and power of a dictator throughout the whole controversy in both houses. The speeches were nothing. It was the marshalling and directing of men, and guarding from attacks, and a ceaseless vigilance preventing surprise," that led to the success of the measure. It is certain that in after-years Douglas came to believe that his doctrine of popular sovereignty was a great political principle; and it is probable that even now he half believed that there was some occult virtue in it as a rule of action. Persistent advocacy often convinces the advocate. Yet, laying aside entirely the moral question, the action of Douglas as a statesman, as a politician and leader of a party, was characterized by a lamentable lack of foresight and the utter absence of the careful reflection which far-reaching measures of legislation demand. Douglas had asserted in 1849 that all the evidences of public opinion seemed to indicate that the Missouri Compromise "had become canonized in the hearts of the American people, as a sacred thing which no ruthless hand would ever be reckless enough to disturb." Having once had that conviction, therefore, he owed it to his country, and to his party as well, not to broach this measure until he had given it deep study and prolonged consideration. For Douglas loved his country; his party was his religion, the Constitution was his creed; and in following the leading of an inordinate ambition he did not imagine that he was sacrificing his party and injuring his country. He made up his mind quickly; confiding, like all spoiled children of fortune who have been endowed with rich natural gifts, in his intuitive judgment, he thought that he had no need to close application and methodical reasoning. "His library was never clear from dust," said a friend and follower; and Greeley, who in these days denounced him without stint, wrote truly after his death that, if Douglas had been a hard student, "it would have been difficult to set limits to his power." He, like his greater Illinois rival, was a good mathematician, but he did not, like Lincoln, wrestle in manhood with the problems of Euclid for mental discipline. He hardly knew any history but that of his own country; he cared not to learn of the development of the world, except when Alexander, Cæsar, and Napoleon were on the stage of action, and of them he could not read too much.

Of all the descriptions of Douglas at this time, none seem to seize the essential characteristics of the man so well as that of a journalist whose soul was wrapped up in the anti-slavery cause. The writer was impressed with his "pluck, persistency, and muscular self-assurance and self-assertion." To see and hear him was to "comprehend the aptness of that title of 'Little Giant.'" Never was a characteristic name better applied. The historian must sympathize with the regret expressed by this journalist that one who championed bad measures with such indomitable ability was not upon the right side; and one cannot but reflect "of what infinite value this remarkable man might

have been to the cause of liberty if the fortune of politics had
made him a leader of it."

Douglas had the quality of attracting men to him; he was
especially fond of young men, and they repaid his complaisance
by devotion. No American statesman but Clay ever had such
a personal following. He now became the leader of the Democratic party; he retained the leadership of the Northern Democrats to the last; and since Andrew Jackson, no man has possessed the influence, received the confidence, or had the support that it was the lot of Douglas to enjoy from the Democrats
in the northern half of the Union. From 1854 to 1858, he was
the centre of the political history of the country; from 1858 to
1860, he was the best-known man in the United States; but
after the contest with Lincoln in 1858, it became apparent that
the "Little Giant" had met his match in that other son of Illinois.

Douglas was generous and faithful to his friends. He had
large ideas in business; he made money easily and spent it lavishly. It was stated during this controversy that he was further-
ing the interests of slavery because he was himself a slave-
holder, but the allegation was untrue. Douglas had, indeed,
been offered a plantation with a large number of slaves by his
father-in-law, but he had declined the gift because he was unwilling to accept the responsibility. He answered this charge in
the Senate with dignity. Indeed, those who sought a mercenary
motive as a key to the course of Douglas strangely misappre-
hended his character.

In comprehensive views he was a true representative of the
West. No public man has ever had more of the spirit of the
boundless prairie or has been such a faithful type of the resistless energy that characterizes the city of Chicago. He understood the West, but it is plain that he had not thought out the
results of the repeal of the Missouri Compromise, for he seemed
to have little apprehension of the political revolution that was
destined to take place in his beloved section of country. On

January 1st, 1854, Indiana, Illinois, Michigan, Wisconsin, and Iowa were Democratic States; all their senators were Democrats; of twenty-nine representatives only five were Whigs. None but Indiana remained reliably Democratic. Michigan, Wisconsin, and Iowa at once became Republican, and Illinois would have immediately ranged herself at their side had it not been for the strong personal influence of Douglas.

Some writers and many men who were contemporary with the event have maintained that the civil war would not have taken place had it not been for the abrogation of the Missouri Compromise. This will probably not be the mature verdict of history. The more the subject is studied, the more profound will appear the prophetic saying of John Quincy Adams: "I am satisfied slavery will not go down until it goes down in blood." Yet it must be adjudged that Douglas hastened the struggle; he precipitated the civil war.

The North was now in a ferment. At the Connecticut State election in April the Democrats had failed to elect the legislature or governor. While both Whig and Democratic conventions had protested against the repeal of the Missouri Compromise, the result of the election was obviously a rebuke to the dominant party for their support of the Kansas-Nebraska bill. The newly elected legislature passed resolutions averse to the proposed measure; these were presented to the House the day on which the concluding vote was taken, and to the Senate before its final action on the bill. The Whig convention of Pennsylvania resolved against the disturbance of the legislation of 1820, while the Democratic convention of that State was silent.

One phase of the public sentiment has been barely alluded to. The foreign immigration had become a factor in politics of which heed must be taken. The Germans and Irish, for the most part, had joined the Democratic party; but the Germans, from the first, were opposed to the repeal of the Missouri Compromise, for they were against the extension of slavery. Of eighty-eight German newspapers, eight were in favor of the Kansas-

Nebraska bill, while eighty were decidedly opposed to it. This change was of enough consequence to determine the political charter of Wisconsin and Iowa, and was a great element of anti-slavery strength in Ohio.

The cannon roared in Washington when the Senate enacted the measure, but gloom overspread the minds of Northern men. Pierce and Douglas, said Greeley, have made more abolitionists in three months than Garrison and Phillips cauld have made in a half century. Crowds of people who had heretofore severely criticised Garrison, Phillips, Parker, and their methods, now flocked to hear them, and were glad to listen to the arguments of these earnest men. It was at once urged by the press and from the platform that an effort should be made to have Kansas enter the Union as a free State, and a systematic movement was begun with this end in view.

The author of the bill was regarded with execration; his middle name was Arnold, and this suggested a comparison to Benedict Arnold. The term which is used in every Christian land as a synonym of traitor was likewise applied to him, and one hundred and three ladies of an Ohio village sent him thirty pieces of silver. He could travel, as he afterwards said, "from Boston to Chicago by the light of his own effigies." Horace Bushnell, a noted preacher in Hartford, applied to Douglas the bitter prophecy of the Hebrew prophet: "Tidings out of the east and out of the north shall trouble him; therefore he shall go forth with great fury to destroy and utterly to make away many, yet he shall come to his end, and none shall help him." A journal which had opposed the Kansas-Nebraska measure with pertinacity asked, in derision, "Who names Douglas for the next President now?" Not a response came from the North.

"Never was an act of Congress so generally and so unanimously hailed with delight at the South" as was the Kansas-Nebraska act, wrote Alexander Stephens six years after its passage. This may be accepted as a fact, although there were some exceptions to the almost universal acclaim. Many people in New Orleans did not like it; such, also, appeared to be the feeling in Texas. Indifference as to the fate of the bill while it was pending was reported from Charleston, from other parts of South Carolina, and from a city of Mississippi. The leading state-rights organ of Charleston did not scruple to condemn the tactics of Stephens as a violation of the rights of the minority and as of a dangerous tendency. But as the measure gradually came to be understood as a victory for slavery and a defeat of the abolitionists, the general feeling fully justified the assertion of Stephens. It was thought in the border States that if a new slave State could be created it would add five per cent to the value of slaves, which was already very high. The planters in the cotton States, being buyers of negroes, did not regard the rise of values as an unmixed good; but they did not grumble: they cast about for a remedy, and did not look for it long. The reopening of the African slave-trade began to be discussed seriously in South Carolina and Mississipi.

There were Southern members of Congress whom Atchison could not convince that Kansas would enter the Union as a slave State. But they felt that if Atchison were too sanguine, and even if the Kansas-Nebraska act did not recognize the Calhoun dogma, it did at any rate make a quietus of the Wilmot proviso doctrine. As the establishment of a principle it was of great benefit to the South; for when the bill was introduced negotiations were in progress which were expected to result in the accession of an important piece of territory from Mexico. That Cuba would be ours by the close of the year was not deemed an unwarranted expectation. Nor was it a wild dream to expect that before many years the United States would extend to the isthmus. The acquisition of Mexico, Central America, and Cuba, to be cut up into slave States, was an object worth striving for, and the Kansas-Nebraska act seemed to assert a principle that could properly be applied if this territory were gained to achieve such a consummation. The better the measure was understood, the more complete seemed the humiliation of the North, and the greater reason there appeared for the exultation of the South.

"The Fugitive law did much to unglue the eyes of men, and now the Nebraska bill leaves us staring," said Emerson. The repeal of the Missouri Compromise emphasized every argument against the Fugitive Slave act, and gave to the story of "Uncle Tom's Cabin" the force of solid reasoning. The uprising against this law of 1850 is a well-known fact of the decade between 1850-60, but the distinction between the excitement which followed its passage and that which grew out of the Kansas-Nebraska act is not always carefully borne in mind. Yet the difference is of transcendent importance. The excitement of 1850 and 1851 was transitory. It was vehement while it lasted, for the abolitionists and extreme anti-slavery men prompted it, but all their agitation did not prevent the public mind from settling into the conviction that the Fugitive Slave law was only one unpalatable article of a good contract. Public opinion at the North in 1852 was well expressed by the Democratic and Whig platforms. Even the brilliant speech of Sumner on the subject did not produce a ripple of excitement, and in 1853 the acquiescence was complete. When the Fugitive Slave law was enforced it was done quietly, with sometimes a lack of zeal on the part of the officers, and with little or no resistance from the people. It seemed to be one of those laws which a law-abiding community believe wrong to resist, though inexpedient to put in force.

But in 1854 there began to be a smarting sense of the injustice of the Fugitive Slave law, which was never allayed until there was no longer reason for its existence. We shall see, in the course of this work, that one political party made, in its political platforms, obedience to this act a test of fidelity, and that the other remained silent on the subject; we shall see that Lincoln, on first taking the oath of his high office, virtually announced his purpose of enforcing it. Yet, after the passage of the Kansas-Nebraska act, the majority of men at the North, and by far the greater number of intelligent and moral people, felt that they had been cheated, and that the Fugitive Slave law was a part of the cheat. They reasoned that the South set aside the Missouri Compromise because it no longer operated in their favor;

and as the Fugitive act was to them the obnoxious part of the compromise of 1850, they would consider the breach of it more honorable than the observance.

In March a colored man had been claimed as a fugitive slave and committed to jail at Milwaukee, Wis. He was rescued by a party of sympathizers. Booth, a journalist, who was one of these, was arrested on a warrant of the United States commissioner; he applied to an associate justice of the State Supreme Court for a writ of habeas corpus and his discharge. The justice ordered his discharge on two grounds, one of which was that the Fugitive Slave law was unsonstitutional. This decision was afterwards affirmed by a full bench of the Wisconsin Supreme Court, only one justice dissenting.

"If the Nebraska bill should be passed, the Fugitive Slave law is a dead letter throughout New England," wrote a Southerner in Boston to a friend. "As easily," he continued, "could a law prohibiting the eating of codfish and pumpkin-pies be enforced as that law executed." The events which followed hard upon the action of the House of Representatives showed that the stranger had accurately judged the drift of opinion.

On the evening of the 24th of May, Anthony Burns, a negro who had esceped from servitude about three months previously, was arrested in the heart of Boston. The next morning he was taken manacled to the United States Courtroom for examination by Commissioner Loring. The news of his arrest had not got into the papers, and the proceedings would have been summary had not Richard H. Dana, Jr., a prominent lawyer of anti-slavery opinions, chanced to pass the court-house at about nine o'clock and receive an intimation of what was going on. He entered the courtroom and offered Burns his professional services. The negro declined them. "It is of no use," he said; "they will swear to me and get me back; and if they do, I shall fare worse if I resist." Meanwhile, Theodore Parker and other gentlemen who had accidentally heard of the arrest had entered the court-room, and Parker had a conference with Burns. He told the frightened fugitive that he was a minister, that by a meeting of citizens he had been appointed the special pastor of fugitive slaves, and he asked whether Burns did not want counsel. The negro replied: "I shall have to go back. My master knows me. His agent knows me. If I must go back, I want to go back as easily as I can." "But surely," rejoined Parker, "it can do you no harm to make a defence." "Well," said Burns, "you may do as you have a mind to about it." "He seemed," Parker afterwards related, "to be stupefied with fear."

The news of the arrest, and the circumstances connected with it, spread quickly through the city and found a great change in public opinion from that which had prevailed three years before, when Sims was arrested. The fugitive had now the active or passive sympathy of nearly every one. Inflammatory handbills were circulated; they were drawn up with skill, appealing at the same time to the fiery abolitionist and to the compromiser of 1850. Invectives against kidnappers and man-stealing were joined to a statement which expressed the overpowering thought in the minds of New England men. "The compromises," one of the placards said, "trampled upon by the slave power when in the path of slavery, are to be crammed down the throat of the North." On Friday morning, the 26th, a call for a meeting at Faneuil Hall that evening was issued, the object of which was stated to be: "To secure justice for a man claimed as a slave by a Virginia kidnapper"; and the notice ended: "Shall he be plunged into the hell of Virginia slavery by a Massachusetts judge of probate?" By Friday evening the city was in a ferment. Not since the massacre in revolutionary days had there been such wild excitement. Agitators were running to and fro, setting all the city in an uproar. The pent-up feeling produced by the repeal of the Missouri Compromise broke forth with fury. The crowd that gathered in Faneuil Hall were agitated by passion; and when Wendell Phillips rose to speak, they were in that state which orators delight to see when they would urge their fellow-men to violent deeds. Phillips had the manner of Brutus, but his words were like those of Mark Antony, fitted to stir up mutiny. "See to it," he said, "that to-morrow, in the streets of

Boston, you ratify the verdict of Faneuil Hall, that Anthony Burns has no master but his God. . . . Will you adhere to the case of Sims and see this man carried down State Street between two hundred men? . . . Nebraska, I call knocking a man down, and this is spitting in his face after he is down." Thus Phillips went on, the audience hanging breathless on his every word.

When he had finished, Theodore Parker delivered a wild, incoherent, and vindictive harangue. "Men and brothers," Parker said, "I am an old man; I have heard hurrahs and cheers for liberty many times; I have not seen a great many *deeds* done for liberty. I ask you are we to have *deeds* as well as words? . . . Gentlemen, there was a Boston once, and you and I had fathers —brave fathers; and mothers who stirred up fathers to manly deeds. . . . They did not obey the stamp-act. . . . You know what they did with the tea." He ended with the proposition that when they adjourned it should be to meet the next morning at nine o'clock in Court-house Square. "To-night," shouted a hundred voices in reply. The excitement was now intense. The people were in a tumult. Above the roar of voices might be heard cries, "To the court-house!" "To the Revere House for the slave-catchers!" Parker tried in vain to still the storm he had raised, but he could not get a hearing. Phillips then ascended the platform and a few well-chosen words sufficed to allay the tumult. He had almost persuaded the audience to disperse quietly, when a man at the entrance of the hall shouted: "Mr. Chairman, I am just informed that a mob of negroes is in Court Square attempting to rescue Burns. I move that we adjourn to Court Square." The hall became quickly empty. The crowd rushed to the scene of action. There they found a small party under the lead of Thomas W. Higginson attempting to break down one of the doors of the court-house with a large stick of timber used as a battering-ram. The Faneuil Hall men lent a hand. Those who could not work rent the air with shouts; others hurled stones or fired pistol-shots at the court house windows. It was an angry, excited crowd of two thousand, bent on the rescue of Burns. At last a breach was made in the door, but the place was defended. In the mêlée one of the marshal's posse was killed, and Higginson was wounded by a sabre-cut. Several of Higginson's companions were arrested, after which no further attempt was made to break into the court-house. Two companies of artillery were immediately ordered out by the mayor to preserve the peace.

This attempt at the rescue of Burns was foolish. Under a government like ours there can be no justification for an attack upon the constituted authorities. It pleased the multitude to call the Boston Court-house the Bastille; but the recollection of the event which was thus conjured up impresses one with the contrast between the Paris of 1789 and the Boston of 1854, and not with their likeness. Yet it is an evidence of the deep feeling that, although this attempt was widely condemned, it did not weaken the public sympathy for the fugitive nor the indignation against the United States functionaries. This attack enabled the marshal to appear as a vindicator of the law; he immediately called out two companies of United States troops, reported his action to the President, and received the reply: "Your conduct is approved. The law must be executed."

On the following Monday the examination began. An eyewitness relates that "the court-house had the air of a beleaguered fortress." Every window was guarded by Massachusetts or United States soldiery. Only one door of the court-house was open, and at that was stationed a strong force of city police. None but functionaries could enter without a permit from the marshal. The counsel for the fugitive made a strong defence. Burns was undeniably the slave of the claimant, although the proofs were clumsy, and on technical grounds he might have been set free. The United States officers, however, were determined to win. On the 2d of June, Commissioner Loring adjudged the negro to his owner.

The most instructive act in the whole drama was now to be played. The fugitive slave must be sent out of Boston. The city was full of people; during the whole week men from the suburban towns and from all parts of Massachusetts had been flocking into Boston. The President had just signed the Kansas-Nebraska act. There was earnest indignation against Congress, the President, and the United States authorities of Boston; but these Massachusetts men were, for the most part, on a peaceful errand bent. The United States district attorney, the marshal, and the mayor of the city were determined, however, to be prepared for a mob and an attempt at rescue. A large body of city police and twenty-two companies of Massachusetts soldiers guarded in detachments the streets through which Burns and his guard must pass. The streets were cleared by a company of cavalry. The procession was made up of one United States artillery battalion, one platoon of United States marines, the marshal's civil posse of one hundred and twenty-five men guarding the fugitive, two platoons of marines, a field-piece, and one platoon of marines as a guard to the field-piece. Windows along the line of march were draped in mourning; from a window opposite the old State-house was suspended a black coffin on which were the words, "The funeral of liberty;" further on was an American flag, the union down, draped in mourning. The solemn procession was witnessed by fifty thousand people, who hissed, groaned, and cried "Shame! shame!" as it went by. A weight of suspense hung over the crowd, and it seemed as if a slight occasion might precipitate an outbreak with terrible consequences. The fugitive was marched to the wharf, and was soon on a United States revenue-cutter, sailing towards Virginia.

To this complexion had it come at last. In a community celebrated all over the world for the respect it yielded to law, and for obedience to those clothed with authority; in a community where the readiness of all citizens to assist the authorities had struck intelligent Europeans with amazement—it now required to execute a law a large body of deputy marshals, the whole force of the city police, eleven hundred and forty soldiers with muskets loaded, supplied with eleven rounds of powder and ball and furnished with a cannon loaded with grape-shot. If anything were needed to heighten the strangeness of the situation, it may be found in the fact that the marshal's deputies were taken from the dregs of society, for no reputable citizen would serve as a slave-catcher.

As the men of Boston and the men of New England reflected on what had taken place, they were persuaded, as they had never been before, that something was rotten in the United States, and that these events boded some strange eruption to our State. Nor was the significance of the transaction entirely lost upon the South. "We rejoice at the recapture of Burns," said a fiery organ of the slavery propaganda, "but a few more such victories and the South is undone."

THE year 1854 was not only that in which Douglas, as chairman of the committee on territories, and leader of most Western Democrats, attempted to carry the Kansas-Nebraska Bill through Congress. It was also the year of a critical Congressional election. The Whig party, since the defeat of its nominee Winfield Scott in 1852, was plainly moribund. The Democratic party was badly divided between Southern Democrats demanding the expansion of slavery and Northern Democrats hostile to it. A great wave of political discontent seemed to be passing over the country. From that wave emerged two new parties; the Republican, destined to early success and a long career, and the Know-Nothing or American, an organization transient and ill-famed.

Some of the Republican leaders were former Whigs; some had been members of the short-lived Free Soil party led by Van Buren in 1848 and John P. Hale in 1852; some were former Democrats. The two most important figures in the formation of the party were Charles Sumner, a Harvard graduate and antislavery attorney who, after denouncing the Mexican War, had been elected senator by a coalition of Free Soilers and Democrats, and Salmon P. Chase, who was sent to the Senate from Ohio by the same combination. These leaders, with others of note, saw that the feeling against the Kansas-Nebraska Act gave them an opportunity to defeat the Northern Democrats and strike a heavy blow against the Southern oligarchy controlling the government.

The autumn elections of 1854 saw four parties in the field; the divided Democrats; the enfeebled Whigs, without leaders or principles; the new nativist or Know-Nothing party created by the great recent increase in European and Catholic immigration; and the Republicans, born of a fusion of various anti-Nebraska elements. The party situation was highly confused. The Know-Nothings carried Massachusetts and polled a strong vote in New York and other Middle Atlantic States. The Republicans won elsewhere in the North. But the important fact was that Democrats lost all along the line from Maine to Iowa, and that the way seemed open for the Republicans, as the most promising coalition of anti-Southern and Free-

soil elements, to make a strong thrust for the Presidency in 1856.

Rhodes effectively describes the confused and anxious situation, and the great opportunity that he believes Seward missed. He might have said more about the psychological complexities evident in the general convulsion of parties; the anti-radicalism evident in some nativist groups, for example; the strong nationalism manifest in various quarters; the not altogether irrational bond of sympathy among antisaloon, antislavery, and antialien elements in the North. He might have said more of the emotions behind Southern attacks upon "Black Republicans" and "Niggerlovers." A fuller analysis of Lincoln's "Peoria Speech" of October, 1854, would be useful. Much new material upon foreign affairs and their place in party developments has also accumulated. Nevertheless, Rhodes's narrative is masterly.

The Birth of the Republican Party

AFTER the passage of the Kansas-Nebraska act, it would seem as if the course of the opposition were plain. In the newspapers and political literature of the time, suggestions are frequent of an obvious and reasonable course to be pursued. The senators and representatives at Washington proposed no plan. They did, indeed, issue an address which was well characterized by a powerful advocate of anti-slavery at Washington. "It is unexceptionable," he wrote, "but hath not the trumpet tone." That the different elements of opposition should be fused into one complete whole seemed political wisdom. That course involved the formation of a new party and was urged warmly and persistently by many newspapers, but by none with such telling influence as by the New York *Tribune*. It had likewise the countenance of Chase, Sumner, and Wade. There were three elements that must be united—the Whigs, the Free-soilers, who were of both Democratic and Whig antecedents, and the anti-

Nebraska Democrats. The Whigs were the most numerous body and as those at the North, to a man, had opposed the repeal of the Missouri Compromise, they thought, with some quality of reason, that the fight might well be made under their banner and with their name. For the organization of a party was not the work of a day; the machinery was complex and costly, and a new national party would not be started without pains and sacrifice. Why then, it was asked, go to all this trouble, when a complete organization is at hand ready for use? This view of the situation was ably argued by the New York *Times* and was supported by Senator Seward. As the New York senator had a position of influence superior to any one who had opposed the Kansas-Nebraska bill, strenuous efforts were made to get his adhesion to a new party movement, but they were without avail. "Seward hangs fire," wrote Dr. Bailey. He agrees with Thurlow Weed; but "God help us if, as a preliminary to a union of the North, we have all to admit that the Whig party is the party of freedom!" "We are not yet ready for a great national convention at Buffalo or elsewhere," wrote Seward to Theodore Parker; "it would bring together only the old veterans. The States are the places for activity, just now." Undoubtedly Seward, Weed, and Raymond sincerely believed that the end desired could be better accomplished if the Whig organization were kept intact. In any event their position and influence were sure. But the lesser lights of the party were of the opinion that to get and hold the national, State, and municipal offices was a function as important for a party as to spread abroad a principle; and if the Whig name and organization were maintained, length of service under the banner would have to be regarded in awarding the spoils.

Yet many Whigs who were not devoted to machine politics, and were therefore able to lay aside all personal and extraneous considerations, saw clearly that a new party must be formed under a new name, and that all the men who thus joined together must stand at the start on the same footing. They differed, however, in regard to the statement of their bond of union.

Some wished to go to the country with simply *Repeal of the Kansas-Nebraska Act* inscribed on their banner. As a new House of Representatives was to be elected in the fall, the aim should be to retire those members who had voted for the bill and to return those who had opposed it. Others wished to go further in the declaration of principles, and plant themselves squarely on the platform of congressional prohibition of slavery in all of the territories. Still others preferred the resolve that not another slave State should be admitted into the Union. Many suggestions, too, were made that broadened the issue. Yet, after all, the differences were only of detail, and the time seemed ripe for the formation of a political party whose cardinal principle might be summed up as opposition to the extension of slavery. The liberal Whigs felt that they could not ask the Free-soilers of Democratic antecedents and the anti-Nebraska Democrats to become Whigs. To the older partisans the name was identified with the United States bank. By all Democrats, Whig principles were understood to comprise a protective tariff and large internal improvements; to enroll themselves under the banner was to endorse principles against which they had always contended.

The first and most effective action to form a new party was taken in the West, where the political machines had not been so highly developed as in the older section of country, and where consequently a people's movement could proceed with greater spontaneity. While the Kansas-Nebraska bill was pending, a meeting of citizens of all parties was held at Ripon, Wisconsin. This differed from other meetings held throughout the North, in that the organization of a new party on the slavery issue was recommended, and the name suggested for it was "Republican." Five weeks after the repeal of the Missouri Compromise had been enacted, authoritative action was taken by a body representing a wider constituency. In response to a call, signed by several thousand leading citizens of Michigan, for a State mass-meeting of all opposed to slavery extension, a large body of earnest, intelligent, and moral men came together at Jackson,

Mich., on the 6th day of July. The largest hall was not sufficient to accommodate the people, and, the day being bright, the convention was held in a stately oak grove in the outskirts of the village. Enthusiasm was unbounded. The reason for a new departure was clearly shown by able men in vigorous speeches. But, in truth, the voters of Michigan fully comprehended the situation. Intelligence of a higher order characterized the population of this State. Already had the educational system been established which has grown into one surpassed by none in the world, and which has become a fruitful model. No people better adapted to set a-going a political movement ever gathered together than those assembled this day "under the oaks" at Jackson. The declaration of principles adopted was long, but all the resolutions, except two which referred to State affairs, were devoted to the slavery question.

It was stated that the freemen of Michigan had met in convention, "to consider upon the measures which duty demands of us, as citizens of a free State, to take in reference to the late acts of Congress on the subject of slavery, and its anticipated further extension." Slavery was declared "a great moral, social, and political evil"; the repeal of the Kansas-Nebraska act and the Fugitive Slave law was demanded; and the abolition of slavery in the District of Columbia was asked for. It was also "Resolved, that, postponing and suspending all differences with regard to political economy or administrative policy . . . we will act cordially and faithfully in unison" to oppose the extension of slavery, and "we will co-operate and be known as 'Republicans' until the contest be terminated." It was further recommended that a general convention should be called of the free States, and of such slave-holding States as wished to be represented, "with a view to the adoption of other more extended and effectual measures in resistance to the encroachments of slavery." Before the convention adjourned a full State ticket was nominated. Three of the candidates were Free soilers, five were Whigs, and two anti-Nebraska Democrats who had voted for Pierce in 1852. The number of voters in the State opposed to the Kansas-Nebraska act was supposed to be forty thousand, of whom it was roughly estimated twenty-five thousand were Whigs, ten thousand Free-soilers, and five thousand anti-Nebraska Democrats. On the 13th of July anti-Nebraska State conventions were held in Wisconsin, Vermont, Ohio, and Indiana. The day was chosen because it was the anniversary of the enactment of the ordinance of 1787. Resolutions similar in tenor to those of Michigan were adopted, and in Wisconsin and Vermont the name "Republican" was assumed.

In 1854, the moral feeling of the community was stirred to its very depths. While the excitement produced by the Kansas-Nebraska legislation had let loose and intensified the agitation of the public mind, yet its whole force was by no means directed to the slavery question. The temperance question began to be a weighty influence in politics. Indeed, from the passage, three years earlier, of the Maine liquor law in the State which gave legislation of this kind its name, it had been generally discussed in New England. Prohibitory laws had been enacted in Massachusetts, Vermont, Rhode Island, Connecticut, and also in Michigan. But now the question began to exercise a powerful sway throughout the North. It was necessarily made an issue in New York, for Governor Seymour had vetoed a prohibitory law; and as a governor and legislature were to be elected in the fall, the temperance men were alive and busy, determined that their doctrine should enter prominently into the canvass. All the influential advocates of a Maine law were anti-slavery men, and it is not apparent that the cause of freedom lost by union with the cause of prohibition. The pleaders for the moral law showed discretion as well as zeal. The journal which, more than all others, spoke for the religious community maintained emphatically that slavery was the first and greatest question at issue in the election.

A far more important element politically was the Know-Nothing movement. The Know-Nothings made their power felt at the municipal elections in the spring and early summer. Their most notable success was achieved in Philadelphia, when the

154 THE BIRTH OF THE REPUBLICAN PARTY

candidate they supported for mayor was elected by a large
majority. These results opened the eyes of the politicians and
of the outside public to the fact that a new force must be taken
into account.

The distrust of Roman Catholicism is a string that can be
artfully played upon in an Anglo-Saxon community. This feeling had been recently increased by the public mission of a papal
nuncio, who came to this country to adjust a difficulty in regard to church property in the city of Buffalo. There had arisen
a controversy on the matter between the bishop and a congregation, and the congregation was backed by a law of New York
State. The nuncio had been received with kindness by the
President, but his visit had excited tumults in Cincinnati, Baltimore, and New York. Moreover, the efforts of Bishop Hughes
and the Catholic clergy to exclude the Bible from the public
schools struck a chord which had not ceased to vibrate. The
ignorant foreign vote had begun to have an important influence on elections, and the result in large cities was anything
but pleasing to the lovers of honest and efficient government. It
was averred that drunken aliens frequently had charge of the
polls; that the intrigue and rowdyism which characterized recent campaigns were the work of foreigners; that the network of
Jesuitism had been cunningly spread; that such was the deep
corruption among politicians that availability in a presidential
candidate had come to mean the man who could secure the foreign vote. Votes were openly bought and sold, and "suckers"
and "strikers" controlled the primary elections of both parties.
These were the abuses. For their remedy it was argued that a
new party must be formed. There were enough of good and
pure men among the Democrats and Whigs to make up an organization which should be patriotic and Christian in character. Then war must be made against French infidelity, German
scepticism and socialism, and the papacy. Of the three evils the
papacy was considered the most dangerous.

The principles of this new party were naturally evolved out
of the ills which were deplored. An order which Washington was

supposed to have given was taken as the keynote. "Put none but Americans on guard to-night," he had said when dangers and difficulties thickened around him; and the shade of the Father of his country seemed to say across the ages, "Americans should rule America." This was the fundamental doctrine of the Know-nothing party. The immediate and practical aim in view was that foreigners and Catholics should be excluded from all national, State, county, and municipal offices; that strenuous efforts should be made to change the naturalization laws, so that the immigrant could not become a citizen until after a residence of twenty-one years in this country.*

No one can deny that ignorant foreign suffrage had grown to be an evil of immense proportions. Had the remedies sought by the Know-nothings been just and practicable and their methods above suspicion, the movement, though ill-timed, might be justified at the bar of history. But when the historian writes that a part of their indictment was true, and that the organization attracted hosts of intelligent and good men, he has said everything creditable that can be said of the Know-nothing party. The crusade against the Catholic Church was contrary to the spirit of the Constitution, and was as unnecessary as it was unwise. The statistics showed plainly that the Catholics were not sufficiently numerous to justify alarm. He who studied the spirit of the times could see this as clearly as he who compared the figures. The Catholic hierarchy can only be dangerous when human reason is repressed, and no one has ever asserted that the last half of the nineteenth century is an age of faith. The purposed exclusion of foreigners from office was illogical and unjust. The proposal to change essentially or repeal the naturalization laws was impracticable. Better means than these could be devised to correct the abuses of naturalization and fraudulent voting.

The methods of the Know-Nothings were more objectionable

* All Know-Nothings were agreed that the time of residence should be extended. The twenty-one years was a favorite period, as the American-born could not vote until they were twenty-one. Some, however, would be satisfied with a fifteen-year limit. *Sons of the Sires*, p. 71.

than their aims. The party was a vast secret society with rami-
fications in every State. Secret lodges were instituted everywhere, with passwords and degrees, grips and signs. The initia-
tion was solemn. The candidate who presented himself for admission to the first degree must, with his right hand upon the
Holy Bible and the cross, take a solemn oath of secrecy. Then,
if he were twenty-one, if he believed in God, if he had been
born in the United States, if neither he himself, nor his parents,
nor his wife were Roman Catholics, and he had been reared
under Protestant influence, he was considered a proper applicant. He was conducted from the ante-room to an inner chamber, where, in his official chair on the raised platform, the
worthy president sat. There, with the right hand upon the Holy
Bible and cross, and the left hand raised towards heaven, the
candidate again took the solemn oath of secrecy, and further
swore not to vote for any man unless he were a Protestant, an
American-born citizen, and in favor of Americans ruling America. Then the term and degree passwords were given to the
newly admitted member. The travelling password and explanation were communicated, and the sign of recognition and
grip were explained. When he challenged a brother, he must
ask, "What time?" The response would be, "Time for work."
Then he should say, "Are you?" The answer would come, "We
are." Then the two were in a position to engage in conversation
in the interests of the order.

The new member was further told that notice of mass-meetings was given by means of a triangular piece of white paper. If
he should wish to know the object of the gathering, he must ask
an undoubted brother, "Have you seen Sam to-day?" and the
information would be imparted. But if the notice were on red
paper, danger was indicated, and the member must come prepared to meet it.

The president then addressed the men who had just joined
the lodge, dilating upon the perils which threatened the country
from the foreign-born and the Romanists. "A sense of danger
has struck the great heart of the nation," he said. "In every city,

town, and hamlet, the danger has been seen and the alarm sounded. And hence true men have devised this order as a means . . . of advancing America and the American interest on the one side, and on the other of checking the stride of the foreigner or alien, of thwarting the machinations and subverting the deadly plans of the Jesuit and the Papist."

After a sufficient probation the member might be admitted to the second degree, where more oaths were taken and another password and countersign were given. But the great mystery was the name of the organization, which the president alone was entitled to communicate. At the proper time he solemnly declared: "Brothers,—You are members in full fellowship of The Supreme Order of the Star-spangled Banner."

For a time the secrets were well kept, but with a membership so large, matters connected with the organization were sure to leak out, and as the theme was susceptible of humorous treatment, people made merry over the supposed revelations. A Philadelphia journal thus exposed the manner of entrance to the local lodge: You must rap at the outer door several times in quick succession, and when the sentinel peeps through the wicket, inquire, "What meets here to-night?" He will answer, "I don't know." You must then reply, "I am one," and he will open the door. At the second door four raps and the password, "Thirteen," will obtain admission. When out in the world, when a brother gives you the grip, you must ask, "Where did you get that?" He will answer, "I don't know." You must reply, "I don't know either," and you may then enter into full fellowship with a member of the mysterious order.

When the curious inquired of the members of this party what were their principles and what their object, the answer invariably was, "I know nothing"; and thus the popular name was given in derision. Yet this was not resented. The appellation expressed mystery, and mystery was aimed at. The real political and official name, however, was The American Party. A prevalent notion was that the Know-Nothings always met at midnight, that they carried dark-lanterns, that they pledged themselves in the dark by the most terrible oaths, and that their proceedings were inscrutable.

The number who joined these secret lodges was very large. They were made up of men who were incensed and alarmed at the power of foreign-born citizens in the elections; of those "whose daily horror and nightly spectre was the pope"; and of others for whom the secret ceremonies and mysterious methods were an attraction. But the most pregnant reason for the transient success of the order arose from the fact that, although the old parties at the North were rent into fragments, there was no ready-made organization to take their place. Men were disgusted and dissatisfied with their political affiliations, and yearned to enlist under a banner that should display positive and sincere aims. If the anti-Nebraska members of Congress had comprehended the situation, as did the freemen of Michigan, a national Republican party would at once have been formed and the Know-Nothings would have lost a large element of strength. The position of the American party on slavery was not clear. Julian, of Indiana, charged that the organization was the result of a deeply laid scheme of the slavery propaganda, whose purpose was to precipitate a new issue upon the North and distract the public mind from the question of pith and moment. Douglas declared that it was simply abolitionism under a new guise. Henry A. Wise, of Virginia, emphatically maintained that the object of the Know-Nothing order was the destruction of slavery. In general, it may be said that although at the North many anti-slavery men were in the organization, those who had the control wished to put forward their distinctive principles and keep the slavery question in abeyance. It seemed, therefore, to the Republicans that the Know-Nothings, not being for them, were against them. At the South the Americans were chiefly represented by those opposed to the formation of a party on the one idea of slavery extension. Thus they incurred the displeasure of the Southerners who had made up their minds that the great issue must be settled before another could be discussed.

The Know-Nothing movement, born of political unrest, augmented the ferment in the country. This was a year of excitement and lawlessness. Riots were frequent. Occasionally a band
of women would make a raid on a bar-room, break the glasses,
stave the whiskey casks, and pour the liquor into the streets.
Garrison, infatuated by his own methods and blind to the trend
of events, burned the Constitution of the United States at an
open-air celebration of the abolitionists in Framingham, Mass.
This action drew forth a few hisses and wrathful exclamations,
but these were overborne by "a tremendous shout of 'Amen.' "
Most of the disturbances, however, grew out of the Know-Nothing crusade. A mob forced their way into the shed near the
Washington monument, and broke to pieces a beautiful block
of marble which came from the Temple of Concord at Rome,
and had been sent by the pope as his tribute to the memory of
Washington. A street preacher, who styled himself the "Angel
Gabriel," excited a crowd at Chelsea, Mass., to deeds of violence. They smashed the windows of the Catholic church, tore
the cross from the gable, and shivered it to atoms. The firemen
and military were called out to aid the police in preserving
order.

On one Sunday, in the City Hall Park of New York, a fight
occurred between the advocates of a street preacher and those
who were determined he should not speak. The latter got the
worse of it, and the self-styled "missionary of the everlasting
gospel," protected by a band of Know-Nothings, was able to
deliver his sermon. On the following Sunday the street preacher
held forth in Brooklyn. When his discourse was finished, he was
escorted to the ferry by about five thousand Know-Nothings,
who, on the way, were set upon by an equally large number of
Irish Catholics. An angry fight ensued, in which volleys of
stones were thrown from one side and bullets fired from the
other. The police were unable to suppress the riot, and the
mayor sent a regiment of military to their aid. During the week
the excitement was intense, and on the next Sunday everything
seemed ready for a violent explosion in Brooklyn. But the

authorities were prepared. The whole of the regular police force was on duty, assisted by a large number of special police and deputy sheriffs. Three regiments of military guarded the streets. The "Angel Gabriel" delivered a fierce invective against the "infernal Jesuit system" and "accursed popery." The precautions taken by the mayor to preserve the peace were so effective that only a slight outbreak took place. A detachment of the Know-Nothing procession was attacked by a gang of Irishmen; but the police fired at the mob, and they quickly dispersed. Similar riots occurred in other cities of the country.

The public mind was so engrossed with political and moral questions that, although cholera was epidemic at the North this summer, it awakened little anxiety and caused no panic.

It is now time to consider the verdict of the Northern people on the Kansas-Nebraska act as evidenced in the elections. The first election after its enactment was in Iowa. Iowa had been a steadfast Democratic State. It had voted for two presidential candidates, Cass and Pierce. In the present Congress it had two Democratic senators, one Democratic and one Whig representative. Both of the senators and the Democratic representative voted for the Kansas-Nebraska bill; the Whig representative did not vote.

A governor was to be elected this year, and the Whigs had nominated James W. Grimes; a Free-soil convention had endorsed the nomination. Grimes issued a spirited manifesto, in which he declared that the extension of slavery was now the most important public question, and that Iowa, the only free child of the Missouri Compromise, should pronounce against its repeal. He made a thorough and vigorous canvass of the State, denouncing everywhere the "Nebraska infamy." The temperance issue entered slightly into the discussion, and the voters favorable to prohibition supported Grimes. The Know-Nothing wave had not reached Iowa. Grimes was elected by two thousand four hundred and eighty-six majority. It was the first time the Democrats had ever been defeated in a State election, and they did not carry Iowa again for thirty-five years. Another result was the choice of a legislature which sent Harlan, an avowed Republican, to the United States Senate. No doubt could exist that the meaning of this election was the condemnation of the Kansas-Nebraska bill. "You have the credit," wrote Senator Chase to Grimes, "of fighting the best battle for freedom yet fought;" and two years later, when the Republican party had become a strong organization, Chase wrote the Iowa governor: "Your election was the morning star. The sun has risen now."

In September, elections were held in Maine and Vermont. In Maine there were four State tickets, the Republican, the Whig, the Democratic, and that popularly termed the rum ticket. The Republican candidate for governor had a handsome plurality. Although there was no choice by the people, the Republicans had the legislature, which insured them the governor. In Vermont the canvass of the anti-Nebraska men was carried on under the name of Fusion; the result was a large majority in their favor. Vermont sent an unbroken anti-Nebraska delegation to the House of Representatives, and Maine, which had hitherto been a reliable Democratic State, only elected one Democratic congressman. The verdict of both of these States was unmistakably adverse to the Nebraska legislation. In neither of them did the temperance question have an important influence, for it had been settled. In Maine the voters of the rum ticket were a corporal's guard. Nor were the Know-Nothings an appreciable element in the result.

In October elections took place in Pennsylvania, Ohio, and Indiana. In Pennsylvania, the Whigs retained their organization, and the Free-soil Democrats ratified that ticket. They made opposition to the Kansas-Nebraska act the main question and elected their governor, but this was due to the assistance of the Know-Nothings. The Know-Nothings elected enough members to the legislature to hold the balance of power between the two parties; and the temperance question entered into the canvass, as a popular vote was taken on a prohibitory law. Yet the best test of sentiment in regard to the Missouri Compromise legislation was shown in the congressional elections. The present delegation consisted of sixteen Democrats and nine Whigs; that chosen this fall was made up of four Nebraska and five anti-Nebraska Democrats, fifteen anti-Nebraska Whigs, and one American.

The anti-Nebraska People's party carried Ohio by seventy-five thousand majority and elected every representative to Congress. The anti-Nebraska party were successful in Indiana by thirteen thousand majority, and chose all the congressmen but two. In both of these States the Know-Nothings co-operated with the anti-Nebraska organization. The temperance question entered into the discussion, and inured to the advantage of the successful party. Yet both the temperance and Know-Nothing ideas were overbalanced by the anti-slavery feeling. The verdict on that was unmistakable. Lincoln, disputing with Douglas at Peoria, commended to him as a refutation of his specious reasoning "the seventy thousand answers just in from Pennsylvania, Ohio, and Indiana."

The contest in Illinois, Douglas's own State, possesses an added interest. Douglas arrived at Chicago, his home, the latter part of August, and gave notice that he would address his constituents on the evening of the 1st of September. Rarely has it been the lot of a senator to speak to a more discontented crowd than he confronted that night. The anti-slavery people were embittered at his course in regard to the Missouri Compromise; the Know-Nothings were incensed at his vigorous denunciation of their order in a speech made at Philadelphia, July 4th; and the commercial interest of the city was indignant because he had opposed the River and Harbor bill. During the afternoon the flags of all the shipping in the harbor were hung at half mast; at dusk the bells of the churches were tolled as if for a funeral, and above the din might be heard the mournful sound of the big city bell. A doleful air pervaded the city. A host of men assembled to hear the justification of the senator, but among them he had hardly a friend. The first few sentences of the speech were heard in silence, but when he made what was considered an offensive remark, a terrible groan rolled up from the whole assemblage, followed by the unearthly Know-Nothing yell. When silence was restored, Douglas continued, but every pro-slavery sentiment was met with long-continued groans. Several statements which the audience doubted were received with derisive laughter. After an hour of interruptions, Douglas lost his temper and abused the crowd, taunting them for being afraid to give him a hearing. This was received with overpowering groans and hisses; and at last Douglas, convinced that further attempt would be useless, yielded to the solicitations of his friends and withdrew from the platform.

In the central part of the State, however, the people heard Douglas gladly. At Springfield, the doughty champion of popular sovereignty met Lincoln in friendly discussion, but, in spite of the prestige his successful career of politician had given him, he was discomfited by the plain Illinois lawyer, the depths of whose nature had been stirred by the repeal of the Missouri Compromise. The fallacy of justifying this action by the plea that it simply instituted the great principle of self-government in the territories was shown by Lincoln in a few words that went to the hearts of the audience. "My distinguished friend," he remarked, "says it is an insult to the emigrants to Kansas and Nebraska to suppose they are not able to govern themselves. We must not slur over an argument of this kind because it happens to tickle the ear. It must be met and answered. I admit that the emigrant to Kansas and Nebraska is competent to govern himself, but I deny his right to govern any other person without that person's consent."

In spite of the vigorous efforts of Douglas, Illinois did not sustain him. It is true that, owing to the popularity of their candidate for State treasurer, the Democrats carried the State ticket, and Douglas made the most of it; but the anti-Nebraska people elected five out of nine congressmen, and their majority in the State on the congressional vote was more than seventeen thousand. They also controlled the legislature, and sent Lyman Trumbull, an anti-Nebraska Democrat, to the Senate. The power of the Know-Nothings was exercised in opposition to the Douglas party.

The course which the canvass took, and the result of the election in New York, exhibit a phase of the political situation different from any that prevailed in the West. An anti-Nebraska convention held in August adopted resolutions, reported by Horace Greeley, which grasped the situation fully and dealt only with the slavery question. In them every one was invited to unite "in the sacred cause of freedom, of free labor and free soil." It was a foregone conclusion that the Whigs would not give up their organization, to the maintenance of which the influence of Seward and Thurlow Weed had been directed. The Whigs, however, in their convention took pronounced ground in opposition to the extension of slavery. They nominated Clark for governor and Henry J. Raymond for lieutenant-governor. Both of these men were anti-slavery Whigs, in full sympathy with Seward. This ticket was adopted by the adjourned anti-Nebraska convention and by the Temperance party. If the fusionists had encountered no opposition save from the Democrats, the result would never have been in doubt. Both factions of this party made nominations. The Hards endorsed the Kansas-Nebraska bill; the Softs approved the policy of Pierce's administration, and nominated Horatio Seymour for governor, thus making a direct issue of prohibition.

But the Know-Nothings were an unknown quantity. They had all along been feared by the Whigs, and when the grand council met at New York City in October, the anxiety knew no bounds. It was a curious political convention. Publicity is desired for ordinary gatherings of the kind; newspaper reporters are welcomed, for it is thought that a detailed account of the proceedings may awaken interest and arouse enthusiasm. But such views did not obtain in the grand council. About eight hundred delegates met at the grand-lodge room of the Independent Order of Odd Fellows. A long file of sentinels guarded the portals; newspaper reporters and outsiders were strictly excluded. The credentials of each delegate were subjected to a rigid scrutiny before he was admitted to the hall. While no authoritative account of the transactions could be given, and profound secrecy was desired by the Know-Nothings in regard to every circumstance, it leaked out that a State ticket had been nominated. Ullman, a conservative Whig, was the candidate for governor. No declaration of principles was published; no public meetings were held to advocate their platform and candidates; they had not the powerful aid of a devoted press; everything was done in the dark. But every Know-Nothing was bound by oath to support any candidate for political office who should be nominated by the order to which he belonged.

When the November election day came the work of this mysterious organization was made manifest. The Know-Nothings, said an apologist, do everything systematically and noiselessly; their votes "fall as the quietly descending dew." Unseen and unknown, wrote an exponent who was elected to Congress, the order "wielded an overwhelming influence wherever it developed its power. . . . In many a district where its existence was unsuspected, it has, in an hour, like the unseen wind, swept the corruptionist from his power and placed in office the unsoliciting but honest and capable citizen."

When the votes were counted, every one but the Know-Nothings themselves was astounded. A current estimate of their strength as sixty thousand had seemed extravagant, but they polled more than double that number. Ullman had 122,282; Clark had 156,804; Seymour had 156,495; and Bronson, the "Hard" candidate, had 33,850. Clark's plurality was 309.

The anti-slavery and temperance sentiment was overshadowed by the American feeling. It was conceded that the Know-Nothings had drawn more from the Whigs than from the Democrats. Yet in the congressional elections the opposition to the repeal of the Missouri Compromise had full play. Twenty-seven out of a total of thirty-three representatives were chosen as anti-Nebraska men.

The election in Massachusetts took place a few days later than in New York. Here the political situation was different from that in any other State. An attempt was made to form a Republican party, and a convention was held under that name. Sumner made a powerful speech, and his influence was dominant. Henry Wilson was nominated for governor. The Whigs would not give up their organization, and the Republicans were therefore nothing but the old Free-soil party under another name. The Whigs adopted strong anti-slavery resolutions, and nominated Emory Washburn for governor. The Know-Nothings, by their secret methods, put Gardner in the field. Gardner had been a conservative Whig, but was now understood to be an anti-slavery man, and the bulk of his supporters were certainly opposed to slavery extension. In truth, the people of Massachusetts were all, with the exception of a few Democrats, so strongly opposed to the repeal of the Missouri Compromise that the question could not be made a political issue. The contest was virtually between the Whigs and Know-Nothings, and the Whig discomfiture was complete. Gardner had more than fifty thousand majority over Washburn. The Whigs had been fairly confident of success, and their amazement was unbounded. But the Know-Nothings knew absolutely what they might reckon upon. Congdon relates that Brewer and he, who were the editors of the Boston *Atlas*, met Gardner in the street shortly before the election. The Know-Nothing candidate said to Brewer: "You had better not abuse me as you are abusing me in the *Atlas*. I shall be elected by a very large majority." To Congdon, the movement seemed like "a huge joke;" and it is undeniable that the humorous side of the organization had attractions for many voters who anticipated amusement from the unlooked-for and startling effects. The Congressmen elected were all Know-Nothings, but all were anti-slavery. The legislature, almost wholly made up of members of the American party, sent Henry Wilson to the Senate.

Wilson's hatred of slavery was greater than his distrust of Irishmen or Catholics. Undoubtedly he would have preferred Republican to Know-Nothing success; but he was ambitious for place, and he saw in the craze of the moment a convenient stepping-stone to political position. Although refused admission to one Know-Nothing lodge, he persisted in his purpose, and succeeded afterwards in getting regularly initiated in another.

The Republicans of Michigan and Wisconsin were eminently successful at their elections, and the results justified the steps which they had taken towards the formation of a new party.

This account of the fall elections may be tedious in its details, but it seems necessary to enter into the matter minutely in order to show whether there were important limitations to the statement that the North in the fall elections emphatically condemned the Kansas-Nebraska legislation. Douglas, with characteristic effrontery, maintained that there had been no anti-Nebraska triumph. The Democrats, he said, had been obliged to contend against a fusion which had been organized by Know-Nothing councils, and their mysterious way of working had taken men by surprise, and was therefore the great reason of success; but it was a Know-Nothing and not an anti-Nebraska victory. The groundlessness and the specious character of this explanation are shown by the detailed recital. And if we view the political revolution with regard to the fortunes of the Democratic party, the results will seem more striking than I have stated them. The Democrats had in the present House of Representatives a majority of eighty-four. In the House which was elected after the passage of the Kansas-Nebraska act, they would be in a minority of seventy-five, and on slavery questions would be obliged to form an alliance with thirty-seven Whigs and Know-Nothings of pro-slavery principles. Of forty-two Northern Democrats who had voted for the Kansas-Nebraska bill, only seven were re-elected. The *National Intelligencer* made a comparison of the elections of 1852 and 1854, showing that without taking into account Massachusetts, the Democratic loss in the Northern States had been 347,742. The most weighty reason for this revulsion of feeling was the repeal of the Missouri Compromise.

Yet, considering the popular sentiment at the time of the enactment of the Nebraska bill, the declaration was not as positive and clear as might have been expected. Public indignation at the breach of plighted faith, dissatisfaction with the old parties, and the resulting political and moral agitation needed a national leader to give them proper direction. Had there been a leader, much of that magnificent moral energy which vented its force against Irishmen and Catholics might have been turned into anti-slavery channels. Two men came out of the congressional contest over the Nebraska bill with apparently sufficient prestige to build up a new party. Chase, indeed, did not object to a new organization, and would have been willing to head such a movement; but the chief element of the new party must come from the Northern Whigs. Chase, having entered public life under Democratic auspices, was obnoxious to the Ohio Whigs, and it would have been impossible even for a man of more tact than he to overcome the personal and political objections to his leadership.

But Seward had the position, the ability, and the character necessary for the leadership of a new party. He was the idol of the anti-slavery Whigs. He was admired and trusted by most of the Free-soilers and anti-Nebraska Democrats. "The repeal of the Missouri Compromise," said the New York *Times*, "has developed a popular sentiment in the North which will probably elect Governor Seward to the Presidency in 1856 by the largest vote from the free States ever cast for any candidate." "Seward is in the ascendency in this State and the North generally," said the Democratic New York *Post*. "The man who should have impelled and guided the general uprising of the free States is W. H. Seward," asserted Greeley.

It was the tide in Seward's affairs, but he did not take it at the flood. "Shall we have a new party?" asked the New York *Independent*. "The leaders for such a party do not appear. Seward adheres to the Whig party."

Perhaps the sympathies of Seward were heartily enlisted in the movement for a new party and he was held back by Thurlow Weed. Perhaps he would have felt less trammeled had not his senatorship been at stake in the fall election. The fact is, however, that the Republican movement in the West and New England received no word of encouragement from him. He did not make a speech, even in the State of New York, during the campaign. His care and attention were engrossed in seeing that members of the legislature were elected who would vote for him for senator. The Know-Nothings were bitterly opposed to him, and he had no sympathy with the organization. Yet it was currently believed that his candidate for governor had endeavored to become a member of a Know-Nothing lodge; it was also charged that emissaries instructed by the followers of Seward had secured admission to the order.

Had Seward sunk the politician in the statesman; had he made a few speeches, such as he well knew how to make, in New York, New England, and the West; had he emphatically denounced Know-Nothingism as Douglas did at Philadelphia, or as he did after he had been chosen senator for another term;* had he vigorously asserted that every cause must be subordinate to union under the banner of opposition to the extension of slavery,—the close of the year 1854 would have seen a triumphant Republican party in every Northern State but California, and Seward its acknowledged leader. Had Douglas been in Seward's place, how quickly would he have grasped the situation, and how skilfully would he have guided public opinion! There was a greater politician and statesman in Illinois than Douglas, who was admirably fitted to head a popular movement; but beyond his own State, Lincoln was unknown: he had not a position from which he could speak with authority and which would obtain him a hearing from the whole people. No man, however, understood the situation better; and of all utterances against the Nebraska legislation, none equalled Lincoln's in making plain to the people the gravity of the step which had been taken and the necessity of united action to undo the wrong.

* Douglas's speech was made July 4th, 1854. See Sheahan, p. 267; Cutts, p. 122. Seward did not criticise the principles and methods of the order until Feb. 23d, 1855, in the Senate. Even then his remarks were characterized by a certain levity which weakened their force. See *Congressional Globe*, vol. xxxi. p. 241.

The speech which he made at Peoria in answer to Douglas tore up the sophistry, political and historical, of the Illinois senator. In it he demonstrated that the ordinance of 1787 had given freedom to their State; he told the history of the Missouri Compromise, and explained the compromise of 1850 in words which were alike clear and profound. This speech, making justly an important epoch in the life of Lincoln, has yet little to do with the history of the country; for it was published in but one Illinois newspaper, and was not known outside of his own State. It made him, indeed, the leader of his party in Illinois, and was therefore an earnest of further advancement. But it is safe to say that had Lincoln been known at the North as were Seward and Chase, and had this speech been delivered in the principal States, it would have acted powerfully to fuse the jarring elements into the union which the logic of the times demanded. Douglas appreciated the force of Lincoln's arguments with the people, and admitted that they were giving him more trouble than all the speeches in the United States Senate. He begged that Lincoln would speak no more during this campaign, he himself agreeing also to desist.

CHARLES SUMNER *was approaching the end of his first term as senator when the presidential campaign of 1856 began. Vehemently assailing the Fugitive Slave Act, characterizing the Kansas-Nebraska Act as an infamous swindle, trying to cut off funds for its enforcement, and denouncing the Know-Nothing party for their equivocal position on slavery, he did a great deal to give the Republican party its early intensity of conviction. His speeches were evidence that the party was thoroughly militant, and meant to meet violence with violence. Congress has seldom heard so bitter a diatribe as his address on "The Crime against Kansas," delivered May 20, 1856, attacking not only the use of fraud and violence to deliver the territory to a proslavery minority, but the personal and public character of Senators Andrew P. Butler of South Carolina and Stephen A. Douglas. Almost immediately he was heavily caned in the Senate chamber by Representative Preston S. Brooks, not so much for his arraignment of Southern offenses against Kansas settlers, as for his slur on South Carolina and on Brooks's kinsman, the South Carolina senator.*

Rhodes, in his spirited account of this episode, might have made more of the fact that a number of Southern newspapers (chiefly Whig sheets) criticized Preston Brooks severely. They held that although he was right to punish Sumner, he chose the wrong time, place, and method. In the North many men were critical of the language that Sumner had used, though public sentiment discouraged outspoken statements to this effect. But, in general, the assault heightened extremist feeling on both sides; it contributed to the division of the nation. The latest and ablest biographer of Sumner, David Donald, shows that in their accounts of the assault, Southerners and Northerners in general spoke an entirely different language. At the time, Emerson wondered whether the Union could or should endure when the two sections were so completely divided in moral feeling, codes of conduct, and attitudes toward law.

The political campaign now under way took on heightened emotion and interest, the Republicans gaining the most immediate profit. They made the

*most of Sumner's prolonged retreat to Europe for
medical treatment. Mr. Donald, who is able to present much fuller material on Sumner's illness, regards it as having mysterious aspects, but rejects as
emphatically as Rhodes the idea that it was in any
way shammed for party purposes. Rhodes might have
said more upon violence as a pervasive element in
national life.*

Brooks Assaults Sumner

THE Kansas question afforded the Republican senators a great
opportunity to define their position and put in concrete shape
their principles before the country. All the troubles, every outrage in Kansas, pointed the argument in favor of congressional
prohibition of slavery in the territories. Hale, of New Hampshire, made, in Greeley's opinion, the best speech of his life.
The new Republican senators from Illinois and Iowa. Trumbull
and Harlan, made their mark. Wade's effort was called by
Simonton "a magnificent invective." Wilson made a stirring
and effective speech, which found favor generally with the
Republicans; ten thousand copies were subscribed for by members of the House before he had finished speaking. It was gall
and wormwood to the Southerners, and many threats of personal violence were made against him. Collamer made a fine
legal argument, and Greeley, who, since dissolving the firm of
Seward, Weed, and Greeley, could not treat the New York
senator fairly, wrote privately to Dana: "Collamer's speech is
better than Seward's, in my humble judgment." The truth is
not always told in confidential correspondence. The personal
feeling of Greeley found vent in communing with his friend,
but he expressed the opinion of the country and the judgment
of the historian when he wrote to his journal that Seward's
speech was "the great argument," and stood "unsurpassed in
its political philosophy." Simonton had heard every speech
which Seward had ever made in the Senate, but he was sure

that this overtopped them all." The praise was merited. The words were those of a great statesman. The thoughtful and reading men of the North could not despair of the republic when their views found such masterly expression in the Senate.

The Republicans, and those inclined in that direction, of every part of the country, were great readers. Men who were wavering needed conviction; men, firm in the faith, needed strong arguments with which they might convince the wavering. Young men who were going to cast their first vote wanted to have the issue set plainly before them. Boys who would soon become voters were deeply interested in the political literature; those who had read *Uncle Tom's Cabin* in 1852 were now reading Republican speeches and newspapers. Never in the world had political thinkers and speakers a more attentive and intelligent public than in the North between 1856 and 1860; and the literature was worthy of the public. As people thought more deeply on the slavery question, the New York *Weekly Tribune* increased its circulation. On the day that it published Seward's speech, one hundred and sixty-two thousand copies were sent out. The Republican Association at Washington printed and sold at a low price a large number of Republican documents. Among them were "Governor Seward's Great Speech on the Immediate Admission of Kansas," Seward's Albany and Buffalo speeches, the speeches on Kansas in the Senate, of Wilson, Hale, Collamer, and Harlan. The supply of this sort of literature makes it evident that the Republican Association knew the people whom it must persuade were those who could be reached only by cogent reasoning; the demand shows the desire for correct political education.

The most startling speech made during the debate, the one which, from the events succeeding, became the most celebrated, was that of Charles Sumner. It was delivered on the 19th and 20th days of May and was published under the title of "The Crime against Kansas." Two days previously he wrote Theodore Parker: "I shall pronounce the most thorough philippic ever uttered in a legislative body." He thought he had girded himself with the spirit of the Athenian, and in one glorious passage his imitation went to the letter of the greatest of orations. Sumner stated the question as one involving "liberty in a broad territory"; a territory which had "advantages of situation," " a soil of unsurpassed richness and a fascinating, undulating beauty of surface, with a health-giving climate," and which was "calculated to nurture a powerful and generous people, worthy to be a central pivot of American institutions. . . . Against this territory," he continued, "a crime has been committed which is without example in the records of the Past." It is greater than the crime of Verres in Sicily. Popular institutions have been desecrated; the ballot-box has been plundered. "Not in any common lust for power did this uncommon tragedy have its origin. It is the rape of a virgin territory, compelling it to the hateful embrace of slavery; and it may be clearly traced to a depraved longing for a new slave State, the hideous offspring of such a crime, in the hope of adding to the power of slavery in the national government. Yes, sir, when the whole world, alike Christian and Turk, is rising up to condemn this wrong, and to make it a hissing to the nations, here in our republic *force*—ay, sir, FORCE—has been openly employed in compelling Kansas to this pollution, and all for the sake of political power. . . . Such is the crime." The criminal is the slave power, and has "an audacity beyond that of Verres, a subtlety beyond that of Machiavel, a meanness beyond that of Bacon, and an ability beyond that of Hastings." Fresh, probably, from reading the entrancing tale of "The Rise of the Dutch Republic" which his friend Motley had just published, Sumner declared that the tyranny now employed to force slavery upon Kansas was kindred to that of Alva, who sought to force the Inquisition upon the Netherlands.

The crime against Kansas is *"the crime of crimes"*; it is *"the crime against nature,* from which the soul recoils, and which language refuses to describe." David R. Atchison, like Catiline, "stalked into this chamber, reeking with conspiracy; and then, like Catiline, he skulked away to join and provoke the conspirators, who at a distance awaited their congenial chief." His followers were "murderous robbers from Missouri"; they were "hirelings picked from the drunken spew and vomit of an uneasy civilization, lashed together by secret signs and lodges," and they "have renewed the incredible atrocities of the assassins and of the Thugs."

The reader may be reminded that although the date of Sumner's speech is later than the time to which I have brought down the history of events in Kansas territory, nothing further of importance occurred until May of this year, and his philippic was based only on those transactions which have already been related in this work. These citations, therefore, will give an idea of his extravagant statements as well as of his turgid rhetoric; and they show the license which he allowed himself in the use of words when wrought up on the subject of slavery.* It is the speech of a sincere man who saw but one side of the question, whose thoughts worked in a single groove, and worked intensely. "There is no other side," he vehemently declared to a friend.

Sumner's speech added nothing of legal or political strength to the controversy. The temperate arguments of the senators who preceded him were of greater weight. But the speech produced a powerful sensation. The bravery with which he hurled defiance towards the South and her institutions challenged admiration. Before this session, on one occasion when he was delivering a fierce invective, Douglas said to a friend: "Do you hear that man? He may be a fool, but I tell you that man has pluck. Nobody can deny that, and I wonder whether he knows himself what he is doing. I am not sure whether I should have courage to say those things to the men who are scowling around him." But Sumner knew not fear; and his sincerity was absolute. His speech was prepared with care. To write out such a philippic in the cool seclusion of the study, and deliver it without flinching, was emphasizing to the Southerners that in

---

* The *Quarterly Review* of London said: "That speech is an example and a proof of the deterioration of American taste."

Sumner they had a persistent antagonist whom the fury of their threats could not frighten.

If there had been no more in Sumner's speech than the invective against the slave power, he would not have been assaulted by Preston Brooks. Nor is it probable that the bitter attack which the senator made on South Carolina would have provoked the violence, had it not been coupled with personal allusions to Senator Butler, who was a kinsman of Brooks. In order that the whole extent of the provocation may be understood, it is necessary to quote Sumner's most exasperating reflections. "The senator from South Carolina [Butler]," he said, "and the senator from Illinois [Douglas], who, though unlike Don Quixote and Sancho Panza, yet, like this couple, sally forth together . . . in championship of human wrongs." "The senator from South Carolina has read many books of chivalry, and believes himself a chivalrous knight, with sentiments of honor and courage. Of course he has chosen a mistress to whom he has made his vows, and who, though ugly to others, is always lovely to him; though polluted in the sight of the world, is chaste in his sight—I mean the harlot slavery. For her his tongue is always profuse in words. Let her be impeached in character, or any proposition made to shut her out from the extension of her wantonness, and no extravagance of manner or hardihood of assertion is then too great for this senator. The frenzy of Don Quixote, in behalf of his wench, Dulcinea del Toboso, is all surpassed." On the second day of his speech Sumner said: "With regret I come again upon the senator from South Carolina [Butler], who, omnipresent in this debate, overflowed with rage at the simple suggestion that Kansas had applied for admission as a State; and, with incoherent phrases, discharged the loose expectoration of his speech, now upon her representative, and then upon her people. There was no extravagance of the ancient parliamentary debate which he did not repeat; nor was there any possible deviation from truth which he did not make. . . . The senator touches nothing which he does not disfigure—with error, sometimes of principle, sometimes of fact. He shows an incapacity of accuracy, whether in stating the Constitution or in stating the law, whether in the details of statistics or the diversions of scholarship. He cannot open his mouth but out there flies a blunder."

A careful persual of Butler's remarks, as published in the *Congressional Globe,* fails to disclose the reason of this bitter personal attack. His remarks were moderate. He made no reference to Sumner. His reply to Hale, though spirited, was dignified and did not transcend the bounds of a fastidious parliamentary taste. Yet it must be said that his defence of Atchison, which today reads as a tribute to a generous, though rough and misguided, man, was very galling to an ardent friend of the free State party of Kansas, such as Sumner. Butler was a man of fine family, older in looks than his sixty years, courteous, a lover of learning, and a jurist of reputation. He was honored with the position of chairman of the Senate judiciary committee. When Sumner first came to the Senate, although he was an avowed Free-soiler, the relations between him and Butler were friendly; they were drawn together by a common love of history and literature. When he made his speech on the Kansas-Nebraska bill, Butler paid him a well-chosen compliment at which he expressed his gratification. In June, 1854, however, the two had a very warm discussion in the Senate on the Fugitive Slave law, growing out of the rendition of Burns, in which Butler replied to Sumner's forcible remarks with indignation. Afterwards Butler sent him word that their personal intercourse must be entirely cut off. The only reason which the South Carolina senator could assign for the present personal attack was that Sumner's vanity had been mortified from thinking that he did not come out of the controversy of 1854 with as much credit as he ought, and this was his opportunity for retaliation.

But no one understanding Sumner's character can accept this as an explanation. There was nothing vindictive or revengeful in his nature. Besides, he was too much wrapped up in his own self-esteem to give more than a passing thought to a social slight from a slave-holding senator, even though he were a leader in the refined and cultivated society of Washington. Sumner's speech seems excessively florid to the more cultivated taste of the present; he might have made a more effective argument, and one stronger in literary quality without giving offence. The speech occasioned resentment not so much on account of the line of personally insulting metaphor. Yet he did not transgress the bounds of parliamentary decorum, for he was not called to order by the President or by any other senator. The vituperation was unworthy of him and his cause, and the allusion to Butler's condition while speaking, ungenerous and pharisaical. The attack was especially unfair, as Butler was not in Washington, and Sumner made note of his absence. It was said that Seward, who read the speech before delivery, advised Sumner to tone down its offensive remarks, and he and Wade regretted the personal attack. But Sumner was not fully "conscious of the stinging force of his language." To that, and because he was terribly in earnest, must be attributed the imperfections of the speech. He would annihilate the slave power, and he selected South Carolina and her senator as vulnerable points of attack.

The whole story of Sumner's philippic, and its results, cannot be told without reference to his sharp criticism of Douglas. "The senator from Illinois," he said, "is the squire of slavery, its very Sancho Panza, ready to do all its humiliating offices. This senator, in his labored address, vindicating his labored report—piling one mass of elaborate error upon another mass—constrained himself to unfamiliar decencies of speech. . . . Standing on this floor, the senator issued his rescript, requiring submission to the usurped power of Kansas; and this was accompanied by a manner—all his own—such as befits the tyrannical threat. Very well. Let the senator try. I tell him now that he cannot enforce any such submission. The senator, with the slave power is back, is strong; but he is not strong enough for this purpose. He is bold. He shrinks from nothing. Like Danton, he may cry: *'L'audace! l'audace! toujours l'audace!'* but even his audacity cannot compass this work. The senator copies the British officer who, with boastful swagger, said that with the hilt of his sword he would cram the 'stamps' down the throats of the American people, and he will meet a similar failure."

When Sumner sat down, Cass, the Nestor of the Senate, rose and said: "I have listened with equal regret and surprise to the speech of the honorable senator from Massachusetts. Such a speech—the most un-American and unpatriotic that ever grated on the ears of the members of this high body—I hope never to hear again here or elsewhere."

When Cass had finished, Douglas spoke of the "depth of malignity that issued from every sentence" of Sumner's speech. "Is it his object," Douglas asked, "to provoke some of us to kick him as we would a dog in the street, that he may get sympathy upon the just chastisement?" If the senator, Douglas continued, had said harsh things on the spur of the moment, and "then apologized for them in his cooler hours, I could respect him much more than if he had never made such a departure from the rules of the Senate. . . . But it has been the subject of conversation for weeks that the senator from Massachusetts had his speech written, printed, committed to memory. . . . The libels, the gross insults, which we have heard to-day have been conned over, written with a cool, deliberate malignity, repeated from night to night in order to catch the appropriate grace; and then he came here to spit forth that malignity upon men who differ from him—for that is their offence." Douglas furthermore charged Sumner with being a perjurer, for he had sworn to support the Constitution and yet publicly denied that he would render obedience to the fugitive law. Sumner's reply was exasperating. "Let the senator remember," he said, "that the bowie-knife and the bludgeon are not the proper emblems of senatorial debate. Let him remember that the swagger of Bob Acres and the ferocity of the Malay cannot add dignity to this body; . . . that no person with the upright form of man can be allowed, without violation of all decency, to switch out from his tongue the perpetual stench of offensive

personality," taking for a model "the noisome squat and name-
less animal." Douglas made an insulting retort, and Sumner
rejoined: "Mr. President, again the senator has switched his
tongue, and again he fills the Senate with its offensive odor."
Douglas ended the angry colloquy by declaring that a man
whom he had branded in the Senate with falsehood was not
worthy of a reply.

Two days after this exciting debate (May 22d), when the
Senate at the close of a short session adjourned, Sumner remained in the Chamber, occupied in writing letters. Becoming
deeply engaged, he drew his arm chair close to his desk, bent
over his writing, and while in this position was approached by
Brooks, a representative from South Carolina and a kinsman
of Senator Butler. Brooks, standing before and directly over
him, said: "I have read your speech twice over carefully. It
is a libel on South Carolina and Mr. Butler, who is a relative
of mine." As he pronounced the last word, he hit Sumner on
the head with his cane with the force that a dragoon would give
to a sabre-blow.* Sumner was more than six feet in height and
of powerful frame, but penned under the desk he could offer
no resistance, and Brooks continued the blows on his defenceless
head. The cane broke, but the South Carolinian went on beating
his victim with the butt. The first blows stunned and blinded
Sumner, but instinctively and with powerful effort he wrenched
the desk from its fastenings, stood up, and with spasmodic and
wildly directed efforts attempted unavailingly to protect himself. Brooks took hold of him, and, while he was reeling and
staggering about, struck him again and again. The assailant
did not desist until his arm was seized by one who rushed to
the spot to stop the assault. At that moment Sumner, reeling,
staggering backwards and sideways, fell to the floor bleeding
profusely and covered with his blood.

* The cane was gutta-percha, one inch in diameter at the larger and
five-eighths of an inch in diameter at the smaller end. Brooks served in
the cavalry during the Mexican war.

The injury received by Sumner was much more severe than was at first thought by his physicians and friends. Four days after the assault, he was able to give at his lodgings his relation of the affair to the committee of the House of Representatives. But, in truth, the blows would have killed most men.* Sumner's iron constitution and perfect health warded off a fatal result; but it soon appeared that the injury had affected the spinal column. The next three years and a half was a search for cure by a man who, with the exception of a severe fever when he was thirty-three, had rarely known what it was to be ill. He submitted himself to medical treatment at Washington, Boston, and London. He was re-elected to the Senate by an almost unanimous vote of the Massachusetts legislature, and tried twice to resume his duties. But Sumner, who was accustomed to ten hours of intellectual work out of the twenty-four, could not now bear the ordinary routine of the day. At last he went to Paris and put himself under the care of Dr. Brown-Séquard, whose treatment of actual cauterization of the back eventually restored him to a fair degree of health; but he never regained his former physical vigor. He was not able to enter regularly again on his senatorial career until December, 1859. He did not speak again until June, 1860, when he described in burning words the "Barbarism of Slavery."

To take a man unawares, in a position where he could not defend himself, and injure the seat of his intellect was truly a dreadful deed.

He who was thus struck down in the strength of a splendid manhood was a man of rare physique, vigorous brain, and pure heart; a senator devoted to his work, punctilious in attentiveness to routine, eager for self-improvement. He so loved intellectual

* Seward wrote his wife, July 5th, 1856: "Sumner is much changed for the worse. His elasticity and vigor are gone. He walks, and in every way moves, like a man who has not altogether recovered from a paralysis, or like a man whose sight is dimmed, and his limbs stiffened with age. . . . His vivacity of spirit and his impatience for study are gone."—*Life of Seward,* vol. ii. p. 282.

labor that he never lost a day. The feeling of revenge was foreign to his nature. Stretched on a bed of pain, compelled by shattered nerves to give up the study and the work that were his life, he felt no resentment towards Brooks.

Full of manly independence, he would submit to no leader, bow to no party, nor solicit any member of the legislature for a vote. His very presence, said a warm political and personal friend, "made you forget the vulgarities of political life." He was the soul of honor; and his absolute integrity extended even to the most trivial affairs of life. Duty was to him sacred, the moral law a daily influence; his thoughts, his deeds, were pure. His faults were venial, and such as we might look for in a spoiled child of a city of culture. He was vain, conceited, fond of flattery, overbearing in manner, and he wore a constant air of superiority.

He was a profound student of words, but he studied them too much in the lifeless pages of dictionaries, and too little in the living discourse of his fellow-men, so that he failed to get an exact impression of their force and color. Consequently, he gave offence at times where none was intended,* a fault for which he greviously answered.

Preston Brooks, the man who did Sumner this lasting injury, was not a ruffian; he came from one of the good South Carolina families. He was well educated, and had been a member of the House of Representatives for three years, where his conduct had been that of a gentleman. He has been called "courteous, accomplished, warm-hearted, and hot-blooded, dear as a friend and fearful as an enemy."

The different manner in which the North and the South regarded this deed is one of the many evidences of the deep gulf between these two people caused by slavery. The North was struck with horror and indignation. The legislature of

---

* Johnson, *Scribner's Magazine*, vol. viii, p. 479. "Sumner's silly way of saying the bitterest things without apparent consciousness of saying anything harmful."—Francis Lieber, *Life of Lieber*, p. 297.

Massachusetts immediately took action, and characterized the assault by resolution in fitting terms. Indignation meetings were held all over the North. Edward Everett, who was a type of Northern conservatism, prefaced the delivery of his oration on Washington at Taunton, Mass., by saying: "The civil war, with its horrid train of fire and slaughter, carried on without the slightest provocation against the infant settlements of our brethren on the frontier of the Union—the worse than civil war which, after raging for months unrebuked at the capital of the Union, has at length, with a lawless violence of which I know no example in the annals of constitutional government, stained the floor of the Senate chamber with the blood of a defenceless man, and he a senator from Massachusetts. . . . O my good friends! these are events which, for the good name, the peace, the safety of the country, it were well worth all the gold of California to blot from the record of the past week." The tendency at the North was to forget entirely the personal provocation, and to regard the assault on Sumner as an outrage by the slave power, because he had so vehemently denounced the South and her institution. Attendant circumstances gave color to this opinion. Keitt, a representative from South Carolina, stood by, during the assault, brandishing his cane in a menacing manner, and threatening Simonton and others who rushed in to interfere. Edmundson, a representative from Virginia, was at hand to render assistance if necessary.

Ever since the excitement growing out of the Burns case, in May and June, 1854, when Sumner had denounced the Fugitive Slave law in vigorous terms, he had been very obnoxious to the South, and at that time he was warned that he stood in personal danger. He was hated by the South much more intensely than any other Republican. The Southern congressmen stood by Brooks, but they justified his action on account of the supposed insult to his kinsman and State, and they endeavored to make out that Sumner's injuries were slight.

The inevitable disagreement of physicians occurred, and there was show of reason, when the excitement ran the highest, for thinking that his hurt would be temporary.

At Washington, congressional propriety, senatorial courtesy, and the conviction that the Senate chamber had been desecrated, modified the public expression of Southern sentiment. But in the slave States themselves the feeling was given full rein, and it was plainly apparent that the assault was approved of by the press and the people.

OPEN *warfare flamed in Kansas even as Sumner delivered his intemperate speech. It had been narrowly averted the previous winter by the action of a new governor appointed by President Pierce. This was Wilson Shannon, neither very able nor fair-minded, who at least curbed some lawless proslavery Missourians ("border ruffians") as they were about to assail the free-state stronghold of Lawrence. Now the proslavery forces launched a new attack on the town. Their object was to discourage Northern immigration, which actually was already certain to fix the ultimate character of Kansas and to cripple the Topeka movement for creating a Free Soil state under Charles Robinson as governor. But the most immediate and important effect of the blow they struck was to arouse John Brown, of the Free Soil settlement called Osawatomie, to reckless activity.*

Writing before a variety of books emphasized the mental instability of "Old John Brown" (actually fifty-six that year) and explored in detail the development of his ideas upon the establishment of a state for escaped slaves and free Negroes somewhere in the Appalachians, Rhodes offers a generally sound and highly readable depiction of this gnarled figure. Kansas that spring, as he says, was in a state of civil war. But the replacement of Shannon as governor by a much stronger man, John W. Geary, made possible the restoration of peace before autumn and strengthened the Democratic party in the presidential campaign.

The "Sack" of Lawrence: John Brown Appears

ON the 11th of May, [1856], the United States marshal for Kansas territory, Donaldson, issued a proclamation to the people stating that he had certain writs to execute in Lawrence; his deputy had been resisted on a similar errand and he had every reason to believe that the attempt to execute the writs would be resisted by a large body of armed men; therefore he commanded all the law-abiding citizens of the territory to appear at Lecompton as soon as possible in sufficient force to execute the law. No call could have better pleased the border ruffians. Now had come the long wished-for opportunity to wipe out the odious town of Lawrence, and send its inhabitants north to Nebraska, where they belonged. Through all the threats and fulminations of the pro-slavery party, it plainly appears that they sincerely thought that the intent of the Kansas-Nebraska act was to give one territory to slavery, the other to freedom; therefore the settlement of Northern people in Kansas was a cheat and an encroachment on their rights. There were probably, however, not more than fifty slave-holders in Kansas, and all that kept the pro-slavery cause alive was the powerful backing it had from western Missouri.

The publication of the marshal's proclamation increased the commotion in eastern Kansas and western Missouri and the alarm of the Lawrence people. Their trusted leader, Robinson, was a prisoner, and there was no one to take his place; but they decided to temporize, which was undoubtedly the best policy. They had already requested Governor Shannon to send them United States troops for protection, but this he refused to do. Now, as they heard of the gathering of the clans on the Missouri border, they held a public meeting and solemnly averred that the statement and inference in Donaldson's proclamation were false. They also endeavored to placate the marshal, but without avail.

The marshal's posse began to collect in the neighborhood of Lawrence. On the 19th of May a young man, returning from Lawrence, was shot by two of the pro-slavery horde, apparently for no other reason than that he was an abolitionist. Three adventurous spirits of Lawrence rode out to avenge his murder, and one of them was killed.

On the 21st of May, the marshal's posse gathered on the bluffs west of the town. It was composed of the Douglas County (Kansas) Militia, the Kickapoo Rangers, other companies from

eastern Kansas led by Stringfellow, the Missouri Platte County
Rifles with two pieces of artillery commanded by Atchison,
three other companies of border ruffians, and Buford and his
men. It was a swearing, whiskey-drinking, ruffianly horde,
seven hundred and fifty in number. The irony of fate had made
them the upholders of the law, while the industrious, frugal
community of Lawrence were the law-breakers. The deputy-
marshal, attended with a small escort, walked into the town
and made some arrests. Not the slightest resistance was offered.
The business of the United States official was soon completed;
but the sheriff of Douglas county had work to do, and Donaldson turned over the posse to Sheriff Jones, saying: "He is a
law-and-order man, and acts under the same authority as the
marshal." Jones, the idol of the pro-slavery party, was received
with wild demonstrations of delight. Under his lead the posse
marched into the town, dragging their five pieces of artillery
and with banners flying. No company, however, carried the
flag of the Union. One banner had a single white star and bore
the inscriptions, "Southern Rights" and "South Carolina;"
another had in blue letters on a white ground—

> Let Yankees tremble, abolitionists fall;
> Our motto is, Give Southern rights to all.

The offices of the obnoxious newspapers were quickly
destroyed; the types and presses were broken, and, with the
books and papers, thrown into the street or carried to the
river. The writ against the splendid stone hotel just completed remained to be executed. At this point Atchison counselled moderation; Buford also disliked to aid in the destruction of property. But Jones was implacable. His wound still
rankled and he was bent on revenge. He demanded of Pomeroy,
the representative of the Emigrant-Aid Company, all the
Sharps rifles and artillery in the town. The rifles were refused
on the ground that they were private property, but a cannon
was given up. Four cannon were then pointed at the hotel and
thirty-two shots were fired, but little damage was done. The

attempt was then made to blow it up with kegs of powder, but without success. At last the torch was applied and the hotel destroyed. The liquors and wines found in the Yankee hotel were not disdained, and the glee felt at the outcome of the movement was increased by frequent potations. The ruffians were ripe for mischief; and when Sheriff Jones said his work was done and the posse dismissed, they sacked the town and set fire to Governor Robinson's house.

The revelry was kept up as those who composed the posse journeyed to their homes. Jubilant border ruffians were everywhere met on the routes of travel, drinking to the victory which had crowned their efforts. But it was a victory worse than a defeat. The attack on Lawrence took place the day before the assault on Sumner; the news of it came to the people of the North a little later. These were two startling events; their coincidence in time was used with great impression by the Republican press. Freedom's representative had been struck down in the Senate chamber; the city dedicated to freedom on the plains of Kansas had been destroyed. Such were the texts on which the liberty-loving journalists wrote, and their masterly pens did full justice to the theme. The first reports were exaggerated. They were to the effect that Lawrence was in ruins, that many persons were killed, and that Pomeroy had been hanged by a mob. Nevertheless, after all misstatements had been corrected and the true history of the affair arrived at, it still remained a most pregnant Republican argument. When President Pierce heard of the motley crowd assembled by the marshal as a posse, he feared the business would be managed badly, and telegraphed Governor Shannon and Colonel Sumner that the United States troops were sufficient to enforce the laws, and that they only should be used. But before this despatch was sent, the mischief had been done.

At no time had the enthusiasm for free Kansas in the North been so great as when the news of this attack on Lawrence became disseminated. Meetings for the aid of Kansas were everywhere held. The burden of the speeches was the attempt to crush out Freedom's stronghold in Kansas and the effort to silence Sumner in the Senate. Men enlisted in the cause, and money was freely subscribed.

In the territory itself, most of the free-State party were at first dismayed; but there were others in whom a spirit of bitter revenge was aroused. John Brown now appeared prominently on the scene. He had come to Kansas the previous October to join his sons, who had settled at Osawatomie, but the motive which led him was his powerful desire to strike a blow at slavery.

John Brown was ascetic in habits, inflexible in temper, upright in intention. In business he was fertile in plans, but their execution brought failure, for he was what people called a visionary man. He raised sheep, cultivated the grape, made wine, and for some years was extensively engaged in partnership with a gentleman of capital in buying and selling, as well as growing, wool. He had good opportunities, but missed them, while his ventures were unprofitable. Being constantly harassed with debts, he could not pay his creditors, and died insolvent.*

John Brown was born out of due time. A stern Calvinist and a Puritan, he would have found the religious wars of Europe or the early days of the Massachusetts colonies an atmosphere suited to his bent. He read the Bible diligently, and drew his inspiration from the Old Testament. His intimate letters, a curious mixture of pious ejaculations and worldly details, of Scripture quotations and the price of farm products, call to mind the puritanical jargon of Cromwell's time. Indeed, the great Protector was his hero: he early imbibed a hatred of slavery, and was eager to earn money not as the price of comforts and luxuries, for his life was of a Spartan frugality, but as the means of freeing the slaves.

Brown, who admired Nat Turner as much as he did George

---

* Brown's plan of grading wool, which engaged the support of Perkins, his wealthy partner in the wool commission business, was, however, based on correct principles, and only failed because it was in advance of his time. When disaster came and the firm was loaded with debts, these were saddled upon Perkins as the responsible partner; and while his loss was heavy, he never had the feeling that Brown's conduct had been other than strictly honest. I am indebted for this information to my friend Mr. Simon Perkins, a son of the gentleman who was in partnership with Brown.

Washington, was tender to the negro, and had brooded for
years over the wrongs of the slaves. With this feeling dominant
in his mind he had come to Kansas and enlisted in the Waka-
rusa war, but denounced the treaty of peace which terminated
it: the action of the free-State party seemed to him pusil-
lanimous. Narrow-minded and of moderate intellectual ability,
Brown despised the ordinary means of educating public sentiment, and had no comprehension of government by discussion.
In his opinion, Kansas could only be made free by the shedding
of blood, and that work ought at once to begin.

When the attack on Lawrence was threatened, the Brown
family and their followers were called upon to aid in the
defence; but, on the way, they heard of the destruction which
had taken place, and turned back. The news made a profound
impression on Brown. He felt that the acts of the pro-slavery
horde must be atoned for. He reckoned up that since and including the murder of Dow, five free-State men had been killed.
Their blood must be expiated by an equal number of victims.
"Without the shedding of blood, there is no remission of sins,"
was one of his favorite texts. A direction was given to his
fanatical thoughts by remembering that threats had been made
against his family by some pro-slavery settlers at Dutch Henry's
crossing of the Pottawatomie. He called for volunteers to go
on a secret expedition. Four sons, a son-in-law, and two other
men accompanied him. John Brown's word was law to his
family. He had the power of communicating to them his enthusiasm for the cause of freedom; but when he declared
that the object of his mission was to sweep off all the pro-
slavery men living on the creek, Townsley, one of the men,
demurred. Brown said: "I have no choice. It has been decreed
by Almighty God, ordained from eternity, that I should make
an example of these men." Yet it took a day to persuade Townsley to continue with the expedition. On Saturday night, May
24th, the blow was struck. Brown and his band went first to
the house of Doyle, and compelled a father and two sons to go
with them. A surviving son afterwards testified under oath

that the next morning "I found my father and one brother, William, lying dead in the road, about two hundred yards from the house. I saw my other brother lying dead on the ground, about one hundred and fifty yards from the house, in the grass, near a ravine; his fingers were cut off and his arms were cut off; his head was cut open; there was a hole in his breast. William's head was cut open, and a hole was in his jaw, as though it was made by a knife; and a hole was also in his side. My father was shot in the forehead and stabbed in the breast." The band then went to Wilkinson's house, reaching there past midnight. They forced him to open the door, and demanded that he should go with them. His wife was sick and helpless, and begged that they should not take her husband away. The prayer was of no avail. The next day Wilkinson was found dead, "a gash in his head and in his side." A little later in the night the band killed William Sherman in like manner. In the morning his body was found. His "skull was split open in two places, and some of his brains was washed out by the water. A large hole was cut in his breast, and his left hand was cut off, except a little piece of skin on one side." The execution was done with short cutlasses which had been brought from Ohio by John Brown. He gave the signal; his devoted followers struck the blows. Townsley, twenty-three years afterwards, stated that Brown shot the elder Doyle, but he himself denied that he had had a hand in the actual killing. The deed was so atrocious that for years his friends and admirers refused to believe that he had been at all concerned in it. They shut their eyes to patent facts, for at the time it was easy to get at the truth. The affidavits in regard to the affair, which Oliver, the Democratic member of the congressional committee, caused to be taken, his speech in the House, explaining and confirming the evidence, the universal belief of free-State and pro-slavery men in the territory, established beyond any reasonable doubt that John Brown and his party were guilty of these assassinations. Considering the general character of the border settlers, those who were killed were not exceptionally bad men. They had made threats against the Browns and maltreated a store-keeper who had sold lead to free-State men. But the Browns had also made threats; and in Kansas, in 1856, threats were common, and frequently unmeaning. If every word spoken by the border ruffians were taken at its proper value, Robinson and Reeded had long stood in jeopardy. It was reported that even John Sherman had been threatened. There was absolutely no justification for these midnight executions.

A tender-hearted son of John Brown, who did not accompany this expedition, said to his father a day or two after the massacre: "Father, did you have anything to do with that bloody affair on the Pottawatomie?" Brown replied: "I approved of it." The son answered: "Whoever did it, the act was uncalled for and wicked." Brown then said: "God is my judge. The people of Kansas will yet justify my course."

In passing judgment at this day, we must emphasize the reproach of the son; yet we should hesitate before measuring the same condemnation to the doer and to the deed. John Brown's God was the God of Joshua and Gideon. To him, as to them, seemed to come the word to go out and slay the enemies of his cause. He had no remorse. It was said that on the next morning when the old man raised his hands to Heaven to ask a blessing, they were still stained with the dried blood of his victims. What the world called murder was for him the execution of a decree of God. But of the sincerity of the man there can be no question.

Of the historical significance of this deed and Brown's subsequent actions we may speak with great positiveness. He has been called the liberator of Kansas, but it may be safely affirmed that Kansas would have become a free State in much the same manner and about the same time that it actually did, had John Brown never appeared on the scene of action. The massacre on the Pottawatomie undoubtedly made the contest more bitter and sanguinary, but there is no reason for thinking that its net results were of advantage to the free-State cause.

As tidings of these executions became known a cry of horror

went up throughout the territory. The squatters on Potta-watomie Creek, without distinction of party, met together and denounced the outrage and its perpetrators. The free-State men everywhere took pains to disavow any connection with such a mode of operation. The border ruffians were wild with fury. While Governor Robinson was at Leavenworth a prisoner, on the way to Lecompton, an excited mob threatened to take him from his guard and lynch him. Threats were also made to hang the free-State prisoners who were at Lecompton.

Governor Shannon promptly sent a military force to the Pottawatomie region to discover, if possible, those who had been engaged in the massacre and arrest them. The border ruffians also took the field, eager to avenge the murder of their friends. Pate, who commanded the sharpshooters of Westport, Missouri, feeling confident that Brown was the author of the outrage, went in search of him. Brown, hearing that he was sought, put himself in the way of the Missourian, gave battle, and captured the border-ruffian company. "I went to take Old Brown," wrote Pate, "and Old Brown took me."

All the military organizations of the free-State party made ready for war. Among the Northern emigrants there were adventurers who were attracted by the prevailing disorder. These, for the most part, came into the territory in the spring of 1856; and there were others who, under ordinary conditions, might have been made steady colonists, but whose natural pugnacity was incited by the attack on Lawrence.

The pro-slavery leaders, alarmed at the flood of Northern emigration that poured into the territory, laid an embargo on the Missouri River, which was the great highway from the East to Kansas. Sharps rifles and other suspicious freight were seized. Travellers bound for Kansas, unable, according to the Missouri standard, to give a good account of themselves, were sent back down the river.

Kansas was now in a state of civil war, a struggle of Guelphs and Ghibellines.

Iᴛ *was clear in advance that the presidential battle of 1856 would be closely fought. Four parties would participate in the contest: the Whigs, now a mere disorganized remnant, who with difficulty brought delegates from twenty-six states to their feeble convention in Baltimore and nominated Millard Fillmore; the Know-Nothings, who in the South accepted the Fillmore ticket but in the North went mainly into the Republican camp; the Democrats, who dropped Pierce and refused to accept Douglas, turning instead to the experienced but pliable James Buchanan; and the Republicans, who in a convention marked by unprecedented enthusiasm selected the dashing explorer John C. Frémont. Many men crossed party lines. In particular, so many Northerners entered the Republican ranks that the outcome was totally uncertain. If Frémont proved able to carry most Northern states, including Pennsylvania, Indiana, and Illinois, he would win.*

Buchanan accepted all the policies inaugurated by the Kansas-Nebraska Act; Frémont stood for its repudiation, for Congressional exclusion of slavery from all the territories, and for the admission of Kansas as a Free Soil state. In these circumstances the South loudly threatened secession. "The election of Frémont," declared Senator Toombs of Georgia, "would be the end of the Union, and ought to be." Many newspapers asserted that Republican victory would mean certain and immediate disruption. Most Republican leaders made light of such threats, and Frémont, who had been born in Savannah and reared in South Carolina, asserted that he could rally family connections in Virginia in a struggle for peace. This son-in-law of Thomas Hart Benton, whose Western exploits appealed to young men, was handicapped by political inexperience, a weak party organization, and the inadequacy of his campaign funds. The campaign was sluggish in the South, but spirited in the border states and the North.

Was the South actually ready to secede in 1856 if Buchanan lost? Rhodes believes that it was; other students of the period are less certain. Rhodes might have brought out more fully the fact that the Republican campaign struck a more thoughtful and intel-

lectual note than had previously been known in such heated party contests. He might have dwelt longer upon Democratic affluence and Republican poverty, especially in Pennsylvania. It is clearer than he suggests that the Whig votes cast for Buchanan and Fillmore on a Union-saving impulse were the decisive factor in the election; and that the result did not carry any approval of the Pierce-Buchanan policy in Kansas.

The Buchanan-Frémont Campaign

ON the part of the Republicans it [the contest] was an educational campaign of high value. Their newspapers in zeal and ability were superior to those of the other side. New York city, then as now, took the lead in journalism, and it is an indication of how the press stood everywhere at the North, except in Pennsylvania, when we note that the four great organs of public opinion, the *Tribune, Times, Herald* and *Post*, supported Frémont. The publication of campaign documents was immense, and great care was taken to circulate them freely. Never before had such serious reading-matter been put into the hands of so many voters, and never before had so many men been willing to take time and pains to arrive at a comprehension of the principles involved in a presidential canvass. An indication of Republican willingness to repose on the wisdom of the fathers is shown by the publication of the Declaration of Independence and the Constitution as a part of a campaign document. The widespread interest is betokened by the appeal of Henry Ward Beecher in the *Independent* for money to print tracts which were to be sent "up and down the hills and valleys of Pennsylvania, carrying truth, by the silent page, to hundreds and thousands of men who have never been reached by the living speaker."

The influence of women was a factor of inestimable value.

The moral side of the political question they were well fitted to grasp. That slavery was wrong, that it ought not to be extended, seemed to them primal truths; and the unobtrusive sway of mothers, wives, and sisters was exerted with greater effect than ever before in public affairs. Certainly government by the people has shown few more inspiring spectacles than the campaign of 1856 at the North.

The conduct of the Republicans during the canvass was almost faultless. The private characters of Buchanan and Fillmore were above reproach; but even had they not been so, their personal affairs would have attracted little attention, for the overpowering sway of the principles at issue was everywhere manifest. Perhaps the only charges that can be made against the Republican press are, exaggeration regarding Kansas affairs and giving currency to a supposed statement of Toombs without sufficient foundation. He was falsely reported to have said that he would yet "call the roll of his slaves under the shadow of Bunker Hill monument." Buchanan's share in the Ostend manifesto was properly used against him, but the Cuban question was so entirely swallowed up in the territorial that this line of attack attracted little attention.

The Democrats, wishing to turn away Northern consideration from the real issue, were free with personal imputations against Frémont. The assertion that he was or had been a Roman Catholic gave the most trouble, for the Republicans desired to gain the Know-Nothing vote. The most authoritative denials did not prevent the reiteration of the charge. Charges were also made against the integrity of Frémont on account of certain operations in California. In the light of his subsequent career, it can not be said that these were disproved to the satisfaction of a judicial mind; but they were not for a moment credited by his supporters, and did not have an appreciable influence on the result. Nor did the apparently admitted story that he was involved in California speculations, and that his notes would not sell in the New York market at even two per cent a month, affect his popularity.

The contest at the South between Buchanan and Fillmore

was sluggish and uninteresting. There were practically but two doubtful States, and the August State election in Kentucky demonstrated that Fillmore could only hope to carry Maryland.

The sagacious politicians of each side stated the problem thus: Of the 149 electoral votes necessary to elect, Buchanan was sure of 112 from the South. He must get, then, the twenty-seven votes of Pennsylvania and ten more. Either Indiana or Illinois would give the required number, or New Jersey and California together. These five were the only doubtful Northern States. Frémont was reasonably certain of 114 electoral votes. To be elected he must also get Pennsylvania and eight more, or else carry all the doubtful States except Pennsylvania; but the chance of securing Pennsylvania was much better than that of getting all of the others. Thus the contest practically settled down to the Keystone State, and it was doubly important because a State election preceded the presidential election of November.

The issue had been made. On both sides the conditions for success were understood. It needed only to persuade and get out the arbiters. A campaign ensued which, for enthusiasm and excitement, surpassed any the country had seen except that of 1840. The old voters were constantly reminded of that memorable year. There was no difficulty in getting up Republican meetings. Processions numbering thousands were common; good music and inspiring campaign songs were constantly heard, and there were few gatherings not graced with the presence of intelligent and devoted women. The meetings were immense. At Pittsburgh, the number assembled was estimated at one hundred thousand freemen. It was said to be a greater gathering than either the Dayton or Tippecanoe meeting of 1840.

"The truth is that the people are much more for us than we have supposed," wrote Dana. "I have been speaking around a good deal in clubs, and am everywhere astonished at the depth and ardor of the popular sentiment. Where we least expect it, large and enthusiastic crowds throng to the meeting and stay for hours with the thermometer at one hundred degrees. It is a great canvass; for genuine inspiration, 1840 could not hold a candle. I am more than ever convinced that Frémont was the man for us." The prominent men of the country could be frequently heard. It is an indication of the varied talent enlisted in the cause that on one evening Hale and Beecher, and on the next Wilson and Raymond, addressed a large crowd of New York city Republicans. Seward did not speak until October 2d. The reason he assigned was that his health was so impaired that he needed rest. Dana wrote confidentially that "Seward was awful grouty." The reflection must have come to him that he, instead of one who only began to labor in the vineyard at the eleventh hour, might have been the embodiment of this magnificent enthusiasm.

In reply to an invitation to attend a meeting in Ohio, Sumner wrote from Philadelphia: "I could not reach Ohio except by slow stages; and were I there, I should not have the sanction of my physician in exposing myself to the excitements of a public meeting, even if I said nothing. This is hard—very hard for me to bear, for I long to do something at this critical moment for the cause." A few days after this letter was published, Republicans had the opportunity of reading an account of a numerously attended banquet in South Carolina given to Preston S. Brooks by the constituents of his district, where, amid vehement cheering, he was presented with a cane on which was inscribed, "Use knock-down arguments."

Banks one afternoon delivered a speech in Wall Street from the balcony of the Merchants' Exchange, and was listened to by twenty thousand men. You ask me "as to Banks's speech," wrote Greeley to an intimate friend. "I think St. Paul on Mars Hill made a better—I mean better for Mars Hill; I am not sure that Banks's is not better adapted to Wall Street. I trust Banks himself does not deem it suited to the latitude of Bunker Hill or Tippecanoe."

Besides reading documents and listening to speeches, the enthusiasm manifested itself in street parades and torchlight processions. Pioneers with glittering axes marched ahead, Rocky-

Mountain glee-clubs sang campaign songs, and the air rang with shouts of "Free speech, free soil, and Frémont," the lusty bands dwelling upon "Frémont" with the staccato cheer. Although in liveliness and enthusiasm this resembled the 1840 campaign, there was a marked difference. The Whigs had then gone to the country without a platform, and the canvass was a frolic; now the Republicans advocated a platform which was so positive in its utterances that no mistake could be made about its meaning. There was, therefore, now a serious devotion to principle, and an earnest determination that the Harrison campaign lacked. The jollity of 1840 is the delight of the humorist; the gravity of 1856 is the study of the political philosopher.

It is difficult to apportion the enthusiasm between a cause and a candidate; but after drinking deep of the campaign literature, one is forced to the conviction that much was for the cause and little for the man; that Republican principles added lustre to the name of Frémont, while Frémont himself gave little strength to the party other than by the romantic interest that was associated with his record as an explorer.* His nomination was indeed received with enthusiasm. Several campaign biographies were published which familiarized the public with the stirring events in his life; but while his "disastrous chances," his "moving accidents by flood and field," and his "hair-breadth 'scapes" made him a hero in the eyes of youth who fed on Cooper and Gilmore Simms, the fuller knowledge of his career was unsatisfactory to many earnest and thoughtful Republicans. The most was made of his being "the brave Pathfinder." The planting of the American flag on the highest peak of the Rocky Mountains was deemed an heroic feat. Yet practical people could not fail to inquire why the qualities of a daring explorer fitted a man to be chief magistrate of the republic at a critical juncture. Little by little, it began to be understood that Frémont was a vulnerable candidate, and, while the charges of corruption were not believed, it was admitted they needed explanation. He

* His romantic marriage added to this interest, and "Frémont and Jessie" was a favorite campaign cry. Jessie Benton was the name of his wife.

did not, therefore, stand before the country with the same character of absolute integrity as did Buchanan and Fillmore.

The Iowa congressional election in August was favorable to the Republicans. In September, Maine and Vermont gave unmistakable evidence of the direction in which the tide was setting in New England. Maine was an old Democratic State; the Republican candidate for governor was Hannibal Hamlin, who, though voting against the Kansas-Nebraska bill, had not formally severed his connection with the Democratic party until June of this year. Then from his place in the Senate he had declared that, as he considered the repeal of the Missouri Compromise the cause of all the present ills, and as the Cincinnati convention had endorsed that repeal, he could no longer act with the Democrats, but must oppose them with all his power. He was now elected governor of Maine by a handsome majority. In Vermont three quarters of the votes were cast for the Republican ticket.

The Republicans were highly elated at these results. All eyes were now turned to the "October States"—Pennsylvania, Ohio, and Indiana. No concern was felt about Ohio, and much less depended upon Indiana than on the Keystone State. The election of October 14th in Pennsylvania was for minor State officers, that of canal commissioner being the most important. There were two tickets in the field—one the regular Democratic, the other the Union, which was supported by Republicans, Americans, Whigs, and anti-Nebraska Democrats; or, stated differently, one ticket had the support of the "Buchaniers," the other that of the "Frémonters," and ostensibly of the "Fillmoreans." The contest was vigorous and excited. The Republicans were aggressive. They pointed to "bleeding Kansas"; they charged that the civil war in that territory was a result of the repeal of the Missouri Compromise, and they demanded a policy which should incontestably make Kansas a free State.

Their best speakers traversed Pennsylvania, making eloquent and able appeals, and the State was flooded with campaign documents. It was clearly discerned where the danger lay. West of the Alleghany Mountains, the enthusiasm for Frémont was like that in New England, New York, and Ohio; but as one travelled eastward a different political atmosphere could easily be felt, and when one reached Philadelphia, which was bound to the South by a lucrative trade, the chill was depressing. The business and social influences of conservative Philadelphia were arrayed against the Frémont movement. The Pennsylvania Dutch, by whom the eastern counties were largely peopled, were set in their way of political thinking; they distrusted change. They were told that Frémont was an abolitionist; they believed that abolitionism was dangerous to the Union; they were attached to the Union, for its existence implied order and security; they were thrifty and prosperous, and much preferred order to the liberty of the black man. Campaign work such as had stirred to the depths New England, New York, Ohio, and the Northwest was carried on by the Republicans to a greater extent in Pennsylvania. They hoped that, while this was a community slower to educate, it would yield to persistent and overflowing effort.

The Democrats dodged the issue. Instead of defending the Douglas and Pierce policy, they averred that the Union was in danger. "I consider," wrote Buchanan, privately, "that all incidental questions are comparatively of little importance in the presidential question, when compared with the grand and appalling issue of union or disunion. . . . In this region the battle is fought mainly on this issue. We have so often cried 'wolf' that now, when the wolf is at the door, it is difficult to make the people believe it; but yet the scene of danger is slowly and surely making its way in this region."

The appeal for the Union was a legitimate party cry, and it answered well in Philadelphia and the Pennsylvania Dutch counties, but there were parts of the State where an additional argument was needed. The manner in which this necessity was met reflects, in the light of subsequent history, discredit on Buchanan or his managers. Howell Cobb, of Georgia, who had the reputation of a straightforward man, and who in 1851 had distinguished himself by a vigorous canvass in his State against the disunion faction, and John Hickman, a congressman from Pennsylvania who had voted for the admission of Kansas under the Topeko Constitution, spoke from the stump all over the Chester Valley, advocating Buchanan's election, and promising fair play in Kansas. At many Democratic mass-meetings in different parts of the State, banners were borne on which was inscribed "Buchanan, Breckinridge, and Free Kansas," the orators maintaining that Kansas was certain to be free if Buchanan were elected. Forney, who was chairman of the Democratic State central committee, and at that time an intimate personal and political friend of Buchanan, avers that this line of argument was based on a positive promise from him that there "should be no interference against the people of Kansas."* The advocacy of the Democratic candidates by Reverdy Johnson, an old-line Whig, and by Barclay, a Democratic congressman from Western Pennsylvania, who had voted for the admission of Kansas under the Topeka Constitution, was an added influence in this direction.

The Democrats had in their campaign the cordial assistance of the President. Shannan's administration of Kansas affairs had become a scandal. Unsteady in habits and purposes, he was execrated by the free-State men; his continuance in office gave additional force to every story of "bleeding Kansas." In August

---

* In a speech at Tarrytown, N. Y., Sept. 2d, 1858, Forney declared that during the canvass of 1856 Buchanan said to him a thousand times: "The South must vote for me, and the North must be secured; and the only way to secure the North is to convince those gentlemen that when I get in the presidential chair I will do right with the people in Kansas. I am now sixty-six years of age. I have reached that time of life when I cannot have any ambition for re-election, and if I have, the only way to secure it is to be strong with my own people at home. I watched this struggle from my retirement in London; I have seen what I conceive to be the mistakes of others. I am not responsible for the administration of President Pierce; therefore I will inaugurate a new system." Forney further said: "I sowed the State with private letters and private pledges upon this question. There is not a county in Pennsylvania in which my letters may not be found, almost by hundreds, pledging Mr. Buchanan, in his name and by his authority, to the full, complete, and practical recognition of the rights of the people of Kansas to decide upon their own affairs."—New York *Tribune,* Sept. 3d, 1858.

he was removed, and John W. Geary, of Pennsylvania, a man of good standing, was appointed in his place. The report went that Geary had said that peace must be restored or Buchanan could not carry Pennsylvania. The difficulty of his mission was emphasized when, on the way to Kansas, he met Shannon fleeing in abject fear, because at the last the pro-slavery leaders had taken offence as their former tool would not do their entire bidding. But the new governor set himself energetically to the work to bring back order. He took an impartial view of the situation; in his effort at pacification, he leaned neither to one side nor to the other, but pursued the course he had marked out with judgment, decision, and success. On the 30th of September he sent the Secretary of State a despatch which was a splendid Democratic argument in the impending contest. "Peace now reigns in Kansas," Geary wrote. "Confidence is gradually being restored. Citizens are returning to their claims. Men are resuming their ordinary pursuits, and a general gladness pervades the entire community. When I arrived here, everything was at the lowest point of depression. Opposing parties saw no hope of peace, save in mutual extermination, and they were taking the most effectual means to produce that terrible result."

The Democratic organization in Pennsylvania was perfect. Unlike other Northern States, Buchanan was there upheld by the most influential newspapers, which were subsidized by "a system of general and liberal advertising." There were many wealthy Democrats in Philadelphia and eastern Pennsylvania, and money flowed in freely from other States. Douglas, while loyally striving to keep Illinois Democratic, was also able to contribute money liberally to aid in carrying the Keystone State. The governor of North Carolina, with other gentlemen, issued a "private and confidential" circular begging for money. "Pennsylvania must be saved at every hazard," they said. "We appeal to you, therefore, as a Democrat and a patriot, to contribute forthwith whatever amount of money you can, and raise what you can from others." The Republican journals charged—probably with truth—that the clerks in the departments at Washington, the officers in the New York City Custom-house, and the laborers in the Brooklyn Navy-yard were assessed for the Pennsylvania campaign fund. It was credibly reported that one hundred and fifty thousand dollars was sent into Pennsylvania from the slave-holding States; that August Belmont contributed fifty thousand dollars; and that other Wall-street bankers and brokers, alarmed at Southern threats and fearing serious financial loss in the event of disunion, put into Forney's hands one hundred thousand dollars more. The allegations of the defeated party regarding the outlay by the other must always be taken with a grain of allowance, yet a fair consideration of all the circumstances makes it reasonable to suppose that the Democrats had much the larger supply of the sinews of war.

It certainly seemed to the Republicans that the Democrats were better provided with means. "We Frémonters of this town," wrote Greeley from New York to an intimate friend, "have not one dollar where the Fillmoreans and Buchaniers have ten each, and we have Pennsylvania and New Jersey both on our shoulders. Each State is utterly miserable, as far as money is concerned; we must supply them with documents, canvass them with our best speakers, and pay for their rooms to speak in and our bills to invite them."

The Democrats were successful in manufacturing enthusiasm for their candidate in his native State, and the abbreviation "Buck and Breck" readily lent itself to a resounding campaign cry. On the eve of election they had a serene confidence of probable success in October and certain victory in November.

Greeley advised his confidant that the fight was "hot and heavy in Pennsylvania. . . . There is everything to do there, with just the meanest set of politicians to do it that you ever heard of." Dana was hopeful. Nine days before the election he wrote: "The election in Pennsylvania week after next will go by from thirty thousand to forty thousand majority against Buchanan, and so on. The tide is rising with a rush, as it does in the Bay of Fundy; and you will hear an awful squealing among the hogs and jackasses when they come to drown. . . . I suppose there are about two hundred orators, great and small, now stumping Pennsylvania for Frémont."

Reeder, who had been a personal and political friend of Buchanan, came out for the Republican candidates, and this was thought good for over three thousand votes in his district. Dana wrote: "The Democrats are terrified and demoralized. . . . My impression now is that every free State will vote for Frémont." Bryant wrote his brother from New York city: "We expect a favorable report from Pennsylvania. The Buchanan men here are desponding, and it seems to be thought that if the State election goes against them, then the presidential election will go against them also. I do not think that certain, however, though it is probable."

The day which terminated this heated contest came, and the result of the voting was awaited with breathless anxiety. Passion had been so wrought up that the timid feared lest the contest of words should be followed by blows. They thanked God that the weather in Philadelphia, which was raw, cold, drizzling, and uncomfortable, kept the turbulent spirits within doors. All felt relief when it passed without bloodshed. Perhaps the tension was increased by the report of the anticipated meeting of fifteen Southern governors at Raleigh to consider what steps should be taken in the event of the election of Frémont.

The excitement in the evening was greatest in Philadelphia. The City of Brotherly Love was in uproar. No one went to bed. The halls where returns were received were crowded; in the streets there was an anxious, excited throng. Several days elapsed before it was certain how the State had gone, but at last it became known that the Buchanan State ticket had been successful by a majority of less than 3000 in a vote of 423,000.

The Republicans charged that the Democrats had carried the State by fraud and bribery. Years afterwards Forney wrote: "We spent a great deal of money, but not one cent selfishly or corruptly." It is indeed difficult to believe that money was not used to purchase voters by some of Forney's henchmen, although he may not have been privy to the transactions, for the astute party manager does not always care to inquire closely into the means by which results are reached. But there is no need of the stale cry, invariably repeated by the defeated party, to account for the later success of the Democrats in the presidential election.

If the State went Democratic, Buchanan's election was certain; if the Union ticket were successful, while a great impetus would be given to the Frémont movement, his election would not be assured. Yet fearing the influence, many conservative Fillmoreans, urged by the sentiments to which Choate had given expression, voted with the Democrats. It is not important whether this was brought about by collusion between the chairman of the American State committee and Forney; but it is certain that, by official direction or tacit consent, many Americans and Whigs bolted their own State ticket.

If the Fusionists had been successful by a small majority, would Frémont have carried Pennsylvania in November and been elected President? Probably not. There was no possibility of getting the bulk of Fillmore's supporters to vote the fusion Frémont-Fillmore electoral ticket which was proposed and actually adopted; and the minute the opposition to Buchanan was divided, he was certain to carry the State by a handsome plurality. Buchanan himself seemed to think that in any event he would receive the electoral vote of Pennsylvania, a confidence based on substantial reasons.

On the 14th of October, State elections were also held in Ohio and Indiana. Ohio went Republican, but Indiana went Democratic, thus making the assurance of Buchanan's election doubly sure.

The November election registered what the October elections had virtually decided. Buchanan carried Pennsylvania, New Jersey, Indiana, Illinois, and California, and all the slave States but Maryland, receiving 174 electoral votes. Frémont had 114 electors, and Fillmore the 8 votes of Maryland.* From the congressional elections it was apparent that the Democrats would also have a majority in the next House of Representatives.

After the disappointment at failing to elect their candidates was over, the Republicans felt that they had reason for self-congratulation. In spite of the complaints of the lack of organization and money in Pennsylvania, the Republicans of a later day could not have wished the campaign different. For it was conducted on the inspiration of a principle, and any manipulation of Pennsylvania voters would have been a blot upon this virgin purity. The immense Frémont vote could be traced along the lines of latitude, springing from New England influence where good and widely extended common-school systems prevailed. The problem now was simply to educate and inspire the people of the Northern States that had voted for Buchanan. Whittier expressed the general feeling when he sang:

> If months have well-nigh won the field,
> What may not four years do?

Considering the weakness of Frémont's character, which later years brought to light, it was fortunate he was not elected President. One shudders to think how he would have met the question of secession, which assuredly would have confronted him at the beginning of his administration.

The cause being much stronger than the candidate, it is probable that Seward or Chase would have carried the same States and received substantially the same votes that went to Frémont. This is an interesting supposition, in view of Seward's

* The popular vote was: Buchanan, 1,838,169; Frémont, 1,341,264; Fillmore, 874,534. Buchanan received in the free States, 1,226,290; in the slave States, 611,879. Fillmore received in the free States, 394,642; in the slave States, 479,892. The vote of South Carolina is not comprised in any of these totals. Those electors were chosen by the legislature. The only votes Frémont received in the slave States were: Delaware, 308; Maryland, 281; Virginia, 291; Kentucky, 314. These figures are based on those given in Stanwood's *History of Presidential Elections.*

ambition for the next presidential nomination; for had he made the run of 1856, he would undoubtedly have been the Republican candidate four years later. Before the smoke of the battle had cleared away, many journals, struck with the astonishing vote Frémont had received, nominated him for the standard-bearer of 1860.

PRESIDENT BUCHANAN *believed when he settled himself in his office that the decision of the Supreme Court in the Dred Scott case, which was delivered within a few days, had rescued his administration from the fierce controversies that had plagued Franklin Pierce and his Cabinet. He quickly found that it had instead plunged him into deeper difficulties than ever. The heart of the decision touched the power of Congress over slavery in the territories in a way that the majority of men in the North could never accept. If the court had merely decided that Dred Scott, a slave under Missouri law, possessed no constitutional right to sue in a federal tribunal, this narrow assertion would have aroused limited controversy. But the court went on to discuss much larger issues, which since the upflare of anger in the North over repeal of the Missouri Compromise and the bloody strife in Kansas, had become inflammatory.*

Two dissenting judges and seven majority judges wrote diverse opinions in the case. The main finding of the court, however, was that Congress had no constitutional power to exclude slavery from the territories of the United States, and therefore had acted unconstitutionally when it had passed the Missouri Compromise. Such was the position taken by five Southern judges and Grier of Pennsylvania. This was a blow at the very citadel of antislavery and Republican doctrine. That it was also a blow at Douglas's popular sovereignty doctrine as laid down in the Kansas-Nebraska Act soon became abundantly plain.

The storm of indignation that swept the North swiftly rose to unprecedented heights. If this decision is to stand for law, declared William Cullen Bryant in the New York Evening Post, *then the United States becomes the land of bondage; then wherever the American flag floats, it is the flag of slavery. If so, it should have the stars and stripes erased; it should be dyed black, and its device should be the whip and fetter. Far from allaying sectional antagonisms, the decision plunged the court into ignominy in the North, brought President Buchanan under suspicion of improperly influencing its members, and made antislavery men determined to offer passive resistance until a new administration could change the character of the court.*

Subsequent students have agreed that Taney was a patriot of high integrity according to his lights but that these lights were dim. They have agreed that Buchanan carried on an extraordinary correspondence before his inauguration with Judge Catron and wrote an improper letter to Judge Grier.

Since Rhodes dealt with this subject, the measured verdict of history has been stated by one learned jurist, E. S. Corwin, and endorsed by another: "The Dred Scott decision cannot be, with accuracy, written down as a usurpation, but it can and must be written down as a gross abuse of trust by the body which rendered it." Its worst result is not noted here by Rhodes. It was the fateful Southern demand in 1858-60 that the Democratic party should be placed upon a Dred Scott platform—it should demand federal protection of slavery throughout the vast territorial domain.

Buchanan and Dred Scott

THE idea one gets of the Buchanan of 1857 from the faithful story of his life by Curtis is that of a man of fair talents working in a groove, filling many public positions respectably, but none brilliantly. Politically, he was always ready to serve his party and willing to follow other leaders. He never desired to branch off independently. While in Congress he did not show ability as a parliamentary leader, and his nature unfitted him to be a vehement advocate. He was an ordinary Secretary of State; he filled the position of minister to England honorably and discreetly, as have many gentlemen before and since. Cold, measured, and reticent, he acquired a reputation for sagacity because he never committed himself until pushed for an answer.

Yet he was a voluminous letter-writer, and filled pages with platitudes and wearisome repetitions. Decorous in manner, he may fitly be called a gentleman of the old school; but he was not a man of culture. Not a gleam of learning appears in his familiar letters. Spending much time in Europe, enjoying the society of distinguished and educated men, the scientific development of his century and the noble literature of his language were to him sealed books. He was inferior in intelligence and power of reasoning to Jefferson Davis, in statesmanship and parliamentary talent to Douglas, in correctness and vigor of judgment to Marcy, while in decision and force of character he was inferior to them all.

When Buchanan wrote his inaugural at Wheatland, he was probably wavering between the policy represented by Jefferson Davis and that represented by Everett and Choate, with an inclination towards the latter. When, after coming to Washington, he inserted a clause in his address referring to the expected decision of the Supreme Court in the Dred Scott case, he may have been still wavering, but the leaning was in the direction of the Southern idea.

He spoke to the sixty-two electoral votes of the doubtful Northern States when he said that he was convinced that he owed his "election to the inherent love for the Constitution and the Union which still animates the hearts of the American people"; and also when he declared that, "having determined not to become a candidate for re-election, I shall have no motive to influence my conduct in administering the government except the desire ably and faithfully to serve my country, and to live in the grateful memory of my countrymen."

He spoke to the one hundred and twelve electoral votes of the South when he said: "A difference of opinion has arisen in regard to the point of time when the people of a territory shall decide this question [of slavery] for themselves. This is happily a matter of but little practical importance. Besides, it is a judicial question, which legitimately belongs to the Supreme Court of the United States, before whom it is now pending, and will, it is understood, be speedily and finally settled. To their decision, in common with all good citizens, I shall cheerfully submit, whatever this may be, though it has ever been my individual opinion that, under the Kansas-Nebraska act, the oppropriate period will be when the number of actual residents in the territory shall justify the formation of a constitution with a view to its admission as a State into the Union."

Buchanan showed astounding complacency when he said: "The whole territorial question being thus settled upon the principle of popular sovereignty—a principle as ancient as free government itself—everything of a practical nature has been decided.... May we not, then, hope that the long agitation on this subject [of slavery] is approaching its end, and that the geographical parties to which it has given birth, so much dreaded by the Father of his country, will speedily become extinct?"

Two days after the inauguration the nominations for the cabinet were sent to the Senate. Cass was Secretary of State; Howell Cobb, of Georgia, had the Treasury department; Floyd, whose chief recommendation seemed to be that he belonged to the first families of Virginia, was Secretary of War; Toucey, of Connecticut, whose senatorial term had just expired and whose strong Southern sympathies had debarred him from any further political preferment which was dependent on the popular voice, was made Secretary of the Navy; Thompson, a Mississippi states-rights man, had the Interior department; Brown, of Tennessee, was Postmaster-General; and Jeremiah S. Black, one of the judges of the Pennsylvania Supreme Court, a jurist of uncommon talent and a man of vigorous mind, was appointed Attorney-General. The new cabinet was far inferior in capacity to the retiring one.

In point of political ability, Howell Cobb dominated his associates, and it was at once prophesied that he would be the master-spirit of the administration. He was a Unionist in 1850, and deemed by the Northern Whigs "sagacious and conservative." He was frank and genial; but it remained a question whether he would like the drudgery of the Treasury department, and it was on all sides admitted that it would be difficult for him to equal the brilliant administration of his predecessor, who had been a master of finance.

Only one member of the cabinet could be said to reflect in any way the Northern conservative feeling typified by Everett and Choate, and that was Cass; but he was nearly seventy-five, and was believed to be an indolent man. Moreover, his speeches in the Senate did not promise a safe and judicious conduct of foreign affairs; still, there seems to have been no alarm on this point, for it was understood that Buchanan would be his own Secretary of State, and Cass merely a first assistant. Cass, like Toucey, was a senator repudiated by his own State. The place he had held for two terms was now filled by a Republican, Zachariah Chandler.

Three members of the cabinet were from the free States, and four from the slave States. The Republicans expected nothing for the cause of freedom from such a cabinet, or from a President whose proclivities were shown in their appointment.

Considering that one Democratic President had succeeded another, the scramble for office was surprising. In less than two months after the election, the conviction was forced upon Buchanan that the pressure would be nearly as great as if he had succeeded a Whig. Rotation in office was advocated as a true Democratic principle. "I cannot mistake," wrote Buchanan in a private letter, "the strong current of public opinion in favor of changing public functionaries, both abroad and at home, who have served a reasonable time. They say, and that too with considerable force, that if the officers under a preceding Democratic administration shall be continued by a succeeding administration of the same political character, this must necessarily destroy the party."

Soon after the inauguration it was evident that Buchanan had committed himself to the principle of rotation in office, and the report went: "The ins look blue, the outs hopeful." When an officer was reappointed it was considered an exception, and reasons were given in the press why a change was not made. Marcy was said to have dryly remarked: "They have it that I am the author of the office-seeker's doctrine that 'to the victors belong the spoils,' but I certainly should never recommend the policy of pillaging my own camp." Northern Democratic senators were active in urging a distribution of the patronage where it would do them the most good, for the current of Northern opinion admonished them that much management was needed to retain their places.

When the great American question of the century had to be grappled with, Buchanan and his cabinet was devoting their time, strength, and ability to investigating the merits of candidates for postmasters, collectors, and tide-waiters. It would not have been so pitiable had the search been simply to find men of business ability and integrity for the positions; but that was not the problem. How could the interest of the Democratic party in this State or that district best be promoted? What could be done with the patronage in the way of preserving the political life of this Northern senator or that Northern representative? These were the questions put to the President for solution. In a short time, Buchanan, who was the very picture of health when he left Wheatland, looked haggard and worn out, largely on account of the pressure from the hungry horde of office-seekers.*

We have seen in the course of this work many attempts of the national legislature and the executive to settle the slavery question. We have now to consider a grave attempt in the same line by the United States Supreme Court. The reverence for this unique and most powerful judicial tribunal of the world was profound. It is possible that from the time of the decision of the Dartmouth College case to the death of Chief Justice Marshall, the court held a loftier place in public opinion than in 1857; for Marshall was one of the world's great judges, and he had forcibly impressed his wonderful legal mind upon the country's jurisprudence. At that time De Tocqueville had written: In the hands of the Supreme Court "repose unceasingly the peace, the prosperity, the existence even, of the Union." But in 1857 the reverence for the Supreme Court was greater than now. In much

---

* Buchanan had what was known as the National-Hotel disease, which was the beginning of his physical disability. "The National-Hotel disease, a disorder which, from no cause that we could then discover, had attacked nearly every guest at the house, and from the dire effects of which many never wholly recovered."—Curtis, vol. ii. p. 188, account of J. B. Henry.

of the political literature of the day it is regarded almost as a fetich; it was looked upon as something beyond the pale of ordinary human institutions. When men became Supreme Court judges, they were believed to be no longer actuated by the prejudices and passions of common humanity. During the slavery agitation there had been propositions of various kinds to refer disputed questions to this court, on the theory that there a wholly impartial and severely just decision might be had. The Democrats who disagreed about the construction of the Kansas-Nebraska act concurred in the proposal to leave the question to the highest judicial tribunal.

In 1857, the Supreme Court was composed of Chief Justice Taney, Justices Wayne, Daniel, Catron, Campbell, Democrats from the slave States; Grier and Nelson, Democrats, and McLean, a Republican, and Curtis, a Whig, from the free States. From the importance of their personality, two of these judges deserve special notice.

Chief Justice Taney belonged to one of the old Roman Catholic families of Maryland, and was himself a devout adherent of that religion. A good student of law, he devoted much time to history and letters; and the thoughts, words, and style of great writers had for him a powerful charm. He especially loved Shakespeare and Macaulay. He rose to eminence at the Maryland bar; he was an untiring worker, and allowed nothing to distract him from his professional duties and domestic life. Of a passionate nature, he had very decided political opinions. President Jackson appointed him Attorney-General, and he soon became the President's trusted and confidential adviser. When Duane, the Secretary of the Treasury, refused to withdraw the government deposits from the United States Bank, Jackson removed him and put Taney in his place. Taney understood banking and finance, and, being a man after Jackson's own heart, supported the President unreservedly in his war against the bank. The Senate refused to confirm Taney as Secretary of the Treasury, and Jackson appointed him Justice of the Supreme Court. Chief Justice Marshall, though disliking the

President and his policy, had a good opinion of Taney's legal ability, and made an effort to secure his confirmation; but action on his nomination was indefinitely postponed. In July, 1835, Marshall died, and Jackson appointed Taney Chief Justice. As the political complexion of the Senate had changed, he did not fail of confirmation, although he had for opponents Webster and Clay.

To fill the place of Chief Justice Marshall was a difficult task, and Taney suffered continually by comparison with his great predecessor; yet as the years went on, he gained solid reputation by accurate knowledge of law, clearness of thought, and absolute purity of life. His written opinions are characterized by vigor of style, reflecting the hours he passed with the masters of our literature.

Curtis had the rich New England culture. By nature a lawyer, he had received at the Harvard law school, sitting at the feet of Judge Story, the training which those who thirsted for legal knowledge could acquire from the instructions of such a teacher. He was thoroughly read in English history. He owed his appointment as justice to Webster, who, when Secretary of State, recommended him most highly to President Fillmore. Curtis was an absolutely impartial judge. His reasoning was clear to laymen and a delight to lawyers. Though his style was a model of compression, he never forgot a point nod failed to be perspicuous. His course on the bench was a fine testimonial to the choice of Webster, whom New England lawyers regarded as the master of their profession.

In the Dred Scott case the opposing principles of slavery and freedom came sharply into conflict in the judicial opinions of Taney and Curtis. The negro Dred Scott had several years previously sued for the freedom of himself and family, and the case came up to the Supreme Court in a regular way. The detailed history of the affair has for our purpose no importance; it went through various stages, and many collateral points were involved. While the freedom or slavery of four negroes was at stake, the interest in their fate is completely overshadowed by the importance of the questions to which the suit gave rise. As a matter of fact, Dred Scott, after being remanded to slavery by the Supreme Court, was emancipated by his master; but he had served as a text for weighty constitutional and political arguments.

Standing out beyond the merits of the case and all other points involved, two questions of vast importance were suggested by the facts. Could a negro whose ancestors had been sold as slaves become a citizen of one of the States of the Union? For if Dred Scott were not a citizen of Missouri, where he had mostly lived, he had no standing in the United States Court.

The second question, Was the Missouri Compromise constitutional? came up in this manner. Dred Scott had been taken by his master, an army surgeon, to Fort Snelling, which was in the northern part of the Louisiana territory, now Minnesota, and had remained there for a period of about two years. In this territory slavery was forever prohibited by the Missouri Compromise, and the counsel for Dred Scott maintained that by virtue of the restriction, residence there conferred freedom on the slave. Thus might arise the question, Was the Missouri Compromise constitutional? and this carried with it the more practical question, Had Congress the power to prohibit slavery in the territories? On the basis of the assertion of this power, the Republican party was builded; and if this power did not inhere in Congress, the Republican party had constitutionally no reason for existence.

The case was first argued in the spring of 1856. Justice Curtis wrote Ticknor, April 8th, the result of the conferences of the judges; "The court will not decide the question of the Missouri-Compromise line—a majority of the judges being of opinion that it is not necessary to do so. (This is confidential.) The one engrossing subject in both houses of Congress, and with all the members, is the presidency; and upon this everything done and omitted, except the most ordinary necessities of the country, depends."

At the term of court, December, 1856, the case was reargued, and the counsel discussed all the questions involved. Still, the judges decided to view the matter only in its narrow aspect, and in its particular bearing on the status of Dred Scott and his family. To Justice Nelson, of New York, was assigned the duty of writing the opinion of the court. He astutely evaded the determination whether the Missouri Compromise act was constitutional; nor did he consider it necessary to pass upon the citizenship of the negro, but in arguing the case on its merits the decision was reached that Dred Scott was still a slave. Had this been the conclusion of the matter, the Dred Scott case would have excited little interest at the time, and would hardly have demanded more than the briefest notice from the historian.

But there now began a pressure on the Southern judges, who constituted a majority of the court, to decide the weighty constitutional question involved in the case. The unceasing inculcation of Calhoun's doctrine regarding slavery in the territories had now brought Southern Democrats, and among them the five Southern judges, round to that notion. Of course the pressure was adroit and considerate, for the judges were honest men impressed with the dignity of their position. The aim was simply to induce them to promulgate officially what they privately thought. It is a tradition that Justice Campbell held back. This is to a certain degree confirmed by a letter of his written long after the event; but if three Southern judges were decidedly in favor of pronouncing a judgment on the constitutional question, it needed only to gain the chief justice to carry along with them Campbell, and perhaps the two Democratic judges from the North. Before the Dred Scott decision was pronounced, Taney, both in character and ability, stood much higher than any other member of the court.

The chief justice was gained. The bait held out to his patriotic soul was that the court had the power and opportunity of settling the slavery question. He had now nearly reached the age of eighty, and, had he been younger, he might have detected the flaws in the reasoning which led him to so decide a position. "Our aged chief justice," wrote Curtis, February 27th, 1857, in a private letter, "grows more feeble in body, but retains his alacrity and force of mind wonderfully," though he "is not able to write much." Certainly the Dred Scott opinion of Taney shows no weakness of memory or abated power of reasoning; but it may have been that age had enfeebled the will and made him more susceptible to influences that were brought to bear upon him.

Before Justice Nelson read his opinion in conference, Justice Wayne, of Georgia, at a meeting of the judges, stated that the case had excited public interest, and that it was expected that the points discussed by counsel would be considered by the court. He therefore moved that the chief justice should "write an opinion on all of the questions as the opinion of the court." This was agreed to, but some of the judges reserved the privilege of qualifying their assent. Justice Wayne had worked industriously to bring this about, and his efforts had an important influence in persuading the chief justice, and Judges Grier, of Pennsylvania, and Catron, of Tennessee, of the expediency of such a course. This determination, though shrouded in the secrecy of Supreme Court consultations, leaked out. Reverdy Johnson, whose constitutional argument had a profound influence on Taney, made his plea December 18th, 1856, and on New Year's Day of 1857, Alexander Stephens wrote to his brother: "The decision [of the Dred Scott case] will be a marked epoch in our history. I feel a deep solicitude as to how it will be. From what I hear, *sub rosa,* it will be according to my own opinion on every point, as abstract political questions. The restriction of 1820 will be held to be unconstitutional. The judges are all writing out their opinions, I believe, seriatim. The chief justice will give an elaborate one." On the 5th of January, Pike wrote the New York *Tribune* that the rumor was current in Washington that the Supreme Court had decided that Congress had no constitutional power to prohibit slavery in the territories.

Two days after the inauguration of Buchanan, Chief Justice Taney delivered the opinion of the court. He stated that one of the questions to be decided was: "Can a negro whose ancestors were imported into this country and sold as slaves become a member of the political community formed and brought into existence by the Constitution of the United States, and as such become entitled to all the rights and privileges and immunities guaranteed by that instrument to the citizen?" The answer is no. Negroes "were not intended to be included under the word 'citizens' in the Constitution, and therefore can claim none of the rights and privileges which that instrument provides for and secures to the citizens of the United States." Moreover, "In the opinion of the court, the legislation and histories of the times, and the language used in the Declaration of Independence, show that neither the class of persons who had been imported as slaves, nor their descendants, whether they had become free or not, were then acknowledged as a part of the people, nor intended to be included in the general words used in that memorable instrument.

"It is difficult, at this day, to realize the state of public opinion in relation to that unfortunate race which prevailed in the civilized and enlightened portions of the world at the time of the Declaration of Independence, and when the Constitution was framed and adopted. But the public history of every European nation displays it in a manner too plain to be mistaken.

"They had for more than a century before been regarded as beings of an inferior order, and altogether unfit to associate with the white race, either in social or political relations; and so far inferior that they had no rights which the white man was bound to respect, and that the negro might justly and lawfully be reduced to slavery for his benefit. He was bought and sold, and treated as an ordinary article of merchandise and traffic, whenever a profit could be made by it. The opinion was at that time fixed and universal in the civilized portion of the white race. It was regarded as an axiom in morals as well as in politics, which no one thought of disputing, or supposed to be open to dispute; and men in every grade and position in society daily and habitually acted upon it in their private pursuits, as well as in matters of public concern, without doubting for a moment the correctness of this opinion."

Citing the famous clause of the Declaration of Independence which asserted "that all men are created equal," the chief justice said: "The general words above quoted would seem to embrace the whole human family, and if they were used in a similar instrument at this day would be so understood. But it is too clear for dispute that the enslaved African race were not intended to be included, and formed no part of the people who framed and adopted this declaration."

The chief justice put the other constitutional question plainly: Was Congress authorized to pass the Missouri Compromise act "under any of the powers granted to it by the Constitution?" The Louisiana territory "was acquired by the general government, as the representative and trustee of the people of the United States, and it must therefore be held in that character for their common and equal benefit. . . . It seems, however, to be supposed that there is a difference between property in a slave and other property, and that different rules may be applied to it in expounding the Constitution of the United States." But "the right of property in a slave is distinctly and expressly affirmed in the Constitution. . . . And no word can be found in the Constitution which gives Congress a greater power over slave property, or which entitles property of that kind to less protection than property of any other description." It is the opinion of the court, therefore, that the Missouri Compromise act "is not warranted by the Constitution, and is therefore void."

All of the judges read opinions. The four Southern judges and Grier distinctly agreed with the chief justice that the Missouri Compromise was unconstitutional; and they concurred sufficiently in the other points to constitute his conclusions the opinion of the court, as it was officially called. It thus received the assent of two-thirds of the judges. Justice Nelson read the opinion he had prepared when it was decided to confine the judgment of the court to the merits of the case, while Justices

McLean and Curtis dissented from the determination of the court. As Curtis covered more fully and cogently the ground, we have now to consider his opinion.

"I dissent," he began, "from the opinion pronounced by the chief justice. . . . The question is, whether any person of African descent whose ancestors were sold as slaves in the United States can be a citizen of the United States. . . . One mode of approaching this question is to inquire who were citizens of the United States at the time of the adoption of the Constitution.

"Citizens of the United States at the time of the adoption of the Constitution can have been no other than citizens of the United States under the confederation. . . . It may safely be said that the citizens of the several States were citizens of the United States under the confederation. . . . To determine whether any free persons descended from Africans held in slavery were citizens of the United States under the confederation, and consequently at the time of the adoption of the Constitution of the United States, it is only necessary to know whether any such persons were citizens of either of the States under the confederation at the time of the adoption of the Constitution.

"Of this there can be no doubt. At the time of the ratification of the Articles of Confederation, all free native-born inhabitants of the States of New Hampshire, Massachusetts, New York, New Jersey, and North Carolina, though descended from African slaves, were not only citizens of those States, but such of them as had the other necessary qualifications possessed the franchise of electors, on equal terms with other citizens. . . . I shall not enter into an examination of the existing opinions of that period respecting the African race, nor into any discussion concerning the meaning of those who asserted in the Declaration of Independence that all men are created equal; that they are endowed by their Creator with certain inalienable rights; that among these are life, liberty, and the pursuit of happiness. My own opinion is that a calm comparison of these assertions of universal abstract truths, and of their own individual opinions and acts, would not leave these men under any reproach of inconsistency; that the great truths they asserted on that solemn occasion they were ready and anxious to make effectual whenever a necessary regard to circumstances, which no statesman can disregard without producing more evil than good, would allow; and that it would not be just to them, nor true in itself, to allege that they intended to say that the Creator of all men had endowed the white race exclusively with the great natural rights which the Declaration of Independence asserts. But this is not the place to vindicate their memory. As I conceive, we should deal here . . . with those substantial facts evinced by the written constitutions of States, and by notorious practice under them. And they show, in a manner which no argument can obscure, that in some of the original thirteen States free colored persons, before and at the time of the formation of the Constitution, were citizens of those States." Therefore, "my opinion is that under the Constitution of the United States every free person born on the soil of a State, who is a citizen of that State by force of its constitution or laws, is also a citizen of the United States."

In considering the power of Congress to prohibit slavery in the territories, Justice Curtis cited "eight distinct instances, beginning with the first Congress, and coming down to the year 1848, in which Congress has excluded slavery from the territory of the United States; and six distinct instances in which Congress organized governments of territories by which slavery was recognized and continued, beginning also with the first Congress and coming down to the year 1822. These acts were severally signed by seven Presidents of the United States, beginning with General Washington and coming regularly down as far as John Quincy Adams, thus including all who were in public life when the Constitution was adopted.

"If the practical construction of the Constitution, contemporaneously with its going into effect, by men intimately acquainted with its history from their personal participation in framing and adopting it, and continued by them through a long series of acts of the gravest importance, be entitled to weight in the judicial mind on a question of construction, it would seem to be difficult to resist the force of the acts above adverted to."

Furthermore, "Slavery, being contrary to natural right, is created only by municipal law." Then, "Is it conceivable that the Constitution has conferred the right on every citizen to become a resident on the territory of the United States with his slaves, and there to hold them as such, but has neither made nor provided for any municipal regulations which are essential to the existence of slavery? . . . Whatever theoretical importance may be now supposed to belong to the maintenance of such a right, I feel a perfect conviction that it would, if ever tried, prove to be as impracticable in fact as it is, in my judgment, monstrous in theory."

Every possible phase of this question was considered by Justice Curtis, and the conclusion arrived at was that the acts of Congress which had prohibited slavery in the territories, including of course the Missouri Compromise, "were constitutional and valid laws."

That a man of the years of Taney could construct so vigorous and so plausible an argument was less remarkable than that a humane Christian man could assert publicly such a monstrous theory. Yet such work was demanded by slavery of her votaries. The opinion of Taney was but the doctrine of Calhoun, announced for the first time in 1847, and now embodied in a judicial decision. As the North grew faster than the South, as freedom was stronger than slavery, it was the only tenable theory on which slavery could be extended. It is a striking historical fact that in but thirteen years of our history, from 1847 to 1860, could such an opinion have been delivered from the Supreme bench. Only by the conviction that slavery was being pushed to the wall, in conjunction with subtle reasoning like that of Calhoun, who tried to obstruct the onward march of the century by a fine-spun theory, could a sentiment have been created which found expression in this opinion of Taney, outraging as it did precedent, history, and justice.

That Taney committed a grievous fault is certain. He is not

to be blamed for embracing the political notions of John C. Calhoun; his environment gave that shape to his thoughts; but he does deserve censure because he allowed himself to make a political argument, when only a judicial decision was called for. The history of the case shows that there was no necessity for passing upon the two questions we have considered at length. Nothing but an imperative need should have led judges, by their training and position presumably conservative, to unsettle a question that had so long been acquiesced in. The strength of a constitutional government lies in the respect paid to settled questions. For the judiciary to weaken that respect undermines the very foundations of the State. As Douglas sinned as a statesman, so Taney sinned as judge; and while patriotism and not self-seeking impelled him, the better motive does not excuse the chief justice; for much is demanded from the man who holds that high office. Posterity must condemn Taney as unqualifiedly as Douglas.

It is probable that Taney in his inmost heart regretted the part he had been made to play, when he saw that his opinion, instead of allaying the slavery agitation, gave it renewed force. The acerbity displayed in his subsequent correspondence with Justice Curtis grates the heart: they are extraordinary letters from a gentleman of high breeding to one with whom he had held friendly and official relations; and it is reasonable to suppose that while Taney bated not a jot of his convictions, he was vexed that he had descended from his high place to no good purpose, and annoyed that so many eminent lawyers thought his argument had been crushed by the rejoinder of Curtis.

If Taney spoke for Calhoun, Curtis spoke for Webster. He had on his side common-sense and justice, even as had his master when disputing with Calhoun. If Taney furnished arguments for the Democrats, Curtis showed that the aim of the Republicans was constitutional. It was a profound remark of Dana on the death of Webster that "he had done more than any living statesman to establish the true Free-soil doctrines."

Pike wrote to the New York *Tribune* that the Supreme Court

of the United States "has abdicated its just functions and descended into the political arena. It has sullied its ermine; it has draggled and polluted its garments in the filth of pro-slavery politics." The opinion of the chief justice deserves "no more respect than any pro-slavery stump-speech made during the late presidential canvass." Rhetoric of this sort made a stirring newspaper letter, and appealed to the radical spirits of the Republican party; but the leaders knew that this opinion of the court was a fact of tremendous import, and must be met by argument and not by declamation. If the opinion of the court were binding on the country, the Republican party must dissolve or give up its fundamental principle, for itwas laboring in an unconstitutional manner. How, then, could the reverence of the Northern people for the highest judicial tribunal be reconciled with a disregard of this opinion? Fortunately, Justice Curtis rose to the height of the situation, and in his opinion gave the key-note to the constitutional argument against the opinion of the court being in any way binding on the political consciences of the people. After mentioning the technical steps by which the court reached the question of the power of Congress to pass the Missouri Compromise act, Curtis said: "On so grave a subject as this, I feel obliged to say that, in my opinion, such an exertion of judicial power transcends the limits of the authority of the court, as described by its repeated decisions, and, as I understand, acknowledged in this opinion of the majority of the court. . . . I do not consider it to be within the scope of the judicial power of the majority of the court to pass upon any question respecting the plaintiff's citizenship in Missouri, save that raised by the plea to the jurisdiction; and I do not hold any opinion of this court or any court binding when expressed on a question not legitimately before it. The judgment of this court is that the case is to be dismissed for want of jurisdiction, because the plaintiff was not a citizen of Missouri, as he alleged in his declaration. Into that judgment, according to the settled course of this court, nothing appearing after a plea to the merits can enter. A great question of constitutional law, deeply affecting the peace and welfare of the country, is not, in my opinion, a fit subject to be thus reached."

Not Republicans alone saw the matter in this light under the guidance of so earnest and able a jurist. Fillmore wrote Curtis that his arguments were unanswerable; and undoubtedly nearly every Northern man who had voted for Fillmore agreed with his chief.

The Southern Democrats were in high glee at the decision. "What are you going to do about it?" they tauntingly asked of the Republicans; and they went to work circulating the opinion of the court as a campaign document. Twenty thousand copies of the opinions of the judges were printed by order of the Democratic Senate. When the Republicans saw clearly their proper course, they vied with the Democrats in giving wide currency to the action of the court. One of their important campaign documents contained the full opinions of Taney and Curtis, and abstracts of the others. People always desire to summarize a long political paper, and Taney's opinion was soon condensed into the aphorism that "negroes had no rights which the white man was bound to respect." This was not fair to Taney, but the dissemination of the saying as the dictum of the court was a most effective weapon in the North against slavery, and had much to do with deepening Northern sentiment in opposition to it.

Douglas soon spoke for the Northern Democrats. He emphatically endorsed the decision of the court, lauded the characters of Taney and the associate judges, and maintained that "whoever resists the final decisions of the highest judicial tribunal aims a deadly blow to our whole republican system of government."

It was perfectly plain to Southern Democrats and Republicans that this decision shattered the doctrine of popular sovereignty; for if Congress could not prohibit slavery in a territory, how could it be done by a territorial legislature, which was but a creature of Congress? And as, according to the decision, slaves were property the same as horses and mules, the Southern emigrant to Kansas had the same right to take his negroes there that the Northern emigrant had to take his live-stock. Both alike claimed the protection of the general government; and if emigration went on under these conditions, the territory was liable to be slave territory before the people could in any manner be called upon to determine the question. A less adroit man than Douglas would have been daunted, but he boldly asserted that the Dred Scott decision and his popular-sovereignty doctrine were entirely consistent. While the master's right to his slave in a territory, he said, "continues in full force under the guarantees of the Constitution, and cannot be divested or alienated by an act of Congress, it necessarily remains a barren and a worthless right, unless sustained, protected, and enforced by appropriate police regulations and local legislation, prescribing adequate remedies for its violation. These regulations and remedies must necessarily depend entirely upon the will and wishes of the people of the territory, as they can only be prescribed by the local legislatures. Hence the great principle of popular sovereignty and self-government is sustained and firmly established by the authority of this decision."

This attempted reconciliation of two irreconcilable principles must have provoked a smile from Southern Democrats and Republicans. But at the North, Douglas had been steadily gaining in popularity since January 1st, 1856; and as he was a consummate party leader, he was nearing the point where he only had to make a daring assertion to have it echoed by his many satellites and believed in by his followers, who were practically the Democratic party of the.North. While he was ordinarily verbose, he cared not to dwell on this point; he passed at once to other points of the decision which he could sincerely advocate. He could not resist referring in a triumphant tone to the fact that the repeal of the Missouri Compromise, for which he had been so much abused, had now turned out to be simply the abrogation of a statute constitutionally null and void.

The reasoning of Taney in regard to the citizenship of the negro was amplified by Douglas in the manner that gave the key-note to his followers. Read at this day, Taney's argument impresses one with its power. It is inhuman. It was effectually refuted. But it was a great piece of specious reasoning, and, translated by Douglas into the language of the stump, it made the staple argument of Northern Democrats from this time to the war. We have seen the course of opinion at the South—how slavery, from having been regarded an abstract evil, came to be looked upon as a positive good. Opinion among the Northern Democrats went through a similar evolution, for the evil was first endured, then pitied, and now embraced. With the approval of the principles of the Dred Scott decision, the last step was taken. Because the negro was inferior to the white man, the Northern Democrats now argued, slavery was his fit condition. This sentiment shows itself in the press, in the friendly discussion at the village store and by the fireside. The Northern Democrats of 1840 to 1850 thought slavery an evil in the abstract; there were even devoted partisans who had conscientious scruples about supporting Polk because he was a slave-holder. Many of these same men were now gravitating to the point of thinking that a favor was done the negro when he was reduced to slavery. This argument, while not unknown in Northern Democratic literature before 1857, becomes prominent after the publication of the Dred Scott decision. Taney's opinion was swallowed by the followers of Douglas, and everywhere reproduced and paraphrased. It was the Kansas-Nebraska act and the Dred Scott opinion which made the national Democrats a pro-slavery party.

Douglas was not left unanswered. Two weeks later Abraham Lincoln, his Illinois rival, then much less widely known, an inferior orator, yet with a greater gift of expression, made a reply. This speech, which was published in the East, states the Republican position in a manner to carry conviction to those who could only be influenced by homely arguments, and at the same time its reasoning strikes the historical student with great force. It therefore deserves more than a passing notice. Who resists the decision? Lincoln asked. "Who has, in spite of the decision, declared Dred Scott free, and resisted the authority of his master over him? . . . But we think the Dred Scott decision is erroneous. We know the court that made it has often overruled its own decisions, and we shall do what we can to have it overrule this. We offer no resistance to it." The condition of the black man, Lincoln asserted, is worse now than at the time of the Declaration of Independence and the adoption of the Constitution. "In those days our Declaration of Independence was held sacred by all, and thought to include all; but now, to aid in making the bondage of the negro universal and eternal, it is assailed and sneered at, and construed and hawked at and torn, till, if its framers could rise from their graves, they could not at all recognize it. All the powers of the earth seem rapidly combining against him [the negro]. Mammon is after him, ambition follows, philosophy follows, and the theology of the day is fast joining the cry. . . . There is a natural disgust in the minds of nearly all white people to the idea of an indiscriminate amalgamation of the white and black races; and Judge Douglas . . . makes an occasion for lugging it in from the opposition to the Dred Scott decision. He finds the Republicans insisting that the Declaration of Independence includes all men, black as well as white, and forthwith he boldly denies that it includes negroes at all, and proceeds to argue gravely that all who contend it does, do so only because they want to vote, and eat, and sleep, and marry with the negroes! . . . Now, I protest against the counterfeit logic which concludes that, because I do not want a black woman for a slave, I must necessarily want her for a wife. I need not have her for either; I can just leave her alone. In some respects she is certainly not my equal; but in her natural right to eat the bread she earns with her own hands, without asking leave of any one else, she is my equal, and the equal of all others."

One widespread charge in reference to the Dred Scott decision must be spoken of. In 1858, it was given the stamp of approval by Seward and Lincoln, who had then become the two leaders of the Republican party. Seward said in the Senate, March 3d: "Before coming into office, Buchanan approached, or was approached by, the Supreme Court of the United States. . . . The court did not hesitate to please the incoming President by . . . pronouncing an opinion that the Missouri prohibition was void. . . . The day of inauguration came— the first one among all the celebrations of that great national pageant that was to be desecrated by a coalition between the executive and judicial departments, to undermine the national legislature and the liberties of the people." The people were "unaware of the import of the whisperings carried on between the President and the chief justice." The President "announced (vaguely indeed, but with self-satisfaction) the forthcoming extra-judicial exposition of the Constitution, and pledged his submission to it as authoritative and final. The chief justice and his associates remained silent." The only evidence for the charge of Seward lay in the statement of the President in his inaugural, that the question as to the time when people of a territory might exclude slavery therefrom was pending before the Supreme Court, and would be speedily settled. Undoubtedly Buchanan then knew what would be substantially the decision of the court on the territorial question, but so did a thousand other men.

As the year 1858 opened, national tensions had increased to an alarming point. Many of the events of the time were connected with healthy growth. The network of railroads was thickening in both North and South and was providing a national market for many products previously sold but locally. The Far West was being bound to the East, not only by transportation lines around Cape Horn and across the Isthmus but by overland stage and telegraph lines, and eventually a fast pony express. Five possible railroad routes were surveyed in the 1850's. The Gila Valley in Arizona was acquired by purchase; naval enterprise opened Japan to a tentative American activity. Yet all the while, in the good times before the panic of 1857 and the hard times afterward, the ulcer of sectional hatred grew more inflamed and painful. It was brought to a more dangerous point when Southern forces, abetted by the timid Buchanan, attempted to bring Kansas into the Union under a dishonest proslavery constitution drawn up by a convention at Lecompton; Douglas in utter disgust allied himself with the Republican leaders to halt this outrage.

The Congressional elections of 1858 assumed intense interest as the crisis deepened. The term of Douglas was drawing to an end. He was anxious to keep his seat in the Senate; he could not obtain a nomination for the presidency in 1860 unless he did. Indomitable in temper, he had incurred the enmity of President Buchanan and the principal Southern leaders by his defiant Lecompton stand. When he returned to Illinois in the early summer of 1858, he knew that he would have to fight for his whole future. An even grimmer battle than he had anticipated opened before him. Lincoln crossed swords with him in the famous "House Divided" speech, and Illinois politicians arranged a series of debates in seven Congressional districts of the State. The encounter of the two leaders reached a crucial point when Lincoln presented Douglas at Freeport with a dilemma: would the Little Giant accept the Dred Scott decision, which meant that the spread of slavery could not be halted in any territory before admission as a state, or would he continue to assert that popular sovereignty might *check it? Douglas presented an answer that most Southerners refused to accept.*

Rhodes does justice to the debates. He shows that while Douglas's speeches were as good as Lincoln's for the purpose of winning immediate votes, Lincoln came off the better for any larger objective. Excellent as his treatment is, Rhodes might have shown more clearly that this was because Lincoln had driven home with memorable force three great conclusions. The first was that slavery had not been a terribly divisive issue early in the history of the republic because the founders had held a faith that the institution would be placed in the path of extinction. The second was that since Southerners and men like Douglas had adopted a new attitude, treating slavery as national and perpetual, the fierce antagonisms it aroused had deepened. The third conclusion was that if men would return to the position that slavery was morally wrong and must be put on the road to gradual abolition, the peril to the Union would disappear. A crisis must be reached and passed; and the time had come to face it courageously.

The Lincoln-Douglas Debates

ABRAHAM LINCOLN had reached eminent rank in his profession, being esteemed the strongest jury-lawyer in the State; but he was a bad advocate in an unjust cause. His clearness of statement was remarkable, and his undoubted sincerity carried conviction.

The repeal of the Missouri Compromise diverted Lincoln's attention from law to politics. Prominent in the Illinois canvass of 1854, he became, on the election of an anti-Nebraska legislature, a candidate for United States senator. But there were five anti-Nebraska Democrats whose choice was Lyman Trumbull. These would not, under any circumstances, vote for Lincoln or another Whig. Although he could control forty-seven votes, which was within tour of the necessary number to elect, yet, rather than risk the election of a Democrat, he, with rare judgment and magnanimity, advised his friends to go for Trumbull, who accordingly was chosen on the tenth ballot.

Lincoln felt deep disappointment at failing to secure the coveted place, for his ambition was great. When a young man, in a fit of profound depression, he said to the most intimate friend he ever had: "I have done nothing to make any human being remember that I have lived. To connect my name with events of my day and generation, and so impress myself upon them as to link my name with something that will rebound to the interest of my fellow-men, is all that I desire to live for." From that time on he had thirsted for fame. He would gladly feed on popularity, and had confidence in his ability to do mighty things, should the opportunity offer. Yet his speech was modest. In the debates of 1858 with Douglas, when seemingly overtopped by the greatness of his rival, his expressions of self-depreciation were so marked as now to strike one painfully, even as with a dim suggestion of the humbleness of Uriah Heep.

How keenly he felt his failure to obtain a hearing is illustrated by an occurrence in 1857. Associated with Edwin M. Stanton and George Harding in a case of great importance that was to be tried in the United States Circuit Court before Judge McLean at Cincinnati, it lay between Lincoln and Stanton as to who should make the second argument. It was finally decided in favor of the Pennsylvanian. Lincoln thought Stanton purposely ignored him and treated him with rudeness; while Stanton was little impressed with the ability of the other, whose appearance, manner, and garb, suited perhaps to the prairie, were but ill adapted for intercourse with the serious attorneys and grave judges of the East.

Ungainly as Lincoln appeared, he had the instincts of a gentleman. In a speech at Springfield this year he said: I shall never be a gentleman "in the outside polish, but that which constitutes the inside of a gentleman I hope I understand, and am not less inclined to practise than others."

When Lincoln entered upon political life he became reticent regarding his religious opinions, for at the age of twenty-five, influenced by Thomas Paine and Volney, he had written an extended essay against Christianity with a view to its publication. A far-seeing friend, however, took the manuscript from him and consigned it to the flames. At the period that our story covers, Lincoln did not believe in the inspiration of the Scriptures or the divinity of Christ, and in moments of gloom, or when wrestling with deep reflection, he doubted the existence of a personal God and a future life. The religious writer whom he chiefly read, and whose influence he felt most, was Theodore Parker. The argument in Chambers's "Vestiges of the Creation" struck him with force; his scientific mind laid fast hold of the doctrine of evolution hinted at in that famous work.

Standing out beyond all other characteristics of Lincoln, manifesting itself in private life, in business, during legal consultation, in forensic contest, and illuminating his strife for political place and power, is his love of truth and justice. When twenty-four years old he was called "honest Abe." At no time, and in no circumstances of his life, did he do aught that threw the faintest taint of suspicion upon this title spontaneously given in a rude village of Illinois.

Such was Lincoln at the age of forty-nine, when he stood forth to contest the senatorship with the most redoubtable debater of the country. He and Douglas had first met in 1834, and the rivalry between them, begun early, did not end until 1860. Both aspired to the hand of the same woman, and Lincoln's manly and rugged qualities proved more attractive than the fascinations of the eloquent and dashing Douglas. Yet in the race for political preferment, Douglas far outstripped the other. Though four years younger, he went to Congress four years earlier; and when Lincoln was a representative, he was a senator, with apparently many years of political honors before him. This greater success was largely due to the fact that Douglas belonged to the dominant party in Illinois. In 1858, Douglas had a great national reputation, while Lincoln's

name had only begun to reach beyond the confines of his own
State. Douglas, however, knew his rival better than did the
people of the East. On hearing that Lincoln would be his opponent, he said to Forney: "I shall have my hands full. He is
the strong man of his party—full of wit, facts, dates—and the
best stump-speaker, with his droll ways and dry jokes, in
the West. He is as honest as he is shrewd; and if I beat him, my
victory will be hardly won." Douglas, in his first speech of the
campaign, paid to Lincoln a generous compliment. "I have
known," said he, "personally and intimately, for about a quarter
of a century, the worthy gentleman who has been nominated
for my place, and I will say that I regard him as a kind, amiable,
and intelligent gentleman, a good citizen, and an honorable
opponent."

The Republican State Convention, meeting at Springfield,
June 16th, unanimously nominated Lincoln as the senatorial
candidate of the party. He addressed the delegates in the most
carefully prepared speech he had ever made. Fully aware for
some time previously what the action of the convention would
be, he had thought earnestly on the principles he should lay
down as the key-note of the campaign. As ideas occurred to him,
he wrote them down on scraps of paper, and when the convention drew near, after weighing every thought, scrutinizing each
sentence, and pondering every word, he fused them together
into a connected whole. Esteeming that this would be for him
a pregnant opportunity, he paid great attention to the art as
well as the matter of his discourse. Drawing inspiration from a
careful reading of the greatest of American orations, he modelled the beginning of his speech after Webster's exordium.

Lincoln began: "If we could first know where we are and
whither we are tending, we could better judge what to do and
how to do it. We are now far into the fifth year since a policy
was initiated with the avowed object, and confident promise,
of putting an end to slavery agitation. Under the operation of
that policy, that agitation has not only not ceased, but has
constantly augmented. In my opinion, it will not cease until a

crisis shall have been reached and passed. 'A house divided against itself cannot stand.' I believe this government cannot endure permanently half slave and half free. I do not expect the Union to be dissolved—I do not expect the house to fall—but I do expect it will cease to be divided. It will become all one thing or all the other. Either the opponents of slavery will arrest the further spread of it, and place it where the public mind shall rest in the belief that it is in the course of ultimate extinction; or its advocates will push it forward till it shall become alike lawful in all the States, old as well as new—North as well as South."

No Republican of prominence and ability had advanced so radical a doctrine. Lincoln knew that to commit the party of his State to that belief was an important step, and ought not to be taken without consultation and careful reflection. He first submitted the speech to his friend and partner, Herndon. Stopping at the end of each paragraph for comments, when he had read, "A house divided against itself cannot stand," Herndon said: "It is true, but is it wise or politic to say so?" Lincoln replied: "That expression is a truth of all human experience, 'A house divided against itself cannot stand.' . . . I want to use some universally known figure expressing in simple language as universally well known, that may strike home to the minds of men in order to raise them up to the peril of the times; I do not believe I would be right in changing or omitting it. I would rather be defeated with this expression in the speech, and uphold and discuss it before the people, than be victorious without it."

When we consider Lincoln's restless ambition, his yearning for the senatorship, and his knowledge that he was starting on an untrodden path, there is nobility in this response. Two years before he had incorporated a similar avowal in a speech, and had struck it out in obedience to the remonstrance of a political friend. Now, however, actuated by devotion to principle, and perhaps feeling that the startling doctrine of 1858 would ere long become the accepted view of the Republican party, he was determined to speak in accordance with his own judgment. Yet as he wanted to hear all that could be said against it, he read the speech to a dozen of his Springfield friends, and invited criticism. None of them approved it. Several severely condemned it. One said it was "a fool utterance," another that the doctrine was "ahead of its time," while a third argued that "it would drive away a good many voters fresh from the Democratic ranks." Herndon, who was an abolitionist, alone approved it, and exclaimed: "Lincoln, deliver that speech as read, and it will make you President."

After listening patiently to the criticisms of his friends, who ardently desired his political advancement, he told them that he had carefully studied the subject and thought on it deeply. "Friends," said he, "this thing has been retarded long enough. The time has come when these sentiments should be uttered; and if it is decreed that I should go down because of this speech, then let me go down linked to the truth—let me die in the advocacy of what is just and right."

After his startling exordium, Lincoln described the advance made by the cause of slavery in virtue of the Dred Scott decision, related how different events led up to the announcement of the opinion of this court, and intimated by his well-known allegory that there was a conspiracy among high parties in the State. He then addressed himself to the argument now frequently maintained, that the slave power could be best opposed by Republicans enrolling themselves under the leadership of Senator Douglas. "There are those who denounce us openly to their own friends," said he, "and yet whisper us softly that Senator Douglas is the aptest instrument there is" to overthrow "the power of the present political dynasty. . . . They wish us to *infer* all from the fact that he now has a little quarrel with the present head of the dynasty; and that he has regularly voted with us on a single point upon which he and we have never differed. They remind us that he is a great man, and that the largest of us are very small ones. Let this be granted. But 'a living dog is better than a dead lion.' Judge Douglas, if not a dead lion for this work, is at least a caged and toothless one. How can he oppose the advance of slavery? He does not care anything about it. His avowed mission is impressing the public heart *to care nothing about it.* . . . He has done all in his power to reduce the whole question of slavery to one of a mere right of property. . . . Clearly he is not now with us—he does not pretend to be, he does not promise ever to be.

"Our cause, then, must be intrusted to, and conducted by, its own undoubted friends—those whose hands are free, whose hearts are in the work—who *do care* for the result. Two years ago the Republicans of the nation mustered over thirteen hundred thousand strong. We did this under the single impulse of resistance to a common danger, with every external circumstance against us. Of strange, discordant, even hostile elements, we gathered from the four winds, and formed and fought the battle through, under the constant hot fire of a disciplined, proud, and pampered enemy. Did we brave all then to falter now?—now when that same enemy is wavering, dissevered, and belligerent? The result is not doubtful. We shall not fail— if we stand firm, *we shall not fail.* Wise counsels may accelerate or mistakes delay it, but, sooner or later, the victory is sure to come."

On the 9th of July, Douglas reached his Chicago home. He had a magnificent and enthusiastic reception, in striking contrast to the one of four years previous. It was a worthy tribute on account of the determined fight he had made against the administration; nor was the friendly feeling towards him confined to the Democrats. Besides his present political popularity, his hold on Chicago people was strong, for he was an eminent citizen of this city of enterprise, devoted to its prosperity, and giving gages of his faith by large investments in its real estate. He was generous, too, and had made a gift of ten acres of valuable land to be used as the site for the University of Chicago. Chicago on this day delighted to do honor to its distinguished citizen, and Douglas was proud of his "magnificent welcome."

His speech was in his best manner. He exulted that the Lecompton battle had been won, and that the Republicans had come around to the doctrine of popular sovereignty. In arguments that are familiar to my readers, he vindicated this principle, and pointed to his record from 1854 as displaying consistency and fidelity. He complimented Lincoln personally and then seized upon his "house-divided-against-itself" doctrine to show the issue that lay between them. With much ingenuity he construed this declaration to mean a desire for uniformity of local institutions all over the country, and as an attack upon State sovereignty and personal liberty. In truth, Douglas averred, "Variety in all our local and domestic institutions is the great safeguard of our liberties." The direct and unequivocal issue between Lincoln and himself was: "He goes for uniformity in our domestic institutions, for a war of sections until one or the other shall be subdued; I go for the great principle of the Kansas-Nebraska bill, the right of the people to decide for themselves."

In regard to Lincoln's criticism of the Dred Scott decision, Douglas said: "I have no idea of appealing from the decision of the Supreme Court upon a constitutional question to the decisions of a tumultuous town meeting;" and "I am free to say to you that, in my opinion, this government of ours is founded on the white basis. It was made by the white man, for the benefit of the white man, to be administered by white men in such manner as they should determine."

Lincoln heard this speech, and the next evening replied to it. But his argument was much inferior in force and in diction to that of his speech at Springfield; it showed a want of careful preparation, without which he was never at his best. Douglas replied to him at Bloomington, July 16th, and had much to say about the doctrine of the "house divided against itself." It invited, he maintained, a warfare of the States. Lincoln "has taken his position," he continued, "in favor of sectional agitation and sectional warfare. I have taken mine in favor of securing peace, harmony, and good-will among all the States."

In this speech, Douglas praised the New York *Tribune* and the
Republicans for the course they had taken during the last
session of Congress.

At Springfield, the next day, Lincoln rejoined. He declared
that the doctrine of popular sovereignty, as expounded by
Douglas, was "the most arrant humbug that had ever been
attempted on an intelligent community." He denied the charge
that he invited a war of sections. He had only expressed his
expectation as to the logical result of the existence of slavery
in the country, and not his wish for such an outcome. Moreover,
he had again and again expressly disclaimed the intention of
interference with slavery in the States. He then charged Douglas himself with being the cause of the present agitation. "Although I have ever been opposed to slavery," said he, "up to
the introduction of the Nebraska bill I rested in the hope and
belief that it was in the course of ultimate extinction. For that
reason it had been a minor question with me. I might have been
mistaken; but I had believed, and now believe, that the whole
public mind—that is, the mind of the great majority—had
rested in that belief up to the repeal of the Missouri Compromise." He again criticised the Dred Scott decision and exclaimed: "I adhere to the Declaration of Independence. If
Judge Douglas and his friends are not willing to stand by it,
let them come up and amend it. Let them make it read that all
men are created equal except negroes."

The opening notes of the campaign were favorable to Douglas. Coming to his home with well-won prestige, the hearty and
sincere reception of Chicago seemed to foreshadow that the
people of Illinois would say by their votes in November, "Well
done, good and faithful servant." The usual means to rouse
campaign enthusiasm were not lacking, and at every place he
had an ovation. Cannon thundered out a welcome, bands of
music greeted him, every evening meeting ended with a display
of fireworks. Special trains were at his disposal, and committees of escort attended his every movement. In the decorations
of the locomotive that hauled his train and the car on which

he rode, on every triumphal arch under which he passed in
the cities that welcomed him, and on the banners borne in the
processions that turned out to do him honor, was emblazoned
the motto "Popular Sovereignty." Money was not lacking to
produce the blare and flare of the campaign; for, lavish himself,
and mortgaging his Chicago real-estate for means to meet his
large expenses, Douglas felt free to accept the contributions of
liberal friends.

Lincoln's "house-divided-against-itself" declaration was received with joy by the Democrats. By the Republican party
workers it was deemed a great mistake. To them, at best, the
contest seemed unequal. Their candidate had no right to handi-
cap himself by the assertion of a principle far in advance of his
party and of what the occasion demanded. It was apparent to
Lincoln and his advisers that the current was setting against
him; nevertheless, he had not the slightest regret for the positive manifesto he had put forth. Thinking that the adroit and
plausible Douglas could be better answered if they spoke from
the same platform, it was determined that Lincoln should
challenge him to a series of joint debates. The challenge was
accepted and the arrangements made for seven meetings—one
in each congressional district, except those districts containing
Chicago and Springfield, where both had already spoken.

The places selected were Ottawa and Freeport, which were
in strong Republican districts, whose congressmen were Lovejoy and Washburne; Galesburg, representing a locality of
moderate Republican strength; Quincy and Charleston, situated in districts that gave fair Democratic majorities; and Alton
and Jonesboro, strong Democratic localities. Jonesboro was in
what was known as "Egypt"; it gave that year to John A.
Logan, the Democratic candidate for congressman, more than
13,000 majority.

In 1856 the vote in Illinois was: For Buchanan, 105,348;
for Frémont, 96,189; and for Fillmore, 37,444. The Republican
hope of success lay in securing a large proportion of the vote
that had been cast for Fillmore. Northern Illinois, in conform-

ity with the general trend of Western settlement, had been peopled from New England, New York, and northern Ohio, and was strongly Republican; while southern Illinois, receiving its population mainly from Virginia and Kentucky, was as strongly Democratic. The central part of this State was the battleground. Douglas had an advantage in that eight of the twelve State senators holding over were Democrats; moreover, the legislative apportionment was based on the census of 1850, but the State census of 1855 had shown a much larger proportional increase in the northern part of the State than in the southern.

Lincoln must win the favor of the abolitionists of whom Lovejoy was a type, of the moderate Republicans, and of the old-line Whigs and Americans. He must contend against the opposition of many Eastern Republicans, of whom Greeley was the most outspoken, and against the lukewarmness of others. But as the canvass proceeded and the issue became clearly defined, the New York *Tribune* could not consistently do aught but give Lincoln a hearty support.

Appreciating the importance of the old Whig vote, and hoping that his former devotion to that party and its principles would prove a potent influence to attract support, Lincoln was grieved when he learned that Senator Crittenden, of Kentucky, whom he highly esteemed, was favorable to the election of Douglas, and would not remain silent when asked for sympathy. Douglas also tried to win the favor of the old-line Whigs, and he gladly referred to his efforts when he "acted side by side with the immortal Clay and the godlike Webster" in favor of the compromise measures of 1850.

It seemed at first as if it would be a desperate struggle to keep intact the Democratic vote; for while Douglas had the machinery of the party and practically all of the Democratic press, the patronage of the administration was powerfully used against him. The proscription of Douglas Democrats holding office was relentless. The organ of the administration saw little choice between Lincoln and Douglas, and thought that true Democrats stood in the position of the woman who looked on at the fight between her husband and the bear. The rancor of Buchanan against Douglas had by no means abated with the adjournment of Congress, and it was whispered that the bitter abuse of the Little Giant in the editorial columns of the *Union* was directly inspired by the President from his summer retreat. The administration party had legislative tickets in nearly every district, and while they avowed that their object and hope were to elect enough members to hold the balance of power and secure an administration Democrat for senator, every one knew that the only appreciable result of their action was to divide the Democratic party and help the Republicans.

Douglas several times spoke bitterly of the war that was made upon him within his party. "The Washington *Union*," he said on one occasion, "is advocating Mr. Lincoln's claim to the Senate. . . . There is an alliance between Lincoln and his supporters, and the federal office-holders of this State and presidential aspirants out of it, to break me down at home." In the last debate, referring to the trouble between Douglas and the administration, Lincoln declared: "All I can say now is to recommend to him and to them to prosecute the war against one another in the most vigorous manner. I say to them, 'Go it, husband! Go it, bear!' "

The two leaders met first at Ottawa, August 21st. That Lincoln was willing to pit himself against Douglas in joint debate showed an abiding confidence in his cause and in his ability to present it. For he had to contend with the ablest debater of the country, the man who in senatorial discussion had overmastered Seward, Chase, and Sumner, and who more recently had discomfited the champions of Lecompton. Lincoln had less of the oratorical gift than Douglas, and he lacked the magnetism that gave the Little Giant such a personal following. Tall, lean, gaunt, and awkward, his appearance as he rose to speak was little fitted to win the sympathy of his hearers. "When he began speaking," writes Herndon, "his voice was shrill, piping, and unpleasant. His manner, attitude, his dark, yellow face, wrinkled and dry, his oddity of pose, his diffident movements"—all seemed against him. But when he got into the heart of his subject, he forgot his ungainly appearance; his soul, exalted by dwelling upon his cause, illumined his face with earnestness, making it lose "the sad, pained look due to habitual melancholy;" and his voice and gestures became effective. From every speech of Lincoln breathed forth sincerity and devotion to right. Whatever other impressions were received by the crowds who gathered to hear him in the summer and fall of 1858, they were at one in the opinion that they had listened to an honest man.

The conditions of the Ottawa debate were that Douglas should open with an hour's speech, Lincoln to follow for one hour and a half, and Douglas to have thirty minutes to close. In the succeeding debates, the time occupied was the same, but the privilege of opening and closing alternated between the two speakers.

In the speech beginning the discussion, Douglas again sneered at the "house-divided-against-itself" doctrine, charged Lincoln with being an abolitionist because he had opposed the Dred Scott decision and had construed the "all-men-are created-equal" clause of the Declaration of Independence to include the negro. "I do not believe," declared Douglas, "that the Almighty ever intended the negro to be the equal of the white man. . . . He belongs to an inferior race, and must always occupy an inferior position."

In calling Lincoln an abolitionist at Ottawa, it was not wholly for the effect it would have on the immediate audience— for the district that sent Lovejoy to Congress, and the people who cheered the doctrine of the "divided house" when Douglas repeated it to condemn it, were not to be affected by that name —but it was rather for the wider audience who would read the speeches in print. If Douglas could fasten on Lincoln the name abolitionist, it would have an influence in the central part of the State, where the old-line Whigs might turn the scale either way. The Illinois abolitionist differed from those who acknowledged Garrison and Phillips as their leaders, in that he believed in political action, and was not a disunionist; yet political definitions are frequently confused, and if a man were deemed an abolitionist, it would not be unnatural to think that he subscribed to Garrison's dogmas—"The United States Constitution is a covenant with death and an agreement with hell," and "No Union with slave-holders." In Illinois as a whole, and, for that matter, generally throughout the North, it was a bar to political preferment to be known as an abolitionist.

Lincoln was not, however, in any sense of the word an abolitionist. He quoted from his Peoria speech of 1854 to show exactly his position, then added: "I have no purpose to introduct political and social equality between the white and black races. There is a physical difference between the two which, in my judgment, will probably forever forbid their living together upon the footing of perfect equality; and inasmuch as it becomes a necessity that there must be a difference, I, as well as Judge Douglas, am in favor of the race to which I belong having the superior position. I have never said anything to the contrary; but I hold that, notwithstanding all this, there is no reason in the world why the negro is not entitled to all the natural rights enumerated in the Declaration of Independence—the right to life, liberty, and the pursuit of happiness. I hold that he is as much entitled to these as the white man." He continued in the strain, and in almost the words, of his Springfield speech of 1857.

Lincoln replied to the criticism on his "house-divided-against-itself" doctrine. "The great variety of the local institutions in the States," said he, "springing from differences in the soil, differences in the face of the country and in the climate, are bonds of union. They do not make 'a house divided against itself,' but they make a house united. If they produce in one section of the country what is called for by the wants of another section, and this other section can supply the wants of the first, they are not matters of discord, but bonds of union—true bonds of union. But can this question of slavery be considered as among these varieties in the institutions of the country? I leave it to you to say whether, in the history of our government, this institution of slavery has not always failed to be a bond of union, and, on the contrary, been an apple of discord, and an element of division in the house."

It was in the Ottawa speech, when alluding to the vast influence of Douglas, that Lincoln made an oft-quoted remark—the assertion, indeed, of an old political truth, yet a truth not always comprehended, and at this time an important lesson for Republicans to learn. The forcible expression of it by their Illinois leader shows how profoundly he had grasped the situation. "In this and like communities," said he, "public sentiment is everything. With public sentiment nothing can fail; without it, nothing can succeed. Consequently, he who moulds public sentiment goes deeper than he who enacts statutes or pronounces decisions. He makes statutes and decisions possible or impossible to be executed."

The importance of the Freeport debate, which occurred six days after that at Ottawa, arises from the catechising of each candidate by the other. Lincoln answered frankly the seven questions put to him by Douglas. The four important statements were: he was not in favor of the unconditional repeal of the Fugitive Slave law, was not pledged to the abolition of slavery in the District of Columbia, nor to the prohibition of the slave-trade between the different States; but he did believe it was the right and duty of Congress to prohibit slavery in all of the territories. The crowd of people that listened to the debate at Freeport inclined as strongly to abolition as any audience that could be gathered in Illinois, and Lincoln's answers regarding his position on the Fugitive Slave law and the abolition of slavery in the District of Columbia must have been unpalatable to many who heard him. It was ground much less radical than Seward, Chase, and Sumner had taken at different times; for the unconditional repeal of the Fugitive Slave law, and the abolition of slavery in the District of Columbia, were, after 1850, the demands of Free-soilers and conscience Whigs. But Lincoln had never been through the Free-soil stage. As a Whig, following Clay and influenced by Webster, he had acquiesced in the compromise of 1850, and his belief in making political action turn on the slavery question was born of the repeal of the Missouri Compromise. His never-varying principle, to which at all times and in all places he adhered, was the prohibition by Congress of slavery in the territories.

Lincoln likewise asked Douglas four questions. In the answer to one, Douglas enunciated what is known as the Freeport doctrine. The question of Lincoln was: "Can the people of a United States territory, in any lawful way, against the wish of any citizen of the United States, exclude slavery from its limits prior to the formation of a State constitution?" It was necessary for Douglas, in his reply, to reconcile his principle of popular sovereignty with the Dred Scott decision. "It matters not," he said, "what way the Supreme Court may hereafter decide as to the abstract question whether slavery may or may not go into a territory under the Constitution; the people have the lawful means to introduce it or exclude it, as they please, for the reason that slavery cannot exist a day or an hour anywhere unless it is supported by local police regulations. Those police regulations can only be established by the local legislature; and if the people are opposed to slavery, they will elect representatives to that body who will by unfriendly legislation effectually prevent the introduction of it into their midst. If, on the contrary, they are for it, their legislation will favor its extension. Hence, no matter what the decision of the Supreme Court may be on that abstract question, still the right of the people to make a slave territory or a free territory is perfect and complete under the Nebraska bill."

This answer attracted more attention throughout the country than any statement of Douglas during the campaign; and, while he could not have been elected senator without taking that position, the enunciation of the doctrine was an insuperable obstacle to cementing the division in the Democratic party.

The influence of this meeting at Freeport is an example of the greater interest incited by a joint debate than by an ordinary canvass, and illustrates the effectiveness of the Socratic method of reasoning. During this same campaign, Douglas had twice before declared the same doctrine in expressions fully as plain and forcible,* but without creating any particular remark; while now the country resounded with discussions of the Freeport theory of "unfriendly legislation."

During this debate, Douglas lost the jaunty air that had characterized his previous efforts. Brought to bay by the remorseless logic of Lincoln, he was nettled to the point of interlarding his argument with misrepresentation; and, as the audience was lacking in sympathy with him, his abuse of the "Black Republican party," and of Lincoln and Trumbull, provoked running comments from the crowd, until, at last, apparently losing his temper, he was drawn into an undignified colloquy with some of his hearers.

A passage from Lincoln's concluding speech at Freeport must be cited, as it shows a prevalent opinion about Douglas in Illinois, and was, moreover, not controverted by him during these debates; it likewise confirms what has been previously stated. Judge Douglas, affirmed Lincoln, at the last session of Congress, "had an eye farther North than he has today. He was then fighting against people who called *him* a Black Republican and an abolitionist. . . . But the judge's eye is farther South now. Then it was very peculiarly and decidedly North. His hope rested on the idea of visiting the great 'Black Republican' party, and making it the tail of his new kite. He knows he was then expecting from day to day to turn Republican and place himself at the head of our organization."

It is interesting to follow these debates in their chronological order as the country in 1858 followed them. It was an intellectual duel between him who represented the best element

---

* At Bloomington, July 16th, where he spoke of legislation being "unfriendly;" and at Springfield, July 17th, when he said, "Slavery cannot exist a day in the midst of an unfriendly people with unfriendly laws."

of the Democratic party and the man who was building up principles, facts, and arguments into a well-defined and harmonious political system. "It was no ordinary contest, in which political opponents skirmished for the amusement of an indifferent audience," said McClernand, who had taken part in the campaign on the side of Douglas; "but it was a great uprising of the people, in which the masses were politically, and to a considerable extent socially, divided and arrayed against each other. In fact, it was a fierce and angry struggle, approximating the character of a revolution."

It is not, however, necessary for our purpose to consider every meeting in detail. There was in the debates much of an ephemeral and personal character. In the personal controversy, Lincoln displayed more acerbity than his opponent. This was not surprising, since Douglas did not show entire fairness. When a charge was refuted, he had a way of making it in another shape, so that it was impossible to get him to admit that he was mistaken. Although frequently exhibiting a hasty temper, he was usually brimming over with good feeling, and this circumstance, together with his effective manner of reiterating a charge, gave him an evident superiority over Lincoln in this feature of the discussion. There was a great desire, on the part of the debaters, to get the better of one another in the immediate judgment of the actual audience; and this gave rise to personal repartees. Here Lincoln did not appear to advantage, on account of his ungainly way of putting things; nor was Douglas altogether happy, because of his great desire to gain immediate points by employing the debater's tricks.

Douglas, better practiced in the amenities of debate, paid Lincoln more than one graceful compliment, but Lincoln had no words of unmeaning praise for his opponent. In his hits at Douglas there are touches of sullen envy mixed with self-depreciation, and laments that fortune should have showered gifts on the Little Giant, while bestowing but meagre favors on himself. He had long envied Douglas, and it galled him that his early rival had succeeded so well in winning fame, while he, conscious of equal intellectual power and of higher moral purpose, should be little known beyond his own State.

But when the discussion turned on principles, the advantage of Lincoln is manifest. As the contest proceeded it grew hotter; and his bursts of eloquence, under the influence of noble passion, are still read with delight by the lovers of humanity and constitutional government. The positions that Douglas had advanced required a cool head to maintain everywhere an appearance of consistency between them. In the increasing heat of the controversy, he sometimes overlooked this, and was influenced too much by his immediate audience, forgetting for the moment that the whole country was looking on, and would read in tranquil hours his every word.

In all the debates, Douglas had little to say on the Lecompton question, although, when he did touch upon it, he spoke well; but, in the main, he seemed again the Douglas of 1854. The radical difference between him and the Republicans appears in every debate; they could agree on anti-Lecompton, but on nothing else; and now that the Lecompton question was settled, it left the former contention in full vigor.

Divested of oratorical flourish, there is little variety in the speeches of Douglas. He scouted continually the idea that the "all-men-are-created-equal" clause of the Declaration of Independence referred to the negro. He charged the Republicans with having formed a sectional party, and in every debate condemned his opponent's doctrine of the "house divided against itself." His most forcible expression on this subject was at Charleston. "Why should this government," he asked, "be divided by a geographical line—arraying all men North in one great hostile party against all men South? Mr. Lincoln tells you that 'a house divided against itself cannot stand.' . . . Why cannot this government endure divided into free and slave States, as our fathers made it? When this government was established by Washington, Jefferson, Madison, Jay, Hamilton, Franklin, and the other sages and patriots of that day, it was composed of free States and slave States, bound together by one common Constitution. We have existed and prospered from that day to this, thus divided. . . . Why can we not thus continue to prosper?"

Lincoln's reply was forcible: "There is no way," he said, "of putting an end to the slavery agitation amongst us but to put it back upon the basis where our fathers placed it; no way but to keep it out of our new territories—to restrict it forever to the old States where it now exists. Then the public mind *will* rest in the belief that it is in the course of ultimate extinction. That is one way of putting an end to the slavery agitation. The other way is for us to surrender and let Judge Douglas and his friends have their way and plant slavery over all the States; cease speaking of it as in any way a wrong; regard slavery as one of the common matters of property, and speak of negroes as we do of our horses and cattle. But while it drives on in its state of progress as it is now driving, and as it has driven for the last five years, I have ventured the opinion, and I say to-day, that we will have no end to the slavery agitation until it takes one turn or the other. I do not mean that when it takes a turn towards ultimate extinction, it will be in a day, nor in a year, nor in two years. I do not suppose that in the most peaceful way ultimate extinction would occur in less than a hundred years at least; but that it will occur in the best way for both races, in God's own good time, I have no doubt."

In the Jonesboro debate, Lincoln had made clear the fallacy of the Freeport doctrine. But in the rejoinder, Douglas showed what a powerful argument the Dred Scott decision was against the cardinal Republican principle of prohibition by Congress of slavery in the territories.

The great historical importance of these debates lies in the prominence they gave Lincoln. The distinction was well deserved. In the Peoria speech of 1854, the Springfield address of 1857, and his published speeches of the 1858 campaign, we have a body of Republican doctrine which in consistency, cogency, and fitness can nowhere be equalled. Lincoln appealed alike to scholars, men of business, and the common people, for such clearness of statement and irrefragable proofs had not been known since the death of Webster. The simple, plain, natural unfolding of ideas is common to both Lincoln and Webster; and their points are made so clear that, while under the spell, the wonder grows how doubts ever could have arisen about the matter. But while it is the sort of reasoning that seems easy for the hearer or reader, it is the result of hard work on the part of the author. A distinguished thinker has said that mathematical studies are of immense benefit to the student "by habituating him to precision. It is one of the peculiar excellencies of mathematical discipline that the mathematician is never satisfied with *à peu près*. He requires the *exact* truth;" and the practice of mathematical reasoning "gives wariness of mind; it accustoms us to demand a sure footing." Undoubtedly the days and nights given by Lincoln to Euclid had much to do with fitting him so well for this contest.

His simple and forcible vocabulary was due to the study of the Bible and Shakespeare. In the habitual use of words that were more common before the eighteenth century than since, Webster and Lincoln are alike. With Webster this was a deliberate choice, but Lincoln had found the Elizabethan language a fit vehicle for his thoughts, and his studies had gone no further.

Some further extracts from Lincoln's speeches are necessary in order fully to understand the historical importance of these debates. He said at Galesburg: "The real difference between Judge Douglas and the Republicans . . . is that the judge is not in favor of making any difference between slavery and liberty— that he is in favor of eradicating, of pressing out of view, the questions of preference in this country for free or slave institutions; and consequently every sentiment he utters discards the idea that there is anything wrong in slavery. Everything that emanates from him or his coadjutors in their course of policy carefully excludes the thought that there is anything wrong in slavery. If you will take the judge's speeches, and select the short and pointed sentences expressed by him—as his declaration that he 'don't care whether slavery is voted up or down'—

you will see at once that this is perfectly logical, if you do not admit that slavery is wrong. If you do admit that it is wrong, Judge Douglas cannot logically say he don't care whether a wrong is voted up or voted down. Judge Douglas declares that if any community want slavery, they have a right to have it. He can say that logically if he says that there is no wrong in slavery; but if you admit that there is a wrong in it, he cannot logically say that anybody has a right to do wrong. He insists that, upon the score of equality, the owners of slaves and owners of property—of horses and every other sort of property—should be alike and hold them alike in a new territory. That is perfectly logical if the two species of property are alike, and are equally founded in right. But if you admit that one of them is wrong, you cannot institute any equality between right and wrong."

Lincoln had no patience with the new construction of the Declaration of Independence. "Three years ago," he declared, "there had never lived a man who had ventured to assail it in the sneaking way of pretending to believe it, and then asserting it did not include the negro. I believe the first man who ever said it was Chief Justice Taney, in the Dred Scott case, and the next to him was our friend Stephen A. Douglas. And now it has become the catchword of the entire party."

This remark was made during the last debate at Alton. In this city, which looked across the river upon the State of Missouri, where Southern sympathy was strong, and which was famous in abolition annals as the place where Lovejoy had been murdered by a pro-slavery mob, Lincoln reached a greater height of moral power and eloquence than he had attained since his opening Springfield speech.

"When that Nebraska bill was brought forward, four years ago last January, was it not," he asked, "for the avowed object of putting an end to the slavery agitation? . . . We were for a little while *quiet* on the troublesome thing, and that very allaying plaster of Judge Douglas's stirred it up again. . . . When was there ever a greater agitation in Congress than last winter?

When was it as great in the country as to-day? There was a collateral object in the introduction of that Nebraska policy, which was to clothe the people of the territories with a superior degree of self-government beyond what they had ever had before. . . . But have you ever heard or known of a people anywhere on earth who had as little to do as, in the first instance of its use, the people of Kansas had with this same right of self-government? In its main policy and in its collateral object, *it has been nothing but a living, creeping lie from the time of its introduction till to-day."*

Lincoln made a good argument drawn from the letter of the Constitution. "The institution of slavery," he said, "is only mentioned in the Constitution of the United States two or three times, and in neither of these cases does the word 'slavery' or 'negro race' occur; but covert language is used each time, and for a purpose full of significance; . . . and that purpose was that in our Constitution, which it was hoped and is still hoped will endure forever—when it should be read by intelligent and patriotic men, after the institution of slavery had passed from among us, there should be nothing on the face of the great charter of Liberty suggesting that such a thing as negro slavery had ever existed among us. This is part of the evidence that the fathers of the government expected and intended the institution of slavery to come to an end. They expected and intended that it should be in the course of ultimate extinction. And when I say that I desire to see the further spread of it arrested, I only say I desire to see that done which the fathers have first done. When I say I desire to see it placed where the public mind will rest in the belief that it is in the course of ultimate extinction, I only say I desire to see it placed where they placed it. It is not true that our fathers, as Judge Douglas assumes, made this government part slave and part free. . . . The exact truth is, they found the institution existing among us, and they left it as they found it. But in making the government they left this institution with many clear marks of disapprobation upon it. They found slavery among them, and they left it among them because of the difficulty, the absolute impossibility, of its immediate removal. And when Judge Douglas asks me why we cannot let it remain part slave and part free, as the fathers of the government made it, he asks a question based upon an assumption which is itself a falsehood; and I turn upon him and ask him the question, when the policy that the fathers of the government had adopted in relation to this element among us was the best policy in the world—the only wise policy—the only policy that we can ever safely continue upon—that will ever give us peace, unless this dangerous element masters us all and becomes a national institution—*I turn upon him and ask him why he could not leave it alone.*"

The stock complaint about the agitation of slavery was effectively answered. "Judge Douglas has intimated," said Lincoln, "that all this difficulty in regard to the institution of slavery is the mere agitation of office-seekers and ambitious Northern politicians. . . . Is that the truth? How many times have we had danger from this question? . . . Is it not this same mighty, deep-seated power that somehow operates on the minds of men, exciting and stirring them up in every avenue of society—in politics, in religion, in literature, in morals, in all the manifold relations of life? Is this the work of politicians? Is that irresistible power which for fifty years has shaken the government and agitated the people to be stilled and subdued by pretending that it is an exceedingly simple thing, and we ought not to talk about it? If you will get everybody else to stop talking about it, I assure you I will quit before they have half done so. But where is the philosophy or statesmanship which assumes that you can quiet that disturbing element in our society which has disturbed us for more than half a century, which has been the only serious danger that has threatened our institutions? I say, where is the philosophy or statesmanship based on the assumption that we are to quit talking about it, and that the public mind is all at once to cease being agitated by it? Yet this is the policy here in the North that Douglas is

advocating—that we are to care nothing about it! I ask you if
this is not a false philosophy? Is it not a false statesmanship
that undertakes to build up a system of policy upon the basis
of caring nothing about *the very thing that everybody does
care the most about?*— a thing which all experience has shown
we care a very great deal about?"

The real issue, Lincoln affirmed, is whether slavery is right or
wrong. "That is the issue that will continue in this country
when these poor tongues of Judge Douglas and myself shall be
silent. It is the eternal struggle between these two principles—
right and wrong—throughout the world. They are the two principles which have stood face to face from the beginning of time,
and will ever continue to struggle. The one is the common right
of humanity, and the other the divine right of kings. It is the
same principle, in whatever shape it develops itself. It is the
same spirit that says, 'You work and toil and earn bread, and
I'll eat it.' No matter in what shape it comes, whether from the
mouth of a king who seeks to bestride the people of his own
nation and live by the fruit of their labor, or from one race
of men as an apology for enslaving another race, it is the same
tyrannical principle."

The excitement in Illinois mounted up to fever heat. Never
had there been such a campaign. That of 1856 was calm by
comparison. The debates did not take place in halls, for no halls
were large enough. These meetings were held in the afternoon,
in groves or on the prairie, and the audiences were from five
thousand to ten thousand. At the Charleston meeting it was
estimated twenty thousand were present. Everywhere women
vied with men in their interest in the contest.

The joint meetings and the speeches of which mention has
been made by no means measure the work of the two candidates.
Lincoln spoke incessantly. In the hundred days of the campaign, Douglas made one hundred and thirty speeches. As the
Little Giant had the Republicans and the influence of the administration to fight, his efforts seemed heroic; and during the

campaign the opinion was universal that, if successful, it would be because his personal prowess had overcome great odds, while defeat might mean his political death.

A host of lesser Illinois aspirants were constantly engaged in campaign work. Members of Congress were to be chosen at the same election, and the candidates stumped thoroughly their districts. Candidates for the legislature occupied a more conspicuous place than usual, for on the successful party would fall the duty and honor of naming for senator one of the two men who were making Illinois famous. Corwin and Chase came from Ohio, and Colfax from Indiana, to assist Lincoln in this memorable struggle. Money was used on both sides more freely than common in a senatorial campaign, but it was employed only for legitimate purposes.* Listening to the arguments of Lincoln and Douglas, the meanest voter of Illinois must have felt that he was one of the jury in a case of transcendent importance, and that, inasmuch as the ablest advocates of the country were appealing to him, he would have deemed it base to traffic in his vote. The party managers knew that success lay only in convincing the minds of men.

The contemplation of such a campaign is inspiriting to those who have faith in the people; for, although Lincoln did not succeed, the Republicans made a material gain over 1856, and paved the way for a triumph in 1860.

X Personal popularity saved Douglas from defeat; he had a majority of eight in the legislature. But the Republican State ticket was elected, the head of it receiving 125,430 votes, while the Douglas Democrat polled 121,609, and the Buchanan Democrat 5071. The total vote had increased over that of the presidential election—an unusual occurrence. This was due

---

* Greeley wrote in 1868: "While Lincoln had spent less than a thousand dollars in all, Douglas in the canvass had borrowed and dispensed no less than eighty thousand dollars, incurring a debt which weighed him down to the grave. I presume no dime of this was used to buy up his competitor's voters, but all to organize and draw out his own; still, the debt so improvidently, if not culpably, incurred remained to harass him out of this mortal life."—*Century Magazine*, July, 1891, p. 375, when this paper of Greeley was first published. I believe this to be a correct statement.

to the great interest awakened by the battle of the giants. The Republicans gained more of the increased vote than the Democrats; but many sincere friends of Lincoln thought that the announcement of the "house-divided-against-itself" doctrine had caused his defeat.

The exultation of Douglas at his triumph was loud and deep. Lincoln ardently desired a seat in the United States Senate, but, accustomed to defeat, he gave way to no expressions of bitter disappointment. Indeed, he had hardly expected a better result, but he was glad he had made the race. He wrote: "It gave me a hearing on the great and durible question of the age which I could have had in no other way; and though I now sink out of view and shall be forgotten, I believe I have made some marks which will tell for the cause of civil liberty long after I am gone."

Lincoln had no regrets about his first Springfield speech. Sumner asked him a few days before his death if at the time he had any doubt about that declaration. He replied: "Not in the least. It was clearly true." Although he had failed to win the senatorship, his speeches had impressed his Illinois friends with the notion that he was a possible candidate for the presidency, and they broached the subject to him. Lincoln's reply was modest and sincere: "What," said he, "is the use of talking of me whilst we have such men as Seward and Chase, and everybody knows them, and scarcely anybody outside of Illinois knows me. Besides, as a matter of justice, is it not due them? . . . I admit that I am ambitious and would like to be President . . . but there is no such good luck in store for me as the presidency of these United States." But there was no question in the mind of Douglas regarding the fitness of Lincoln. Being asked his opinion of his late antagonist by Senator Wilson on the first opportunity after the election, Douglas said: "Lincoln is an able and honest man, one of the ablest men of the nation. I have been in Congress sixteen years, and there is not a man in the Senate I would not rather encounter in debate."

Important in its bearing on the future was the impression

made by these debates beyond the State of Illinois. The speeches were published in full in the Chicago journals; many of them found a place in the St. Louis, Cincinnati, and New York newspapers, and beyond all else, a Western Republican looked for the verdict of New York and New England. Illinois, in 1858, was politically and socially as far from New York city and Boston as Nebraska is to-day. The readers of the New York journals were, however, kept well informed as to the progress of the campaign, and enough speeches on each side were published to convey a correct idea of the issue between the debaters.

THE *Democrats met in convention in Charleston in April, 1860, with their ranks hopelessly divided between adherents of Douglas and his Popular Sovereignty principle on one side, and aggressive Southern Rights men on the other. One of the stormiest gatherings in political history ended in an irreparable schism. Failing to agree on candidate or platform, the convention broke up. The main body adjourned to meet again in Baltimore, where by overwhelming vote it nominated Douglas. The aggressive Southerners gathered in Richmond, where they unanimously selected John C. Breckinridge of Kentucky, asserting "that it is the duty of the federal government, in all its departments, to protect, when necessary, the rights of persons and property in the territories." The division meant that the party had been wrecked. Southern extremists hailed this ominous event with joy; the break-up of the Democratic Party was an indispensable step toward the break-up of the Union.*

Meanwhile, the Republicans held in mid-May in Chicago a tumultuous convention of delegates from all the free states and the borderland. Most Eastern delegates favored the nomination of Seward of New York, or Simon Cameron of Pennsylvania. The largest body of Westerners stood behind Lincoln, although Chase of Ohio had at first about fifty votes. It was the Westerners who filled the galleries and provided the loudest noise. It was they, too, who showed the greatest proficiency in organizing undecided delegations, bargaining for votes, and making the most of Lincoln's unblemished political reputation, which stood in contrast to the spotty record of the Seward-Thurlow Weed machine in New York. They were assisted by the wide and favorable publicity that Lincoln had obtained by his recent Cooper Union address in New York. On the third ballot Lincoln won, with a confident and almost completely united party behind him.

Rhodes has written a spirited narrative of the campaign, catching well its combination of practical politics and high idealism. Subsequent writers have made more than he did of economic issues—the tariff plank, the pledge of free homesteads, the promise of financial support for a Pacific railroad. But they were really of

*minor importance in comparison with the great over-
riding question of slavery. The only serious fault that
more recent students of the campaign of 1860 could
find with Rhodes's narrative is that he does less than
justice to the desperation that Douglas put into his
speeches and the reason for his despairing earnestness. For by election day Douglas had become convinced that the nation faced a deadly conspiracy to
dissever and ruin it. Nobody, of course, can suppose
that the final uprising of several million people against
the Union represented a conspiracy. But Douglas
fully believed that the division of the Democratic
party in Charleston had been brought about by a
conspiracy of Yancey, Rhett, Slidell, and a few other
extremists; he was convinced that their intent had
been to make certain the election of a Republican,
and when that was accomplished, to precipitate the
South into secession; he strongly suspected that they
meant to follow secession by an effort to seize Washington. Of conspiracy in this narrower sense he saw
many evidences.*

The Triumph of Lincoln

It became early apparent [in the convention] that the followers
of Seward in Pennsylvania were few, and that her second choice
lay between Lincoln and Bates, a vote of the delegates being
60 for Lincoln to 45 for Bates as their second choice.

To win the support of the close followers of Cameron, David
Davis promised that he should have a cabinet position in the
event of Lincoln's election; and this, in addition to the other
influences that had been used, secured nearly the whole vote
of Pennsylvania. Lincoln himself knew nothing of these bargains at the time, and they were made against his positive direction. A careful and anxious observer of what was taking
place at Chicago, he sent to his friends this word in writing,
which reached them the day before the nomination: "I agree,"
he said, "with Seward in his 'irrepressible conflict,' but I do not

endorsed his 'higher-law' doctrine"; then, underscoring the words, he wrote: "Make no contracts that will bind me."

Greeley, either ignorant of these bargains, or distrusting that the Pennsylvania and Indiana delegations could be brought to fulfil their part, thought, when the convention met Friday morning, that there could be no concentration of the anti-Seward forces. The Seward managers themselves felt so confident that they sincerely asked, and with no idea of bravado, whom the opposition would like for Vice-President.

The convention met and the candidates were put in nomination without the speeches of eulogy that have since become the rule. At the mention of the name of Seward or Lincoln, the great hall resounded with applause and cheers; but the Lincoln yell far surpassed the other in vigor. Tom Hyer's men had this morning marched through the street to the music of victorious strains, and had so prolonged their march that when they came to the wigwam they found the best places occupied by sturdy Lincoln men; all of Seward's followers were not able to get into the wigwam, and much of the effect of their lusty shouts was therefore lost.

In many contemporaneous and subsequent accounts of this convention, it is set down as an important fact, contributing to the nomination of Lincoln, that on this day the Lincoln men out-shouted the supporters of Seward. One wonders if those wise and experienced delegates interpreted this manipulated noise as the voice of the people. While the shouts for "old Abe" were in a considerable degree spontaneous, due to the fact that the convention was held in his own State, art was not lacking in the production of these manifestations. The Lincoln managers, determined that the voice of Illinois should be literally heard, engaged a Chicago man whose shout, it was said, could be heard above the howling of the most violent tempest on Lake Michigan, and a Doctor Ames, a Democrat living on the Illinois river, who had similar gifts, to organize a *claque* and lead the cheering and applause in the convention hall.

"As long as conventions shall be held, I believe," wrote

Greeley, "no abler, wiser, more unselfish body of delegates from the various States will ever be assembled than that which met at Chicago." The vigor of the young men was tempered by caution and experience of the graybeards. Sixty of the delegates, then unknown beyond their respective districts, were afterwards sent to Congress, and many of them became governors of their States.* That a convention composed of such men—men who had looked behind the scenes and understood the springs of this enthusiasm—should have had its choice of a candidate dictated by the cheers and shouts of a mob, is difficult to believe.

The convention was now ready to ballot. As the calling of the roll proceeded, intense interest was manifested by leaders, by delegates, and by spectators. New England came first, and did not give the number of votes for Seward that had been anticipated, but New York's plumper of 70, announced dramatically by Evarts, almost neutralized this effect. All but 6½ votes of Pennsylvania went to Cameron. Virginia gave surprise by casting 14 votes out of her 23 for Lincoln; and the entire Indiana delegation (26 in number), declaring for the railsplitter of Illinois caused a great sensation. The secretary announced the result of the first ballot: Seward, 173½; Lincoln, 102; Cameron, 50½; Chase, 49; Bates, 48; scattering, 42; necessary to a choice, 233.

The confidence of the Seward managers was not shaken. Intense excitement prevailed. "Call the roll! Call the roll!" fairly hissed through the teeth of the delegates, fiercely im-

* See *Twenty Years of Congress*, Blaine, vol. i. p. 164. There were many noted men, or men who afterwards became so, in the convention. Among them were E. H. Rollins, of New Hampshire; John A. Andrew, Geo. S. Boutwell Edw. L. Pierce, and Samuel Hooper, of Massachusetts; Senator Simmons, of Rhode Island; Gideon Welles, of Connecticut; Evarts, Preston King, and Geo. W. Curtis, of New York; Fred T. Frelinghuysen, of New Jersey; Wilmot, Thaddeus Stevens, and Reeder, of Pennsylvania; Francis P. Blair and Montgomery Blair, of Maryland; Cartter, Corwin, Monroe, Delano, and Giddings, of Ohio; Judd, David Davis, and Browning, of Illinois; Schurz, of Wisconsin; John A. Kasson, of Iowa; Caleb B. Smith, of Indiana; Austin Blair and T. W. Ferry, of Michigan; Francis P. Blair, Jr. and B. Gratz Brown, of Missouri. Greeley and Eli Thayer sat for Oregon.

patient for the second trial. Vermont gave the first surprise by throwing her whole vote, which before had complimented Senator Collamer, to Lincoln; Pennsylvania gave him 48, and Ohio 14. The secretary announced the second ballot. Seward had 184½; Lincoln, 181; and all the rest, 99½ votes. Seward's hopes were blasted. On the third ballot he had 180, while Lincoln had 231½, lacking but 1½ votes of the necessary number to nominate. Before the result was declared, Cartter, of Ohio, mounted his chair, and, gaining the breathless attention of the convention, announced the change of four votes of Ohio from Chase to Lincoln. Many delegates then changed their votes to the successful candidate, and as soon as Evarts could obtain the floor he moved, in melancholy tones, to make the nomination unanimous.

A confidential letter of Greeley to Pike, written three days after the nomination, gives an inkling of the fluctuations of the contest. "Massachusetts," he wrote, "was right in Weed's hands, contrary to all reasonable expectation. . . . It was all we could do to hold Vermont by the most desperate exertions; and I at some times despaired of it. The rest of New England was pretty sound, but part of New Jersey was somehow inclined to sin against light and knowledge. If you had seen the Pennsylvania delegation, and known how much money Weed had in hand, you would not have believed we could do so well as we did. Give Curtin thanks for that. Ohio looked very bad, yet turned out well, and Virginia had been regularly sold out; but the seller could not deliver. We had to rain red-hot bolts on them, however, to keep the majority from going for Seward, who got eight votes here as it was. Indiana was our right bower, and Missouri above praise. It was a fearful week, such as I hope and trust I shall never see repeated."

The nomination of Lincoln was received in the wigwam with such shouts, cheers, and thunders of applause that the report of the cannon on the roof of the building, signalling the event, could at times hardly be heard inside. The excited masses in the street about the wigwam cried out with delight. Chicago was wild with joy. One hundred guns were fired from the top of the Tremont House. Processions of "Old Abe" men bearing rails were everywhere to be seen, and they celebrated their victory by deep potations of their native beverage.

The sorrow and gloom of Seward's supporters were profound and sincere. Thurlow Weed shed bitter tears. Men thought that talent and long service had been set aside in favor of merely an available man borne into undue prominence by the enthusiasm of the mass over a rail-splitting episode; and that the party of moral ideas had sacrificed principle for the sake of success.

Hannibal Hamlin, of Maine, was nominated for Vice-President, and the work of the convention was done.

General delight prevailed in Illinois, Indiana, Ohio, and Iowa at the nominations; Pennsylvania regarded gleefully the defeat of Seward, but the first feeling among the Republicans of the other States was one of disappointment that the New York senator had not been chosen.

Lowell spoke for a large number when, in the October *Atlantic Monthly,* he wrote: "We are of those who at first regretted that another candidate was not nominated at Chicago. ... We should have been pleased with Mr. Seward's nomination for the very reason we have seen assigned for passing him by— that he represented the most advanced doctrines of his party."

On hearing of the nomination, Douglas said to a knot of Republicans who gathered round him in the Capitol: "Gentlemen, you have nominated a very able and a very honest man." Nevertheless, at that time no high opinion of Lincoln's ability existed outside of Illinois. But it was not long before the North came to regard the choice at Chicago as the wisest that could have been made. . . .

The campaign of 1860 was not so animated as that of 1856, yet the problem concerning the division of the electoral votes was substantially the same. Frémont had had 114 electors; of these, and of the 4 of Minnesota, Lincoln was reasonably certain, but he needed 34 more, which must be had from some combination of the votes of the following States: Pennsylvania, which cast 27; New Jersey, 7; Indiana, 13; Illinois, 11; Oregon, 3; California, 4. While not arithmetically necessary to carry Pennsylvania, it was, as in 1856, practically so; for if the Republicans could not obtain the vote of Pennsylvania, they certainly could not hope for that of New Jersey, and one or the other was absolutely required. Had Douglas been the candidate of the united Democracy on the Cincinnati platform, the contest would have been close and exciting and the result doubtful. Douglas himself boasted that had that been the case he would have beaten Lincoln in every State of the Union except Vermont and Massachusetts. Had the Democrats been united on Breckinridge and the Southern platform, the only conceivably different result would have been larger Lincoln majorities in the Northern States. But with the actual state of affairs, after the two nominations at Baltimore, the success of the Republicans seemed to be assured. The split in the Democratic party doomed it to certain defeat before the people; but as the contest went on, a glimmer of hope arose that while it was absolutely impossible for Douglas, Breckinridge, or Bell to obtain a majority of the electoral votes, it was within the bounds of possibility to defeat Lincoln and throw the election into the House of Representatives. Then Breckinridge might be elected, or, the House failing to make a choice, Lane would become President by virtue of having been chosen Vice-President by the Senate.

This contingency created some alarm among the Republicans, whose elation had been great at the failure of the Democrats to cement at Baltimore their divided party. Pennsylvania and Indiana still held their State elections in October, and it was generally conceded that if they went Republican, nothing could prevent the election of Lincoln. Pennsylvania was the more important, and at first the more doubtful, of the two; so that, as in 1856, the contest again hinged on the State election in the Keystone State. Now, however, a new issue had been brought into the canvass. A sequence of the panic of 1857 was great depression in the iron trade. As the Democrats in Congress had voted almost unanimously against the Morrill tariff bill, which, from the Pennsylvania point of view, was expected to cure the present trouble, Democrats in that State were lukewarm. Republicans, on the other hand, were aggressive and went to work in earnest to secure the doubtful vote, by showing the greater devotion of their party to the material interests of the State. The Chicago convention, as we have seen, recognized this sentiment by adopting a tariff plank, which, although it was called ambiguous in expression, had been satisfactory to the Pennsylvania delegation.* But there was no doubt about the Democratic position. Both the Douglas and the Breckinridge conventions had reaffirmed the Cincinnati platform of 1856, which declared in favor of "progressive free trade throughout the world." Andrew G. Curtin, the People's candidate for governor, a man of ability and energy, and a thorough-going protectionist, gave the key-note to the Pennsylvania campaign by pushing into prominence the tariff question. Protection to home industry, and freedom in the territories, were the watchwords; but the promise of higher duties on iron appealed more powerfully to the doubtful voters than did the plea for free soil. Many speeches were made in which the sole issue discussed was the tariff, and it is safe to say that no Pennsylvania advocate of Lincoln and Curtin made a speech in his State without some mention of the question that now dominated all others in the Pennsylvania mind. The effect of this mode of conducting the canvass was so marked that by September it became apparent that, although the Democratic candidate for governor was supported by the adherents of Douglas, Breckinridge, and Bell, the chance of election lay decidedly on the side of Curtin. The fusion in 1856 had been against the Democrats; now the Lincoln party breasted the combined opposition. Douglas himself was affected by the drift of sentiment. Although he had always

* "The *Evening Post* says the tariff plank in the Chicago platform means free trade; the *Tribune* says it means protection. . . . The tariff resolution was intended to conciliate support in Pennsylvania and New Jersey without offending free-trade Republicans in other States."—New York *World*, Oct. 19th, then an independent journal inclining to Bell.

been regarded as inclining to free trade, he argued in a speech made in Pennsylvania in favor of protection to the industries of that great manufacturing State.

But outside of Pennsylvania and New Jersey, one hardly heard the tariff question mentioned. The theoretical difference between the contending parties was regarding slavery in the territories; but so far as the existing territory of the country was concerned, it can hardly be called a practical issue.* No "bleeding Kansas" gave point to Republican arguments as had been the case in 1856. Yet the Republican canvass was a protest against the policy of Pierce and Buchanan, who had used the executive influence invariably against freedom; it was opposition to acquiring more slave territory; it was opposition to the revival in any shape of the African slave-trade, which, if accomplished, would make the territorial question as vital as ever Kansas affairs had done. The speech of Gaulden, a Georgia delegate in the Charleston convention, which had been received with demonstrations of approval, was widely published at the North, and, being regarded as the sincere avowal of one who spoke for many planters, it had produced a marked effect on Northern sentiment. "I am a Southern states-rights man," he had said; "I am an African slave-trader. I am one of those Southern men who believe that slavery is right, morally, religiously, socially, and politically. I believe that the institution of slavery has done more for this country, more for civilization, than all other interests put together. . . . I believe that this doctrine of protection to slavery in the territories is a mere theory, a mere abstraction. . . . We have no slaves to carry to

* The editor of the Memphis *Appeal*, after a trip to New Orleans, wrote a well-considered article from which I extract: "There are not enough slaves in the slave States to cultivate the States which border on the inland sea, two-thirds of the area of each of which has never yet been pressed by the foot of a slave. For centuries to come, unless other sources of supply of Southern labor are opened up, there cannot and will not be, in the possibility of things, another slave territory added to the Union. . . . If men must extend slavery, let them come out for the African slave-trade, but do not be quarrelling about the miserable twaddle of slavery protection by Breckinridge, or of intervention to destroy it, on the other hand, by Lincoln."—Cited by New York *World*, Oct. 8th.

these territories. We can never make another slave State with our present supply of slaves. . . . I would ask my friends of the South to come up in a proper spirit, ask our Northern friends to give us all our rights, and take off the ruthless restrictions which cut off the supply of slaves from foreign lands. . . . I tell you, fellow-Democrats, that the African slave-trader is the true Union man. . . . If any of you Northern Democrats will go home with me to my plantation in Georgia, I will show you some darkies that I bought in Maryland, some that I bought in Virginia, some in Delaware, some in Florida, some in North Carolina, and I will also show you the pure African, the noblest Roman of them all."

"We can extend slavery into new territories," said Seward, at Detroit, September 4th, "and create new slave States only by reopening the African slave-trade." "The same power that abrogated the Missouri Compromise in 1854," said he at Madison, September 12th, "would, if the efforts to establish slavery in Kansas had been successful, have been, after a short time, bold enough, daring enough, desperate enough, to have repealed the prohibition of the African slave-trade. And, indeed, that is yet a possibility now." "I have said that this battle was fought and this victory won," declared Seward, at St. Paul, September 18th. "There is one danger remaining—one only. Slavery can never more force itself or be forced, from the stock that exists among us, into the territories of the United States. But the cupidity of trade and the ambition of those whose interests are identified with slavery are such that they may clandestinely and surreptitiously reopen, either within the forms of law or without them, the African slave-trade, and may bring in new cargoes of African slaves at one hundred dollars a head, and scatter them into the territories; and once getting possession of new domain, they may again renew their operations against the patriotism of the American people." The slave States, Seward averred at New York city, November 2d, "are going to say next, as they logically must, that they should reopen the African slave-trade, and so furnish the supplies for slavery."

While the divided opposition made Republican success almost certain, the lack of a common enemy, who took the same form and advocated the same principles everywhere, deprived the canvass of the vigor and excitement that prevail when a line is sharply drawn between two parties on one decided issue. In New England—excepting Connecticut—and in the Northwest, the contest lay between Lincoln and Douglas. The other candidates were barely mentioned, and as Douglas had no chance whatever of election, the contest could not be called spirited. In New York, Pennsylvania, New Jersey, and Connecticut, Breckinridge and Bell had a following; but in those States there was little enthusiasm, except that drawn out by Republican meetings. In the slave States outside of Missouri, the contest lay between Breckinridge and Bell. Douglas had supporters everywhere, but it was recognized he could carry no slave State but Missouri, and his candidacy in the South resulted only as a diversion which redounded to the advantage of Bell, for the supporters of Douglas and Bell agreed in pronounced devotion to the Union; while it was practically true, which Douglas intimated at Baltimore, that, although every Breckinridge man was not a disunionist, every disunionist in America was a Breckinridge man. As the canvass proceeded, Lincoln, as representing the more positive resistance to Southern domination, drew to himself Douglas Democrats at the North; while Breckinridge, as representing the logical Southern doctrine, drew from the adherents of Douglas at the South.

More political machinery was employed in the Republican canvass than in 1856. Office-seekers had been present in force at the Chicago convention, and, as the prospect of success increased, their number grew and they were on hand everywhere to do the necessary work of party organization. The Wide-awakes, in their inception merely a happy accident, were turned to good account in arousing enthusiasm. Companies and battalions of them, wearing capes and bearing torches, were a necessary feature of every Republican demonstration. Lincoln's early occupation was glorified, and men bearing fence-rails might be seen in every procession. In Boston, a significant feature of a parade was a rail-splitters' battalion composed of men averaging six feet two inches in height. The Sumner Blues, a company of colored men from Portland, took part in the same procession, for it was not overlooked that the result of the election might affect the lot of the negro. Lincoln meetings, large and small, addressed by men of character and ability, were a feature of the summer and autumn; in every village, town, and county, there was frequent opportunity for the inquiring voter to familiarize himself with the issue before the people. Nearly all the educational features of the campaign of 1856 were repeated; the published debates of Lincoln and Douglas were read with interest and effect; yet less reliance was placed on newspapers and campaign documents than in the previous presidential canvass. The religious element, with the active personal participation of the clergy, which was one of the characteristics of 1856, was not now so obtrusive or pronounced; but in New England and along the lines of New England influence, the hearty wishes and fervent prayers of most Protestant ministers were for Republican success. Henry Ward Beecher, and Dr. Chapin, the eminent Universalist, did not scruple to deliver political speeches from their pulpits the Sunday evening before the election. The young men and first voters, who had been studying the slavery question since 1852, took a vital interest in this campaign. They read the political literature with avidity. Filled with enthusiasm, they were glad to enroll themselves in the Wide-awake order, and make manifest their determination to do all in their power to avert the longer misrule of the Southern oligarchy. "The Republican party," said Seward at Cleveland, October 4th, "is a party chiefly of young men. Each successive year brings into its ranks an increasing proportion of the young men of this country." Northern school-teachers, under the inspiration of the moral principle at stake, impressed upon eager listening boys that they were living in historic times, and that a great question, fraught with weal or woe to the country, was about to be decided. The torch-bearers of literature were on the side of Lincoln. "I vote with the Republican party," wrote Holmes to

Motley; "I cannot hesitate between them and the Democrats." Whittier offered the resolutions at a Republican meeting at Amesbury; William Cullen Bryant was at the head of the
Lincoln electoral ticket of New York, and George William
Curtis spoke frequently from the stump. Few political arguments have been more cogent, or expressed in choicer phrase,
than that of James Russell Lowell, published in the *Atlantic
Monthly* for October. It may be said to represent the opinion of
the men of thought and culture of the country. "The slave-holding interest," he wrote, "has gone on step by step, forcing concession after concession, till it needs but little to secure it forever in the political supremacy of the country. Yield to its latest
demand—let it mould the evil destiny of the territories—and
the thing is done past recall. The next presidential election is to
say yes or no. . . . We believe this election is a turning-point in
our history. . . . In point of fact . . . we have only two parties in
the field: those who favor the extension of slavery, and those
who oppose it." The Republican party "is not unanimous about
the tariff, about State rights, about many other questions of
policy. What unites the Republicans is . . . a common resolve to
resist the encroachments of slavery everywhen and everywhere. . . . It is in a moral aversion to slavery as a great wrong
that the chief strength of the Republican party lies." The question that needs an answer in the election is: "What policy will
secure the most prosperous future to the helpless territories
which our decision is to make or mar for all coming time? What
will save the country from a Senate and Supreme Court where
freedom shall be forever at a disadvantage?"

Dr. Francis Lieber, who for years held a chair in the University of South Carolina, and was now a professor in Columbia
College, presided over a German Republican meeting in New
York city. When the news reached South Carolina, the Euphra-
dian Society of the college expelled him from honorary membership, and his bust and portrait were removed from the halls
of the society. "I am denounced at this moment at the South in
very virulent language," wrote Lieber to his son.

But one argument was used with any show of success by the

opponents of the Republicans at the North. The sectional character of the Republican party was urged, with the averment that if Lincoln were elected, the cotton States would certainly secede from the Union. Southern speakers of ability and influence made such declarations freely, and the press teemed with threats of like tenor. The menaces were no more arrogant than those of 1856, but they seemed more grave and sincere. It may be that the Southern leaders had little idea that Lincoln could be elected, and used the threats of disunion as an electioneering cry; but the less prominent speakers were terribly in earnest, and avowed themselves ready to make good their words. The slave-holders whom they addressed were persuaded that Lincoln's election would mean emancipation; the poor whites were convinced that negro equality and citizenship would follow. At the South, the Wide-awakes were regarded as a semi-military organization whose determination was to see Lincoln inaugurated if elected; and soon companies of minute-men as a counter-demonstration began forming in the cotton States.

In judging these events, it is impossible to divest ourselves of the knowledge of the end, yet there certainly seems in the Southern threats a seriousness that foreboded trouble, and thus to many well-informed men they appeared in 1860.

Douglas, since his nomination, had spoken in several Southern States. He knew more of the aims of the secessionists than any other Northern man, and he was sincere when he declared at Chicago: "I believe that this country is in more danger now than at any other moment since I have known anything of public life." The supporters of Douglas and Bell made no attempt to conceal their fears, but the cry of "wolf" was so obviously in their interest that Republicans could not be blamed for regarding it as an effort to frighten people from voting for Lincoln. And for the most part it was so looked upon. Seward said at St. Paul: "Slavery to-day is for the first time not only powerless, but without influence in the American republic. For the first time in the history of the United States, no man in a free State can be bribed to vote for slavery. . . . For the first time in the history of the republic, the slave power has not even the ability to terrify or alarm the freeman so as to make him submit, or even to compromise. It rails now with a feeble voice, instead of thundering as it did in our ears for twenty or thirty years past. With a feeble and muttering voice they cry out that they will tear the Union to pieces. . . . 'Who's afraid?' Nobody's afraid. Nobody can be bought." "For ten, aye for twenty, years," declared Seward at New York, four days before the election, "these threats have been renewed, in the same language and in the same form, about the first day of November every four years when it happened to come before the day of the presidential election. I do not doubt but that these Southern statesmen and politicians think they are going to dissolve the Union, but I think they are going to do no such thing." Lowell spoke of "the hollowness of those fears for the safety of the Union in case of Mr. Lincoln's election," and called to mind that false alarms had been sounded before. "The old Mumbo-Jumbo," he asserted, "is occasionally paraded at the North, but, however many old women may be frightened, the pulse of the stock-market remains provokingly calm." A certain support for this view was found in the expression of the Douglas and Bell newspapers at the South that deprecated any move in the direction of secession until an overt act had been committed by the coming Republican administration.

There were Republicans who knew too much of the South to regard these threats as gasconade, yet who were determined to force the issue. They had not forgotten that the cry of "The Union is in danger" had elected Buchanan; and they could see no hope for the country if the Southern party were always going to be able to frighten voters from opposing the extension of slavery. Therefore, in their opinion, the North was bound to answer the threat of the South by a defiance. "We are summoned to surrender," said Carl Schurz at St. Louis. "And what price do they offer to pay us for all our sacrifices if we submit? Why, slavery can then be preserved!"

Dr. Lieber, who knew by long actual contact the people of

both sections, and who was linked to the South and the North by ties of family and friendship, judged the situation with remarkable insight. "As to the threats of dissolution of the Union should Mr. Lincoln be elected," he wrote to his son, "I do not reply, 'Try it, let us see'; on the contrary, I believe the threat is made in good earnest, and that it is quite possible to carry it into execution. . . . It sometimes has occurred to me that what Thucydides said of the Greeks at the time of the Peloponnesian War applies to us at present. 'The Greeks,' he said, did not understand each other any longer, though they spoke the same language; words received a different meaning in different parts.' "

In truth, when Senator Hammond wrote, "Every sensible man in the country must know that the election of Mr. Lincoln will put the Union at imminent and instant hazard;" when James L. Orr said that "the honor and safety of the South required its prompt secession from the Union in the event of the election of a Black Republican to the presidency;" and when Alexander Stephens declared that the success of Lincoln was certain, and the result would be "undoubtedly an attempt at secession and revolution," Northern men of discretion were forced to pause and ask whether there were not as much sincerity as bravado in the threats that were heard from all parts of the South.

Efforts were not lacking to bring about a union of the opponents of the Republicans. As has been stated, the followers of Douglas and of Bell and Breckinridge supported the same ticket in Pennsylvania. In Indiana, where Bell had but little support, the Douglas and Breckinridge factions united on a candidate for governor. A partial fusion on an electoral ticket was accomplished in Pennsylvania and New Jersey; a more perfect one in New York. Jefferson Davis tried to concentrate the opposition to Lincoln on a single candidate. Bell, "profoundly impressed by the danger which threatened the country," was willing to withdraw in conjunction with Douglas and Breckinridge, provided some man more acceptable than any of the three could be put forward, and he gave Davis an authorization to open negotiations with that end in view. Breckinridge gave Davis similar authority. The matter was broached in an amicable spirit to Douglas. "He replied that the scheme proposed was impracticable, because his friends, mainly Northern Democrats, if he were withdrawn, would join in the support of Lincoln rather than of any one who should supplant him; that he was in the hands of his friends, and was sure they would not accept the proposition." But at no time had Douglas any hope of election. Early in the canvass he told Wilson and Burlingame that Lincoln would be elected; and we may believe him sincere when in September he declared: "Believing that the Union is in danger, I will make any personal sacrifice to preserve it. If the withdrawal of my name would tend to defeat Mr. Lincoln, I would this moment withdraw it." When he had this conference with Wilson and Burlingame, he told them that he was going South to urge submission to the probable verdict, and after his stumping tour in New England he wended his way southward. At Norfolk, Virginia, he had an opportunity to avow his sentiments. The head of the Breckinridge electoral ticket for Virginia asked him: "If Abraham Lincoln be elected President, will the Southern States be justified in seceding from the Union?"

"To this I answer emphatically no," said Douglas. "The election of a man to the presidency by the American people, in conformity with the Constitution of the United States, would not justify any attempt at dissolving this glorious confederacy."

Another question was put: "If they, the Southern States, secede from the Union upon the inauguration of Abraham Lincoln, before he commits an overt act against their constitutional rights, will you advise or vindicate resistance by force to their secession?" Douglas replied: "I answer emphatically that it is the duty of the President of the United States, and all others in authority under him, to enforce the laws of the United States as passed by Congress and as the court expound them. And I, as in duty bound by my oath of fidelity to the Constitution, would do all in my power to aid the government of the United States

in maintaining the supremacy of the laws against all resistance
to them, come from what quarter it might. In other words, I
think the President of the United States, whoever he may be,
should treat all attempts to break up the Union by resistance to
its laws as Old Hickory treated the nullifiers of 1832. . . . I
acknowledge the inherent and inalienable right to revolution
whenever a grievance becomes too burdensome to be borne."
But the election of Lincoln "is not such a grievance as would
justify revolution or secession." This declaration brought down
upon the head of Douglas a shower of abuse from the secessionist faction at the South. The Charleston *Mercury* contemp-
tuously called him "a regular old John Adams federalist and
consolidationist." Nothing daunted, however, and in spite of the
remonstrance of Senator Clingman, a political friend, Douglas
repeated assertions similar in emphasis and vigor at other places
in the South. At Baltimore he still further elaborated his position and warned his hearers of impending danger. "States that
secede," he declared, "cannot screen themselves under the pretence that resistance to their acts 'would be making war upon
sovereign States.' Sovereign States cannot commit treason. In-
dividuals may. . . . I tell you, my fellow-citizens," he continued,
"I believe this Union is in danger. In my opinion, there is a
mature plan through the Southern States to break up the Union.
I believe the election of a Black Republican is to be the signal
for that attempt, and that the leaders of the scheme desire the
election of Lincoln so as to have an excuse for disunion."

Douglas took the unusual course for a presidential candidate
of visiting different parts of the country and discussing the
political issues and their personal bearing. Speaking on all occasions—from the platform of the railroad car, the balcony of
the hotel, at monster mass-meetings, frequently jaded from
travel, many times without preparation and on the suggestion of
the moment—he said much that was trivial and undignified; but
he also said much that was patriotic, unselfish, and pregnant
with constitutional wisdom. His love for the Union and devotion to the Constitution inspired all his utterances. The cyno-

sure of all eyes, he taught lessons that were destined to bear important fruit. Coldly received at the South, looked upon as a renegade, he aroused great enthusiasm everywhere at the North, and his personal presence was the only feature that gave any life to the struggle against the Republicans.

Apart from the rail-splitting episode, the personality of Lincoln counted for little in the campaign. It was everywhere conceded that he was thoroughly honest, but his opponents sneered at his reputed capacity, and, outside of his own State, few regarded his nomination as other than the sacrifice of commanding ability in favor of respectable mediocrity. In popular estimation his great merit consisted in being able to carry the doubtful States. Schurz deemed it necessary to assure his constituents at Milwaukee that Lincoln was not merely an available candidate, "a second or third rate man like Polk or Pierce," but that the debate with Douglas had shown that he had a "lucid mind and honest heart." The campaign went on without direction, with hardly a suggestion even, from the Republican standard-bearer. Seward filled the minds of Republicans, attracting such attention and honor, and arousing such enthusiasm, that the closing months of the campaign were the most brilliant epoch of his life. It was then he reached the climax of his career. His grief and sense of humiliation at not receiving the nomination in Chicago were poignant. "I am," he wrote, "a leader deposed by my own party, in the hour of organization for decisive battle." In common with his intimate friends, he charged his defeat chiefly to Greeley. He felt towards that influential editor as much vindictiveness as was possible in a man of so amiable a nature. But he did not retire to his tent. At the time of the meeting of the convention he had left the Senate and gone to his home in Auburn, where he expected to receive the news of his success surrounded by the friends and neighbors whom he loved, and who repaid his love by veneration. When the news of Lincoln's nomination came, and when his friends were quivering with disappointment, and no one in Auburn had the heart to write the conventional editorial endorsing the nomination,

Seward, smiling, took pen in hand and wrote the article for the Republican evening journal. "No truer or firmer defenders of the Republican faith," he declared, "could have been found in the Union than the distinguished and esteemed citizens on whom the honors of nomination have fallen." He also gave at once, over his own signature, a public and emphatic support to platform and candidates; and, while then of the opinion that he would soon seek the repose of private life, he came, when time had assuaged his grief, to a better conclusion, and devoted his hearty and energetic efforts to the success of the cause. "The magnanimity of Mr. Seward, since the result of the convention was known," wrote Lowell, "has been a greater ornament to him and a greater honor to his party than his election to the presidency would have been." Seward's friends followed the example set them. "We all feel that New York and the friends of Seward have acted nobly," wrote Swett to Weed, after the election.

In the early part of September, Seward began a tour of speech-making at Detroit. He went as far west as St. Paul and Lawrence, Kansas, ending with an address to his townsmen the night before election. The sincere and hearty demonstrations wherever he went were an "earnest tribute." The crowds that gathered to hear him felt what Schurz had put in words, that Seward was "the intellectual head of the political anti-slavery movement," and had "in the hearts of his friends a place which hardly another man in the nation could fill." As the people of the sure Republican States, where he for the most part spoke, heard the words of wisdom, they could not but feel a profound regret that he was not their standard-bearer. When we consider the great moral question involved, the variety of presentation, the many-sided treatment, the fearlessness of statement, the appeal to reason and the highest feelings, the absence of any attempt to delude the people by the smallest misrepresentation, Seward's efforts in this campaign are the most remarkable stump-speeches ever delivered in this country. While he paid Lincoln well-chosen compliments, the references to the opposing candidates were courteous. The speeches are a fit type of the campaign—a campaign conducted on a great moral principle. Seward reaffirmed almost everywhere the declaration of the "irrepressible conflict," maintaining that the Republicans simply reverted to the theory and practice of the fathers. He made appear at all times the political, social, and moral evil of slavery. "There is no man," he said, "who has an enlightened conscience who is indifferent on the subject of human bondage." Yet he spoke with forbearance of the people of the South. "You must demonstrate the wisdom of our cause," he affirmed, "with gentleness, with patience, with loving-kindness, to your brethren of the slave States." He maintained that "most men . . . are content to keep the Union with slavery if it cannot be kept otherwise." At Chicago he showed what a bulwark of freedom was the great Northwest, by its prosperity and commercial importance; and he prophesied that "the last Democrat is born in this nation . . . who will maintain the Democratic principles which constitute the present creed of the Democratic party." The night before election he averred that the question to be decided was: "Shall freedom, justice, and humanity ultimately and in the end prevail; are these republican institutions of ours safe and permanent?" He referred to the threats of disunion, and while expressing no defiance, he declared: "Fellow-citizens, it is time, high time, that we know whether this is a constitutional government under which we live. It is high time that we know, since the Union is threatened, who are its friends and who are its enemies."

At the beginning of the canvass no doubt existed on the part of the Republican managers of any of the important States but Pennsylvania and Indiana. Occasional fears were expressed about Indiana as late as August, but that State soon came to be regarded as reasonably sure. By the latter part of August, also, owing to the vigorous and effective canvass under the leadership of Curtin and McClure, there were adequate grounds for believing that Pennsylvania would elect the People's candidate for governor in October, and choose Lincoln electors in Novem-

ber. Then Republican alarm began to be excited in regard to the
State of New York. "Brethren in the doubtful States, trust New
York; you may do it undoubtingly," said the *Tribune* in July;
but a different tale had to be told in September, when it announced that "the opposition are going to concentrate their
efforts on New York." "I think," wrote Lincoln to Thurlow
Weed, "there will be the most extraordinary effort ever made to
carry New York for Douglas. You and all others who write me
from your State think the effort cannot succeed, and I hope you
are right. Still, it will require close watching and great efforts on
the other side."

Without the thirty-five electoral votes of the Empire State,
Lincoln could not be chosen President; and a determined effort
now began to be made to carry that State against him. Negotiations were had with a view of a fusion electoral ticket; and after
protracted conferences, some ending in failure, but renewed
again with hope, a scheme of fusion was at last completed. Supporters of Douglas, Bell, and Breckinridge were to vote for common electors; of these, eighteen were apportioned to Douglas,
ten to Bell, and seven to Breckinridge.* This combination had
a show of success, but it had the faults of a negative programme.
No intelligent opponent of Lincoln could for a moment think it
possible to elect by the people any one of the other candidates,
and the movement, divested of subterfuge, was simply one to
throw the election into the House of Representatives. Many
men, alarmed at the condition of affairs, thought the election of
Lincoln a lesser evil than to have the contest continued in Congress. In spite of the union of the opposition, the chances were
all with the Republicans. "I find no reason to doubt," wrote
Seward to Lincoln, after his return from the Western tour, "that
this State will redeem all the promises we have made." The Germans strongly supported Lincoln. Carl Schurz was making
speeches everywhere in his favor. The majority of the Fill-

* New York *Tribune*, Sept. 25th: "New York, especially, was the arena
of a struggle as intense, as vehement and energetic, as had ever been
known."—Greeley's American Conflict, vol. i. 326. "It was only after
a most determined canvass that fusion was defeated in New York."—
Recollections of a Busy Life, Greeley, p. 392.

moreans of 1856 were also on his side. The elections of Maine and Vermont in September increased the encouragement of the Republicans, but as New England was considered strongly Republican, the result had little effect on the opposition.

Although great confidence was felt and expressed in the success of Curtin at the October State election, so much depended on the result in Pennsylvania that the Republicans felt a nervous anxiety until the votes had been counted. This was especially the case, since the week before election the Democrats had sent considerable money into Pennsylvania, making a last desperate effort to carry the State. But October 9th decided the contest. Curtin carried Pennsylvania by thirty-two thousand majority, and Lane in Indiana had nine thousand seven hundred and fifty-seven more votes than his competitor. The prominence given the tariff question, and the undoubted position of the supporters of Lincoln on that issue, contributed more than any other one factor to the result in Pennsylvania. After the October elections it was conceded, South as well as North, that nothing could prevent the election of Lincoln. "Emancipation or revolution is now upon us," said the Charleston *Mercury*. There began a stampede of floating voters, whose desire to be on the winning side overpowered other motives. The Republican National Committee in a public address considered that the October elections settled the presidential contest, but urged unabated effort in order that a majority of the House of Representatives in the next Congress might be secured. From this time on the contest had the flavor rather of a congressional than a presidential canvass, except in so far as imposing Wide-awake demonstrations implied larger contrivance and greater expense than usual.

The conditions in New York were somewhat different from those existing in the other Northern States. A faint hope lingered that the fusionists might there be successful. The commercial and property interests of New York city, honestly fearing secession in the event of Republican success, bestirred themselves to use their most potent weapon in averting the threatened danger. It was reported that William B. Astor had contributed one million dollars, and wealthy merchants a second million, in aid of the fusion ticket. A systematic effort to frighten business and financial interests was made with the result of causing a stock-panic in Wall Street during the last days of October. The grave charge was made that the Secretary of the Treasury, on a visit to New York city at this time, had abetted this movement by avowing repeatedly, and with no attempt at concealment, that Lincoln's election would be followed by disunion and a general derangement of the monetary concerns of the country.

Three days before the election Thurlow Weed wrote Lincoln: "Since writing you last Sunday, the fusion leaders have largely increased their fund, and they are now using money lavishly. This stimulates and to some extent inspires confidence, and all the confederates are at work. Some of our friends are nervous. But I have no fear of the result in this State."

Election day came and passed off quickly. In New York city, where excitement and trouble were expected—for in the decade between 1850-60 turbulent elections were not infrequent—the election was the most orderly and quiet that could be remembered. Even the newspaper reporters were forced to confess that the day was intolerably dull. The Republicans were successful. Lincoln and Hamlin carried States which would give them one hundred and eighty electoral votes; Douglas would receive twelve, Breckinridge seventy-two, and Bell thirty-nine. Lincoln had carried every free State but New Jersey, whose electoral vote was divided, Lincoln receiving four, and Douglas three of her votes. Of the popular vote Lincoln had 1,857,610; Douglas, 1,291,574; Breckinridge, 850,082; Bell, 646,124. Lincoln had 930,170 votes less than all his opponents combined.* But while all the members of the next Congress had not been elected,

* Greeley's *American Conflict,* vol. i. p. 328, where a sufficiently exact attempt is made to apportion the fusion vote. Other interesting data are given. Lincoln received in the slave States 26,430; Douglas, 163,525. Breckinridge received in the free States 279,211; Bell, 130,151. Lincoln's majority over Douglas was 566,036. Breckinridge lacked 135,057 of a majority in the slave States.

enough was known to make it certain that in neither the House nor the Senate would the Republicans have a majority. This was understood and admitted to be the case at the South.

While the electoral vote Douglas received was insignificant, his popular vote was a triumph. With the influence and patronage of the administration against him, holding the machinery of the party in most of the Northern States only by protracted struggles, fighting Breckinridge at the South and Lincoln at the North, waging a hopeless battle, and attracting hardly any votes by the prospect of success, it was a high tribute that so many turned out on election day to show their confidence and do him honor.

On election day, Longfellow wrote in his journal: "Voted early," and the day after: "Lincoln is elected; overwhelming majorities in New York and Pennsylvania. This is a great victory; one can hardly overrate its importance. It is the redemption of the country. Freedom is triumphant." Motley, from across the sea, wrote, when the news reached him: "Although I have felt little doubt as to the result for months past, . . . yet as I was so intensely anxious for the success of the Republican cause, I was on tenterhooks till I actually knew the result. I rejoice at last in the triumph of freedom over slavery more than I can express. Thank God it can no longer be said, after the great verdict just pronounced, that the common law of my country is slavery, and that the American flag carries slavery with it wherever it goes.

The meaning of the election was that the great and powerful North declared slavery an evil, and insisted that it should not be extended; that while the institution would be sacredly respected where it existed, the conduct of the national government must revert to the policy of the fathers and confine slavery within bounds; that they hoped, if it were restricted, the time might come when the Southern people would themselves acknowledge that they were out of tune with the enlightened world and take steps gradually to abolish the system. The persistent and emphatic statement by the opposition that the Republicans were the radical party had fixed that idea in the public mind; but in truth they represented the noblest conservatism. They simply advocated a return to the policy of Washington, Jefferson, and Madison.

The North had spoken. In every man's mind rose unbidden the question, What would be the answer of the South?

SINCE *Rhodes wrote the third volume of his* History, *more elaborate and searching studies of the culture and social life of the period have been published. Historians of literature in particular have done justice to the novelists, essayists, and poets of the fifties, one of the richest decades in our annals. When Rhodes wrote, the greatness of Herman Melville, for example, was quite unrecognized, and the depth as well as social variety to be found in the writings of the novelists, poets, travel writers, and memoirists of the period were not comprehended as they can be since the publication of Van Wyck Brooks's volumes and Edmund Wilson's* Patriotic Gore. *On the debit side, Rhodes found a great deal of political corruption, much that was meretricious in taste, especially among fashionable people, too much violence all along the frontier, and so much dullness in the large towns that one caustic Frenchman remarked that the most cheerful place he could find in one of them was the cemetery. Men sought money all too avidly, and large fortunes were becoming numerous. As a result, the fashionable watering places like Saratoga and Newport required of their sojourners not only good manners and respectability but wealth. The country still had an amount of uncouth deportment, vulgar speech, and tobacco spitting that shocked Europeans, but it was becoming distinctly less provincial. It made its own standards, and observed them; it cared less about the opinion of foreigners.*

No doubt Rhodes was correct in finding that Americans were an especially religious people, conservative in matters of faith and dogma. The Bible held a potent place in education, letters, and morals. He was probably justified in asserting that the sexual morality of the country was higher than in Europe; Tocqueville had said this at an earlier date, as Bryce said it later. Nor, in spite of the cheapness of whiskey, did Americans drink as habitually and heavily as the people of Continental Europe. The position of women was high, and in the North and West they lived a freer, more vigorous life than abroad; for in new communities struggling with the wilderness, they simply had to show more independence and initiative. But Rhodes presents all his generalizations with moderation, sup-

porting them not with statistical tables or the fruit of questionnaires but with the statements of shrewd observers. One of his most positive passages offers a denial of the frequent charge that Americans worked too hard. They did not take enough exercise, he granted, but he thought that their hard work protected them from vice and slackness.

Rhodes would have dealt more incisively with the influence of the frontier on American life had he possessed some of the later works on Frederick Jackson Turner, Mark Twain, and their ideas. He could have written a sharper delineation of the American mind of the time had he possessed some of the books of a subsequent date analyzing the democratic faith in America and on romanticism, pragmatism, the conflict between idealism and materialism, and the idea of progress. Most later students would agree that Rhodes gives too little attention to the gospel of success as a dominant agent in shaping American society. With the limited tools that he possessed, however, the historian ably summarized the surface aspects of his subject.

American Society, 1850–60

To contrast society, in the sense in which the word is used by the sociologist, of the decade of 1850-60 with that of our own day, is for the student an easy task: two remarkable books furnish him complete and well-digested materials. Fortunate the country that has two such eulogists as De Tocqueville and Bryce! They had philosophic minds; and, loving America and loving the truth, they were correct delineators. The earlier traveller has described us as we were in 1832; the later has depicted the America of 1880-90. While the United States of 1850-60 is neither the United States of De Tocqueville nor the United States of Bryce, the development of one into the other was going on, and, in noting how some phases of the earlier life were disappearing, or were being merged into that of our own time, we may grasp the salient points that distinguish the decade we are studying.

The changes have been indeed great. The time before the war seems far removed from our present generation. the civil conflict is a sharp dividing line between two characteristically distinct periods, and it has been considered the cause of the transformation. If we confine our attention to the South, whose territory was devastated, whose property and the flower of whose youth were spent, and whose social system was revolutionized, we need seek no further reason; for in the States that seceded, the chronology of "before the war" or "since the war" has a living meaning such as it has never obtained at the North. A study of contemporary Europe, a close examination of social forces, will show us causes more potent than the civil commotion in bringing about the alteration that is so striking a fact of the last half of our century. These far-reaching forces are the railroad and its adjunct the telegraph.

Effects not infrequently attributed to the war and to the legislation which grew out of it had begun to show themselves before 1860. The executive and legislative departments of the national government were undoubtedly as much tainted with corruption between 1850-60 as they are at the present time. This will be clearly illustrated if we recall the scandal of the Galpin claim, and mention that, in 1857, three members of the House of Representatives were proved guilty of corrupt practices, and resigned their seats to avoid expulsion. Plentiful evidence of the popular opinion that dishonesty prevailed may be found in the literature of the time.

It was the common belief in the decade we are studying that, except in New York, New Jersey, and Pennsylvania, there was little or no bribery in the legislatures of the States. One does not often meet the charge that a candidate for United States senator had bought enough members of a caucus or a legislature to insure his election. But from that time to this the deterioration of our legislatures is striking.

Municipal rottenness already existed in New York, and perhaps in some other Eastern cities. New England, the States west of Pennsylvania, and the Southern States do not appear to have been infected. The condition of New York may have been as bad as it is to-day; but the general complaint, now heard in almost every city having a population of more than 200,000, of bribery, jobbing, and misused funds, is not a feature of the decade of 1850–60.*

* The New York *Tribune* of June 29, 1860, has a noteworthy article, entitled "New York and Her Rulers." The writer (probably Greeley) said: "For mayor we have Fernando Wood; for chief dispensers of criminal justice, George G. Barnard and Abraham D. Russell. . . . The law is ostentatiously, persistently defied, in order that the alderman and their confederates may steal a good share of the money. Jobs are got up and 'put through' the two boards merely as cover for such division of the spoils; operators divide with aldermen and councilmen. . . . Our great tax-payers look on at all this with stolid apathy, or bribe the requisite functionaries to undervalue their property. . . . The men of property, of culture, of leisure, having abdicated, the actual government of our city to-day rests on this basis:

"1. A conspiracy of ten thousand rumsellers to get rich or live uselessly at the general cost. . . .

"2. Next in order come the great army of roughs sympathizing and co-operating with the rum-sellers."

Bryce truly wrote: "There is no denying that the government of cities is the one conspicuous failure of the United States. . . . In New York, extravagance, corruption, and mismanagement have revealed themselves on the largest scale. . . . But there is not a city with a population exceeding 200,000 where the poison germs have not sprung into a vigorous life; and in some of the smaller ones, down to 70,000, it needs no microscope to note the results of their growth. Even in cities of the third rank, similar phenomena may occasionally be discerned."—Vol. i. p. 608.

For a dark picture of public corruption based on an article in the New York *Herald*, May, 1858, and the report of the Bremen consul in New York, see *Geschichte der Handelskrisen*, Wirth, pp. 346, 347.

The New York *Herald* of June 6, 1856, in making the comparison of municipal regulations in Paris, London, Berlin, and Vienna with that of New York, to the striking disadvantage of the latter, says: "The only city in Europe where corruption and filth and disorder hold as much sway as they do in New York is the city of Rome, which is under an ecclesiastical government."

Andrew D. White wrote in the *Forum* for Dec., 1890, p. 361: "About a year since I stood upon the wharves and in the streets of Constantinople. I had passed from one end of Europe to the other: these were the worst I had seen since I left home, and a spasm of homesickness came over me. During all my residence in foreign cities, never before had the remembrance of New York, Philadelphia, and other American towns been so vividly brought back to me. There in Constantinople, as the result of Turkish despotism, was the same hap-hazard, careless, dirty, corrupt system which we in America know so well as the result of mob despotism; the same tumble-down wharves, the same sewage in the docks, the same

Outside of three or four of the largest Eastern cities, the direct use of money to buy voters was substantially unknown.

President Buchanan wrote, in 1858, that "we never heard until within a recent period of the employment of money to carry elections." Wherever, outside of New York City, this form of bribery was practised, it was done irregularly and in a bungling way. The present system, which, combining business and military methods, has decided many important elections, and seems able to circumvent any laws, did not then exist. Men did not boast of how the floating vote had been caught by the buying of captains of tens and of fifties; and it is safe to say that no man elected to high national office, when making a post-prandial speech, gloried in his party's and his own success by the judicious use of money in a close and seemingly purchasable State.

Yet the United States of 1860 was more corrupt than the United States of De Tocqueville. De Tocqueville visited this country when the peculiar conditions that mark the Jacksonian era were seen in their pristine vigor; but, although he learned that the honesty of public functionaries was often doubted, he did not hear that voters were bought with money. The testimony of Pike is of great weight, for, although an ardent Republican, he at this time looked on passing events with the eye of a philosopher. "There can be no doubt in any reasonable mind," he wrote from Niagara Falls, June 1, 1860, "that we are entered in this country upon what may be fairly termed the Era of Corruption in the administration of public affairs. We have reached it by rapid and, in some sort, natural stages. Not that all the corruption of mankind has at once centered upon our time, but circumstances have conspired to give it a remarkable development at this period. I confidently assume that the mu-

---

'pavements fanged with murderous stones,' the same filth, the same ob-stacles to travel and traffic. . . . At various times it has been my lot to sojourn in nearly every one of the greater European municipalities, from Edinburg to Athens, from St. Petersburg to Naples, from Paris to Buda-Pesth. . . . In every respect for which a city exists, they are vastly supe-rior to our own."

nicipal government of New York City, the legislature of New York State (as well as some other States), and the action of federal authority during the two past administrations are so well known to the public that this declaration will, without more elaborate proof, pass unchallenged by the intelligent reader."

By the decade of 1850-60, the accumulation of large fortunes had begun. This tendency was not a feature of the United States of De Tocqueville; it was coeval with the extension of railroads and the telegraph. If it be true that, with this growth of enormous fortunes, poverty has become more abject, this tendency had begun before the war, and has been the result rather of the constantly deteriorating character of the European immigration than of industrial changes on our own soil. *

The student of morals and manners is fortunate in possessing, in addition to the incomparable works of De Tocqueville and Bryce, the recorded observations of many foreign travellers. On the whole, our country has been fairly treated. The captious

* "With the princely fortunes accumulating on the one hand, and the stream of black poverty pouring in on the other, contrasts of condition are springing up as hideous as those of the Old World."—New York *Tribune*, April 21, 1854, cited by Chambers, Things in America, p. 199. David A. Wells wrote in 1876: "It cannot . . . be doubted that the general tendency of events during the last quarter of a century of our national history has been to more unequally distribute the results of industrial effort, to accumulate great fortunes in a few hands—in short, to cause the rich to grow richer and the poor poorer."—*First Century of the Republic,* p. 172. Atkinson came to a different conclusion. "Is it not true," he asks, "that while the rich may have become relatively no poorer, the poor have been steadily growing richer, not so much in the accumulation of personal wealth, as in the power of commanding the service of capital in ever-increasing measure at a less proportionate charge? Can it be denied that labor as distinguished from capital has been and is securing to its own use an increasing share of an increasing product?"—*The Industrial Progress of the Nation,* p. 79. It is impossible for any man to present all the evidence by which he arrives at such a conviction. It comes from much reading, observation, reflection, and a comparison of views with other observers. My own notion is, that Atkinson is nearer right than Wells. The different years in which Wells and Atkinson wrote may account in some degree for their opposite conclusions. Atkinson wrote in 1887. While there are now many fortunes which have been accumulated in a lifetime, and which could not under a perfect system have been amassed in that time, I incline to the opinion that most of them have been made at the expense of men of middling fortunes, and of men whose business and manufacturing operations are comparatively small, and not at the expense of those who work with their hands.

criticisms of Basil Hall, Mrs. Trollope, and Dickens may be set off by the books of Grund, Lady Wortley, and Chambers. These last came to admire the United States, and succeeded in their purpose. They make excuses for the faults and ordinary annoyances of travel; they see merits that the average American could not discern; they even depreciate their own country to praise America. Delighting in the journey, they show a charming disposition of mind, and take thoroughly optimistic views. They display an amiability that should be the special envy of travellers, receiving pleasure from almost every experience, and undoubtedly communicating their own charm of manner to their entertainers. Their books, with the exception of Chambers's description of a slave auction, are now of little value, but the temper of the writers is admirable. Other works which take a middle course between carping and indiscriminate praise are those of Harriet Martineau, Lyell, Ampère, and Mackay.

English travellers, with hardly an exception, were struck with the poor health of Americans. "An Englishman," wrote Lyell, "is usually recognized at once in a party by a more robust look, and greater clearness and ruddiness of complexion." He also noted "a careworn expression in the countenances of the New-Englanders." Harriet Martineau said we were distinguished for "spare forms and pallid complexions," and that "the feeling of vigorous health" was almost unknown. Thackeray wrote from New York, "Most of the ladies are as lean as greyhounds." Our shortcomings in this respect were fully appreciated by ourselves. The *Atlantic Monthly* pointed out that in the appearance of health and in bodily vigor we compared very unfavorably with English men and women. George William Curtis spoke of the typical American as "sharp-faced, thought-furrowed, hard-handed," with "anxious eye and sallow complexion, nervous motion, and concentrated expression;" and he averred that we were "lantern-jawed, lean, sickly, and serious of aspect." Emerson mentioned "that depression of spirits, that furrow of care, said to mark every American brow"; and on another occasion he referred to "the invalid habits of this country;" when in England, in 1847, he wrote home: "When I see my muscular neighbors day by day I say, Had I been born in England, with but one chip of English oak in my willowy constitution!" The *Atlantic Monthly* declared that, "in truth, we are a nation of health-hunters, betraying the want by the search."* It was admitted that the young men were coming up badly. Holmes wrote: "I am satisfied that such a set of black-coated, stiff-jointed, soft-muscled, paste-complexioned youth as we can boast in our Atlantic cities never before sprang from loins of Anglo-Saxon lineage." In the "Easy Chair" Curtis observed, "In the proportion that the physique of Young America diminishes, its clothes enlarge."† The students in the colleges were no better than the young men of the cities.‡ The women

* Oct. 1858, p. 529. A writer in *Harper's Magazine* for Dec., 1856, p. 60, says: "The American's lungs are never inflated with a full breath, and his chest accordingly contracts, and his shoulders bend under their own weight; his muscles shrink, and his legs become lank from disuse; his face waxes pale from indoor life; his brain grows languid from exhaustion, and his nerves are raw and irritable from excitement. All the succulency of health is burnt out of him." An editorial in the New York *Times* for March 9, 1855, states: "Strange that we do not see in our pale, waxen-faced men the signs of our growing impotence, and in our delicate, blood-less women tokens that the race degenerates." "Foreigners see in us a degenerate offspring of a nobler race, and with them a skeleton-frame, a yellow-dyed, bilious face, an uncomfortable, dyspeptic expression, an uneasy, spasmodic motion, and a general ghost-like, charnel-house aspect, serve to make up a type of the species Yankee."—*Harper's Magazine*, Oct., 1856, p. 643. The same writer speaks of "the excitability which is the characteristic of the fast-moving American," and of "the universal irritability and restlessness of our people," and adds: "A foreign medical adviser while travelling in this country remarked that the whole nation seemed to be suffering from a paroxysm of St. Vitus's dance."

† "Easy Chair," *Harper's Magazine*, Oct., 1853, p. 701. "Young America —a man before he is out of his teens, a score of years ahead of his age. He never trundled a hoop nor spun a top, but he can handle the cue with the skill of a master."—*Harper's Magazine*, Dec., 1856, p. 58. "Look at our young men of fortune. Were there ever such weaklings? An apathetic-brained, a pale, pasty-faced, narrow-chested, spindle-shanked, dwarfed race—mere walking manikins to advertise the last cut of the fashionable tailor!"—*Ibid.*, Oct. 1856, p. 646.

‡ "Contrast the life of the American with that of the English student. Look at that pale-faced, dirty-complexioned youth, flitting like the ghost of a monk from his college cell to chapel or recitation hall. His very dress is shadowy and unsubstantial. His meagre frame is hung with a limp cal-ico gown, and his feet drag after him in slouchy slippers. Follow him to his room, where he lives his life almost unconscious of the air, earth, or sky, and you see him subside suddenly into that American abomination, a

sadly lacked physical tone. Dr. Holmes spoke of the "American female constitution, which collapses just in the middle third of life, and comes out vulcanized india-rubber, if it happen to live through the period when health and strength are most wanted."*

Curiously enough, we advertised our ailments. The hearty English salutation of "good-morning" had given way to an inquiry about one's health, which, instead of being conventional, like that of the French and the Germans, was a question requiring an answer about one's physical feelings and condition.† Pleas of ill-health in the national Senate and the House of Representatives were not infrequent.‡

---

rocking-chair, or fall upon his bed, where, with his pipe and a book wearily conned, he awaits the unwelcome call of the bell to lecture. To move he is indisposed; and yet when at rest he seems exhausted. He does not sit, but sprawls; and he and his fellows, in their loose and fusty dress, as they listlessly lounge or drawl out their recitations, might readily pass for so many captives of a watch-house, half-awakened into sobriety from a night's debauch."—*Harper's Magazine,* Dec., 1856, p. 59.

* *The Autocrat of the Breakfast-Table,* p. 47; see article, "Our Daughters," *Harper's Magazine,* Dec., 1857; New York *Times,* March 9, 1855; *Our Old Home,* Hawthorne, p. 59; see also *ibid.,* p. 368, where Hawthorne writes: "I often found, or seemed to find, . . . in the persons of such of my dear countrywomen as I now occasionally met, a certain meagreness (Heaven forbid that I should call it scrawniness!), a deficiency of physical development, a scantiness, so to speak, in the pattern of their material make, a paleness of complexion, a thinness of voice."

† An anecdote illustrating this is thus told in the "Easy Chair" of *Harper's Magazine,* Dec., 1857, p. 123: "It is related to Mr. Webster that, being once in a great Western city, waiting for the cars, he was entreated by the mayor to devote the hour he had on his hands to the business of being introduced to the citizens. Somewhat reluctantly, being jaded by travel, Mr. Webster consented. The first gentleman led up was Mr. Janes—a thousand closely treading on his heels, all anxious to take the great man by the hand, and only an hour for the whole to do it in. 'Mr. Webster,' said the mayor, 'allow me to introduce to you Mr. Janes, one of our most distinguished citizens.' 'How do you do, Mr. Janes?' said Mr. Webster, in a tone not calculated to attract much confidence. 'The truth is, Mr. Webster,' replied Janes, 'I am not very well.' 'I hope nothing serious is the matter,' sternly answered Mr. Webster. 'Well, I don't know that, Mr. Webster. I think it's rheumatiz, but my wife—' Here the mayor rapidly interposed with the next citizen."

‡ "My health for a long time has been bad."—Senator Dixon, Feb. 4, 1854. "Being somewhat indisposed."—Senator Toombs, Feb. 23, 1854. "If my health and strength and voice will permit."—Douglas, March 12, 1856. "If I were to consult my feelings, my strength and physical ability, I should not trespass upon the patience of the House."—Stephens, July

Our physical degeneracy was attributed to the climate. Yet it is difficult to reconcile this opinion with the enthusiasm of many European travellers over certain aspects of nature in America. The bright sunshine, the blue sky, the golden, Oriental sunsets, the exhilarating air were an astonishment and delight. "The climate of the Union," wrote De Tocqueville, "is upon the whole preferable to that of Europe." We have now come to recognize the fact that a climate to be salubrious need not be moist; that between the dryness of Colorado and the humidity of England, there may be a mean—such as is found in the larger part of the Northern States—better adapted to health than either and that the greater amount of sunshine compensates for the wider variations in temperature.

But without begging the question of American ill-health by ascribing it to climate, it may unquestionably be found to be due to a bad diet, bad cooking, fast eating, and insufficient exercise in the open air. The appetizing forms in which the genius of New England cookery displayed itself provoked an inordinate consumption of sweets, hot breads, and cakes. With what surprise does this generation read that our greatest philosopher always ate pie for breakfast! The use of the frying-pan in the West and the South pointed well the quaint remark that "God sends meat and the Devil sends cooks." Men ate too much animal food and especially too much pork. The cooking and the service at hotels and other public places made dinner "the seed-time of dyspepsia." A fashionable tendency prevailing in the cities to live in hotels and large boarding-houses, promoted unwhole-

31, 1856. "I have suffered all day with a severe headache."—Senator Bigler, Feb. 26, 1857. "My system is so reduced that it is with difficulty I can speak at all."—Senator Bayard, Feb. 26, 1857. "I know not that my strength is sufficient to enable me to be present to-night."—Douglas, March 22, 1858. Even Sumner early caught the infection. He said, July 28, 1852: "My bodily health for some time past down to this very week has not been equal to the service I have undertaken." These are some of many such expressions that I have noted. I have only come across one similar statement in English reported speeches. Burke, in his speech on the impeachment of Warren Hastings, said: "Your lordships will have the goodness to consult the strength which, from late indisposition, begins almost to fail me." Mr. Shepherd, a student of history at Oxford, informed me that, in an extensive reading of the House of Commons debates, he did not recollect of ever meeting with such excuses.

some living. The use of wine at table was rare, the drinking of drams before dinner habitual. Tobacco was used to excess, and chewing was as common as smoking.*

Boys at schools and colleges, young men who were clerks and salesmen in the cities, and the sons of rich parents alike formed these bad habits.† Neither men nor women took exercise in the open air. No one walked when he could ride. The trotting buggy took the place of the horse's back. The Americans were gregarious, and loved town life, having no taste for healthful country recreations. Their idea of the country was the veranda of a large

---

* See *Society in America,* Martineau, vol. ii. p. 264; *The Homes of the New World,* Bremer, vol. i. pp. 142, 152; Dickens's *American Notes; The Upper Ten Thousand,* Bristed; The *Atlantic Monthly,* Oct. 1858, p. 529; *Harper's Magazine,* Sept. 1858, p. 491. Sam Slick has a lesson from Abernethy: "The Hon. Alden Gobble was dyspeptic, and he suffered great uneasiness after eating; so he goes to Abernethy for advice. 'What's the matter with you?' said the doctor. 'Why,' says Alden, 'I presume I have the dyspepsy.' 'Ah!' said he, 'I see—a Yankee—swallowed more dollars and cents than he can digest.' 'I am an American citizen,' says Alden, with great dignity; 'I am Secretary to our legation at the Court of St. James.' 'The devil you are,' said Abernethy; 'then you'll soon get rid of your dyspepsy.' 'I don't see that inference,' said Alden; 'it don't follow from what you predicate at all; it ain't a natural consequence, I guess, that a man should cease to be ill because he is called by the voice of a free and enlightened people to fill an important office.' 'But I tell you it does follow,' said the doctor, 'for in the company you'll have to keep you'll have to eat like a Christian.' It was an everlasting pity that Alden contradicted him, for he broke out like one moon-distracted mad. 'I'll be d—d,' said he, 'if I ever saw a Yankee that don't bolt his food whole, like a boa-constrictor. How the devil can you expect to digest food that you neither take the trouble to dissect nor the time to masticate? It's no wonder you lose your teeth, for you never use them; nor your digestion, for you overload it; nor your saliva, for you expend it on the carpets instead of on your food. It's disgusting; it's beastly. You Yankees load your stomachs as a Devonshire man does his cart, as full as it can hold, and as fast as he can pitch it in with a dung-fork, and drive off; and then you complain that such a load of compost is too heavy for you. Dyspepsy, eh? Infernal guzzling, you mean. I'll tell you what, Mr. Secretary of Legation, take half the time to eat that you do to drawl out your words, chew your food half as much as you do your filthy tobacco, and you'll be well in a month.' "—Cited in *Harper's Magazine,* Dec., 1858, p. 66.

† Young America smokes regalias, drinks brandy-and-water; "can stand more drinks than would stagger a coal-heaver; he becomes pale and pasty in the face, like badly-baked pie-crust, weak in the back, dwarfish in stature, and shaky in the limbs."—*Harper's Magazine,* Dec., 1856, p. 58; see also *The Upper Ten Thousand,* Bristed, p. 19. " 'Who cares' says Young America, and straightway he goes on chewing his tobacco, thrusting his feet through hotel windows, burning his vitals with coarse brandy."— "Easy Chair" of *Harper's Magazine,* Sept., 1856, p. 561.

caravansary at Saratoga or Newport. Athletics were almost unknown. "There is no lack," said Edward Everett, in 1856, "of a
few tasteless and soulless dissipations which are called amusements, but noble, athletic sports, manly out-door exercises,
which strengthen the mind by strengthening the body, and
bring man into a generous and exhilarating communion with
nature, are too little cultivated in town or country." "We have
a few good boatmen," wrote Holmes, in 1858—"no good horsemen that I hear of—I cannot speak for cricketing—but as for
any great athletic feat performed by a gentleman in these lati-
tudes, society would drop a man who should run around the
Common in five minutes." Athletics were not a prominent feature even of college life.

The improvement in these respects since the decade of 1850-
60 is marked, and despite the large element of truth in the precise observations of Emerson, Everett, Holmes, and Curtis, they
do not embrace with scientific breadth the whole subject, for the
experience of our Civil War gave little indication of physical degeneracy in the Northern people: signs of improvement were already manifest before this period closed. The gospel of physical
culture had been preached with effect, and "Muscular Christianity" was set up as an ideal worth striving to realize. "Health
is the condition of wisdom," declared Emerson in 1858, and not
long after the world of fashion, discarding the Parisian model of
life and beginning the imitation of the English, shortened the
city season, acquired a love for the country, for out-door exercise and athletic sports. But the French cuisine, almost the sole
outward trace left of the period of French domination, was a
potent and enduring influence. Any one who considers the difference between the cooking and the service of a dinner at a
hotel or restaurant before the war and now, will appreciate what
a practical apostle of health and decent living has been Del-
monico, who deserves canonization in the American calendar.
With better digestion and more robust bodies, the use of stimulants has decreased. While wine at the table is more common,
tippling at bars has come to be frowned upon; lager beer and
native wines have to a considerable extent taken the place of

spirituous liquors; hard drinkers are less numerous, total abstainers are probably on the increase, and tobacco-chewing is dying out. The duration of life is now at least as long in America as it is in Europe.

During the last forty years the American physique has unquestionably improved. A philosopher now, contrasting Englishmen and ourselves, would not make the comparison to our so great disadvantage as did Emerson from his observations in 1848, when he wrote: "The English, at the present day, have great vigor of body and endurance. Other countrymen look slight and undersized beside them, and invalids. They are bigger men than the Americans. I suppose a hundred English, taken at random out of the street, would weigh a fourth more than so many Americans. Yet, I am told, the skeleton is not larger."* "I used to think myself," said Edward Atkinson, "only an average man in size, height, and weight at home, but when I made my first visit to England (in 1877), I was rather surprised to find myself a tall and large man by comparison with those whom I passed in the streets."† The American school-boy and college student are to-day equal in physical development to

---

* *English Traits,* chap. iv. "It is good to see," wrote Hawthorne, "how stanch they [the English] are after fifty or sixty years of heroic eating, still relying upon their digestive powers, and indulging a vigorous appetite; whereas an American has generally lost the one and learned to distrust the other long before reaching the earliest decline of life; and thenceforward he makes little account of his dinner, and dines at his peril, if at all."— *Our Old Home,* p. 343. "Comparing him [the Englishman] with an American, I really thought that our national paleness and lean habit of flesh gave us greatly the advantage in an æsthetic point of view. . . . I fancied that not merely the Suffolk bar, but the bar of any inland county in New England, might show a set of thin-visaged men, looking wretchedly worn, sallow, deeply wrinkled across the forehead, and grimly furrowed about the mouth, with whom these heavy-cheeked English lawyers, slow-paced and fat-witted as they must needs be, would stand very little chance in a professional contest."—*Ibid.,* p. 352.

† *The Industrial Progress of the Nation,* p. 23. Mr. Atkinson informs me that when this visit was made he weighed about 185 pounds, and was 5 feet 8½ inches high; and he further writes me: "The impression that I then obtained of my relative height, as compared to the great body of the English, has been confirmed by subsequent visits." In *Science* for Nov. 11, 1887, he gives a number of interesting facts collected from clothiers, which show that "the American man is decidedly gaining in size and weight;" see also chapter entitled "English and American Health," in T. W. Higginson's *Concerning All of Us.*

the English youth. This is due in some degree to the growth of athletics. But an advance in the physique of American students as compared with English was observed as early as 1877. . . .*

The *Independent* spoke for many men and women when it declared the theatre "an unmitigated evil." While in the smaller towns of the North theatrical performances were given at irregular intervals, if at all, the lecture, the concert, and the minstrel show formed substantially the only public amusements of people outside of the largest cities. In the decade of 1850-60 the lecture system reached its height. As the lecture was instructive and moral, it received the support of religious people; also, it served a good purpose as an entertainment for the long winter evenings. Of the two hundred lecturers who were in request in many parts of the country, only a few might boast of eloquence, and still fewer spoke with a voice of power. Much that was ephemeral and commonplace was discoursed from the platform in an oracular manner. Yet chief of those who always drew a crowd, and whose utterances in the lyceum are notes of the intellectual and moral development of the time, was Emerson. "I

* *The Industrial Progress of the Nation,* Atkinson, p. 23; Eighth Annual Report of the Massachusetts State Board of Health, January, 1877, where Dr. Henry P. Bowditch says: "A comparison of the pupils of the selected Boston schools [the Public Latin School, the Private Latin School, the Massachusetts Institute of Technology] with the children of the English non-laboring classes at the public schools and universities, shows that the former are in general heavier in proportion to their height than the latter. . . . The Boston boy is therefore by no means to be described as tall and thin in comparison with his English cousin. Dr. Baxter's conclusion, that 'the mean weight of the white native of the United States is not disproportionate to his stature,' seems, therefore, as far as these boys are concerned, as applicable to growing children as to adults. It will thus be seen that the theory of the gradual physical degeneration of the Anglo-Saxon race in America derives no support from this investigation" (p. 304). Dr. Bowditch writes me April 15, 1892: "Some tables furnished me by Mr. Roberts, after the publication of my paper, showing the height and weight of English boys at Marlborough, Eton, Oxford, Cambridge, etc., seem to show that there is no great difference between English and American boys. The question therefore arises, whether these later figures represent a class of boys more truly comparable with those whom I measured than were the first ones which I used. It is very difficult to decide this question, but I think it may be safely said that, judging by the physique of the children, the Anglo-Saxon race has not undergone any important change in being transplanted to New England. It certainly has not degenerated physically."

have heard," wrote Lowell, "some great speakers and some accomplished orators, but never any that so moved and persuaded men as he." His hearers owed much "to the benign impersonality, the quiet scorn of everything ignoble, the never-sated hunger of self-culture that were personified in the man before them." Much of the "country's intellectual emancipation was due to the stimulus of his teaching and example," and because "he had kept burning the beacon of an ideal life above our lower region of turmoil."

In 1852 Thackeray came to this country and "preached," as he called it, on "The English Humorists of the Eighteenth Century." "The lectures," he wrote, "are enormously *suivies,* and I read at the rate of a pound a minute nearly." The great novelist was pleased to find how much his books were read and liked. He wrote home: "The prettiest girl in Philadelphia, poor soul, has read 'Vanity Fair' twelve times." Two great orators are identified with the lyceum, Henry Ward Beecher and Wendell Phillips. Beecher, who was looked up to as the apostle of a great congregation, swayed powerfully immense audiences; Phillips, who spoke oftener and more willingly on the slavery question than on any other subject, owed to the lecture system his frequent opportunity to address people in various parts of the country. While Edward Everett was not a lyceum orator, his oration on Washington, heard as it was by vast numbers, deserves mention as one of the events of this character.

To eke out a scanty income was the inducement which led most of the platform speakers to traverse the country and deliver lectures. The writing of the lecture was perhaps not difficult; the delivery of it might be an agreeable task; but the getting from place to place was hard work indeed. Emerson, on returning from one of these winter journeys, wrote in his diary: " 'Twas tedious, the obstructions and squalor of travel. The advantage of these offers made it needful to go. It was, in short —this dragging a decorous old gentleman out of home and out of position, to this juvenile career—tantamount to this: 'I'll bet you fifty dollars a day for three weeks that you will not leave your library, and wade, and freeze, and ride, and run, and suffer all manner of indignities, and stand up for an hour each night reading in a hall;' and I answer, 'I'll bet I will.' I do it and win the nine hundred dollars."*

The period we are reviewing may be called the golden age of American literature. Irving was still writing, and, although his best work had been done, his great fame cast a halo around our literature and was the inspiration of many. Prescott won his laurel wreath before 1850, but his singularly patient and diligent life did not come to an end until 1859. He was then at work on "Philip the Second," which had he been able to finish it, would have proved a fitting and brilliant close to his useful career.

Rather as journalist than poet did Bryant make his mark on this era, for his noted poems were written before 1850. But the renown he had acquired as poet gave meaning and power to his journalistic pen, and literature claimed him as one of its lights. Longfellow, the most popular of American poets, living a serene and beautiful life, shed his radiance over this period. He had already won fame, but the poems which gave him that fame were now read and re-read: they had entered into the life of the people as a wholesome influence. When this loved and admired poet came to publish "The Courtship of Miles Standish," he created a sensation and conferred a pure delight such as has fallen to few in the literary world of

* Cabot, p. 565, see also p. 567; New York *Tribune*, Sept. 9, 1859. "The years when Youmans was travelling and lecturing were the years when the old lyceum system of popular lectures was still in its vigor. The kind of life led by the energetic lecturer in those days was not that of a Sybarite, as may be seen from a passage in one of his letters: 'I lectured at Sandusky and had to get up at five o'clock to reach Elyria; I had had but very little sleep. To get from Elyria to Pittsburgh, I must take the five o'clock A.M. train, and the hotel darky said he would try to awaken me. I knew what that meant, so I did not get a wink of sleep that night. Rode all day to Pittsburgh, and had to lecture in the great Academy of Music over footlights. The train that left for Zanesville departed at two in the morning. Was assured there would be a sleeping-car on the train, but found none.' "—John Fiske on "Youmans," *Popular Science Monthly*, May, 1890.

America.* He told a simple tale of love, wherein the Plymouth colony was the scene, and the beautiful Puritan maiden, the doughty captain, the fair-haired, azure-eyed lover were the actors. That this unaffected story should have appealed so powerfully to the Northern people was a tribute not only to the art of the poet, but a tribute to his readers as well, and was an indication of the profound interest inspired by the Pilgrims of the *Mayflower*. It was declaimed from the platform by elocutionists, read by school-teachers to their pupils, and it made an evening entertainment at many a family fireside. Whittier, who, of all the poets, took rank in popularity next to Longfellow, fired the hearts of many citizens with manly purpose. To him is the honor of having been the pre-eminent poet of the anti-slavery cause.

During the decade of 1850-60, Bancroft published several volumes of his monumental work. At the close of the year 1849, Ticknor's "History of Spanish Literature" appeared.† In 1856, Motley burst upon the world with "The Rise of the Dutch Republic," which achieved an immediate success and a lasting recognition. His enthusiasm for liberty and human rights found a response in the temper of the time.

For the great works of Lowell we must look before 1850 and

* In Longfellow's journal we find these entries: "Oct. 16, 1858. The Courtship of Miles Standish published. At noon, Ticknor told me he had sold 5000 in Boston, besides the orders from a distance. He had printed 10,000, and has another 10,000 in press. Met George Vandenhoff, who reads the poem in public to-night.

"Oct. 23d. Between these two Saturdays Miles Standish has marched steadily on. Another 5000 are in press, in all an army of 25,000 in one week. Fields tells me that in London 10,000 were sold the first day."— *Life by S. Longfellow*, vol. ii. p. 327. "Mrs. George Vandenhoff is announced to read Longfellow's forthcoming poem, The Courtship of Miles Standish, at Springfield, on Saturday evening, the day of its publication."—New York *Tribune*, Oct. 13, 1858.

† Ticknor is a fine example of a generous-principled scholar, anxious to assist the human intellect in its efforts and researches. Methinks he must have spent a happy life (as happiness goes among mortals), writing his great three-volumed book for twenty years; writing it, not for bread, nor with an uneasy desire of fame, but only with a purpose to achieve something true and enduring."—*American Note-Books*, Hawthorne, vol. ii. p. 159.

after 1860. But in spirit, though not in time, "The Biglow Papers" belong to the period of our review. With some of the enduring qualities of a classic, this satire combines a point and freshness that were felt more keenly in the days of slavery and Southern domination than now. "The Autocrat of the Breakfast Table" delivered his oracular discourses at the end of this decade. "The Autocrat," wrote Motley to Holmes, "is an inseparable companion. . . . It is of the small and rare class to which 'Montaigne's Essays,' 'Elia,' and one or two other books belong, which one wishes to have forever under one's thumb." In this same period came "The Scarlet Letter," "The House of the Seven Gables," "The Blithedale Romance," and "The Marble Faun." The teaching of Emerson's long life can be limited to no decade, though he undoubtedly spoke with the greatest vigor in the ten years before the war. In those lectures and essays he is speaking still. The Christian, the agnostic, the transcendentalist, the scientific investigator alike learn from him wisdom. The apostle of literature and the apostle of science both do him honor.

The Americans of the decade we are studying were great readers. Of periodicals—an embarrassment of wealth in our day—there were but three which may be called characteristic of the period, and these occupied a larger space in the public mind than they or any similar magazines occupy at this time. "Dear old 'Easy Chair,'" a letter from Springfield, Illinois, said, "I am a school-mistress out West, and it is a bright day when *Harper's* comes." George William Curtis, whose eloquence as an orator is overshadowed by his brilliancy as an essayist, began writing the "Easy Chair" in October, 1853. The nineteenth century Addison had a million readers. To what an audience did those words of wholesome morality, healthy criticism on literature and art, and acute observations on society appeal! His ability, combined with literary urbanity, gave him unbounded influence; his monthly essays must be reckoned among the educating and refining influences of the decade. The works of fiction spread by *Harper's Magazine* before its readers deserve mention. When Dickens's "Bleak House" was finished, Thackeray's "Newcomes" was begun. To have the first reading in serial of "The Newcomes" seems almost as delightful as it would have been to see the first representation of "The Merry Wives of Windsor." "The Newcomes" was followed by Dickens's "Little Dorrit," and that by Thackeray's "Virginians," "Lovel the Widower," and "The Four Georges." The first instance perhaps of the publication in the United States of an extensive historical work as a serial in a magazine was that of John S. C. Abbott's "Life of Napoleon," which began in August, 1851, and was continued for nearly four years. This work, reflecting the enthusiasm of Thiers, presented a view of Napoleon radically different from that which had been familiar to American readers, and implanted in the minds of the youth of the decade an admiration for his career..

Putnam's Magazine, instead of reprinting English works, aimed at the development of American literature; thus it served as a medium of expression for writers full of ideas and eager to get a hearing. As one now turns over the volumes of this magazine, refinement and good taste seem to exhale from their pages, and the student of this surging decade, of this period of storm and stress, after wading through a mass of polemical literature, feels a calming influence when he reads *Putnam's,* where political and social reforms are advocated in the language of literature, and in a tone which appears to indicate that one is moving in the best society. George William Curtis again appears as a laborer, and Parke Godwin was an intimate associate. Godwin wrote a series of political articles remarkable for their high character and moral elevation. They treated of the necessity for ridding the nation of slavery, and convinced many people of culture, to whom the rugged arguments of the *Tribune* and the powerful invective of the *Liberator* would have appealed in vain.

The starting of *The Atlantic Monthly,* in November, 1857, with Emerson, Lowell, Longfellow, and Holmes as its sponsors, was a literary event of the first order. Lowell was editor. He wrote literary criticisms, and in his political articles brought to bear upon the questions of the day rare insight, clear statement, and vigorous expression. Emerson's voice came to the cultivated readers of this magazine in poetry and prose. Longfellow contributed poems; while the merry vein of Holmes in "The Autocrat" and "The Professor at the Breakfast Table" cast a lightsome charm over people whose religious and political lives tended to deep seriousness.

When we know what a reading people like the Americans read, we have an index to their moral life. Men and women whose intellectual pabulum was of the character I have spoken of above could not fail to have sound ideas of conduct and a sincere desire to live up to them. The cleanness of the three popular magazines which have been mentioned, any article in which a young girl might read, is certainly an ethical measure.

By *the middle of December, 1860 it was clear that South Carolina was about to secede from the Union, and that unless some prompt remedy was adopted other states of the lower South would quickly follow her. Various proposals were made to bridge the gulf between the North and South. Henry Clay was dead, but he had a lineal successor in the Senate in John J. Crittenden, whom Kentucky had elected as a Whig in 1835 and had kept in a seat most of the years since. A man of conservative temper, detesting the extremists on both sides, he was now ready for the supreme effort of his career.*

His compromise proposal embodied six articles which he thought might well be added to the Constitution as amendments. Chief among them was one which provided that in all the territories then held or thereafter acquired north of the Missouri Compromise line of 36° 30', slavery should be forbidden; south of it slave property was to be legal and to enjoy national protection. This plan went before a Senate committee of thirteen, and a House committee of thirty-three. The really potent voice in pronouncing upon it, however, as Rhodes emphasizes, was that of the president-elect. He refused to yield an inch on his contention that slavery had no proper place outside the older states where it existed, and that the natural and right status of all territories was that intended by the framers of the Constitution, a thoroughgoing devotion to freedom. Rhodes's summary of the discussion is clear and impartial, and his statement of Lincoln's position—which he approves—is unexceptionable.

Historians of a later date have divided sharply on the question whether the Republican leaders should not have consented to the Crittenden Compromise. Had they done so, might not time, and the unfitness of the Southwest for slave labor, and the fast-increasing preponderance of the North in population, wealth, and political power have settled the issue peaceably in their favor? Nobody could say. What is certain is that Lincoln would have been recreant to his principles—sound and just principles—had he yielded. He had insisted that a crisis must be reached and passed—that is, passed with a decision that slavery must be forbidden to expand and put in the path of ultimate extinction. It would not do to reach the crisis—and evade it again.

Secession

THE presidential election took place November 6; the South Carolina legislature passed the act calling a convention November 10. No man of judgment and public experience could now longer doubt that South Carolina would secede soon after December 17, the day fixed for the assembling of the convention. November 8 the war department received a letter from Colonel Gardner, then in command at Fort Moultrie, advising that the garrison be strengthened in Moultrie, and that a company of soldiers be sent to Fort Sumter and another to Castle Pinckney. November 9, if Floyd's diary is genuine and correct, Attorney-General Black, in cabinet meeting, earnestly urged "sending at once a strong force into the forts in Charleston Harbor"; and Secretary Cass substantially agreed with him. Never in our history in a trying time has the course which the executive should pursue been less open to doubt than in the situation which now confronted President Buchanan. In addition to the actual facts clearly indicating the correct policy, a precedent of the highest value existed. In every step which he ought to have taken, he had before him the example of President Jackson, the great hero of his own party, whose action had been supported by all but four States of the country. Moreover, Jackson had been Buchanan's trusted political leader, and had written him while he was in Russia a confidential letter, giving him some account of the trouble of 1832-33, and saying, "I met nullification at the threshold." Before the South Carolina convention of 1832, which passed the ordinance of nullification, met, Jackson sent for General Scott and asked his advice as to what should be done to carry out his determination that "The Union must and shall be preserved." The counsel of Scott was: Garrison strongly Fort Moultrie and Castle Pinckney ("Sumter was not quite above ground"); have a sloop-of-war and some revenue-cutters in Charleston "to enforce the collection of duties." "Proceed at once," was the prompt reply of President Jackson, "and execute these views. You have my *carte blanche* in respect to troops; the vessels shall be there."

It was gross dereliction of duty on the part of President Buchanan that he did not at once send for General Scott, and discuss with him in detail the action of Jackson, and then decide to carry out a similar policy. For—in spite of the verbose reasoning with which Buchanan and his defenders have confused the question, by insisting that what was involved was really the coercion of a State, and then proceeding to discuss the right and the expediency of such action, and his lack of authority—the course that the executive should have pursued is as clear as day. Buchanan denied the right of secession, and acknowledged that it was his duty to enforce the laws in South Carolina in so far as he was able. November 17 he asked for an opinion of his attorney-general. This move was proper, but, like most of his proper actions in this crisis, tardy. Yet when the opinion came giving him warrant for the Jacksonian policy, it was not too late to follow it. Attorney-General Black, as sound a jurist as ever advised a President, replied in three days to his request. "You can now," he wrote Buchanan, "if necessary, order the duties to be collected on board a vessel inside of any established port of entry. . . . Your right to take such measures as may seem to be necessary for the protection of the public property is very clear." When we brush away all extraneous considerations, when we isolate the question of executive duty from party disputes and constitutional theories, it is surprising what unanimity existed at the North in regard to the matter of the greatest practical moment. Not a lawyer in the North would have denied the powers of the President as thus laid down by Black. Had Buchanan decided promptly to act with energy on that line of duty, every Northern man who had voted for Lincoln, Douglas, or Bell, and nearly every Northern man who had voted for Breckinridge would have sustained him with enthusiastic zeal. No more scathing criticism on the President can be pronounced than that of Black himself who, forty days later, spoke of "the fatal error which the administration have committed in not sending down troops enough to hold *all* the forts" in Charleston Harbor.

The means at the President's command to carry out a Jacksonian policy may be gathered from the controversy between him and General Scott, which was printed in the columns of the *National Intelligencer* in 1862, and continued in their respective books. It appears, according to Scott, that 1000 soldiers of the regular army were disposable, and, while this is denied by Buchanan, we shall have no difficulty in believing Scott's statement to be correct, when we remember that the army had 16,000 effective men. It is true that the American army was then, as it always has been in time of peace, small for the duty imposed upon it; but we may be sure that if the will to do so had existed, there would have been no great difficulty in placing 1000 men during the month of November in Southern forts where they were most needed. That there were 400 soldiers ready October 29 every one admits; and it would have been a good beginning of a policy of action had the President, after the South Carolina legislature called the convention, sent these troops to Charleston.

That to garrison the Southern forts would have increased the irritation of Southern Carolina and would have driven the other cotton States onward in the path of secession, as the defenders of the President maintain, is possible. On the other hand, a determination on the part of the administration to protect the public property and collect the duties, accompanied by the proposal of a compromise to allay the disaffection of the South, might have caused the remainder of the Southern States to delay their movements. For it must be borne in mind that this matter of plain executive duty had not in November become confounded in the Southern mind with the coercion of a State, as it did two months later. Yet, whatever may have been the weight of probability as to the effect of such a vigorous step, the case was one of those where the executive officer should have done his duty regardless of the consequences.

It is true that the crisis was a much greater one than that which Jackson had to meet. Then, although the disunion party had a large majority in South Carolina, and she had the tacit sympathy of three sister States, the case was vastly different from the present situation where unanimity prevailed within her confines, and she had the avowed sympathy of all the cotton States. In 1832, Louisiana and the border States were against South Carolina; now Louisiana was getting ready to follow her, while the border States, though deprecating her precipitate movement, shared her feeling as to the aggression of the North. Yet, if the crisis was greater, greater would have been the glory to him who met it in the way unerringly pointed out by precedent, law, and devotion to the Union. It was a pregnant opportunity for an executive gifted with singleness of purpose, a dauntless temper of mind, and a wisdom to guide his valor to act in safety. But on such a man as Buchanan fortune lavishes her favors in vain. Vacillating and obstinate by turns, yet lacking firmness when the occasion demanded firmness, he foundered about in a sea of perplexity, throwing away chance after chance, and, though not wanting in good intentions and sincere patriotism, he laid himself open to the undisguised contempt of all sections and all parties. In but one respect has the later differed from the contemporary judgment of him. From an oft-repeated Northern charge that he was actuated by treachery to his own section, he has been fully absolved. When, however, we compare what he did with what he ought to have done, we may affirm with reason that of all of our Presidents, with perhaps a single exception, Buchanan made the most miserable failure. He had been so long under Southern domination that he could not now throw it off. Common prudence required that he should keep in his cabinet none but stanch Union men; this test would have resulted in the retirement of Cobb and Thompson, and probably a reconstruction of the whole cabinet in the middle of November, such as took place late in December and in January. According to Floyd's diary, a difference developed itself in cabinet meeting as early as November 10, on the question of the South's submission to Lincoln's election and the right of secession, in which dispute Cobb, Thompson, and Floyd ranged themselves on one side, and Cass, Toucey, Black, Holt, and the President on the other.

At a time when a plan of resolute action should have been the daily and nightly thought of Buchanan, he sat himself down to write an essay on constitutional law, which he sent to Congress as his annual message. While engaged in this work, the War Department received a letter from Major Robert Anderson, who, on account of his high reputation, had been selected to command Fort Moultrie. The recommendation in this letter, in addition to previous advice and entreaties, should have come to the President with such a cumulative force that even he could no longer fail to appreciate that which nearly every Union man in the country saw as an imperative necessity. November 23, Anderson suggested that Moultrie be reinforced. He added: "Fort Sumter and Castle Pinckney *must* be garrisoned immediately, if the government determines to keep command of this harbor." This native of Kentucky, who had taken a wife from Georgia, then went on: "I need not say how anxious I am— indeed, determined, so far as honor will permit—to avoid collision with the citizens of South Carolina. Nothing, however, will be better calculated to prevent bloodshed than our being found in such an attitude that it would be madness and folly to attack us. There is not so much of feverish excitement as there was last week, but that there is a settled determination to leave the Union, and to obtain possession of this work, is apparent to all." Before the President's message went to Congress, Anderson iterated these suggestions, and in this last letter he showed that the administration could depend on him to act with moderation as well as firmness. Making a requisition for howitzers, heavy revolvers, and muskets, he added, "God forbid, though, that I *should*" have to use them.

But the President, instead of accepting the advice of Major Anderson, was taking counsel with Jefferson Davis in regard to the message, and modifying it in deference to his suggestions.* The original draft of it was read to the cabinet, receiving in the main the approval of all but Cobb and Thompson, who objected to the denial of the right of secession. Four days after the President sent his message to Congress, Secretary Cobb resigned his position, and, in honor, Thompson should have done likewise, but he clung to his place a month longer. A President made of sterner stuff would certainly have demanded his resignation.

The annual message was read to Congress, December 4. We may pass over without criticism the assertion therein contained that the Southern discontent was due to the Northern agitation of slavery. Because Buchanan was Buchanan, it would have been sinning against his nature and the convictions of many years had he neglected this occasion to tell the North how much it had been in the wrong. Nor can fault be found with the expression of his hope that the Northern States which had offended would repeal their Personal Liberty laws. The parts of the message that we may commend set a standard to which we can hold the President, and they indicate a policy which, carried out logically in word and deed, would have made the name Buchanan in America a far different household word. He denied the right of secession. The framers of this government, he said, "never intended to implant in its bosom the seeds of its own destruction, nor were they at its creation guilty of the absurdity of providing for its own dissolution. . . Secession is neither more nor less than revolution." Congress had not en-

* *Rise and Fall of the Confederate Government,* Jefferson Davis, vol. i. p. 59. The author adds: "The message was, however, somewhat changed, and . . . I must say that in my judgment the last alterations were unfortunate—so much so that when it was read in the Senate I was reluctantly constrained to criticise it."

croached upon a right of the South, and the threatened dissolution of the Union proceeded from an apprehension of future danger, which was no just cause of revolution. He asserted the unquestioned right of property of the United States in the forts, magazines, and arsenals in South Carolina; "the officer in command of the forts has received orders to act strictly on the defensive"; if the forts are attacked, "the responsibility for consequences would rightfully rest upon the assailants." Then the President began to falter, entering upon an extended argument to prove that Congress had no right to coerce a State. While in this reasoning he had the support of his attorney-general, and undoubtedly that of many of the best lawyers in the North, irrespective of their party attachment, the introduction of the subject was unwise, for, as Black pointed out, the coercion of a State, as jurists understood it, would be apt to become confounded in the popular mind with the enforcement of the laws. This was actually the case, and became the source of much mischief. The discussion of coercion was, moreover, irrelevant to the emergency. No one of any political standing or following called for such a policy.

When on the subject of the forts, the President should have stated that it was his firm intention to hold them; and, when announcing that "the revenue still continues to be collected as heretofore at the custom-house in Charleston"—knowing that the collector had determined to resign when South Carolina passed the ordinance of secession—he should have asserted emphatically that, no matter what took place, he should collect the duties in the custom-house, on board of a revenue-cutter in the harbor, or, as Jackson had done, in Castle Pinckney. Had the forts in Charleston Harbor been properly garrisoned, the declaration of such a policy could only have been received in South Carolina, and in the communities that sympathized with her, as the assertion of a solemn duty; it might have met with the approval of a considerable minority in the border States, and it surely would have caused a thrill of patriotism at the North that could not have failed to unite it almost to a man.

The great need of the time was the assertion of a vigorous nationality on some point that people could rally around without being hampered by constitutional quibbles and legal technicalities. The President should further have indicated to Congress with some detail what additional legislation he needed for the present exigency. Hand in hand with the recommendation of some action for the purpose of allaying Southern discontent should have gone the express determination to use all the power at his command to defend the public property and collect the duties. Had the President thus acted as became a sterling Union man, the country would have forgiven his bootless suggestion of compromise—his proposal to have incorporated into the Constitution what was substantially the important article of the Breckenridge platform, an article which had been resisted by the Douglas Democrats in the Charleston convention to the disruption of their party, and had been declared against by every Northern State.

That Buchanan deserves historical censure for not having pursued the Jacksonian policy seems to me beyond question; for the path of duty was so plain that he should have walket in it, and accepted whatever consequences came from right-doing. Yet what the consequences might have been is a fair subject of historical inquiry. That firm and prompt action on the part of the President would have been alone sufficient to nip secession in the bud, as it did nullification in 1832, I cannot bring myself to believe, although it so appeared to some contemporary actors, and although such a view has been urged with persistence by later writers. It does, however, seem possible that such vigor might have led, in December, to a compromise of a sort to prevent the secession of any State but South Carolina. Yet those of us who hold to the idea of the irrepressible conflict can see in the success of such a project no more than the delay of a war that was inevitable, a postponement proper indeed, if the compromise were not dishonorable—for the stars in their courses were fighting on the side of the North. Yet the weight of probability tends to the view that the day of compromise was past, and that the collision of sentiment, shaping the ends of the North and the South, had now brought them both to the last resort of earnest men. That Buchanan feared a conflict is evident: the mainspring of his wavering course was his feverish desire that the war should not begin under a Democratic administration, nor while he was in the Presidential chair. His policy was guided by the thought of after me the deluge, and must be classed among the wrecks with which the vacillation of irresolute men have strewn the coasts of time.* Assuming that war was probably inevitable in 1861, and that Buchanan believed it to be so, a grave indictment against him is that he threw away many of the advantages which the North had in the possession of the national government and in an established administrative system. During the last four months of his presidency, inaction was the course pursued by the North, busy preparation that pursued by the South. Since destiny pointed to certain war and the doom of the Southern cause, the better the preparation of the North the shorter would have been the conflict and the less the suffering. But Buchanan could not forget his party interests when he should have sunk all else in the feeling that he was an American and a disciple of Jackson and of Webster. Had he risen to that height the war might have begun under his presidency, but he would have had a united North at his back; and when he retired to private life with the approval of a grateful people, he might have handed over to his successor, with the advantage of a continuity of administration, a well-defined policy.

Buchanan's message, like all non-committal executive papers in a crisis of affairs, failed to satisfy positive men in either section. His subserviency to the South had so alienated most of the Northern people from him that only a most decided revolt against those who had been his masters—such as Douglas had achieved in 1857—would have brought him their hearty sup-

---

* In his speech in the House, Feb. 7, 1861, Henry Winter Davis spoke of the President as muttering: "Not in my time, not in my time; after me the deluge!"

port. Seward's criticism was made in a private letter, but the substance of it got into the newspapers, and struck the popular note. The message, he said in writing to his wife, "shows conclusively that it is the duty of the President to execute the laws —unless somebody opposes him; and that no State has a right to go out of the Union—unless it wants to." As was foreseen by Black, the President entangled the general understanding by his unnecessary attempt to make clear the difference between the coercion of a seceding State and upholding within her limits some striking symbol of national authority. Yet there were many men at the North who could appreciate the distinction that he made, and who felt that the message was by no means an entire surrender to Southern demands; there were also timorous souls, with anxiety reasonable and just, who saw in the President's course a possible chance of averting civil war: these wrote him letters of approbation.

On the first of November, 1860, Buchanan was popular at the South, and his administration received a certain measure of approval. He had served that section well, and his name ought to have inspired enthusiasm; but he had suffered in its estimation because his policy of making Kansas a slave State had not been a success. His message failed to satisfy the South. The Disunionists did not like the denial of the right of secession. Yet some so-called Unionists in the cotton States were pleased with the position he had taken. There were steadfast Union men in the border States—and these may have been many—to whose idea of nationality the President's abnegation of his own authority and his denial of the power of Congress came with a shock. The pity of it was that he made no ringing declaration of what he proposed to do in the way of executing the laws—such a declaration as would have served as a common rallying-point for them and for the people of the North.

Immediately after the election the Republicans were in high glee at their success. Their companies and battalions of Wide-awakes lent themselves handily to the enthusiastic dem-

onstrations. For the moment it seemed as if nearly every one
at the North was of their party. But their joy was short-lived,
for it began to be apparent that the Republican contest for the
possession of the government had only begun. In less than a
week men who were not blinded by preconceived ideas were
convinced that South Carolina would certainly secede, and
that there was danger of the other cotton States following her
example. The question arose, What would the Republicans do
to prevent disunion? They·were the arbiters of the situation, and
—assuming what was undoubted, that the sentiment of South
Carolina would drive her to secession—on their action depended
whether the outcome should be disunion, and, in case of disunion, whether it should be war or peace. There were some
who blinked the fact, and asserted stoutly that the declarations of the Southerners were idle threats, but a disposition to
look matters squarely in the face prevailed. When men met
in the streets, in public places, or in society, the common salutation of the day and the usual talk gave way to the question that
rose in every mind, "Do you think the South will secede?" Not
many answered as Beecher did this question: "I don't believe
they will; and I don't care if they do."

Opinion of the way in which the crisis should be met formed
on three distinct lines. A spontaneous feeling existed that the
election had been fair, that the decision had been reached in a
constitutional manner, and that it was the duty of the South to
submit to the election of Lincoln as the Northern Democrats
were submitting to it, and as Republicans had acquiesced to the
election of Buchanan. This seemed especially incumbent upon
the Southern people, for, to the pro-slavery policy of the present
administration, carried out at their dictates, was due the Republican success of 1860.* Many of those belonging to the

* "The chief virtue of Republican success was in its condemnation of the
narrow sectionalism of Buchanan's administration, and the corruptions by
which he attempted to sustain his policy. Who doubts but that if he had
been true to his promises in submitting the controversy in Kansas to its
own people, and had closed it by admitting Kansas as a free State, that the
Democratic party would have retained its power? It was his infernal policy
in Kansas . . . that drove off Douglas and led to the division of the

victorious party, who held decidedly the belief that submission was a moral and political obligation resting on the South, and that the United States was a nation, went the whole length which their position logically required. To secede and do any act of violence was, in their view, treason, and men who engaged in such work were traitors. Those who were reading men—and the majority of Republicans in 1860 were such—fed on literature adapted to sustain this opinion. Jackson's proclamation against the nullifiers and Webster's speech advocating the Force bill were published in a convenient form to supply a popular demand. About this time appeared the last volume of Parton's picturesque "Life of Jackson," and the graphic story of the way in which the sturdy general met nullification at the threshold had an effect in shaping public sentiment. Dwelling upon this episode of our history and despairing because of the imbecility of Buchanan prompted the North to burst forth almost in one voice: "Oh, for an hour of Andrew Jackson!"

Another phase of opinion was both represented and led by Horace Greeley. Three days after the election the New York *Tribune,* in a leading article, said: "If the cotton States shall decide that they can do better out of the Union than in it, we insist on letting them go in peace. The right to secede may be a revolutionary one, but it exists nevertheless. . . . Whenever a considerable section of our Union shall deliberately resolve to go out, we shall resist all coercive measures designed to keep it in. We hope never to live in a republic, whereof one section is pinned to the residue by bayonets." The *Tribune* was the most influential journal of the Republican party, and, next to Seward and Lincoln, Greeley was the most powerful leader of opinion in that party. This view had its greatest popularity in November and in the first part of December, 1860; it received

Democratic party and the consequent election of Lincoln."—Letter of John Sherman to General Sherman, Nov. 26, 1860, *Century Magazine,* Nov. 1892, p. 92. "We owe the election of Lincoln only to the misrule of the present administration, and to the unfortunate dissensions in our own party."—August Belmont to John Forsyth of Alabama, Dec. 19, *Letters of Belmont,* privately printed, p. 21.

the countenance of other Republican newspapers; it prevailed with Henry Ward Beecher, whose consummate oratory swayed many audiences; it won, also, a certain adherence from the Garrison abolitionists, who saw in the accomplishment of it the realization of their dream of many years. The tendency of Southern and Democratic writers has been, not unnaturally, to overrate the strength of this opinion at the North; on the other hand, because of its speedy decline in public estimation after the middle of December, as well as for the further reason that the war was prosecuted on a theory diametrically opposed to it, we are liable to fall into the error that it was merely the erratic outburst of an eccentric thinker, having no root in public sentiment. It seems clear to me, however, that a respectable minority of Republicans were inclined to a similar view in the last months of 1860. That Greeley came near being nominated United States senator by the New York Republican caucus in February, 1861, and that his strength forced the followers of Seward and Weed to drop their candidate, Evarts, and unite on Harris as the only means of defeating Greeley, shows that advocating acquiescence in peaceable secession did not forfeit a leader's standing in the Republican party. Yet it is also true that, after January 1, the *Tribune* in a measure recanted, and it is quite possible that its articles of November, 1860, cost Greeley the senatorship. For peaceable disunion, when it came to be thoroughly discussed, was seen to be a geographical and military impossibility; it did violence to the Union feeling, the strongest political sentiment at the North; it wounded those who had a strong idea of nationality, and who loved to boast of the country which extended from ocean to ocean, from the Lakes to the Gulf, and whose great river rose amid the snows of the North to end its course in the land of the sugar-cane.

What we may properly call the Greeley policy obtained its strength largely on account of a general repugnance to the coercion of a State. If South Carolinians were almost unanimous for secession, the impracticability of any plan of coercion seemed manifest whenever the enforcement of it came to be discussed. One strong tie that bound the States together, a daily reminder of the federal authority, was not at this time in question. The government duly transmitted the mails to South Carolina, and to the other States bent on secession, until Fort Sumter was fired upon; the Southern postmasters did not resign, but continued to account to the post-office department at Washington. The resignation of the United States judge and district attorney, at Charleston, prevented the holding of the federal courts, but this was not a matter requiring instant remedy. Even if successors were appointed, they could not conduct the judicial business without juries, and on these no South Carolinian would serve. Did coercion mean the sending of troops to Charleston to force men to do jury duty, to constrain the legislature to choose United States senators, to tear down the palmetto flags flying in the streets of Charleston, and to prevent the assembling of the convention that would surely adopt an ordinance of secession? The moment these questions were asked it was seen that coercion was neither possible nor desirable. Yet there existed the clear distinction drawn by Attorney-General Black between the collection of the revenue and the protection of public property, and what he termed "an offensive war to punish the people for the political misdeeds of their State government, or to enforce an acknowledgment that the government of the United States is supreme." Buchanan's policy of letting I dare not wait upon I would encourage the dogmatic assumptions of the secessionists to the point of maintaining that any move towards the collection of the duties or the reinforcement of the forts would be coercion; while the Northern advocates of a heroic course, thinking perhaps there was virtue in a name that implied physical force, continued to employ the word coercion when, according to the distinction of Black, they meant no more than the use of that authority which he had without reservation ascribed to the President. The progress of events gave a certain justification to this confusion of thought. An act of executive duty, which would have occasioned only an emphatic protest from South Carolina in November, caused a demonstration of war in January. This perplexity would not have arisen at the North had Buchanan seized his great opportunity and made himself the national hero.

A third phase of Republican opinion found expression in the advocacy of a compromise. Many who had voted for Lincoln, believing with the generality of their party that the Southern menaces of disunion were largely gasconade, were now, since they had awakened to the seriousness of the situation, frightened at the result of their own work. August Belmont, in writing to John Forsyth of Alabama in November, spoke of "the reaction which has already taken place among thousands who voted for Lincoln," and in December he wrote: "I meet daily now with men who confess the error they have been led into, and almost with tears in their eyes wish they could undo what they helped to do." There were, indeed, Republicans who felt that they might offer without dishonor a compromise that would retain the cotton States excepting South Carolina, yet who had no craven regrets at the election of Lincoln, and who were willing, if need were, to fight for the Union. The most eminent exponent of such an opinion was Thurlow Weed, whose adroitness in practical politics had hitherto been his chief distinction, but who now rose almost to the height of statesmanship. With judicial purpose he brought himself to look upon the Southern side of the question, and with magnanimity he urged, "They who are conscious of least wrong can best afford to manifest a spirit of conciliation." Weed was now sixty-three years old; he had that intense love for the Union characteristic of Whigs whose ideas had been moulded by Webster and Clay. The danger of disunion and how to avert it were his daily and nightly thoughts. By the end of November he had matured in his mind a plan of compromise, which he suggested in his newspaper, the Albany *Evening Journal*—at this time, probably, the most powerful organ of public opinion outside of New York City. He proposed, in the place of the actual "vindictive Fugitive Slave law," one that should provide for the payment for rescued slaves by the counties in which the violation of the law had taken place. In regard to the "vexed" territorial question, he asked, "Why not restore the Missouri Compromise line?" By this he meant the extension of that line to the Pacific Ocean, allowing slavery south and prohibiting slavery north of it. In an article which he wrote advocating this plan of conciliation, Weed showed a rare comprehension of Southern sentiment; he urged his plan with cogent reasoning, the result of profound reflection irradiated by his long public experience. It was a bold step for a partisan Republican to take, and this he appreciated; he thought the suggestions would at first be unpopular with his political friends, but he deemed it his duty as a leader of opinion to express his views frankly, hoping that his party would come to regard the situation as he did, or, at all events, that from the discussion to which his articles would give rise, the Republicans might work out a plan to ward off disunion.

To Greeley and to Thurlow Weed, the great journalist and the great politician, praise is due because, at a crisis when it was easier and safer to criticise and object, they did not hesitate to express their positive convictions. Greeley's policy, when ventilated, was seen to be impossible. Yet at first it appeared to be a solution worthy of consideration; and had a sea as wide as that between England and Ireland flowed between the cotton States and the rest of the Union, it might have been a wise settlement of the difficulty. Thurlow Weed's policy gained strength with the discussion of it in the light of the progress of events. The general tendency being towards the effacement of former party lines, this policy received the approval of those at the North who voted for Douglas, Breckinridge, and Bell. Douglas, beginning now that last and most glorious portion of his career, on which his admirers love to dwell, spoke at New Orleans, two days after the election, against secession; November 13, he wrote a formal letter to the business men of New Orleans, showing from the Southern point of view the folly of it; and on the way north he addressed with the same purpose a Virginian audience. His course was calculated to foster among the Southern people a sentiment that should induce them to meet half-way the overtures of Republicans disposed to follow Thurlow Weed.

Thus stood affairs on December 3, when Congress met. South Carolina was practically unanimous for secession; the President had failed utterly to rise to the emergency, while at the North there existed an overwhelming desire to preserve the Union. All eyes were directed towards Congress. Would it avert the threatened danger? As the persistent attitude of South Carolina and the warm sympathy with her of her sister States were fixed facts, the question was, What would the Republicans in Congress be willing to do to satisfy the South? Compromise had solved the difficulty in 1820, in 1833, and in 1850; and it was now apparent that the border State men and the Northern Democrats could unite on a plan which would prevent the secession of all the States except South Carolina. Would the Republicans go as far as that? Properly to judge their action in this crisis, we must first inquire, what were the grievances of the South as made known to Congress?

The tangible grievances were the interference with the execution of the Fugitive Slave act by the Personal Liberty laws, and the denial by the North to the owners of negro slaves of the common rights of property in the territories. The wrong done the South by the Personal Liberty laws was dwelt upon by men who were opposed to secession, and who, taking an impregnable position, were willing to rest their case upon a remedial complaint. Their conspicuous exponent was Alexander H. Stephens. In the famous speech which he made before the Georgia legislature, November 14, he thrust this view into prominence. His words gave rise to much discussion. It may be positively affirmed that, if the sole grievance of the South had been the alleged nullification of the Fugitive Slave act by many Northern States, there would have been no secession but that of South Carolina. For this grievance would certainly have been redressed. Vermont, the pioneer in this sort of legislation, had already taken steps towards the revision of her Personal Liberty act. On December 17 the national House of Representatives, in which the Republicans and anti-Lecompton Democrats had a clear majority, earnestly recommended, by a vote of 153 to 14, the

repeal of the Personal Liberty laws in conflict with the Constitution. These facts, with others that will be mentioned later,
show that, if it would have appeased the South, every State, with
the possible exception of Massachusetts, either would have
rescinded this legislation, or so modified it that it no longer
would have been an offence. Early in the session of Congress,
however, the Republicans were told that this would not settle
the difficulty. "You talk about repealing the Personal Liberty
bills as a concession to the South," said Senator Iverson of
Georgia. "Repeal them all tomorrow, sir, and it would not stop
the progress of this revolution." Iverson spoke for a large party
in the empire State of the South. Since the secession of South
Carolina had become a foregone conclusion, the action of
Georgia was awaited with breathless interest, and every indication of her sentiment was scanned with care. "What though all
the Personal Liberty bills were repealed," asked Jefferson Davis,
the leader of the cotton States; "would that secure our rights?"

The other tangible grievance—the refusal of the North to
recognize that the slaveholder's human chattels had the common
attributes of other property in the territories—was urged with
emphasis by Davis and by Toombs. It was indeed replied that
the Dred Scott decision gave them all that they claimed, but to
this it was naturally rejoined that the President-elect did not
accept as binding the general principle in regard to slave property as asserted by Chief-Justice Taney. The experience of the
last seven years had made patent to each party the importance
of a friendly executive, when the issue of freedom and slavery
should come to be fought out in the territories.

The intangible grievance of the South was the sentiment
of the North in regard to slavery. In most of the public declarations and confidential letters one is struck with the influence
which the stigma cast by Republicans upon the slave-holders
had on the Southern mind. This sensitiveness proved to be a
heavy obstacle in the way of compromise. Between the idea
that slavery was right, or, at least, the only suitable condition
of the negro, and the idea that slavery was a blot upon the na-

tion, it seemed wellnigh impossible to hit upon the common ground of opinion which was a necessary antecedent to compromise. "The true cause of our danger," declared Jefferson Davis, "I believe to be that a sectional hostility has been substituted for a general fraternity. . . . Where is the remedy?" he asked. "In the hearts of the people" is the ready reply.

The election of Lincoln seemed to the Southerners a declaration of hostility to their institution by the Republican party. When they read his speeches in the Lincoln-Douglas debates, they saw that he clearly stood for the conviction that slavery is wrong, and that the government could not endure permanently half slave and half free. Yet, despite the misunderstanding of one section by the other, a compromise on the lines laid down by Thurlow Weed was possible in December. Many schemes were proposed, but the most famous of them is that of Senator Crittenden of Kentucky; of those which would have been acceptable to the cotton States other than South Carolina, this plan was the one fairest to the North. Crittenden had now reached the age of seventy-three. An old Whig and a lover of the Union of the Henry Clay sort, actuated by sincere patriotism, having the confidence of all parties in the Senate, adapted by the character of his mind and by his residence in a Union-loving border slave State to look in some degree upon both sides of the question, it was fitting that in his last years of public service he should do all in his power to cure the breach between the two sections. He introduced his plan of compromise in the Senate, December 18. Its salient feature was the disposition of the territorial question. Could that have been agreed to, an accommodation on the other points of difference would not have been difficult. Crittenden proposed as a constitutional amendment that slavery should be prohibited "in all the territory of the United States now held, or hereafter acquired, situated north of latitude 36° 30′. . . . In all the territory south of said line of latitude . . . slavery is hereby recognized as existing, and shall not be interfered with by Congress, but shall be protected as property by all the departments of the territorial government during its continuance." States should be admitted from the territory either north or south of that line with or without slavery, as their constitutions might provide.*

On the same day that Crittenden proposed his compromise, the Senate adopted the resolution of Powell of Kentucky, which provided for a special committee of thirteen to consider "the grievances between the slave-holding and the non-slave-holding States," and to suggest, if possible, a remedy. Two days later the Vice-President named the committee: Powell of Kentucky, Hunter of Virginia, Crittenden of Kentucky, Seward of New York, Toombs of Georgia, Douglas of Illinois, Collamer of Vermont, Davis of Mississippi, Wade of Ohio, Bigler of Pennsylvania, Rice of Minnesota, Doolittle of Wisconsin, Grimes of Iowa. Three of the senators were from the border slave States, two from the cotton States, three were Northern Democrats, and five were Republicans. The constitution of the committee was eminently fair, the distribution according to parties and sections just. In ability, character, and influence all the senators stood high; three of them were leaders of public sentiment. There was warrant for believing that, if the Union could be saved by act of Congress, these senators would discover the way. On the day that they first met in committee, December 21, the news recently received must have heightened their impression of the gravity of the situation and added to their sense of responsi-

---

* This was called Article 1. The Crittenden compromise provided for other constitutional amendments:

Article 2. "Congress shall have no power to abolish slavery in places under its exclusive jurisdiction, and situate within the limits of States that permit the holding of slaves."

Article 3. Congress shall have no power to abolish slavery in the District of Columbia without compensation, and without the consent of its inhabitants, of Virginia, and of Maryland.

Article 4. Congress shall have no power to prohibit or hinder the transportation of slaves between slave-holding States and territories.

Article 5. A provision for the payment of the owners by the United States for rescued fugitive slaves.

Article 6. "No future amendment of the Constitution shall affect the five preceding articles . . . and no amendment shall be made to the Constitution which will authorize or give to Congress any power to abolish or interfere with slavery in any of the States by whose laws it is or may be allowed or permitted."

bility. December 20, the South Carolina convention had unanimously adopted the ordinance of secession, an action which kindled enthusiasm in the cotton States, and awakened some demonstrations of approval in North Carolina and Virginia. It was believed that unless a composition could be effected, Georgia, Florida, Alabama, and Mississippi would certainly secede, and that Louisiana and Texas would probably follow their example. The stake which the North had to play for was these six cotton States. If they were not won, might not the game be shifted to a contest where the border slave States would be at hazard? This was well understood by the Northern senators when the members of the committee came together and conversed informally on their first day of meeting. The people of the North for the most part had some notion of the peril in which the Union lay; but they felt that if these thirteen men could not agree on an acceptable compromise, there was not elsewhere in the country wisdom to devise a plan and influence to get it adopted. On one day they read of the secession of South Carolina; on the next, that there had been "a free interchange of opinion" among the members of "the select committee of the Senate on the crisis"; and it might have seemed to augur well that these gentlemen who met on a high social footing could begin their proceedings by a sincere endeavor to understand one another's position, rather than by presenting cut-and-dried ultimatums. This fact was the more noteworthy, as the session had been remarkable for an almost complete cessation of social intercourse between Northern and Southern senators. It was, indeed, a rare committee. On election day no two men in public life had stood for sentiments so diametrically opposed as Seward and Jefferson Davis, and yet they were on friendly social terms and had been intimate. The incessant and bitter party and factional warfare of seven years could not sour the genial nature of Douglas, who was disposed to extend the right hand of fellowship to every man on the committee, with the possible exception of Davis. In addition to a willingness to sink any personal animosities, he also stood ready to yield somewhat of his political views for the purpose of avoiding disunion. Crittenden was the Nestor of the Senate. Collamer, Grimes, and Doolittle were Republicans of sound judgment, and, we may believe, loved their country better than their party. Union-loving Kentucky had both of her senators on the committee, Union-loving Virginia had one.

December 22, the committee got fairly to work. On the motion of Davis, it was decided that no report should be adopted unless it had the assent of a majority of the Republican senators, and also a majority of the other eight members of the committee. This was a wise and even necessary arrangement. It was reasonably certain that no compromise could be carried through Congress without the concurrence of at least three of the Republican members of the committee; and as the different propositions comprised constitutional amendments which required the approval of three fourths of the States, time would be wasted in presenting to the country any compromise not sustained in the manner called for by the Davis resolution. Crittenden now introduced his compromise, and the committee with praiseworthy speed proceeded to vote upon it. On the first article of the proposed constitutional amendment—the one having for its scope the settlement of the slavery question in the territories, of which an abstract has been given in the text—the vote stood: Yeas, Bigler, Crittenden, Douglas, Hunter, Powell, Rice—6. Nays, Collamer, Davis, Doolittle, Grimes, Seward, Toombs, Wade—7. The senators from the border slave States and the Northern Democrats voted for it; the senators from the cotton States and the Republicans against it. All the Republicans of the committee voted against the rest of the proposed articles amending the Constitution; all the other members of the committee voted for them. On the first and second resolutions, the Republicans are recorded in the negative; the Democrats and Crittenden, in the affirmative. The third and fourth resolutions, which were favorable to the North, had the unanimous vote of a full committee.

The first article of the proposed constitutional amendment,

the one devoted to the territorial question, was of all by far the most important. Unless an agreement could be reached on this point, no compromise was possible. As Davis and Toombs voted with the Republicans against that proposition, it is often asserted that they, jointly with the Republicans, are responsible for the defeat of the Crittenden compromise; but this is a mistake, for the evidence is undoubted that, if a majority of the Republican members of the committee had indicated their intention to accept that as a settlement, Davis and Toombs would also have supported it. No fact is clearer than that the Republicans in December defeated the Crittenden compromise; few historic probabilities have better evidence to support them than the one which asserts that the adoption of this measure would have prevented the secession of the cotton States, other than South Carolina, and the beginning of the civil war in 1861. It is worth while, therefore, to inquire by what influences the Republicans were led to take this position, and to consider whether their course can be justified at the judgment-bar of history.

To answer the first part of this proposed inquiry the course of Seward and of Lincoln, the leaders of the Republican party, demands our attention. On the day after that on which Lincoln was elected, Seward possessed a more powerful influence than any one in the Republican party. This influence became somewhat weakened with the Republican senators and representatives by the time that Congress met, for Seward was naturally supposed to favor the compromise suggested by his faithful friend and political partner, Thurlow Weed. That supposition had received much credence from the sanction of the plan by the New York *Times* and the New York *Courier and Enquirer*, journals which had steadily supported Seward, and the editors of which were his warm personal and political friends. Moreover, Dana had told some Republican members, who called at the *Tribune* office on their way to Washington, and expressed regret at the overtures of Weed, that the articles were Seward's, and that he "wanted to make a great compromise like Clay and

Webster." The first part of Dana's statement we must regard as a mistake; and, while the evidence is not positive that Seward contemplated heading a movement of Republicans that would have resulted in the acceptance by them of a plan similar in essence to the Crittenden compromise, yet his private correspondence from December 1 to December 13 shows that he was wavering, and gives rise to the belief that the pressure of Weed, Raymond, and Webb, backed as they were by powerful New York men of their party,* would have outweighed that of his radical Republican colleagues if he had not been restrained by the unequivocal declarations of Lincoln. "No one has any system, few any courage or confidence in the Union in this emergency," he wrote home December 2; "I am engaged busily in studying and gathering my thoughts for the Union." I told the Republican caucus of senators, he wrote Weed, that "they would know what I think and what I propose when I do myself. . . . The Republican party today is as uncompromising as the Secessionists in South Carolina. A month hence each may come to think that moderation is wiser." "Our senators," he said, in a letter to his wife, December 7, "agree with me to practice reticence and kindness. But others fear that I will figure, and so interfere and derange all." "The debates in the Senate," he wrote, three days later, "are hasty, feeble, inconclusive, and unsatisfactory; presumptuous on the part of the ill-tempered South; feeble and frivolous on the part of the North."

Lincoln's influence on the march of events must now be taken into account. A letter tendering Seward the position of Secretary of State was delivered to him December 13. In it the

* August Belmont wrote Governor William Sprague of Rhode Island, Dec. 13: "I can assure you that all the leaders of the Republican party in our State and city, with a few exceptions of the ultra radicals, are in favor of concessions, and that the popular mind of the North is ripe for them"; and Dec. 19: "Last evening I was present at an informal meeting of about thirty gentlemen, comprising our leading men, Republicans, Union men, and Democrats, composed of such names as Astor, Aspinwall, Moses H. Grinnell, Hamilton Fish, R. M. Blatchford, etc. They were unanimous in their voice for reconciliation, and that the first steps have to be taken by the North."—*Letters of August Belmont*, privately printed, pp. 15, 16.

President-elect said that this had been his "purpose from the day of the nomination at Chicago," and he had "the belief that your position in the public eye, your integrity, ability, learning, and great experience all combine to render it an appointment pre-eminently fit to be made." Seward did not immediately accept the offer. In a polite and considerate letter he replied that he should like time for reflection and to consult his friends; of all persons, he desired most the counsel of his wife and of Thurlow Weed. Leaving Washington December 14, he arrived at Albany the next day, and remained there long enough to have a full consultation with Weed, in which we may be sure that his probable colleagues in the cabinet, as well as the affairs of the country, were discussed. Much as he wished to, he had not deemed it prudent to visit Lincoln, but while at Albany he either suggested or fell in with the idea that Weed should go to Springfield on his behalf. He and Weed conferred together December 15 and 16. December 17, the Albany *Evening Journal* had a carefully studied editorial, in which, asserting that the "question must have a violent or peaceful solution," it urged the Republicans to accept as a settlement of the dispute regarding the territories what was substantially the Crittenden proposition. Weed then went to Springfield; Seward went to his home at Auburn, there to await the return of his friend. Weed's consultation with Lincoln took place December 20. His article in the *Evening Journal* having reached there at about the same time, served as a fitting text for a discussion of the critical state of affairs, and, before the conference ended, the news that South Carolina had passed the ordinance of secession furnished important material for it.

Lincoln's mind was made up. Naturally, no man in the country had watched with greater anxiety than he the course of events in South Carolina, or had studied more carefully the trend of Northern sentiment and the disposition to compromise. His first belief, "that this government posesses both the authority and the power to maintain its own integrity," was confirmed by his mature thought; but, in holding to this legitimate conviction, he did not lose sight of an equally important fact. "The

ugly point," he said, in private conversation, "is the necessity
of keeping the government together by force, as ours should
be a government of fraternity." A statesman at such a crisis
would naturally cast about for a policy that might peacefully
preserve the Union; and a statesman such as was the President-
elect, who had been devoted to peaceful pursuits, would have
deemed it wicked to conjure up visions of military power and
glory, and would shrink from beginning his administration with
a civil war on his hands. There is no doubt that, if the Crittenden compromise had been put forward as an ordinary congressional enactment instead of a constitutional amendment,
Lincoln would have accepted every article of it except the one
that proposed the settlement of the territorial question. Touching the cardinal principle of the Republican party, the principle
that explained the reason of the party's existence, he was firm.
"Entertain no proposition for a compromise in regard to the
extension of slavery," he wrote, December 11, to Kellogg, the
Illinois member of the House committee of thirty-three on the
crisis. "The instant you do, they have us under again: all our
labor is lost, and sooner or later must be done over. . . . The
tug has to come, and better now than later. You know I think
the Fugitive Slave clause of the Constitution ought to be
enforced—to put it in its mildest form, ought not to be resisted."
Two days later, in a letter to E. B. Washburne, also a member
of Congress from Illinois, he repeats the same idea and objects
to the scheme for dividing the territory between slavery and
freedom by the Missouri line. "Let that be done," he writes,
"and immediately filibustering and extending slavery recom-
mences. On that point hold firm as a chain of steel." Lincoln's
letter to John A. Gilmer of North Carolina, written December
15, shows not only judicious constancy, but a largeness of
political comprehension that is admirable. "On the territorial
question I am inflexible," he said. "On that there is a difference
between you and us; and it is the only substantial difference.
You think slavery is right and ought to be extended; we think
it is wrong and ought to be restricted. For this, neither has any
just occasion to be angry with the other."

LINCOLN'S *speeches on his journey to Washington did not lift him in the esteem of the nation. He spoke extemporaneously, too often in trite terms, and obviously under constraint; he had to give reassurance to the South while offering some show of resolution to the North, and so could hardly avoid an evasive tone. Moreover, he had all too little assistance or advice. Rhodes might have said more upon the green inexperience of his secretarial aides, John Hay and John G. Nicolay; more upon the selfish designs of Seward, Simon Cameron, and Montgomery Blair, whom he chose to be secretary of state, secretary of war, and postmaster-general respectively; and more upon the reawakened ambitions of Douglas, who was now trying to pull the Democratic party together again, and who indicated that he might assail the administration mercilessly. But once in Washington, Lincoln began to show his latent strength. One veteran Free Soiler assured a friend: "His backbone is pronounced good by the best judges." In his inaugural address he showed backbone, stating categorically: "No State, upon its own mere motion, can lawfully get out of the Union." On this principle, Douglas stood squarely behind him.*

The president's Cabinet made up a coalition government. It included men who had been conservative Whigs and radical Whigs, Union Democrats of Jacksonian views, and radical exponents of new Republican ideas. Lincoln, like other leaders of coalitions—such as Lloyd George in Britain during the First World War—had to fight to exert his own authority, and fortunately had the fighting power that men like Franklin Pierce and Buchanan had lacked. Rhodes describes the differences of view in the Cabinet well, though with less emphasis on Blair's Jacksonian firmness than it merits. Less ability was found in the Cabinet which President Jefferson Davis hastily assembled. His first secretary of war, Leroy Pope Walker, was characterized by Vice-President Alexander E. Stephens as "rash in counsel, irresolute in action." The secretary of the Treasury, Christopher G. Memminger, was a methodical, hard-working man who lacked expertness in finance, and unfortunately thought in terms of a short war. Robert Toombs

*proved unfit for the hopeless tasks of the state depart-
ment. For it and the whole government, as Rhodes
might have brought out more forcibly, were crippled
by the allegiance of the Confederacy to slavery, an
institution from which other civilized and progressive
nations recoiled.*

*The major strength of the North lay in its civil
leaders; the major strength of the South, as Rhodes
shows in his vigorous narrative, in its military leaders
—although Davis was doubtless the ablest and most
devoted chieftain whom it could have chosen.*

Lincoln Takes Over:
Confederacy Organized

Two days before his election was officially declared Lincoln
started on his journey from Springfield to Washington. Having
received many invitations from States and cities offering their
hospitality, he stopped frequently, and made many speeches as
he proceeded along his circuitous route. Greeted everywhere
with enthusiasm, and listened to with profound respect, he may
at this time have laid the foundations of that hold on the plain
people which was to be of such rich benefit to him and to his
country in the years that were to come. But if the purpose in
view was to convince the reflecting Union men of the North that
he was equal to the task before him which he himself thought
"greater than that which rested upon Washington," the journey can only be looked upon as a sad failure, and his speeches,
except his touching farewell to his old friends and neighbors at
Springfield, and his noble address in Independence Hall, Philadelphia, had better not have been delivered. To acquit himself
with dignity in that position were difficult for any man; and
Lincoln, now the cynosure of all eyes, did not have the knack of
saying the graceful nothings which are so well fitted for the occasions on which he spoke. In his speeches the commonplace
abounds, and though he had a keen sense of humor, his sallies of

wit grated on earnest men who read in quiet his daily utterances. The ridiculous, which lies so near the sublime, was
reached when this man, proceeding to grave duties, and the
great fame that falls to few in the whole world, asked at the
town of Westfield for a little girl correspondent of his, at whose
suggestion he had made a change in his personal appearance,
and when she came, he kissed her, and said, "You see I have let
these whiskers grow for you, Grace." The next day's journal
headed the account, "Old Abe Kissed by a Pretty Girl."

Lincoln could indeed have spoken well of the serious matters of which his mind was full, but prudence and propriety forbade that he should anticipate his inaugural address, which had
been already prepared. At Indianapolis, while declining to commit himself, he threw out intimations indicating that he saw a
clear distinction between the coercion of a State on the one
hand, and the holding and retaking the United States forts and
the collection of duties on the other; but his comparison of a
Union on the Southern theory to a "free-love arrangement,"
differing from the true relation of a "regular marriage," while it
might have been effective in private conversation, was not a
dignified illustration for the President-elect to use when addressing the people of a nation chaste in thought and prudish in
expression. Lincoln enounced many good ideas, but it was one
of the hardships of his position that his misses were dwelt upon,
and his hits ignored. His remarks at Columbus: "There is nothing going wrong. . . . There is nothing that really hurts anybody;" and that at Pittsburgh, when, his features lighting up
with a smile, he said: "There is no crisis but an artificial one,"
created a painful impression; yet such utterances were dictated by a worthy motive; he really felt more anxiety about the
outlook than he deemed it wise to show. His declaration in
Independence Hall ought to have compensated for all such slips.
"There will be no bloodshed," he assured the country, "unless
it be forced upon the government. The government will not use
force unless force is used against it."

Lincoln's ignorance of the ways of the fashionable world told against him in New York city, where the tendency of refined people is to judge new men at first rather by their manners than by their qualities, and his wearing black kid gloves at the opera on a gala night gave rise to sarcastic comment. Receiving warnings at Philadelphia which he could not afford to disregard from General Scott, Seward, and two other friends that a plot had been concocted to assassinate him in Baltimore, he deviated from the published plan of going through that city by day, and proceeded secretly to Washington by night. This drew ridicule from his enemies, and expressions of sincere regret from many of his well-wishers, and augmented the prejudice against him which he must surmount. Nor did his bearing in Washington between his arrival and the inauguration do anything to dispel the unfavorable impression that especially prevailed in the East touching his ability to cope with the difficulties he must meet. When Bowles, in a private letter to Dawes, wrote, "Lincoln is a 'Simple Susan,'" he expressed a silent but a commonly held opinion. The hearts of many thoughtful persons must have failed as they contrasted Jefferson Davis, with his large public experience and high reputation, with this untried man from Illinois. Curiously enough, Thurlow Weed, whose grief at the nomination of Lincoln had been of surpassing bitterness, was now one of the few in the East who seemed to have full faith that he would prove adequate to the duty imposed upon him.

Meanwhile the Peace Convention at Washington, sitting with closed doors, ex-President Tyler being in the chair, was with patriotic purpose laboring diligently to save the Union. Among the delegates were many men of character, ability, and distinction. While the proceedings were not published and secrecy was enjoined upon the members, the points of the important debates and the doings leaked out from time to time and—such was the shrinking of the country from civil war—occupied a larger space in the public mind than a due regard for historical proportion can accord to them. February 27, the nineteenth day of its session, the convention recommended to Congress a constitutional amendment as a plan of adjustment; but the important section, that relating to slavery in the territories, had been carried, the convention voting by States, by a majority of one only, the votes of three States which were divided not being counted. Moreover, several prominent members publicly announced their dissent from the prevailing voice of their respective delegations. The plan, being less favorable to the South than the Crittenden compromise and yet not satisfactory to the radical Republicans, lacked the support of a homogeneous majority, and went to Congress with no force behind it. On the morning of March 4, in the last hours of the Senate session, Crittenden offered the project of the Peace Conference. It came to a vote, receiving, however, only seven yeas, Crittenden and Douglas and two Republicans being among the number.

The radical Republicans had from the first been opposed to the Peace Convention. Lowell represents well a phase of thoughtful sentiment. "The usual panacea of palaver was tried," he wrote; "Congress did its best to add to the general confusion of thought; and, as if that were not enough, a convention of notables was called simultaneously to thresh the straw of debate anew and to convince thoughtful persons that men do not grow wiser as they grow older." Those who represented Michigan at Washington and at her State capital were opposed to compromise, therefore she had not appointed commissioners to the Peace Convention; but after it had been in session a week, her senators, at the request of Massachusetts and New York, advised her governor to send delegates. Senator Chandler's letter, which was made public before the convention adjourned, may be reckoned as one of the influences of the time. "I hope you will send," he wrote, "*stiff-backed* men or none. The whole thing (i.e., the convention) was gotten up against my judgment and advice, and will end in thin smoke. . . . Some of the manufacturing States think that a fight would be awful. Without a little bloodletting this Union will not, in my estimation, be worth a rush." This letter affected painfully the Unionists of the border States and the conservative Republicans, but some hard-headed

Northern men had arrived at this conviction, although few thought there was wisdom in giving vent to it.

Virginia voted in the Peace Convention against the section relating to slavery in the territories, her senators opposed the plan in the Senate, and ex-President Tyler, who had much to do with bringing about this conference, repudiated its action in a public speech at Richmond. The plan not being satisfactory to Virginia, it was idle to think that North Carolina, Tennessee, and Arkansas would consider it a sufficient guarantee for their remaining in the Union, or that it would bring back the cotton States.

The historical significance of the Peace Convention consists in the evidence it affords of the attachment of the border slave States to the Union, and the lingering hope of readjustment in North Carolina and Tennessee. The different ways in which it was regarded brings out the contrast between the sentiment of these communities and that of the cotton States. . . .

Jefferson Davis in his book intimates that the South would gladly have welcomed a general convention of the States for the consideration of differences and the amendment of the Constitution, but that this boon was denied them by the representatives of the North. This is obviously an error in memory, not unnatural considering the way in which Davis's work was written, and it would be unfair to assume that it was one of the arguments officially put forth to justify disunion, since the statement is so palpably untrue that no Southern writer would urge it after he had examined the evidence. Seward, Chase, and Lincoln advocated a national convention. The leader of the conservative Republicans, the exponent of the radicals, and the President-elect all agreed on this point, and such a project would have met with unanimous favor in the North. But the cotton States would not listen to it.

On the 4th of March Lincoln was peacefully inaugurated. His address, to which careful heed was given by an anxious and eager crowd, had been carefully prepared at Springfield. With

the Constitution, Henry Clay's speech of 1850, Jackson's proclamation against nullification, and Webster's reply to Hayne as
authorities, "he locked himself up in a room up-stairs over a
store across the street from the statehouse," and amidst dingy
surroundings wrote an immortal state-paper. He submitted it to
friends for approval and advice; from Seward he received many
suggestions, some of which he adopted. Lincoln now proclaimed
to the country that he had no purpose to interfere directly or
indirectly with slavery in the States; he intimated that he
should enforce the Fugitive Slave law;* he held "that in contemplation of universal law and of the Constitution, the union
of these States is perpetual." "No state," he continued, "upon
its own mere motion, can lawfully get out of the Union; resolves
and ordinances to that effect are legally void; and acts of violence within any State or States, against the authority of the
United States, are insurrectionary or revolutionary, according
to circumstances. . . . To the extent of my ability I shall take
care, as the Constitution itself expressly enjoins upon me, that
the laws of the Union be faithfully executed in all the States. . . .
In doing this there need be no bloodshed or violence; and there
shall be none, unless it be forced upon the national authority.
The power confided to me will be used to hold, occupy, and
possess the property and places belonging to the government,
and to collect the duties and imposts; but beyond what may be
necessary for these objects there will be no invasion, no using
of force against or among the people anywhere. . . . The mails,
unless repelled, will continue to be furnished in all parts of the
Union. . . .

"One section of our country believes slavery is right and
ought to be extended, while the other believes it is wrong and
ought not to be extended. This is the only substantial dispute. . . .

"Physically speaking, we cannot separate. . . In your hands,

* "When," asked Douglas, at Springfield, April 25, "was the Fugitive
Slave law executed with more fidelity than since the inauguration of the
present incumbent of the presidential office?"—Chicago *Tribune*, June 6;
New York *Tribune*, May 1.

my dissatisfied fellow-countrymen, and not in mine, is the momentous issue of civil war. The government will not assail you. You can have no conflict without being yourselves the aggressors. . . . We are not enemies, but friends. We must not be enemies. Though passion may have strained, it must not break our bonds of affection. The mystic cords of memory, stretching from every battlefield and patriot grave to every living heart and hearthstone all over this broad land, will yet swell the chorus of the Union, when again touched, as surely they will be, by the better angels of our nature."

Purposely conspicuous on the platform where Lincoln stood was Senator Douglas, for he wished to give notice to his followers and the country that he proposed to support the President in his efforts to maintain the Union. The inaugural was generally satisfactory to the Northern people. Conservative and radical Republicans and Douglas Democrats alike approved it. Its power to win popularity lay in its being a straightforward and not uncertain expression of the predominating Union sentiment of the North. It was a paper such as Jackson, Clay, and Webster would have sanctioned had they been living, and nearly every voter at the North owned one of these statesmen as his political teacher and guide. But in the Confederate States Lincoln's inaugural was construed to mean war. It was similarly regarded in Virginia, and only the unconditional Unionists liked it in Maryland. This feeling was reflected in Wall Street in a decided downward movement of stocks.

On the next day after the inauguration the President sent the names of his proposed cabinet to the Senate. Seward was named for the State Department and Chase for the Treasury; Simon Cameron, of Pennsylvania, as Secretary of War; Gideon Welles, of Connecticut, as Secretary of the Navy; Caleb B. Smith, of Indiana, as Secretary of the Interior. Edward Bates, of Missouri, was appointed Attorney-General, and Montgomery Blair, of Maryland, Postmaster-General. As the intentions of Lincoln in regard to his cabinet became known the war of factions raged. The most important contest turned on Seward and Chase, for it was one in which opposing opinions in the Republican party clashed. Seward stood for a policy of peace, of conciliation, perhaps of compromise. Chase had made no secret of his opinion—"Inauguration first, adjustment afterwards." To Seward himself little or no objection was made. All conceded that his position in the party, his ability, his fitness entitled him to the first place in the cabinet. But he was hit by the fight made against his follower Cameron, and by the failure of his friends to prevent the appointment of Chase. Cameron agreed with Seward that conciliation was the correct policy. On this account the radicals opposed him. Governor Curtin and A. K. McClure, of Pennsylvania, strenuously objected to him on account of his personal character and a long-standing factional feud. Many were the considerations for and against Cameron, but in the end the scale was probably turned in his favor by the powerful advocacy of Weed and Seward. Seward's friends, however, were not successful in the exclusion of Chase, and on that account, two days before the inauguration, Seward withdrew his acceptance of the position of Secretary of State. "The President is determined that he will have a compound cabinet," he wrote to his wife. "I was at one time on the point of refusing—nay, I did refuse for a time to hazard myself in the experiment." Nicolay and Hay have told of the infinite tact with which on this occasion Lincoln treated Seward; and if talent, as Chateaubriand said, is only long patience, what a talent for political affairs this inexperienced man from Illinois displayed at the outset of his executive career!

Pennsylvanians protested against the appointment of Chase, for in their view he was not sound on the tariff question. Conservatives objected to Blair, because he was radical and uncompromising, and because, being a true disciple of Andrew Jackson, he was ready to fight at once if need be for the restoration of the national authority. Lincoln listened to all objections and all protests; he gave heed to all arguments, and though at times he hesitated and was on the point of changing his mind in regard to some of the appointments, the names he finally sent to the Senate made up the cabinet substantially as he had framed it in his mind the night of his election.

Meanwhile the Confederate congress and executive were diligently at work at Montgomery. Beauregard had been made a brigadier-general, and sent to Charleston to take charge of the military operations in the name and by the authority of the Confederate States. On the day of Lincoln's inauguration the Confederate flag was raised over the Montgomery capitol, and two days later it was displayed from the Charleston custom-house. It had three broad stripes—the one in the centre white, the others red, with a blue union containing seven white stars. Davis was reluctant to give up the old national flag, asserting that in the event of war a different battle-flag would make a sufficient distinction between the combatants. The Confederate provisional congress remained in session until March 16. It authorized the raising of a military force of 100,000 volunteers to serve for twelve months, and the issue of $1,000,000 in treasury notes, bearing interest at the rate of one cent per day per $100, redeemable after one year. It passed acts to organize and support a navy; to organize a post-office department; to establish judicial courts. It passed the necessary appropriation bills. A commission of three, with Yancy at its head, was sent to Europe to obtain recognition for the new government, and to make treaties of amity, commerce, and international copyrights. The different States turned over to the Confederacy the property of the national government which they had taken, the State of Louisiana receiving a special vote of thanks from the Confederate congress for the transfer of $536,000 in coin, which she had seized in the United States mint and custom-house at New Orleans.

Before the Confederate congress adjourned it adopted a permanent constitution.* It was the Constitution of the United States, with but three essential differences. It expressly affirmed the right of property in negro slaves; it made the recognition

* The government of the Confederacy was carried on for one year under the provisional constitution, and the legislative body was called the provisional congress. The first congress under the permanent constitution met Feb. 18, 1862.

and protection of slavery in any new territory that might be acquired mandatory on congress; and in the different provisions touching the peculiar institution, seeking no refuge in the ingenious circumlocution of the federal Constitution, it used the words "slave" and "slavery." In the preamble it asserted the doctrine of the sovereignty of the States. It forbade congress to lay duties on foreign importations for the purpose of fostering any branch of industry. In two of these changes lay the essence of the secession; the other change gave expression to a largely held construction of the Constitution of the United States. Still another alteration was made, which, in view of the strong sentiment existing in the cotton States in 1859 favorable to the reopening of the African slave-trade, may seem extraordinary. The Confederate constitution prohibited the importation of negroes from any foreign country except the slave-holding States of the old Union. This clause was adopted by the vote of four States to two, South Carolina and Florida opposing it. It showed the respect Southern statesmen had for the opinion of the enlightened world, and was thrown out as an allurement to foreign powers for their recognition, and as an inducement for the border slave States to join the Confederacy. It is probable that Southern senators and representatives would have objected to such a provision in the old Constitution, for, although urged to it by Winthrop, Crittenden did not deem it wise to make the article of his compromise that dealt with the foreign slave-trade a constitutional amendment, but offered it as one of the joint resolutions. Further alterations were made, all of which are of great interest to students of political science, and which are generally considered by them as improvements on the Constitution of 1787.

The religious character of the people manifested itself in the preamble to their organic instrument by "invoking the favor and guidance of Almighty God."

The permanent constitution was adopted on March 11, by a unanimous vote of the seven States represented, and was promptly ratified by the different State conventions.

When one thinks of the many fruitless attempts of peoples to devise wise systems of government, and of the many admirable constitutions on paper which have been adopted, but which have failed to find a response in the character and political habits of the men for whom they were intended, one might be lost in admiration at the orderly manner in which the Southerners proceeded, at the excellent organic instrument they adopted, at the ready acceptance of the work of their representatives, were it not that they were running amuck against the civilized world in their attempt to bolster up human slavery, and in their theory of governmental particularism, when the spirit of the age was tending to freedom and to unity. The sincerest and frankest public man in the Southern Confederacy, Alexander H. Stephens, told the true story. "The new constitution has put at rest forever," he declared, "all the agitating questions relating to our peculiar institution—African slavery as it exists amongst us—the proper status of the negro in our form of civilization. This was the immediate cause of the late rupture and present revolution. . . . The prevailing ideas entertained by Jefferson and most of the leading statesmen at the time of the formation of the old Constitution were, that the enslavement of the African was in violation of the laws of nature; that it was wrong in principle socially, morally, and politically. . . .

"Our new government is founded upon exactly the opposite idea; its foundations are laid, its corner-stone rests, upon the great truth that the negro is not equal to the white man; that slavery—subordination to the superior race—is his natural and normal condition. This, our new government, is the first in the history of the world based upon this great physical, philosophical, and moral truth. . . .

"The great objects of humanity are best attained when there is conformity to the Creator's laws and decrees, in the formation of governments as well as in all things else. Our confederacy is founded upon principles in strict conformity with these laws. This stone, which was rejected by the first builders, 'is become the chief of the corner'—the real 'corner-stone'—in our new edifice."

It is obvious that when Lincoln took the oath of office he had two distinct purposes in his mind; to hold forts Sumter and Pickens, and to use all means short of the compromise of principle to retain the border slave States and North Carolina, Tennessee, and Arkansas in the Union. On going to his office the morning of March 5 he found that the Sumter question was more perplexing than he had imagined. A letter from Holt, still acting as Secretary of War, gave the information that Anderson had written that his provisions would last only a few weeks longer, and that to reinforce the fort successfully with a view of holding it would require an army of 20,000 disciplined men. While the federal government, waiting the issue of the Peace Convention, had pursued a policy of inaction, the South Carolinians had been steadily at work on the islands in Charleston harbor, erecting batteries and strengthening the forts which bore on Sumter.

As *Webster and Clay had repeatedly warned the South, a peaceable separation was impossible. If war had not come at one point and for one immediate provocation, it would have begun elsewhere on the long boundary and as a result of other collisions. How could the Mississippi be divided? If the government had accepted the principle of peaceable secession, other fissions might soon have occurred. Lincoln proved his firmness on two vital issues. He had refused to consider any compromise plan which permitted an extension of slavery, thus surrendering the very platform position on which he had been elected. He had also asserted flatly in his inaugural address that he would maintain the national property confided to him, including the Southern forts. It might have been possible to prolong an uneasy truce for a time by yielding ground, and Seward wished to do this, in the fatuous belief that a revival of Union sentiment in the South would bring the seceded states back into the fold. But Lincoln and eventually a majority of his Cabinet saw that such a course would betray the basic principles of national existence, lose nearly every hope of the future, and in the end gain nothing. He decided to provision and hold Fort Sumter.*

The Confederate authorities might have waited in the belief that by deferring hostilities they could strengthen the position of their section. But the pride and impatience of radical Southern leaders conspired with the hope many entertained of a great and immediate gain from open war. Strike a blow! the hotter Southerners urged; this will bring hesitant Virginia under the Confederate banner, and other laggard states—North Carolina, Tennessee, Arkansas—after her. Thus it was that when the leaders of the government just organized in Montgomery learned that Lincoln's relief expedition was on its way to Sumter, they ordered their troops in Charleston to demand the surrender of the fort, and if the demand was refused, batter it into submission. Neither side coolly planned the conflict which thus began. But given the geography of the country, a variety of factors—pride, political pressures, angry sectional resentments, and the precipitate Southern temper—made it inevitable.

Rhode's narrative provides a temperate outline of

the main points of negotiation between the North and South, although subsequent students have given us fuller detail and a deeper analysis of the discussions on both sides. The honesty and candor of Lincoln have been vindicated against the attacks of sympathizers with the South who have vainly striven to convict him of a provocative course. Rhodes's position here is quite unassailable. But Rhodes was hardly in a position to do justice to the power struggle behind the scenes inside the Lincoln administration. It has since been shown that the devious Seward had a more subtle plan than that of embroiling the North in a conflict with Europe in the hope that the South would come to her side. His plan was to take steps for a Northern war with Spain and seizure of Cuba, an island the South had long coveted; then if France entered the conflict, the North could also take the French islands. He intended a closer relationship with Britain, but thought the South might readily join in gaining Cuba. In his folly, however, Seward coolly proposed that Lincoln divest himself of his constitutional powers and hand them over to Seward himself. Lincoln quietly but emphatically put the secretary in his place.

Fort Sumter

As early as April 4 the President decided to send to the succor of Fort Sumter the expedition which, March 29, he had ordered to be got ready. For several days there had been unusual stir in the War and Navy departments. It was known that they were preparing an expedition at the Brooklyn Navy-yard. It took air that the government had decided not to withdraw Anderson, that Sumter would be provisioned and Pickens reinforced. These reports coming to the ears of Campbell, he asked Seward by letter, April 7, whether they "were well or ill founded." The secretary replied, "Faith as to Sumter fully kept—wait and see," meaning that the government would not make an attempt to supply the fort without giving notice to Governor Pickens. April 6, Robert S. Chew, a clerk in the State Department, was sent to Charleston with instructions drafted by Lincoln's own hand to give the proper notification. Arriving there the evening of April 8, and being at once accorded an interview, he read to Governor Pickens what the President had written: "I am directed by the President of the United States to notify you to expect an attempt will be made to supply Fort Sumter with provisions only; and that if such attempt be not resisted, no effort to throw in men, arms, or ammunition will be made without further notice, or in case of an attack upon the fort."

I have related with considerable detail the story of the Seward-Campbell negotiations, for the reason that Jefferson Davis and Alexander H. Stephens in their books have urged the duplicity of the Washington authorities in this affair as contributing justification to the Confederate attack on Fort Sumter, and for the further reason that Justice Campbell, whose sincerity and straightforwardness cannot be questioned, averred that "the equivocating conduct of the administration" was the "proximate cause" of the commencement of the war in Charleston harbor. If, as these gentlemen more or less distinctly assume, the President consented to this negotiation, and knew of the assurances which Seward gave, his course cannot successfully be defended. Nicolay and Hay do not tell us in set terms how far he was privy to the quasi-promises of his secretary, but from their narrative it is a reasonable inference that he knew little or nothing about them. Secretary Welles, writing in 1873, says emphatically that the President did not know of Seward's assurance that Fort Sumter would be evacuated, and never gave it his sanction. Considering Lincoln's character and manner of action, nothing but the most positive evidence should convince us that he was in any way a party to this negotiation, and of this there is none. His disturbance at the effusive and unauthorized representations of Lamon goes to show that if he had become aware of the lengths to which his secretary was going, he would have called a halt and insisted that those who had been

misled sould be undeceived. The truth is that the assurances to
Campbell were simply those of an officious Secretary of State
whose vanity had grown by what it fed on, until now he deluded
himself with the idea that he and not another was the executive
of the nation. He had strenuously objected to the part of Lincoln's inaugural which asserted, "The power confided to me will
be used to hold, occupy, and possess the property and places
belonging to the government;" he seemed to see so clearly the
political wisdom of giving up Sumter that, when he came to
have on his side General Scott and the majority of the cabinet,
he did not for a moment suppose that the President would act
contrary to counsel of such preponderating weight, and in his
expressions to Campbell he was absolutely sincere. But Jefferson Davis was not deceived. He knew Seward through and
through, for when in the Senate the two had been intimate; and
although at this time he fell into the mistake of regarding the
secretary as the power behind the throne, he was not misled in
the affair of Sumter. At this time Davis worked in his office
from nine to six, and having been used to executive business, we
may be sure that no important despatch went out from Montgomery the substance of which he did not know. "The government," wrote Walker, Secretary of War, to Beauregard, April
2, "has at no time placed any reliance on assurances by the government at Washington in respect to the evacuation of Fort
Sumter, or entertained any confidence in the disposition of the
latter to make any concession or yield any point to which it is
not driven by absolute necessity." The secret instructions from
Montgomery to the commissioners were "to play with Seward,
to delay and gain time until the South was ready." The commissioners were little if at all deceived. They, like every one
who had facilities for getting correct information, were aware
that there was a decided difference of opinion in the cabinet,
and that if the peace party prevailed, the Confederacy would
obtain Fort Sumter without firing a shot; they thought, as did
Stanton and many others, that the Seward action would carry
the day, but regarding the Secretary of State as unscrupulous,

they did not place absolute reliance on his assurances. Justice Campbell, believing that Seward was the President in fact, and trusting him implicitly, was the only sufferer on the part of the South.

Whether in private conversation with Lincoln Seward received any intimation which with rash assumption he construed into an adoption of his own views, neither the biographies of Lincoln nor of Seward disclose. Douglas said that the President had assured him that Sumter would be evacuated as soon as possible; but as he was eager for such action, we may readily believe that he gave to some indirect or qualified statement of Lincoln a positive interpretation. I feel quite sure that the President gave to no one a more certain expression of his thoughts than he did to Francis P. Blair, to whom, after the cabinet meeting of March 15, he said that it had not been fully determined to withdraw Anderson, but he thought such would be the result. Between March 5 and March 29 the President hesitated; he looked on both sides of the question, heard all arguments, and weighed every consideration. The difficulties of the situation were great, and they were made greater because the three men, General Scott, Seward, and Chase, in whose experience or ability he had great confidence, and on whom he was disposed to lean, proved, so far as concerned the important question in March, broken reeds. General Scott again tried his hand at state-craft, and proposed to Seward four alternative policies. The two which he thought the most desirable were to offer the Crittenden compromise to the South, or to say, "Wayward sisters, depart in peace."

Of the impracticable and optimistic notions of the Secretary of State we have seen much. "Seward is infatuated," wrote Sumner; "he says in sixty days all will be well." But all that I have related is as nothing in folly compared to the "Thoughts for the President's consideration," submitted April 1. "We are at the end of a month's administration," Seward wrote, "and yet without a policy, either domestic or foreign." For the home policy he proposed: "Change the question before the public from one

upon slavery or about slavery for a question upon union or disunion;" evacuate Fort Sumter; "defend and reinforce all the
forts in the Gulf."

For the foreign policy: "I would demand explanations from
Spain and France categorically at once. I would seek explanations from Great Britain and Russia. . . . And if satisfactory
explanations are not received from Spain and France, would
convene Congress and declare war against them. But whatever
policy we adopt, there must be an energetic prosecution of it.
. . . Either the President must do it himself . . . or devolve it on
some member of his cabinet. . . . It is not in my especial province.
But I neither seek to evade nor assume responsibility." Egregi-
ous folly this seems to us to-day. Wild, erratic, and indefensible
would such a policy have been in 1861. Yet it is true that a popular notion then prevailed to some extent—though it was not,
so far as I know, held by any able public man except Seward—
that if a foreign war were brought about, the alienated sections
would unite in amity, and like brothers fight the common foe
under the old flag. The President's reply showed Seward that
Lincoln was determined to be the master; yet he argued kindly
the question of domestic affairs, ignored with rare consideration
the wild foreign policy suggested, and with magnanimity kept
secret this correspondence.

Chase clearly comprehended the situation. He saw there were
but two alternatives, war or peaceable separation. But while he
estimated aright the horrors of civil war, he did not perceive
that it was practically impossible for the two governments to
remain long at peace even if disunion were now agreed to. When,
therefore, of the two evils he preferred to recognize "the organization of actual government by the seven seceded States as *an
accomplished revolution*," he put himself out of sympathy with
the policy the President had set forth in the inaugural address.
It is not probable that Lincoln thought out the only two alternatives as logically as did Chase. With true greatness he did not
shake his own judgment by peering into a future full of trouble.
As a result of mature reflection he had declared, "Physically

speaking we cannot separate." To this truth he was determined
to hold, and in conformity with it he proposed to conduct the
affairs of the nation. Yet, for the very reason that in his deal-
ings with the seceded States he was inflexible in his purpose to
preserve the Union, so, with the aim of retaining Virginia, he
was willing to go to the utmost verge of conciliation. He fully
appreciated that to save her from secession would insure Maryland and Kentucky, and bring a lever to bear upon North Carolina and Tennessee. Virginia's convention had met February
13. It was plainly apparent that while a majority of the delegates were opposed to the secession of their State, they were
equally strong in their resistance to a policy of coercion on the
part of the federal government towards the Confederate States.
After the declaration of policy in the President's inaugural address, the sentiment favorable to secession increased in Virginia. What Lincoln called the execution of the laws, the Virginians denominated coercion. Seward, however, thought much
good could be accomplished by working on the Union men of
the convention. In this he had the opproval of the President,
who, knowing that the Unionists were anxious for the withdrawal of Anderson, probably intended to use the evacuation of
Sumter, if he should be forced to it by military necessity, as an
inducement for them to adjourn the convention *sine die,* which
would retard for a while the secession movement. The report
that the troops were to be withdrawn from Charleston harbor
was good news to the Union men of Virginia, though unwelcome
to the precipitators, and caused a reaction of sentiment friendly
to the North. But when it became apparent that Sumter would
not be evacuated the secession wave rose again. Nevertheless,
as late as April 4 the convention voted down by 89 to 45 a resolution to submit an ordinance of secession to the popular vote.

March 31 the President determined to send an expedition
from New York to reinforce Fort Pickens, in conformity with
a plan submitted to him by Captain Meigs. Captain Fox was
busy preparing the Sumter expedition, and while Lincoln had
virtually decided, April 4, to send it, yet, as the earliest mo-

ment that it could be ready was the 6th, he reserved in his mind the privilege of countermanding it or changing its destination, should he hear that his former order touching Fort Pickens had been executed. For what was needed for the effect it would have on the North and on Europe was a vigorous assertion at some point of the national authority. The question naturally arose, Could not this be done at Pickens, and the tender susceptibilities of the Virginia Unionists nursed by the withdrawal of the troops from Sumter? April 6 the President heard that the order of March 11 for the reinforcement of Fort Pickens had not been carried out. He no longer hesitated. As he said later, when he took the people of the North into his confidence, "The strongest anticipated case for using it (the expedition to supply Fort Sumter) was now presented, and it was resolved to send it forward." The President's decision was right. It would have been also right had Vogdes landed his company at Pickens; and while, all the circumstances considered, no blame can attach to him for being tardy, it would have been better if he had come sooner to this determination. It was apparent that public opinion at the North would sustain the administration in any measure for the relief of Major Anderson. Since the night when he transferred his force from Moultrie to Sumter he had been her hero. That movement represented the time when the government had ceased to be swayed by Southern ideas and influences, and had come under the direction of men of national opinions. Moreover, South Carolina had begun the revolution; Charleston was its centre. For its influence on the North and on Europe one expedition to Sumter were worth a dozen to Pickens. Lincoln had to contend with a united people in dealing with the Southern Confederacy; but he had not a united North at his back. Clearly the best chance of uniting the North lay in some just assertion of national authority in the harbor of Charleston. He had been elected President of the United States, and with his view of the indissolubility of the Union, he owed it to his country to make the attempt to keep its flag waving where the revolution had commenced. He owed it to himself as well, for the world does not forgive the man who, when the extremity comes, will not fight for the throne or the chief power of the State to which his title is clear.

To a hard-headed thinker like Lincoln it must have been patent that the surrender of Sumter would only adjourn the difficulty. Sumter obtained, the Confederate States would demand Pickens; Pickens in their possession, they would ask for the recognition of their government. The Virginia, North Carolina, and Tennessee Unionists would urge the giving up of Pickens, and in case the North did not make concessions which she had already repeatedly refused, they would press the policy of peaceful separation, and thus shaking a rod over Lincoln's head, make his position intolerable, and lose him the respect of the North and of Europe.

April 6, Judge Magrath, of Charleston, was advised by a friend in Washington that an attempt would be made to supply Fort Sumter. On the next day Anderson's purchases of fresh provisions were stopped by General Beauregard, who at the same time called out the rest of the contingent troops. April 9 the Sumter mails were taken possession of, and the official letters sent to Montgomery. The President's formal notification of his design to send provisions to Anderson was immediately telegraphed by Beauregard to the Confederate Secretary of War. Jefferson Davis and his cabinet now had a momentous question to decide, and they gave it a long and profound consideration. Toombs at first said, "The firing upon that fort will inaugurate a civil war greater than any the world has yet seen; and I do not feel competent to advise you." Later during the council he opposed the attack. "Mr. President," he declared, "at this time it is suicide, murder, and will lose us every friend at the North. You will wantonly strike a hornet's nest which extends from mountain to ocean, and legions now quiet will swarm out and sting us to death. It is unnecessary; it puts us in the wrong; it is fatal." Yet the Confederate States, as they had assumed the position of an independent nation, could not brook it that a foreign power should retain a strong fortress commanding one of their important harbors. To South Carolina this occupation of territory over which she held sovereignty was intolerable, and to the people of Charleston the flaunting of the Stars and Stripes before their eyes was a daily insult. The pressure of the State and the city on the Confederate government for the possession of Fort Sumter had already been importunate, and now that the hope of obtaining it by negotiation was gone, Davis could no longer resist the current; but in allowing himself to be carried along with it, he committed a stupendous blunder.

Two days after Governor Pickens had received notice of the intention to send supplies to Anderson, Davis ordered Beauregard to demand the evacuation of Fort Sumter, and, if it was refused, to proceed "to reduce it." In accordance with the order Beauregard sent, on the afternoon of April 11, three aides to make the demand of Anderson, who, after consultation with his officers, refused compliance; but when he handed the aides his written reply he said, "Gentlemen, if you do not batter the fort to pieces about us, we shall be starved out in a few days." This remark was deemed by Beauregard so important that he telegraphed it to Montgomery in connection with Anderson's formal refusal to evacuate Sumter. Walker, the Secretary of War, by direction of Davis, immediately replied: "Do not desire needlessly to bombard Fort Sumter. If Major Anderson will state the time at which, as indicated by him, he will evacuate, and agree that in the meantime he will not use his guns against us unless ours should be employed against Sumter, you are authorized thus to avoid the effusion of blood. If this or its equivalent be refused, reduce the fort as your judgment decides to be most practicable." Four aides at once took this proposition to Anderson, handing it to him three-quarters of an hour after midnight of April 11. He had a long conference with his officers, and gave his answer at 3:15 on the morning of the 12th. "I will," he wrote, . . . "evacuate Fort Sumter by noon on the 15th instant, and I will not in the meantime open my fires upon your forces unless compelled to do so by some hostile act against this fort or the flag of my government, . . . should I not receive prior to that time controlling instructions from my government or additional supplies." The aides, in accordance with their instructions from Beauregard, read the letter, promptly refused Anderson's terms, and notified him that in an hour their batteries would open fire on the fort. The four men who in the last resort made the decision that began the war were ex-Senator Chesnut, Lieutenant-Colonel Chisholm, Captain Lee, all three South Carolinians, and Roger A. Pryor, a Virginia secessionist, who two days before in a speech at the Charleston Hotel had said, "I will tell your governor what will put Virginia in the Southern Confederacy in less than an hour by Shrewsbury clock. Strike a blow!" The aides went immediately to Fort Johnson and gave the order to fire. At 4:30 A.M. a shell fired from a mortar of that battery "rose high in air," writes Crawford, who was standing on the parapet of Sumter, "and, curving in its course, burst almost directly over the fort." This was the signal for the bombardment to begin.

With Anderson's last response before them, would General Beauregard or Jefferson Davis have given the word to commence the attack? As affairs turned out it was an equivalent of Davis's conditions. As things were, it was an endeavor of Anderson to meet Beauregard half way, for he disapproved of the Fox expedition, and on both military and political grounds believed that his government ought to give him the order to evacuate the fort. It was impetuosity, not sound judgment, which impelled Chesnut and his companions to make a peremptory decision instead of consulting their chief, which would have involved only an hour's delay.

Beauregard, his officers, and Governor Pickens were needlessly alarmed about the relief expedition. It was three days late in getting off from New York. Fox had arranged that it should consist of the war-ships *Powhatan, Pawnee, Pocahontas,* and *Harriet Lane;* the steam-tugs *Uncle Ben, Yankee* and *Freeborn;* and the merchant steamer *Baltic,* with two hundred men and the necessary supplies on board. The *Powhatan* carried the

armed launches and the sailors to man them; the tugs were intended to convey the provisions to the fort and tow the launches.
The *Baltic,* on board of which was Fox, arrived off Charleston
at three o'clock on the morning of April 12, and found only the
Harriet Lane. The two stood in towards the bar to make, under
a flag of truce, an offer of provisions to the fort, but as they drew
near they observed that the bombardment of Sumter had commenced. Though the *Pawnee* arrived at seven, war having actually begun, nothing could be accomplished without the tugs and
the *Powhatan.* One tug had been detained in New York by her
owner. By a heavy northeast gale the *Uncle Ben* had been driven
into Wilmington, and the *Yankee* as far south as the entrance
to Savannah. Owing to a confused and unsystematic administration of affairs at Washington and to the meddling of Seward
the *Powhatan* had been detached from the Sumter expedition
and had joined that destined for the reinforcement of Pickens.
It was impossible even to attempt the execution of Fox's plan.
The expedition was a failure. Fox and his companions watched
the bombardment, chafing at their powerlessness to render their
brothers-in-arms any assistance.

Had Chesnut brought Anderson's last communication to
Beauregard, he, being a careful man, might have submitted it to
Davis, and it is more than probable that the Confederate President would have said, Wait. That the Montgomery government
was solicitous to avoid the attack is evident from the anxious
inquiry of Walker the morning of April 12, "What was Major
Anderson's reply to the proposition contained in my despatch
of last night?" For it must not be forgotten that the primary object of the Sumter expedition was not to bring troops and munitions of war, but merely to furnish the garrison with a necessary
supply of food. By this time both Lincoln and Davis undoubtedly felt that war was inevitable, and on account of the influence
on public sentiment at the North both were anxious to avoid
striking the first blow, and disposed to proceed with the utmost
caution. Davis had good reason to regret that matters so fell
out that the South became the aggressor; while Lincoln might

well thank his stars for that blunder, since is gave him in his time of trouble a united North.

Half an hour after Fort Johnson gave the signal the fire from the Confederate batteries became general. Sumter remained silent for two hours. The garrison were on half-rations; their bread exhausted, they breakfasted on pork and damaged rice. At seven o'clock they began returning the fire of the Confederates. An artillery duel followed. There being no great disparity in the armament of the two forces, the contest would not have been unequal had Anderson possessed a full garrison. His force of officers, privates, musicians, and non-combatant laborers was a total of 128. Opposed to him was the South Carolina army of from 5000 to 6000 men. It was made up largely of the best blood of the State. Planters and their sons, men of wealth and family of Charleston, did not scruple to serve in the ranks. In the gray of the morning, when the roar of the cannon was heard, the city poured out its people. They thronged to the wharves and the Battery. On no gala occasion had the reporter seen so many ladies on this favorite promenade as now turned out to witness the opening scene of the great tragedy of the Civil War. As they gazed upon their beautiful bay what a spectacle they beheld! Fort Johnson, Fort Moultrie, the Cumming's Point, and the other batteries were firing continuously at Sumter. When Anderson began, he replied first to Cumming's Point, then to the enfilade battery on Sullivan's Island, and "next opened on Fort Moultrie, between which and Fort Sumter a steady and almost constant fire was kept up throughout the day." What war ever had a more dramatic beginning! Charleston, reflecting on the history of South Carolina in union with the other states since 1776, and on the crowded hours of stirring events from the November election of 1860 to this 12th day of April, now saw the "circumstance of glorious war," and heard in hostile array

> the mortal engines whose rude throats
> The immortal Jove's dread clamors counterfeit.

The duel continued all day. In the afternoon, owing to an insufficient supply of cartridges, the fire on Sumter slackened; after dark it entirely ceased. The Confederate mortars threw shells at intervals of a quarter of an hour during the whole of the night. The night was dark and rainy, the wind and tide were high. Beauregard, afraid that troops and supplies might be thrown into Sumter from the fleet, commanded the utmost vigilance at the channel batteries and on Morris and Sullivan's islands. Early on the morning of the 13th the bombardment was renewed. "Fort Sumter," wrote Moultrie's commandant, "opened early and spitefully, and paid especial attention to Fort Moultrie." At about nine o'clock the officers' quarters in Sumter took fire from the shells or hot shot of the Confederates, who thereupon redoubled the rapidity of their fire. The flames spread to the barracks; by noon they had enveloped all of the wood-work, and made it evident that the powder-magazine would have to be closed. Anderson gave the order to remove as much powder as possible, and by great exertion fifty barrels were taken out and distributed around the casemates. The doors of the magazine were shut and earth was packed against them. But now the fire spread with such swiftness that the powder in the casemates was in danger, and all but five barrels were thrown into the sea. The cloud of smoke and cinders almost suffocated the men; they threw themselves upon the ground and covered their faces with wet cloths, or crept to the embrasures for a breath of fresh air. The flames reached the magazine of grenades, and explosion after explosion followed. The fire of Sumter ceased; that of the Confederates came thick and fast. To show that the Union soldiers were undaunted, Captain Doubleday ordered that a few rounds be fired. At each discharge the Confederates "cheered the garrison for its pluck and gallantry, and hooted the fleet lying inactive just outside the bar." At 1:30 in the afternoon the flag-staff was shot away and fell to the ground; with all possible promptness the flag was raised again. In the interval the fire of the Confederates slackened. The disappearance of the flag prompted ex-Senator Wigfall to go from

Cumming's Point to Sumter in a small boat, under a flag of truce, with a request for the suspension of hostilities, and, leading Beauregard to think that Anderson was in distress, caused him to send three other aides with an offer of assistance. These visits resulted in terms of evacuation being offered by Beauregard and accepted by Anderson. The story is told in the report of Anderson, written on board the steamship *Baltic*, off Sandy Hook: "Having defended Fort Sumter for thirty-four hours, until the quarters were entirely burned, the main gates destroyed by fire, the gorge walls seriously injured, the magazine surrounded by flames, and its door closed from the effects of heat, four barrels and three cartridges of powder only being available, and no provisions remaining but pork, I accepted terms of evacuation offered by General Beauregard, being the same offered by him . . . prior to the commencement of hostilities, and marched out of the fort Sunday afternoon, the 14th instant, with colors flying and drums beating, bringing away company and private property, and saluting my flag with fifty guns."

Judged by loss of life, no battle could be more insignificant; not a man on either side was killed. Judged by the train of events which ensued, few contests in our history have been more momentous.

Charleston gave itself up to joy. The Confederate flag waving over Sumter seemed to its people a glorious sight. The churches were crowded. At the Catholic cathedral a *Te Deum* was celebrated with great pomp. The venerable Episcopal bishop at St. Philip's and the rector at St. Michael's attributed "this signal and bloodless victory to the infinite mercy of God, who specially interposed his hand in behalf of their righteous cause." During the week rejoicing of a more profane character was prolonged. Montgomery celebrated with enthusiasm the first triumph of the Confederate arms.

ONE of the engaging qualities of Rhodes as historian was his warm appreciation of moral greatness in the heroes he depicted. He never lacked enthusiasm for qualities of generosity, courage, and fidelity to principle. Early in his story of the war he has to present three men of memorable distinction of character as well as intellect—Robert E. Lee, who took his stand with his state; Stephen A. Douglas, who hurried back to Illinois to rally the Middle West to the Union cause; and Charles Francis Adams, who, as son of a president and close friend of Secretary Seward, voyaged to London when European intervention in the conflict might have been fatal to the United States. Rhodes presents these three men with accuracy, but also with enthusiasm for the noble part that each played in the stormy era.

Lee, it should be made plain—perhaps plainer than Rhodes thought fitting—had no loyalty whatever to the South as a whole or to basic Confederate principles. He disapproved of slavery and disliked the doctrine of secession. His attachment was to the proud Old Dominion with which the Lee family had been associated for nearly two and a half centuries. His devotion to duty stands unquestioned; Winfield Scott correctly declared, "He is true as steel, sir! true as steel!" Whether he might not have felt devotion to a somewhat larger range of ideas and a deeper concept of moral obligation is a moot question. Douglas, who had served his country sometimes well and sometimes ill, now responded to the sternest dictates of nationalism and patriotism. Had he survived, he would have fought to the end for the Union and the supremacy of the Constitution. Whether he would have labored with equal devotion to purge the land from the divisive curse of slavery, we shall never know. No minister to a foreign land ever served the United States more vigilantly and unbendingly than Charles Francis Adams. He had patent faults of temper that would have been less evident had they not matched similar faults on the part of Palmerston and Russell, the heads of the British government; but his honesty, sincerity, and bulldog tenacity commanded the respect of the government he faced, which has always admired character. Rhodes does justice to these three leaders.

Lee, Douglas, and Charles Francis Adams Face the Crisis

THE Confederates had an advantage in that Robert E. Lee espoused their cause; to some extent appreciated at the time, this in reality was an advantage beyond computation. Had he followed the example of Scott and Thomas, and remained in service under the old flag, in active command of the Army of the Potomac, how differently might events have turned out!

Lee, now fifty-four years old, his face exhibiting the ruddy glow of health and his head without a gray hair, was physically and morally a splendid example of manhood. Able to trace his lineage far back in the mother-country, he had the best blood of Virginia in his veins. The founder of the Virginia family, who emigrated in the time of Charles I., was a cavalier in sentiment; "Light-horse Harry" of the Revolution was the father of Robert E. Lee. Drawing from a knightly race all their virtues, he had inherited none of their vices. Honest, sincere, simple, magnanimous, forbearing, refined, courteous, yet dignified and proud, never lacking self-command, he was in all respects a true man. Graduating from West Point, his life had been exclusively that of a soldier, yet he had none of the soldier's bad habits. He used neither liquor or tobacco, indulged rarely in a social glass of wine, and cared nothing for the pleasures of the table. He was a good engineer, and under General Scott had won distinction in Mexico. The work that had fallen to his lot he had performed in a systematic manner and with conscientious care. "Duty is the sublimest word in our language," he wrote to his son. Sincerely religious, Providence to him was a verity, and it may be truly said he walked with God.

A serious man, he anxiously watched from his station in Texas the progress of events since Lincoln's election. Thinking "slavery as an institution a moral and political evil," having a soldier's devotion to his flag and a warm attachment to General

Scott, he loved the Union, and it was especially dear to him as the fruit of the mighty labors of Washington. Although believing that the South had just grievances due to the aggression of the North, he did not think these evils great enough to resort to the remedy of revolution, and to him secession was nothing less. "Still," he wrote in January, 1861, "a Union that can only be maintained by swords and bayonets, and in which strife and civil war are to take the place of brotherly love and kindness, has no charm for me. . . . If the Union is dissolved and the government is disrupted, I shall return to my native State and share the miseries of my people, and, save in defence, will draw my sword on none." Summoned to Washington by his chief, Lee had arrived there a few days before the inauguration of Lincoln, and he had to make the decision, after the bombardment of Sumter and the President's call for troops, whether he should serve the national government or Virginia. The active command of the federal army with the succession to the chief place was virtually offered to him, but, with his notion of state-rights and his allegiance to Virginia, his decision, though it cost him pain to make it, could have been no other than it was. He could not lead an army of invasion into his native State, and after the ordinance of secession had been passed by the Virginia convention he resigned his position and accepted the command of the Virginia forces.

Northern men may regret that Lee did not see his duty in the same light as did two other Virginians, Scott and Thomas, but censure's voice upon the action of such a noble soul is hushed. A careful survey of his character and life must lead the student of men and affairs to see that the course he took was, from his point of view and judged by his inexorable and pure conscience, the path of duty to which a high sense of honor called him. Could we share the thoughts of that high-minded man as he paced the broad pillared veranda of his stately Arlington house, his eyes glancing across the river at the flag of his country waving above the dome of the Capitol, and then resting on the soil of his native Virginia, we should be willing now to recognize in him one of the finest products of American life. For surely, as the years go on, we shall see that such a life can be judged by no partisan measure, and we shall come to look upon him as the English of our day regard Washington, whom little more than a century ago they delighted to call a rebel. Indeed in all essential characteristics Lee resembled Washington, and had the great work of his life been crowned with success or had he chosen the winning side, the world would have acknowledged that Virginia could in a century produce two men who were the embodiment of public and private virtue.

The contemplation of Lee's course at the parting of the ways has another lesson for us of the North: it should teach us to regard with the utmost charity other officers in the army and men in civil life who either did not believe in the constitutional right of secession or in the expediency of exercising it, yet who deemed it the path of duty to follow the fortunes of their States when they, in the parlance of the day, resumed their full sovereign powers.

"The loss of Stephen A. Douglas at this crisis must be regarded as a national calamity," wrote Greeley, while Douglas was lying on his death-bed in Chicago. Leaving Washington soon after pledging his support to the President, he had on his way home spoken words of wise and pure patriotism to the citizens of Wheeling, to the people of Columbus, and to the legislature of his own State. The last time that he addressed his countrymen from the platform, always a labor of love, was on his arrival, the 1st day of May, at Chicago, when a concourse of all parties met him at the depot and escorted him to the wigwam in which Lincoln had been nominated, now, as then, crowded with ten thousand people. In his emphatic way Douglas declared: "There are only two sides to the question. Every man must be for the United States or against it. There can be no neutrals in this war; *only patriots—or traitors.* . . . It is a sad task to discuss questions so fearful as civil war, but sad as it is, bloody and disastrous as I expect it will be, I express it as my conviction before God that it is the duty of every American citizen to rally round the flag of his country." His work, however, was done. Worn out and sick, he took to his bed to die. His last thoughts were of his country; his dying message to his sons came with a full voice. "Tell them," he said, "to obey the laws and support the Constitution of the United States." With all his failings he lacked not patriotism. His ambition had wrecked himself and his party; but he had done much to retrieve his great error, and the nation, in sorrowing at his loss, forgot the Kansas-Nebraska bill or forgave its author.

The solidarity of Christendom is such that the nations across the water could not look on the struggle in America unmoved. The North and the South appealed to Europe, the one for sympathy, the other for material aid; and such was the connection between the English-speaking peoples, that to each the attitude of all the rest of Europe together was unimportant compared with what they expected from England. The people of the Confederacy not only asked her assistance, but confidently believed that the want of cotton would compel her recognition of their independence and the eventual breaking of the federal blockade;*

* "By the end of this summer the stock of cotton and tobacco in Europe will be exhausted. Europe must have more, or witness the commencement of the most terrible of revolutions at home—a revolution arising from starvation. It is therefore a matter of compulsion that they should break through the blockade and obtain our crop under the right of their neutral flag."—Richmond *Examiner*, July 2. Aug. 9 the same journal commended united voluntary withholding of cotton from the market. Action by the Confederate government would be ill advised from a diplomatic standpoint; comp. Charleston *Courier* of July 30. The Charleston *Courier* declared, Sept. 21, "that honor and duty and policy and patriotism require that not a bale of cotton should leave a Southern port . . . until it can be exported legally and regularly after a recognition of the Confederacy." "The American crop is grown and gathered, but its proprietors threaten to withhold it from our markets."— London *Times*, Sept. 19. "The Confederate States have presumed upon their monopoly so far as to make it an engine of coercion. They have declared, though perhaps without much sincerity, that they will hold back their crops and leave Europe to see what can be done without them." —*Ibid.*, Sept. 21. The Richmond *Dispatch*, Oct. 1, 1861, expressed surprise that a single man in the South could entertain the notion "that it would be good policy to permit England to purchase the entire cotton crop." Professor Sumner says in regard to this view, which seems to have had more currency at this time in private circles than among the Confederate statesmen: "Perhaps the grandest case of delusion from the fallacy of commercial war which can be mentioned is the South in 1860. They undertook

that she would not hesitate to adopt that policy when she comprehended the situation, and knew that the South offered her cotton in exchange for her manufactured goods, which would be subject only to a simple revenue tariff. Nor, indeed, in their opinion, had she a choice in the matter; for so many of her operatives were dependent for bread on a constant supply of the Southern staple that if it were not to be had a revolution would break out in Great Britain. " 'Look out there,' a Charleston merchant said to William H. Russell, pointing to the wharf on which were piled some cotton bales; 'there's the key that will open all our ports, and put us into John Bull's strong-box as well.' " "Rhett," Russell wrote, "is also persuaded that the Lord Chancellor sits on a cotton bale. 'You must recognize us, sir, before the end of October.' " Jefferson Davis did not share the overweening confidence of his people. The *Times* correspondent, arriving at Montgomery early in May, noted his anxious expression, his "haggard, care-worn, and pain-drawn look," and set down in the diary that the Confederate President "was quite aware of the difficulty of conquering the repugnance which exists (in Europe) to slavery." Benjamin, the attorney-general of the Confederacy, felt sure, however, that cotton would prove to be the king over Great Britain. "All this coyness about acknowledging a slave power will come right at last," he declared with a jaunty air.

Both the North and the South were disappointed at the action of England. Lord John Russell, the foreign minister, received unofficially the Confederate commissioners, but gave them no encouragement. In May the British government decided that a due regard to the commercial interests of its subjects required that it should take notice of affairs in America, and accordingly it issued, May 13, "The Queen's Proclamation of Neutrality." "Whereas," it said, "hostilities have unhappily commenced be-

---

secession in the faith that 'cotton is king,' and they had come to believe that they had a means to coerce the rest of the world by refusing to sell cotton. As soon as they undertook secession their direst necessity was to sell cotton. Their error came down to them in direct descent from 1774 and Jefferson's embargo."—Alexander Hamilton, p. 65.

tween the government of the United States of America and certain States styling themselves the Confederate States of America," it declared the "royal determination to maintain a strict and impartial neutrality in the contest between said contending parties." The proclamation, modelled after that issued in 1859 on the commencement of the war between Austria and France and Sardinia, with the usual whereases, recitals of statutes, warnings, and commands—an official matter-of-course on the occasion of a war between two friendly nations—derived now great importance for the reason that its issuance and the nature of its terms were the recognition of the Confederate States as a belligerent power. To regard the Confederate States as a belligerent conflicted with the theory of the Lincoln administration that the Southerners were insurgents, and with the largely prevailing notion at the North that they should be treated as rebels and traitors; and it placed in the eyes of nations—for all the important powers of Europe substantially followed the example of Great Britain—the vessels that should accept letters of marque from the Confederate government on the level of privateers, instead of considering them pirates and the men on board amenable to punishment for piracy, as the President's proclamation of April 19 had declared them to be. By Davis's inviting application for letters of marque, and by Lincoln's proclamation of blockade, it seemed probable to the English government that a maritime war would result; and the declaration of neutrality appeared necessary for the protection of British interests on the high seas as well as "an endeavor, so far as possible, to bring the management of it (i.e., 'a war of two sides') within the rules of modern civilized warfare."* It was a decided disadvantage to the Union that the probable Confed-

* Lord John Russell's statement in conversation to Adams, Adams to Seward, May 21. Russell also stated: "The fact was that a necessity seemed to exist to define the course of the government in regard to the participation of the subjects of Great Britain in the impending conflict. To that end the legal questions involved had been referred to those officers most conversant with them, and their advice had been taken in shaping the result. Their conclusion had been that, as a question merely of *fact*, a war existed."—*Message and Documents*, p. 92.

erate cruisers were at once given the quality of privateers instead of having the hand of every maritime power raised against them as pirates; but the English then, and have since, made out a good case.* It was a stubborn fact that the United States had, in 1856, refused its unconditional assent to a proposition, agreed to by the larger number of civilized nations, that "privateering is and remains abolished." Nevertheless, the American government and people felt honestly aggrieved at this action of Great Britain. Seward wrote that the queen's proclamation was "exceptionable," on account of its being issued on the very day of the arrival in England of Charles Francis Adams, the minister to the Court of St. James appointed by President Lincoln, and also for the matter of it; and Adams, in a conversation with Lord John Russell, "conducted in the most friendly spirit," after hearing his assignment of the reasons for the government's course, remarked "that the action taken seemed . . . a little more rapid than was absolutely called for by the occasion."

Northern men, feeling in every nerve that slavery was the single cause of the trouble, and deeming it impossible that England could shut her eyes to the patent fact that the peculiar insituation was the corner-stone of the Confederacy, looked to her, on account of her honorable and praiseworthy position towards negro slavery since 1833, for generous sympathy. The appar-

* Lord Russell, in conversation already cited and in that reported by Adams to Seward, June 14; Lord Russell to Lord Lyons, May 21, June 21, British and Foreign State Papers, 1860-61, pp. 192, 198; debate in the House of Lords, May 16. The London *Times* of May 15 said: "Being no longer able to deny the existence of a dreadful civil war, we are compelled to take official notice of it. . . . Our foreign relations are too extensive, the stake we hold in the commerce of the world is too vast, and, we may add, our attitude is a matter of too much importance for us to allow ourselves the gratification of saying 'Peace, when there is no peace,' so largely indulged in up to the very latest moment by the statesmen of America herself. Yes, there is war. . . . Eteocles and Polynices are confronting each other with hostile weapons, and England, like the venerable queen of Thebes, stands by to behold the unnatural combat of her children. From acknowledging the state of war the next step is to acknowledging the belligerent rights of the contending parties. . . . As belligerents they are as equal in our eyes as Trojan or Tyrian was in the eyes of Queen Dido. We are bound equally to respect their blockades and equally to abstain from any act which may violate the conditions of the most impartial and undiscriminating neutrality;" see, also, Earl Russell to Adams, Aug. 30, 1865.

ently undue haste, therefore, with which her government placed the Confederate States on an equality with the Union as to belligerent rights was galling; and it seemed to presage the recognition of their independence at the earliest opportune moment. There is, wrote Motley from his home, June 14, "a deep and intense feeling of bitterness and resentment towards England just now in Boston. . . . The most warm-hearted, England-loving men in this England-loving part of the country are full of sorrow at the attitude taken up by England. It would be difficult to exaggerate the poisonous effects produced by the long-continued, stinging, hostile articles in the *Times*. The declaration of Lord John Russell that the Southern privateers were to be considered belligerents, was received, as I knew and said it would be, with great indignation. . . . This, then, is the value, men say to me every moment, of the anti-slavery sentiment of England, of which she has boasted so much to mankind. This is the end of all the taunts and reproaches which she has flung at the United States government for being perpetually controlled by the slavery power, and for allowing its policy to be constantly directed towards extending that institution." The irritation at the North came largely from the belief that the Queen's Proclamation represented an evident desire on the part of the ruling classes of Great Britain to aid the South. The sending of the *Great Eastern* with troops to Canada fostered this impression. The concession of belligerent rights to the Confederates raised their hopes, and seemed to them to imply that they had not reckoned in vain on the support of England.

It cannot be averred that at this time our Secretary of State conducted foreign affairs with tact and wisdom. His despatch of May 21, even in the shape that it reached Adams, might, in the hands of a less competent and prudent minister, have led to serious difficulty; but had it been sent as Seward first wrote it— without the modifications and suggestions of the President, with the instruction to deliver to the British foreign minister a copy of it if he continued even unofficial intercourse with the Confederate commissioners; menacing, as it did, Great Britain for this and her presaged acknowledgment of the Southern privateers as lawful belligerents; threatening her categorically with war if she should recognize the Confederacy, and intimating that "the result of the debate in which we are engaged" may be war "between the United States and one, two, or even more European nations," in which the United States will come out of it very much better than Europe—the game would then have been in England's hands. To repel Seward's reckless language would be easy; to carry out the policy of acknowledging the independence of the Confederate States or of breaking the blockade, demanded by what then would have grown to be an irresistible sentiment, would have been grateful work for the English government. In turn, Northern public opinion might have exacted a declaration of war against Great Britain, which would also mean war with France, as the two European nations were then on a friendly footing and were acting together in American affairs. The infatuation of Seward is hard to understand; it shows that the notion which had prompted the "Thoughts for the President's consideration" still lodged in his brain, and that he dreamed that if the United States made war on England because she helped the Confederacy, the Southerners, by some occult emotional change, would sink their animosity to the North, and join with it for the sake of overcoming the traditional enemy. His unconcern at the prospect of serious trouble with England was not courage, but a recklessness which made him obvious of what all discerning Northern statesmen knew— that the people devoted to the Union had undertaken quite enough, in their endeavor to preserve the nation from destruction by its internal foes. "Great Britain," Seward wrote to his wife, "is in great danger of sympathizing so much with the South, for the sake of peace and cotton, as to drive us to make war against her as the ally of the traitors. If that comes, it will be the strife of the younger branch of the British stock for freedom against the older for slavery. It will be dreadful, but the end will be sure and swift." It is no wonder that Thurlow Weed, his friend and mentor, apprehended that he was "too decisive" with the European powers. The course of Seward was all the more dangerous in that it represented the defiant sentiment of many Northern people, and one can hardly exaggerate the evil it might have brought upon us had he not been restrained by the President, whose native good sense was instructed by the intelligence and discretion of Sumner. It produced mischief in England, where, sympathy being divided between the North and the South, it tended to make the position of the friends of the Union more difficult to maintain. "I earnestly entreat," wrote to Sumner the Duke of Argyll, a member of the British cabinet, and thoroughly friendly to the North, "that you will use your influence and official authority to induce your government, and especially Mr. Seward, to act in a more liberal and a less reckless spirit than he is supposed here to indicate towards foreign governments, and especially towards ourselves. I find much uneasiness prevailing here lest things should be done which would arouse a hostile spirit in this country. . . . I believe there is no desire stronger here than that of maintaining friendly relations with America. But there are points on which our people are very sensitive; and if they saw themselves touched on these points in honor or interest, the irritation would be extreme and could not be controlled." Fortunately, the position of minister to England was filled by a man who had extraordinary qualifications for the place. Charles Francis Adams —the selection of Seward, and thoroughly loyal to his chief— whose distinguished ancestry gave him especial welcome in a country where birth is highly esteemed, translated the harsh language of the Secretary of State into courteous but forcible reasoning: menace became remonstrance, and without taking a radical, or what might have proved an untenable, position, he persistently urged the claims of his government. If it be good diplomacy to see your own side of the question intensely, and your opponent's side with sufficient distinctness to repel his arguments, but not clearly enough to sympathize in the least with his standpoint, and, moreover, to present your case with candor and firmness, then Adams, in these first negotiations with Lord John Russell, showed himself a good diplomat, winning admiration from his own countrymen and respect from England.

While Adams was exhibiting our position in the most favorable light to the government and to "persons of weight in Great Britain," sober second thought had come to the administration and people in America. "There has nothing occurred here," wrote Schleiden from Washington, June 5, to Sumner, "in regard to Great Britain; and the President, who last night entertained the whole diplomatic body at dinner, told me, when I alluded to these relations, in a very sensible manner, that it appeared to him as if this government had no reason to complain of any European power in this contest, all of them having, by the long-continuing want of any distinct policy on the part of the United States, been induced more or less to believe the Union weaker, and the seceded States stronger, than was really the fact. He seemed not, at least, to be apprehensive, neither was Lord Lyons." A leading article in the New York *Tribune* of June 3, when compared with preceding expressions of opinion, showed either that it was inspired in high official quarters and was an effort to lead opinion, or else that it represented a changing public sentiment. This journal argued that the "evident desire" of the western European powers to maintain amicable relations with us had not been fairly met on this side of the water; defending England in some measure for her recognition of the belligerent rights of the Confederate States, it excused the unofficial reception of their commissioners by Lord John Russell. Returning to the subject the following day, it said that even if Great Britain or France should open one of the blockaded ports and load a merchant fleet with cotton, we had better pocket the insult for the supreme reason of necessity, for our war with the South was a "life-and-death struggle." As the scope of the Queen's Proclamation of Neutrality came to be more clearly understood, sentiment in the Union certainly grew more favorable towards Great Britain. The letters of Belmont and of Motley, representing as they did a wide range of opinion, reflect this improved feeling. Motley, while in Washington, had an hour's talk with Lincoln, and he spoke out of his large knowledge of the subject with friendliness and warm sympathy of the English government and people—to good purpose, he thought. The President's remark in his Fourth-of-July message was a sincere expression, and stated with reasonable exactness the sentiment of the public. "The sovereignty and rights of the United States," he declared, "are now everywhere practically respected by foreign powers, and a general sympathy with the country is manifested throughout the world."

With the change of feeling towards England, opinions altered touching the treatment of the Confederates. That severe punishment should be visited upon them had been the common desire. "I have seen it placarded in the streets of Boston," wrote George Ticknor, "that we should hang the secession leaders as fast as we can get them into our power. I have found this course openly urged in leading papers in New York and Boston. It is even said that the government at Washington is now considering the expediency of adopting it." No one, indeed, had seriously proposed that a traitor's doom should be meted out to the rank and file; and by the 4th of July it became apparent that prisoners taken in battle must be exchanged, and the war in other respects conducted on the same principles as war with a foreign nation. It was then seen that executions of the leaders would be revolting to humanity, and, moreover, that the Confederate States were strong enough to make reprisals. While I have not been able to trace the matter, it seems reasonable to believe that the declarations of the European powers had an influence in modifying public sentiment in this regard. Not that these declarations affected the law in the case, for legally as well as according to the popular notion the Confederates were rebels and traitors, but the nations of Europe expressed the opinion that they had shown sufficient strength to have conceded to them the rights of belligerents. Chase accurately described the course of the administration when, as chief-justice, he afterwards said, in a judgment delivered from the bench, "The rights and obligations of a belligerent were conceded to it [the Confederacy] in its military character very soon after the war began, from motives of humanity and expediency, by the United States." A fair statement of Northern sentiment by the 4th of July is that, although most of the rebels would be pardoned by a gracious government, Jefferson Davis and the men captured on board of vessels bearing his letters of marque should be hanged.

Adams wrote from London, May 31: "The feeling towards the United States is improving in the higher circles here. It was never otherwise than favorable among the people at large." Of the same tenor were his despatches of a week and a fortnight later. June 1 the English government interdicted the armed ships and privateers of both parties from carrying the prizes made by them into any British ports. This order in its operation would hurt the Confederacy, but not the Union, which had commissioned no privateers; it caused expostulations from the Confederate agents in London, and drew from Seward the remark that "it would probably prove a death-blow to Southern privateering."

THE *Mason and Slidell affair—the seizure by an American warship of Confederate envoys to Britain and France, taken by force from a British mail steamer on the high seas—caused great excitement in Europe and America. Rhodes uses his careful account of it as part of a study of British sentiment and British official attitudes. In this he showed a much more judicial attitude than most Northerners of his generation, who had deeply resented the position taken by the British upper classes and their leading organ, the London* Times. *It hurt many Americans to learn, as Rhodes pointed out with emphasis, that Seward had at first taken an incorrect stand, defending the seizure of Mason and Slidell when that act was quite indefensible under the terms of international law. Fortunately Lincoln was hesitant and moderate from the beginning, and some leading Americans proclaimed that the United States had been in the wrong. If Lincoln did not at first grasp the propriety of giving up Mason and Slidell, Charles Francis Adams and Sumner did, and helped bring Seward and Lincoln to the right decision.*

For the time when it was written, Rhodes's study of British neutrality marked a tremendous advance toward a just assessment of the foreign situation. He did not give sufficient weight to British middle-class sentiment, which was friendly from the beginning, and which after the Emancipation Proclamation became adamant against any unfriendly action—such action as Napoleon III was all too ready to take. Rhodes makes a few mistakes of fact. He thought that the whole British press was united in a determination to support the Palmerston government when the two envoys were captured, although actually important newspapers in London and Manchester refused to do so. He gave credit to British workingmen for their general adherence to the Northern side, even in the stricken cotton textile districts; but he paid too little attention to the religious press, especially on the nonconformist side, and to the influential London Daily News *and weekly* Spectator. *Yet in a complicated situation he picked his way well.*

It was not until 1925 that Ephraim D. Adams brought out a study of Great Britain and the Civil

War which treated the whole subject as primarily a chapter in British history, and which made use of much new material preserved in the British archives. On this work all subsequent treatments have relied heavily. It is noteworthy, however, that Adams made considerable use of the earlier investigations by Rhodes.

Mason and Slidell

ENGLISH sentiment up to late in the summer [of 1861] was favorable to the federal government. "I have not seen or heard of a soul," wrote Darwin, June 5, to Asa Gray, "who is not with the North." But when the detailed news of the battle of Bull Run became fully understood, when the full effect of it was comprehended, a marked revulsion of feeling took place. It is easy to classify the many manifestations of opinion, from the day that the tale of Bull Run was told in England to that on which London heard of the capture of Mason and Slidell. There were outspoken friends of the North, and men distinctly favorable to the South; but the dominant sentiment was that of the main body of the aristocracy and middle class, who, seeing clearly, as they thought, that the Union could not conquer the Confederacy, earnestly longed for the war to cease. The aristocracy had no tears to shed that the great and powerful democracy, rent by internal feud, was going the way of all democracies; they felt that a divided Union would be less of a moral menace than a compact democratic federal government to the intrenched rights on which most European governments, and particularly that of Great Britain, were based. The middle class, devoted to commerce and manufactures, were disturbed that the supply of cotton was cut off. Business became deranged. Hunger stared thousands of laborers in the face. Higher in the social scale, the fear of curtailed incomes and of the sacrifice of luxuries and necessaries may be plainly seen. Goldwin Smith, a friend to the North, described the situation in terms

none too strong: "The awful peril, not only commercial but
social, with which the cotton famine threatened us, and the
thrill of alarm and horror which upon the dawning of that peril
ran through the whole land."* Peace would open the Southern
ports, would restore comfort to the British householder; and
as it seemed to him that the South was in the end certain to
gain her independence, the sooner the fact was acknowledged
by the North, the sooner would the disturbed equilibrium be
restored. This was the opinion of the great body of voting
Whigs and of such Conservatives as did not distinctly sympathize with the South, and it found fitting representation in
Palmerston and Russell, the two leading men of the cabinet.
Earl Russell, in a speech at Newcastle in October, told the
British public that the American civil war did not turn on the
question of slavery, "though that, I believe," he added, "was
the original cause of the quarrel;" neither was the strife about
free trade or protection; but the two parties were "contending,
as so many States in the old world have contended, the one for
empire and the other for independence." To what good result,
he asked, can the contest lead? He answered his own question,
to the effect that a separation of the two sections was the only
logical and permanent settlement of the controversy. The notion
that the Union could never be restored found expression in the
Times and the *Saturday Review,* which, gravitating naturally
to the representation of the opinion of the majority of the English public, made, by reason of the ability with which they ham-
mered away, many converts from among the waverers. The
laboring class, so far as they thought at all, sympathized with

* *Macmillan's Magazine,* Dec., 1865, p. 167. See detailed figures in London *Times* of Sept. 7. "The reports from Lancashire apprise us that the
first mutterings of the long-expected storm are already heard. Mills are
working short time, manufacturers are reducing wages, and operatives
assembling in trouble and alarm to discuss the prospects before them.
. . . The fact is that our stocks of cotton are rapidly sinking, while the
supplies on the road to us are of uncertain quality and insufficient
amount. . . . So a manufacture which pays upward of £ 11,000,000 in
wages, and supports a fifth part of our whole population, is coming gradually to a stand."—London *Times,* Sept. 19. "Lancashire calls for so many
million bales of cotton, but these bales are paid for with so many millions
of pounds. In fact, it is a trade of some £ 40,000,000 a year."—*Ibid.,* Sept.
21.

the United States. They saw clearly, as did the aristocracy, that the cause of the North was the cause of democracy in England; but they counted little in making up the sum of public sentiment, for parliamentary representation was based upon the reform bill of 1832, which gave them no share in the suffrage.

It is not the least of the glories of England that when public opinion veers strongly in one direction, she has men who see clearer than the mass, and set themselves at work to stem the current; who speak boldly and with no uncertain sound; whose boldness, whose resistance to the tyranny of the majority, if joined to ability and honesty, rarely if ever—such is the wholesomeness of English political life—compel them to retirement. Most conspicuous of these men, who at this time were unreservedly on the side of the North, was John Bright. September 6 he wrote Sumner from Rochdale, giving his own opinion and an exposition of the sentiment of the country. "The *Times* newspaper, as you know," he said, "will willingly make mischief if its patrons want mischief, and on your side you have the New York *Herald* doing Southern work when it dares to do it, and stirring up ill-blood with England as the best mode of helping its Southern friends. Public opinion here is in a languid and confused state. The upper and ruling class have some satisfaction, I suspect, in your troubles—they think two nations on your northern continent more easy to deal with than one, and they see, without grief, that democracy may get into trouble and war and debt and taxes, as aristocracy has done for this country. The middle class wish abolition to come out of your contentions, but they are irritated by your foolish tariff, and having so lately become free-traders themselves, of course they are great purists now, and severely condemn you. In this district we have a good many friends of the South—the men who go South every year to buy cotton for our spinners, and those among our spinners and merchants who care little for facts and right, and go just where their interest seems to point. I have not, so far, seen any considerable manifestation of a disposition to urge our government to interfere in your affairs; and yet with some, doubtless, there is a hope that France and

England will not permit their cotton manufacture to be starved out by your contest. There is a great anxiety as to what is coming. Our mills are just now reducing their working time to four days and some of them to three days in the week; this is not universal or general, but it is spreading, and will soon become general, I cannot doubt. Working half-time we can go on till April or May perhaps, but this will cause suffering and discontent, and it is possible pressure may be put upon the government to take some step supposed likely to bring about a change. I preach the doctrine that the success of the North is our nearest way to a remedy, but there are those who hold a contrary opinion. . . . With our upper-class hostility to your country and government, with the wonderful folly of your tariff telling against you here, and with the damage arising from the blockade of the Southern ports, you will easily understand that the feeling here is not so thorough and cordial with you as I could wish it to be."

Bright was the ablest and best-known exponent of the friendly feeling towards the North, but he had many sympathizing friends. Cobden, William E. Forster, the Duke of Argyll, and Thomas Hughes are not only men of grateful memory to the North, but they reflect honor on their own land. The *Daily News* and the *Spectator* urged the cause of the North without ceasing, with signal ability uniting large information to correct judgment.* The sentiment towards America in England depended

* "We believe, as we always did, that the South cannot hold out."— *Daily News*, Sept. 17. "The Southern States are, according to their own formal declaration, fighting not only to perpetuate, but to extend the institution of slavery."—*Ibid.*, Oct. 10; see, also, Sept. 18, Oct. 2, 3, 4. "The news of every succeeding mail from America makes it more and more evident that the slavery issue is the practical hinge of the civil war. . . . The view taken by the conservatives, whether avowed or concealed under the cloak of moderate liberalism, is . . . that the North are fighting for an impossibility. . . . This impossibility is rather a new invention; it dates from the battle of Bull Run. . . . To talk of the endeavor [of the North] as an impossibility is an abuse of human language." —London *Spectator*, Sept. 14; see, also, Sept. 28, Nov. 16. The London *Star* was also strong in its sympathy with the North. I have read many extracts from it, but have not consulted its files, for the reason that, as it was the reputed organ of Cobden and Bright, I have preferred to show this phase of sentiment by their private letters.

to some extent on differences of political opinion. The war and the Northern conduct of it were used with effect by the *Times* and the *Saturday Review* to point the moral of the failure of the great democracy to realize the hopes of its English advocates. "Help us to a breath of generous strengthening sympathy from Old England," wrote Sumner to William H. Russell, "which will cheer the good cause, and teach everybody that there can be no terms of any kind with a swarm of traitors trying to build a State on human slavery." "I do not approve," wrote Russell in reply, "of the tone of many papers in Great Britain in reference to American matters; but do not forget, I pray you, that in reality it is Brightism and republicanism at home which most of those remarks are meant to smite. America is the shield under which the blow is dealt.* In the light of succeeding events and the well-rounded career of John Bright, we may venture to assert that he had high moral and political wisdom and chose the right side, and that the dominant English opinion was wrong and did harm to Great Britain, to America, and to civilization. "Some friends of mine in this town," he wrote Sumner from Rochdale, November 20, "have invited me to a public dinner on the 4th of December. I intend to take that opportunity for saying something on your great political earthquake, and I need not tell you that I shall not abandon the faith I have in the greatness of the free North. It has been a misfortune here that so little has been said to instruct the public on the true bearings of your question, for it is incredible almost how densely ignorant even our middle and upper class is with regard to your position. The sympathies of the great body of the people here are, I think, quite right, although some papers supposed to be read by them are wrong. I suspect there has been some tampering with a certain accessible portion of the press. I am very anxious that your affairs should take some more de-

* Letter of Oct. 2, Pierce-Sumner Papers, MS.; see the London *Times* of Aug. 19. "The real secret of the exultation which manifests itself in the *Times* and other organs over our troubles and disasters, is their hatred, not to America so much as to democracy in England."—Motley to his mother from England, Sept. 22, *Correspondence,* vol. ii. p. 35.

cided turn before our Parliament meets about the 1st of February. When a mob of 650 men get together with party objects and
little sympathy for you or for the right anywhere, there is no
knowing what mischief may come out of foolish and wicked
speeches, with a ministry led by such a man as the present Prime
Minister of England. However, I will hope for the best."

If, with the results before us, we extol the political percep-
tions of the few, fairness demands that we examine the contemporary evidence to ascertain what may excuse the mistake
of the majority. That Earl Russell, the *Times,* and the *Saturday Review* made out an apparently good case, hardly needs
stating. The iterated and reiterated argument ran that, as the
Confederacy was certain to gain its independence, the sooner
the disturbance was put an end to the better. "The people of
the Southern States," declared the *Times,* "may be wrong, but
they are ten millions." This summed up the political philosophy of the British public; yet the notion that the North
could not conquer the South was shared by many of our friends.
"Judging from this distance," wrote Bright to Sumner, September 6, "I confess I am unable to see any prospect of reunion
through a conquest of the South, and I should grieve to see it
through any degrading concessions on the part of the North.
I confess I am surprised at the difficulties you meet with even
in the border States. It would seem that the separation in regard to feeling and interests had made a fatal progress before
secession was openly proclaimed; for surely, if there was a
large and preponderating sympathy for the Union in those
States, the Northern forces would have great advantages over
the South in the conduct of their operations which they do not
now appear to have. . . . I cannot see how the South, with its
vast territory, is to be subdued, if there be any of that unanimity among its population which is said to exist, and of which
there are some proofs. If it be subdued, I cannot see in the future a contented section of your great country made up of
States now passing through the crisis of a civil war, with every
ferocious passion excited against the North; and the prospect

being so dark, looking through the storm of war, I am hoping
for something that will enable you to negotiate." "The belief
is largely held," he wrote, November 20, that the subjugation
of the South "is barely, if at all, possible, and that a restoration
of the Union is not to be looked for." Cobden did not believe
that the North and the South could "ever lie in the same bed
again." "I hope to God," wrote Darwin, "we English are
utterly wrong in doubting whether the North can conquer
the South." On our side of the water the letter of William M.
Evarts to Thurlow Weed, purporting to give "about the staple
of opinion and conversation when men talked freely," breathed
out despair of the Union being able to conquer the Confederacy.

It was frequently asserted that if the North, in 1861, had
avowed the war to be against slavery, we should have had the
warm sympathy of the British public.* The proclamation of
emancipation, if issued a year earlier, would undoubtedly have
increased the enthusiasm of our English friends,† and lent

* "If the issue of forcible and total emancipation is raised, the United
States will have no reason hereafter to complain of a want of popular sympathy in England."—London *Saturday Review*, Sept. 28; see, also, Oct. 5,
Nov. 9. "That the doctrine of emancipation, if always and sincerely
professed by the Northern States, would have strongly commended their
cause to the sympathies of this country, is not for a moment to be doubted.
. . . The public in this country would rejoice to see an end made of
slave-holding, and so far the North might gain."—London *Times*, Sept. 30.
"There would perhaps be an overwhelming sentiment of popular sympathy with the North in this conflict if they were fighting for freedom; but
the pretence that this is an anti-slavery war cannot be sustained for a moment, and is sedulously disavowed by the government itself."—W. H.
Russell to Sumner, Oct. 14, Pierce-Sumner Papers, MS.; see also New
York *Tribune*, Aug. 11.

† Bright wrote Sumner, Sept. 6: "Many console themselves with the
hope that the great question of the future condition of your four million
negroes is about to be solved. I do not see how you can move for emancipation within your Constitution, or without giving to the South a complete cause in favor of their insurrection; but if necessity or the popular
feeling should drive you to it, then there will, I think, be no power in this
country able to give any support to the South. Many who cavil at you now
say, 'If the war was for liberating the slave, then we could see something
worth fighting for, and we could sympathize with the North.' I cannot
urge you to this cause. The remedy for slavery would be almost worse
than the disease, and yet how can such a disease be got rid of without
some desperate remedy?" Harriet Martineau wrote Sumner, Nov. 14:

augmented potency to their arguments; but the course of English opinion after September, 1862, may well raise the doubt whether it would have helped us with the aristocracy and the bulk of the middle class. . . .

The irritation caused by the ungenerous criticism of the London journals was cast back by the recrimination of our own press. Chief in truculence was the New York *Herald.* "We first unmasked it," it said, "and then spiked the battery which English aristocrats were preparing against this country and its liberties. . . . We notified the English government and aristocracy that we were prepared to resent the insults they seemed disposed to offer us, and have thus far kept England in abeyance;" and seven weeks later it declared, "Let England and Spain look well to their conduct, or we may bring them to a reckoning." Such writing did harm to our cause. "It is unfortunate," said John Bright, in a letter to Sumner of November 20, "that nothing is done to change the reckless tone of your New York *Herald;* between it and the *Times* of London there is great mischief done in both countries." As friends of the North in England endeavored to depreciate the influence of the London *Times,* so did friends of England in America underrate the power of the New York *Herald.* But, in truth, this journal spoke for a potent public sentiment outside of New England. By its large news-gathering agencies, and by its

---

"Whenever the anti-slavery view is adopted and acted upon at Washington in any preponderant way, you will have no reason to complain of coldness on this side of the water. . . . I need not explain that I, with my American friendships and sympathies, am eager and constant in speaking up for what you and I consider the right, and in hoping for the best; but the pottering at Washington is infinitely damaging here to your cause."— Pierce-Sumner Papers, MS. Darwin wrote Asa Gray, June 5: "Some few, and I am one of them, even wish to God, though at the loss of millions of lives, that the North would proclaim a crusade against slavery. In the long-run, a million horrid deaths would be amply repaid in the cause of humanity."—*Life and Letters,* vol. ii. p. 166. "We can wait till the occasion arises for showing how England can sympathize with a people who have a purpose to abolish slavery."—London *Daily News,* Sept. 17. "We have no hesitation in saying that we believe the boldest course would be the wisest. The Union can never be restored again with the old canker at the roots."—London *Spectator,* Oct. 5.

unvarying support of the administration, it had a large and increasing circulaticn. Men who were eager for the latest and fullest news from the field, and who wished to stand loyally by Lincoln against the fault-finding of peace Democrats on one side and of Frémont radicals on the other, read it gladly. It had a body of devoted readers whom it could influence, and in working up animosity towards England it played upon an oft-used string. The American voter of 1861 had learned at school, from his crude historical study of the Revolution and the War of 1812, that England was a natural enemy; and failing now, in his own country's death-grapple, to make proper allowance for the difficulties of her situation, he was ready and apt to mis-judge her. Thus censure and recrimination went on between the two countries.

The English public had facts enough for a correct judgment. The *Times* and *Daily News* were full of trustworthy informa-tion, and a cereful reading of them, with a fairly enlightened judgment, ought to have led to the conviction that, although the success of the North would not necessarily bring about the abolition of slavery, it was certain to deprive that institution of its political and social power, and eventually destroy it, while the success of the South was sure to extend negro slavery and reopen the African slave-trade. To deny this was to shut the eyes to patent facts. Yet the English would not believe there was a moral question involved in the contest,* because, under the influence of their hatred of democracy and their desire for good trade and prosperous manufactures, they did not wish to believe it; and the thought that the South would probably succeed developed into a wish for its success. Nevertheless, it

---

* Edward Dicey wrote: "I have often heard it asserted, and I have seen the statement constantly repeated in the English press, that slavery had nothing to do with the questions at issue between the North and the South. I can only say that during my residence in Washington [the early part of 1862] I heard little talked about except the question of slavery."—*Federal States*, vol. i. p. 190. Anthony Trollope wrote: "It is vain to say that slavery has not caused secession, and that slavery has not caused the war. That, and that only, has been the real cause of this conflict, though other small collateral issues may now be put forward to bear the blame."—*North America* (1862), vol. ii. p. 61.

may not be becoming for an American to pass condemnation, for, being true children of the mother-country, it may be suspected that, in similar circumstances, we should have likewise erred; that, had England been engaged in a war in which justice, supported by the monarchy and the aristocracy, was on one side, and American dollars and a plausible case on the other, the dominant sympathy in our country would have been with the cause which seemed linked with our commercial prosperity.

Great Britain preserved a strict neutrality. What Motley wrote from Paris may, in the light of the later evidence, be affirmed as true up to the last of November. "The present English government," he said, "has thus far given us no just cause of offence." Louis Napoleon, the emperor of the French, though in his American policy he did not represent the intelligent and liberal sentiment of his country, had officially asked England to co-operate with him in recognizing the Confederacy and breaking the blockade, but this she had refused to do. Motley saw the English Foreign Secretary in September, and gave to Holmes an account of his visit. "I think I made some impression on Lord John Russell," he wrote, "with whom I spent two days soon after my arrival in England; and I talked very frankly and as strongly as I could to Lord Palmerston. . . . For this year there will be no foreign interference with us, and and I do not anticipate it at any time, unless we bring it on ourselves by bad management. . . . Our fate is in our own hands, and Europe is looking on to see which side is the strongest. When it has made the discovery, it will back it as also the best and the most moral." The impression which Motley made was not lasting. In October Earl Russell proposed to Palmerston that England unite with France in an offer of mediation between the North and the South, with the implied understanding that a refusal of it by the United States would make these two European countries her enemies. Palmerston did not agree with Russell, but thought their true policy was to keep clear of the conflict; his opinion determined the course of the government, which was in harmony with the prevailing sentiment of the country, although the disposition of the Emperor Napoleon was a matter of public knowledge.

Such was the state of public sentiment in England, and of feeling in the United States in regard to it, when an over-zealous American naval commander brought the two countries to the brink of war. James M. Mason and John Slidell, who had been appointed commissioners from the Southern Confederacy to Great Britain and France, reached Havana on a little steamer which had successfully run the blockade, and there they took passage for Southampton in the British mail steamship *Trent*. November 8, the next day after she left Havana, she was overhauled in the Bahama Channel by the American man-of-war *San Jacinto,* under the command of Captain Wilkes. He fired a shot across her bow without result, and then a shell; this brought her to. The lieutenant of the *San Jacinto* with a number of sailors and marines boarded the *Trent,* and took from her by force Mason, Slidell, and their secretaries, in spite of their appeal to the British flag for protection, and in spite of the protest of Captain Williams, of the royal navy, in charge of the mails. The prisoners were taken to Fort Warren in Boston harbor.

The news of this transaction was received in New York November 16. The country went wild with jubilant delight as if it had gained a signal victory in the field. The Northern people had waited and watched so long for some result from the immense levies of men and of money that it is no wonder they gave way to extravagant joy when the two men, who of all the Confederates except Davis and Floyd were hated the worst, were delivered into their hands. Blended with the feeling that Mason and Slidell would now be prevented from doing us mischief abroad was the thought that they would serve as important hostages. Fourteen federal officers, prisoners of war at Richmond and Charleston, had been selected by lot to be hanged in case the pirate's doom should be meted out to the same number of privateersmen confined at the North, and carrying out the plan of treating them as common felons, they

had been incarcerated in the county jail. It was now proposed
that, in retalitation, Mason and Slidell be sent to the Tombs,
and that if the hanging began, it should not end until these men
of distinction had died on the scaffold. It was understood that
Great Britain had to be reckoned with, but in the flush of excitement war with her was looked at without trepidation; for
the belief existed that if half a million men could be raised to
battle for the Union, double that number would enlist to fight
the traditional enemy. As representing the prevalent sentiment,
Secretary Welles sent a congratulatory letter to Captain Wilkes;
Boston gave him a banquet at which Governor Andrew and the
Chief Justice of the Massachusetts Supreme Court spoke with
enthusiasm; he was a guest at the dinner of the Boston Saturday Club; and the National House of Representatives on the
first day of its session thanked him. It also requested the President to confine Mason as a convicted felon. Edward Everett,
Caleb Cushing, and Richard H. Dana, Jr., justified the act of
Wilkes. The press teemed with discussions of the legal points
involved, and with citations from the authorities on international law tending to show that the American captain had acted
within proper limits.

Secretary Welles is authority for the statement that all the
members of the cabinet, except Blair, shared his own jubilation
and that of the House and the country at the arrest of Mason
and Slidell. Lincoln was not carried away by the general joy.
He knew that the act of Wilkes was not in line with principles
for which he had contended, and for this reason, and for the
further one that it might be hard to resist the popular clamor
for their summary punishment, he feared that they would
"prove to be white elephants." Of all the men in responsible
positions Sumner and Blair saw the clearest; they were in
favor of at once surrendering to England the Confederate commissioners. Had Lincoln understood international law as well
as Sumner, and had he felt that confidence of public support
which he did later, he might have directed this, for in doing
a rightful act he was capable of breasting popular sentiment.

His sense of the feeling of the people was keener than his knowledge of international law, and knowing he had alienated the
radicals by his treatment of Frémont, he held back with his
habitual caution from a peremptory move which might also
lose him the support of that body of conservative Republicans
and war Democrats whose ideas were fairly espoused by the
New York *Herald*. Yet at this time four men could have led
public opinion. If Lincoln, Seward, Chase, and Sumner had
declared that the act of Wilkes was contrary to the law of nations and our own precedents, that Great Britain had been
wronged, and that the injury could be atoned only by the surrender of Mason and Slidell, the country would have acquiesced
in it. Policy as well as justice dictated such a course. It was
true, as the London *Times* affirmed, that "the voices of these
Southern commissioners, sounding from their captivity, are a
thousand times more eloquent in London and in Paris than
they would have been if heard at St. James's and the Tuileries."
The American government, not being able to rise to the height
of giving up these captives before they were demanded, did the
next best thing. If, as Welles asserts, Seward was at first as elated
as any one, reflection changed his mind, for his despatch to
Adams of November 30 was prudent, and seems to indicate that
he believed the surrender of Mason and Slidell to be the probable solution of the difficulty.* The secretary informed Adams
that Captain Wilkes had acted "without any instruction from
the government," and gave him permission to impart this fact,
and to read the whole of his friendly, confidential note to Earl
Russell and Lord Palmerston. In his annual message the President made no allusion to the affair. November 27 England
received the news of the arrest of Mason and Slidell. The opin-

---

* It seems to me clear from Seward's letters to Weed (Dec. 27, 1861, and
Jan. 22, 1862, *Life of Seward,* vol. iii. pp. 34, 43) that he was determined,
after he had carefully considered the matter, to urge the surrender of the
commissioners, if Great Britain demanded them; and although his letter to
Weed of March 7, 1862 (*Galaxy*, March, 1870), is somewhat inconsistent
with this view, it does not necessarily contravene it. This is all the more
creditable to Seward on account of the Jingo policy he had pursued, and
on account of his bitterness towards England.

ion was general that it was an outrage to her flag. Liverpool, strong in sympathy with the South, held a crowded and influential indignation meeting. It "has made a great sensation here," wrote John Bright to Sumner from London, "and the ignorant and passionate and 'Rule Britannia' class are angry and insolent as usual. The ministers meet at this moment on the case." The next day Bright wrote from Manchester: "A cabinet council was held yesterday. The chancellor, attorney, and solicitor-general were agreed, and decided that you have done an illegal act in seizing the commissioners. . . . I have urged that . . . nothing should be asked from your government that you could not easily comply with. The tone of the ministers is not violent, and I hope they will be moderate." At that meeting the cabinet decided that the act of Captain Wilkes was "a clear violation of the law of nations, and one for which reparation must be at once demanded." Earl Russell prepared a despatch to Lord Lyons, the language of which was softened and made more friendly on the suggestion of the Queen and the prince consort; but as modified, the British government demanded the liberation of Mason, Slidell, and their secretaries, and "a suitable apology for the aggression." Seward was to have seven days, if necessary, to make a reply; but if at the end of that time no answer or an unfavorable one should be received, Lord Lyons was instructed to leave Washington and "to repair immediately to London." On Sunday, December 1, a Queen's messenger bearing this despatch was on his way to Washington. The admiralty began making extensive naval preparations; eight thousand troops were sent to Canada; the Queen by proclamation prohibited the export of arms and ammunition.

"England's attitude," wrote Martin Farquhar Tupper, a friend of the North, "is that of calm, sorrowful, astonished determination." This well expresses the sentiment of the majority of Englishmen who had property and intelligence. They felt that the United States "had invaded the sanctuary which England extends to all political exiles who seek her protection," and that it had, moreover, insulted her flag. Though

averse to war, they agreed that if adequate reparation were
not made they must resort to the ultimate argument of nations.
War meant the decimation of families and increased taxation,
yet while Great Britain could inflict injury on the United
States, such a war could bring no glory. Neither could it be
ignored that she would be the ally of a slave power, nor that her
merchant marine could be harmed beyond measure by American privateers. The longing that the Washington government
would so act that this public woe might be averted was earnest
and sincere. That such a war would open the Southern ports and
give them the much-needed supply of cotton, was far from
being deemed a sufficient compensation for the damage to
England which would ensue. The question still pending made
the usual merry Christmas a gloomy festival.*

A certain set in England, however, strong in social influence
and position, had so ardent and active a sympathy with the
South that they were for war at any price, and they did their
best to embroil the two countries. "The excitement here
has been and is great," wrote John Bright to Sumner, December 5, "and it is fed, as usual, by newspapers, who seem
to imagine a cause of war discovered to be something like
'treasure-trove.'" Two days later he said: "There is more calm-
ness here in the public mind—which is natural after last week's
explosion—but I fear the military and naval demonstrations
of our government point to trouble, and I am not sure that it
would grieve certain parties here if any decent excuse could be
found for a quarrel with you. You know the instinct of aristocracy and of powerful military services, and an ignorant people
is easily led astray on questions foreign to their usual modes of

* "Christmas comes this year on a country bright with sun and frost,
but on a people oppressed with a national loss and threatened with a
formidable war. Already closed mills and short time have given some part
of our population an earnest of what they may hereafter expect; already
speculation is more careful than it has been for many years, and the sombre
appearance of our churches and chapels last Sunday portends a bad season
next spring for the many trades concerned in female attire. The prospect
of an aggravated income-tax sits like a nightmare on many households."—
London *Times*, Dec. 27.

thought." In his letter of December 5 he described the sentiment of a majority of his countrymen much as it seems to me to have been from a study of the London press and the other evidence. "Our law officers," he wrote from Rochdale, "are agreed and strong in their opinion of the illegality of the seizure of the commissioners. . . . All the people here, of course, accept their opinion as conclusive as to the law of the case. . . . Now, notwithstanding the war spirit here, I am sure, even in this district where your civil strife is most injuriously felt, that all thoughtful and serious men, and indeed the great majority of the people, will be delighted if some way can be found out of the present difficulty. . . . Nations *drift* into wars—as we drifted into the late war with Russia—often through the want of a resolute hand at some moment early in the quarrel. So, now, a courageous stroke, not of arms, but of moral action, may save you and us. . . . It is common here to say that your government cannot resist the mob violence by which it is surrounded. I do not believe this, and I know that our government is often driven along by the force of the genteel and aristocratic mob which it mainly represents. But now in this crisis I fervently hope that you may act firmly and courteously; any moderate course you may take will meet with great support here, and in the English cabinet there are, as I certainly know, some who will gladly accept any fair proposition for friendly arrangement from your side."

An offset to the war-at-any-price faction was the group represented by Bright, Cobden, and Forster. They urged the treatment of the matter in an amicable way; should the federal government maintain that its act was legal and right, they were ready to accept arbitration, or even propose it, rather than go to war. At Rochdale, December 4, Bright made a noble, sympathetic, and convincing speech, reaching a moral height which few public men ever attain. "This steamer will take out a report of Bright's speech," wrote Cobden to Sumner, December 5, "and my letter of excuse for not being able to attend. You will see that we stand in the breach, as usual, to stem the tide of passion. But you know that we don't represent all England at such a moment. . . . You will see a new feature in this disagreeable matter in the ardor with which the French press takes up the cry against you. Some of the papers most eager to push us to extremities are those which are conducted by parties who are supposed to be in the confidence of the emperor."

On the whole, the attitude of the majority of the English pending the difficulty was dignified, although they showed some acerbity upon hearing the news of the way in which Wilkes's action had been received in the United States—"the outburst of hilarity," as the *Times* described it. The Southern sympathizers, however, were active and aggressive, using arguments which had considerable power over the English mind. The pressure of the blockade, the proposal of the federal government to sink in the channels leading to the Southern ports vessels laden with stone, the animosity of Seward to Great Britain, were urged as fortifying reasons to the outrage committed on board the steamer *Trent,* all of which together would justify a declaration of war. Seward's course irritated English opinion, and made the position of our friends and that of the larger number of Englishmen who desired to preserve a strict neutrality harder to maintain. "There is a feeling among our ministers," wrote Bright to Sumner, November 29, "that Mr. Seward is not so friendly in his transactions with them as they could wish." This feeling was shared by the public. A remark he was said to have made to the Duke of Newcastle, who accompanied the Prince of Wales to America in 1860, went the rounds. Seward told the duke, at a dinner given by Governor Morgan to the prince, that in the next administration he should probably occupy high office; that "it would become his duty to insult England, and that he should insult her accordingly." The remark—supposing that the duke understood it correctly—was probably an attempt at facetiousness, but he took the very poor joke in sober earnest, and gave the story to the ministry; afterwards it got into the newspapers, and at this time had considerable influence on public opinion. The subsequent acts of Seward seemed to confirm the accuracy of the report. It was also believed that, soon after his accession to office, he had proposed to the North and the South that they sink their differences and unite in an attack on Canada. His public circular of October 14 to the governors of all the States on the seaboard and lakes, urging them to put their ports and harbors in a condition of complete defence in order to guard against attack from foreign nations, when joined to all the other circumstances, seemed to show that, for his own behoof, he was determined to provoke a war with Great Britain. "There is general distrust and hostility to yourself," said Thurlow Weed, in a letter from London of December 6 to Seward. "There is an impression, I know, in high quarters here," wrote Cobden to Sumner, November 29, "that Mr. Seward wishes to quarrel with this country. This seems absurd enough. I confess I have as little confidence in him as I have in Lord Palmerston. Both will consult bunkum for the moment, without much regard, I fear, for the future." We may, I think, accept as faithful this characterization.

Yet in the Mason and Slidell affair Seward behaved better than Palmerston. We have seen that the secretary wrote Adams, November 30, that he might assure Lord Palmerston and Earl Russell that Captain Wilkes had acted without any authority whatever from the government. December 19 Adams imparted this to Russell, and although the American minister took great care that the despatch and his conference with the British foreign secretary should be kept strictly private, an inkling of them in some manner leaked out, and the funds rose one per cent. on the next day. In the meantime popular opinion took an admirable turn. The Bright and Cobden party had gained on the British public at the expense of the sympathizers with the Southern Confederacy. The feeling became strong that if agreement could not be reached by negotiation, arbitration were preferable to war. The giving out of the virtual contents of Seward's despatch by Palmerston would have been proper, and would have caused joy in the financial and commercial circles of London. But not only did he fail to confirm the pleasant rumor which had obtained currency, but he suffered his accredited organ, the *Morning Post,* to assert more than once, without correction, that while Adams had indeed communicated a despatch to the British government, it "in no way related to the difficulty about the *Trent.*" It is possible that Palmerston, with an eye to his majority in the House of Commons, soon to assemble, saw fit to cajole the war party, in which were many members of Parliament, while other members of the cabinet sympathized with the dominant opinion for peace. "I *suspect,*" wrote Bright to Sumner, December 21, "there is a section of our government disposed for war, but I *know* there is another section disposed for peace."* "We in England," said Cobden in a letter to Sumner, "have ready a fleet surpassing in destructive force any naval armament the world ever saw, exceeding greatly the British navy in the great French war in 1810. *This force has been got up under false pretences.* There is always a desire on the part of governments to use such armaments, by way of proving that they were necessary. *France* was the pretence, and now we have plenty of people who would be content to see this fleet turned against you."†

* Pierce-Sumner Papers, MS. Bright had written, Dec. 14: "The unfavorable symptom is the war preparations of the government and the sending of troops to Canada and the favor shown to the excitement which so generally precedes war. This convinces us either that this government believes that you intend war with England, or that itself intends war with you. The first supposition is scarcely credible—unless the New York *Herald* be accepted as the confidential organ of your government (!), or that Lord Lyons has misrepresented the feeling of the Washington cabinet. The second supposition may be true—for it may be imagined that by a war got up on some recent pretence, such as your steamer *San Jacinto* is supposed to have given, we may have cotton sooner than by waiting for your success against the South. I know nothing but what is in the papers, but I conclude that this government is ready for war if an excuse can be found for it. I need not tell you that at a certain point the moderate opinion of a country is borne down by the passion which arises and which takes the name of patriotism, and that the good men here who abhor war may have no influence if a blow is once struck."—*Ibid.*

† Letter of Dec. 12, Pierce-Sumner Papers, MS. Cobden wrote, Jan., 1862: "Palmerston ought to be turned out for the reckless expense to which he has put us. . . . Then came Seward's despatch to Adams on the 19th December, which virtually settled the matter. To keep alive the wicked passions in this country as Palmerston and his *Post* did was like the man, and that is the worst that can be said of it."—Morley's *Cobden,* p. 572; see, also, Goldwin Smith's article, *Macmillan's Magazine,* Dec. 1865.

The Queen's messenger delivered Earl Russell's despatch of November 30 to the British minister at Washington at half-past eleven on the night of December 18. Lord Lyons saw Seward the next day, and, in accordance with private instructions, did not read Russell's despatch, but acquainted him with the tenor of it, saying that her majesty's government would be satisfied with nothing less than the liberation of the captive commissioners. The Secretary of State asked for a little delay. December 23 Lyons read to Seward England's formal demand, and left him a copy of it. It does not appear that the British minister stated that unless he received a satisfactory answer in seven days he should close his legation and leave Washington, nor that Seward asked what would be the consequence should the United States refuse compliance. In a private note from Russell to Lyons the desire of the English government "to abstain from anything like menace" was expressed. Courtesy and a conciliatory manner marked the conduct of the Englishman, dignity and gravity that of the American during these negotiations. On Christmas morning the President assembled his cabinet. Earl Russell's despatch was read. The Secretary of State submitted the draft of his answer proposing to surrender Mason and Slidell to the British authorities. Sumner came by invitation to the cabinet meeting, and read to the gentlemen assembled the letters of John Bright, and the most important of those from Cobden. While the discussion to which these papers gave rise was going on, a despatch from the Minister of Foreign Affairs of France to Mercier, her representative at Washington, was sent into the council-room. This asserted that England had made a just demand, and urged that the federal government comply with it. The despatch had been received only that morning by Mercier. Impressed by its importance he had hurried to the White House, and begged that it be submitted at once to Seward. The discussion went on until two o'clock, and was continued the next day. Seward maintained that, Wilkes having clearly violated the law of nations, England had a right to ask for the restoration of the Confederate commissioners. Sumner, either in the cabinet meeting or out of it, strongly supported this view of the Secretary of State. The President and some members of the cabinet hesitated. Lincoln had entertained the notion of proposing arbitration; perhaps it had been suggested to him by one of Bright's letters. While he cared little about keeping Mason and Slidell, and was earnestly anxious to avoid war with Great Britain, he feared the sentiment of the people. In the end, however, from the considerations that the United States did not have a good case and that it could not afford a war with Great Britain, all came to Seward's position and approved his answer. His letter, dated December 26, was a lengthy discussion of the law, obviously written for its effect at home. The best and perhaps the only necessary parts were: This government cannot deny the justice of the claim presented by the British government, which "is not made in a discourteous manner," and "the four persons in question . . . will be cheerfully liberated." Mason, Slidell, and their secretaries were delivered to an English steamer at Provincetown. The disavowal of the act was accepted as a sufficient apology.

THE *first strong gleam of sunshine for the North, wiping out the memories of the defeats at Bull Run, Ball's Bluff, and Wilson's Creek, came in Tennessee. Ulysses S. Grant, a capable veteran of the Mexican War but a dreary failure for years afterward, had been appointed a colonel of Illinois volunteers soon after Fort Sumter, and began a rise of astonishing swiftness. In August, 1861, he was made brigadier-general and given command of a district with headquarters at Cairo. Here he faced the Confederate commander, Albert Sidney Johnston, who had far greater prestige than his own. The Union forces managed, with the aid of river gunboats, to gain and keep control of most of western Kentucky. It became evident to a number of officers and civilians that while the Confederates' line of defense, protecting their main depots at Nashville, was strong at its well-fortified extremities, it was weak in the center. It could withstand attack at Columbus on the Mississippi, and at Bowling Green deep within Kentucky. But two rivers pierced the line, and both Fort Henry on the Tennessee and Fort Donelson on the Cumberland, only eleven miles apart, seemed vulnerable. Spies had reported their weakness to Union headquarters. While McClellan still stood inert, despite an order by Lincoln to undertake active operations on February 22, 1862, Grant and Flag Officer Andrew H. Foote of the navy moved energetically.*

Using sources that by later standards would seem thin, Rhodes gives a memorable account of the operations raising Grant to the eminence of a national hero. The country thrilled to Grant's reply to the Confederate request for an armistice at Donelson: "No terms except unconditional and immediate surrender." Rhodes takes up the story just after Foote and his gunboats, by reducing Fort Henry, had opened the way for the far more difficult advance upon Donelson. Then, as Jefferson Davis's formal assumption of the leadership of the Confederates occurred immediately afterward, he gives a description of that dramatic scene.

Grant Takes Donelson

THE inaction of the Army of the Potomac, due at first to McClellan's incompetence, and afterwards to his illness during the fine weather and smooth roads of December and the first half of January, was a deep disappointment to the people. The senators and representatives were full of it. "We are in a condition now where we must stir ourselves on account of the expense," said Senator Wade to General McDowell, December 26, 1861. "It is awful; and we are endeavoring to see if there is any way in God's world to get rid of the capital besieged, while Europe is looking down upon us as almost a conquered people." "It is no wonder," declared Lovejoy in the House, January 6, 1862, "that the people are growing impatient; it is no wonder that that impatience is becoming earnest in many portions of the country, and is almost reaching a point beyond that of passive emotion. The whole nation is waiting for the army to move forward. They have furnished the men and money, and why does not the army move?" Writing from the office of the *Evening Post,* New York, Parke Godwin asked Sumner, "what the awful and disastrous inaction of our military men means? People here are rapidly becoming disgusted," he added, "even the most patient are losing heart; and all see that unless some grand blows are struck the war is gone." "When," asked John Bigelow, despairingly, from over the sea, "are we to stop hearing of the great things our army and our navy and our young Napoleon are *going to do,* and to begin to hear of what they *have done?*" Anthony Trollope read public opinion correctly when he concluded that "belief in McClellan seemed to be slipping away." Chase had lost confidence in the general of the army. Lincoln stood by McClellan, but he was convinced that Seward's diplomacy, Chase's finance, and his own hold on the people could be sustained only by military victories, or at all events by an earnest effort to win them. January 10 he called a council at the White House of Generals McDowell and Frank-

lin, Seward, Chase, and the assistant Secretary of War; Mc-
Clellan, not having yet recovered from his illness, was not
present. The President said: "I am in great distress. If something is not done soon, the bottom will be out of the whole
affair; and if General McClellan does not want to use the
army I would like to *borrow* it, provided I could see how it could
be made to do something. What can be done with the army
soon?" he asked McDowell. The general replied that it was
feasible to attack the enemy at Centreville and Manassas, and
he verbally outlined a plan of operation; this, further developed
in writing, he read the next evening to the council. His conclusion as then stated was: "It seems to me the army should
be ready to move in all of next week." Monday, January 13,
McClellan met at the White House these gentlemen and also
Montgomery Blair and General Meigs. The President explained
how and why the advice of the two generals had been demanded,
and requested McDowell again to expose his plan. This he did,
ending with a natural apology to his superior officer for his
action, which McClellan received coldly. The President then
asked what and when anything could be done? McClellan replied that "the case was so clear that a blind man could see it,"
and then, discussing matters of detail, made difficulties and be-
fogged the issue. Chase, undoubtedly with impatience, put the
direct question to the general what he intended doing with his
army, and when he intended doing it? A long silence ensued.
McClellan broke it at last, saying that it was his intention to
have the general operations of the armies begin by a movement
of Buell in Kentucky. He paused; then resuming speech said:
"I am very unwilling to develop my plans, for I believe that in
military matters the fewer persons to whom they are known the
better. I will tell them if *ordered* to do so." The President asked:
"Do you count upon any particular time? I do not ask what that
time is, but have you in your own mind any particular time fixed
when a movement can be commenced?" McClellan replied, "I
have." "Then," rejoined the President, "I will adjourn this
meeting."

A fortnight passed away, and still the story ran, "All quiet on the Potomac." January 27 the President issued his "General War Order Number 1"; this "ordered that the 22d of February, 1862, be the day for a general movement of the land and naval forces of the United States against the insurgent forces." He followed this up with his "Special War Order Number 1;" this directed "that all the disposable force of the Army of the Potomac . . . be formed into an expedition for the immediate object of seizing . . . Manassas Junction."

Meanwhile General George H. Thomas defeated a superior force of Confederates at Mill Spring, Kentucky. A little later General Burnside, in co-operation with Commodore Goldsborough, took Roanoke Island, North Carolina. Eclipsing far, however, every success on the federal side, and in its importance and influence matching the Confederate victory of Bull Run, was an achievement of General Grant in Tennessee.

In the West the Confederate line of defence was from Columbus, on the Mississippi River, to Bowling Green. Both of these places were in Kentucky: the first was called a "Gibraltar," the second the "Manassas of the West." Two other important points on this line in the State of Tennessee were Fort Henry, which defended the Tennessee River, and Fort Donelson, which commanded the Cumberland, the two rivers here being but eleven miles apart. If these forts were captured, two important gateways would be open to the heart of the Confederacy. The troops in this field of operation were under the command of Albert Sidney Johnston, then esteemed the ablest general of the South. Halleck, with headquarters at St. Louis, had control of the Union forces in this department; Grant, under him, was at Cairo. The notion that this line ought to be broken occurred to several federal generals; that it entered into the minds of Grant and Flag-officer Foote is of the highest moment, for by their position and character they were fit men to head an expedition to break it. Acting upon reconnoissances made by General C. F. Smith and Foote, Grant urged Halleck that he be permitted to capture Fort Henry, and in this request for authority he was

joined by Foote January 28. January 30 Halleck telegraphed
the desired permission. February 1 Grant received by mail the
detailed instructions; on the 2d the expedition of iron-clad and
wooden gun-boats, and transports carrying the troops, started
from Cairo under his and Foote's command. On the 6th he telegraphed Halleck: "Fort Henry is ours. . . . I shall take and destroy Fort Donelson on the 8th." The business had been done by
Foote and his iron-clads. Owing to the badness of the roads, the
troops were unable to make in time the march which was necessary for co-operation, and most of the Confederate garrison
escaped to Donelson.

Albert Sidney Johnston heard with dismay of the fall of Fort
Henry. "I determined," he afterwards wrote Davis, "to fight for
Nashville at Donelson, and gave the best part of my army to do
it, retaining only 14,000 men to cover my front, and giving
16,000 to defend Donelson." On account of the heavy rains,
which made the roads impassable for artillery and wagons,
Grant was unable to carry out his prophecy to the letter; but
having sent the gun-boats and some of the troops around by
water, he left Fort Henry on the morning of February 12 with
about 15,000 men, including eight batteries and part of a regiment of cavalry, and marched across the country towards Donelson, arriving in front of the enemy about noon. "That afternoon and the next day," writes Grant, "were spent in taking up
ground to make the investment as complete as possible." On the
13th there was some fighting, in which the Union troops got the
worse of it. That night Foote with his gun-boats and reinforcements arrived. "On the 14th," wrote Grant, "a gallant attack
was made by Flag-officer Foote upon the enemy's works with
the fleet. The engagement lasted probably an hour and a half,
and bid fair to result favorably in the cause of the Union, when
two unlucky shots disabled two of the armored boats, so that
they were carried back by the current. The remaining two were
very much disabled also, having received a number of heavy
shots about the pilot-houses and other parts of the vessels. After
these mishaps I concluded to make the investment of Fort Don-

elson as perfect as possible, and partially fortify and await repairs to the gun-boats." Foote had been wounded. Discouragement and discomfort were supreme in the Union ranks that night. When the soldiers quitted Fort Henry the weather was springlike and warm; many of them had left behind their blankets and overcoats. Now a storm of sleet and snow prevailed. They had no tents, they were so near the enemy that they dared not light their fires, and their sufferings during that cold and pitiless night were intense.

The Confederate generals were Floyd—Buchanan's Secretary of War—Pillow, and Buckner. They and their men had been cast down by the fall of Fort Henry, but their spirits had risen with the repulse of the gun-boats, which had not cost them the injury of a battery of the death of a man. They saw, however, the arrival of the federal reinforcements with concern. That evening they held a council of war, and they were of one mind that Grant, with a constantly increasing force, would soon be able completely to beleaguer the fort, and that nothing remained for them but to make an attempt to cut their way through the besiegers and recover the road to Nashville. They determined to attack early the next morning.

Reinforcements had increased Grant's army to 27,000. McClernand's division was on the right, holding the Nashville road; Lew. Wallace's was in the centre, and C. F. Smith's on the left.

Extending beyond the earthwork of Fort Donelson was a winding line of intrenchments nearly two miles in length, defended on the outside at some points with abatis. These intrenchments were fully occupied by the Confederates. At five o'clock on the morning of February 15 Pillow's division sallied out and fell upon McClernand. The Union troops were not surprised, and made a stubborn resistance. The fight was hot, the snow was red with blood. McClernand sent to Grant's headquarters and then to Lew. Wallace for assistance, but Wallace decided that his instructions required him to maintain his actual position. Meanwhile Buckner, who commanded the

Confederate right wing, had sent troops to Pillow. A second message reached Lew. Wallace, saying that McClernand's command was endangered. So Wallace, having learned that Grant was on a gun-boat more than five miles away, sent forward his first brigade, which, however, being imperfectly directed by a guide, did not reach a position to render effective help. McClernand, bearing the brunt of the battle, was outnumbered, his ammunition failed, and he was obliged to fall back. The fugitives who crowded up the hill in the rear of Lew. Wallace's line brought "unmistakable signs of disaster. . . . A mounted officer galloped down the road shouting 'We are cut to pieces.' " The Confederates, having possession of the Nashville road, had a chance of escape, but they made no attempt to avail themselves of it. They continued to advance on their retreating foes, when Lew. Wallace ordered his third brigade to check their onset; this was done with vigor; the charge of the enemy was repelled.

Early that morning Foote had requested Grant to come to his flag-ship for consultation, he himself being too badly injured to leave the boat. Complying with this request, the commanding general of the Union army was not, therefore, during this attack, on the field where he could direct operations. His conference with Foote terminated, he met, on going ashore, Captain Hillyer, of his staff, "white with fear . . . for the safety of the national troops." The roads, which had been deep with mud, were now frozen hard. Travel on horseback was slow. The fight had been on the Union right of a line three miles long. Grant "was some four or five miles north of our left." He made his way back with the utmost possible speed. "I saw everything favorable for us along the line of our left and centre," he says. On the right, however, there was confusion. The fighting had ceased.

It was the intensest moment in Grant's life. The war had given him an opportunity to amend a broken career; should he fail in this supreme hour, another chance might never come to him. His unfortunate absence during the morning's battle would certainly be misconstrued. Yet he was equal to the emergency. He showed himself a true soldier and a compeller of men. "Wholly

unexcited, he saluted and received salutations of his subordinates," writes Lew. Wallace, who was in conversation with Mc-
Clernand when Grant rode up. "It cannot be doubted that he
saw with painful distinctness the effect of the disaster to his
right wing. His face flushed slightly. With a sudden grip he
crushed the papers (which looked like telegrams) in his hand.
But in an instant these signs of disappointment or hesitation
cleared away. In his ordinary quiet voice he said, addressing
himself to both officers, 'Gentlemen, the position on the right
must be retaken.' "

Grant tells in an unaffected manner the story of his action.
"I heard some of the men say," he writes, "that the enemy had
come out with knapsacks and haversacks filled with rations. . . .
I turned to Colonel Webster, of my staff, and said: 'Some of
our men are pretty badly demoralized, but the enemy must be
more so, for he has attempted to force his way out, but has
fallen back; the one who attacks first now will be victorious,
and the enemy will have to be in a hurry if he gets ahead
of me.' I determined to make the assault at once on our left.
. . . I directed Colonel Webster to ride with me and call out
to the men as we passed: 'Fill your cartridge-boxes quick and
get into line; the enemy is trying to escape, and he must not
be permitted to do so.' This acted like a charm. The men only
wanted some one to give them a command. We rode rapidly to
Smith's quarters, when I explained the situation to him, and
directed him to charge the enemy's works in his front with his
whole division, saying at the same time that he would find
nothing but a very thin line to contend with. The general was
off in an incredibly short time."

It is seldom that a writer of the remarkable powers of description which Lew. Wallace possesses sees a decisive battle
from the stand-point of a general; it is, therefore, fitting that he
should tell the story of this glorious charge. "Taking Lauman's
brigade" he writes, "General Smith began the advance. They
were under fire instantly. The guns in the fort joined in with
the infantry, who were at the time in the rifle-pits, the great

body of the Confederate right wing being with General Buckner. The defence was greatly favored by the ground, which subjected the assailants to a double fire from the beginning of the
abatis. The men have said that 'it looked too thick for a rabbit
to get through.' General Smith, on his horse, took position in the
front and centre of the line. Occasionally he turned in the saddle
to see how the alignment was kept. For the most part, however,
he held his face steadily towards the enemy. He was, of course,
a conspicuous object for the sharp-shooters in the rifle-pits. The
air around him twittered with minie-bullets. Erect as if on review he rode on, timing the gait of his horse with the movement
of his colors. A soldier said, 'I was nearly scared to death, but I
saw the old man's white mustache over his shoulder, and
went on.'

"On to the abatis the regiments moved without hesitation,
leaving a trail of dead and wounded behind. There the fire
seemed to get trebly hot, and there some of the men halted,
whereupon, seeing the hesitation, General Smith put his cap
on the point of his sword, held it aloft, and called out, 'No
flinching now, my lads! Here—this is the way! Come on!' He
picked a path through the jagged limbs of the trees, holding his
cap all the time in sight; and the effect was magical. The men
swarmed in after him, and got through in the best order they
could—not all of them, alas! On the other side of the obstruction
they took the semblance of re-formation and charged in after
their chief, who found himself then between the two fires. Up
the ascent he rode; up they followed. At the last moment the
keepers of the rifle-pits clambered out and fled. The four regiments engaged in the feat planted their colors on the breast-
work. Later in the day Buckner came back with his division,
but all his efforts to dislodge Smith were in vain." That night a
large part of Smith's division bivouacked within the Confederate lines.

After he had commenced his advance Grant ordered a charge
on the enemy's left, which was undertaken by Lew. Wallace. A
hill had to be won. When he made known the desperate char-

acter of the enterprise to his regiments, the men "answered with cheers and cries of 'Forward, forward!' and I gave the word." The charge was successful, the hill was gained. The sortie had cost the Confederates about 2000 killed and wounded; the loss of the Federals was somewhat greater. The night closed with the Union troops in possession of the Nashville road. There was no way of escape from Fort Donelson except by the river and by a road submerged from the river's overflow. Grant made arrangements for an assault at daylight the next morning. Hardly a doubt of its success could exist.

Inside the fort there was dismay. An hour after midnight the three generals took counsel together. "I am confident," said Buckner, "that the enemy will attack my line by light, and I cannot hold them for half an hour." "Why so; why so, general?" Pillow demanded. "Because I can bring into action not over 4000 men, and they demoralized by long and uninterrupted exposure and fighting, while they can bring any number of fresh troops to the attack." Pillow rejoined: "I differ with you. I think you can hold your lines; I think you can, sir." "I know my position," exclaimed Buckner, "and I know that the lines cannot be held with my troops in their present condition." Floyd, who outranked the others, broke in: "Then, gentlemen, a capitulation is all that is left us." This Pillow denied. "I do not think so," he said; "at any rate, we can cut our way out." Buckner replied: "To cut our way out would cost three-fourths of our men, and I do not think any commander has a right to sacrifice three-fourths of his men to save one fourth." To which Floyd replied: "Certainly not. We will have to capitulate; but, gentlemen, I cannot surrender; you know my position with the Federals; it wouldn't do; it wouldn't do." "I will not surrender myself nor the command," declared Pillow, "will die first." "Then I suppose, gentlemen," said Buckner, "the surrender will devolve upon me." Floyd asked Buckner, "General, if you are put in command, will you allow me to take out by the river my brigade?" "Yes, sir," was the reply; "if you move your command before the enemy act upon my communication offering to capitulate." Then Floyd turned to Pillow and said, "I turn the command over, sir." Pillow replied, promptly, "I pass it." This drew from Buckner the remark: "I assume it. Give me pen, ink, and paper, and send for a bugler."

Two small steamers, which arrived at the fort about day-break, furnished Floyd and about 1500 of his Virginia troops a means of escape. Pillow crossed the river in a skiff. Colonel Forrest took out 500 of his cavalry and a number of men from the infantry and artillery regiments, mounted on the artillery horses, over the road which was submerged by the overflow of the Cumberland.

Early Sunday morning, February 16, Buckner sent the Union general a letter, which brought forth the famous reply that gave him, by a play upon his initials, the name of Unconditional Surrender Grant. "Yours of this date," he wrote Buckner, "proposing armistice and appointment of commissioners to settle terms of capitulation, is just received. No terms except unconditional and immediate surrender can be accepted. I propose to move immediately upon your works." The Confederate general was compelled to accept what he called "the ungenerous and unchivalrous terms." The surrender of Fort Donelson included 12,000 to 15,000 men, "at least forty pieces of artillery, and a large amount of stores, horses, mules, and other public property."

Men of the Northwest and men of the Southwest met here for the first time in battle on a large scale. Both armies were made up of raw troops; both fought well. The generalship on the Union side was distinctly superior. On account of their environment Western men were at the start better fitted to endure the hardships and adapt themselves to the conditions of soldiering in a rough country, than were men from the cities, the trim villages, and the rural districts, fairly provided with good roads, of New England and New York, and of such the Army of the Potomac was largely composed. But the main reason for the greater success of the Western armies cannot be found in any such slight differences in surroundings between peoples so homogeneous; and, making further allowance for the relief of the Western troops from the ever-present responsibility of defending the capital, we are forced to the conviction that in the chance of becoming skilled and self-reliant soldiers, the tremendous odds in favor of the three-years' men of the West over those of the East lay in their being led by Grant instead of by McClellan. Striking and refreshing to the student is it to turn from the excuses and subterfuges of McClellan's reports and letters to the direct and prompt manner in writing and action of Grant.

Ulysses S. Grant is one of the most interesting men whom the war brought out of obscurity. In his "Personal Memoirs" he has told with fascinating simplicity the story of his education and training in boyhood and youth. There was manual labor on the farm as well as attendance at the school; he broke horses and took care of them, he studied under the ordinary teachers, and in the crude text-books of the day. Matthew Arnold, attracted by his early history, makes the comment, "What a wholesome bringing up it was!" He had no desire to go to West Point, but went there because his father insisted on it. He took little interest in the studies or the life of the Military Academy, and showed aptitude for nothing but mathematics. Nevertheless he was graduated twenty-first in a class of thirty-nine, and went into the army. He was twenty-four years old when the Mexican War began, and served with credit through the whole of it under Taylor and Scott. Here we get glimpses of his self-education induced by contact with men and affairs. He was not a man who assimilated a variety of knowledge; he had, in fact, a mind the reverse of encyclopædic, but by careful observation and systematic thinking he made certain truths his own; these became ingrained in the fibre of his brain, guiding his action in the supreme moment of opportunity.

Returning from the Mexican campaign he married a woman whom he had long loved. Remaining in the army, he passed nearly four years at Detroit and Sackett's Harbor, when his regiment was ordered to the Pacific coast. This occasioned a separation from his family, and a cloud came over his life. He fell into habits of intemperance. In 1854 he resigned from the army and rejoined his family. "I was now to commence," he writes, "at the age of thirty-two, a new struggle for our support." On his wife's farm, near St. Louis, he endeavored to gain their livelihood. He lacked capital, but struggled on with indifferent success. One of the pictures of this time of his life is his loading of a cord of wood on a wagon, and taking it to the city for sale. At last he had a tedious attack of ague, which partially incapacitated him for work, and he gave up farming. He became a real-estate agent in St. Louis, but in this venture did not prosper. When thirty-eight years old he came for advice and assistance to his father, who was in comfortable circumstances, and had a hardware and leather store in Galena, Illinois. "I referred him to Simpson," the father writes, "my next oldest son, who had charge of my Galena business. . . . Simpson sent him to the Galena store to stay until something else might turn up in his favor, and told him he must confine his wants within $800 a year; that if that would not support him, he must draw what it lacked from the rent of his house and the hire of his negroes in St. Louis. . . . That amount would have supported his family then, but he owed debts at St. Louis, and did draw $1500 a year, but he paid back the balance after he went into the army." Did it not throw light on his later career, it would be unnecessary to refer to a phase of his life in Missouri and in Galena. He had not thrown off the bad habits he had acquired in the army, and with them went impecuniosity and shiftlessness. Acquaintances in St. Louis and in Galena used to cross the street to avoid meeting Grant, and being solicited for the loan of small sums of money. "Among his old army acquaintances," says a well-informed writer in the *Nation* "and particularly in the staff corps, the impression was prevalent that his life was hopelessly wrecked." Breaking through this wretchedness, however, there were gleams of true manhood. He was honest and truthful, and he had the instincts of a gentleman, which prevented him from becoming a loafer. He never used profane language; he did not tell obscene stories; and this was not from refinement of taste, for that he lacked, but from his purity of soul.

Such was Ulysses S. Grant when he had reached the age of thirty-nine, and when, in April, 1861, after the firing on Sumter, he was called upon to preside over a war meeting in Galena. He declined to be a candidate for the captaincy of the company enlisted in his town, but he never went back to the leather store. He drilled these men and accompanied them to Springfield, remaining with them until they were mustered into the United States service. Governor Yates, of Illinois, then employed him in the adjutant-general's office of the State. In May he wrote the adjutant-general of the army, offering his services to his country, saying that he thought himself "competent to command a regiment." "I felt some hesitation," he writes in his book, "in suggesting rank as high as the colonelcy of a regiment, feeling somewhat doubtful whether I would be equal to the position." But no notice whatever was taken of his letter. He then went to Cincinnati and called at the headquarters of the Department of Ohio, on McClellan, whom he had known slightly at West Point and in Mexico, hoping he would be offered a position on the general's staff. "I called on two successive days at his office, but failed to see him on either occasion," is his record. In June he was appointed colonel of an Illinois regiment of three-years' men, and in August a brigadier-general of volunteers. From a military experience in Missouri he had learned a lesson which always seemed beyond McClellan. Advancing on a Confederate force, he was feeling much afraid of the enemy, but kept on, and when he reached the camp found that they had fled, showing that they had been equally afraid of him. "From that event to the close of the war," he says, "I never experienced trepidation upon confronting an enemy, though I always felt more or less anxiety. I never forgot that he had as much reason to fear my forces as I had his." In November, 1861, he attacked a Confederate camp at Belmont; a battle ensued which was without result, but it served as an education for Grant and his soldiers, and demonstrated his coolness in the time of danger. At

Donelson he showed intellectual qualities of a high order. He knew Floyd was no soldier, he had a poor opinion of Pillow's military ability, and made the disposition of his forces accordingly. Had Buckner been in command, Grant's plan of investment would have been different. His physical courage was rare even among soldiers, who regard the virtue as nothing extraordinary. "I can recall only two persons," writes Horace Porter, "who throughout a rattling musketry fire always sat in their saddles without moving a muscle or winking an eye; one was a bugler and the other was General Grant." But the sight of a bull-fight in Mexico was sickening to him.

The capture of Fort Donelson was indeed a great victory; it caused the Confederates to abandon Bowling Green and Columbus, and to evacuate Nashville; it resulted in a Union advance of over two hundred miles of territory before the enemy could rally or reorganize. It set at rest all doubts, if any still existed, as to the permanent position of Kentucky in the civil conflict, and it was a step towards the recovery of Tennessee, in the eastern part of which a formidable Union sentiment existed. The North rejoiced with exceeding great joy. "The underpinning of the rebellion seems to be knocked out from under it," wrote Chase. In an article in the *Evening Post*, Bryant maintained that "the victories we have gained are equal at least to five hundred million dollars poured at once into the public exchequer;" and he therefore urged the President to veto the Legal-tender bill. Holmes wrote Motley: "Never was such ecstasy, such delirium of excitement, as last Monday, when we got the news from Fort Donelson. Why, to give you an instance from my own experience, when I, a grave college professor, went into my lecture-room, the class, which had first got the news a little before, began clapping and clapping louder and louder, then cheering, until I had to give in myself, and flourishing my wand in the air, joined with the boys in their rousing hurrahs, after which I went on with my lecture as usual. The almost universal feeling is that the rebellion is knocked on the head, that it may kick hard, even rise and stagger a few paces, but that its *os frontis* is beaten in."

The capture of Fort Donelson was in England regarded as a victory of high importance, and helped much the cause of the North. Even before the news of it was received sentiment favorable to the Union had been growing. "Before our Parliament met," wrote John Bright to Sumner, February 27, "there was much talk of interference with the blockade, and much was still said in favor of the South. All that has passed away. In London all has changed, and it is difficult to find a noisy advocate of the secession theory. The press has become much more moderate, and the great party that was to have driven the government into hostilities with you is nowhere to be found. Even the hot Mr. Gregory, the Southern advocate in the House of Commons, is very slow at taking any step in the direction of his known sympathies, and has contented himself with a notice that, at some time not yet fixed, he will call the attention of the House to the state of the blockade." When the particulars of Grant's victory became known, it could no longer be asserted that the South had a monopoly of competent officers and of good and brave soldiers. Confidence in the ability of the Confederates was shaken. The friends of the North felt that at last the United States had demonstrated that it had the stronger battalions.

The fall of Donelson gave the South the bitterness of defeat which the North had felt after Bull Run, and it was doubly bitter, as the Confederates had begun to think that in the field they were invincible. No one appreciated the magnitude of the disaster better than the commanding general in the West. "The blow was most disastrous," wrote Albert Sidney Johnston to Davis, "and almost without remedy." When the governor of Tennessee proclaimed that the troops must evacuate Nashville, and adjourned the legislature to Memphis, panic seized upon the people, and disorder, turbulence, and rapine ensued. At Richmond consternation reigned. The management of the campaign was on all sides found fault with, and Davis at once ordered that Floyd and Pillow be relieved from command. The pressure from the people and the Confederate congress upon Davis for the removal of Johnston was strong, but he resisted it and stood by his favorite general. Shortly after the fall of Donelson came the day appointed for the provisional government to give place to the permanent government of the Confederacy, and for the inauguration of its president and vice-president for the term of six˙ years. This was February 22, and one is struck with the emphasis that all the contemporary and subsequent accounts give to the dismalness of the day. The heavens were black and the rain poured down. Davis, pale and emaciated, delivered his inaugural address, at the foot of the Washington monument in Capitol Square, to a crowd of people, the gloom in whose hearts was fitly reflected by nature's sombre hue. All minds were full of the defeats suffered by the Confederate arms. "At the darkest hour of our struggle," their president declared, "the provisional gives place to the permanent government. After a series of successes and victories which covered our arms with glory, we have recently met with serious disasters. But in the heart of a people resolved to be free, these disasters tend but to stimulate to increased resistance. . . . With humble gratitude and adoration," he concluded, "acknowledging the Providence which has so visibly-protected the Confederacy during its brief but eventful career, to thee, O God! I trustingly commit myself, and prayerfully invoke Thy blessing on my country and its cause."

Reflecting in scathing terms on the arbitrary acts and violations of the Constitution and the law by the Lincoln government, Davis boasted "that, through all the necessities of an unequal struggle, there has been no act on our part to impair personal liberty or the freedom of speech, of thought, or of the press. The courts have been open, the judicial functions fully executed, and every right of the peaceful citizen maintained as securely as if a war of invasion had not disturbed the land." This might Davis truthfully say on the 22d of February, but not for many days longer. The Confederates stood adversity no better than had the Federals. By authority of an act of Congress, passed in secret session, the Confederate president, March 1, proclaimed martial law in the city of Richmond and the adjoining country to the distance of ten miles, and declared the suspension of the privilege of the writ of *habeas corpus*. At first the law-abiding citizens were well pleased with this action. One morning, shortly after the inauguration, the walls in different parts of the city were "scrawled over with inflammatory and treasonable mottoes"; these were interpreted to mean a call upon the Unionists to co-operate in resistance to the Confederate government, and caused alarm. When, therefore, under the operation of martial law, several notorious Unionists, who were regarded in this time of distress as traitors, were arrested, the people applauded the vigor of their government. Moreover, the municipal administration and police system, which had served well the quiet and refined Virginia capital, had broken down under the growth of the city and the influx of soldiers, gamblers, and adventurers. General Winder, to whom was delegated practically unlimited power, positively prohibited the distillation of spiritous liquors, and ordered all the dram-shops closed. He established a military police, and strictly enforced this and other orders, restoring peace to the city where had been confusion and turbulence. Rowdies, drunkards, and idle soldiers disappeared from the streets. Ladies could now walk out without fear of insult, and gentlemen could go out at night without danger of being robbed.

But the delight of the people was short-lived. General Winder did not use his arbitrary power with mildness and discretion. The well-grounded belief obtained that he employed it for private oppression and the gratification of personal malice. Extraordinary arrests of respectable citizens were made, capricious acts of tyranny were done, and it was impossible for the sufferers to get redress. A vexatious passport system was established. The Richmond *Whig*, on account of its criticisms of the administration, was obnoxious to Winder, and one day when an article appeared which he supposed to be a violation of one of his orders, he gave the command to arrest the editor and close the office. This order was not carried out, however, owing to the dissuasion of Jones, a clerk in the Confederate war-office, who maintained that no offence had been committed. Jones's entry of April 17 in his diary is: "The press has taken the alarm, and several of the publishers have confessed a fear of having their offices closed if they dare to speak the sentiments struggling for utterance. It is indeed a reign of terror! Every Virginian and other loyal citizens of the South—members of Congress and all —must now, before obtaining General Winder's permission to leave the city for their homes, bow down before the aliens in the provost-marshal's office and subscribe to an oath of allegiance, while a file of bayonets are pointed at their backs." This much one may gather from the contemporary evidence, but Pollard asserts that the half was not told in the newspapers of the day, that Winder exercised the powers of a viceroy in a terrible manner. His police was largely composed of disreputable men; he gave employment to two hundred spies, on whose reports of private conversations good citizens were imprisoned, and then had to depend for their release on the whim of the tyrant. Not only men but women suffered indignities at his hands. His rule was indeed a despotism of the worst kind. He was responsible to no one but Davis, who sustained him, or at all events kept him in his place. Public opinion, however, asserted itself so strongly that Congress modified the law under which the President had exercised these extraordinary powers.

It was now that a party in opposition to Davis, with powerful exponents in Congress and in the press, was formed. Owing to changes in the cabinet, Benjamin now held both the state and war portfolios; he was the chief adviser of the Confederate president and his confidential friend. The blame for the disasters of the early part of 1862 was largely imputed to Benjamin, and at the same time much criticism intended for Davis was showered upon the secretary's head. The permanent congress was composed of a Senate and House of Representatives, but, since the army attracted the best talent of the Confederacy, it was in ability not up to the level of the provisional congress, nor to the representation which the South used to send to the national legislature. "This is a very poor congress," Stephens said, confidentially. "There are few men of ability in the House. In the Senate not more than two or three."

Lincoln's war orders were probably designed as much for assuring the people that something would be done as for commands to his generals. But as affairs turned out, his "Special War Order Number 1," issued January 31, which directed McClellan to begin a forward movement February 22, whose object should be the seizure of Manassas Junction, was the highest strategy. McClellan had an army three times as large as Johnston's, better equipped, better fed, in better health, and full of confidence on account of the victories which had been gained for the Union; while Johnston's army was almost as much demoralized as were the Richmond government and people, and the time of enlistment of a large number of his men had nearly expired. Had McClellan advanced February 22 a cheap victory awaited him. An intelligent study of the internal affairs of the Confederacy, a reasonable knowledge of the force of the enemy —which might have been easily gained—could not fail to convince a man who was fit to command an army that now was the supreme moment to strike a series of blows, that it was the time when the tide of affairs should be taken at its flood. Only one obstacle existed. The roads were bad, but not impassable. Edward Dicey saw them when they were at the worst, and his testimony is that "they were not worse than many of the roads in the south of Italy, over which the Sardinian army marched in 1860." Moreover, McClellan would have had a railroad behind him to transport his supplies. Of the army of the Potomac, Dicey wrote: "I have seen the armies of most European countries, and I have no hesitation in saying that, as far as the average raw material of the rank and file is concerned, the American army is the finest." These magnificent men, full of courage and desire to end the war speedily, panted to be led against the enemy; but their general, instead of giving the word, haggled with the President over a plan of campaign. It is certain that if the Grant of Donelson had been in command, he would have fought Johnston's army and beaten it, and it is possible he might have captured it, or Richmond, or both, thus shortening the war at least a year, and putting an end to the probability of foreign interference.

Meanwhile the astute Confederate general, finding it impossible to conjecture that McClellan would not take advantage of the peculiarly favorable conditions, and aware that in that event he stood in jeopardy, was making preparations to withdraw his army to a more secure position. Beginning his preparations February 22, he commenced the retreat March 7, and four days later had his army safely on the south bank of the Rappahannock River. Constantly expecting an attack, he had deemed it impossible to remove all the property accumulated at Manassas Junction, and therefore a large amount of stores, provisions, clothing, blankets, and baggage were burned. March 9 McClellan heard of Johnston's movement, and immediately gave the order for the occupation of Centreville and Manassas. The Union army found that they had been fronting phantom ordnance as well as phantom soldiers. Being deficient in artillery, Johnston had made "rough wooden imitations of guns," which were "kept near the embrasures in readiness for exhibition"—"Quaker guns," our newspapers called them. Hawthorne was in Washington at this time, and has with exquisite skill described this advance. "On the very day of our arrival," he wrote, "sixty thousand men had crossed the Potomac on their march towards Manassas, and almost with their first step into Virginia mud the phantasmagoria of a countless host and impregnable ramparts, before which they had so long remained quiescent, dissolved quite away. It was as if General McClellan had thrust his sword into a gigantic enemy, and, beholding him suddenly collapse, had discovered to himself and the world that he had merely punctured an enormous swollen bladder."

INTO *some twenty pages Rhodes compresses a record of the dramatic encounter of the* Merrimac *and the* Monitor; Shiloh *and the angry controversies it engendered; and the capture of New Orleans, with its potent effects abroad and at home. These events in the spring of 1862 had the highest importance—such importance, indeed, that Rhodes could well have given more space to them. But so far as it extends, his treatment is sound. He did not make the error so frequent in earlier writers of exaggerating the value of Ericsson's invention of the ironclad monitor. Ironclads had appeared earlier in the French and British navies, and the monitors—as Admiral S. F. Du Pont found when he attacked Charleston with them in April, 1863, and suffered a heavy disaster—were not a sound basis for an ironclad sea-going navy.*

Shiloh, which represented Albert Sidney Johnston's counterstroke after Donelson, proved that Union strength on the Tennessee River was too great to be shaken even by Grant's careless overconfidence and erratic generalship. As Rhodes states, the troops of Grant and Sherman were most lamentably surprised. But after Buell's timely arrival helped win a victory, the conquest of the West became possible; and except for the delays and blunders of Halleck, the chief commander in the area, and the widespread doubts about Grant's capacity, it might have been more rapidly achieved. As for the capture of New Orleans, it crowned a remarkably bold and brilliant display of leadership by Farragut. And it came in the nick of time to help keep European powers neutral when McClellan failed in his campaign in Virginia, as he immediately did.

During the spring, encouraged by Shiloh and New Orleans, Lincoln pressed upon the Congressional leaders of the border states his far-reaching proposals for compensated emancipation. They unfortunately met a shortsighted and stubborn rejection. This rejection, however, helped lay the foundation on which Lincoln was later to build his Emancipation Proclamation. All parts of this story have been treated in detail by various writers since Rhodes's narrative appeared; al-

*though his treatment can no longer be termed con-
clusive on any of them, it offered a sound foundation
for more thorough study.*

Monitor; Shiloh; New Orleans

ON Sunday, the 9th of March, the day that the news of the
evacuation of Manassas came, the President received the startling intelligence of the havoc done the day previous in Hampton Roads by the Confederate iron-clad *Merrimac.* On this
Saturday began a new chapter in naval warfare, the introduction to which had come from the hands of two friendly but rival
powers of Europe. In 1858 France built an armor-plated steam
frigate, and speedily thereafter England had constructed another. Their success was sufficient to render "armor-plating an
essential feature in the construction of vessels of war." In the
dissolution of the Union the Confederacy got its share of competent naval officers, and they at once turned their attention to
this new invention. In July, 1861, the Confederate Secretary of
the Navy gave the order to raise the United States steam frigate *Merrimac*—which was one of the ships burned and sunk at
the time of the destruction of the Gosport navy-yard—and convert her into an iron-clad; this work proceeded as rapidly as
could be expected under the imperfect manufacturing and mechanical conditions which prevailed in the South. Not until
October did the Navy Department at Washington let the contract for the building of an iron-clad on a plan submitted by
John Ericsson. The necessity for rapid construction, that she
might be ready as soon as the *Merrimac,* on which he knew
work was progressing, the desire to have a vessel of light
draught, together with some other reasons, had induced Ericsson to design the peculiar type of the *Monitor,* instead of following the French and English models. Work on the *Merrimac*
at Gosport and work on the *Monitor* at Brooklyn went on;
it was a race to get ready first, and each side had an inkling of

what the other was doing. The *Merrimac* appeared upon the scene of action a few hours before the *Monitor*.

About noon on Saturday March 8, the *Merrimac* with several tenders steamed into Hampton Roads. The officers of the blockading squadron knew her at once and prepared for action. The frigates *Minnesota, St. Lawrence,* and *Roanoke,* anchored at Fortress Monroe, headed for the enemy, which to them looked "like a huge half-submerged crocodile," but the water being low, they grounded. The sailing frigate *Congress* of fifty guns, and the *Cumberland,* a sloop-of-war of twenty-four guns, at Newport News made ready for the *Merrimac,* and as she approached discharged their broadsides, the shore batteries opening fire immediately after. The balls rebounded from her iron sides as if they had been of india-rubber. She reserved her fire until within easy range, gave the *Congress* a broadside as she passed, then, steering directly for the *Cumberland,* brought her guns to bear upon the Union sloop-of-war killing and wounding men at every shot, and proceeding on under full headway, rammed the *Cumberland,* "knocking a hole in the side near the water line as large as the head of a hogshead." Backing clear she continued her fire. The water rushed into the hole in the *Cumberland,* but she kept up the fight, discharging her cannon until they reached the water's edge, and going down with colors flying. The commander of the *Congress,* seeing the fate of her sister ship, ran her aground to escape destruction, but she was attacked vigorously by the *Merrimac* and the Confederate gunboats. The fight was unequal, she being able to make little resistance; at last hot shot from the *Merrimac* set her on fire and completed her destruction. The *Minnesota* was aground and at the mercy of the iron-clad, but although there remained nearly two hours of daylight, the pilots were afraid to attempt the channel at ebb tide, the *Merrimac* drawing twenty-two feet; she therefore returned to Sewell's Point and anchored, to wait the light of the next day, when her officers expected to return and destroy the *Minnesota.*

That night the consternation in the Union fleet and among

the Union troops was profound. The stately wooden frigates, deemed in the morning powerful men-of-war, had been shown to be absolutely useless to cope with this new engine of destruction. The next morning, in Washington, Seward, Chase, Stanton, and Welles hastened to the White House to confer with the President. Alarm pervaded their discussion; their prognostications were gloomy. Stanton was especially excited and declared: "The *Merrimac* will change the whole character of the war; she will destroy *seriatim* every naval vessel; she will lay all the cities on the seaboard under contribution. . . . I will notify the governors and municipal authorities in the North to take instant measures to protect their harbors." I have no doubt, he said, that the monster is at this moment on her way to Washington. Looking out of the window, which commanded a view of the Potomac for many miles, he continued, "not unlikely we shall have from one of her guns a shell or cannon-ball in the White House before we leave this room." The dispatches from the War Department reflect the same anxiety. Besides other measures of precaution, a fleet of canal-boats loaded with stone were sent down the Potomac to be sunk, if it was found necessary to obstruct the channel. The terror, though natural, was extreme. The *Merrimac* had, however, broken the blockade at Norfolk, and she could do likewise at other ports—a consideration of utmost importance.

While, on this Sunday morning, March 9, the President and the other authorities were a prey to keen anxiety, bounds were set to the *Merrimac's* power for ruin by John Ericsson's *Monitor*. Barely escaping shipwreck twice on her voyage from New York, she arrived at Hampton Roads at ten o'clock on the evening of the 8th, and took a position which protected the *Minnesota*. Early in the morning of the 9th the *Merrimac* stood for the *Minnesota* and opened fire on her. The *Monitor*, which was commanded by Lieutenant John L. Worden, steered directly for the *Merrimac* and commenced firing. Then ensued, for four hours, a hand-to-hand fight. The *Monitor*, appropriately described as a "cheese-box on a raft," was of 900 tons, the *Merri-*

mac of 3500. The *Monitor* had two 11-inch Dahlgren guns, fired from a revolving turret; the other had six 9-inch Dahlgren guns and two 32-pounder Brooke rifles in broadside, and 7-inch Brooke rifles on pivots in the bow and stern. Men said at the time a pygmy strove against a giant; David had come out to encounter Goliath. Shot after shot struck the *Merrimac* and the turret of the *Monitor* without injury; the armor was superior to the projectiles. At one time Lieutenant Jones, who was in command of the *Merrimac*, inquired, "Why are you not firing, Mr. Eggleston?" "Why, our powder is very precious," was the reply; "and after two hours' incessant firing I find I can do her about as much damage by snapping my thumb at her every two minutes and a half." The *Merrimac* tried to ram her antagonist, but she herself was unwieldy, and the *Monitor,* being easily handled, got out of her way without difficulty, receiving only a glancing blow which affected nothing. The *Monitor* then "came up on our quarter," Wood relates, "her bow against our side, and at this distance fired twice." The impact of the shots "forced the side in bodily two or three inches. All the crews of the after-guns were knocked over by the concussion, and bled from the nose or ears. Another shot at the same place would have penetrated." At another time Greene, who was in the turret of the *Monitor,* writes, the *Monitor* made a dash at the *Merrimac's* stern, hoping to disable her screw, which Worden thinks he missed by not more than two feet. "Soon after noon," as Greene relates the story, "a shell from the enemy's gun, the muzzle not ten yards distant, struck the forward side of the pilot-house directly in the sight-hole or slit, and exploded, cracking the second iron log and partly lifting the top, leaving an opening. Worden was standing immediately behind this spot, and received in his face the force of the blow, which partly stunned him, and filled his eyes with powder, utterly blinded him." This caused the *Monitor* to withdraw temporarily from the action. The commander of the *Merrimac,* perhaps thinking that she had given up the contest, or because his own boat was leaking badly, steered towards Norfolk, and the struggle was over. Only a few had been wounded on the *Merrimac;* with the exception of the injury to Worden, there was no casualty of account on the *Monitor*.

It had been a wonderfully picturesque fight. Holmes, in a letter to Motley, spoke of the *Monitor's* "appearance in front of the great megalosaurus or deinotherium, which came out in its scaly armor that no one could pierce, breathing fire and smoke from its nostrils; is it not the age of fables and of heroes and demigods over again?" The relief of the Union government and people was great. The power of the *Merrimac* was broken; she did no further mischief.* This first encounter between ironclads determined that they alone would be of avail in the naval warfare of the future. The English government and people showed intense interest in the accounts of the contest, and it was the subject of a long debate in the House of Commons. The admirable performance of the *Monitor*, and the intelligence that the United States purposed building a fleet of such boats, increased their respect for its blockade of the Southern ports.†

The President, having consented to McClellan's Peninsula

* When Norfolk was evacuated in May by the Confederates, they destroyed the *Merrimac*. In Dec. the *Monitor* foundered off Cape Hatteras.

† Hansard, March 31, 1862. The London *Times* of March 25 said: "Who would have thought it possible that after England and France had theorized so long on iron-plated and iron-powered vessels, the first real trial should be made by the inhabitants of the peaceful New World met in unnatural strife? . . . Nothing now remains for our Admiralty but to discontinue the building of wooden vessels, and to convert all that will bear it into machines of war resembling the Confederate frigate." See, also, the London *Daily News*, March 29, the London *Spectator* of March 29, April 5. The London *Saturday Review* of March 29 said: "Not more than a year ago the *Times* dwelt with much emphasis on the fact that the Americans had steadily refused to avail themselves of the new-fangled device of iron-plated ships. That a people so adventurous and skilful in mechanical appliances should have pronounced the new invention a chimera, was supposed to be a serious ground for doubting the wisdom of the course which France had initiated and England sluggishly followed. No one could then have imagined that the first real test of armor–plated ships in actual warfare would be furnished by America. It is only within a few weeks that either of the belligerents has had a plated ship ready for sea; and, as if to supply the crucial experiment which was wanting to build up the confidence of our naval architects, the *Merrimac* and the *Monitor* have exhibited their powers of attack and defence, and proved that even imperfect specimens (as they probably are) of their class are quite capable of sweeping from the ocean whole fleets of the old wooden liners."

plan of campaign, issued an order March 8, dividing the Army
of the Potomac into four army corps, to be commanded, respectively, by Generals McDowell, Sumner, Heintzelman, and
Keyes. General Wadsworth was to have command of the forces
in and about Washington. March 11 another presidential order
relieved McClellan of the command of all military departments
except that of the Potomac. The ostensible reason for this
was that the general would be actively engaged in the field; at
the bottom it represented the waning confidence of Lincoln and
Congress in him, for their trust had received a shock from his
being outgeneralled by Johnston, when he allowed the Confederate commander to steal away from Manassas unimpeded
and without harm. March 13 he and his corps commanders had
a council at Fairfax Court-house, where they decided in favor of
the Peninsula plan of campaign, provided—besides other conditions not necessary to be mentioned for our purpose—that the
aid of the navy could be had in silencing the batteries of the
enemy on York River, and determined that "the force to be
left to cover Washington shall be such as to give an entire feeling of security for its safety from menace." When the plan was
submitted to the President, he, in a communication from the
War Department, made no objection to it, but stipulated again
that Washington be left entirely secure. The embarkation of the
troops began. McClellan himself reached Fortress Monroe on
the afternoon of April 2. Part of his army was there, and the
rest of it was on the way. Directly after his departure there
cropped out a serious misunderstanding between the President
and the War Department on one side, and McClellan on the
other, in reference to what they understood to be necessary to
make the capital entirely secure. It was not so much a difference
regarding the number of troops needed, but McClellan counted
Banks's army in the Shenandoah as part of the covering force
required. The President did not so understand it, and, alarmed
at the dispositions the general had made, directed that Mc--
Dowell's corps be detained at Washington. This was an exceedingly unfortunate misunderstanding. Too much depended

on the federal possession of Washington for Lincoln to take the slightest chance touching its safety, and yet the withdrawal of 35,000 men was naturally a serious disappointment to the general. He was more to blame, probably, than any one else for this misapprehension. The idea one gets of McClellan from his book and reports is that of a man who does not think straight and work out matters to a logical conclusion. There is a lack of precision and an inconsistency in his statements which indicate a want of clear and concentrated thinking. Such men go through life victims to frequent and honest misunderstandings. Possibly Lincoln may have been at fault in not fully entering into the details with his general, for relations between Stanton and McClellan had already become so inharmonious that no efficient and generous co-operation between them could be expected.

McClellan's plan was a good one, but in the execution of it he showed neither promptness nor ability. Magruder, the Confederate general in command, held a fortified line of thirteen miles from the York River to the James, to defend which he had 11,000 men; 6000 of these were at Yorktown on the York River, and at Mulberry Island on the James; 5000 were posted at the assailable points along his front. McClellan, with his overwhelming force, could easily have broken the Confederate line within a week after the arrival of his army on the Peninsula, and Yorktown would have fallen into his hands. Lincoln's letter of April 9, urging immediate action, is pathetic in its display of his yearning for his general's success, and his desire to furnish abundant means to secure it. "I suppose," he wrote, "the whole force which had gone forward for you is with you by this time, and if so, I think it is the precise time for you to strike a blow. By delay the enemy will relatively gain upon you; that is, he will gain faster by fortifications and reinforcements than you can by reinforcements alone. And once more let me tell you it is indispensable to you that you strike a blow. I am powerless to help this. You will do me the justice to remember I always insisted that going down the bay in search of a field, instead of fighting at or near Manassas, was only shifting, and not surmounting, a difficulty; that we would find the same enemy and the same or equal intrenchments at either place. The country will not fail to note, is now noting, that the present hesitation to move upon an intrenched enemy is but the story of Manassas repeated. I beg to assure you that I have never written you or spoken to you in greater kindness of feeling than now, nor with a fuller purpose to sustain you so far as, in my most anxious judgment, I consistently can. But you must act." Instead, however, of piercing the Confederate line by assault, McClellan sat down before Yorktown, and began the siege of it in a deliberate and scientific manner, probably losing more men by disease in the swamps of Virginia than an assault would have cost him; meanwhile complaining of the lack of his expected co-operation of the navy and of the withdrawal of McDowell's corps, begging the President and the Secretary of War for more troops, and hugging the delusion that Stanton and the radical Republicans at heart desired the failure of his campaign. He gave the Confederates what of all things they most desired—time to recover from their early discouragement, time to bring about the recuperation which shattered the sanguine hopes of the North. While he was erecting most formidable siege works before Yorktown, the Confederate congress, perhaps influenced by fears for the safety of their capital, passed the conscription act, giving an additional impetus to the reorganization of their army.

Meanwhile at the West the cause of the Union was gaining ground. General Curtis had driven the Confederates out of Missouri into Arkansas. But the victory of Donelson had not been followed up to its full fruition. It was Grant's opinion that "if one general, who would have taken the responsibility, had been in command of all the troops west of the Alleghanies, he could have marched to Chattanooga, Corinth, Memphis, and Vicksburg with the troops we then had; and as volunteering was going on rapidly over the North, there would soon have been force enough at all these centres to operate offensively against any body of the enemy that might be found near them." Such an occupation would have precluded the operation of the Confederate conscription act in a large extent of territory, and prevented a considerable increase of the Southern army. His actual success pointed out Grant for such a command, and, considering what a tremendous advance the insignificant victories in western Virginia gained for McClellan, it might seem astonishing that his ability as a soldier, testified to by the capture of Donelson, was not sooner recognized. Such an arrangement, however, would have supplanted Halleck, which, as he shared with Grant and Foote the glory of Forts Henry and Donelson, would have been unnatural, and was probably not entertained by any one in authority at Washington. There was, moreover, a general distrust of Grant. Owing, probably, to defective means of communication, Halleck did not get as full and prompt reports from Grant as he deemed necessary, and he complained of this to McClellan, who still had command of all the Union armies. "I have had no communication with General Grant for more than a week," he telegraphed March 3. "He left his command without my authority and went to Nashville. His army seems to be as much demoralized by the victory of Fort Donelson as was that of the Potomac by the defeat of Bull Run. . . . I can get no returns, no reports, no information of any kind from him. Satisfied with his victory, he sits down and enjoys it without any regard to the future." "Do not hesitate to arrest him at once if the good of the service requires it, and place C. F. Smith in command," promptly replied McClellan. Halleck the next day rejoined: "A rumor has just reached me that since the taking of Fort Donelson General Grant has resumed his former bad habits. If so, it will account for his neglect of my often-repeated orders. I do not deem it advisable to arrest him at present, but have placed General Smith in command of the expedition up the Tennessee." This was an injustice to Grant. Halleck condemned the victor of Donelson without a hearing and on insufficient and untrustworthy evidence, thus displaying a disposition to supersede him on a mere pretext. Grant was ordered to remain at Fort Henry. Hurt by the reprimands he received from Halleck, and also at being superseded, he asked, after explaining why his reports had not been regularly received, to be relieved from further duty in that department, a request which he twice repeated. Halleck was satisfied with his explanations, so advised the War Department, and sent Grant a despatch expressive of trust. This was glad tidings to him, and he at once replied that he would "give every effort to the success of our cause." General Smith, on account of an injury received at Pittsburg Landing, was incapacitated for active exertion, and this occurring at the time that Grant gained the favor of Halleck, he was restored to the command of the Army of the Tennessee. He arrived at Savannah, in western Tennessee, March 17, and soon had five divisions of his army in camp at Pittsburg Landing, nine miles above Savannah, on the Tennessee River and south of it; Lew. Wallace's division was stationed at Crump's Landing, five miles below Pittsburg and on the same side of the river. The Army of the Ohio, under General Buell, which occupied Nashville and middle Tennessee, had been ordered to join the Army of the Tennessee at Savannah. The plan of campaign was an offensive movement against the Confederates, who were in force at or near Corinth, Mississippi.

After the battle of Mill Spring, Beauregard had been sent to the West to assist Albert Sidney Johnston in what was recognized as a grave situation, and now he had fixed upon Corinth as the base of operations. He used the utmost exertion to collect an army, calling upon the governors of Alabama, Louisiana, Mississippi, and Tennessee, and the generals of other departments, for help in the most earnest manner; he even appealed to the people of the Southwest to send their church-bells to be manufactured into cannon, an appeal which met with a prompt response. March 25 Johnston's army joined Beauregard's at Corinth, and the Confederate generals determined to attack Grant before Buell should join him, hoping by a quick movement to surprise his forces at Pittsburg Landing. April 3 the Confederate army left Corinth, but the weather was stormy and the roads were bad, causing the usual delays in the movement of troops, so that the attack planned for April 5 could not be made until Sunday the 6th.

Grant was so bent on his projected offensive movement, and

so confident that Johnston would not assume the aggressive so soon after the long and apparently demoralized retreat from Bowling Green and Columbus, that he had neglected all defensive measures; he had, indeed, some apprehension of an attack on Crump's Landing, but none for one on Pittsburg Landing. He was careless about the disposition of his forces; he threw up no intrenchments, although he had been ordered by Halleck to fortify his position, and although he had a swollen river at his back which separated him from his expected reinforcements, while he himself had his headquarters at Savannah; but at this time he would have moved them to Pittsburg Landing had he not expected Buell at Savannah on the 6th.

The Confederates were now face to face with their foe. Beauregard, disappointed at the delay, fearing that the chance to surprise Grant had been lost and that Buell might join him at any moment, favored giving up the attack and retiring to Corinth. Johnston overruled his second in command, and said to Beauregard and his corps commanders, "Gentlemen, we shall attack at daylight to-morrow. I would fight them if they were a million." In the early morning of April 6 the Confederates made the onslaught with vigor.

Few if any battles of our Civil War have given rise to so much controversy as this of Shiloh, for so the contest is now generally known. One of the points of dispute is whether the federal troops were surprised. That they were surprised was the current opinion at the North, largely based, it is true, on the accounts of newspaper correspondents. Halleck, who went to Pittsburg Landing soon after the battle, and had no desire to screen Grant, telegraphed Stanton from there, May 2: "The newspaper accounts that our divisions were surprised are utterly false. Every division had notice of the enemy's approach hours before the battle commenced;" and after "a patient and careful inquiry and investigation" he reiterated this in a letter of June 15 from Corinth. Grant and Sherman have maintained the same. The evidence is, indeed, conflicting, but it is clear enough that at least a portion of the Union army was on the alert, and that a reconnaissance had been made to discover the force of the enemy; it seems equally clear that few, if any, of the federal officers suspected that the whole Confederate army of 40,000 men was before them. That Johnston had not succeeded in effecting a complete surprise was due to the vigilance of the division, brigade, and regimental commanders, and not to the foresight of the commanding general. April 5 Grant telegraphed Halleck, "The main force of the enemy is at Corinth"; and later on the same day he said, "I have scarcely the faintest idea of an attack (general one) being made upon us, but will be prepared should such a thing take place." Colonel Ammen, who commanded a brigade of Nelson's division in Buell's army, which division had arrived at Savannah at noon of the 5th, saw Grant, as he recorded in his diary, at about three o'clock in the afternoon of that day, and said to the general that his troops could march on to Pittsburg Landing, if necessary. Grant replied: "You cannot march through the swamps; make the troops comfortable; I will send boats for you Monday or Tuesday, or some time early in the week. There will be no fight at Pittsburg Landing; we will have to go to Corinth, where the rebels are fortified. If they come to attack us we can whip them, as I have more than twice as many troops as I had at Fort Donelson." Had Grant suspected that 40,000 Confederates confronted his army of 33,000, he certainly would have slept at Pittsburg Landing that night. In an air line Savannah was only six miles from Pittsburg Landing, and while eating his breakfast he heard the firing. Sending an order to Nelson to march his division up the river to a point opposite Pittsburg Landing, the general took boat for the scene of action, stopping on the way at Crump's Landing, to tell Lew. Wallace to hold himself in readiness for an order to come to the assistance of the rest of the army. Arriving at Pittsburg Landing, and finding a tremendous battle in progress, he sent the anticipated order to Wallace, and pressed Nelson to hasten. Although he visited the several divisions, and made perhaps the best disposition he could, it was a battle in which the commanding general on the Union side counted for little; the division, brigade, and regimental commanders did the work. General William Tecumseh Sherman was the hero of the day. He was wounded twice, and had several horses shot under him. McClernand did valiant service. Hurlbut, W. H. L. Wallace, and Prentiss (these five led divisions) were equal to the demands upon them. Wallace and Prentiss were surrounded. Wallace, in attempting to cut his way out, fell mortally wounded. Prentiss, to save a useless and complete sacrifice, surrendered with 2200 men.

The most pathetic incident on the Confederate side was the death of Albert Sidney Johnston. He had felt keenly the strictures on his generalship for the loss of Donelson, and yet in a measure he admitted their justice. "The test of merit in my profession with the people is success," he wrote Davis. "It is a hard rule, but I think it right." He could not help seeing that Beauregard had accomplished results in rallying the people of the Southwest which, with his loss of prestige, he could not have attained. At Corinth he proposed to turn over the command to Beauregard, confining himself to the duties of a department commander, an unselfish offer which Beauregard at once refused. When the battle began he left his second at the headquarters in the field, while he himself rode forward to the front, and cutting loose from communication with his corps commanders, fought as a volunteer of high rank in the line, without attempting to keep his hand on the general control of the army. His seeming disposition was to win a signal victory or die in the attempt. At a critical moment in the afternoon, while leading a charge of a Tennessee regiment, he received a ball in his leg which cut an artery; he soon bled to death. The wound was not necessarily fatal, and had his surgeon, who had attended him most of the morning, been with him he might have been saved; but seeing a large number of wounded men, he had ordered the surgeon to establish a hospital and care for them. His death was a severe blow to the Confederate army.

The battle of Shiloh was a fierce fight. It is described by Force as "a combat made up of numberless separate encounters

of detached portions of broken lines, continually shifting position and changing direction in the forest and across ravines."
The contest of the first day lasted twelve hours and was a Confederate victory, in that the Union troops were driven back one
mile and a half and lost Shiloh church, the point which, Grant
writes, "was the key to our position." Beauregard's headquarters on the night of April 6 were where Sherman's had
been the night before. Nevertheless the result utterly failed to
meet the expectations of Johnston and Beauregard; they had
hoped to capture the Union army, or at any rate to drive it
from the field in complete rout. Lew. Wallace's division, through
a misunderstanding of orders, did not get to the field until
Sunday's battle was over. Colonel Ammen's brigade of Buell's
army reached the Landing in the afternoon and was ferried
across the river, arriving in time to take part in the last minutes of the contest. Ten thousand stragglers from the Union
army cowered under the high bank of the river. Many of the
troops were raw and fled panic-stricken at the first charge; some
of the officers showed cowardice as well as inefficiency. Stragglers from the Confederate ranks were numerous. Nearly ten
thousand Union soldiers were killed, wounded, or captured; the
Confederate loss in killed and wounded was as great as the
Union, but the loss in prisoners was small. Through it all Grant
preserved his imperturbability. "The tremendous roar to the
left," writes Whitelaw Reid, who, as a newspaper correspondent,
saw the battle, "momentarily nearer and nearer, told of an effort
to cut him off from the river and from retreat. Grant sat on his
horse quiet, thoughtful, almost stolid. Said one to him, 'Does not
the prospect begin to look gloomy?' 'Not at all,' was the quiet
reply. 'They can't force our lines around these batteries to-night
—it is too late. Delay counts everything with us. To-morrow we
shall attack them with fresh troops, and drive them, of course.' "

The night of the battle a heavy rain poured down on the un-
sheltered soldiers of both armies as they slept on their arms.
The Union gun-boats fired at regular intervals heavy shells over
the woods towards the point where the Confederates had biv-

ouacked, for the purpose of disturbing their rest. Beauregard's disorganized and shattered army, worn out with the exertions of Sunday, was little fitted to cope with the body of fresh troops that had joined Grant. Lew. Wallace had arrived with 6500 men. The rest of Nelson's division, Crittenden's, and part of McCook's division of Buell's army, amounting in all to about 20,000, had reached the scene of action. Buell himself had been on the field of battle Sunday. He and Grant met that night, and determined to make a simultaneous attack on the Confederates early Monday morning. The onslaught was made and resulted in victory. At two o'clock, after eight hours of fighting, Beauregard gave the order to retire; this was accomplished in good order. That night again it rained heavily, making the bad roads worse. Owing to the fatigue of the Army of the Tennessee Grant ordered no immediate pursuit; the later pursuit was not effective. The loss of Grant's army was 1513 killed, 6601 wounded, 2830 captured or missing, a total of 10,944; the casualties in Buell's army was 241 killed, 1807 wounded, and 55 captured or missing, a total of 2103. The whole union loss amounted to 13,047. In the Confederate army, as officially reported, there were 1728 killed, 8012 wounded, and 959 missing. Never before had a battle of such magnitude been fought in America. It was a desperate effort of the Confederates to retrieve what they had lost by the capture of Donelson, but their advance northward was for the time effectually repelled.

General C. F. Smith, who had done such heroic service at Donelson, did not share in the battle of Shiloh. He was in bed at Savannah, owing to an abrasion on the leg received as he was getting into a small boat at Pittsburg Landing; the wound mortified, and he died April 25. In his death the Union army suffered a great loss. Grant writes that, at the time he was superseded by Smith, Halleck's opinion and that of the generality undoubtedly was that Smith had greater fitness for the command of the Army of the Tennessee than he himself had, and in fact he rather inclined to that opinion himself.

The general notion at the North was that only the arrival of

Buell's army saved Grant from a second and more disastrous defeat. Whether that judgment be correct has since become a matter of controversy. Grant and Sherman have affirmed that, with Lew. Wallace's division of fresh troops, they would on Monday have driven the Confederates from the field. Bearing on this dispute, the remarks of General Sherman, in his official report of April 10, 1862, are significant. At about ten A.M. Monday, he wrote, "I saw for the first time the well-ordered and compact columns of General Buell's Kentucky forces, whose soldierly movements at once gave confidence to our newer and less-disciplined forces. . . . I concede that General McCook's splendid division from Kentucky drove back the enemy along the Corinth road, which was the great central line of this battle." It is safe, at all events, to say that the arrival of Buell converted what would have been at best a doubtful result into an almost absolute certainty. Considering the bad roads, the obstacles encountered, the orders received that haste was unnecessary, and that the soldiers were not veterans, Buell and his officers showed energy and celerity in their march from Nashville to Pittsburg Landing.

The laurels which Grant had won at Donelson were faded by his carelessness at Shiloh. That the battle had been a useless slaughter was the opinion of many of his officers and soldiers; and as the details of it became known, and as private letters began to be received from the army, the feeling towards him in the Western States, from which his troops came, was full of bitterness. The press faithfully reflected this sentiment, and members of Congress shared it. Elihu B. Washburne, in the House, and John Sherman, in the Senate, alone defended him. "You will see, from Harlan's remarks," wrote Sherman to his brother, the general, "there is much feeling against Grant, and I try to defend him, but with little success." All sorts of charges against him were made; that he had been reckless could not be gainsaid with much show of reason. The pressure on the President for his removal was great. A. K. McClure relates that, carried along by the overwhelming "tide of popular sentiment," and backed by "the almost universal conviction of the President's friends," he urged this course upon Lincoln. Going to the White House at eleven o'clock one night, in a private interview of two hours, in which he did most of the talking, McClure advocated with earnestness the removal of Grant as necessary for the President to retain the confidence of the country. "When I had said everything that could be said from my standpoint," McClure proceeds with his story, "we lapsed into silence. Lincoln remained silent for what seemed a very long time. He then gathered himself up in his chair and said, in a tone of earnestness that I shall never forget, '*I can't spare this man; he fights.*' " The result demonstrated what a clear perception of military ability Lincoln had in this case, when he determined to save Grant from removal and disgrace.

April 7, the second day of the battle of Shiloh, General John Pope, in conjunction with two of Foote's gun-boats, captured Island No. 10 with 6000 or 7000 prisoners; this was a fortress commanding the Mississippi River, and the next one below Columbus. Halleck went to Pittsburg Landing, arriving there April 11, and ordered Pope and his army to join him. Receiving also other reinforcements, he soon had 100,000 effective troops. Appointing General Thomas commander of the right wing, Buell of the centre, and Pope of the left, he named Grant his second in command; but as there went with it no precise duty, this assignment of position was really a displacement. Grant chafed under this, asked several times to be relieved from duty, and would have left the army had he not been dissuaded by Sherman, with whom he had already begun that fast friendship which endured throughout his whole life. Beauregard had been reinforced, and had an effective strength of 50,000. Towards the close of April Halleck began his move on Corinth, marching slowly and cautiously, and intrenching at every halt. The enemy's outposts hovered near the advancing army, but Halleck's orders to his subordinate commanders were to bring on no engagement. He was more than a month advancing the twenty-three miles from Pittsburg Landing to Corinth, and as soon as he arrived before the Confederate intrenchments Beauregard evacuated the place, of which the Union army then took peaceful possession. Grant, Sherman, and Pope had been anxious to fight the enemy, but Halleck discouraged all such suggestions and efforts. Corinth being a strategic point, on account of the junction there of the Mobile and Ohio Railroad running north and south, and the Memphis and Charleston Railroad running east and west, was worth having; but a victory over Beauregard's army would have been worth vastly more.

In the last days of April New Orleans was surrendered to Flag-officer Farragut, and the Union flag waved over the city. This result had been attained by an expedition of men-of-war under the command of Farragut, and a fleet of mortar boats under David D. Porter, which had bombarded with effect Forts St. Philip and Jackson; these forts were depended on as the main defences of New Orleans, although seventy-five miles below it. After five days of bombardment without reducing the forts, Farragut decided to make an attempt to run by them, and at two o'clock, on the morning of April 24, he gave the signal to advance, Porter, in the meanwhile, opening fire with fury from his mortar boats. Farragut, returning vigorously the fire of the forts, succeeded in getting past them with the largest portion of his fleet; he then attacked the Confederate gun-boats, which disputed the passage of the river above the forts, and, owing to the superiority of his vessels and the better discipline of his men, he easily defeated them in the naval battle which ensued, consigning most of them to destruction. He then steamed up the river without further serious molestation. When the news spread in New Orleans that the federal fleet was coming, hundreds of drays were set to work to haul the cotton in the presses and the yards to the levee; here patriotism applied the torch to the staple so eagerly desired at the North and in Europe. May 1 General Butler with 2500 troops occupied the city; Forts St. Philip and Jackson had surrendered to Commander Porter three days previously. The taking of New Orleans, a city of 160,000 inhabitants, the chief commercial port and the largest city of the South, a place well known in Europe as an important trading point, had a profound effect on opinion in England and France. May 15 Slidell wrote Benjamin from Paris that a conversation with Thouvenel, the French Minister of Foreign Affairs, led him "fairly to infer that if New Orleans had not been taken, and we suffered no very serious reverses in Virginia and Tennessee, our recognition would very soon have been declared." On the next day he had a conversation with Billanet, "minister *sans* portfolio, especially charged to represent the government in the Chambers on all subjects connected with foreign affairs. . . . In reply to my suggestions," Slidell wrote, "that the war could only be brought to a close by the intervention of European powers, which should be preceded by our recognition and a renewed proffer of mediation, he said that France could not act without the co-operation of England, but that within the last few days there seemed to be a change in the tone of the English cabinet; that if New Orleans had not fallen, our recognition could not have been much longer delayed." Mason wrote Benjamin from London, "The occupation of the principal Southern ports by the enemy, and the increased rigor of the blockade of those remaining to us, resulting from it, give little hope now of any interference in regard to the blockade, and leave only the question of recognition."

FOR *the South, the most glorious event of the year 1862 was the success of their incomparable military leaders, Lee and Jackson, in defeating McClellan before Richmond. Despite disaster at Shiloh, the loss of New Orleans, and the tightening of the blockade, the Confederates could rejoice in holding their capital so safe that they were able to invade Maryland in an effort that, if successful, would probably have brought foreign recognition of their government. And then they closed the year by a smashing victory at Fredericksburg on the Rappahannock that almost forced Lincoln to reorganize his government. For the North, the frustration of McClellan's march upon Richmond with what had seemed an overwhelming array was the bitterest of disappointments. Many people had confidently expected him to crush Lee's smaller and more poorly equipped Army of Northern Virginia, to drive Jefferson Davis and his cabinet back to Montgomery, and to send a wave of despair across the whole South. If McClellan had taken Richmond, and if at the same time Halleck and Grant had followed the victory at Shiloh with swift marches upon Chattanooga or Vicksburg (or possibly even both), the North might have won the war. Two tremendous "ifs"! In the large view of national history, however, such an early termination of the conflict could well have been unfortunate. It would have left slavery shaken but not overthrown. It was the prolongation of the war that made Lincoln's Emancipation Proclamation, which became effective on New Year's Day in 1863, an imperative step; and time proved it a momentous step, not alone in American annals, but in the history of civilization.*

*Before Rhodes published his story of the abortive Peninsular Campaign, the journalist William Swinton had brought out a narrative of McClellan's campaigns and an analysis of his mind and character that steered a middle path between malicious detraction on one side, and uncritical eulogy on the other (*The Army of the Potomac, 1866*). Swinton wrote: "He was assuredly not a great general; for he had the pedantry of war rather than the inspiration of war." The Comte de Paris had also provided a careful record of McClellan's operations, in the second volume of his work on the Civil War (1876), which possessed judicial qual-*

ity. Both writers emphasized the errors of the President in his interferences with military affairs; he was "extremely ill-advised at times," wrote the Comte de Paris. Historians since Rhodes have in general taken much his view of the Peninsular Campaign and agreed with his conclusions upon the Union general. McClellan has had his earnest defenders; but he was clearly a failure, and his excursions into politics were (it is now generally agreed) even more censurable than Rhodes pronounces them. No author has better caught the imposing drama of the situation as McClellan, at the head of the mightiest armed host that the continent had ever seen, pushed within sight of the Richmond spires.

McClellan Fails before Richmond

JUNE 1   Robert E. Lee was placed in command of the Confederate army, but did not assume the direction of affairs until the fighting of that day was over. While Davis had unbounded confidence in Lee, and Stonewall Jackson thought that he had military talents of a high order, no one could at that time have dreamed of his latent genius. The Army of Northern Virginia (by this name it became known shortly afterwards) regarded him as the most distinguished of engineers, but they retained a vivid impression of his failure the previous autumn in western Virginia, and neither officers nor men were hopeful that he would direct with energy and ability operations in the field. Johnston had won their confidence and respect; all looked upon his hurt as a calamity, and few, if any, believed that his loss had been repaired. Lee at once summoned his general officers in council. Longstreet, the commander of a division, did not regard this as reassuring; he thought secrecy in war was necessary, and that a discussion of plans with brigadiers was either harmful or useless. Lee listened intently to their accounts of the late battle and to their present opinions; he disclosed nothing, but, when the tone of the conversation became despondent at the progress of the siege which the invaders were conducting he endeavored to cheer up his officers, and in this was assisted by Davis, who joined the council before its members separated. Afterwards Lee made a careful survey of the position of his army, and directed that it be at once strongly fortified. He had some difficulty in overcoming the aversion to manual labor which obtained among the Southern soldiers, but his constant personal superintendence combined with his pleasing authoritative manner to push things forward, so that he soon had his defensive works well under way. In one respect at least the substitution of Lee for Johnston was a gain for the Southern cause. Johnston and Davis could not work together, and while the fault lay more with the Confederate President, the general was not wholly blameless. Johnston's letters at this time are marked by an acerbity which is not absent even when he is writing to Lee, for whom he had undoubtedly a profound respect. No one could quarrel with Lee, who in his magnanimity and his deference to his fellow-workers resembles Lincoln. Between the courtly Virginia gentleman, proud of his lineage, and the Illinois backwoodsman who came out of the depths, the likeness, in this respect, is as true as it is striking.

The harmony between Davis and Lee was complete. Something had already been done in the way of bringing reinforcements from the South, and under the new command this movement went on with vigor. In reading the orders, the despatches, the history of the army at this time, one seems to feel that a new energy has been infused into the management of affairs. Lee had a talent for organization equal to that of McClellan. In a few days he had matters well in hand and had gained the respect of the officers of his army. Unremitting in industry, he rode over his lines nearly every day. June 6 he noted "the enemy working like beavers," and wrote Longstreet: "Our people seem to think he will advance to-morrow morning. If so, I directed that he should be resisted." Longstreet, who commanded the Confederate right, had expected an attack at any moment since the battle of Fair Oaks. In six days subsequent to that battle the Confederate defences were so far advanced that Lee had good ground for his hope that he could repel an assault.

Although McClellan was in sight of the spires of Richmond, he had no intention of attempting to break through by storm the Confederate line of intrenchments. The weather was unfavorable. The heavy rains continued, and the Chickahominy became a flood interfering with the desired crossing of troops from the north to the south side of the river. The roads were so bad that the movement of artillery—an arm in which the Federals excelled—was extremely difficult if not impossible. The freshet in the James River was the greatest that had been known since 1847. In one street of Richmond the water came nearly up to the hubs of wagon-wheels, and owing to the condition of the roads the task of supplying the Confederate army was laborious and irksome. When Burnside visited, June 10, McClellan's headquarters, it took him four and a half hours to cover nine miles. He reported to Stanton that it was impossible to move artillery, and "but for the railroad the army could not be subsisted and foraged."

McClellan was begging for reinforcements, and the War Department did its best to comply with his demands. McCall's division of McDowell's corps was ordered to join him, and regiments were sent him from Baltimore, Washington, and Fort Monroe. These troops went forward by water as McClellan desired. It had been intended to send him the residue of McDowell's army, and this general wrote: "I go with the greatest satisfaction, and hope to arrive with my main body in time to be of service." The President strained every nerve to help McClellan, but was unable to do all that he wished. June 15 he wrote: I now fear that McDowell cannot get to you either by water or by land in time. "Shields's division has got so terribly out of shape, out at elbows and out at toes, that it will require a long time to get it in again." At the time the order was given McCall to join the Army of the Potomac, Stanton telegraphed McClellan: "Please state whether you will feel sufficiently

strong for your final movement when McCall reaches you."
The reply came promptly: "I shall be in perfect readiness to
move forward and take Richmond the moment McCall reaches
here and the ground will admit the passage of artillery." June
12 and 13 McCall's division joined him: this with the troops
from Baltimore, Washington, and Fort Monroe gave him a
total reinforcement, since the battle of Fair Oaks, of 21,000.
The weather had now become fine. The roads were dry. It
actually looked as if McClellan were going to give battle. June
13 his adjutant telegraphed Burnside: "General McClellan
desires me to say that there is a prospect of an engagement
here shortly"; and five days later he himself telegraphed the
President: "After to-morrow we shall fight the rebel army as
soon as Providence will permit." But a preposterous overestimate of the enemy's force and a shrinking from an order
that would result in the profuse shedding of blood led him again
to hesitate: he did not give the word that would have brought on
a desperate battle. Perhaps at this time his irresolution and
timidity stood his army in good stead. McClellan had 105,000
to Lee's 64,000, and when we take into account that a portion
of his force was necessary to guard his communications on the
north side of the Chickahominy, he had not preponderance
enough to justify a direct attack on an army strongly intrenched.
It is evident from Lee's and Davis's letters that nothing would
have gratified them more. Whatever discouragement had prevailed immediately after the battle of Fair Oaks had vanished.
"We are better prepared now than we were on the first of the
month," wrote Jefferson Davis, June 23, "and with God's
blessing will beat the enemy as soon as we can get at him."

As McClellan gave expression in writing to his many vacillating moods, it is difficult to know exactly what was his real
plan, but we may accept the one which he outlined to his wife.
"I shall probably," he gave her to understand, "make my first
advance June 17 or 18. The next battle will be fought at 'Old
Tavern,' on the road from New Bridge to Richmond. I think the
rebels will make a desperate fight, but I feel sure that we will

gain our point. . . . I shall make the first battle mainly an artillery combat. As soon as I gain possession of the 'Old Tavern' I will push them in upon Richmond and behind their works; then I will bring up my heavy guns, shell the city, and carry it by assault." It was substantially this same plan that Lee, who seemed to know McClellan as well as did McClellan himself, divined and undertook to thwart. "Unless McClellan can be driven out of his intrenchments," he wrote Jackson, "he will move by positions ("gradual approaches" is the expression Lee employs in a previous letter) under cover of his heavy guns within shelling distance of Richmond." It was apparently the conventional design of an engineer officer, and was foreseen independently by Davis, Longstreet, and D. H. Hill. Knowing the Federal superiority in artillery, it is little wonder that they regarded the movements of the Union army with apprehension. Perhaps they did not guess what Lee seemingly took for granted, that McClellan's procrastination would bring to naught his strategy. Nothing indeed could have been more dangerous to the Union forces. Encamped in the swamps of the Chickahominy, unaccustomed to an atmosphere so damp and malarious, drinking the water of the marshes, his soldiers suffered from diarrhœa and fevers, many of them also from scurvy, with the natural result that the morale of his army had lowered distinctly from the 1st to the 20th of June. But more than this, his delay was even fatal in that it afforded Lee time to mature and execute a project which needed a greater genius than McClellan to frustrate. Davis visited the lines of the army frequently, and from his own observations and friendly intercourse with the commanding general, comprehended the situation and saw clearly the problem to be solved. "The enemy," he wrote June 13, "keeps close under cover, is probably waiting for reinforcements, or resolved to fight only behind his own intrenchment. We must find if possible the means to get at him without putting the breasts of our men in antagonism to his heaps of earth." As a measure towards this end, Lee decided to reinforce with two brigades Jackson, who was still in the Shenandoah

valley, directing him with his main body to "move rapidly to
Ashland by rail or otherwise . . . and sweep down between the
Chickahominy and Pamunkey, cutting up the enemy's communications." Lee, having made up his mind that a direct assault upon McClellan's left wing was "injudicious if not impracticable," would, with the larger part of his force, cross the
Chickahominy and fall upon Porter, who commanded the right
wing of the Union army. Proceeding with caution, he ordered
Stuart with his cavalry to make a reconnaissance "around the
rear of the Federal army to ascertain its position and movements." Having now some apprehension that McClellan, if
aware of the weakening of his force by the reinforcement to
Jackson, might attack the Confederates, he asked the Secretary of War to influence the Richmond newspapers not to
mention the project. June 16 Lee made a personal reconnaissance of the Federal position north of the Chickahominy, and
the question to his military secretary, "Now, Colonel Long,
how can we get at those people?" showed that he was still
revolving the details of his plan. Shortly after this he submitted
his ripened project to his President, showing that the successful
execution of it depended upon the ability of the small Confederate force left before Richmond to hold in check the more
powerful left wing of the Federal army which was on the south
side of the Chickahominy. "I pointed out to him," writes Davis,
in his relation of the interview, "that our force and intrenched
line between that left wing and Richmond was too weak for a
protracted resistance, and, if McClellan was the man I took
him for, . . . as soon as he found that the bulk of our army was
on the north side of the Chickahominy, he would not stop to try
conclusions with it there, but would immediately move upon his
objective point, the city of Richmond. If, on the other hand, he
should behave like an engineer officer and deem it his first
duty to protect his line of communication, I thought the plan
proposed was not only the best, but would be a success. Something of his old *esprit de corps* manifested itself in General
Lee's first response, that he did not know engineer officers were

more likely than others to make such mistakes, but immediately passing to the main subject, he added, 'If you will hold him as long as you can at the intrenchment, and then fall back on the detached works around the city, I will be upon the enemy's heels before he gets there.' " Not long after this interview Jefferson Davis wrote his wife: "I wish General J. E. Johnston were able to take the field. Despite the critics who know military affairs by instinct, he is a good soldier, never brags of what he did do, and could at this time render most valuable service."

One week after he had given the order for the reinforcement of Jackson, Lee, apparently reckoning on McClellan's certain inaction, played upon the credulity of his adversary and the fears of the authorities in Washington. He knew that McClellan was in the habit of reading the Richmond journals, which, in view of their faithful regard of his former request, were now asked to publish the news that strong reinforcements had been sent to the Shenandoah valley. One newspaper asserted that Jackson, who now had as many men as he wanted, would drive Frémont and Shields across the Potomac, or, if they made a stand, would gain over them another glorious victory. This was evidence, the editor continued, of the immense military resources of the South; there were men enough to defend Richmond and to swell Jackson's army. McClellan, who had received the same intelligence from deserters, fell into the trap and telegraphed the President, "If 10,000 or 15,000 men have left Richmond to reinforce Jackson, it illustrates their strength and confidence." The War Department had like information from other sources, and induced the President to withhold troops from the Army of the Potomac that otherwise would have been sent. Yet Lincoln suspected this action of the Confederates to be a "contrivance for deception," but seems to have been alone in his suspicion.

Meanwhile Jackson was swiftly and stealthily moving his army towards the Chickahominy. To be present at the personal conference which Lee desired, he left his troops fifty miles from Richmond with orders to continue their progress; and, riding with haste, met in council at mid-day on June 23 the commanding general, Longstreet, D. H. Hill, and A. P. Hill. Lee set forth his plan of battle, and assigned to each of his generals the part he should play. Jackson said that he would be ready to begin his attack on the morning of the 26th.

While these astute soldiers were constructing this snare, what was McClellan doing? He had noted, June 23, the "rather mysterious movements" of the enemy; he had heard the next day that Jackson was marching towards him with the intention of attacking his rear, and that Confederate troops from Richmond intended to cross the Chickahominy near Meadow Bridge. He ought to have been cudgelling his brains to guess Lee's plan and to devise measures to thwart it; yet there is no evidence that McClellan was at this time gravely anxious. He had been engaged in writing an essay in the form of a long letter to the President, instructing him in the matter of military arrests and the exercise of military power in general, dictating to him what should be the course of the government in dealing with slavery: in short, the general admonished the chief magistrate with regard to his civil and military policy in the conduct of the war. Those parts of the letter that were not insolent were platitudes, and denoted a scattering of thought which augured ill in a man who had supreme responsibility. The injunctions that trenched upon the ground of the President would have been unbecoming in a general flushed with victory; in a commander who was not backed up by success they were outrageous. Not Lee nor Grant in any portion of his brilliant career can be conceived to have written to his President this letter of McClellan's.

McClellan was getting ready for his gradual advance. The first step, which was taken by Heintzelman June 25 in front of Seven Pines, resulted in a skirmish, but led to nothing further. All attention is now concentrated on the north side of the Chickahominy. On the evening of the 25th, McClellan visited Fitz John Porter's headquarters, where he was confirmed in the impression that Jackson would assail his rear;

and detecting indications of an attack on his front, he made arrangements accordingly.

Through unavoidable delays Jackson was half a day late. A. P. Hill with five brigades waited at Meadow Bridge until three o'clock in the afternoon of this June 26 for Jackson to perform his part; then fearing longer delay, he crossed the river and came directly in front of Porter. This brought on a battle in which the Confederates met with a bloody repulse. In the mean time D. H. Hill and Longstreet, with their divisions, had gone over the Machanicsville bridge to the north bank of the Chickahominy, but arriving at a late hour of the day, only D. H. Hill's leading brigade took part in the engagement.

McClellan went to Porter's headquarters that afternoon or early evening, while the battle was still on. Obtaining a better idea of Jackson's object, his fear for the communications with his base at White House increased, and that apprehension doubtless entered largely into the consultation with his favorite general. Porter, full of energy and ambition, proposed that he should be slightly reinforced, with the purpose of holding his own on Beaver Dam creek, while McClellan with the main body of the army moved upon Richmond. His alternative was to fall back with his corps to a safer position. While McClellan was with Porter, he came to no decision, but on returning to his own headquarters, he arrived at the conclusion, either from a fuller knowledge of Jackson's movements or from reflection on what he already knew, that Porter's position was untenable, and ordered him to withdraw his troops to the selected ground east of Gaines's Mill, where he could protect the bridges across the Chickahominy which connected the Union right and left wings and were indispensable should a further retreat become necessary. Porter received this command at two o'clock in the morning, and at daylight began the movement, which was executed without serious molestation and in perfect order. At first he had hoped to get along without aid, although he requested McClellan to have Franklin's corps ready to reinforce him, but on posting his army in position he made up his mind

that his force was too small to defend successfully so long a
line, and therefore asked Barnard, the chief engineer of the
army, who had conducted him to the new position, to represent
to the commanding general the necessity of reinforcement, and
also to send him felling axes for defensive purposes. Barnard
went to the headquarters of the army on the south side of the
Chickahominy at nine or ten in the morning, and being informed that the commanding general was reposing, failed to
see McClellan and to deliver any word to him, so that he
never received this appeal of Porter for additional troops. This
was a grave mischance, and may have lost the Union army the
day. Nevertheless, at seven in the morning, Franklin did receive
an order to send Slocum's division to assist Porter; but at nine
or ten o'clock, when part of the division had crossed the Chickahominy, the order was countermanded, and the troops who had
gone over returned to their original position on the south side
of the river.

On this Friday, June 27, was fought the battle of Gaines's
Mill. Porter, who had at the commencement of the battle
20,000 to 25,000 men, contended against Jackson, Longstreet,
and the two Hills, whose combined forces amounted to 55,000.
Lee was in immediate command, and Jefferson Davis was on
the battlefield. In their first onset the Confederates met with
an obstinate resistance and were driven back. At two o'clock
in the afternoon Porter called for reinforcements; and McClellan, who did not visit the field of battle that day, but remained
at the army headquarters on the south side of the Chickahominy, ordered Slocum's division of 9000 men to his support. This
time they joined him. Porter, who was making a magnificent
fight and undoubtedly believed that he held in check the larger
part of Lee's army, supposed that his commanding general with
the 55,000 troops remaining on the south side of the river would
embrace an occasion so conspicuous to overpower Magruder's
25,000 that stood between the Union left wing and Richmond,
and to accomplish by a bold stroke the object of the campaign.
In balancing the chances, the weight of authority, both North-

ern and Southern, is that success would have attended this operation. At the Union headquarters it was expected; by the Confederate generals it was feared. But in McClellan's orders and despatches, either official or private, there is no inkling that he pondered at any time that day so bold a project. Indeed, his estimate of the Confederate force precluded the barest consideration of it. He believed that Lee had 180,000 men, of whom 70,000 had assailed Porter, leaving between McClellan and Richmond, behind intrenchments, 110,000, on whom none but a foolhardy general would think of making a direct attack with an army only half as large. His attitude was confessedly defensive, and he measured the situation as if the Shakespearean saying,

> In cases of defense 't is best to weigh
> The enemy more mighty than he seems,

were a maxim of war.

Magruder deceived McClellan, as he had done when the Union army lay before Yorktown; he also misled Franklin, Sumner, and Hooker, by attacking their pickets from time to time, and by opening a frequest fire of artillery on their works. At about five o'clock in the afternoon McClellan, hearing that Porter was hotly pressed, asked Franklin and Sumner if they could spare men for his assistance. Franklin, having now but one division, did not deem it prudent further to weaken his force, and Sumner reluctantly proffered two brigades, which were ordered across the Chickahominy. Nothing shows McClellan's timid tactics more clearly than his hesitation in reinforcing Porter. He loved Porter and would have rejoiced, without a spark of envy, to see him win a glorious victory. His despatches make evident how anxious he was to give efficient support to his right wing, yet, swayed by his overestimate of the enemy's force, he apparently accepted the judgment of his corps commanders without question, when considerations, both military and personal, should have led him to send one half of his left wing to Porter's aid. His telegram to the Secretary of

War at the close of the day, "that he was attacked by greatly superior numbers in all directions on this side" (the Richmond side of the Chickahominy), remains an ineffaceable record of his misapprehension.

Meanwhile Fitz John Porter, as cool as if he were on parade, his tactics seemingly without defect, himself in the thick of the fight inspiriting his officers and men, repelled the assaults of nearly double his numbers, directed by the genius of Lee and Stonewall Jackson, led on by the courage and determination of the Hills and Longstreet. Higher praise can come to no general than that which Lee and Jackson unconsciously gave Porter in their reports. "The principal part of the Federal army was now on the north side of the Chickahominy," wrote Lee; both speak of the "superior force of the enemy." All accounts agree as to the discipline and bravery of the soldiers of both armies. When we consider their small experience in battle, we may describe the impetuous attack of the Confederates as did Jackson the charge of one of their regiments, speaking of it as an "almost matchless display of daring and valor." We may also borrow from him the words "stubborn resistance" and "sullen obstinacy" to describe the work of defence. On the Union side Meade and John F. Reynolds, commanders of brigades, made their mark that day. But skilful as was the general, brave as were the soldiers, 31,000 men, with no intrenchments, with barriers erected along a small portion only of their front, could not finally prevail against 55,000 equally brave and as skilfully led. The end came at about seven o'clock. Lee and Jackson ordered a general assault; the Confederates broke the Federal line, captured many cannon, and forced Porter's troops back to the woods on the bank of the Chickahominy. Then cheering shouts were heard; they came from the brigades of French and Meagher of Sumner's corps which had been sent to the support of their comrades. They came too late to save the day, but they efficiently covered the retreat of Porter's exhausted and shattered regiments, who withdrew dejectedly to the south side of the river.

In his despatches during the battle McClellan does not display bewilderment. At five o'clock he thought Porter might hold his own until dark, and three hours later his confidence was only a little disturbed, but by midnight he had reached a state of demoralization which revealed itself in his famous Savage Station despatch to the Secretary of War. "I now know the full history of the day," he wrote. "On this side of the river (the right bank) we repulsed several strong attacks. On the left bank our men did all that men could do, all that soldiers could accomplish, but they were overwhelmed by vastly superior numbers, even after I brought my last reserves into action. The loss on both sides is terrible. . . . The sad remnants of my men behave as men. . . . I have lost this battle because my force was too small. . . . I feel too earnestly to-night. I have seen too many dead and wounded comrades to feel otherwise than that the government has not sustained this army. If you do not do so now, the game is lost. If I save this army now, I tell you plainly that I owe no thanks to you or to any other persons in Washington. You have done your best to sacrifice this army."

The news was a terrible blow to the President. The finely equipped army which had cost so much exertion and money, had gone forward with high hopes of conquest, and apparently bore the fate of the Union, had been defeated, and was now in danger of destruction or surrender. This calamity the head of the nation must face, and he failed not. Overlooking the spirit of insubordination in his general's despatch, with equal forbearance and wisdom, he sent McClellan a reply which, mingling circumspection with gentleness of spirit, offers the most charitable explanation possible of the disaster. "Save your army at all events," he wrote. "Will sent reinforcements as fast as we can. . . . I feel any misfortune to you and your army quite as keenly as you feel it yourself. If you have had a drawn battle or a repulse, it is the price we pay for the enemy not being in Washington. We protected Washington and the enemy concentrated on you. Had we stripped Washington he would have been upon us before the troops could have gotten to you. . . . It is the nature of the case, and neither you nor the government are to blame."

The Peninsular campaign was a failure, and the chief cause of its failure may be ascribed to McClellan. I have spoken of the mistakes of Lincoln and Stanton, wherein they contributed to the embarrassment of the Union army in its operations before Richmond, but it is not just to weigh their errors as heavily as we do those of the commanding general. Lincoln was a civilian called by the voice of the people to a place which on the occurrence of the war became one of unprecedented difficulty. That he would gladly have thrown all responsibility of the movement of armies on a man of military training, is shown by his whole treatment of McClellan. But McClellan was not equal to the position of commander-in-chief, and because of his incompetence the President was forced little by little to invade his province and assume unwonted duties with a result that is not surprising. Lincoln's care to avail himself of all sources of enlightenment is shown by his night journey, June 23, on a quick special train to West Point for the purpose of consulting General Scott, who was too infirm to visit Washington. The traditions of the country were favorable to the occupancy of the War Department by a civilian, and Stanton brought to this office ability, energy, and honesty. The mistakes of Lincoln and Stanton were those of civilians who were constrained by force of circumstances to intervene in military business, while McClellan's trade was war; and when offensive operations had to be conducted on a large scale, he showed himself to be incompetent in his trade. It is no longer necessary to bring proof, indeed it is hardly necessary even to state, that Lincoln desired sincerely and ardently the success of his general. To me it is equally clear that Stanton shared this feeling. The very nature of the case, the combination of patriotism and self-interest, must have made the Secretary eager for victories no matter by what general won. His letters, despatches, and verbal assurances are evidence either that he did all in his power to aid McClellan, consistent with what he deemed his duty elsewhere, and that he would have rejoiced with no feeling of envy at the success of the Peninsular campaign, or that he was black-hearted and treacherous, to a degree inconceivable of one trusted by the most honest and magnanimous of men, Abraham Lincoln.

McClellan's failure was due largely to his absurd overestimate of the enemy, which unnerved him when active operations were needed.

IN a dark hour—the hour in which the blundering John Pope took control of the Union forces before Washington, in which McClellan dragged his feet in getting troops back north from the Richmond area and some subordinates like Fitz-John Porter played malign parts, the hour of defeat at Second Bull Run and of a new invasion of Kentucky by the Confederates under General Braxton Bragg—Lincoln had to devote himself in great part to political measures. The Army of the Potomac was pretty well demoralized by exhausting efforts that had ended in humiliating failure. More troops had to be called out—"three hundred thousand more." Something had to be done to satisfy the rising demand for action against slavery. The Radical Republicans who had tried in vain to force Seward out of the Cabinet demanded a decisive step toward emancipation; general public sentiment in the North was veering in that direction; and Lincoln himself, after the rebuff given his plan of compensated emancipation by the leaders of the border states, saw that emancipation was becoming a necessity. It would hearten Northern sentiment, dismay and weaken the South, and open the gate to a large-scale enlistment of Negroes in the army. Congress was constantly threatening to press ahead of him. Congress was ready to tax the country heavily, to pass a stringent act for the confiscation of rebel property, and to vote such constructive measures as the Homestead law and Pacific Railroad bill. Congress had taken steps to free the slaves in the District of Columbia and to affirm the fact of universal freedom in the territories.

Lincoln now proved himself ready to move more promptly than most of his advisers in the government had been. He knew that he must lead the public sentiment of the North. He fully realized, too, the importance of meeting the demands of the great body of foreign opinion—especially British working-class and middle-class opinion—which had hoped from the outset for the extinction of slavery. He was ready to double the objects of the war: it must vindicate both Union and freedom.

Lincoln, Greeley, and Slavery

BRIEF reflection convinced President Lincoln . . . that the Union armies must be increased if the end were to be attained towards which the Northern people strove. With a view to starting fresh enlistments, Secretary Seward, furnished with a letter in which the President made clear the need of additional troops, went to New York City, Boston, and Cleveland to confer with men of influence and with as many governors of States as possible. In this letter Lincoln declared: "I expect to maintain this contest until successful, or till I die, or am conquered, or my term expires, or Congress or the country forsakes me; and I would publicly appeal to the country for this new force, were it not that I fear a general panic and stampede would follow, so hard is it to have a thing understood as it really is." After Seward had conferred in New York City with men of weight and taken counsel by wire in cipher with the President and Secretary of War, it was determined to issue a circular to the governors of the States of the Union, exposing the situation and asking them to offer the President the needed reinforcements. On July 2, in accordance with the secret arrangements, there appeared in the newspapers, in the words of the draft which Seward had made, a letter from the governors requesting the President to call upon the several States for men enough "to speedily crush the rebellion." The President's reply, which was also printed, follows substantially Seward's draft, except that during the negotiations the necessity of the country on one hand and the willing co-operation of the governors on the other had combined to increase the number of troops at first proposed, and the call went forth for 300,000 three years' men. Sumner wrote John Bright: "The last call for three hundred thousand men is received by the people with enthusiasm, because it seems to them a purpose to push the war vigorously. There is no thought in the Cabinet or the President of abandoning the contest." "We shall easily obtain the new levy," said

Lincoln in a private letter. It was evident from the first that the people would give the government efficient support, although the call came upon them during a period of painful suspense when they were without news from McClellan's army. The War Department did not hear from McClellan from June 28 to July 1, and not until July 3 could the President have felt sure that his army was safe. Lincoln grew thin and haggard, and his despatches from the first of these days are an avowal of defeat. Stanton, on the other hand, did not realize the truth. June 29 he telegraphed Seward, "My inference is that General McClellan will probably be in Richmond within two days." Had the Secretary of War been given to dissimulation, or had he not sent a similar despatch to General Wool at Baltimore, we might suppose that he intended to mislead the men of influence and the governors with whom Seward was conferring, in order that the promise for additional troops might be more easily obtained. Seward took the cue readily, and in his draft of the governors' letter explained that the fresh recruits were needed to follow-up "the recent successes of the Federal arms." But the Northern people were not deceived. Learning after five days of suspense that McClellan's army had reached the James River, they recognized that it had been defeated and forced to retreat. The event was spoken of as a disaster, the news of it causing at once a panic in Wall Street. Days of gloom followed. "Give me a victory and I will give you a poem," wrote Lowell to his publisher; "but I am now clear down in the bottom of the well, where I see the Truth too near to make verses of." There was a noticeable disposition to find fault with Stanton, whose folly in stopping recruiting at the time of the Union successes in the spring was bewailed. Not nearly so marked was the disposition to censure McClellan for the misfortune that had befallen the North, while Lincoln escaped with less criticism from the country at large than either.

Meanwhile Congress was in session, an observer of military events and a diligent worker in its sphere, though exercising less relative sway and attracting less attention than in a time

458 LINCOLN, GREELEY, AND SLAVERY

of peace, for the war caused the executive to trench upon its
power and directed all eyes to his acts and the work of his
armies. Nevertheless the senators and representatives labored
with zeal, sagacity, and effect. The laws of this session show how
much an able and honest Congress may accomplish when
possessed of an earnestness and singleness of purpose that will
prevail against the cumbrous rules which hedge about the action
of a democracy's legislative body, unfitting it for the management of a war.

Congress at this session authorized the President to take
possession of the railroads and the telegraph lines when the
public safety required it, recognized the governments of Hayti
and Liberia, passed a Homestead Act, established a Department of Agriculture, donated public lands to the several States
and Territories for the purpose of founding agricultural colleges, and authorizing the construction of a railroad to the
Pacific Ocean, giving it aid in land and in government bonds.
It created a comprehensive and searching scheme of internal
taxation which became a law by the President's approval July
1. This might be briefly described with a near approach to
accuracy as an act which taxed everything. So impressed are two
writers with its burdensome character that they have added to
their summary of its provisions, as an apt description of it,
Sydney Smith's well-known humorous account of British
taxation in 1820.* Under this act of Congress, distillers of spirits, brewers of ale, beer, and porter, all other manufacturers,

* Blaine, *Twenty Years of Congress*, vol. i. p. 433; W. C. Ford, *Lalor's
Cyclopædia,* vol. ii. p. 577. Their citation is from Sydney Smith's article
on America, *Edinburgh Review,* Jan., 1820. Smith wrote: "Taxes upon
every article which enters into the mouth, or covers the back, or is placed
under the foot—taxes upon everything which it is pleasant to see, hear,
feel, smell, or taste—taxes upon warmth, light, and locomotion—taxes on
everything on earth, and the waters under the earth—on everything that
comes from abroad, or is grown at home—taxes on the raw material—taxes
on every fresh value that is added to it by the industry of man—taxes on
the sauce which pampers man's appetite, and the drug that restores him to
health—on the ermine which decorates the judge, and the rope which hangs
the criminal—on the poor man's salt, and the rich man's spice—on the
brass nails of the coffin, and the ribands of the bride—at bed or board,
couchant or levant, we must pay."—P. 77.

wholesale and retail dealers, men in all kinds of business, whether their trade was to supply necessaries or luxuries, or to furnish amusements (such as proprietors of theatres and circuses and jugglers), lawyers, physicians, surgeons, and dentists were required to pay for licenses. A duty of twenty cents per gallon was imposed on spirits, one dollar per barrel on malt liquors, and that on tobacco and cigars was heavy. Many products and nearly all manufactures and articles were taxed, and carriages, yachts, billiard-tables, and plate, also slaughtered cattle, hogs, and sheep, railroad bonds, passports, legacies, and distributive shares of personal property. A duty of three per cent. was laid on the gross receipts of railroads, steamboats, and toll-bridges, on dividends of banks, savings institutions, trust and insurance companies, on the gross receipts from advertisements in newspapers, etc., and on the salaries and pay of officers and persons in the service of the United States above an exemption of $600. On the gross receipts of railroads using other power than steam and of ferry-boats the duty was one and one-half per cent. One tenth of one per cent. was exacted on the gross amount of auction sales. A tax of three per cent. on incomes less than $10,000, and of five per cent. on incomes over $10,000 with an exemption of $600 was imposed, although certain deductions were allowable in making the return. Upon the income of citizens residing abroad, there was laid a tax of five per cent. without the usual exemption. Stamp duties were imposed upon every species of paper used to represent or transfer property, on medicines or preparations, perfumery, cosmetics, and playing-cards. The duties on imports were increased by an act approved by the President, July 14.

Next to the tax and appropriation bills, the most important measure of this session of Congress, the Confiscation Act, dealt with a subject which attracted during the whole course of its consideration much attention from both Senate and House. The act as finally passed and approved iterated the penalty of death for treason, but allowed the court at its discretion to commute the punishment to fine and imprisonment; defined the crime of rebellion and annexed a penalty to it; directed the President "to cause the seizure of all the estate and property, money, stocks, credits, and effects," of all military and civil officers of the Southern Confederacy or of any of the States thereof, and, after sixty days of public warning, confiscate likewise the property of all "engaged in armed rebellion" against the United States "or aiding or abetting such rebellion"; freed forever the slaves of those convicted of treason or rebellion, and also the slaves of "rebel owners" who took "refuge within the lines of the [Union] army" or in any way came under the control of the Federal government; denied the protection of the Fugitive Slave Act to any owners of escaped slaves except those loyal to the Union, and forbade any military or naval officer to surrender any fugitive to the claimant;* gave authority for the colonization of "persons of the African race made free" by this act; authorized the President to employ negroes as soldiers; and gave him power to amnesty the rebels by proclamation and to make exceptions from a general pardon.

The bill which had been reported by Senator Trumbull from the Judiciary Committee and the one which the House had originally passed were more stringent in their provisions,

* Congress did not repeal the Fugitive Slave Law, although Sumner would have been glad to propose it had there been a chance of success.— Pierce's *Sumner*, vol. iv. p. 71. June 9 Julian offered a resolution in the House instructing the Judiciary Committee to report a bill to repeal it, and, although the House was disposed to go further in striking at slavery than the Senate, this resolution was laid on the table, 17 Republicans voting with 19 Unionists (all but two of these from the border slave States) and 30 Democrats, making a total of 66 for such action to 51 against.—*Cong. Globe*, p. 2623; *Julian's Polit. Rec.*, P. 218.

The Fugitive Slave Law continued to be enforced where legal processes could apply. The Washington despatch to the New York *Herald*, May 16, said: "The Fugitive Slave Law is being quietly enforced in this district to-day, the military authorities not interfering with the judicial process. There are at least four hundred cases pending." See *Life of Garrison*, vol. iv. p. 51, note 1. General J. D. Cox writes me, under date of March 26, 1896: "The anti-slavery sentiment grew so rapidly in the field that the right to reclaim a fugitive slave in camp was never of any use to slaveholders. Officers said 'You may take him if you can find him,' but the rank and file took care that he should not be found." See paper "Dealing with Slavery," by Channing Richards, *Sketches of War History*, vol iv., *Ohio Commandery of the Loyal Legion*.

and therefore more satisfactory to the radicals of the Senate, of whom Sumner, Wade, and Chandler were the leaders, than the act finally agreed to; but even this act was more acceptable to them than the measure which the conservative Republicans of the Senate with the aid of the Democrats and the Unionists of the border States, had, on a decisive vote, succeeded in adopting. Of this Chandler declared, June 28, the day on which McClellan began his retreat to the James: "I do not believe the bill is worth one stiver. It is utterly worthless as a bill to confiscate property." The subject went to a committee of conference, and while it was pending, senators and representatives were in gloom over the misfortune and failure of the Army of the Potomac.

The bill "was at last passed," wrote Sumner, "under the pressure from our reverses at Richmond." It is, he added, "a practical act of emancipation. It was only in this respect that I valued it. The Western men were earnest for reaching the property of the rebels. To this I was indifferent except so far as it was necessary to break up the stronghold of slavery." That "the Confiscation Act was more useful as a declaration of policy than as an act to be enforced" is the mature judgment of John Sherman, who in the Senate took an active part in the discussion of the measure. Yet the clause which affirmed the death penalty for treason was no empty form of words, for many Republicans, Unionists, and Democrats at this time thought that the "leaders of the rebellion" ought to be hanged, and that such in the end would be their fate.

The Confiscation bill agreed upon in conference was enacted by the House July 11, and by the Senate one day later. It now became bruited abroad that the President would veto the bill, and many legislators were anxious lest Congress and perhaps the people should come into collision with the Executive. To ascertain in view of the many dangers thickening about the country, if this might not be avoided, Senator Fessenden and another gentleman had a consultation with the President. They found the rumor to be true. Lincoln's

chief objection arose from his interpretation of the act to mean
that offenders might be forever divested of their title to real
estate. Confiscation to this extent was, in his view, clearly
opposed to the explicit assertion of the Constitution, "No
attainder of treason shall work corruption of blood or forfeiture
except during the life of the person attainted." So strenuous
was his opposition to this feature that he had decided to veto
the bill, and had prepared a message pointing out his objections, and ending with, "I return the bill to the House in which
it originated." Many regarded this measure of confiscation as
one of the highest importance. Trumbull declared: "I believe
that the passage of the bill and its fair execution is worth more
towards crushing the rebellion than would be the capture of
Richmond and the destruction of the whole rebel army that is
around it to-day." Wade spoke of it as "the most useful of all
bills, one that lies deeper in the hearts of the people than anything we have done during the session or can do. If it should
fail to meet the approbation of the President of the United
States, I can tell him it will be the saddest announcement that
ever went out from the Capitol." The tone of some of the radical
senators toward the President in the debate of July 16 was
bitter, and by the veto of the bill the suppressed opposition to
him in his own party would undoubtedly have been forced to
an open rupture. The misfortune was obviated by Congress
passing, the day previous to its adjournment, an explanatory
joint resolution which removed Lincoln's main objection and
was signed by him at the same time with the Confiscation Act
itself. His draft of the proposed veto message which he sent
to the House with the announcement of his approval of the
bill and the joint resolution showed that his construction of the
act was different from that of the radical senators, and that its
execution in his hands might be attended with a greater regard
for the forms of law and the letter of the Constitution than, according to their view, ought to obtain in this time of real danger
to the Republic.

The disaster to McClellan's army increased the criticism of

the radical Republicans, who did not believe that the President was conducting the war with vigor. They found fault with him chiefly because he did not remove McClellan from command and because he did not strike at slavery.* That they were restive at the President's encroachment on the powers of Congress and his failure to exercise his authority by some measure of liberation, had already become apparent in the Senate. Inasmuch as Congress had been called upon by the explanatory joint resolution to shape its action in accordance with the wish of the Executive conveyed in a channel unknown to the Constitution, the feeling broke out, in the debate of July 16, that the President had magnified his office. Sherman intimated that they were acting under "duress," while Lane, of Indiana, further declared that the duress was the "threat of a veto from the President." Preston King, of New York, and Trumbull thought that Congress was coerced by this mode of proceeding; and Wade sneered at the practice of learning the "royal pleasure" before they could pass a bill. When Congress adjourned the next day, some of the radical senators and representatives went home with a feeling of hostility to Lincoln, and of despair for the Republic.

They misjudged him, but not unnaturally, for although he was thinking about slavery as earnestly as any of them, the indiscretion of a general had obliged him to take a position

* Adams S. Hill, Washington correspondent New York *Tribune,* at about this time wrote to Sydney Howard Gay, managing editor: "Ten minutes' talk last night with Gen. Wadsworth. The result this. He is cheerful in view of military prospects, but thinks political signs gloomy. I value his testimony because he has, as he says, been with the President and Stanton every day at the War Department—frequently for five or six hours—during several months. He says that the President is not with us; has no Antislavery instincts. He never heard him speak of Anti-slavery men, otherwise than as 'radicals,' 'abolitionists,' and of the 'nigger question,' he frequently speaks. Talking against McClellan with Blair, in Lincoln's presence, Wadsworth was met by Blair with the remark, 'He'd have been all right if he'd stolen a couple of niggers.' A general laugh, in which Lincoln laughed, as if it were an argument. W. believes that if emancipation comes at all it will be from the rebels, or in consequence of their protracting the war."—A. S. Hill Papers, MS. In this manner I shall indicate the private correspondence which has been kindly placed at my disposal by Professor Hill.

which seemed to them to indicate a reactionary policy. Hunter, who commanded the Department of the South, issued an order, May 9, declaring free all the slaves in South Carolina, Florida, and Georgia. The first knowledge of this came to Lincoln through the newspapers one week later. Chase urged him to let the order stand. "No commanding general shall do such a thing upon *my* responsibility without consulting me," was the President's reply. May 19 he declared Hunter's order void, and in his proclamation appealed to the people of the border slave States to adopt some measure for the gradual abolishment of slavery, and accept the compensation for their slaves proffered them by the President and by Congress. "I do not argue," he said,—"I beseech you to make arguments for yourselves. You cannot, if you would, be blind to the signs of the times. I beg of you a calm and enlarged consideration of them, ranging, if it may be, far above personal and partisan politics. This proposal makes common cause for a common object, casting no reproaches upon any. It acts not the Pharisee. The change it contemplates would come gently as the dews of heaven, not rending or wrecking anything. Will you not embrace it? So much good has not been done by one effort in all past time, as in the providence of God it is now your high privilege to do. May the vast future not have to lament that you have neglected it." This fervent and reasonable appeal did not convince those to whom it was addressed, but it showed the people of the North that the President desired to rid the nation of slavery if it could be done in a constitutional manner. In spite of the muttering at Washington, the declaration that Hunter's emancipation order was void received general approval throughout the country, since many Republicans, who were eager to see blows struck at slavery from any quarter, felt that they must yield to Lincoln, who had the power and responsibility.*

Two events happening previously to this indicated that the

* New York *Herald,* May 17, 20, *Tribune,* May 19, 20. R. H. Dana wrote Sumner, June 7: "If two papers were opened—one for Hunter's proclamation and the other for the President's present position on that point—to be signed *only by voters,* the latter would have three to one in Massachusetts."—Pierce-Sumner Papers, MS. But see Gov. Andrew's opinion

administration was keeping step with the march of human freedom. The first man in our history to suffer death for violating the laws against the foreign slave trade was hanged at New York in February. In April Secretary Seward concluded and honorable and efficient treaty with Great Britain for the suppression of the African slave trade.

How the government could treat slavery and the slaves to redound to the advantage of the Union cause was made the overpowering question in Lincoln's mind by his visit of July 8 to the Army of the Potomac at Harrison's Landing, which brought home to him with telling force the disastrous event of the Peninsular campaign. Gradual emancipation of the slaves, compensation of their owners, and colonization of the freed negroes,—this is the policy that he adopted. So vital did he deem some action of this kind that he could not allow the senators and representatives of the border slave States to go home on the adjournment of Congress before he had brought the matter again to their attention. July 12 he called them to the White House, and asked them earnestly if they would not adopt his policy and accept compensation for their slaves. He spoke of the hope entertained by "the States which are in rebellion" that their sister slave communities would join their Confederacy. "You and I know what the lever of their power is. Break that lever before their faces and they can shake you no more forever. . . . If the war continues long . . . the institution in your States will be extinguished by mere friction and abrasion—by the mere incidents of war. . . . Much of its value is gone already. How much better for you and for your people to take the step which at once shortens the war and secures sub-

---

in his letter to Stanton, May 19, Schouler's *Massachusetts in the Civil War*, p. 333. Chase, urging the President to let Hunter's order stand, had written: "It will be cordially approved, I am sure, by more than nine-tenths of the people on whom you must rely for support of your administration."—Warden, p. 434. Senator Grimes wrote his wife: "The President has to-day rescinded Hunter's proclamation. The result will be a general row in the country. All the radical Republicans are indignant but me, and I am not, because I have expected it and was ready for it. . . . But the end must come, protracted by the obstinacy and stupidity of rulers it may be, but come it will nevertheless."—Salter, p. 196.

stantial compensation for that which is sure to be wholly lost in any other event." He then told them and the public of a difficulty he had to contend with,—"one which threatens division among those who, united, are none too strong." Out of General Hunter's order the discord had lately arisen. "In repudiating it," Lincoln continued, "I gave dissatisfaction if not offence to many whose support the country cannot afford to lose. And this is not the end of it. The pressure in this direction is still upon me and increasing." In conclusion he averred that "our common country is in great peril," and besought them to help save our form of government. A majority of the representatives of Kentucky, Virginia, Missouri, and Maryland in the two houses of Congress, twenty in number, replied that the policy advocated seemed like an interference of the national government in a matter belonging exclusively to the States; they questioned the constitutional power of Congress to make an appropriation of money for such a purpose; they did not believe that the country could bear the expense proposed; they doubted the sincerity of Congress in making the offer, and thought that funds for the compensation of slave owners should be placed at the disposal of the President before the border States were called upon to entertain such a proposition.* One

* McPherson, *Political History of the Great Rebellion,* p. 215. In the course of their reply they said: "It seems to us that this resolution [of March, see vol. iii. p. 631] was but the annunciation of a sentiment which could not or was not likely to be reduced to an actual tangible proposition. No movement was then made to provide and appropriate the funds required to carry it into effect; and we were not encouraged to believe that funds would be provided." Senator Henderson, who made an individual reply favorable to the President's views, wrote: "I gave it [the resolution of March] a most cheerful support, and I am satisfied it would have received the approbation of a large majority of the border States delegations in both branches of Congress, if, in the first place, they had believed the war with its continued evils—the most prominent of which, in a material point of view, is its injurious effect on the institution of slavery in our States— could possibly have been protracted for another twelve months; and if in the second place they had felt assured that the party having the majority in Congress would, like yourself, be equally prompt in practical action as in the expression of a sentiment."

Minority replies favorable to the President's position were made by seven representatives and by Horace Maynard of Tennessee, as well as by Senator Henderson. McPherson, p. 217 *et seq.*

other objection must have weighed with them, which is only hinted at in their reply. It was a part of the plan that payment for the slaves should be made in United States bonds, and while negro property had become admittedly precarious the question must have suggested itself, whether, in view of the enormous expenditure of the government, the recent military reverses, and the present strength of the Confederacy, the nation's promises to pay were any more valuable. Gold, which June 2 was at three and one-half per cent. premium, fetched now, owing to McClellan's defeat and the further authorized issue of paper money, seventeen per cent.: its price from this time forward measures the fortunes of the Union cause.

During a drive to the funeral of Secretary Stanton's infant son, the day after his interview with the border State representatives, Lincoln opened the subject, which was uppermost in his mind, to Seward and to Welles. The reverses before Richmond, the formidable power of the Confederacy, made him earnest in the conviction that something must be done in the line of a new policy. Since the slaves were growing the food for the Confederate soldiers, and served as teamsters and laborers on intrenchments in the army service, the President had "about come to the conclusion that it was a military necessity, absolutely essential for the salvation of the nation, that we must free the slaves or be ourselves subdued." In truth, he was prepared to go as far in the path to liberation as were the radical Republicans of Congress. The inquiry therefore is worth making, why he did not recommend to Congress some measure to this end, which, with his support, would undoubtedly have been carried. It would appear reasonable that if the President under the rights of war could emancipate the slaves, Congress with the executive approval should have the same power; but Lincoln evidently believed action in this matter to lie outside the province of the legislative body. Ready as he himself was to declare free the slaves in all the States which continued "in rebellion" after Jan. 1, 1863, he remarked in the message submitted with the proposed veto of the Confiscation

Act, "It is startling to say that Congress can free a slave within a State."* An edict of the President would be more impressive and would influence public opinion in the country and in Europe more than could a legislative act that was passed only after long debate and the consideration of various amendments, and was in the end perhaps a compromise in conference committee. Moreover a sagacious statesman in the position of chief magistrate, could better time the stroke. Again it is possible that Lincoln intended to secure gradually the co-operation of Congress in his policy, and began by proposing this further step towards compensation—for the offer of compensation was an indispensable part of his plan—which would meet one objection of the border State men. July 14, the day after his conversation with Seward and Welles, he asked the Senate and the House to pass a bill placing at his disposal a certain sum in six per cent. bonds to be used by him in paying for slaves in any State that should lawfully abolish slavery. This request was not well received in the Senate. Grimes and Sherman did not recognize the right of the President "to introduce a bill here," and it was only after an effort on the part of Sumner that the message and the bill were referred to the Committee on Finance. Sumner also proposed that Congress defer their adjournment in order to consider the subject, but could not get his resolution before the Senate. On the day before the adjournment of Congress there was introduced in the House of Representatives from the select committee of emancipation a bill pro-

---

* As an indication of sentiment in Congress, I quote from Sumner's speech in the Senate of June 27: "There are senators who claim these vast War Powers for the President and deny them to Congress. The President, it is said, as commander-in-chief may seize, confiscate, and liberate under the Rights of War, but Congress cannot direct these things to be done. . . . Of the pretension that all these enormous powers belong to the President and not to Congress I try to speak calmly and within bounds. . . . But a pretension so irrational and unconstitutional, so absurd and tyrannical, is not entitled to respect. The Senator from Ohio [Mr. Wade] . . . has branded it as slavish. . . . Such a pretension would change the National Government from a government of law to that of a military dictator. . . . That this pretension should be put forward in the name of the Constitution is only another illustration of the effrontery with which the Constitution is made responsible for the ignorance, the conceit, and the passions of men."
—*Works,* vol. vii. p. 139.

viding for the issue of bonds to the amount of $180,000,000 to be used for the compensation of loyal owners of slaves in the border States and in Tennessee, when any one of them should by law abolish slavery, and for the appropriation of $20,000,000 to be expended in colonizing the freed negroes. Owing to the lateness of the session, the bill was not considered.

July 17 Congress adjourned. Five days later Lincoln read to his cabinet, to the surprise of all, probably except Seward and Welles, a proclamation of emancipation which he purposed to issue. In it he said that he intended to recommend to Congress, at its next meeting, the adoption of a practical measure of compensation. He reiterated that the object of the war was the restoration of the Union; "and as a fit and necessary military measure for effecting this object," he dclared that on January 1, 1863, all slaves in States wherein the constitutional authority of the United States was not recognized should be thenceforward and forever free. Various suggestions were offered, but all of the cabinet except Blair gave the policy proposed a full or qualified support. Blair demurred, on the ground that it would cost the administration the fall elections. Seward pleaded for delay, saying, in substance: "Mr. President, I approve of the proclamation, but I question the expediency of its issue at this juncture. The depression of the public mind, consequent upon our repeated reverses, is so great that I fear the effect of so important a step. It may be viewed as the last measure of an exhausted government, a cry for help; the government stretching forth its hands to Ethiopia, instead of Ethiopia stretching forth her hands to the government. It will be considered our last *shriek* on the retreat. Now, while I approve the measure, I suggest, sir, that you postpone its issue until you can give it to the country supported by military success, instead of issuing it, as would be the case now, upon the greatest disasters of the war." The President had not seen the matter in this light; the wisdom of Seward's objection struck him with force; and he "put the draft of the proclamation aside, waiting for a victory."

The secret of this conference was well kept. The radical Republicans, ignorant of the President's determination to strike at slavery when the proper time should arrive, continued their criticisms of his policy. His order of August 4 for a draft of 300,000 nine-months militia combined with the general gloom that deepened as the summer went on, to intensify this fault-finding, which culminated in The Prayer of Twenty Millions, written by Greeley and printed in the New York *Tribune* of August 20. All who supported your election, he said, and desire the suppression of the rebellion, are sorely disappointed by the policy you seem to be pursuing with regard to the slaves of rebels. "We require of you, as the first servant of the republic, charged especially and pre-eminently with this duty, that you EXECUTE THE LAWS. We think you are strangely and disastrously remiss in the discharge of your official and imperative duty with regard to the emancipating provisions of the new Confiscation act; [that] you are unduly influenced by the counsels, the representations, the menaces of certain fossil politicians hailing from the border slave States; [that] timid counsels in such a crisis [are] calculated to prove perilous and probably disastrous. We complain that the Union cause has suffered and is now suffering immensely from your mistaken deference to rebel slavery. We complain that the Confiscation act which you approved is habitually disregarded by your generals, and that no word of rebuke for them has yet reached the public ear. Frémont's proclamation and Hunter's order were promptly annulled by you, while Halleck's No. 3, with scores of like tendency, have never provoked even your remonstrance. We complain that a large proportion of our regular army officers with many of the volunteers evince far more solicitude to uphold slavery than to put down the rebellion. I close as I began, with the statement that what an immense majority of the loyal millions of your countrymen require of you is a frank, declared, unqualified, ungrudging execution of the laws of the land, more especially of the Confiscation act.

Lincoln did not read this open letter, which was addressed to him only through the columns of the New York *Tribune,* until August 22. He replied at once in a letter which was printed the next day in the *National Intelligencer* of Washington, and was also telegraphed to Greeley, appearing in the evening edition of the *Tribune*. The President said: "If there be in it [your letter] any statements or assumptions of facts which I may know to be erroneous, I do not, now and here, controvert them. If there be in it any inferences which I may believe to be falsely drawn, I do not, now and here, argue against them. If there be perceptible in it an impatient and dictatorial tone, I waive it in deference to an old friend whose heart I have always supposed to be right.

As to the policy I 'seem to be pursuing,' as you say, I have not meant to leave any one in doubt.

I would save the Union. I would save it the shortest way under the Constitution. The sooner the national authority can be restored, the nearer the Union will be 'the Union as it was.' If there be those who would not save the Union unless they could at the same time save slavery, I do not agree with them. If there be those who would not save the Union unless they could at the same time destroy slavery, I do not agree with them. My paramount object in this struggle is to save the Union, and is not either to save or to destroy slavery. If I could save the Union without freeing any slave, I would do it; and if I could save it by freeing all the slaves, I would do it; and if I could save it by freeing some and leaving others alone, I would also do that. What I do about slavery and the colored race, I do because I believe it helps to save the Union; and what I forbear, I forbear because I do not believe it would help to save the Union. I shall do less whenever I shall believe what I am doing hurts the cause, and I shall do more whenever I shall believe doing more will help the cause. I shall try to correct errors when shown to be errors, and I shall adopt new views so fast as they shall appear to be true views.

I have here stated my purpose according to my view of official duty; and I intend no modification of my oft-expressed personal wish that all men everywhere could be free."

Lincoln and Greeley may be looked upon as representative exponents of the two policies here outlined. There was in their personal relations a lack of sympathy, because they did not see things alike. Lincoln knew men, Greeley did not; Lincoln had a keen sense of humor, Greeley had none; indeed, in all their intercourse of many years, Lincoln never told the serious-minded editor an anecdote or joke, for he knew it would be thrown away. Greeley and the *Tribune,* though not so power-ful at this time in forming public opinion as they had been from 1854 to 1860, exerted still a far-reaching influence and gave ex-pression to thoughts rising in the minds of many earnest men. No one knew this better than the President, who, in stating his policy in a public despatch to Greeley, flattered the editor and those for whom the *Tribune* spoke. His words received the wid-est publication, and were undoubtedly read by nearly every man and woman at the North. They were sound indeed. His position could not have been more cogently put. His policy was right and expedient, appealed to the reason of his people and inspired their hopes.

How large a following Greeley had cannot be set down with exactitude. His letter was more than a petition like that of "the three tailors of Tooley Street," which one of his rivals deemed modesty itself compared with Greeley's, yet it was far from being the prayer of twenty millions. Lincoln had a ma-jority with him before his reply, and his reply made many friends. In spite of the misfortune of the Army of the Potomac, he still had only to announce clearly his policy to obtain for it the support of a host of plain people. An enthusiastic mass-meeting in Chicago listened to the reading of a poem whose theme was the July call for troops. "We are coming, Father Abraham, three hundred thousand more," now became the song of the soldiers and the watchword of the people.

Until the spring of 1862 the government of Great Britain pre-served the neutrality which had been declared by the Queen's proclamation at the beginning of the war. As we have now come to the period when this neutrality was violated to the injury of the United States, and as it certainly would not have been violated had the feeling of the dominant classes been friendly to the North, reference must again be made to English sentiment on our Civil War. In classifying English sentiment as it prevailed in the autumn of 1861, and in suggesting certain excuses for the preponderating opinion of those whose political and social position was high, I omitted a consideration of weight. The sympathy of the British government and public with Italy during the war of 1859, and the progress made in that war towards Italian liberty, impressed upon the English mind the doctrine that a body of people who should seek to throw off an obnoxious dominion and form an orderly government of their own, deserved the best wishes of the civilized world for their success. Why, it was asked in England, if we were right to sympathize with Italy against Austria, should we not likewise sympathize with the Southern Confederacy, whose people were resisting the subjugation of the North? This argument swayed the judgment of the liberal-minded Grote, and colored other opinion which was really dictated by interests of rank or of commerce and manufactures.

The divisions of sentiment in the spring of 1862 were the same as in the preceding autumn. The "Torifying influence" which had affected English Liberals as a result of the Trent affair had been modified by victories of the Union armies in the Southwest. The belief obtained that the North would win and that England would get cotton; but as the spring wore on and no further progress was made, as the stock of cotton diminished and as the distress of the operatives in Lancashire increased, sympathy turned again to the South. Those who favored action on the part of the government, first by mediation, which, if not accepted by the North, should be succeeded by the recognition of the Southern Confederacy and the breaking of the blockade, grew stronger in their expressions. Men of this opinion watched the Emperor of the French, hoping that he might initiate the policy dear to their hearts which they could not persuade their own government to venture upon. The main body of the aristocracy and the highest of the middle class desired that the great democracy should fail, partly because it was a democracy, partly because it enacted high protective tariffs, partly because the division of a great power like the United States which had constantly threatened Great Britain with war would rebound to their political advantage; but with that portion of the middle class engaged in commerce and manufactures the desire that overshadowed all else was that the war should come to an end so that England could get cotton and resume the export of her manufactured goods to America. The reports of the burning of cotton at the South, and the falling off in the demand of the North for English merchandise consequent on the enforced economy of the times, intensified this feeling. The North could terminate the war by the recognition of the Southern Confederacy; and the irritation was great over her persistence in the seemingly impossible task of conquering five and one-half millions of people. "Conquer a free population of 3,000,000 souls? the thing is impossible," Chatham had said; and this was applied with force to the case in hand.

The friends of the North remained as sincere and active as in the previous autumn, but like the patriots at home they had days of discouragement at the small progress made towards a restoration of the Union. The most significant and touching feature of the situation is that the operatives of the North of England, who suffered most from the lack of cotton, were frankly on the side of the United States. They knew that their misery came from the war, and were repeatedly told that it would cease in a day if the North would accept an accomplished fact; but discerning, in spite of their meagre intelligence, that the struggle was one of democracy against privilege, of freedom against slavery, they resisted all attempts to excite them to a demonstration against its continuance. They saw their work fall off, their savings dwindle, their families in want even to the prospect of lacking bread, yet they desired the North to fight out the contest.

LINCOLN'S *ill fortune with commanders in the East continued until the middle of 1863. After the bloody defeat of Burnside on the Rappahannock he had turned to "Fighting Joe" Hooker, another Mexican War veteran who had distinguished himself as a corps commander at Antietam, and who was especially liked by Secretary of the Treasury Chase and other Radical Republicans. Hooker devised an able piece of strategy for his advance in Virginia and, with a superiority of nearly two to one over Lee, seemed about to win a great victory at Chancellorsville. Then in the battle at the beginning of May, 1863, a sudden loss of nerve, and confusion heightened by a stunning concussion under cannon fire, involved him in a costly defeat. At once Lee planned another thrust into Pennsylvania, although Stonewall Jackson had been slain in a night melee at Chancellorsville. As his march got under way, Hooker, to the relief of Lincoln, Stanton, and Halleck in Washington, resigned. On the very eve of Gettysburg, George Gordon Meade, a Pennsylvanian who had been wounded in the McClellan Peninsular Campaign and had fought well since, was placed in command.*

Rhodes's account of the battle that followed—a battle in which corps commanders displayed the ablest leadership on the Northern side and Lee committed several crippling mistakes on the Southern—remains generally valid. Meade's management of the army was adequate, though he displayed none of the dash and spirit of another Pennsylvanian, Hancock. Like Lincoln and the North generally, Rhodes found it hard to forgive Meade for not following up his success with vigor and crushing Lee on the retreat. He could hardly have attacked the defeated Confederates immediately, but with energy and resolution he could have struck them hard before they recrossed the rain-swollen Potomac. Perhaps, as Lincoln believed, he might have ended the war then and there—for Grant was achieving an even greater success on the Mississippi.

Gettysburg

BY the middle of June the movements of Lee in Virginia warned the North of the approaching invasion. The President called for 100,000 militia from Maryland, Pennsylvania, Ohio, and West Virginia, the States regarded as in immediate danger. The Secretary of War asked help from the governors of thirteen of the other States. No response was so prompt, no action so effective, as that of Horatio Seymour of New York. "I will spare no effort to send you troops at once" was the word which came from him over the wires. June 16 the Confederate cavalry were heard of at Chambersburg, and busy preparations were made to defend the threatened points. At first the surmise gained ground that Pittsburg was in jeopardy. Alarm spread through the city, business was suspended, shops were closed, factories stopped. The citizens turned out in crowds to throw up intrenchments on the surrounding hills. One day it was reported that 14,000 were at work with picks and shovels, and these men were ready to take up rifles or man the batteries should the enemy appear. Mill-owners organized their laborers into companies, and the government furnished them arms and ammunition. A number of prominent citizens, representing the committee of public safety, requested the President to authorize Brooks, the general in command, to declare martial law, although Brooks thought this step unnecessary and unwise. Some desired that McClellan be placed in command of the militia for home defence; others urged the President to give them Frémont, who would inspire confidence and enthusiasm, and bring forward many thousand volunteers.

At one time there was some anxiety for Washington and Baltimore. Stuart in a cavalry raid passed between the Union army and these cities. It was in the Cumberland valley of Pennsylvania, however, that the presence of the enemy was actually and painfully felt. Yet the Confederates under the immediate command of Lee committed little or no depredation and mischief.

Before he himself crossed the river into Maryland, he wrote to Davis, "I shall continue to purchase all the supplies that are furnished me while north of the Potomac, impressing only where necessary," and he exerted himself to the utmost to have his wishes in this regard observed. His order of June 21 enjoined scrupulous respect for private property, and that of the 27th, after he had reached Chambersburg, manifested his satisfaction with his troops for their general good behavior, but mentioned that there had been "instances of forgetfulness," and warned them that such offenders should be brought to summary punishment. Military discipline, mercy, and the desire to do everything possible "to promote the pacific feeling" at the North prompted him to such a course. It is true that the payment for supplies was made in Confederate money which turned out to be worthless, but in estimating his motives it must be remembered that he paid with the only currency that he had, a currency which bade fair to have a considerable value should his confident expectation of defeating the Union army on Pennsylvania soil be realized. No attestation of Lee's sincerity in issuing these orders is needed, but it is grateful to read in various Northern journals of the time words of praise of the Southern commanders for restraining their soldiers from "acts of wanton mischief and rapine."

No matter how mercifully war may be carried on, it is at the best a rude game. At first the raid of the Confederate horsemen caused excitement in the Cumberland valley. The feeling of relief when they fell back was only temporary, and gave place to alarm and distress as Ewell's corps advanced, and later the rest of Lee's army. The country was wild with rumors. Men, women, and children fled before the enemy, and care was taken to run their horses out of the way of the invader. The refugees deemed themselves and their property safe when they had crossed the broad Susquehanna. The bridge over the river, the communication of the Cumberland valley with Harrisburg, was thronged with wagons laden with household goods and furniture. Negroes fled before the advancing host, fearing that they might be dragged back to slavery. June 26 Curtin, the governor of Pennsylvania, issued a proclamation calling for 60,000 men to come forward promptly "to defend their soil, their families, and their firesides." Harrisburg, the capital of the State, was indeed in danger, as was realized by the authorities and the citizens. Thirty regiments of Pennsylvania militia, besides artillery and cavalry, and nineteen regiments from New York assembled under the command of General Couch, who disposed his forces to the best advantage, stationing a large portion of them for the defence of Harrisburg. In the city all places of business were closed, and citizens labored on the fortifications with the pick and spade. Men were enrolled by wards and drilled in the park and on the streets. The railroad depot was a scene of excitement, caused by the arrival in large numbers of volunteers and the departure of women and frightened men. The progress of the enemy was pretty accurately known. Reports ran that he was twenty-three miles from the city, then eighteen. June 28 cannonading was heard for two hours, and every one knew that the Confederates were within four miles of the Capitol. Harrisburg would probably have been taken had not Ewell's corps been called back by Lee.

If Harrisburg were captured it was thought that the Confederates would march on Philadelphia. Men well informed believed that Lee had nearly 100,000 men and 250 pieces of artillery. A strong pressure in Philadelphia and elsewhere was brought to bear upon the President to place McClellan in command of the Army of the Potomac, or, at all events, of the militia for the defence of Pennsylvania. The Washington *National Intelligencer,* in an article entitled "A Calm Appeal," said, "After much reflection and with a full sense of the responsibility which it involves, we feel it our solemn duty at this juncture to avow the deliberate but earnest conviction that the President cannot by any one act do so much to restore the confidence of the nation as by the recall of General McClellen to the Army of the Potomac." These words were the expression of a serious and powerful sentiment at the North. The board of

Councilmen of New York City passed unanimously a resolution, Republicans as well as Democrats voting for it, asking for the restoration of McClellan to the command. It was reported that certain prominent citizens of Philadelphia had requested him to come to their city and "take military charge of things generally." Governor Parker telegraphed to the President that "The people of New Jersey want McClellan at the head of the Army of the Potomac. If that cannot be done, then we ask" that he be placed in command of the militia from New Jersey, New York, and Pennsylvania "defending these Middle States from invasion. If either appointment be made the people would rise *en masse.*" A. K. McClure, a steadfast Republican and friend of the administration, urged that McClellan be given a command. The Common Council of Philadelphia asked it. When Governor Curtin made a speech in that city to rouse its citizens, he was interrupted by cries, "Give us McClellan." A rumor got abroad in New York City that he had been made general-in-chief in the place of Halleck. He chanced to come to town that day from New Jersey, and was greeted with cheers from crowds of enthusiastic people. But there was probably no thought of placing him at the head of the Army of the Potomac or of the militia in Pennsylvania. Lincoln replied kindly to Governor Parker: "I beg you to be assured that no one out of my position can know so well as if he were in it, the difficulties and involvements of replacing General McClellan in command, and this aside from any imputations upon him."

On the evening of June 28 the rumor circulated in Philadelphia that the Confederates were shelling Harrisburg. Chestnut and Market streets were thronged with thousands of men eager for news. The next day two prominent citizens telegraphed to the President that they had reliable information that the enemy in large force was marching upon Philadelphia. Other men of influence desired him to give the general in command authority to declare martial law. Business stopped. The merchants, the manufacturers of iron, the proprietors of machine shops, the coal operators held meetings, and offered inducements to their workmen to enlist for the defence of the State. The members of the Corn Exchange furnished five companies. A meeting of the soldiers of the War of 1812 and another of clergymen were held to offer their services for home defence. It was said that bankers and merchants were making preparations to remove specie and other valuables from the city. Receipts and shipments on the Pennsylvania Railroad were suspended. With all the disturbance and alarm there was no panic. The excitement was at its height from June 27 to July 1. July 1 the sale of government five-twenties for the day amounted to $1,700,000. Few trains were running on the eastern division of the Pennsylvania Railroad, and it was expected that the track would in many places be destroyed, yet the shares of this company sold in Philadelphia at 61¾ June 27, and at 60 July 1, on a par basis of 50,—a fact as worthy of report as the story of Livy that the ground on which Hannibal encamped his army three miles from Rome, happening at that very time to be sold, brought a price none lower on account of its possession by the invader. While gold advanced in New York, there was no panic in the stock market.

When the alarm at the invasion of Pennsylvania was at its height, when every man in the North tremblingly took up his morning newspaper and with a sinking heart watched the daily bulletins, the intelligence came that there had been a change in commanders of the Army of the Potomac. Those in authority depended for the salvation of Harrisburg, Baltimore, and Washington on this army, which the public with its half-knowledge of the situation also felt to be their mainstay.

Hooker, following upon Lee's right flank and covering Washington, crossed the Potomac, and June 27 made his headquarters at Frederick, Maryland. He proposed to strike Lee's line of communications with Richmond, and desired the garrison of 10,000, holding Maryland Heights, which commanded Harper's Ferry, as a reinforcement to the corps he had ordered to march west for that purpose. "Is there any reason why Maryland Heights should not be abandoned?" he asked Halleck. "I cannot approve their abandonment," was the answer, "except in case of absolute necessity." Hooker wrote a reply proving that the troops in question were "of no earthly account at Harper's Ferry," while, if placed at his disposition, they might be used to advantage. He ended his despatch with begging that it be presented to the President and the Secretary of War. Immediately after he had sent it, his growing anger at what he considered the unwise and shackling instructions of the general-in-chief prompted him to write, apparently in a fit of petulance, a second despatch asking to be relieved of his position. Halleck received the second telegram five minutes after the first, and referred it to the President. Lincoln made up his mind quickly, and sent an officer to the Army of the Potomac with an order relieving Hooker and appointing in his place George G. Meade. It was an excellent choice. Meade looked like a student, had scholarly habits, was an officer of courage and ability, and commanded now the Fifth Corps, having served in the Potomac army with credit, even distinction. Receiving the communication from the President late on the night of June 27 or early the next morning, he answered it at 7 A.M. in a tone of genuineness which betokened confidence. "As a soldier," he said, "I obey the order placing me in command of this army, and to the utmost of my ability will execute it." The appointment was satisfactory to the officers of the army. Although the risk was great in making a change of generals at so critical a moment, Fortune attended the step and smiled on the new commander during the next five days which gave him fame.

"You are intrusted," wrote Halleck to Meade, "with all the power which the President, the Secretary of War, or the General-in-Chief can confer upon you, and you may rely upon our full support." In answer to a specific inquiry, Meade received for a second time the permission to do as he pleased with the garrison on Maryland Heights. He withdrew it, and posted the larger part of the troops at Frederick as a reserve.

He estimated Lee's force at 80,000 to 100,000; his own he placed at the larger number. His resolution was prompt. June

29 and 30 he advanced northward, and by the evening of the 30th the First Corps had crossed the Pennsylvania line, while the Third and Eleventh were in the northern part of Maryland; these three constituting the left wing of the army under the command of General Reynolds. The Twelfth Corps lay in Pennsylvania, but at some distance east of the First. Meade established headquarters at Taneytown, Maryland, thirteen miles south of Gettysburg, retaining the Second and Fifth Corps within easy reach. The Sixth Corps was likewise in Maryland, but lay farther to the eastward, thirty-four miles from Gettysburg. Meade had been prompt to command, his subordinates zealous to obey. The officers, sinking for the moment all their rivalries and jealousies, were careful and untiring in their efforts, while the soldiers did wonders in making long and rapid marches in the hot sun and sultry air of the last days of June. The main idea of Meade had been "to find and fight the enemy," at the same time covering Baltimore and Washington. Hearing now that Lee was falling back and concentrating his army, he announced his present design in a despatch to Halleck. "The news proves my advance has answered its purpose," he said. "I shall not advance any, but prepare to receive an attack in case Lee makes one. A battle-field is being selected to the rear on which the army can be rapidly concentrated."

The first mistake in Lee's campaign arose from the absence of Stuart's cavalry. He had no accurate and speedy knowledge of the movements of the Federals. His own and Longstreet's instructions to Stuart lacked precision, and Stuart made an unwise use of his discretion. Forgetting perhaps that the main use of horsemen in an enemy's country is to serve as the eyes of the army, the spirit of adventure led him into a raid about the Union troops which lost him all communication with the Confederate army, so that Lee was in the dark as to the progress of his adversary. On the night of June 28 a scout brought word to him that the Union army had crossed the Potomac and was advancing northward. His communications with Virginia were menaced, and he did not dare to let them be intercepted. He might indeed for a while live upon the country, but he could not in his position suffer the interruption of his supplies of ammunition. He called Ewell back from his projected attack upon Harrisburg, and ordered him as well as Longstreet and Hill to march to Gettysburg, on the east side of the South Mountain range.

July 1 Reynolds came in contact with the Confederates. Buford with his cavalry having the day before taken possession of Gettysburg and occupied Seminary Ridge west of the town was resisting their advance when Reynolds with the First Corps came to his assistance. Sending orders to Howard to advance promptly with the Eleventh, Reynolds selected the battle-field and opened the battle of Gettysburg, but he did not live to see the result of his heroic stand. Before noon he received a bullet in his brain and died instantly. "The death of this splendid officer," writes Fitzhugh Lee with grace, "was regretted by friend and foe," and borrowing the words of another, he adds, "No man died on that field with more glory than he; yet many died, and there was much glory!"

After Reynolds's death matters went badly for the First and Eleventh Corps. They were "overborne by superior numbers and forced back through Gettysburg with great slaughter." Buford's despatch of 3:20 P.M. points out an important reason for the defeat. "In my opinion," he said, "there seems to be no directing person." All was confusion and looked like disaster when Hancock arrived on the field. On hearing that Reynolds was killed, Meade, with his excellent judgment of the right man for the place, sent Hancock forward to take the command. He restored order and inspired confidence while the Union troops were placed in a strong position on Cemetery Hill east of the town. It is thought that if the Confederates had been prompt they might have carried the height, but the order to do so from Lee to Ewell was conditional, and with his force then present he did not deem the attempt practicable. Nevertheless, the first day of the battle of Gettysburg was a Confederate success.

Late in the afternoon of July 1 Slocum with the Twelfth

Corps had arrived at Gettysburg. Sickles with the Third Corps marched thither with celerity and zeal. The reports of Hancock, Howard, and others decided Meade that Gettysburg was a good place to fight his battle, and he issued orders to all of his corps to concentrate at that point. He himself arrived upon the battle-field at one in the morning, pale, tired-looking, hollow-eyed, and worn out from want of sleep, anxiety, and the weight of responsibility.

By the afternoon of July 2, Lee and Meade had their whole forces on the field, the armies being about a mile apart. Lee had 70,000, Meade 93,500, less the losses of the first day, which had been much greater on the Union than on the Confederate side. The Confederates occupied Seminary Ridge in a line concave in form, the Federals Cemetery Ridge in a convex line, a position admirably adapted for defence. Meade decided to await attack, and if he had studied closely the character and history of his energetic adversary, he might have been almost certain that it would come. Longstreet, however, differed with his commander. In a conversation at the close of the first day's fight, he expressed a desire that their troops be thrown around the left of the Union army, interposing themselves between it and Washington and forcing Meade to take the offensive. The anxiety of Lee at receiving no information from his cavalry had become excitement, and, somewhat irritated at a suggestion contrary to what he had determined upon, he said, "No, the enemy is there and I am going to attack him." From the commencement of his invasion, he had shown contempt of his foe. The stretching of his line from Fredericksburg to Winchester in the face of an opponent who had greater numbers can bear no other construction. While he deemed Meade a better general than Hooker, he thought that the change in commanders at this critical moment counter-balanced the advantage in generalship; and while he was astonished at the rapid and efficient movements of the Army of the Potomac after Meade took command, he had undoubtedly become convinced from his almost unvarying success that he and his army were invincible—a confidence shared by nearly all of his officers and men. His victories on his own soil were extraordinary, but if we compare his campaigns of invasion with those of Napoleon we shall see how far he fell short when he undertook operations in an unfriendly country, although the troops that followed him were in fighting qualities unsurpassed. "Except in equipment," writes General Alexander, "I think a better army, better nerved up to its work, never marched upon a battle-field." With such soldiers, if Lee had been as great a general as Napoleon, Gettysburg had been an Austerlitz, Washington and the Union had fallen.

Lee was up betimes on the morning of July 2, but the movements of his soldiers were slow, and he lost much of the advantage of his more speedy concentration than Meade's. The afternoon was well advanced when he began his attack, and by that time the last of the Union army, the Sixth Corps, which had marched thirty-four miles in eighteen hours, was arriving. There was tremendous fighting and heavy loss that afternoon on both wings of each army. On the Union side Warren and Humphreys distinguished themselves. Sickles was struck by a cannon ball that caused the loss of a leg and was borne from the field. The result of the day is accurately told by Lee: "We attempted to dislodge the enemy, and, though we gained some ground, we were unable to get possession of his position." The Confederate assaults had been disjointed: to that mistake is ascribed their small success.

The feeling among the officers in Meade's camp that night was one of gloom. On the first day of the battle the First and Eleventh corps had been almost annihilated. On the second day the Fifth and part of the Second had been shattered; the Third, in the words of its commander who succeeded Sickles, was "used up and not in good condition to fight." The loss of the army had been 20,000 men. Only the Sixth and Twelfth corps were fresh. But the generals had not lost spirit, and in the council of war called by Meade all voted to "stay and fight it out." The rank and file fought as Anglo-Saxons nearly always fight on their own soil. On the first day and the morning of the second the

martial ardor of many of the men had been mingled with cheer-
fulness at the report that McClellan had been restored to his
old command. "The boys are all jubilant over it," said a soldier
to General Hunt, "for they know that if *he* takes command
everything will go right." We may guess that on this gloomy
night the men went over again in their minds the fate of their
army when under Pope, Burnside, and Hooker it had encountered the veterans of Lee, but in spite of this doleful retrospect
they must have felt in some measure "the spirit that animated
general headquarters," the energy of Meade and the faithful
co-operation of his generals.

Meade had no thought of taking the offensive, and was busy
in improving the natural defences of his position with earthworks. The partial successes of the Confederates determined
Lee to continue the attack on the 3d of July. In the early morning there was fighting on the right of the Union line. Then followed an unnatural stillness. "The whole field became as silent
as a churchyard until one o'clock." Suddenly came from the
Confederate side the reports of two signal guns in quick succession. A bombardment from one hundred and fifteen cannon
commenced, and was replied to by eighty guns of the Union
army, whose convex line, advantageous in other respects, did
not admit of their bringing into action a large part of their artillery. "It was a most terrific and appalling cannonade," said
Hancock. But it did little damage. The Union soldiers lay under the protection of stone walls, swells of the ground, and
earthworks, and the projectiles of the enemy passed over their
heads, sweeping the open ground in their rear. Everybody from
the commanding general to the privates felt that this was only
preliminary to an infantry charge, and all braced themselves
for the tug of war. Hancock with his staff, his corps flag flying,
rode deliberately along the front of his line, and by his coolness
and his magnificent presence inspired his men with courage and
determination. For an hour and a half this raging cannonade
was kept up, when Hunt, the chief of the Union artillery, finding his ammunition running low, gave the order to cease firing.

The Confederates thought that they had silenced the Federal batteries, and made preparation for their next move.

Longstreet had no sympathy with the vigorous offensive tactics of his chief; and when Lee on the morning of this July 3 directed him to be ready after the bombardment had done its work to make an attack with Pickett's fresh division reinforced from Hill's corps up to 15,000 men, he demurred, arguing that the assault could not succeed. Lee showed a little impatience, apparently made no reply, and by silence insisted on the execution of his order. Longstreet took Pickett to the crest of Seminary Ridge, pointed out to him what was to be done, and left him with a heavy heart. Alexander of the artillery was directed to note carefully the effect of his fire, and when the favorable moment came to give Pickett the order to charge. He did not like this responsibility, and asked Longstreet for specific instructions, but the reply which came lacked precision. Still the artillery must open, and when the fire of the Federal guns had ceased, as has been related, Alexander, looking anxiously through his glass at the points whence it had proceeded, and observing no sign of life in the five minutes that followed, sent word to Pickett: "For God's sake, come quick. . . . Come quick, or my ammunition won't let me support you properly." Pickett went to Longstreet. "General, shall I advance?" he asked. Longstreet could not speak, but bowed in answer. "Sir," said Pickett, with a determined voice, "I shall lead my division forward." Alexander had ceased firing. Longstreet rode to where he stood, and exclaimed: "I don't want to make this attack. I would stop it now but that General Lee ordered it and expects it to go on. I don't see how it can succeed." But as he spoke Pickett at the head of his troops rode over the crest of Seminary Ridge and began his descent down the slope. "As he passed me," writes Longstreet, "he rode gracefully, with his jaunty cap raked well over on his right ear, and his long auburn locks, nicely dressed, hanging almost to his shoulders. He seemed a holiday soldier." From the other side the Union soldiers watched the advance of Pickett and his fifteen thousand with suspense, with admiration. As they came forward steadily and in perfect order with banners flying, those who looked on might for the moment have thought it a Fourth of July parade.

The Confederates had nearly a mile to go across the valley. As they descended the slope on that clear afternoon under the July sun in full view of their foe, they received a dreadful fire from the Union batteries, which had been put in entire readiness to check such an onset. Steadily and coolly they advanced. After they had got away, the Confederate artillery reopened over their heads, in the effort to draw the deadly fire directed at them from Cemetery Ridge; but the Union guns made no change in aim, and went on mowing down Pickett's men. Half-way across there was the shelter of a ravine. They stopped for a moment to breathe, then advanced again, still in good order. A storm of canister came. The slaughter was terrible. The left staggered; but, nothing daunted, Pickett and what was left of his own division of forty-nine hundred pressed on in the lead. The other divisions followed. Now the Union infantry opened fire. Pickett halted at musket range and discharged a volley, then rushed on up the slope. Near the Federal lines he made a pause "to close ranks and mass for a final plunge." In the last assault Armistead, a brigade commander, pressed forward, leaped the stone wall, waved his sword with his hat on it, shouted, "Give them the cold steel, boys!" and laid his hands upon a gun. A hundred of his men had followed. They planted the Confederate battle-flags on Cemetery Ridge among the cannon they had captured and for the moment held. Armistead was shot down; Garnett and Kemper, Pickett's other brigadiers, fell. The wavering divisions of Hill's corps "seemed appalled, broke their ranks," and fell back. "The Federals swarmed around Pickett," writes Longstreet, "attacking on all sides, enveloped and broke up his command. They drove the fragments back upon our lines." Pickett gave the word to retreat.

The Confederates in their charge had struck the front of the Second Corps. Hancock, its commander, "the best tactician of the Potomac army," showed the same reckless courage as Armistead, and seemed to be everywhere directing and encouraging his troops. Struck by a ball, he fell from his horse; and lying on the ground, "his wound spouting blood," he raised himself on his elbow and gave the order, "Go in, Colonel, and give it to them on the flank." Not until the battle of Gettysburg was over did he resign himself to his surgeon, and shortly afterwards he dictated this despatch to Meade: "I have never seen a more formidable attack, and if the Sixth and Fifth corps have pressed up, the enemy will be destroyed. The enemy must be short of ammunition, as I was shot with a tenpenny nail. I did not leave the field till the victory was entirely secured and the enemy no longer in sight. I am badly wounded, though I trust not seriously. I had to break the line to attack the enemy in flank on my right, where the enemy was most persistent after the front attack was repelled. Not a rebel was in sight upright when I left."

Decry war as we may and ought, "breathes there the man with soul so dead" who would not thrill with emotion to claim for his countrymen the men who made that charge and the men who met it?

Longstreet, calm and self-possessed, meriting the name "bulldog," applied to him by his soldiers, expected a counter attack, and made ready for it. Lee, entirely alone, rode up to encourage his broken troops. "His face did not show signs of the slightest disappointment, care, or annoyance," recorded an English officer in his diary on the day of the battle, "and he was addressing to every soldier he met a few words of encouragement, such as, 'All this will come right in the end: we'll talk it over afterwards, but in the mean time all good men must rally. We want all good and true men just now.' He spoke to all the wounded men that passed him, and the slightly wounded he exhorted 'to bind up their hurts and take up a musket' in this emergency. Very few failed to answer his appeal, and I saw many badly wounded men take off their hats and cheer him. He said to me, 'This has been a sad day for us, Colonel—a sad day; but we can't expect always to gain victories.'

Notwithstanding the misfortune which had so suddenly befallen him, General Lee seemed to observe everything, however
trivial. When a mounted officer began licking his horse for shy-
ing at the bursting of a shell, he called out, 'Don't whip him,
Captain; don't whip him. I've got just such another foolish.
horse myself, and whipping does no good.' "

An officer almost angry came up to report the state of his
brigade. "General Lee immediately shook hands with him and
said cheerfully, 'Never mind, General, *all this has been* MY
fault—it is *I* that have lost this fight, and you must help me
out of it in the best way you can.' "

The Books are full of the discussion whether or not Meade
should have made a counter-attack. Those who say he ought to
have done this maintain that the Confederate army might have
been destroyed. It is true that he did not appreciate the magnitude of his victory, but ought the critic to demand from him any
greater military sagacity than from Lee? The Confederate general under similar circumstances did not comprehend how badly
he had beaten Burnside at Fredericksburg and did not follow
up his great success.

We need concern ourselves only for a moment with the controversy between Longstreet and the friends of Lee. It is clear
that Longstreet did not give his commander the hearty co-
operation which the occasion demanded. On the other hand,
it is difficult, if not impossible, to traverse his argument that Lee
should have put some officer in charge of the movement
who had confidence in the plan of attack, or, as so much depended on it, that the commander himself should have given
to the operations of the third day his personal attention. The
champions of Lee maintain that his orders required the charge
of Pickett to be made by a more powerful column than was sent
across the valley under the murderous fire of the foe, and that
Longstreet was at fault for neglecting to supply his remaining
two divisions for the attack. Reduced to figures, it means that
23,000 instead of 15,000 should have made the assault. They
would have had to contend with 70,000 men, strongly in-

trenched, of whom two corps were fresh, whose generals were prepared and alert. There is no reason for thinking that the result would have been different. The comparison which is frequently made between Lee's attack at Gettysburg on the third day and Burnside's storming of Marye's Heights is a reproach to the generalship of the Confederate commander, and is keenly felt by his friends, who would all regard him infallible. Had it not been for the Gettysburg campaign, the intimations in Southern literature would be more frequent than they are that he is entitled to rank with Napoleon in the class of great commanders. But the likeness in military ability will halt before it is pushed far. Nevertheless, let the comparison of the emotions of Napoleon and Lee after disaster be made, and his countrymen will perceive what reason they have to revere the memory of the American. Thus he wrote, July 9, to Pickett: "No one grieves more than I do at the loss suffered by your noble division in the recent conflict, or honors it more for its bravery and gallantry." At the end of the account, said Napoleon in 1813, what has the Russian campaign cost me? 300,000 men, and what are the lives of a million to a man like me!

On the morning of the Fourth of July the people of the North received this word: "The President announces to the country that news from the Army of the Potomac, up to 10 P.M. of the 3d, is such as to cover that army with the highest honor, to promise a great success to the cause of the Union, and to claim the condolence of all for the many gallant fallen, and that for this he especially desires that on this day He whose will, not ours, should ever be done be everywhere remembered and reverenced with profoundest gratitude." The rejoicing of the people was not boisterous; it took the character of supreme thankfulness for a great deliverance. The victory of Gettysburg demonstrated that Lee and his army were not invincible, and that the Confederates had lost in playing the card of an invasion of the North. Nothing now remained to them but a policy of stubborn defence. That this would likewise end in ruin was foreshadowed by the fateful event of the Fourth of July. Vicksburg surrendered to General Grant. Meade's sturdy and victorious resistance to attack was followed by the glorious end of the most brilliant offensive campaign of the war. Had the war been one between two nations, it would now have undoubtedly terminated in a treaty of peace, with conditions imposed largely by the more successful contestant.

The Fourth of July at Gettysburg passed in tranquillity. "Under the cover of the night and heavy rain," Lee began his retreat. Meade followed. The President comprehended the importance and moral effect of the victory better than did his general. He may nct have seen the remark of Napoleon in 1809, "In war the moral element and public opinion are half the battle;" but the fact he knew well. Nevertheless, he wrote Halleck at seven in the evening of July 6 from his country residence at the Soldiers' Home: "I left the telegraph office a good deal dissatisfied. You know I did not like the phrase [Meade's] 'Drive the invaders from our soil.' " Mentioning other circumstances, he added: "These things all appear to me to be connected with a purpose to cover Baltimore and Washington, and to get the enemy across the river again without a further collision, and they do not appear connected with a purpose to prevent his crossing and to destroy him. I do fear the former purpose is acted upon and the latter rejected." The next day he sent this word to Halleck: "We have certain information that Vicksburg surrendered to General Grant on the 4th of July. Now, if General Meade can complete his work, so gloriously prosecuted thus far, by the literal or substantial destruction of Lee's army, the rebellion will be over." At the same time Halleck telegraphed Meade: "Push forward and fight Lee before he can cross the Potomac." He sent other telegrams, probably on the prompting of the President, urging Meade to attack the enemy, but forwarded two despatches inconsistent with the importunity of the others. "Do not be influenced by any despatch from here against your own judgment," he said. "Regard them as suggestions only." Again he wrote: "I think it will be best for you to postpone a general battle" until everything is ready. Perhaps all of those telegrams which urged prompt action were the President's.

By July 11 Lee in his retreat had reached the Potomac, his army covering the river from Williamsport to Falling Waters. Three days before he had written Davis: "A series of storms . . . has placed the river beyond fording stage, and the present storm will keep it so for at least a week. I shall therefore have to accept battle if the enemy offers it, whether I wish to or not. . . . I hope your Excellency will understand that I am not in the least discouraged, or that my faith in the protection of an all-merciful Providence or in the fortitude of this army is at all shaken." The condition of the army "is good, and its confidence unimpaired." July 10 he sent confidentially this word to Stuart: "We must prepare for a vigorous battle, and trust in the mercy of God and the valor of our troops." July 12, after he had taken up his very strong position on the Potomac, he wrote Davis: "But for the power the enemy possesses of accumulating troops I should be willing to await his attack, excepting that in our restricted limits the means of obtaining subsistence are becoming precarious. The river has now fallen to four feet, and a bridge, which is being constructed, I hope will be passable by to-morrow."

By July 11 Meade in his pursuit had come within striking distance of Lee. Reinforced by some fresh troops, he might have attacked on the 12th or 13th and ought to have done so. Defeat could not result in disaster. A success no greater than Antietam would be a help to the cause, and a complete victory was possible that might end the war. While proceeding with great caution, Meade had determined to make an attack July 13; but, wavering in mind and weighed down with responsibility, he called, contrary to the best military maxims, a council of war. Five out of seven of his corps commanders were opposed to the projected attack, which influenced him to delay giving the orders for it. He devoted July 13 to an examination of the enemy's position, strength, and defensive works, and the next day advanced his army for a reconnaissance in force or an assault if conditions justified it, when he ascertained that during the night previous the Confederate army had crossed the Potomac. "The escape of Lee's army without another battle has created great dissatisfaction in the mind of the President," telegraphed Halleck. Meade asked to be relieved of the command of the army: his application was refused.

During the 12th and 13th of July Lincoln was a prey to intense anxiety, and when he got the intelligence, soon after noon of the 14th, that Lee and his army were safely across the river, he could hardly restrain his irritation within bounds. "We had them within our grasp," he declared; "we had only to stretch forth our hands and they were ours, and nothing I could say or do could make the army move." I regret that I did not myself go to the army and personally issue the order for an attack. On the spur of the moment he gave vent to his feelings in a letter to Meade which on second thoughts he did not sign or send. Prefacing his censure with "I am sorry now to be the author of the slightest pain to you," he wrote: "You fought and beat the enemy at Gettysburg; and of course, to say the least, his loss was as great as yours. He retreated, and you did not, as it seemed to me, pressingly pursue him; but a flood in the river detained him, till by slow degrees you were again upon him. You had at least twenty thousand veteran troops directly with you, and as many more raw ones within supporting distance, all in addition to those who fought with you at Gettysburg; while it was not possible that he had received a single recruit; and yet you stood and let the flood run down, bridges be built, and the enemy move away at his leisure without attacking him."

GRANT *had done badly in the Shiloh campaign, displaying little generalship. It was with some difficulty that Lincoln kept him in command in the West. His first attempts to reach and take Vicksburg were failures of a highly discouraging nature. But not only did he have indomitable fighting capacity; he had endless persistence. His fortunes and those of the war in the West changed when in the spring of 1863 he undertook one of the boldest movements in the history of modern warfare. Leaving his communications, and throwing his army (with naval help) down the river below Vicksburg, he prepared to attack it from the east and the south. The result was complete success, achieved in time to make July 4, 1863, one of the memorable days of the war for the North.*

Vicksburg

BEFORE and during the war the Mississippi River possessed, as a channel of communication and commerce, a great importance, which has steadily diminished with the development of the railroad system of the West. The importance of gaining the control of it was from the first appreciated at the North. Looked upon in the East as a military advantage, it was deemed by the people of the Western States indispensable to their existence as an outlet to their products, an artery for their supply. "The free navigation of the Mississippi" were words to conjure with, not only in the Southwest, but everywhere west of the Alleghanies, except in the region directly tributary to the great lakes. From the location of his home Lincoln was brought up with this sentiment, he had his mind impregnated with it in manhood, and now he did not for a moment lose sight of its military and commercial consequence. The capture of Forts Henry and Donelson and the resulting operations had freed the Mississippi north of Vicksburg; the capture of New Orleans had given us its mouth. But the Confederates had practical possession of it between their two strong fortresses of Vicksburg and Port Hudson, a distance of about two hundred miles, and thereby retained communication between Louisiana and Texas on one side and the rest of the Confederacy on the other. Louisiana supplied them with sugar, and the great State of Texas furnished quantities of grain and beef, besides affording, by virtue of its contiguity to Mexico, an avenue for munitions of war received from Europe at the Mexican port of Matamoras,—a consideration of weight, for the ports of the Southern States were now pretty effectually sealed by the Federal blockade. Of the two fastnesses Vicksburg was by far the more important, and the desire in the Confederacy to keep it was ardent. Sentiment as well as military judgment inclined Jefferson Davis to make a strenuous effort for its defence. It was in his own State, whose notables were dear to him not only because in his view they were patriots, but because most of them were personal acquaintances or friends. His own plantation, too, was in the neighborhood of Vicksburg. He had in December, 1862, paid a visit to the State of Mississippi, and inspected with his soldier's eye the fortifications of the city, and, tarrying in Jackson to address the legislature, had urged them fervently to do their utmost in cooperation with the Confederate government to preserve this stronghold and their State from the inroads of the enemy.

From the Union point of view the three most important strategic points in the South were Richmond, Vicksburg, and Chattanooga. Vicksburg ranked second, for its capture would give the United States the control of the Mississippi River and cut the Confederacy asunder. One attempt had been made to take it by a bombardment from gun-boats and mortar-vessels, and later another by an assault of the army. Both had failed. Nevertheless, the government, the army, and the navy determined to persevere. Since it was within his province, Grant assumed, January 30, 1863, "the immediate command of the expedition against Vicksburg."

Vicksburg, which for the most part was built upon a bluff two hundred feet above high-water mark of the river, was a natural stronghold, strengthened by art and unassailable from the front. The problem was to reach the high ground on the east bank of the river so that it might be attacked or besieged from the side or rear. Grant prosecuted the work on a canal which had been begun with the object of making a channel across the peninsula opposite Vicksburg, by which transports might pass below it, carrying troops and supplies to a new base. With the same purpose he endeavored to open a route through the bayous from Milliken's Bend on the north to New Carthage on the south. Other devices of artificial channels connecting natural water-courses above Vicksburg were tried; apparently, indeed, every experiment was made that engineering skill or military initiative could suggest. Nearly two months were spent in such operations, and all of them failed.

It had been a winter of heavy and continuous rains. The river had risen to an unusual height, and in places the levees had given way. "The whole country was covered with water. Troops could scarcely find dry ground on which to pitch their tents. Malarial fevers, measles, and small-pox broke out among the men." From newspaper correspondents, from letters which the soldiers wrote home, from reports of visitors to the camps, the people of the North knew in detail of the many attempts and failures, of the exceeding discomfort of the army, and received exaggerated accounts of the sickness which prevailed. Having in mind the Grant of Shiloh rather than the Grant of Donelson, they looked upon his actions in a fault-finding mood, and believed the stories of his intemperance which were now in large measure revived. McClernand, one of his corps commanders who had hoped to head the expedition against Vicksburg, a patriotic War Democrat, a clever politician, and a man of influence in the West, was a mover in the intrigue for his displacement. An able Western journalist who swayed public opinion maintained, in a letter to the Secretary of the Treasury, that Grant was incompetent, accused him of gross misconduct, and demanded, "in the name of the Western people and the Western troops, that his command should be taken from him and given to Rosecrans." Chase sent this letter to the President with his sanction, and added that reports inculpating General Grant "are too common to be safely or even prudently disregarded." Nevertheless, Lincoln stood by his general faithfully.*

Grant was slandered. To Rawlins, his assistant adjutant-general, his true friend and mentor, he had early in March given a pledge on his honor that he would drink no more during the war, and at this time he was adhering to the pledge with rigor. His despatches and letters exhibit a cool brain, his actions show a steady judgment and unremitting energy. Since the battle of Shiloh he had most of the time had a responsible command, but had done nothing to attract public attention. Useful as the commander of a department, his service in the field had been small and inconspicuous, but in these ten months he had observed much and thought much about the conflict that tore his country. He was not a reader of military books, nor a close student of the campaigns of the great masters of his art, nor did he con the principles of strategy and the rules of tactics; but he was in his own way and within certain lines a deep thinker. After we read the despatches and comprehend the aim of such accomplished soldiers as McClellan and Meade, what refreshment there is in the grasp of the absolute purpose of the war shown in these words of Grant: "Rebellion has assumed that shape now that it can only terminate by the complete subjugation of the South or the overthrow of the government." There must have passed through his mind the thought that if the chance came he could

* It is to this period that Nicolay and Hay assign the retort of Lincoln to the zealous persons who demanded Grant's removal because he drank too much whiskey: "If I knew what brand of whiskey he drinks, I would send a barrel or so to some other generals."—*Ibid.*; Richardson's *Life of Grant,* p. 299; *Anecdotes of A. Lincoln,* J. R. McClure, p. 94. Nicolay and Hay do not vouch absolutely for the authenticity of this anecdote, and I doubt it, for the reason that if the traditions be true the President and Stanton were disturbed at the reports of Grant's intemperance. In his Reminiscences, Charles A. Dana gives a partial confirmation of this. "Stanton sent for me to come to Washington," Dana writes. "He wanted some one to go to Grant's army, he said, to report daily to him the military proceedings and to give such information as would enable Mr. Lincoln and him to settle their minds as to Grant, about whom at that time there were many doubts and against whom there was some complaint." The letter sending Dana his appointment is dated March 12.—*McClure's Magazine,* Nov. 1897, p. 29. See Dana to Ştanton, July 13, *ibid.,* Jan. 1898, p. 254.

show the stuff that was in him. In taking command of the expedition against Vicksburg, he created the opportunity and
began with two months of failures. Sensitive to detraction, he
felt the calumnies propagated at the North, and was undoubtedly annoyed that, held in no higher estimation than Hooker
and Rosecrans, he was with them on trial at the bar of public
opinion, and in Washington, too, was regarded only as an equal
contestant for a prize offered by the government.* This was in
the last days of March, 1863, after Rosecrans had won his victory of Stone's River and before Hooker had met with his defeat
at Chancellorsville.

The failure of the engineering expedients to turn or to supplement the courses of the waters, the necessity of accommodat-
ing himself to the natural features of the country, brought home
to Grant the question, What was to be done? "The strategical
way according to the rule," he writes, "would have been to go
back to Memphis; establish that as a base of supplies . . . and
move from there along the line of the railroad." This was the
advice of Sherman, his ablest and most trusted lieutenant. But,
reasoned Grant, that is a backward movement and gravely objectionable, because it will intensify the discouragement with
the war prevailing at the North. "There was nothing left to be
done," he said, "but to *go forward to a decisive victory.*" Without a council of war, without consulting any of his able officers,
he formed his plan, and hoped for approval from Washington
after he had begun to carry it out. He told it to his government
in his despatches to Halleck, all of which are marked by courtesy and respect. From the confident and masterly tone of his
communications, we may imagine with what satisfaction they
were read by the President, who at first consented by silence,
and, before the news of any signal success was received, authorized a despatch which gave Grant "full and absolute authority

* Halleck to each, Hooker, Rosecrans, and Grant, March 1: "General:
There is a vacant major-generalcy in the Regular Army, and I am authorized to say that it will be given to the general in the field who first wins an
important and decisive victory." Of course this was by direction of the
President.

to enforce his own commands," and bore this further assurance: "He has the full confidence of the government."*

His execution was as prompt as his conception was bold. March 23 he ordered the concentration of his army at Milliken's Bend. The roads having dried up somewhat, although still "intolerably bad," he ordered, March 29, McClernand's corps to march to New Carthage, while Sherman and McPherson with their corps were in due time to follow. The movement was slow, the transportation of supplies and ammunition and the progress of the artillery were difficult. For the success of the enterprise, the co-operation of the navy was necessary, and from Admiral Porter Grant received efficient and generous support. Gun-boats and other craft were needed for service below Vicksburg, more rations than could be hauled over a "single narrow and almost impassable road" were wanted, hence gun-boats and transports must run the batteries. On the night of April 16 such a movement was made. In utter darkness the fleet started; but the Confederates fired houses on the Louisiana side, and lighted bonfires on the east side of the river, disclosing to their view and aim seven iron-clads, three steamers with ten barges in tow,— these last heavily loaded with supplies. The Vicksburg batteries opened with shot and shell, and the gun-boats returned the fire. All the vessels were struck, but only one was disabled. A shell burst in the cotton surrounding the boilers of the steamer *Henry Clay,* set her on fire, and she burned to the water's edge. "I was out in the stream when the fleet passed Vicksburg," writes Sherman, "and the scene was truly sublime." "The sight was magnificent but terrible," are the words of Grant. The run-

* Stanton to Charles A. Dana, May 5, O. R., vol. xxiv. part i. p. 84. Dana, as special commissioner of the U. S. War Department, was now at Grant's headquarters, and made frequent reports to Stanton. He filled the position with cleverness and discretion. He estimated correctly Grant, Admiral Porter, Sherman, and McPherson, seems to have received their confidence, and did not abuse it. His despatches, written in the clear, terse English of which he was a master, are an excellent history of the progress of the campaign. The words of Stanton (June 5) to him are none too strong: "Your telegrams are a great obligation and are looked for with deep interest. I cannot thank you as much as I feel for the service you are now rendering."—*Ibid.,* p. 93.

ning of the batteries had been a success, and again on the night of April 22 six steamers towing twelve barges loaded with hay, corn, and provisions steamed and drifted past Vicksburg, bringing an abundance of supplies to the army south of this stronghold.

Still remained the problem how to get on the high ground on the east bank of the river. McClernand's and McPherson's corps were set in motion for Hard Times, part of them in the steamers and barges, the others afoot. To mask the main movement, Sherman made a demonstration on Haynes's Bluff above Vicksburg. April 29 Porter's gun-boats attacked the fortress of Grand Gulf. Hoping that these would silence the enemy's batteries, Grant had ten thousand troops on board the steamers and barges, while he himself was in a tug-boat out in the stream, watching the assault, and ready, if the conditions warranted, to give the order to the troops to land and take the place by storm. But Grand Gulf was too high above the river, and its fortifications too strong to be captured by a front attack, and after five hours of bombardment the attempt was abandoned. "I immediately decided," wrote Grant, "upon landing my forces on the Louisiana shore and march them across the point to below the Gulf. At night the gun-boats made another vigorous attack, and in the din the transports safely ran the blockade." The vantage-ground on the east bank of the Mississippi was determined by intelligence from a negro who told Grant that there was a good road from Bruinsburg to Port Gibson. At daylight in the morning of April 30, employing the iron-clads and steamers as ferry-boats, he began the work of transferring the troops to Bruinsburg, on the east side of the river. Once across they commenced their march, and in two miles reached high ground. As soon as Grant had made sure that he would effect this landing, he had telegraphed Halleck, "I feel that the battle is now more than half won." Yet all the obstacles of nature had not been overcome. The country with its bayous, swamps, and ravines, its timber, undergrowth, and almost impenetrable vines and canebrakes, rendered offensive operations difficult and hazardous. But, urged by their general, the soldiers pressed on. At two o'clock in the morning of May 1, on the road to Port Gibson they met the Confederates, whom they outnumbered. Skirmishing began, developing, as it grew light, into battle. "The fighting continued all day," said Grant, "and until after dark, over the most broken country I ever saw. . . . The enemy was driven from point to point." They were "sent in full retreat." The next day Port Gibson was ours. The Confederates evacuated Grand Gulf. From that fortress Grant wrote a long despatch to Halleck, giving an account of his success. "This army is in the highest health and spirits," he said. "Since leaving Milliken's Bend they have marched as much by night as by day, through mud and rain, without tents or much other baggage and on irregular rations, without a complaint and with less straggling than I have ever before witnessed." Could the army have transmitted a collective despatch, they might have said, Our general has been subject to the same discomforts as we, he has shared all our hardships.

Grant had now a secure base of supplies at Grand Gulf. He had intended to co-operate with General Banks in the reduction of Port Hudson, and after its capture move with the united armies against Vicksburg; but he now learned that Banks had not made the progress expected, and, on the other hand, that General Joe Johnston was on his way to Jackson to take charge of the defence of Vicksburg, for which, as the South had taken alarm, reinforcements were constantly arriving. "Under this state of facts, I could not afford to delay," was his after explanation. May 3 he announced his purpose to Halleck thus: "I shall not bring my troops into this place [Grand Gulf], but immediately follow the enemy, and, if all promises as favorable hereafter as it does now, not stop until Vicksburg is in our possession." He was soon joined by Sherman's corps, and had a force of about 43,000. Opposed to him was Pemberton with 40,000 in Vicksburg and along the line of the railroad, and Johnston with about 15,000 in Jackson. With the Napoleonic idea Grant proposed to beat these forces in detail. He moved with amazing celerity. With only a single road leading from Grand Gulf, he knew that he could not supply his army from that point, and therefore stopped long enough to arrange for the transport of his ammunition and to get up what rations he could of hard bread, coffee, and salt, intending for the rest to live upon the country. He cut loose from his base and moved forward. "As I shall communicate with Grand Gulf no more . . . you may not hear from me again for several days," was his laconic despatch to his government. May 12, outnumbering the enemy, he beat him at Raymond after "a brisk fight of more than two hours." "I will attack the State capital to-day," he said in his telegram announcing this victory. He was as good as his word. May 15 he telegraphed: Jackson "fell into our hands yesterday after a fight of about three hours. Joe Johnston was in command. The enemy retreated north, evidently with the design of joining the Vicksburg forces. I am concentrating my forces at Bolton to cut them off if possible."

From an intercepted despatch he knew correctly the intentions of Johnston, who before the loss of the State capital had ordered Pemberton to come up if practicable, on the rear of the Union army at once. Pemberton with a large part of his force had reached Edwards Station, but deemed the movement ordered by his superior "suicidal." Not comprehending that in Grant he had a man of original mind to contend with, one who had got from his West Point training mental discipline and not merely a set of rules, he moved south of the railroad, intending to get between the Union army and its base on the Mississippi, —a useless movement, for, as we have seen, the great general had some days before abandoned his base of supplies. Owing to the heavy rains and high water in the creek which he had to cross, Pemberton had not proceeded far with his southward march when he received a despatch from Johnston, who was ten miles north of Jackson, saying, "The only mode by which we can unite is by your moving directly to Clinton." He made a retrograde movement with the design of taking a road north of the railroad to Clinton, when he encountered the forces of

Grant, who, after his victory over Johnston, had set out to vanquish the other Confederate host. May 16 the two armies met in the battle of Champion's Hill. Again the Union force was the larger, again the Confederates were discomfited. They fled, and Grant pursued them. The next day they made a stand at Big Black River bridge. He attacked. They had lost heart and were filled with consternation at the swift movements and impetuous onsets of Grant. Let Pemberton tell the story of the day: "The enemy . . . advanced at a run with loud cheers. Our troops in their front did not remain to receive them, but broke and fled precipitately. One portion of the line being broken, it very soon became a matter of *sauve qui peut*." Himself depressed and his troops demoralized, he retired within the defences of Vicksburg.

As soon as he could get across the Big Black River, Grant followed and took possession of the long-coveted heights of Walnut Hills and Haynes's Bluff, securing a base of supplies which had safe and unobstructed water communication with the North. As Grant and Sherman together rode up on the dry high ground north of Vicksburg and looked down upon the Confederate fortress and then upon the Federal fleet within easy distance, Sherman, perceiving the full force of what they had gained, and overcome with the recollection of the time when he had panted for that position, broke out into enthusiasm which knew no bounds, while Grant, imperturbable, thought and smoked on. There was reason for rejoicing. In nineteen days Grant had crossed the great river into the enemy's territory, had marched one hundred and eighty miles through a most difficult country, skirmishing constantly, had fought and won five distinct battles, inflicting a greater loss upon the enemy than he himself sustained and capturing many cannon and fieldpieces, had taken the capital of the State and destroyed its arsenals and military manufactories, and was now in the rear of Vicksburg.

From the demoralization of the Confederates, he hoped that he might carry their works by storm, and made an assault,

which was unsuccessful. He then commenced the investment of
the city. Since he had crossed the Mississippi only five days'
rations had been issued from the commissary department; but
the troops, drawing the rest of their supplies from the country,
had lived fairly well, although they had suffered from the want
of bread, as the cry from the private soldiers of "Hardtack! hardtack!" informed Grant as he rode one day along the lines.
Solicitous for the comfort of the men, he soon made arrangements by which they had a full supply of coffee and bread.

May 18 Pemberton received a despatch from Johnston, saying that if Vicksburg were invested it must surrender ultimately: "instead of losing both troops and place, we must if possible save the troops. If it is not too late, evacuate Vicksburg and
march to the northeast." By immediate compliance with this
order there is a bare chance that Pemberton might have saved
a part of his army, but, after a council of war, he decided to
make the attempt to hold Vicksburg.

Grant still hoped that he might take the place by storm. His
soldiers were eager, and the advantages of a speedy capture
were great. May 22 he ordered an assault in force: this failed,
with a loss of 3199. On the evening of that day he wrote, "I now
find the position of the enemy so strong that I shall be compelled to regularly besiege the city." "I intend to lose no more
men," he said on the morrow, "but to force the enemy from one
position to another without exposing my troops." "The position
is as strong by nature as can possibly be conceived of, and is well
fortified," he advised Halleck. . . . "The enemy are now undoubtedly in our grasp. The fall of Vicksburg and the capture
of most of the garrison can only be a question of time. I hear a
great deal of the enemy bringing a large force from the East to
effect a raising of the siege." His next despatch shows watchful-
ness as well as confidence: "I can manage the force in Vicksburg and an attacking force on the rear of 30,000, but may have
more to contend against. Vicksburg will have to be reduced by
regular siege. My effective force here is about 50,000, and can be
increased 10,000 more from my own command." Halleck had

anticipated his desire for reinforcements, and had ordered troops to him from Missouri and Kentucky, so that by the time he was ready for a final assault he had an army of 75,000.

The hard-work of the siege fell largely upon the engineers, who were too few in number. Therefore all the officers who were graduates of West Point were pressed into this branch of the service, and their academic knowledge of military engineering was made of avail. Grant, Sherman, and McPherson did double duty, counting no labor too mean which would contribute to the glorious result in view. Much of the drudgery was performed by negroes, who, attracted by the promise of wages ushered in by the new era, flocked into the Union lines. "We are now approaching with pick and shovel," wrote General Sherman to his brother, the Senator. . . . "In the mean time we are daily pouring into the city a perfect storm of shot and shells, and our sharp-shooters are close up and fire at any head that is rash enough to show itself above ground." "The approaches are gradually nearing the enemy's fortifications," said Grant in his despatch to Halleck, June 3. . . . "We shell the town a little every day and keep the enemy constantly on the alert. We but seldom lose a man now. The best of health and spirits prevail among the troops." "Vicksburg is closely invested" is, five days later, the report of his progress. "I have a spare force of about 30,000 men with which to repel anything from the rear. . . . Johnston is concentrating a force at Canton." June 18 he wrote, "Deserters come out daily. All report rations short."

The situation of the besieged was pitiable. The mass of de-moralized soldiers who poured into the city, fleeing from the victorious Union army after the battle of Big Black River bridge, was a bad augury, and, while the feeling was for the moment relieved by the repulse of the two assaults of Grant, gloom settled down upon soldiers and people before the steady systematic work of the investing army. The "tumultuous, joyous city full of stirs" became a camp and a trench. In the town were many non-combatants, some of whom were women and children; and while the casualties among them were not many, the nervous strain from the continual bombardment by the fleet on one side and the Federal artillery on the other was great. One soldier remarked the demoralizing effect of the howling and bursting shells, another the intense and hideous hiss of the conical balls from the heavy rifled-guns of the steamer *Cincinnati*, and a lady tells of the fearful noise, the wild screams, the whizzing and clattering sound of the shrapnel-shells that struck terror to the heart. The lie of the ground lent itself to the building of caves which served as a refuge for women and children. The caves soon became dwelling-places where they ate and slept. Their fathers, husbands, and sons were on duty in the trenches. The bombardment from the mortars across the Mississippi, the constant fire on the Confederate lines by artillery and sharpshooters, caused the loss of many officers and men, and immediate anguish to their households. "The screams of the women of Vicksburg," writes one of them, "were the saddest I have ever heard. The wailings over the dead seemed full of a heart-sick agony. I cannot attempt to describe the thrill of pity, mingled with fear, that pierced my soul, as suddenly vibrating through the air would come these sorrowful shrieks!—these pitiful moans!—sometimes almost simultaneously with the explosion of a shell." Grief, anxiety, sordid cares, and suffering at the deprivation of the necessaries and conveniences of life made up the existence of the citizens and the women. Soon there was lack of the proper kind of food, then hunger stared them in the face.

The sole hope was that Johnston would break the investment, and the appeals of Pemberton, which were sent to him with great difficulty, were urgent. Jefferson Davis was in deep concern at the impending fate of Vicksburg, and did his utmost to forward reinforcements from all available points, but, after draining the resources of the Confederacy, he was able to increase Johnston's army to a total of only 24,000 to 34,000 men. The reinforcements to Grant were coming more rapidly and in greater numbers, and there was no time when Johnston could have brought more than an equal force to attack that which

Grant had set apart to frustrate any attempt to break the siege. The Union troops would fight behind breastworks with the probability of repulsing the Confederates with great slaughter. Johnston was wise when he refused to give battle with an inadequate army. The acrimony exhibited in the correspondence between him and his President is apt to induce friends of the South to impute a share of the blame for their great disaster to one or the other, but, it seems to me, with little reason. Johnston ought, indeed, to have proceeded in person to join Pemberton as soon as he arrived at Jackson, but he offers the excuse that he was too weak physically to attempt such a ride. With that exception he seems to have done everything possible,* and Davis in Richmond wrought in his sphere with energy and zeal. The superior resources of the North were bound to tell whenever a great military leader should arise. The leader had arisen, the government furnished him everything, and he bore full sway. Despatches were so long in transmission from Washington to his headquarters that the orders or the wishes of the President or Halleck were ineffectual when received. Halleck directed him to unite, if possible, his forces with Banks's in order to attack Vicksburg and Port Hudson separately with the combined armies, but he received the despatch on the battle-field of the Big Black just before his soldiers charged the enemy, and, flushed with his victories, he knew that by the logic of events he should disregard the order. Against this able handling of abundant resources the efforts of the Confederates were vain. Johnston comprehended the situation, and placed the dilemma before the authorities in Richmond. "Without some great blunder of the enemy we cannot hold both Mississippi and Tennessee," he telegraphed June 15; "which it is best to hold is for the Government to determine. . . . I consider saving Vicksburg

* After the war Grant said: "I have had nearly all of the Southern generals in high command in front of me, and Joe Johnston gave me more anxiety than any of the others. I was never half so anxious about Lee. . . . Take it all in all, the South, in my opinion, had no better soldier than Joe Johnston—none at least that gave me more trouble."—J. R. Young, *Around the World with General Grant*, vol. ii. pp. 212, 213.

hopeless." With so difficult a choice before him, Jefferson Davis may not be blamed that he did not order Bragg's army to Mississippi, leaving Tennessee open to Rosecrans.

The communication between Johnston and Pemberton was irregular and precarious. One courier availing himself of the river went as far as he dared in his skiff, then landed and waited for the darkness of night. He removed all his clothes, fastened his despatches securely within them, and bound them in turn firmly to a plank. This he pushed into the stream, and floated with it down the river past the gun-boats to Confederate ground. June 14 Johnston sent this word: "All that we can attempt to do is to save you and your garrison. . . . Our joint forces cannot raise the siege of Vicksburg." This was received within a week, and Pemberton in reply suggested a plan for this relief.

Meanwhile the garrison was suffering from fatigue, lack of food, enfeeblement, and sickness. Soon after the commencement of the siege the meat ration was reduced one half, and in lieu thereof, that of sugar, beans, and rice was increased. As an encouragement to the troops Pemberton impressed the chewing tobacco in the city, and issued it to them; this, he said, "had a very beneficial influence." The meat became almost exhausted, bacon gave out. Recourse was had to the flesh of horses and mules. It is said that the Frenchmen among the Louisiana troops prepared a toothsome dish of rats. Corn meal ran low, and the supply was eked out by a mixture of dried peas ground up. The incessant work of countermining against the greater number of besiegers who pushed operations night and day, the labor of defence, the exposure in the trenches "to burning suns, drenching rains, damp fogs and heavy dews," wore the men out, and, together with a growing want of confidence in their commander, caused a loss of morale. Of this, the conversations of pickets during their temporary truces and the reports of deserters gave Grant an inkling, as he steadily and grimly closed about the beleaguered city and made ready for a final assault. Pemberton, who seems to have been a brave and conscientious officer, saw his power of resistance declining day by day. June

28 he received an "appeal for help" from many soldiers in the trenches, which from its sincerity must have moved his feelings and may have been an influence in determining his action. "Our rations," it said, "have been cut down to one biscuit and a small bit of bacon per day, not enough scarcely to keep soul and body together, much less to stand the hardships we are called upon to stand. . . . If you can't feed us, you had better surrender us, horrible as the idea is, than suffer this noble army to disgrace themselves by desertion. . . . Men are not going to lie here and perish if they do love their country dearly. . . . Hunger will compel a man to do almost anything. . . . This army is now ripe for mutiny unless it can be fed."

When July 1 came, Pemberton made up his mind that he could not repel another assault, which he knew was at hand, and that he must surrender or endeavor to cut his way out. He submitted the question by confidential notes to his division commanders, and afterwards held with them a council of war; all being unanimous for capitulation, he decided on opening negotiations with Grant. July 3 white flags denoting his desire for a parley were raised on his works, causing hostilities thereabouts to cease. Two officers bearing a flag of truce with a letter from him asking for terms wended their way toward the Union lines. This resulted in a conference that afternoon between Grant and Pemberton, who were old acquaintances, having served in the same division during a part of the Mexican war. They met on a hillside, near a stunted oak-tree, a few hundred feet from the Confederate lines, and after their interchange of views Grant wrote that evening a letter offering terms of capitulation which, after a little delay, were accepted. At 10:30 on the morning of July 4, in the self-same hour that Lincoln announced to the country the result of Gettysburg, he sent this word to his government: "The enemy surrendered this morning. The only terms allowed is their parole as prisoners of war." "Glory, hallelujah!" wrote General Sherman to Grant, "the best Fourth of July since 1776." The number of prisoners taken was 29,491, while the Confederate loss up to that time had probably reached

10,000. Besides, 170 cannon and 50,000 small arms were captured. The muskets, being of an improved make recently received from Europe, were used to replace the inferior arms of many regiments of the Union army. The result had been gained at small cost: Grant's loss during his whole campaign was 9362.

"In boldness of plan, rapidity of execution, and brilliancy of results," wrote Halleck, a scholar in military affairs, your "operations will compare most favorably with those of Napoleon about Ulm." Others of his friends have drawn a parallel with the Italian campaign of 1796. On the day that the news was received in Washington the government conferred on him the honor of a major-generalship in the regular army; and later, on his recommendation, made Sherman and McPherson, his efficient and faithful lieutenants, brigadiers in the regular service.

Of what occurred when the Federal troops took possession of the city and the Confederates marched out, accounts differ in detail but agree in essence. Grant wrote, "Not a cheer went up, not a remark was made that would give pain." A Confederate officer of high rank recollects a hearty cheer from a division of the Union army, but it was given "for the gallant defenders of Vicksburg."

When the news of the victory reached Port Hudson, the Confederate commander surrendered it to General Banks, who had invested it with his army. July 16 the steamboat *Imperial*, which had come directly from St. Louis, landed its commercial cargo on the levee at New Orleans. As Lincoln said, "The Father of Waters again goes unvexed to the sea."

THE *last great crisis of the war period in foreign af-*
fairs was precipitated by the success of Confederate
agents in getting control, in 1863, of two powerful
armored warships with heavy prows or rams that were
being built at Birkenhead on the Mersey. The vigi-
lance of the American consul in Liverpool and of
Charles Francis Adams in London met the danger.
Had one or both cruisers escaped to the high seas, as
the Alabama *had done, they might have broken the*
blockade of the South, placed Northern ports in peril,
and brought on a war between the United States and
Great Britain—with Napoleon III supporting the
British. Fortunately, the British Foreign Office had
already determined to maintain its neutral position.
Lord John Russell had to move cautiously, for he
could not seize ships without a proper legal basis. His
deliberation gave Adams some days of great anxiety;
but he issued orders to stop the rams in time. Rhodes
tells this exciting story with facts that were first re-
vealed in his pages.

The British Rams

IN the mean time work was proceeding on the two steam iron-
clad rams which the Lairds were building at Birkenhead for the
Confederates. Adams was diligent in calling the attention of
Earl Russell to the transaction, and in furnishing him evidence,
supplied by Dudley, our consul at Liverpool, which showed the
character and destination of these vessels; and, should a grave
contingency arise, he had for his guidance an unequivocal despatch from the Secretary of State. If more vessels which become
armed cruisers get away, Seward wrote, rendering it evident
that the laws of Great Britain, or their administration, or the
judicial construction of them is not sufficient to insure a proper
observance of neutrality, then the United States must protect
themselves. Being brought to a condition of things where war
is waged against them "by a portion, at least, of the British
nation," the President may decide to order the navy to pursue

these "pirates" into the British ports, and while perceiving the "risks and hazards" consequent on such a determination he does not think that the responsibility of war will fall upon the United States.

In pursuance of the communications of Adams, Earl Russell, with honest intent, set affairs in train to ascertain for whom these iron-clad rams were building, with the design of stopping them should there be, under the law, warrant for such action. While their construction was a matter of common knowledge, and while, as the *Times* remarked, "ninety-nine people out of a hundred believe that these steam rams are 'intended to carry on hostilities sooner or later against the Federals,'" Captain Bulloch, the able naval representative of the Southern Confederacy, who had contracted for these war-ships as well as for the *Alabama,* and had been enlightened by the seizure of the *Alexandria,* was managing the business astutely, with the sympathetic co-operation of the Lairds. To a report that they were for the Emperor of the French, Palmerston, in an allusion in the House of Commons, gave some credence: when this was shown to be without foundation, it was stated to the English government that they were for the viceroy of Egypt. This was in turn denied. Representations were then made to the officials who were investigating the matter, that they were owned by a firm of French merchants, and for this there was a legal basis. Fearing that they might be seized, Bulloch had in June sold the ships to a French firm who had engaged to resell them to him when they should get beyond British jurisdiction. He had no idea that the Lairds suspected that the sale was not a *bona fide* transfer: indeed, they wrote to the English Foreign Office that they were building the vessels for a Paris copartnery.

Earl Russell caused all the facts which were submitted to him to be sifted with care by the Law officers of the Crown, who gave him two positive opinions nearly a month apart, that there was "no evidence capable of being presented to a Court of Justice" that the ships were intended for the Confederates, but that, on the other hand, the claim of French ownership seemed to be legally sustained; they could not, therefore, advise the Government to detain the vessels. Still Russell was not satisfied, and he he continued his inquiries, leaving no stone unturned to arrive at the truth; but in spite of his suspicions he could not get over the palpable tokens that they belonged to a firm of Paris merchants. He therefore wrote Adams, September 1, that the government was advised that they could not in any way interfere with these ships, but he promised that they would maintain a careful watch, and be ready to stop them, should trustworthy evidence show any proceeding contrary to the statute. At this time he was at his country-seat in Scotland, and his letter did not reach Adams until four o'clock of September 4.

Our minister had returned from his outing, cheered by his friendly intercourse with members of the government; but on his arrival in London he was immediately confronted with the critical question of the iron-clad rams, one of which Dudley had good reason to believe would at any time go to sea. September 3 Adams wrote Russell, transmitting copies of further depositions, and averring that there were no reasonable grounds for doubt that these iron-clad rams were intended for the Confederate service; and the next day, hearing from Dudley that one of them was about to depart, he sent to the Foreign Office a "last solemn protest against the commission of such an act of hostility against a friendly nation." Soon afterwards he received Russell's note of September 1, which, he wrote in his diary, "affected me deeply. I clearly foresee that a collision must now come out of it. I must not, however, do anything to accelerate it, and yet must maintain the honor of my country with proper spirit. The issue must be properly made up before the world on its merits. The prospect is dark for poor America." After a night given to such reflections, "My thoughts turned strongly upon the present crisis. . . . My conclusion was that another note must be addressed to Lord Russell. So I drew one which I intended only to gain time previous to the inevitable result." This was his celebrated despatch of September 5: "My Lord," he wrote: "At this moment, when one of the iron-clad vessels is on the point of departure from this kingdom, on its hostile errand against the United States, I am honored" with yours of the 1st instant. "I trust I need not express how profound is my regret at the conclusion to which Her Majesty's Government have arrived. I can regard it no otherwise than as practically opening to the insurgents free liberty in this kingdom to execute a policy" of attacking New York, Boston, and Portland, and of breaking our blockade. "It would be superfluous in me to point out to your lordship that this is war. . . . I prefer to desist from communicating to your lordship even such portions of my existing instructions as are suited to the case, lest I should contribute to aggravate difficulties already far too serious. I therefore content myself with informing your lordship that I transmit by the present steamer a copy of your note for the consideration of my government, and shall await the more specific directions that will be contained in the reply."

If Russell had been in London, the tale of the iron-clad rams would have been simple and brief: one friendly interview between him and Adams would have cleared up the matter, for both had the same end in view. It is the crossing of their letters which makes the story complex, and which necessitates a close attention to the dates when the notes were received as well as when they were sent. Had the Foreign Secretary been of the mind to admit our minister somewhat more to his confidence, such an unravelling of the correspondence would not be required to manifest that Russell deserves applause for his methodical straightforwardness and his honest purpose in this affair where action was hedged about with difficulties, owing to the evasion of the true ownership and to the force of the precedent made by the narrow and doubtful construction of the statute in the case of the *Alexandra*.

As early as September 1 he was better than his word to Adams. Layard, the Under Secretary for Foreign Affairs, who was in London, wrote on that day to the Treasury: "I am directed by Earl Russell to request that you will state to the Lords Commissioners of her Majesty's Treasury that so much suspicion attaches to the iron-clad vessels at Birkenhead, that if sufficient evidence can be obtained to lead to the belief that they are intended for the Confederate States Lord Russell thinks the vessels ought to be detained until further examination can be made." Reflection, in which the belief that he had been tricked in the escape of the *Alabama* undoubtedly played a part, led him, two days later [September 3], to direct that the iron-clad rams be stopped.* On this day he wrote from Meikleour, Scotland: "My dear Palmerston,—The conduct of the gentlemen who have contracted for the two iron-clads at Birkenhead is so very suspicious that I have thought it necessary to direct that they should be detained. The Solicitor-General has been consulted, and concurs in the measure, as one of

---

* I have adopted this explanation of Russell's apparently sudden change in two days only after a very careful consideration. From the whole correspondence it seems to me that he was gradually-working to this point. The steps are exactly those which a very honorable man given somewhat to vacillation would take. The additional evidence which Adams sent to the Foreign Office had not yet reached him.

Another explanation may be suggested which it might be assumed that I should adopt in order to be consistent with my treatment of his alteration of opinion in October, 1862. Adams, on a visit to the Duke of Argyll at Inverary Castle, Scotland, makes this entry in his diary, Aug. 28: "In the evening a little conversation with the Duke of Argyll about the fitting out of the iron-clad vessels. He said that he had received a letter from Mr. Sumner, dwelling very strongly on the danger of war from this cause. I said that I felt the same apprehension. He wanted to know something of the French claim. I replied that I had exposed the motive of that pretence. . . . The Ministry dislikes to assume a responsibility which may make it the object of popular attack at home. It thus hazards the evil of war upon a doubt. He seemed a little impressed with my earnestness. I told him I had instructions on the subject far more stringent than I had yet been disposed to execute. My own inclinations had been to make as little of the difficulty as I could. But I could not fail to regard the question as grave and critical." It is no unnatural supposition that the Duke should have communicated this conversation to Earl Russell by letter, and it may have been a slight contributing cause to the decision, but the main reason seems to me to have been that, full of regret at the escape of the *Alabama* and her depredations, he was determined not to give our country another similar cause of offence.

The difference of feeling too in England after McClellan's reverses before Richmond, and after Gettysburg and Vicksburg, is an element to be taken into consideration. "The progress of the Federal arms," wrote Cobden to Bright, Sept. 8, "will help the Cabinet over some of the legal technicalities of the enlistment act."—Morley, p. 589. The Northern victories undoubtedly strengthened Russell's arm to do what he considered right. The feeling of the ministry is probably well expressed by the Duchess of Argyll to Sumner, Sept. 8: "I have just heard that the iron-clads are to be arrested. I trust there may be evidence sufficient to do what we wish to do."—Pierce-Sumner Papers, MS.

policy, though not of strict law. We shall thus test the law, and, if we have to pay damages, we have satisfied the opinion, which prevails here as well as in America, that that kind of neutral hostility should not be allowed to go on without some attempt to stop it. If you do not approve, pray appoint a Cabinet for Tuesday or Wednesday next [the 8th or 9th]." Palmerston did not dissent, and therefore called no meeting of the Cabinet. But Russell was not content to wait the slow course of the post or the approval of the Prime Minister, and on the same day [September 3] telegraphed to Layard to give directions to stop the iron-clads "as soon as there is reason to believe that they are actually about to put to sea, and to detain them until further orders." September 4 he sent word to Adams that "the matter is under the serious and anxious consideration of Her Majesty's Government;" but this the minister did not receive until after he had despatched his note, saying, "It would be superfluous in me to point out to your lordship that this is war." September 5 Russell ordered that the vessels "be prevented from leaving Liverpool" on a trial trip "or on any other pretext" "until satisfactory evidence can be given as to their destination," and on the same day he sent a confidential note to the *chargé d'affaires* in Washington, requesting that Secretary Seward be apprised that they had been stopped from leaving port; but for some unexplained reason he did not advise Adams of this action until three days later.

After the iron-clad rams were "detained," the Foreign Secretary employed the utmost circumspection to prevent the one almost ready for slipping away to sea through any artifice. While two different constructions may be drawn from the correspondence, it seems, on the whole, that he had confidence in the honor of the Lairds, although it was at times clouded with suspicions, born of the escape of the *Alabama* and augmented by their persistence in asking permission for a trial trip, that, if the steamer went out to test her machinery, she would never come back, through causes ostensibly beyond their control. A large body of seamen from the Confederate cruiser *Florida* had recently come to Liverpool for the purpose, it was suspected, of carrying out a plan for the "forcible abduction of the vessel," and to checkmate this game Russell had moved the Board of Admiralty to authorize the Admiral of the Channel fleet, then in the Mersey, to place "on board the iron-clad, about to be tried, a sufficient force of seamen and marines in her Majesty's naval service to defeat any attempt to run away with the vessel." But it then turned out that the ship was not ready, and the trial trip was postponed.

In the mean time the Foreign Office made a systematic and careful investigation, demonstrating, to a moral certainty, that the French ownership was a blind, and that the iron-clad rams were intended for the Confederates. October 8, by the order of Earl Russell, the vessel the more advanced in her construction was seized, and the next day the *Broad Arrow* was likewise put upon the other. The Lairds were annoyed at this action, and their operatives showed much ill feeling. To ward off any attempt at a rescue, the ships were watched by a powerful naval force. The question whether the iron-clads should be condemned was never passed upon by the courts. Neither the government nor the owners were eager to run the chances of a trial. In the end, as the best way out of the complication, the vessels were purchased by the British Admiralty.

These iron-clad rams were formidable vessels of war, and had they got away they would undoubtedly have broken the blockade at Charleston and Wilmington;* and as the blockade,

---

* Through the kindness of Mr. Charles F. Adams and Mr. S. A. B. Abbott, I have received the following statement made in Jan., 1898, from Captain Page, who had been selected as the commander of these vessels: I never received from the Confederate government any instructions, written or of any other kind, as to the course I should pursue after taking command of the rams, but I had outlined in my own mind a plan of operations. My intention was to sail at once to Wilmington and to raise the blockade there and at Charleston. Having accomplished this, I intended to raise the blockade of the gulf ports and cut off all communications of the North by water with New Orleans. I had at the time perfect confidence in my ability to accomplish my purposes, and I now believe, in the light of what I have since learned, that if the rams had been permitted to leave England I would have been successful. I never had any intention of attacking New York, Boston, or Hampton Roads, or any Northern port, as I did not believe in that kind of warfare.

constantly growing in efficiency, was a potent weapon on the Northern side, the harm would have been incalculable: the victories even of Gettysburg and Vicksburg might have been neutralized. Bulloch dreamed that "our iron-clads" might "sweep the blockading fleet from the sea front of every harbor," "ascend the Potomac," and "render Washington itself untenable," and lay Portsmouth (N. H.) and Philadelphia under contribution. From some such damage Earl Russell, by his careful and decisive action, saved the North, and thereby prevented a war between the United States and Great Britain, which the energy of Bulloch and the sympathy and cupidity of a firm of Birkenhead ship-builders came near bringing about. The seizure of the rams was a blow to the Confederate cause.

The debate in the House of Commons, June 30, made it evident that England would not recognize, singly or jointly, the Southern Confederacy, or offer to mediate between the two belligerents; and the proceedings which I have just related showed that the Confederates could no longer hope to build and get away from England vessels of war. The contrast of the action now, and that in regard to the *Alabama* was marked, especially as the case against the cruiser was the stronger of the two. Her depredations, the claims for damages, urged persistently by our government, the Proclamation of Emancipation, Gettysburg and Vicksburg, invigorated the friendship of Russell, and added to his supporters in the Cabinet.

As early as January, Benjamin, the Confederate Secretary of State, complained, when writing to Slidell, that Mason had "been discourteously treated by Earl Russell," in March, that "the irritation against Great Britain is fast increasing;" and in June he indulged in words almost abusive of the English government. August 4 he wrote Mason that the President was convinced, from the recent debates in Parliament, that England would not recognize the Confederacy, and he therefore instructed him to consider his mission at an end, and withdraw from London. Mason received this despatch September 14, and after waiting a week to consult with Slidell, notified Earl Rus-

sell that in accordance with his instructions he should terminate his mission. Jefferson Davis, in his message to his Congress in December, gave vent to his "dissatisfaction with the
conduct of the British government," two of his many grievances
being that they respected the Federal blockade, and had seized
the iron-clad rams.

While Seward's diplomacy after the *Trent* affair may, on the
whole, be commended in the view of the results accomplished,
there was in it so much of the "claim everything" principle that
it is not extolled by adepts in international law. The course
of Adams was well-nigh faultless. There being no Atlantic cable,
it took from three weeks to a month to obtain instructions that
he asked for. In an exigency therefore he could not wait for
these, and was forced many times to act on his own judgment,
with a result, since his knowledge was larger and his vision
clearer than Seward's, that was beneficial to our cause. As I
have told the story of the iron-clad rams, his language in the
celebrated despatch of September 5 may seem more peremptory
than the occasion required, but he must be judged in the light
of the facts he himself knew. Applying that test, we perceive
that his action, which showed both decision and reserve, denoted
diplomatic ability of the highest order.

Russell lacked the force of Palmerston, the many-sidedness
and the promptitude of initiative of Gladstone; he belonged to
that class of honorable gentlemen whose service to their country
and their order is safe rather than impressive, and if his conduct
be estimated, not by a hard and fast line which the historian
with the knowledge of the after event may draw in his study,
but with a due allowance for the difficulties which beset the path
of a practical statesman, it may be asserted, in spite of his devi-
ations from a consistent course, that he deserved well of both
English-speaking nations. While the course of England towards
us was not as just as ours towards her during the Crimean War,
it must be borne in mind that "our only well-wisher in Europe"
was Russia, and that if a contrast be instituted with the policy
of France, the action of the government of Great Britain will

appear to border on friendliness. England, indeed, was the insurmountable obstacle to the recognition of the Southern Confederacy by France and other European nations. While the English Cabinet looked with regret on the operations of English merchants and ship-builders who, by selling arms, munitions, and vessels to the South, entangled Great Britain in its relations with the United States, Louis Napoleon instigated the Confederates to construct two iron-clads and four clipper corvettes in France, giving indirectly the assurance that they might be armed and equipped, and permitted upon a plausible pretext to leave his ports. While Russell declined to see Mason, subsequent to their first meeting, shortly after his arrival in February, 1862, and Palmerston saw him only twice, at a time when all danger of foreign interference had passed, the Emperor accorded three interviews to Slidell, and the Minister of Foreign Affairs and other members of the imperial ministry and household held with him unrestrained intercourse. Moreover, Louis Napoleon conquered Mexico, and placed a European monarch on her throne. Notwithstanding his designs were not so clear in 1863 as they are now, enough was known to arouse in the mind of the American public a suspicion that was undoubtedly shared by Seward, although the tone of his despatches to France, either from motives of policy, or because he was influenced by the traditional amity of that nation and the sympathy of liberal Frenchmen, was considerate and kindly, in striking contrast with his roughness to England.

After October, 1863, there was no danger of foreign intervention in our struggle.

WHEN *William S. Rosecrans, commanding Union forces in Tennessee, was defeated in September, 1863, with terrible loss, at Chickamauga—the last really impressive Confederate triumph of the war—his army was saved by General George H. Thomas. Grant then took charge, ordering a concentration of Union troops in and about the vital railroad center of Chattanooga. Before long Grant was ready for an offensive with four famous commanders, Sherman, Thomas, Sheridan, and Hooker, under his direction. In the brilliant operations that ensued, the Union armies won two spectacular positions, Lookout Mountain and Missionary Ridge, and were ready to press into Georgia as soon as the weather and the repair of communications permitted. By the early part of 1864 the Western command was in highly efficient order. But in the East a stronger leader than Meade, who still headed the Army of the Potomac, was clearly needed.*

Lincoln recognized that this leader was available. He and his associates in the war department and Congress took precisely the right step. They revived the grade of lieutenant-general, previously held only by Washington and Scott, for Grant. They called him East and agreed that he should be given unhampered control of all the armies of the Union. Lincoln trusted Grant so completely that he knew that political interference would not be needed. Grant made his headquarters in the field in close proximity to Meade. As May opened in 1864 the armies both east and west were set in motion, the Army of the Potomac crossing the Rapidan River and pushing southeast through the wilderness toward Richmond. Controversy still exists about Grant's plan of action. He was bloodily checked in the Wilderness, checked again with heavy losses at Spotsylvania, and checked once more with a frightful list of dead and wounded at Cold Harbor; but after each check he pressed on by an undaunted flank march until he decided to move to the James River as a base. Terrible as his losses were, he could afford them; the Confederates could not afford their smaller but nevertheless severe casualties.

Grant Takes the High Command

In a military point of view, thank Heaven!" Motley wrote, "the 'coming man,' for whom we have so long been waiting, seems really to have come." Exactly so, thought the President, Congress, and the people. By an act of February 29, Congress revived the grade of Lieutenant-General, and authorized the President to place the General, whom he should so appoint, in command of the armies of the United States under his direction and during his pleasure. It was understood on all sides that the man whom the nation's representatives desired to honor and upon whom they wished to devolve the burden of military affairs was Grant. This action fell in with the ideas of Lincoln. From the first he would have been glad to have some general on whom he could rely, on whom he could throw the responsibility of military operations. Scott failed him, on account of the infirmities of age; McClellan lacked the requisite ability; and Halleck, who was likewise deficient, shrunk from the burden after the disaster to Pope, and became merely the President's chief-of-staff. It was a welcome function for him to send to the Senate at once the nomination of Grant as Lieutenant-General. It was immediately confirmed.

Grant received orders from the department to report at Washington, and the day that he left Nashville to assume his new duties he wrote General Sherman a private letter, which brings into view the sublime friendship between these two soldiers, always marked by consideration and loyalty, and never to be alloyed with jealousy on the one side or envy on the other. Thus he wrote to his bosom companion-in-arms: "While I have been eminently successful in this war, in at least gaining the confidence of the public, no one feels more than I how much of this success is due to the energy, skill, and the harmonious putting forth of that energy and skill, of those whom it has been my good fortune to have occupying subordinate positions under me. There are many officers to whom these remarks are applicable to a greater or less degree, proportionate to their ability as soldiers; but what I want is to express my thanks to you and McPherson, as *the men* to whom, above all others, I feel indebted for whatever I have had of success. How far your advice and suggestions have been of assistance, you know. How far your execution of whatever has been given you to do entitles you to the reward I am receiving, you cannot know as well as I do. I feel all the gratitude this letter would express, giving it the most flattering construction. The word *you* I use in the plural, intending it for McPherson also."

Sherman replied: "You do yourself injustice and us too much honor in assigning to us so large a share of the merits which have led to your high advancement. . . . You are now Washington's legitimate successor, and occupy a position of almost dangerous elevation; but if you can continue, as heretofore, to be yourself, simple, honest, and unpretending, you will enjoy through life the respect and love of friends, and the homage of millions of human beings who will award to you a large share for securing to them and their descendants a government of law and stability. I repeat, you do General McPherson and myself too much honor. At Belmont you manifested your traits, neither of us being near; at Donelson also you illustrated your whole character. I was not near, and General McPherson in too subordinate a capacity to influence you. Until you had won Donelson, I confess I was almost cowed by the terrible array of anarchical elements that presented themselevs at every point; but that victory admitted the ray of light which I have followed ever since. I believe you are as brave, patriotic, and just as the great prototype Washington; as unselfish, kind-hearted, and honest as a man should be; but the chief characteristic in your nature is the simple faith in success you have always maifested, which I can liken to nothing else than the faith a Christian has in his Saviour. This faith gave you victory at Shiloh and Vicksburg. Also, when you have completed your best preparations, you go into battle without hesitation, as at Chattanooga—no doubts, no reserve; and I tell you that it was this that made us act with confidence. I knew wherever I was you thought of me, and if I got in a tight place you would come—if alive. My only points of doubt were as to your knowledge of grand strategy, and the books of science and history; but I confess your common-sense seems to have supplied all this. Now, as to the future. Do not stay in Washington. Halleck is better qualified than you are to stand the buffets of intrigue and policy. Come out West; take to yourself the whole Mississippi Valley; let us make it dead sure, and I tell you the Atlantic slope and Pacific shores will follow its destiny as sure as the limbs of a tree live or die with the main trunk! We have done much; still much remains to be done. Time and time's influences are all with us; we could almost afford to sit still and let these influences work. Even in the seceded States your word now would go further than a President's proclamation or an act of Congress. For God's sake, and for your country's sake, come out of Washington! I foretold to General Halleck before he left Corinth the inevitable result to him, and I now exhort you to come out West. Here lies the seat of the coming empire; and from the West, when our task is done, we will make short work of Charleston and Richmond, and the impoverished coast of the Atlantic."

Arriving in Washington, Grant met Lincoln for the first time at a crowded reception at the White House. An appointment between the two was made for the next day, when, in the presence of the Cabinet, General Halleck, and a few others, the President said: "General Grant, the nation's appreciation of what you have done, and its reliance upon you for what remains to do in the existing great struggle, are now presented, with this commission constituting you Lieutenant-General in the Army of the United States. With this high honor devolves upon you also a corresponding responsibility. As the country herein trusts you, so, under God, it will sustain you. I scarcely need to add that with what I here speak for the nation goes my own hearty personal concurrence."

Grant replied: "Mr. President, I accept this commission with gratitude for the high honor conferred. With the aid of the noble armies that have fought on so many fields for our common country, it will be my earnest endeavor not to disappoint your expectations. I feel the full weight of the responsibilities now devolving on me; and I know that if they are met, it will be due to those armies, and, above all, to the favor of that Providence which leads both nations and men."

The next day Grant was formally assigned to the command of the armies of the United States. Until his visit to Washington he had the intention of remaining in the West, but he now saw that his place was with the Army of the Potomac. He went to the front, and had a conference with Meade, at which, after an interchange of views creditable to both, he decided that Meade should retain his present command. He then went to Nashville, and discussed with Sherman, who succeeded him as chief of the Western army, the plan of operations in Tennessee and Georgia, returning, March 23, to Washington. He was now by all odds the most popular man in the United States.* Both parties and all factions vied with one another in his praise. He had met with obstacles in working up to the present position, which was the meed of his genius and character, and had suffered many hours of pain at the obloquy with which he had been pursued. But Vicksburg and Chattanooga were victories the cumulative force of which not only bore down all detraction, but raised the general who won them to a height of glory. It falls to few men of action to receive in their lifetime such plau-

* John Sherman, in a letter to his brother, March 26, gives an account of the homage paid Grant in Washington. "General Grant is all the rage. He is subjected to the disgusting but dangerous process of being lionized. He is followed by crowds, and is cheered everywhere. While he must despise the fickle fools who run after him, he, like most others, may be spoiled by this excess of flattery. He may be so elated as to forget the uncertain tenure upon which he holds and stakes his really well-earned laurels. . . . The opinion I form of him from his appearance is this,—his will and common-sense are the strongest features of his character. He is plain and modest, and so far bears himself well."—*Letters*, p. 224. General Sherman replied, April 5: "Grant is as good a leader as we can find. He has honesty, simplicity of character, singleness of purpose, and no hope or claim to usurp civil power. His character, more than his genius, will reconcile armies and attach the people. Let him alone. Don't disgust him by flattery or importunity. Let him alone. . . . If bothered, hampered, or embarrassed, he would drop you all in disgust, and let you slide into anarchy."—*Ibid.*, p. 225.

dits, with hardly a murmur, with scarcely a grudge, as fell to the happy lot of Grant in the winter and early spring of 1864. His modest bearing and unaffected demeanor induced respect for his character, as his great deeds and won admiration for his military genius. Striking, indeed, is it to one who immerses himself in the writings of the time to contrast this almost universal applause of Grant with the abuse of Lincoln by the Democrats, the caustic criticism of him by some of the radical Republicans, the damning him with faint praise by others of the same faction.

Grant had the charm of simplicity of character, and in common with Lincoln he possessed the sentiment that he was one of the plain people, and would fain keep in touch with them. The two furnished, in this respect, a pattern for the great men of a democracy which is constituted of educated and moral persons. But he lacked the external manners, the aloofness of person, the quality of being niggard of his time, the dignity of bearing that should go with the commander of over half a million of soldiers to whom the nation looked for its salvation. Richard H. Dana, with that power of seeing things keenly, and describing them vividly, which he had exhibited in his early life in the story of "Two Years Before the Mast," shows us Grant as he beheld him before he left finally for the field, when his mind was engrossed with the great plans of the campaign. Dana had arrived at Willard's Hotel, Washington, and had gone to the office to inquire for his luggage, when, as he tells the story, "a short, round-shouldered man, in a very tarnished major-general's uniform came up, and asked about his card for General Dana, which led me to look at him. There was nothing marked in his appearance. He had no gait, no *station,* no manner, rough, light-brown whiskers, a blue eye, and rather a scrubby look withal. A crowd formed round him; men looked, stared at him, as if they were taking his likeness, and two generals were introduced. Still, I could not get his name. It was not Hooker. Who could it be? He had a cigar in his mouth, and rather the look of a man who did, or once did, take a little too much to drink. I inquired of the bookkeeper. 'That is General Grant.' I joined the starers. I saw that the ordinary, scrubby-looking man, with a slightly seedy look, as if he was out of office and on half pay, and nothing to do but hang round the entry of Willard's, cigar in mouth, had a clear blue eye, and a look of resolution, as if he could not be trifled with, and an entire indifference to the crowd about him. Straight nose, too. Still, to see him talking and smoking in the lower entry of Willard's, in that crowd, in such times,—the generalissimo of our armies, on whom the destiny of the empire seemed to hang!"

The next morning Dana, having met Grant at breakfast, thus completes his account: "He was just leaving the table, and going to the front for the great movement. I said, 'I suppose, General, you don't mean to breakfast again until the war is over.' 'Not here, I sha'n't.' He gets over the ground queerly. He does not march, nor quite walk, but pitches along as if the next step would bring him on his nose. But his face looks firm and hard, and his eye is clear and resolute, and he is certainly natural, and clear of all appearance of self-consciousness. How war, how all great crises, bring us to the one-man power!"

I have now brought the story down to the last year of the war, and from this time onward I shall treat military affairs only in a general way. "It was not till after both Gettysburg and Vicksburg," wrote General Sherman, "that the war professionally began."* In 1864 and 1865 the campaigns and the battles were, as in the previous years, the events on which all else depended; but now that the President and generals had learned well the lessons of war, and began to conduct it with professional skill,

---

* W. T. Sherman wrote R. N. Scott, Sept. 6, 1885: "I contend and have contended with European officers of world-wide fame that the military profession of America was not responsible for the loose preliminary operations of 1862, and that it was not till after both Gettysburg and Vicksburg that the war professionally began. Then our men had learned in the dearest school of earth the simple lesson of war. Then we had brigades, divisions, and corps which could be handled professionally, and it was then that we as professional soldiers could rightfully be held to a just responsibility."— *North American Review*, March, 1886, p. 302.

there is a measure of justification for the writer who prefers henceforth to dwell upon the political and social side of the conflict to the dwarfing of the military picture.

The details of Grant's plan need not concern us. The two salient features of it are simple and of the utmost importance; they were the destruction or capture of Lee's army by himself and his force of 122,000 men, and the crushing of Joseph E. Johnston by Sherman with his army of 100,000. From the nature of the situation a second objective point in the one case was Richmond, in the other, Atlanta. The winter and early spring had been spent largely in systematic and effective preparation. The confidence of the people in Grant was so great that many were sanguine that the war would be over by midsummer.

On the night of May 3 the Army of the Potomac began its advance by crossing the Rapidan without molestation, and encamping the next day in the Wilderness, where one year before Hooker had come to grief. Grant had no desire to fight a battle in this tangled jungle; but Lee, who had watched him intently, permitted him to traverse the river unopposed, thinking that, when he halted in the dense thicket, every inch of which was known to the Confederate general and soldiers, the Lord had delivered him into their hands. Lee ordered at once the concentration of his army, and with Napoleonic swiftness marched forward to dispute the advance of his enemy. May 5 the forces came together in the Wilderness, and a hot battle raged. The Confederates were in number only half of the Union troops, but the difficulties of the battle-ground which their leader had chosen, their better topographical knowledge, the circumstance that the superior Federal artillery could be little used made it an equal contest, neither side gaining the advantage.

Grant perceived that he must fight his way through the Wilderness, and prepared to take the offensive the next day; but Lee had likewise determined on attack. Both desiring the initiative, the battle was on at an early hour. It progressed with varying fortune, each force gaining successes at different moments, and at different parts of the line. At one time the Confederate right wing was driven back, and disaster seemed imminent, when Longstreet came up and saved the day. A Texas brigade of Longstreet's corps went forward to the charge, and Lee, who like his exemplar Washington was an eager warrior, and loved the noise and excitement of battle, spurred onward his horse, and, intensely anxious for the result, started to follow the Texans as they advanced in regular order. He was recognized, and from the entire line came the cry, "Go back, General Lee! go back!" This movement of the Confederates was stopped by the wounding of Longstreet by a shot from his own men, an accident similiar to that by which Stonewall Jackson one year before had received his mortal hurt.

The fighting of these two days is called the Battle of the Wilderness. Both generals claimed the advantage; both were disappointed in the result. Grant, who had expected that the passage of the Rapidan and turning of the right of the Confederates would compel them to fall back, had hoped to march through the Wilderness unopposed, fight them in more open country, and inflict upon them a heavy blow. Lee, in no way daunted because Grant had taken command in person of the Army of the Potomac, thought, undoubtedly, that his victories in the West had been due more to the lack of skill of his opponents than to able generalship, and had hoped to beat Grant as he had beaten McClellan, Pope, Burnside, and Hooker, drive him back across the Rapidan, and constrain him, like his predecessors, to abandon his campaign. Measured by casualties, the Confederates came the nearer to victory. The Union loss was 17,666; that of the Confederates was certainly less, although an accurate report of it is lacking. It is stated as half, and, again, as nearly two-thirds of that of the Federals. The Army of the Potomac had the death of the brave General Wadsworth to deplore.

May 7 neither general showed a disposition to attack. Grant decided to continue the movement by the left, and march by night to Spotsylvania Court House. His army started without knowing whether or not it had been beaten, but aware of the great slaughter; and when they came to the parting of the ways, the question in all minds arose, would the orders be to turn northward and recross the river? The columns filed to the right, the faces of the men were set towards Richmond, and Grant, in their estimation, was exalted. The soldiers sang and stepped forward with elastic tread. "The spirits of men and officers are of the highest pitch of animation," was the word which Dana sent Stanton. Grant rode by, and in spite of the darkness was recognized. The men burst out into cheers, swung their hats, clapped their hands, threw up their arms, and greeted their general as a comrade. They were glad that he was leading them onward to Richmond instead of ordering them to fall back to the camp which they had just abandoned.

The Confederate soldiers, believing in their invincibility on their own soil, thought that Grant, like the other Federal generals, would give it up and fall back; and Lee at one time held the opinion that he was retiring on Fredericksburg. But the Confederate general was too sagacious to base his entire action on one supposition, and surmising that Grant might move to Spotsylvania, he sent thither part of his force, which, having the shorter and easier line of march, reached there first, and took position across the path of the Union army. The armies coming in contact, there were several days of fighting; at times raging and bloody battles, again naught but skirmishing and the firing of sharpshooters. It was on a day of this desultory work when Sedgwick, the commander of the Sixth Corps, fell. He was mourned by both friend and foe. May 11 Grant sent his celebrated despatch to Halleck. "We have now ended the sixth day of very heavy fighting. . . . I . . . propose to fight it out on this line if it takes all summer." After the furious battle the next day at the Salient—"the bloody angle"—there was a lull, due principally to the heavy and constant rains, which made the roads deep with mud and impassable. It is true, however, that the Union army needed rest, and that Grant was desirous of reinforcements to fill the gaps in his ranks caused by his heavy losses. In these battles at Spotsylvania he was almost invariably the attacking party; he assailed in front the Confederates, whose intrenchments, defended by rifled muskets and by artillery throughout, quadrupled their strength. It is said that the hurling of his men against Lee in chosen and fortified positions was unnecessary, as the roads in number and in direction lent themselves to the operation of turning either flank of the Confederate army. "To assault 'all along the line,' " writes General Walker, "as was so often done in the summer of 1864, is the very abdication of leadership." But Grant was essentially an aggressive soldier, and an important feature of his plan of operations was, as he himself has stated it, "to hammer continually against the armed force of the enemy and his resources until by mere attrition, if in no other way," the South should be subdued. Circumstances similar to the one which occurred in the Wilderness are to be noted. On May 10, and again on the 12th, at the fight at the "bloody angle," when the Confederates were on the verge of disaster, Lee rode to the head of a column, intending to lead a charge which he deemed might be necessary to save the day. On both occasions the soldiers refused to advance unless their general should go to the rear. Lee did not court danger, and was apparently reckless in the one case only after his lines had been broken, and in the other when the struggle for the Salient demanded the utmost from general and men. It is worthy of record that such incidents in the life of Lee did not take place until Grant came to direct the movements of the Army of the Potomac.

May 18 Grant attacked again, but failed to carry the Confederate intrenchments. On the next day part of Lee's force in making a demonstration was met and repulsed. Several days later Grant crossed the North Anna River. Lee, concentrating his troops, interposed them between the two wings of the Union army, which were widely separated, and could reinforce neither the other without passing over the river twice. "Grant," write Nicolay and Hay, "was completely checkmated." Lee begrudged every step Grant took towards Richmond, and had

planned now to assume the offensive, when he fell ill. He declared impatiently on his sick-bed in his tent, "We must strike
them, we must never let them pass us again;" but before he had
recovered sufficiently to take personal charge of an attack,
Grant, "finding the enemy's position on the North Anna
stronger than either of his previous ones," withdrew, unmo-
lested, to the north bank of the river. Meanwhile Butler, with
an army, was moving up the James River, and, taking the Confederates by surprise, occupied, without opposition, City Point
and Bermuda Hundred. It was in the chances that a skilful and
daring general might have captured Petersburg or Richmond.
Butler was neither, and dallied while Beauregard energetically
gathered together the loose forces in North and South Carolina,
and brought them to the defence of the two places. The result
of his operations is thus accurately related by Grant: "His
[Butler's] army, therefore, though in a position of great security, was as completely shut off from further operations directly
against Richmond as if it had been in a bottle strongly corked."

Marching forward, and fighting on the way, Grant, by June
2, had gone a considerable distance farther south, had reached
the ground which one wing of McClellan's army had occupied
in May and June, 1862, and was in position near the scene of
Fitz John Porter's gallant fight of Gaines's Mill, almost in sight
of the spires of the Confederate capital. Lee, about six miles
from the exterior fortifications of Richmond, held a position
naturally strong, which by intrenchments he had made practically impregnable. Flanking movements being apparently at an
end, Grant, with unjustifiable precipitation, ordered an assault
in front. This was made at 4:30 in the morning of June 3, and
constituted the Battle of Cold Harbor, the greatest blemish on
his reputation as a general. The order having at first been given
for the attack on the afternoon of the 2d, and then postponed
for the morrow, officers and men had a chance to chew upon it,
and both knew that the undertaking was hopeless. Horace Porter, an aide-de-camp of Grant, relates that when walking among
the troops on staff duty the evening before the battle, he noticed

many soldiers of one of the regiments designated for the assault pinning on the back of their coats slips of paper on which were written their names and home addresses, so that their dead bodies might be rocognized on the field, and their fate be known to their families at the North.

The soldiers sprang promptly to the assault. The history of Hancock's corps, the Second, is an epitome of the action. In about twenty-two minutes its repulse was complete. It had "lost over 3000 of its bravest and best, both of officers and men." The true story of the day is told by General Lee: At one part of the Confederate line the Federals were "repulsed without difficulty;" at another, having penetrated a salient, they were driven out "with severe loss," at still another their "repeated attacks . . . were met with great steadiness and repulsed in every instance. The attack extended to our extreme left . . . with like results." Thus he concluded his despatch: "Our loss to-day has been small, and our success, under the blessing of God, all that we could expect." The casualties in the Union army were probably 7000. Grant at that time regretted the attack, as he did also near the close of his life, when he gave expression to his perpetual regret in his Personal Memoirs. "No advantage whatever," he added, "was gained to compensate for the heavy loss we sustained." After the Battle of Cold Harbor he determined to move his army south of the James, and June 12 took up his march, the advance corps reaching the river on the next night.

The loss of Grant from May 4 to June 12 in the campaign from the Rapidan to the James was 54,929, a number nearly equal to Lee's whole army at the commencement of the Union advance; that of the Confederates is not known, but it was certainly very much less. Nor do the bare figures tell the whole story. Of this enormous loss the flower of the Army of the Potomac contributed a disproportionate share. Fighting against such odds of position and strategy, the high-spirited and capable officers were in the thick of danger, and of the rank and file the veterans were always at the front: they were the forlorn hope. The bounty-jumpers and mercenaries skulked to the rear. The morale of the soldiers was much lower than on the day when, in high spirits, they had crossed the Rapidan. The confidence in Grant of many officers and of most of the men had been shaken.

In the judgment of many military critics, Grant had not been equal to his opportunities, had not made the best use of his advantages, and had secured no gain commensurate with his loss. Yet the friends of McClellan who maintain that because McClellan reached the same ground near Richmond with comparatively little sacrifice of life, his campaign had the greater merit, miss the main point of the situation, that the incessant hammering of Lee's army was a necessary concomitant of success. They attach to the capture of the Confederate capital the subjugation of the South, ignoring that Grant was supremely right in making Lee's army his first objective and Richmond only his second. His strategy was superior to McClellan's in that he grasped the aim of the war, and resolutely and grimly stuck to his purpose in spite of defeats and losses which would have dismayed any but the stoutest soul; and criticism of him is not sound unless it proves, as perhaps it does, that there might have been the same persistent fighting of the Army of Northern Virginia without so great a slaughter of Northern soldiers. The case is certainly stronger for Grant if we compare his work even thus far with the operations of Pope, Burnside, and Hooker. As for Meade, his name is so gratefully associated with the magnificent victory of Gettysburg that our judgment leans in his favor, and would fain rate at the highest his achievements; but it is difficult to see aught that he did afterwards in independent command towards bringing the war to a close. If the narrative be anticipated, and the comparison be made of Grant's total losses to the day on which he received the surrender of Lee's army, with the combined losses of the rest of the commanders of the Army of the Potomac, the result arrived at is that his aggregate was less than theirs, and his was the great achievement. The military literature of the South directly and by implication breathes a constant tribute to the effectiveness of his plan and his execution of it. It must not, however, be forgotten that McClellan and Meade had weakened in some measure the power of resistance of the Army of Northern Virginia.

NOBODY *in the North, no matter what his party or political creed, thought for a moment, as 1864 dawned, of postponing the presidential election; the Republicans, who were certain to renominate Lincoln, and the Democrats, who were almost certain to nominate George B. McClellan, would fight it out just as if peace reigned. But down to the last few weeks it seemed a highly uncertain contest. For one reason, the prestige of the President rested largely upon the progress that the armed forces were making toward final victory, and until late summer that progress was discouragingly slow. For another reason, both major parties were so deeply divided that it was difficult to measure their strength. In the Republican ranks the radical element, demanding harsh terms of peace and reconstruction, and condemning the administration for what impatient men termed its slowness, stood earnestly opposed to the moderate or conservative element; many of its leaders would gladly have discarded Lincoln altogether. On the Democratic side the War Democrats, who wished to fight stubbornly for the restoration of the Union, were bitterly opposed by the Peace Democrats, who stood for negotiations with the Confederacy and a compromise peace. Many of the Peace Democrats were almost as antagonistic to McClellan as to Lincoln, especially after Little Mac repudiated a defeatist plank in the platform.*

The capture of Atlanta by Sherman at the beginning of September and the victory of Sheridan at Cedar Creek in Virginia on October 19 marked a turn in the tide of public sentiment. Victory was coming within sight; the assertion of the Democratic platform that the war was a failure seemed increasingly fatuous. The government took action that ensured a vote for many soldiers in the field, and most of them voted for Lincoln. On election day, November 8, he was returned to power by a four-hundred-thousand popular majority and an overwhelming lead in the electoral college.

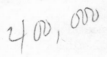

The Re-election of Lincoln

McCLELLAN accepted the nomination of the Democrats, but repudiated the pivotal resolution of their platform. Grant furnished a strong campaign document, in a private letter to E. B. Washburne, written August 16, but not published until twenty-four days later. "I state to all citizens who visit me," he wrote, "that all we want now to insure an early restoration of the Union is a determined unity of sentiment North. The rebels have now in their ranks their last man. The little boys and old men are guarding prisoners, guarding railroad bridges, and forming a good part of their garrisons for entrenched positions. A man lost by them cannot be replaced. They have robbed the cradle and the grave equally to get their present force. Besides what they lose in frequent skirmishes and battles, they are now losing, from desertions and other causes, at least one regiment per day. With this drain upon them the end is not far distant, if we will only be true to ourselves. Their only hope now is in a divided North. This might give them reinforcements from Tennessee, Kentucky, Maryland, and Missouri, while it would weaken us. With the draft quickly enforced, the enemy would become despondent, and would make but little resistance. I have no doubt but the enemy are exceedingly anxious to hold out until after the presidential election. They have many hopes from its effects. They hope a counter-revolution; they hope the election of the Peace candidate. In fact, like 'Micawber,' they hope for something to 'turn up.' Our Peace friends, if they expect peace from separation, are much mistaken. It would but be the beginning of war with thousands of Northern men joining the South because of our disgrace in allowing separation. To have 'peace on any terms,' the South would demand the restoration of their slaves already freed; they would demand indemnity for losses sustained, and they would demand a treaty which would make the North slave-hunters for the South. They would demand pay for the restoration of every slave escaping to the North."

Vol. IV, pp. 525–39.

The State elections in Vermont and Maine, during the first half of September, showed that the disaffection with the administration was small, and indicated a favorable result for Lincoln in November.

During the month of August, Sheridan, who, it will be remembered, had been placed in command of the army in the Shenandoah valley, accomplished no positive results, but in his marches and countermarches, in his advance and retreat, he was learning the ground and studying his adversary. Grant, watching all the movements, and alive to the importance of the valley, paid his lieutenant a visit, September 15, and gave him an order in the two words, "Go in!" Four days later Sheridan gained a brilliant victory over Early at Winchester, announcing it in these words to Grant: "I attacked the forces of General Early . . . and after a most stubborn and saguinary engagement, which lasted from early in the morning until five o'clock in the evening, completely defeated him, and, driving him through Winchester, captured about 2500 prisoners, 5 pieces of artillery, 9 army flags, and most of their wounded." September 20 Lincoln sent this hearty message to Sheridan: "Have just heard of your great victory. God bless you all, officers and men." The Confederates "rallied and made a stand in a strong position at Fisher's Hill," where Sheridan again attacked them and put them to rout. "I achieved a most signal victory over the army of General Early at Fisher's Hill to-day," he telegraphed to Grant, September 22; ". . . only darkness has saved the whole of Early's army from total destruction. My attack could not be made until four o'clock in the evening, which left but little daylight to operate in. . . . The victory was very complete."

These victories of Sheridan appealed to the popular imagination, as had those of Stonewall Jackson in 1862; but now it was the North which rejoiced that the commander who united dash and prudence was on their side, giving them long-wished-for but unexpected victories in the Shenandoah valley, which had been the death of so many hopes, and the open door to the invasions of the North. What campaign speeches were Sheridan's despatches, telling the stories of Winchester and Fisher's Hill! How they contrasted with the declaration of the Chicago platform that there had been "four years of failure to restore the Union by the experiment of war," and with its demand that there should be "a cessation of hostilities"! While such victories are gained, said one citizen to another as they shook hands and rejoiced, the war is not a failure; and victors in such battles do not ask for an armistice.

The political campaign was now prosecuted with vigor. Secretary Seward, in a brief speech at Washington, said, "Sherman and Farragut have knocked the bottom out of the Chicago nominations." Chase, who during July and August had been sulky and wavering, and had sneered at the President, now announced his support of Lincoln, went on the stump, and made effective speeches for the Union candidate. Dickson wrote: "I make no doubt of Lincoln's triumphant election." Whitelaw Reid, in a newspaper despatch from Washington, said that the radicals had returned to their old allegiance, and would fight in the van. *
Governor Andrew, in a private letter, wrote that the plain duty for them as practical men was to give to Lincoln their energetic support. The tide having turned, the President helped the movement with the art of the politician. The sixth resolution of the Union National Convention virtually called for the removal of Montgomery Blair from the cabinet. During the gloomy

* To the St. Louis *Democrat*, Sept. 21: "A private letter received here to-day from one of the prominent leaders in the radical movement now abandoned for another convention in Cincinnati, says: 'The conditions under which that call was issued were the general apathy and discontent, and the apparent certainty of Mr. Lincoln's defeat. All this is changed. The outrage on the nation perpetrated at Chicago, the fall of Atlanta, the success of the cause in Vermont and Maine, render that impossible and unreasonable which then seemed our only safety. We must now place ourselves in the van of the fight; we shall not enjoy its honors, but we will do what we may to save the country; it shall not be said of us that we have played in this contest the part of Fitz John Porter at the Second Battle of Bull Run.' This statement, I have reason to know, fairly represents the views of the entire body of earnest Unionists with and for whom he has been acting, from Ben Wade and Winter Davis down. Whoever among our foes counts on disaffection or lukewarmness in our ranks in the coming contest reckons without his host."—New York *Sun,* June 30, 1889.

summer, when everything seemed going wrong, when a smaller man would have complied with this demand, Lincoln did nothing, knowing that such an effort would be compared to the drowning man clutching at straws. But when the current began to run in his favor, he was willing to make assurance doubly sure by lending himself to a bargain which should win the support of the still disaffected radicals who had placed Frémont in nomination, and of Wade and Davis, the authors of the manifesto and the most bitter of his opponents, who had influence and a considerable following. Frémont was withdrawn from the field, and the President was to request the resignation of Blair. The bargain was faithfully carried out. Frémont's letter of withdrawal to do his "part toward preventing the election of the Democratic candidate" was published in the evening journals of September 22, and the next day the President requested the resignation of Blair.

To seal such a bargain was not a dignified proceeding on the part of the President of the United States, but it was a politic move. When we take into account the history of the candidacies of third parties, the earnest following of Frémont, and the estimated closeness of the vote in certain important States, the political shrewdness of Lincoln will be apparent. To consolidate the Republican party against its old-time opponent, to secure the energetic service of Wade on the stump, and the silence of Henry Winter Davis by a concession which had in it nothing of dishonor, and involved no injury to the public service, was a course to be adopted, without hesitation, by a master politician. Blair, with generosity and patriotism, made the sacrifice, and began at once to speak publicly and labor earnestly for the re-election of Lincoln. The Union and Republican party, being now united, made an aggressive fight. Their epigrammatic interpretation of the Democratic platform, Resolved that the war is a failure, was put forth on all occasions with the taunt that Farragut, Sherman, Sheridan, and Grant had made this declaration forever and completely false; for Grant, the general of all the armies, shone in the reflected glory of his two lieutenants. Nothing could be more effective with the mass of the people than the contrast of these words of despair, written out carefully by Vallandigham, the most unpopular man of eminence in the country, with the victories on sea and land won by the ability and persistence of the admiral and generals who had been sustained by the hopefulness of the President and the people. In vain did Robert C. Winthrop argue, "If anybody is disposed to cavil with you about your platform, tell him that General McClellan has made his own platform, and that it is broad enough and comprehensive enough for every patriot in the land to stand upon." His supporters for the presidency, Winthrop continued, are not "scared from their position by any paper pellets of the brain, wise or otherwise, which ever came from the midnight sessions of a resolution committee in the hurly-burly of a National Convention." But the record could not be blotted out. The salient resolution of the Democratic platform, or the epitome of it uttered every day by every Union newspaper and stump-speaker in all the villages, towns, and cities, was a damning argument which could not be overthrown. By way of parrying it, the Democrats glorified the generalship of McClellan, and made much of the alleged ill treatment of him by Lincoln, Stanton, and Halleck, when he was in command of the Army of the Potomac. During July and August, when military reverses were the food of reflection, there was a point to these arguments; but the glory of Antietam paled when compared with the Atlanta campaign and the victories of Sheridan in the Shenandoah. The desperate character of the canvass for McClellan led the New York *World,* the ablest and most influential Democratic journal of the country, into an unworthy line of argument. Not content with the general charges of the "ignorance, incompetency, and corruption of Mr. Lincoln's administration," it cast imputations upon the personal honesty of the President. It asked the questions: "Mr. Lincoln, has he or has he not an interest in the profits of public contracts?" "Is Mr. Lincoln honest?" and gave these answers: "That Lincoln had succumbed to the . . . opportunities and temptations of his present place is capable of the easiest proof," and "This claim of honesty will not bear examination." Again it made this assertion, " 'Honest Old Abe' has few honest men to defend his honesty." If anything in history be true, not only was there no just ground at this time for the slightest suspicions of the personal integrity of Lincoln, but it is, furthermore, certain that no more honest man than he ever lived.

From such campaign slanders it is agreeable to turn to the speeches of Horatio Seymour and Robert C. Winthrop, who advocated the election of a gentleman of honor in manner and words befitting their own high characters. At the end of the campaign, Winthrop quoted the injunction of an English orator and statesman, that "we should so be patriots as not to forget that we are gentlemen"; and while there may have been a tinge of sarcasm in this allusion, he himself did not depart from the rule by a hair. Paying tribute to the strongest sentiment in the country at that time, love for the Union, both Seymour and Winthrop tried to impress it upon their hearers that the restoration of the Union would be more surely and quickly accomplished under the Democrats than by a continuance of the administration of Lincoln; and both gave their adherence to the party cry, "The Constitution as it is, and the Union as it was." "Good Heavens!" exclaimed Winthrop, "what are we fighting for?" Both urged with force that Lincoln's "To Whom it may Concern" letter, in insisting upon the abandonment of slavery made an uneccessary and insuperable condition to the re-establishment of the Union, and both expressed their sincere belief that the Republican policy of emancipation and subjugation was an effectual hindrance to the pacification of the South.

It is perhaps unnecessary to say that the historian whose faith is in the anti-slavery cause can have no sympathy with the main line of Seymour's and Winthrop's arguments, but he will be recreant to his duty should he leave the impression that he approves the doctrine that in the stress of the nation criticism of the faults of the administration should be silent. Believing, as he must, from the political literature of the day and the sequence of events, that the good of the country and the good of mankind demanded the re-election of Lincoln, and that Seymour and Winthrop had chosen the wrong part, he may rejoice that on collateral points they spoke words of warning and of wisdom on which lovers of our country will do well to ponder. Seymour mentioned "the frauds and failures that in an unusual degree have marked the conduct of affairs during the last three and a half years. I do not mean to say," he continued, "that the administration is to be condemned because, under circumstances so unusual as those which have existed during this war, bad men have taken advantage of the confusion in affairs to do acts of wrong. But I do complain that when these wrongs are done, the government deliberately passes laws that protect the doer, and thus makes wrongdoing its own act. Moreover, in an election like this, when the government is spending such an enormous amount of money, and the liability to peculation is so great, the administration that will say to contractors, as has been openly said in circulars: 'You have had a good contract, out of which you have made money, and we expect you to use a part of that money to assist to replace us in power,' renders itself a partner in fraud and corruption. The contractor will say to this government: 'You shall not make a peace that shall put an end to all my profits.' " "The Republican party," declared Winthrop, "have so thriven and fattened on this rebellion, and it has brought them such an overflowing harvest of power, patronage, offices, contracts, and spoils, and they have become so enamoured of the vast and overshadowing influence which belongs to an existing administration at such an hour, that they are in danger of forgetting that their country is bleeding and dying on their hands."

Worthy of note, too, is what both Seymour and Winthrop said, respecting the suppression of newspapers and arbitrary arrests. "In Great Britain," asserted Seymour, "the humblest hut in the kingdom, although it may be open to the winds and rains of heaven, is to the occupant a castle impregnable even to the monarch, while in our country the meanest and most unworthy underling of power is licensed to break within the sacred precincts of our homes." "When martial law," said Winthrop, "is deliberately and permanently substituted for almost every other kind of law; when it is promulgated and enforced in places and under circumstances where it has no relation whatever to military affairs; when this extreme medicine of government is adopted and administered as its daily bread; when we see persons arrested and imprisoned . . . without examination or trial; . . . when we see newspapers silenced and suppressed at the tinkling of an Executive bell, a thousand miles away from the scene of hostilities; . . . when we hear those who have solemnly sworn to support the Constitution, proclaiming a prospective and permanent policy in utter disregard and defiance of that great charter of free government, and deriding and denouncing all who are for holding fast to it as it is,—who can help being alarmed for the future?" *

The speeches of Winthrop and Seymour, however logical in appearance and finished in expression, were answered in the common mind by the bulletins of Sherman and Sheridan, the decline in gold and in the necessaries of life, and the advance in price and continued large purchase of our bonds in Germany. But persons given to reflection, who liked to see argument met

* Winthrop wrote in a private letter, Oct. 23: "The McClellan managers think so well of my New London speech that they have had it stereotyped, and besides my own edition, 200,000 copies are being circulated as campaign documents. My nomination at the head of the Democratic electoral ticket in this State was without my knowledge, but, feeling as I did, I could not refuse it, though I was sorry to be placed in a sort of antagonistic position to Everett" (who was at the head of the Union ticket.)—*Memoir,* p. 258. He wrote, Dec. 10: "I dined yesterday with William Amory—the Friday Club—all of whom, as it turned out, had voted McClellan except Agassiz and Chief Justice Bigelow. Caleb Cushing was there as a guest, but his politics I doubt if any one can accurately define except himself. He and I walked home together about midnight, when he volunteered the remark that my New London speech was the most effective one on that side, and that if McClellan's cause had been uniformly advocated in the same spirit, and the campaign run on those lines, he might have been triumphantly elected. I had already learned, on good authority, that both Lincoln and Seward had expressed a substantially similar opinion, which I consider one of the greatest compliments ever paid me, there being no better judges of the ability of campaign speeches than these three men."— *Ibid.,* p. 261.

by argument, found matter to their satisfaction in the campaign speeches of Carl Schurz, which, though not seemingly purposed as a direct answer to Winthrop and Seymour, shook their positions, demonstrating clearly and cogently the necessity for the re-election of Lincoln. Schurz maintained that the evidence was abundant and clear that the Confederates would not come back on the basis of reunion; that "the recognition of the independence of the Confederacy was a condition *sine quâ non* for all peace negotiations;" and that the Democratic argument, "while the rebel government is for war the Southern people are for peace," although specious, was in reality destitute of foundation. The sentiment which pervaded Winthrop's and Seymour's speeches he showed to be merely a "vague impression . . . that the union and universal good feeling may be restored by a policy of conciliation and compromise." But nothing could be clearer than that the only course to be pursued was to fight the war out. "We went into the war," he declared, "for the purpose of maintaining the Union and preserving our nationality. . . . Gradually it became clear to every candid mind that slavery untouched constituted the strength of the rebellion, but that slavery touched would constitute its weakness. . . . It became a question of life or death—the death of the nation or the death of slavery. Then the government chose. It chose the life of the nation by the death of slavery. . . . As soon as a man throws his whole heart into the struggle for the Union, he throws, at the same time, his whole heart into the struggle against slavery." It is useless to talk of restoring the Union as it was. "Thank God, it is impossible" to revive slavery.

"There is not, now, the slightest uncertainty about the re-election of Mr. Lincoln," wrote Chase to John Sherman, October 2. "The only question is, by what popular and what electoral majority. God grant that both may be so decisive as to turn every hope of rebellion to despair!"

October 11 State and congressional elections took place in Pennsylvania, Ohio, and Indiana. Ohio went Union by a majority of 54,751; Indiana gave Morton, for governor, 20,883 more votes than were received by his Democratic opponent, and all three States made material gains in Union members of Congress. These elections manifested a tendency of public opinion which gave an almost unerring indication of the election of Lincoln in November. Sheridan conveyed an augmented force to the movement, and infused enthusiasm into the last weeks of the canvass. In a despatch to Grant, at ten in the evening of October 19, he thus tells the story: "My army at Cedar Creek was attacked this morning before daylight, and my left was turned and driven in confusion; in fact, most of the line was driven in confusion with the loss of twenty pieces of artillery. I hastened from Winchester, where I was on my return from Washington, and found the armies between Middletown and Newtown, having been driven back about four miles. I here took the affair in hand, and quickly united the corps, formed a compact line of battle just in time to repulse an attack of the enemy, which was handsomely done at about 1 P.M. At 3 P.M., after some changes of the cavalry from the left to the right flank, I attacked, with great vigor, driving and routing the enemy, capturing, according to the last report, forty-three pieces of artillery and very many prisoners. . . . Affairs at times looked badly, but by the gallantry of our brave officers and men disaster has been converted into a splendid victory."

"With great pleasure," telegraphed Lincoln to Sheridan, "I tender to you and your brave army the thanks of the nation, and my own personal admiration and gratitude for the month's operations in the Shenandoah valley; and especially for the splendid work of October 19, 1864." "The nation rings with praises of Phil Sheridan," said the Chicago *Tribune*. In New York City his exploit was "recited in prose and chanted in verse." The most famous poem called forth by the battle was "Sheridan's Ride," written on the impulse of the moment by Thomas Buchanan Read, and delivered immediately after it was written to a large audience in Cincinnati by James E. Murdoch, a retired actor and celebrated reader, whose declamation in the dramatic style eight days before the election stirred the crowd and served as effective last words of the political campaign.

November 8 the presidential election took place. Lincoln carried States sufficient to give him 212 electoral votes, while McClellan would receive only 21,—those of New Jersey, Delaware, and Kentucky. In but one large State, New York, was there a close contest; Lincoln had a majority of the popular vote, in the whole country, of 494,567. Another result of the elections of the year was that enough Republican and Unionist members of the House of Representatives had been elected to insure the requisite majority of two-thirds for the constitutional amendment abolishing slavery.

"I give you joy of the election," wrote Emerson to a friend. "Seldom in history was so much staked on a popular vote. I suppose never in history." "I thought that I should have much to say about the result of the election," wrote Motley from Vienna to his daughter. "But I am, as it were, struck dumb. The more than realization of my highest hopes leaves me with no power of expression except to repeat over and over again,—

O Grosser Gott in Staube danke ich dir.

Even with the wealth of experience which his country's history has since furnished him, the historian can add nothing to the fervor of these expressions of men who lived in the spirit. In the first election of Lincoln, the people of the North had spoken, had declared their antagonism to slavery; did they remain true to their highest aspirations, they could not turn back, but must go forward. In spite of burdensome taxation, weariness of the war, and mourning in every household, they decided on this election day of 1864 to finish the work they had begun.

*In mid-December, 1864, Thomas inflicted a crushing
defeat upon the Confederate forces under Hood in the
decisive battle of Nashville; on December 10, Sherman compelled Hardee to evacuate the city of Savannah; the Union lines about Petersburg and Richmond
were steadily tightening. Lee, forced upon the defensive, saw his supplies of food, arms, and ammunition more and more seriously depleted. He was made
general-in-chief of the Confederate armies on February 6, 1865, but the Confederate situation was then
beyond rescue. Rhodes ably tells the story of his final
retreat and surrender. Then hard on the heels of victory came the great tragedy of the conflict—the murder of Lincoln.*

Appomattox and the
Assassination of Lincoln

AT an early hour April 3 a brigade of the Ninth Corps, Army of
the Potomac, took possession of Petersburg, and the President,
who was still at City Point, telegraphed to Stanton that he was
going to the front to see General Grant. The despatch drew
from the Secretary these anxious words: "Allow me respectfully
to ask you to consider whether you ought to expose the nation to
the consequence of any disaster to yourself in the pursuit of a
treacherous and dangerous enemy like the rebel army." In the
afternoon Lincoln replied: "Thanks for your caution but I have
already been to Petersburg. Stayed with General Grant an hour
and a half and returned here. It is certain now that Richmond
is in our hands and I think I will go there tomorrow. I will take
care of myself."

Although at different times since February 20 alarm had been
felt for the fate of the capital, the Richmond newspapers for
four days preceding the evacuation gave no idea of the impending disaster. "Failure," said the *Whig* of March 30, "attends
Grant in all his plans and enterprises." The Richmond *Dispatch*

appeared Saturday, April 1 for the last time in the Southern
Confederacy. This Journal for that day and previously and the
other journals for March 29, 30, 31 convey the impression that
matters in the city were going on much the same as for many
months past. The advertisements in their columns indicate a
fairly permanent state of society in which plans pertaining to
the common affairs of life are laid ahead. Candidates put themselves forward in "election notices" for the different offices at
the next municipal election and beg the support of their fellow-citizens. A teacher of music, a dressmaker and a chiropodist
ask for business patronage. There are marriage and death notices, even "personals." In the country is wanted a teacher "competent to teach the English language." Houses and rooms are
advertised to rent. March 21 Jones notes "many red flags"
which are auction notices "for sales of furniture and the renting
of houses to the highest bidders." The owners he says have postponed offering their property "until the last moment" in order
to take advantage of some favourable turn in affairs to realize
the "extortionate prices" that they demanded. He thinks they
will get what they ask on account "of Johnston's success,* which
revives the conviction that Richmond will not be evacuated."
The *Dispatch* of April 1 advertises real estate for sale, an auction of 1000 books to take place Wednesday, April 5, and other
auctions on several days of the coming week. March 30, the
mayor's court deals with petty offences; and in a higher court a
man convicted of "voluntary manslaughter" is sent to the peni-
tentiary for three years. Regular trains for Danville and Lynchburg are announced as late as April 1, and there are other indications of travellers arriving from the South; but three days
earlier the notice of trains northward on the Richmond and
Potomac Railroad failed to appear in the *Dispatch*. Of the six
or seven hotels only two—the Spotswood and American—remained open. Public entertainments continue as usual. If you
are charitably disposed you can go to a concert at St. James's

---

* At Bentonville, a temporary success which was exaggerated in the
Confederacy.

church for the benefit of the orphans. The Richmond theatre is open, the play being a dramatization of "Aurora Floyd," and other attractions are promised for next week. At another place of amusement "Budd and Buckley's Minstrels and Brass Band" are "received nightly with shouts of applause"; but here is a reminder of the cordon drawing around the Confederacy in the notice ending, "Highest price paid for old and new cork at the hall." The most curious advertisements are those connected with the institution of slavery. There is printed a list of slaves, thirty-nine in number, remaining at the Eastern District Military prison, Richmond. Rewards offered for the return of runaway slaves are common. Besides those of the usual sort in the time of peace are some growing out of the state of war. One owner offers "$5000 reward for the capture of sixteen negroes who ran off from my plantation in Buckingham . . . for the purpose of joining the enemy in his recent raid"; another desires information of "three negro boys seized and carried off by the Yankees." Yet there are many still in bonds. Slaves are offered for hire, a characteristic notice being, "For hire, a negro woman, a good washer and ironer for the remainder of the year." There are persons willing to exchange their Confederate paper money for negroes. Advertisements frequently appearing from two different parties are, "Wanted to purchase a good cook." Other property owners are willing to sell their slaves. One notice runs "For sale privately, a qualified servant woman, twenty-eight years old with three healthy children. . . . The woman is a No. 1 house servant, fine seamstress and sold for no fault." There is still considerable buying and selling, writes Jones in his Diary of March 22, for what are called "dollars," and although slave property is manifestly precarious "yet a negro man will bring $10,000 at auction" which, however, is equivalent to only about $100 in coin.

The newspapers during these last days of the Confederacy furnish striking instances of devotion to the declining cause. Under authority of a joint resolution of Congress the Secretary of the Treasury asked for contributions to the public treasury, and received a noteworthy response. He himself gave $100,000 in bonds and the same amount in currency and Benjamin, the Secretary of State, gave $7500 in bonds. A North Carolina soldier's wife contributed her mite of $50 in Confederate money (worth about fifty cents in silver). A gentleman of North Carolina sent a diamond ring and $221.40 in coin. Some North Carolina and Virginia women gave their jewels and silver plate. In reading the list of articles of use and of ornament, one may imagine that among them were keepsakes, family presents and many trifling objects dear to womankind. In itself it is a prosaic roll, but as each little thing is the symbol of tears and of hopes it is impossible to read it without emotion.

As late as April 1, Davis apparently thought that there was no immediate necessity for the abandonment of Richmond. On the morning of the 2d, which was Sunday, he was at St. Paul's listening to the noble liturgy of the Episcopal Church, when the clergyman was reading for the last time in his ministry the prayer for the President of the Confederate States. Here Davis was apprised by a messenger from the War Department of the gravity of the military situation. He left his pew quietly and walked out of the church with dignity, learning soon the contents of Lee's despatch which gave an account of his disaster and advised that Richmond be abandoned. The news spread rapidly, and so unexpectedly had it come upon the city that the greatest confusion and excitement prevailed as functionaries and citizens made ready for flight. Davis with all the members of his cabinet except Breckinridge, a number of his staff and other officials, got away at eleven o'clock in the evening on a train of the Richmond and Danville Railroad and reached Danville the next afternoon in safety. Under a previous order of Lee Ewell who was in command of the troops in Richmond directed that the tobacco in the city should be burned and that all stores which could not be removed should be destroyed. It is probable that the fires lighted in pursuance of this order spread to shops and houses and it is certain that a mob of both sexes and colours in the early morning of April 3 set fire to buildings and "began to plunder the city." Ewell says in his report that by daylight the riot was subdued and Jones writes that at seven o'clock in the morning men went to the liquor shops in execution of an order of the city government and commanded that the spirits be poured into the streets. The gutters ran with liquor from which pitchers and buckets were filled by black and white women and boys. By seven o'clock also the evacuation of Richmond by the Confederates had been completed.

The Union troops passed cautiously the first line of Confederate works but as they met with no opposition, they went by the next lines at a double-quick, and when the spires of the city came into view, they unfurled the national banner, and, their bands striking up "Rally round the flag," they sent up cheer on cheer as they marched in triumph through the streets. But they found confusion, an extensive conflagration, and a reign of pillage and disorder. Their commander Weitzel received the surrender of Richmond at the city hall at quarter past eight, and, by two o'clock in the afternoon they had quelled the tumult and put out the fires but not before a considerable portion of the city had been destroyed.

The Union soldiers were received by the white people gratefully and by the negroes with joy. Full of meaning was the visit of President Lincoln to Richmond which was made from City Point the next day in an unostentatious and careless manner and in utter disregard of Stanton's warning. Proper arrangements for his conveyance and escort had been made but, owing to two accidents the President completed his river journey in a twelve-oared barge and walked about a mile and a half through the streets of Richmond accompanied by Admiral Porter and three other officers with a guard of only ten sailors armed with carbines. He was received with demonstrations of joy by the negroes and, though the city was full of drunken Confederates, he met with neither molestation nor indignity. He went to the house which Davis had occupied as a residence, now the headquarters of Weitzel and, if we may believe some personal recollections, he looked about the house and sat in Davis's chair with boyish delight. Lincoln passed the night in Richmond and April 5 returned to City Point. Under that date Jones reported perfect order in the city and Dana telegraphed from Richmond, "*Whig* appeared yesterday as Union paper" and the "theatre opens here to-night."

Now the Confederates had evacuated Richmond and Petersburg during the night of April 2 and the early morning of the 3d. Grant without tarrying for a visit to Richmond set after them in hot pursuit. On the 4th he sent this despatch to Stanton from Wilson's Station: "The army is pushing forward in the hope of overtaking or dispersing the remainder of Lee's army. Sheridan with his cavalry and the Fifth Corps is between this and the Appomattox; General Meade with the Second and Sixth following; General Ord is following the line of the South Side Railroad." On the next day Sheridan reported that the "whole of Lee's army is at or near Amelia Court-House." Lee gives this account; "Upon arriving at Amelia Court-House on the morning of the 4th with the advance of the army, on the retreat from the lines in front of Richmond and Petersburg, and not finding the supplies ordered to be placed there, nearly twenty-four hours were lost in endeavoring to collect in the country subsistence for men and horses. This delay was fatal and could not be retrieved." On moving forward on the 5th, his troops, "wearied by continual fighting and marching" and not able to obtain rest or refreshment, found that Sheridan had possession of the Richmond and Danville Railroad which cut off their retreat to Danville, therefore they were ordered to march towards Lynchburg. From Jetersville Sheridan telegraphed Grant on the 5th, "From present indications the retreat of the enemy is rapidly becoming a rout;" but somewhat later he said, "I wish you were here yourself. I feel confident of capturing the Army of Northern Virginia if we exert ourselves. I see no escape for Lee." Grant with four of his staff and a mounted escort of fourteen men started at once to ride the sixteen miles which separated him from Sheridan. Darkness had come on and, his route lying through the woods, he did not reach Sheridan's camp until about half-past ten. As he and his companions picked their way to headquarters the awakened troopers, recognizing Grant, gave vent to their astonishment at the uncommon occurrence of the General-in-Chief appearing at that late hour so near the enemy's lines. "Why there's the old man," said one. "Boys this means business." "Great Scott!" exclaimed another, "the old chief's out here himself. The rebs are going to get busted to-morrow certain." Grant, having acquired from Sheridan a thorough knowledge of the situation, made a midnight visit to Meade and ordered the movements for the next day with the design of heading off Lee.

The result of the plans laid for April 6 is told best by Sheridan. At noon his report is, "the enemy are moving to our left with their trains and whole army." They "were moving all last night and are very short of provisions and very tired indeed. . . . They are reported to have begged provisions from the people of the country all along the road as they passed. I am working around farther to our left." Later in the same day he sent this word to Grant: "The enemy made a stand. . . . I attacked them with two divisions of the Sixth Army Corps, and routed them handsomely. . . . If the thing is pressed I think that Lee will surrender." Let Lee take up the story: "The army continued its march during the night [April 6] and every effort was made to reorganize the divisions which had been shattered by the day's operations; but the men being depressed by fatigue and hunger, many threw away their arms, while others followed the wagon trains and embarrassed their progress. On the morning of the 7th rations were issued to the troops as they passed Farmville, but the safety of the trains requiring their removal upon the approach of the enemy all could not be supplied. The army reduced to two corps under Longstreet and Gordon moved steadily on the road to Appomattox Court-House." Then Grant: "On the morning of the 7th the pursuit was renewed. . . . It was soon found that the enemy had crossed to the north side of the Appomattox; but so close was the pursuit that the Second Corps got possession of the common bridge at High Bridge before the enemy could destroy it and immediately crossed over.

The Sixth Corps and a division of cavalry crossed at Farmville to its support. Feeling now that General Lee's chance of escape was utterly hopeless I addressed him the following communication from Farmville: 'April 7. General: The result of the last week must convince you of the hopelessness of further resistance on the part of the Army of Northern Virginia in this struggle. I feel that it is so, and regard it as my duty to shift from myself the responsibility of any further effusion of blood, by asking of you the surrender of that portion of the C. S. army known as the Army of Northern Virginia.' " Lee replied inquiring what terms Grant would offer. To this communication came promptly the answer: "Peace being my great desire there is but one condition I would insist upon, namely, that the men and officers surrendered shall be disqualified for taking up arms again against the Government of the United States until properly exchanged." "Early on the morning of the 8th the pursuit was resumed," continues Grant. "General Meade followed north of the Appomattox and General Sheridan with all the cavalry pushed straight for Appomattox Station followed by General Ord's command and the Fifth Corps. During the day General Meade's advance had considerable fighting with the enemy's read guard but was unable to bring on a general engagement. Late in the evening General Sheridan struck the railroad at Appomattox Station, drove the enemy from there, and captured twenty-five pieces of artillery, a hospital train, and four trains of cars loaded with supplies for Lee's army."

Sheridan was alive to the situation; he telegraphed to Grant at twenty minutes past nine on the evening of the 8th, "we will perhaps finish the job in the morning. I do not think Lee means to surrender until compelled to do so." Lee gives this account of that day: "By great efforts the head of the column reached Appomattox Court-House on the evening of the 8th and the troops were halted for rest." Still clinging to the hope that he might yet escape, he wrote Grant in his second communication that he had not intended to propose the surrender of the Army of Northern Virginia, as in his opinion no such emergency had arisen, but that he would like to meet Grant to confer with him touching the restoration of peace. Grant was too wary to be entrapped in a fruitless negotiation which might serve for delay and replying, "I have no authority to treat on the subject of peace," pushed forward his operations. On the morning of April 9 Lee made "a desperate effort to break through" Sheridan's cavalry which had formed in his front across the road on which he must continue his march. Sheridan fell back gradually. General Ord, who with two corps had marched from daylight on the 8th until the morning of the 9th with a rest of only three hours, now deployed his men and barred the way of the Confederates. In order to learn whether or not his situation was hopeless Lee despatched one of his staff to Gordon who sent back this word: "Tell General Lee I have fought my corps to a frazzle and I fear I can do nothing unless I am heavily supported by Longstreet's corps." Longstreet was in the rear with Meade close upon him and not available for an attack in front. The Army of Northern Virginia was hemmed in and had no alternative but surrender. After receiving the message from Gordon, Lee was convinced and said: "Then there is nothing left me but to go and see General Grant and I would rather die a thousand deaths."

He ordered the white flag to be displayed, requested by letter a suspension of hostilities and an interview with Grant. The two generals met at McLean's house in the little village of Appomattox Court-House. Lee wore a new, full-dress uniform of Confederate gray "buttoned to the throat" and a handsome sword, the hilt of which was studded with jewels, while Grant had on "a blouse of dark-blue flannel unbuttoned in front" and carried no sword. "In my rough travelling suit," wrote Grant, "the uniform of a private with the straps of a lieutenant-general, I must have contrasted very strangely with a man so handsomely dressed, six feet high and of faultless form."* The two

---

* *Personal Memoirs*, vol. ii. p. 490. Porter writes that Lee's "hair and full beard were a silver gray." Cf. description in vol. iii. p. 411. Grant stooped slightly. "His hair and full beard were nut-brown without a trace of gray."—*Century Magazine*, Oct. 1897, p. 883. Lee was fifty-eight, Grant nearly forty-three.

generals had met while in the old army during the Mexican War, and Lee, fifteen years the senior and of higher rank, had made a distinct impression on Grant.

Twenty years later (1885) when he knew that what remained to him of life was but a span to be measured by weeks if not by days Grant wrote an account of this interview, giving us an insight into his soul which exacts our admiration and which we ought not to forget when in future pages we are contemplating another side of the man. "My own feelings," said Grant, "which had been quite jubilant on the receipt of Lee's letter were sad and depressed. I felt like anything rather than rejoicing at the downfall of a foe who had fought so long and valiantly. . . . We soon fell into a conversation about old army times. . . ." This "grew so pleasant that I almost forgot the object of our meeting." He was brought to the business in hand by Lee who suggested that he write out the terms on which he proposed to receive the surrender of the Army of Northern Virginia. Grant set down these conditions: "the officers to give their individual paroles not to take up arms against the Government of the United States until properly exchanged; and each company or regimental commander sign a like parole for the men of their commands. The arms, artillery and public property to be parked and stacked and turned over to the officers appointed by me to receive them. This will not embrace the sidearms of the officers nor their private horses or baggage. This done, each officer and man will be allowed to return to their homes, not to be disturbed by U. S. authority so long as they observe their paroles and the laws in force where they may reside." Grant tells us how he composed this letter: "When I put my pen to the paper I did not know the first word that I should make use of in writing the terms. I only knew what was in my mind and I wished to express it clearly so that there could be no mistaking it. As I wrote on the thought occurred to me that the officers had their own private horses and effects, which were important to them but of no value to us; also that it would be an unnecessary humiliation to call upon them to deliver their side-arms. . . .

When General Lee read over that part . . . he remarked with some feeling, I thought, that this would have a happy effect upon his army."

I shall continue the account of this interview from the article of Horace Porter which is written largely from contemporary memoranda. Shortly after Lee had read the proposition he said: " 'There is one thing I should like to mention. The cavalrymen and artillerists own their own horses in our army. Its organization in this respect differs from that of the United States. . . . I should like to understand whether these men will be permitted to retain their horses.'

" 'You will find that the terms as written do not allow this,' General Grant replied; 'only the officers are permitted to take their private property.'

"Lee read over the second page of the letter again, and then said: 'No, I see the terms do not allow it; that is clear.' His face showed plainly that he was quite anxious to have this concession made; and Grant said very promptly, and without giving Lee time to make a direct request:

" 'Well, the subject is quite new to me. Of course I did not know that any private soldiers owned their animals; but I think we have fought the last battle of the war,—I sincerely hope so,— and that the surrender of this army will be followed soon by that of all the others; and I take it that most of the men in the ranks are small farmers, and as the country has been so raided by the two armies, it is doubtful whether they will be able to put in a crop to carry themselves and their families through the next winter without the aid of the horses they are now riding, and I will arrange it in this way. I will not change the terms as now written, but I will instruct the officers I shall appoint to receive the paroles to let all the men who claim to own a horse or mule take the animals home with them to work their little farms. . . .'

"Lee now looked greatly relieved, and though anything but a demonstrative man, he gave every evidence of his appreciation of this concession, and said: 'This will have the best possible effect upon the men. It will be very gratifying, and will do much toward conciliating our people.' "

Lee then accepted the proposition. The number of men surrendered was 26,765. The Confederates had "been living for the last few days principally upon parched corn" and were badly in need of food. Grant supplied them with rations. As soon as the Union soldiers heard of the surrender they commenced firing salutes at different points along the lines. He ordered them stopped, saying, "The war is over; the rebels are our countrymen again: and the best sign of rejoicing after the victory will be to abstain from all demonstrations in the field."

Lee rode back sorrowfully to his soldiers. "The men gathered round him," writes Cooke, "wrung his hand and in broken words called upon God to help him. . . . The tears came to his eyes and looking at the men with a glance of proud feeling, he said, in suppressed tones, which trembled slightly: 'We have fought through the war together. I have done the best I could for you. My heart is too full to say more.' " On the morrow he issued a farewell address to the Army of Northern Virginia and rode away to Richmond. The army disbanded and dispersed to their homes.

On the day after the surrender Grant had an interview with Lee and suggested that he use his great influence in advising the capitulation of the remaining Southern armies. The Union general did not enter the Confederate lines, did not go to Richmond and gave no sign of exultation. He went back to City Point and thence to Washington in order to stop further military preparations. The day of his arrival there, four days after the surrender of Lee, he and the War Department came to the determination, "to stop all drafting and recruiting, to curtail purchases for arms, ammunition," etc.; "to reduce the number of general and staff officers to the actual necessities of the service," and "to remove all military restrictions upon trade and commerce so far as may be consistent with public safety."

Having spoken freely of the mistakes of Grant in the Virginia campaign of 1864 I must in candour express the opinion that in these final operations he outgeneralled Lee. The conditions were not unequal; 49,000 men opposed 113,000 and the game was escape or surrender. Lee's force was dispersed by defeat, weakened by captures and the shattered and discouraged remnant of it was forced to capitulate. That Lee was outgeneralled in this Appomattox campaign is a judgment supported by the intimations of some Confederate writers, made with the utmost deference to their general, that if everything had been managed properly the Army of Northern Virginia might have eluded surrender and protracted the war.

The news of the surrender of Lee was received in Washington at nine o'clock Sunday evening April 9 and at a somewhat later hour in other cities of the land. While the people had exulted at the occupation of Richmond they perceived that the possession of the capital of the Confederacy did not imply the end of the war. But now, it was in everybody's mouth, "the great captain of the rebellion had surrendered": this imported that slavery was dead, the Union restored and that the nation lived. So pregnant an event ought speedily to be known to Europe and the Inman line despatched a special steamer on the Monday to carry the intelligence across the ocean. The people of the North rejoiced on the night of the 9th and during the day and evening of the 10th as they had never rejoiced before nor did they during the remainder of the century on any occasion show such an exuberance of gladness. Business was suspended and the courts adjourned. Cannons fired, bells rang, flags floated, houses and shops were gay with the red, white and blue. There were illuminations and bonfires. The streets of the cities and towns were filled with men, who shook hands warmly, embraced each other, shouted, laughed and cheered and were indeed beside themselves in their great joy. There were pledges in generous wines and much common drinking in bar-rooms and liquor shops. There were fantastic processions, grotesque performances and some tomfoolery. Grave and old gentlemen forgot their age and dignity and played the pranks of schoolboys. But always above these foolish and bibulous excesses sounded the patriotic and

religious note of the jubilee. "Praise God from whom all blessings flow" were the words most frequently sung in the street, the
Board of Trade and on the Stock Exchange. One writer records
that in the bar-room of Willard's Hotel, Washington, when the
news arrived, an elderly gentleman sprang upon the bar and led
the crowd in singing with unwonted fervour the well-known
doxology. "Twenty thousand men in the busiest haunts of
trade in one of the most thronged cities of the world," Motley
wrote, uncovered their heads spontaneously and sang the psalm
of thanksgiving, "Praise God." Noteworthy was the service in
Trinity Church, New York, one hour after midday of the Tuesday following the surrender, when the church overflowed with
worshippers, who were in the main people of distinction. The
choir chanted the "Te Deum" and at the bidding of the clergyman, the congregation rose, and, inspired by the great organ
and guided by the choir, sang the noble anthem "Gloria in
Excelsis." These opening words, "Glory be to God on high and
on earth peace, good will towards men," had a peculiar significance to the Northern people who during these days of rejoicing
were for the most part full of generous feeling for the South.
Patriotism expressed itself in the songs "John Brown's Body,"
"My country, 'tis of thee," "Rally round the flag" and the
"Star-spangled Banner." Lowell instinctively put into words
what his countrymen had in their hearts: "The news, my dear
Charles, is from Heaven. I felt a strange and tender exaltation.
I wanted to laugh and I wanted to cry, and ended by holding my
peace and feeling devoutly thankful. There is something mag-
nificent in having a country to love."

Before I proceed to relate how this universal rejoicing was
quickly followed by horror and deep mourning I shall give an
account of Lincoln's attitude towards reconstruction during the
last days of his life.

While the President was in Richmond (April 4, 5) he had
two interviews with Judge Campbell, in the last of which he
gave to this self-constituted representative of the Southern people a written memorandum, stating the three indispensable

conditions of peace: the national authority must be restored throughout the States; the Executive will make no recession concerning slavery; and all forces hostile to the government must disband. On his return to City Point, as a result of his deliberation, he wrote to General Weitzel, April 6, that he might permit "the gentlemen who have acted as the legislature of Virginia . . . to assemble at Richmond and take measures to withdraw the Virginia troops and other support from resistance to the general government." Nothing came of this. The surrender of Lee and Campbell's misconstruction of Lincoln's letter to Weitzel incited the President to telegraph to his general withdrawing both his letter and memorandum. This was not done however before there had been published, in the Richmond *Whig*, with the approval of Weitzel, an address to the people of Virginia signed by many of the State senators and representatives and a number of citizens, who solicited that the governor, the members of the legislature and certain men of prominence should come together in Richmond by the 25th of April, in order that from such a conference might ensue an immediate meeting of the General Assembly and the restoration of peace to their commonwealth. The interest of this circumstance in its bearing on the after history lies in the opposition of the radical Republicans to any such mode of reconstruction. Stanton in cabinet meeting showed that he was disturbed by the President's action; and the committee on the conduct of the war, who were on a visit to Richmond at the time the address appeared, "were all thunderstruck and fully sympathized with the hot indignation and wrathful words of" their chairman Senator Wade.

One loves to linger over the last days of Lincoln. He had nothing but mercy and kindness for his bygone enemies. "Do not allow Jefferson Davis to escape the law; he must be hanged," was said to him. "Judge not that ye be not judged" came the reply. On the boat journey from City Point to Washington (April 8, 9) he and his companions, among whom was Sumner, conversed with the freedom of a "small family party" and were happy that the end of the war was in sight. On the Sunday (the 9th) he read to them from his favourite play, "Macbeth,"

Duncan is in his grave;
After life's fitful fever he sleeps well;
Treason has done his worst: nor steel, nor poison,
Malice domestic, foreign levy, nothing
can touch him further.

A second time he read these words aloud.

On Tuesday evening, April 11, Lincoln made to the rejoicing people who had come to the White House to hear him his last public speech. "By these recent successes," he said, "the reinauguration of the national authority—reconstruction—which has had a large share of thought from the first, is pressed much more closely upon our attention. It is fraught with great difficulty." He then proceeded to defend his action in regard to the government of Louisiana. "As to sustaining it [the Louisiana government]," he continued, "my promise is out. But as bad promises are better broken than kept, I shall treat this as a bad promise, and break it whenever I shall be convinced that keeping it is adverse to the public interest; but I have not yet been so convinced. I have been shown a letter on this subject, supposed to be an able one, in which the writer expresses regret that my mind has not seemed to be definitely fixed on the question whether the seceded States, so called, are in the Union or out of it. It would perhaps add astonishment to his regret were he to learn that since I have found professed Union men endeavoring to make that question, I have purposely forborne any public expression upon it. As appears to me, that question has not been, nor yet is, a practically material one, and that any discussion of it, while it thus remains practically immaterial, could have no effect other than the mischievous one of dividing our friends. As yet, whatever it may hereafter become, that question is bad as the basis of a controversy, and good for nothing at all—a merely pernicious abstraction.

"We all agree that the seceded States, so called, are out of their proper practical relation with the Union, and that the sole object of the government, civil and military, in regard to those States is to again get them into that proper practical relation. I believe that it is not only possible, but in fact easier, to do this without deciding or even considering whether these States have ever been out of the Union, than with it. Finding themselves safely at home, it would be utterly immaterial whether they had ever been abroad. . . . The amount of constituency, so to speak, on which the new Louisiana government rests, would be more satisfactory to all if it contained 50,000, or 30,000, or even 20,000, instead of only about 12,000, as it does. It is also unsatisfactory to some that the elective franchise is not given to the colored man. I would myself prefer that it were now conferred on the very intelligent and on those who serve our cause as soldiers.

"Still, the question is not whether the Louisiana government, as it stands, is quite all that is desirable. The question is, will it be wiser to take it as it is and help to improve it, or to reject and disperse it? Can Louisiana be brought into proper, practical relations with the Union sooner by sustaining or by discarding her new State government? Some 12,000 voters in the heretofore slave State of Louisiana have sworn allegiance to the Union, assumed to be the rightful political power of the State, held elections, organized a State government, adopted a free-State constitution, giving the benefit of public schools equally to black and white and empowering the legislature to confer the elective franchise upon the colored man. Their legislature has already voted to ratify the constitutional amendment recently passed by Congress, abolishing slavery throughout the nation. These 12,000 persons are thus fully committed to the Union and to perpetual freedom in the State—committed to the very things, and nearly all the things, the nation wants—and they ask the nation's recognition and its assistance to make good their committal. Now, if we reject and spurn them, we do our utmost to disorganize and disperse them. We, in effect, say to the white man: You are worthless or worse; we will neither help you nor be helped by you. To the blacks we say: This cup of liberty which these, your old masters, hold to your lips we will dash from you, and leave you to the chances of gathering the spilled and scattered contents in some vague and undefined when, where and how. . . . Concede that the new government of Louisiana is only to what it should be as the egg is to the fowl, we shall sooner have the fowl by hatching the egg than by smashing it. . . . What has been said of Louisiana will apply generally to other States. . . . In the present situation, as the phrase goes, it may be my duty to make some new announcement to the people of the South. I am considering, and shall not fail to act when satisfied that action will be proper."

Of this speech Sumner wrote to Lieber: "The President's speech and other things augur confusion and uncertainty in the future, with hot controversy. Alas! alas!"

Friday, April 14 Lincoln held his last cabinet meeting. General Grant was present and said that he was anxious in his continual expectation of hearing from Sherman. The President replied: "I have no doubt that favorable news will soon come for I had last night my usual dream which has preceded nearly every important event of the war. I seemed to be in a singular and indescribable vessel, but always the same and to be moving with great rapidity toward a dark and indefinite shore." Matters of routine were disposed of and then the subject of reconstruction was taken up. After some discussion the President said: "I think it providential that this great rebellion is crushed just as Congress has adjourned and there are none of the disturbing elements of that body to hinder and embarrass us. If we are wise and discreet we shall reanimate the States and get their governments in successful operation, with order prevailing and the Union re-established before Congress comes together in December. . . . I hope there will be no persecution, no bloody work after the war is over. No one need expect me to take any part in hanging or killing those men, even the worst of them. Frighten them out of the country, open the gates, let down the bars, scare them off [throwing up his hands as if scaring sheep]. Enough lives have been sacrificed. We must extinguish our resentments if we expect harmony and union. There is too much of a desire on the part of some of our very good friends to be masters, to interfere with and dictate to those States, to treat the people not as fellow-citizens; there is too little respect for their rights. I do not sympathize in these feelings." He then spoke of the Louisiana government, joined in the discussion regarding the status of Virginia and said at the close of the meeting: Reconstruction "is the great question pending and we must now begin to act in the interest of peace."* Stanton gave two accounts of this council. "At a cabinet meeting yesterday," he wrote at half-past one in the morning of April 15, "the President was very cheerful and hopeful; spoke very kindly of General Lee and others of the Confederacy and the establishment of government in Virginia." At 11.40 the same morning he said in a letter to Adams: "The President was more cheerful and happy than I had ever seen [him], rejoiced at the near prospect of firm and durable peace at home and abroad, manifested in marked degree the kindness and humanity of his disposition and the tender and forgiving spirit that so eminently distinguished him."

Rejoicing over Lee's surrender which began on Sunday night continued through the week but by Friday it had abated in the Northern cities leaving in its train a serene content. The most significant celebration took place at Charleston, South Carolina and had been arranged sometime beforehand for the purpose of hoisting the flag over Fort Sumter four years from the day on which it fell; but much was added to the joyful anniversary by the intelligence of Lee's surrender which was learned on their arrival by the distinguished visitors from the North who went there to participate in what Beecher called "a grand national event." The religious exercises at the fort were marked by a puritanical fervour; and distinct efforts were made to evoke the memories of the past. The chaplain who had thanked God at the flag-raising December 27, 1860 now offered a prayer. General Robert Anderson made a brief speech with deep feeling and

* Welles in *The Galaxy*, April, 1872, pp. 525-527. I have altered the account from the third person to the first. After mature consideration I have adopted these recollections as a substantially exact account of this meeting. Welles had an accurate memory and his story fits into the situation. My own judgment is confirmed by Nicolay and Hay who are acute critics of the authenticity of reported private conversations of Lincoln (see vol. x. p. 282), and by Stanton's general accounts which follow in the text.

raised the same United States flag over the ruins of Fort Sumter which he had lowered April 14, 1861. Sumter saluted the flag with one hundred guns and every fort and battery which had fired upon the little garrison at the commencement of the war now gave a national salute. The people sang the "Star-spangled Banner." Henry Ward Beecher delivered an impressive oration. At the banquet at the Charleston Hotel in the town one of the speakers was William Lloyd Garrison, who had been hanged and burned in effigy at Charleston thirty years before, and on whose head the South had set a price.

While the rejoicing went on in Charleston and echoes of the jubilation of the early week resounded throughout the North, Lincoln was assassinated. Walt Whitman has told the story of the exultation over the end of the war and of the death of the Captain with the peaceful haven in sight:

O Captain! my Captain! our fearful trip is done,
The ship has weather'd every rack, the prize we sought is won,
The port is near, the bells I hear, the people all exulting,
While follow eyes the steady keel, the vessel grim and daring.

. . . .

O Captain! my Captain! rise up and hear the bells;
Rise up—for you the flag is hung—for you the bugle trills,
For you bouquets and ribboned wreaths—for you the shores
　　a-crowding,
For you they call, the swaying mass, their eager faces turning.

. . . .

My Captain does not answer, his lips are pale and still,
My father does not feel my arm, he has no pulse nor will,
The ship is anchored safe and sound, its voyage closed and
　　done,
From fearful trip the victor ship comes in with object won;

Exult O shores and ring O bells!
But I with mournful tread,
Walk the deck my Captain lies,
Fallen cold and dead.

Somewhat after two o'clock on the afternoon of April 14 General Grant bade the President good-by having declined his invitation to accompany him to the theatre that evening, the desire of seeing their children taking Mrs. Grant and himself to New Jersey. Lincoln spent an agreeable afternoon. He had an hour's chat with his son Robert (who for a short time had been a captain on Grant's staff), and then took a long drive with his wife, his happy and tender mood colouring his review of the past and anticipation of the future. Schuyler Colfax, Speaker of the last House and prospective Speaker of the next, was unable to join the theatre party but called at the White House at half-past seven in the evening in order to have a few last words before setting out on his journey to the Pacific coast. At ten minutes past eight the President rose and said to his wife, "Mother, I suppose it's time to go though I would rather stay;" then grasping Colfax's hand with, "Pleasant journey to you, I'll telegraph you at San Francisco, good-by" he went with Mrs. Lincoln, Miss Harris and Major Rathbone to Ford's theatre to see Laura Keene's company play the comedy "Our American Cousin."

John Wilkes Booth, an erratic actor delighting in the gloom of "Richard III." and Schiller's "Robbers," a man of intemperate habits, and a fanatical sympathizer with the South, had organized a conspiracy for the murder of the President, Vice-President, General Grant and Secretary Seward, in which he had chosen for his part the assassination of the President. Between ten o'clock and half-past, Booth, fortified by liquor, showed a card to the servant sitting outside of the President's box, was allowed to pass, entered the box stealthily, put a pistol to Lincoln's head and shouting *Sic semper tyrannis,* fired. Dropping his pistol he struck with a knife at Rathbone, who was endeavouring to seize him, and jumped from the box to the stage. Although a high leap it would not have been difficult for an actor of Booth's training had not his spur caught in the folds of the flag with which the Presidential box was draped. He fell to the stage, breaking his leg, rose immediately, and, turning to the audience, brandished his knife, rushed out of the theatre, and, mounting a fleet horse rode away.

The ball had entered Lincoln's brain, at once rendering him

insensible. He was taken to a house opposite, lay in a state of coma all night and died at twenty-two minutes past seven in the morning.

In Stanton's account of the tragedy, he said, the door of the President's private box "was unguarded." Had one of the million soldiers which Lincoln commanded been on guard with proper orders, by far the most precious life in the country, the one life absolutely necessary to the nation, would have been saved. There is but one other historic assassination fraught with such consequence to country, perhaps to civilization—that of Julius Cæsar. "And when some of his friends did counsel Cæsar," wrote Plutarch, "to have a guard for the safety of his person and some also did offer to serve him: he would never consent to it but said, It was better to die once than always to be afraid of death." Such was the attitude of Lincoln.

"Cæsar was the entire and perfect man," wrote Mommsen. ". . . But in this very circumstance lies the difficulty, we may perhaps say the impossibility, of depicting Cæsar to the life. As the artist can paint everything save only consummate beauty, so the historian, when once in a thousand years he encounters the perfect, can only be silent regarding it." This were truer of Lincoln than of Cæsar, yet it is true of neither. In intellect Cæsar surpassed Lincoln. Yet it remained for Washington and Lincoln to render false for the first time in history the generalization of Montesquieu: "Constant experience shows us that every man invested with power is apt to abuse it; he pushes on till he comes to something that limits him. Is it not strange though true to say that virtue itself has need of limits!"

Poet, preacher and orator have said all that can be said of Lincoln. It were too much to claim for him a world glory alongside of those men of titanic intellects who have bestrode the Old World, and whose deeds have amazed the New. It is enough that he is dear to Americans and enshrined next to Washington in their hearts.

Bibliographical Note

History of the United States from the Compromise of 1850 to the Final Restoration of Home Rule in the South in 1877.
Vol. I, 1850–54. New York: Harper & Bros., 1892.
Vol. II, 1854–60. New York: Harper & Bros., 1892.
Vol. III, 1860–62. New York: Harper & Bros., 1895.
Vol. IV, 1862–64. New York: Harper & Bros., 1899.
Vol. V, 1864–66. New York: Macmillan Co., 1904.
Vol. VI, 1866–72. New York: Macmillan Co., 1906.
Vol. VII, 1872–77. New York: Macmillan Company, 1906.
Vol. VIII, *History of the United States from Hayes to McKinley,* 1877–96. New York: Macmillan Co., 1919.
Vol. IX, *The McKinley and Roosevelt Administrations,* 1897–1909. New York: Macmillan Co., 1922.

The first seven volumes have been reprinted several times, always from the same plates but with some changes in pagination.

Index

DATE DUE

OCT 31 '68			
DEC 2 '68			
FEB 24 '69			
DEC 2 '69			
FEB 16 '71			
DEC 13 '71			
OCT 24 '72			
NOV 9 '72			
MAR 20 '75			
NOV 3 '76			
NOV 17 '78			
DE 5'80			
MAR 25 '87			
GAYLORD			PRINTED IN U.S.A.